NEW NEGRO ARTISTS IN PARIS

NEW NEGRO ARTISTS IN PARIS

AFRICAN AMERICAN PAINTERS AND SCULPTORS IN THE CITY OF LIGHT, 1922–1934

THERESA LEININGER-MILLER

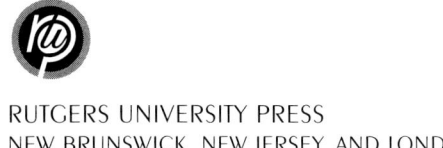

RUTGERS UNIVERSITY PRESS
NEW BRUNSWICK, NEW JERSEY, AND LONDON

Library of Congress Cataloging-in-Publication Data

Leininger-Miller, Theresa A.
    New Negro artists in Paris : African-American painters and sculptors in the city of light, 1922–1934 /
Theresa Leininger-Miller.
        p.   cm.
    Includes bibliographical references and index.
    ISBN 0-8135-2857-7 (cloth : alk. paper) — ISBN 0-8135-3858-5 (pbk : alk. paper)
    1. Expatriate artists—France—Paris. 2. Afro-American art—France—Paris. 3. Afro-American
artists—France—Paris. 4. Art, American—France—Paris. 4. Art, Modern—20th century—France—
Paris. I. Title.

    N6850.L45   2000
    704.03'96073044361—dc21   00-024449

British Cataloging-in-Publication data for this book is available from the British Library

Manufactured in the United States of America

CONTENTS

LIST OF ILLUSTRATIONS

ACKNOWLEDGMENTS

This book, which began as a dissertation at Yale University in 1990, would not have been possible without the aid of many people. I wish to thank my advisor, Robert Farris Thompson, for his enthusiastic support and encouragement. I am especially grateful to committee member Richard J. Powell of Duke University, who provided the most specific suggestions for improvement and the most intriguing conversations. I am indebted to him for paving the way for scholarly study on African American artists abroad with his excellent dissertation, at Yale, and book on William H. Johnson, as well as his fascinating work on diasporic studies and the Harlem Renaissance. Colloquium members at Yale, Ann E. Gibson and Robert L. Herbert, were also very helpful as models of intellectual thought and writing. Additionally, Ann offered very thoughtful and incisive comments later, on the book manuscript, as well as kind words of motivation. Judith Wilson, now at the University of California, Irvine, was also an excellent source of information and insights in the early stages of the study. More recently, Julie Aronson, Curator of American Painting and Sculpture at the Cincinnati Art Museum, suggested improvements for the chapters on sculptors.

My mother, Carol Leininger, my classmate Julie Nicoletta, and my husband, Brian S. Miller, all read the manuscript at various stages, made useful suggestions, and gave pep talks. I am especially grateful to Brian, whose deep love, warm laughter, and unflagging good humor and interest pulled the study on to completion. Our son Nicholas was always a source of delight and inspiration with his heart-melting smiles and hugs. And baby Jacob timed his arrival into the world just as I was getting the last reprint permissions for illustrations. His playful cooing was a welcome break from last-minute tasks.

Thanks to the following fellowships, I was able concentrate on the dissertation research and writing for extended periods of time—Full Yale University Fellowship, 1987–1991; Ten-Week Graduate Student Fellowship, Smithsonian Institution, 1990; Henry R. Luce Fellowship in American Art History and Samuel H. Kress Foundation Fellowships, 1990–1991; Predoctoral Fellowship, Smithsonian Institution, 1991–1992; John F. Enders Research Assistance Grants, 1992, 1990; and the Dr. Renton K. Brodie Predoctoral Fellowship, University of Cincinnati, 1993. Travel funds from the Lehman Fellowship Foundation, the Charles D. Cuttler Fellowship, and the women's studies program at the University of Cincinnati (1993–1995), allowed me to deliver papers on topics in the dissertation at the College Art Association and the Midwest Art History Society annual conferences and the Gender and National Identity conference at the University of Cincinnati.

At the National Museum of American Art, where I was a predoctoral fellow (summer 1990 and 1991–1992), I was particularly grateful for the advice, feedback, and encouragement that I received from Lynda Roscoe Hartigan, curator of paintings, and from Lois Marie Fink, curator of research and now Curator Emerita, and for the great moral support from fellow fellows (sisters) Elizabeth O'Leary, Christine Bell, Juanita Holland, and Winnie Owens-Hart. At the Archives of American Art, Liza Kirwin and Arthur Breton brought important sources to my attention. I also thank librarians Cecilia Chin and Virginia Mecklenburg. I especially recognize Rita Pierson for being such a great part-time roommate in Alexandria.

The staffs at the Beinecke Rare Book and Manuscript Library, Yale University; Howard University, especially Esme Bahn; the Schomburg Center for Research in Black Culture, New York Public Library; the Rare Book and Manuscript Library, Columbia University; the Amistad Research Center; and Rhode Island College were all very helpful. Also, in New York, Camille Billops and James Hatch allowed me to transcribe various interviews and photocopy their files, and Corrine Jennings shared her knowledge about Nancy Elizabeth Prophet and Hale Woodruff and lent me photographs of the artists' works. For special access to the Guggenheim files, I am grateful to G. Thomas Tanselle.

Many people throughout the country shared their private collections with me. In Baltimore, Madeline Murphy kindly allowed me to transcribe Laura Wheeler Waring's diary and offered room and board on several occasions. In Providence, George Proffitt graciously opened his files on Nancy Elizabeth Prophet. In Croton-on-Hudson, Harry Henderson shared the many files he had compiled with Romare Bearden and nudged me along via the telephone over the years. In Boston, John Axelrod ordered a photograph of his Hayden painting for the book.

At Fisk University, head librarian Jessie Carney Smith courteously brought me a flashlight to read manuscripts by, and ice water to combat the heat, when a power outage knocked out the lights and air conditioning for days during the summer of 1990. She also published my first study on Prophet in *Notable Black American Women* (1992) and shared her research on Augusta Savage.

In Paris, Michel Fabre kindly extended an associate research fellowship to me at the Centre d'Etudes Afro-Américaines et des Nouvelles Littératures en Anglais, Université de la

Sorbonne Nouvelle, allowed me to have access to his wonderful private library, and helped me track down some information. Lynne Thornton and Elisabeth Fraser also facilitated my research endeavors in various ways.

For additional assistance from scholars and supporters, I thank Asake Bomani, Patricia Brady, Karen C. C. Dalton, David Driskell, Wendy Greenhouse, Dagmar Schulz Hagenkötter, Michael Harris, Amy Kirschke, Samella Lewis (who loaned photographs of Hayden's watercolors of the Colonial Exposition of 1931), Dominique Malaquais, Archibald Motley Jr., Jontyle Theresa Robinson, Linda Nieman, Janie Stevens, Joseph Szasafi, and William E. Taylor, and the graduate and undergraduate students in my African American art history classes at Wesleyan University and the University of Cincinnati.

At the University of Cincinnati, in the College of Design, Architecture, Art, and Planning (DAAP), fellow art history faculty members Jonathan Riess and Lloyd Engelbrecht supported the completion of the dissertation and the search for a publisher, which was facilitated by a reduced teaching load in fall 1992, and special-duty leaves of absence in winter 1995 and fall 1997. These were approved by Dean Jay Chatterjee, Associate Dean Kristi Nelson (now Vice Provost), and School of Art Directors Derrick Woodham and Wayne Enstice. Jonathan and Lloyd were especially encouraging and provided pivotal letters of recommendation for awards. DAAP librarians Jane Carlin, Steve Welker, and Nanda Araujo provided fast and efficient service by helping to track down last-minute research details.

At Rutgers University Press, I was very fortunate in having an excellent, discerning, and very understanding editor in Leslie Mitchner, who believed in the potential of the manuscript from the beginning, and who, along with her able assistant, Paula Kantenwein, smoothly facilitated its completion in a timely manner. Copyeditor Romaine Perin's expertise, efficiency, and sharp eye for detail greatly assisted refinement, as did production editor Brigitte Goldstein's skillful supervision.

My husband, Brian S. Miller, and my parents, Carol and Edward Leininger, have been most supportive throughout the long writing process and I am especially grateful for their love and patience.

INTRODUCTION

"*I*n the very process of being transplanted," wrote Alain Locke in 1925, "the Negro is becoming transformed."[1] Although Locke was speaking of the Great Migration in the early twentieth century, when some four hundred thousand African Americans left the rural South for the urban North in search of greater opportunities, his words also ring true for Negro artists who studied in Paris. This was especially the case for the African American painters and sculptors who launched their careers in that city in the late 1920s and early 1930s; there they were transformed into New Negro artists—black modernists.

In 1903, in his book *The Souls of Black Folk,* W.E.B. Du Bois wrote eloquently about the dual heritage of African Americans. The following passage has since been much quoted:

> After the Egyptian and Indian, the Greek and Roman, the Teuton and Mongolian, the Negro is a sort of seventh son, born with a veil, and gifted with second-sight in this American world,—a world which yields him no true self-consciousness, but only lets him see himself through the revelation of the other world. It is a peculiar sensation, this double consciousness, this sense of always looking at one's self through the eyes of others, of measuring one's soul by the tape of a world that looks on in amused contempt and pity. One ever feels his twoness,—an American, a Negro; two souls, two thoughts, two unreconciled strivings; two warring ideals in one dark body, whose dogged strength alone keeps it from being torn asunder.
>
> The history of the American Negro is the history of this strife,—this longing to attain self-conscious manhood, to merge his double self into a better and truer self. In this merging he wishes neither of the older selves to be lost. He would not Africanize America, for America has much to teach the world and Africa. He would not bleach his Negro soul in a flood of white Americanism, for he knows that Negro blood has a

message for the world. He simply wishes to make it possible for a man to be both a Negro and an American, without having the doors of Opportunity closed roughly in his face.

This, then, is the end of his striving; to be a co-worker in the kingdom of culture, to husband and use his best powers and his latent genius.

The innate love of harmony and beauty that set the souls of his people a-dancing and a-singing raised but confusion and doubt in the soul of the black artist; for the beauty revealed to him was the soul-beauty of a race which a larger audience despised, and he could not articulate the message of another people.[2]

Going abroad gave African American artists the opportunity to view their dual heritage, their split subjectivity, through a wider lens in the culture kingdom's capital of Paris. There, they began to articulate their own complex and diverse messages about the "soul-beauty" of a race.

New York has long been seen as the locus for the Harlem Renaissance, yet the movement was hardly confined to northern Manhattan. Significant events took place elsewhere in the United States, Europe, Africa, and the Caribbean. In terms of the visual arts, Paris played a pivotal role in the development of some of the leading Harlem Renaissance artists.

While Harlem may have been the "Mecca for the New Negro," as described by Alain Locke in the March 1925 issue of the mainstream magazine *Survey Graphic,* Paris was Mecca for New Negro visual artists and many other foreigners. The city attracted a "lost generation" of Americans in the 1920s and 1930s, and hundreds of artists, musicians, and writers from all over the world flocked to the French capital in search of a sense of community and the freedom to be creative. For African Americans, the lure of Paris was enhanced by fear of and disgust with the widespread racial discrimination that they experienced in the United States. They sought a more nurturant environment where their work would receive serious attention, as well as the chance to study many of the world's greatest cultural achievements. France offered all this, as well as an active black diasporal community with a growing sense of Pan-Africanism.

At least twelve documented African American artists—four women, two of whom were sculptors, and eight men, all painters, including one who was a printmaker, thrived in the bohemian atmosphere of Paris, studying at the finest academies, exhibiting at respected salons, winning awards, seeing choice art collections, mingling with people of diverse ethnic origins, dancing to jazz, and fervently discussing art, race, literature, philosophy, and politics. Although their individual experiences differed widely, they had much in common, including exposure to traditional European art, African art, modern art, and proto-Négritude ideas.

The African American artists who went to Paris between 1922 and 1934 constitute a diverse group. Gwendolyn Bennett (1902–1981), Aaron Douglas (1899–1979), William Thompson Goss (b. 1894), William Emmett Grant (active 1929–1931), Palmer Hayden (1890–1973), William Henry Johnson (1901–1970), Archibald J. Motley Jr. (1891–1981),

Elizabeth Prophet (1890–1960), Augusta Savage (1892–1962), Albert Alexander Smith (1896–1940), Laura Wheeler Waring (1887–1948), and Hale Woodruff (1900–1980) came from all over the United States, from Green Cove Springs, Florida; to Giddings, Texas; to Widewater, Virginia. Almost all moved from their small hometowns to attend art schools in larger cities. Few, though, attended the same institution. Johnson and Smith graduated from the prestigious National Academy of Design in New York, and Motley and Grant went to the Art Institute of Chicago. The rest took classes around the country—at the Pennsylvania Academy of Fine Arts (Waring), Rhode Island School of Design (Prophet), John Herron Art Institute (Woodruff), University of Nebraska (Douglas), Commonwealth Art Colony in Boothbay, Maine (Hayden), Cooper Union (Savage), and Pratt Institute (Bennett). These artists had in common dedicated teachers who had studied in Paris and who urged their students to do the same. Additionally, nearly all put themselves through school by working a variety of odd jobs. Making a living generally slowed down their formal education, and all but two of the artists were more than thirty-two years of age by the time they went to Europe. Most could scarcely afford to travel, in contrast to many white Americans who made the same pilgrimage.

Fortunately, after 1919, the burgeoning postwar economy permitted both increased scholarship aid from private patrons and institutions, and less expensive transatlantic travel. William E. Harmon, a real estate investor and philanthropist, established the Harmon Foundation in 1922 to support black artists. His first monetary awards went to Woodruff and Hayden in 1926 and aided their travel abroad. Julius Rosenwald, the Sears Roebuck magnate, founded a scholarship program in 1929 specifically to aid African Americans, and both Douglas and Savage received fellowships from his foundation. Other wealthy business-men offered scholarships through national competition. The Carnegie Corporation supported both Savage and Prophet, and the Guggenheim Foundation sponsored Motley's one-year stay in Paris. Educators also worked to give African Americans the European experi-ence. Waring won a Cresson Traveling Fellowship from the Pennsylvania Academy of Fine Arts in 1914, painter Charles Webster Hawthorne raised funds for his student Johnson in 1926, and teachers at Florida Agricultural and Mechanical School raised fifty dollars to aid Savage in 1929. In addition, small groups of private citizens funded artists. For example, several white women in Providence backed Prophet, a theater group in Indianapolis donated money to Woodruff, and the Delta Sigma Theta sorority gave Bennett a thousand dollars. Supplemented by hard-earned savings, these twelve artists separately boarded ship for the French capital during the following decade. There, they produced a remarkable number of paintings, sculpture, and prints of great variety that were exhibited in France and in the United States. Study abroad won for these artists the critical acclaim that established their reputations as some of the most significant leaders of the international New Negro move-ment in the visual arts.

The experiences of African American artists in Paris, ca. 1922–1934, were distinc-tive, yet they shared some of the same benefits and challenges as other foreign artists there at the same time, such as a loose sense of community and an ambivalence about the city and their place in it. What made them unique was the kind of art they produced and the ways in which they marketed those images. Ever aware of multiple audiences—French and European jurors and patrons, writers from the African diaspora, and Americans, both black and white, who were viewers, jurors, patrons, critics, and readers of black periodicals, in the United States—they created diverse works. Their stylistic approaches, although mostly academic and rarely avant-garde, were less exciting than the subjects they tackled. These ranged from conservative landscapes and depictions of French landmarks, to Cubist and near-abstract compositions, to genre scenes of rural African Americans, to meditative busts of black men, to sleek portrayals of androgynous figures, to cartoonlike renderings of African dancers, to fantasies of ancient African kingdoms, to sophisticated nightclub revelers. As Richard Powell has argued about the Harlem Renaissance in general, "This new, diaspora-informed, black visual modernism developed out of an inherent contradiction: a celebration of skyscrapers, Cadillacs, and progressivism that existed alongside indelible memories of rural shacks and mule-drawn wagons."[3] In a sense, these artists also explored two main themes that were occupying French artists at the same time, those of modernity and nostalgia.[4] The concept of nostalgia, or more specifically, romanticism, of longing for both an earlier, mythical time in America's folk history and a grand, exotic vision of Africa, is all the more intriguing given the use of stereotypes by these painters and sculptors. The reliance, expansion, and subversion of black stereotypes were certainly conditioned and affirmed in large part by white American and European patronage. Yet there was considerable agency and choice on the part of the producers as well. This study is an initial attempt to analyze the connections between those factors in Paris in the 1920s and early 1930s.

A SURVEY OF THE LITERATURE AND RESEARCH
ON AFRICAN AMERICAN ARTISTS IN PARIS

While there is a plethora of publications on white Americans in Paris, there has been no comprehensive study on African American artists in Paris, until now. The earliest study on the subject is a small exhibition catalog from 1989 by Catherine Bernard, *Afro-American Artists in Paris: 1919–1939*. The publication includes a brief, nine-page essay and one-paragraph biographies on eight artists. In 1992, the Bomani Gallery in San Francisco sponsored the exhibition and catalog, *Paris Connections: African American Artists in Paris,* which covered the subject from 1830 to the present and included my essay "The Transatlantic Tradition: African-American Artists in Paris, 1830–1940." This was the first publication to look at the phenomenon from its presumed inception until World War II.

Michel Fabre of the Sorbonne has amassed a marvelous private collection on the broader subject of African Americans in Paris, which he graciously shared with me; the fruits of his decades-long work are evident in his publications *From Harlem to Paris: Black American Writers in France, 1840–1980* (1991) and *Way B(l)ack Then and Now: A Street Guide to African Americans in Paris* (1992), this latter coauthored with John A. Williams. While groundbreaking, in neither the book nor the compilation are the visual arts discussed in depth. Only two books, published in conjunction with major monographic exhibitions, contain a thorough analysis of an African American artist abroad during the 1920s and 1930s. Richard Powell's outstanding *Homecoming: The Art and Life of William H. Johnson* (1991), an expansion of his dissertation from 1988, covers Johnson's entire life, highlighting the few months that the artist spent in Paris, the two years in the south of France, and the eight years in Scandinavia. Dewey Mosby and Darrel Sewell's excellent retrospective exhibition catalog *Henry Ossawa Tanner* (1991) also encompasses a life's work and necessarily focuses on the French experience; Tanner became an expatriate to Paris in 1891 and passed away there in 1937. Because both of these studies are monographic (and because Tanner was a generation older than those artists who went abroad after World War I), they do not fully explore the community of African American artists in Paris in the 1920s and 1930s.

The subject of African Americans in Europe is of increasing interest to scholars and the general public. The Center for the Study of Black Literature and Culture held the first international conference on the topic, "Black Artists in France: A Symposium," at the University of Pennsylvania in March 1991. Despite the title, the meeting dealt primarily with literature and film and very little with the visual arts. The next international conference, "African-Americans and Europe," sponsored by the Centre d'Etudes Afro-Américaines de la Sorbonne Nouvelle, Harvard and Columbia Universities, and the University of Mississippi, took place at the Sorbonne, University of Paris, in February 1992. Two of the fifty panel sessions dealt with the fine arts. There, I gave the paper "Roots of Black Modernism? African-American Artists in Paris, 1922–1932." Next, the international conference "A Visual Encounter: African-Americans and Europe" took place at the Palais du Luxembourg in Paris in February 1994. This colloquium focused on contemporary cultural politics and included presentations on the visual arts by several art historians and many contemporary African American artists. In 1996, the Studio Museum in Harlem held the exhibition "Explorations in the City of Light: African-American Artists in Paris, 1945–1965" and Tyler Stovall published his book *Paris Noir: African Americans in the City of Light*.

In the past two decades, numerous scholars have produced articles and exhibition catalogs on African American art, but there is still only a handful of monographs and very few scholarly articles on individual artists. In the present volume, then, I rely heavily on primary source material—artists' correspondence, diaries, published statements, sketchbooks, and taped interviews, and contemporary articles from newspapers and periodicals. There is no single source for these documents. For those African American artists who traveled abroad, only the collected papers of Palmer Hayden, William Henry Johnson, Henry Ossawa Tanner, and Hale Woodruff are in the Archives of American Art. Information by and about the other artists exists in collections all over the country—at Howard University, the National Archives, the Library of Congress, the Schomburg Center for Research in Black Culture of the New York Public Library, the New York Public Library Artists Index, the Hatch-Billops Archives, Rhode Island College, Brown University, Fisk University, the Museum of African-American Art in Los Angeles, the Amistad Collection in New Orleans, and Atlanta University, and in private collections, to name just a few of the places. What does exist in these archives is fragmentary at best. Most newspaper and magazine articles are not properly identified with full bibliographic information, making the establishment of exact chronologies difficult. Further, much of what has been published contains conflicting information and many inaccuracies. In order to create skeletal biographies, then, I checked and rechecked facts, cross-indexing all available material and utilizing such basic documents as census records, birth and death certificates, and obituaries. However, some errors may still remain.

To complicate matters, most of the works created by African American artists in Paris have never been published. Some are in public museums—the National Museum of American Art probably has the largest holdings—and private collections, but many are lost. Discussion of those works, therefore, is often limited to contemporary descriptions, photographs in archives, or analysis based on reproductions in periodicals, seen only on microfilm or photocopies. (That is also why some of the existing reproductions are not of the highest quality.) I have been able to locate only a few reproductions of works by six of the artists in Paris between the world wars—Waring, Bennett, Douglas, Johnson, Goss, and Grant—whose time abroad was a year or less. For that reason, I have chosen to focus on the remaining six artists, whose Parisian sojourn was longer. The time in which Prophet, Hayden, Woodruff, Motley, Savage, and Smith were in France ranged from one to fourteen years, and each produced at least twelve works abroad.

Scholarly work on these six artists is scant, despite the fact that these were among the best-known visual artists of the Harlem Renaissance. No one has published an article on Smith since his death in France in 1940. The most comprehensive biographical essays on Prophet and Savage were both published in *Notable Black Americans* (1992), edited by Jessie Carney Smith (I wrote the entry on Prophet, and Smith penned that on Savage). Small exhibition catalogs do exist on Savage (Deidre Bibby, *Augusta Savage and the Art Schools of Harlem,* 1988), Hayden (Allan Gordon, *Echoes of Our Past: The Narrative Artistry of Palmer C. Hayden,* 1988), Woodruff (Mary Schmidt Campbell, *Hale Woodruff: Fifty Years of His Art,* 1979), and Motley (Jontyle Theresa Robinson and Wendy Greenhouse, *The Art of Archibald J. Motley, Jr.,* 1991). The latter work is exemplary for its insightful and well-documented essays by Wendy Greenhouse and Jontyle Robinson, but even here only a page is devoted to Motley's year in Paris. Academic studies also exist on Woodruff (Winifred Stoelting's Ph.D. dissertation in liberal arts at Emory University, 1978), Motley (Elaine D. Woodall's M.A. thesis in art history from Pennsylvania State University, 1977), and Aaron Douglas (Amy Kirschke's dissertation in history and art history at Tulane University, 1991; and her book *Aaron Douglas: Art, Race, and the Harlem Renaissance,* 1995). None of these investigations encompasses the artists' full lives. Woodall's investigation ends just before Motley went abroad. Stoelting did outline Woodruff's activity in Paris in depth, but because her degree was in liberal studies, it was not her intention to do art historical analysis on the works that Woodruff produced abroad. Kirschke could do little more in this regard, given the paucity of information on Douglas's time in France. The present volume, then, is the first extensive scholarly examination of the experience and work of African American artists in Paris, 1922–1934.

A NOTE ABOUT THE STRUCTURE OF THE BOOK

The book is composed of seven chapters. The first is a brief survey of the debut of African American artists in Paris from 1830 to 1914, concluding with a brief analysis of the important role of Henry O. Tanner in the lives of several artists abroad at the turn of the century. I have not dwelt on Tanner in depth because of the substantial amount of published research readily available on him. In each of the six subsequent chapters, I focus on a single artist during the 1920s and early 1930s. Because Prophet's time abroad, 1922 to 1934, brackets that of all the other artists, aside from expatriate Smith, in France then, and because she was the first to actively work and exhibit in Paris, the study begins with her and then follows the chronological order in which the other artists arrived in the city: Hayden, 1927–1932; Woodruff, 1927–1931; Motley, 1929–1930; Savage, 1929–1931; and Smith, 1920–1940. Although Smith arrived in France in 1920, two years before Prophet, he spent most of the early 1920s traveling throughout Europe, performing with various jazz bands before truly settling in Paris near the end of 1924. Aside from Tanner, he stayed abroad the longest; Smith passed away in France in 1940. Since only very limited biographies exist on these six artists, in the chapter on each, I analyze their lives from birth until the end of their time in France.[5]

While the artist-by-artist approach has its limitations, it has been used to good effect by other scholars whose books concern Americans in Paris between the world wars; for example, Michel Fabre, *From Harlem to Paris: Black American Writers in France, 1840–1980* (1991), Elizabeth Hutton Turner, *American Artists in Paris, 1919–1929* (1988), and Shari Benstock, *Women of the Left Bank: Paris, 1900–1940* (1986). Especially because so few scholarly studies exist on any of these African American artists, it is necessary to understand each artist's individual experiences before effective comparisons about their work can be made. In the conclusion I examine the artists' shared backgrounds, patronage in the United States and in France, similar experiences in Paris, and artistic developments, and the impact that study abroad had on the rest of their careers.

This book may well have been a broader study of the experiences and work of all African American artists in Paris between the world wars. However, the strongest sense of community took place ca. 1927–1932, when most of these artists were there, and it seems as though there were no exhibitions by "New Negro" artists in Paris after 1932. Beginning in 1935, a few African American artists traveled abroad to study in more or less consecutive years—Rex Gorleigh and James Porter (ca. 1935–1936), Selma Burke (ca. 1936–1937), Lois Mailou Jones (1937–1938), and Clarence Lawson (ca. 1938–1939).[6] None of these seems to have interacted with any of the others while in Paris except in the most limited fashion, and Tanner no longer served as the unofficial host to aspiring African American artists; he had passed away in 1937 three months before the arrival of Jones. Further, aside from Jones, whose time in the French capital is well documented, there is very little material, verbal or visual, from or about the other artists' time in France. They did not receive significant critical attention in either France or the United States. Beyond this, 1935 marked the beginning of a new consciousness in the form of Négritude, with the publication of *L'étudiant noir* by Léopold Sédar Senghor, Aimé Césaire, and Léon Damas. Thus, this study focuses on the six artists who spent a substantial amount of time in Paris in the 1920s and 1930s, who produced important works of art there, who were identified as leading visual artists of the Harlem Renaissance, and who left an important legacy of their achievements for their students and others.

The subject of this volume has obvious connections to other issues such as European and European American depictions of black culture between the world wars; the French reception of black culture from the entire diaspora (especially vis-à-vis Josephine Baker); African American writers, musicians, and entertainers in Paris; the Pan-African movement in France; the broader context of the Harlem Renaissance; the role of French artists, critics, and patrons who were in tune with the African American community; the response of Africans, West Indians, and other black French citizens to African American artists in Paris; the experiences of expatriate artists in other countries; and so forth. Scholars have already published some of this material, and some of it may never be examined fully for lack of adequate resources. Given these factors, as well as space restrictions, this study necessarily has a specific focus, and only tangentially includes discussion of some of the above topics.

This is clearly an initial study, subject to revision and expansion as more information becomes available. Even as the book was going to press, I learned of additional works produced in Paris by Hayden and Woodruff in the private collections of Derrick Joshua Beard, the Hatch-Billops Collection, Corinne Jennings, and Michael Rosenfeld. It is hoped that a more comprehensive analysis of African American artists in Paris will include such images.

NEW NEGRO ARTISTS IN PARIS

1

THE DEBUT OF AFRICAN AMERICAN ARTISTS
IN PARIS, 1830–1914

*T*HE NEW ORLEANS CONNECTION, 1830–1855

In the early nineteenth century, when transatlantic travel was limited to the wealthy, the strongest connection between African Americans and France was in the New Orleans elite—*gens de couleur libres*—who by 1840 made up 20 percent of the population of one hundred thousand in the former colonial capital.[1] As literary scholar Michel Fabre has pointed out, the culture of free persons of color in New Orleans derived more from French traditions than from the New World context.[2] Although a 1724 law forbade French settlers to marry or cohabit with their female slaves, miscegenation (both voluntary and forced) was common in the eighteenth century. Since wealthy white immigrants often left fortunes to their children born out of wedlock, the *gens de couleur libres* gained powerful economic status in Louisiana, but were discriminated against by southern practice. Because there were few qualified black teachers and French whites were reluctant to instruct free black students, wealthy whites and mulattos sent their children of mixed descent to France for formal education. Several Creole writers, all French-speaking and many of French descent, among them B. Valcour, studied in Paris, and some, such as Victor Séjour and Louis and Camille Thierry, became expatriates in France.

At least four New Orleans Creole artists—Florville Foy, Julien Hudson, Jules Lion, and Eugène Warburg—studied in Paris before the Civil War.[3] They all had unmarried parents—prosperous, white, European-born fathers and mothers of African descent. Unfortunately, since few records about these artists have survived, little is known about their lives and work. In fact, there are fewer than two dozen pieces extant that are known to have

1

been produced by all African American artists in France in the nineteenth century. Art historical discourse on these artists has thus been limited to mostly biographical sketches. A brief look at the cultural and social situations of these Louisianian men will demonstrate that they held much in common, although they barely, if ever, interacted.

Florville Foy (1820–1903) was the son of Azélie Aubry (ca. 1795–1870), a free woman of color, and Prosper Foy (1787–1854), a white French-born marble cutter, sculptor, engraver, teacher of architecture, and slaveholder. Foy's father sent him to Paris in the mid-1830s, but where and with whom he studied is a mystery.[4] It is likely, however, that he was influenced by grave designs at the Père Lachaise cemetery. Upon his return to New Orleans, Foy took up his father's trade and became one of the leading marble-tomb cutters in Louisiana for the following sixty-five years, producing wall vaults, utilitarian tombs, and such funerary sculptures such as plaques, bas-reliefs, and carved decorative ornaments. His many commissions and transactions are well documented and his numerous signed works (mostly classical) can be found in the Saint Louis I, II, and III cemeteries and the Lafayette I, Cypress Grove, Greenwood, and Odd Fellows cemeteries in New Orleans.[5] Currently, only one of Foy's nonfunerary works, the charming neoclassical marble *Child with Drum*, ca. 1838, is known; it is now in the State Museum of Louisiana.

Jules Lion (ca. 1809–1866), a prolific printmaker, was born in France.[6] His lithographs were exhibited at the prestigious Paris Salons of 1831 (three prints), 1833 (*Affût aux canards* [Duck blind], which won honorable mention),[7] 1834 (four works, including a scene based on Victor Hugo's *Notre Dame de Paris*), and 1836 (prints after Van Dyck, Jacquand, Waltier, and Boulanger).

Lion immigrated to New Orleans, where the 1837 city directory lists him as a free man of color, a painter, and a lithographer; he worked in a lithography shop opened by *L'Abeille* (The bee) newspaper office. Lion visited Paris during the summer of 1839 when Louis-Jacques-Mandé Daguerre distributed a pamphlet detailing his invention of early photographic methods. By September, Lion was back in New Orleans producing daguerrean views of the city. Within months newspapers were praising the clear images he exhibited at the Saint Charles Museum. While Lion was credited with introducing the daguerreotype to New Orleans and he produced city scapes and sheet music illustrations,[8] his best-known work was a series of more than 150 fine lithographs of prominent Louisianians and other leaders, including Andrew Jackson, that he executed between 1837 and 1847.

Lion's only pastel work, *Asher Moses Nathan and Son* (1845, fig. 1), is a double portrait of a mulatto man and his white father. Art historian Regenia Perry suggests that the youth is Achille Lion, born out of wedlock to a woman of color who later became Jules Lion's wife, and Nathan (1784–1864), a Dutch Jewish immigrant and wealthy dry-goods merchant.[9] Perhaps to spare his white wife embarrassment and to give his children a European education, Nathan sent Achille and his sister, Anna, to Paris. After Nathan's wife died, he legally adopted Achille Lion and left his fortune to him and Anna.[10] Jules Lion portrayed his affluent stepson and natural father embracing; they seem to have had a cordial

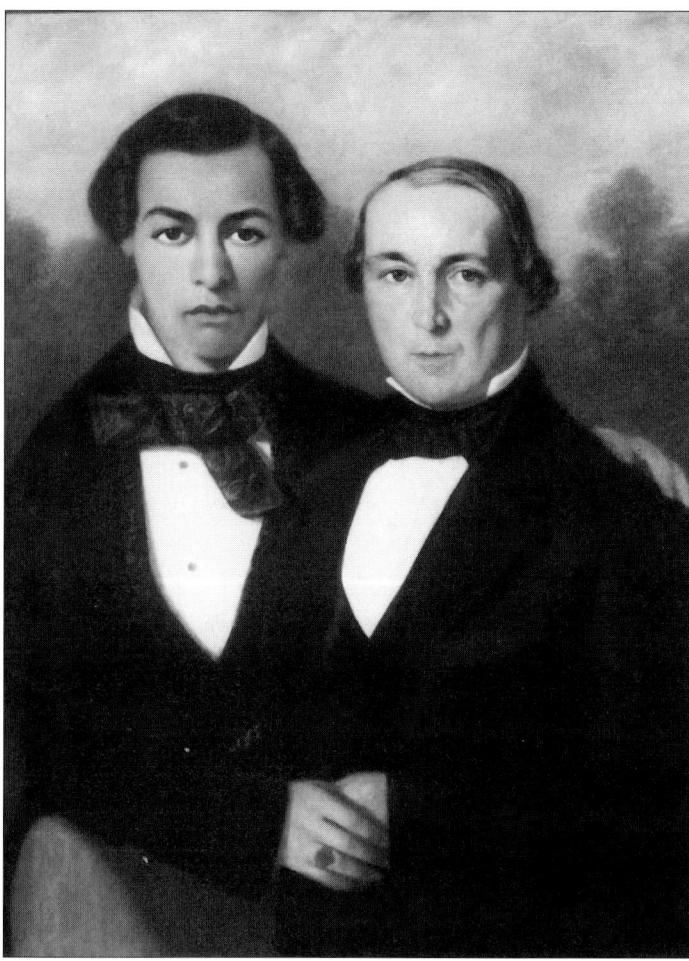

FIGURE 1
Jules Lion,
*Asher Moses Nathan
and Son,* 1845, pastel
on paper, 26 x 36 in.
Collection of Mr. and Mrs.
Jack O. Brittain Sr.

relationship. Art historian Judith Wilson suggests that the composition not only documents the actual paternity of Lion's stepson, but may also refer to the biracial artist's own mixed heritage.[11]

While both Lion and Foy were supported by their bourgeois, white fathers, who helped finance their education in Paris, and they developed highly successful businesses in New Orleans upon their return to the United States, there is no evidence that they ever met. Yet they were not alone; there were many other black artists in antebellum New Orleans, among them scenograph and ornamental painter Louis Pepite (active mid-1820s), sculptor Alexander Nelder (ca. 1823–ca. 1868); painters Alexandre Pickhil (active 1840s–1850s), known as the "Titian of New Orleans," and Felix Deville (active 1850s–1860s); and lithographer Louis Lucien Pessou (ca. 1825–1886).[12] It is not yet known whether any of these men traveled abroad, but many other black men in the arts did, such as actor Ira Aldridge and New Orleans musicians Eulalie de Mandeville, Lucien and Sidney Lambert, and Edmond Dédé.[13]

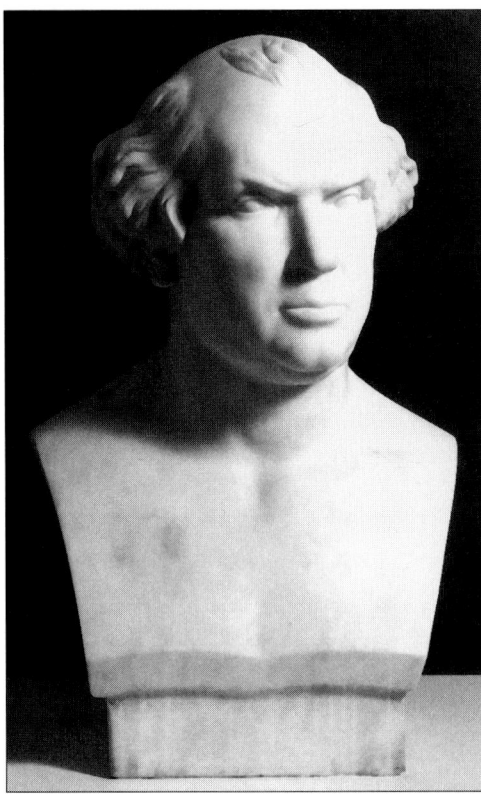

FIGURE 2
Eugène Warburg, *Portrait de S.E.*
[Son Excellence, John Young Mason],
le ministre des Etats-Unis à Paris, ca. 1855,
marble, 22½ in. (h).
Virginia Historical Society. Gift of Mrs. Fanny
Mason Cooke, 1927.21.

Sculptor Eugène Warburg (1826–1859), like Foy, was the son of a white immigrant, Daniel Warburg, and a Cuban mulatto slave, Marie Rose Blondeau, who was freed in the 1830s. He began his career as a marble cutter, along with his brother Daniel.[14] Warburg executed funerary sculpture, religious works, and busts of generals, magistrates, and other notables.[15] He also depicted Greek mythological subjects, such as Ganymede presenting nectar to Jove.[16] In the 1840s he studied in New Orleans with Philippe Garbeille, a French sculptor whose specialty was portrait busts, who no doubt encouraged his student to continue his training in France. Aided by an inheritance from the sale of his mother's slaves, Warburg set sail in late 1853. He soon found a studio in Montparnasse and began classes at the Ecole Nationale des Beaux-Arts under the direction of François Jouffroy. In 1855, four of his works were accepted by the Salon de Paris. These were two plaster pieces, *Un jeune pêcheur jouant avec un crabe* (A young fisherman playing with a crab) and *Un portrait,* and two marble busts, *Un portrait* and *Portrait de S.E. le ministre des Etats-Unis à Paris* (fig. 2).[17] The latter bust became Warburg's best known and only surviving work. The United States minister to France was "his excellency," John Young Mason (1799–1859), appointed by President Franklin Pierce in 1853. The Neoclassical portrait, executed from life, depicts Mason as a stern-faced, middle-aged man with a receding hair line and double chin.

Warburg received this commission from Mason through the aid of Pierre Soulé, a family friend, who provided the sculptor with a letter of introduction to the minister. In

1854 the three men were in Ostend, Belgium; Warburg probably modeled the bust at that time. Soulé, the U.S. minister to Spain, was working with Mason on the Ostend Manifesto in connection with the American acquisition of Cuba. Soulé feared the "Africanization" of Cuba and defended slavery in the United States.[18] Ironically, he supported Warburg, a man born a slave to a Cuban mulatto but freed by his German Jewish father when a young child.[19]

THE LURE OF ENGLAND, ITALY, CANADA, AND HAITI, 1856–1890

Unlike his predecessors who returned to New Orleans in the 1830s, Warburg remained in Europe for the rest of his life. From France, he traveled to England in 1856. There a British group sponsored by the Duchess of Sutherland commissioned him to design a series of bas-relief plaques depicting scenes from Harriet Beecher Stowe's novel *Uncle Tom's Cabin*. The following year, Warburg left London for Florence with letters of recommendation from the duchess, Stowe, and Soulé.[20] The Tuscan capital was renowned for its white American expatriate sculptors, among them Horatio Greenough, Hiram Powers, and others, but gradually became a way station for sculptors such as Randolph Rogers, William Wetmore Story, and William Henry Rinehart, who would stay longer in Rome.[21] Warburg soon moved there with his wife, only to die in January 1859. He may well have been the first expatriate African American artist.

Warburg's death just before the Civil War marked the end of an era of a racially based caste system in which free people of color enjoyed greater opportunities than did slaves. During the reconstruction period this boundary disappeared and it was extremely difficult for any black artist to make a living in the United States. Yet, more than two decades would pass before the next African American artist ventured to Paris. From 1860 to 1880, the Civil War and the Franco-Prussian War, among other events, prevented most American artists from studying in France. Americans continued to travel abroad, however, making the Grand Tour of Europe and lingering in England and Italy.[22] London had been the common destination abroad of American painters since the late eighteenth century. Benjamin West, John Singleton Copley, Mather Brown, John Trumbull, and others briefly visited Paris while touring the Continent, they but formed a community in London.[23] That situation was reversed by the end of the nineteenth century; London became a gateway for sculptors and painters en route to Rome and Paris, the new artistic centers of Europe.

About the middle of the nineteenth century, several British and American abolitionist groups began to back the work of African American artists at home and abroad. Antislavery patrons funded the artistic studies of Philadelphian portrait painter and daguerreotypist Robert M. Douglass Jr. (1809–1887).[24] He traveled to England with a letter of recommendation from the well-known white portrait painter Thomas Sully and with the support of the Grimké family.[25] Douglass also traveled frequently to the French-speaking West Indies from the late 1830s through the 1860s.[26] There, he completed a portrait of Nicolas Fabre Geffrard, president of the Republic of Haiti (1859–1867) and produced drawings of missionary stations in Jamaica.[27]

Cincinnati abolitionists supported Robert S. Duncanson when he made his Grand Tour of England, France, Switzerland, and Italy in 1853.[28] Duncanson would leave the United States again for three years to escape the Civil War; from 1863 until 1866, he traveled throughout Canada, Scotland, and England.[29] He would return to Canada for sketching trips in the summers of 1869 and 1870.[30] One of Duncanson's colleagues in Cincinnati, the highly successful daguerreotypist James P. Ball, sojourned in Paris and London in 1856, where he is said to have photographed Queen Victoria.[31] Ball may have taken his enormous antislavery panorama, *Ball's Splendid, Mammoth Pictorial Tour of the United States Comprising Views of the African Slave Trade; of Northern and Southern Cities; of Cotton and Sugar Plantations; of the Mississippi, Ohio and Susquehanna Rivers, Niagara Falls &C.*, painted by a number of African American artists, abroad for exhibition after showing it in Boston's Armory Hall in the spring of 1855 (the work has since disappeared).[32] It is possible that he was in London when Warburg was working on his series of bas-reliefs depicting scenes from *Uncle Tom's Cabin* and received a welcome from abolitionists in Britain, as he did in Massachusetts.[33]

Antislavery support primarily underwrote sculptor Edmonia Lewis's European travel in 1865. She sold sculptures and plaster copies of Colonel Robert Gould Shaw, the leader of black Civil War troops, and medallion portraits of John Brown. Unknowingly following Warburg's path, Lewis toured London, Paris, and Florence, then settled in Rome.[34] Although she returned to the United States in 1870–1871, 1873, 1876, and 1878,[35] she would remain a celebrated expatriate in Italy, producing works depicting emancipated African Americans, literary images of Native Americans, classical and Biblical figures, and historical scenes, such as the death of Cleopatra. Lewis, Ball, and Duncanson enjoyed exceptional patronage, but their success was atypical. Aside from Tanner, they seem to have been the only African American artists who spent significant periods in Western countries other than the United States and France before 1945. Some artists, such as landscapist Edward Mitchell Bannister (1828–1901) in Providence, Rhode Island, longed to go abroad during the 1870s and 1880s, but could not get the financial backing.[36]

By the 1880s, Americans were filtering back to France. After briefly visiting London in November 1881, Charles Ethan Porter (1847?–1923) went to Paris with a letter of introduction from American writer and humorist Mark Twain, a fellow resident of Connecticut.[37] In Hartford, Porter had auctioned off his still lifes and landscape paintings to raise money for a European sojourn.[38] Porter most likely hoped to develop his skill at such works at the renowned Ecole des Beaux-Arts. He lived on the same avenue as the école in Paris; however, no record exists for Porter's attendance at the institution and he did not exhibit his work in France.[39] While abroad, Porter executed angular nudes, a shimmering landscape of haystacks, and floral still lifes.[40] *Still Life with Flowers* (ca. 1883), with its full pink blossoms casually dropping from a glistening vase on a table before a neutral background, is reminiscent of still life compositions by Henri Fantin-Latour. It is likely that Porter was familiar with the French flower painter's work; they both lived on the rue des Beaux-Arts and Fantin-Latour regularly exhibited at the Salon.[41] However, further information is necessary to determine Porter's mentors abroad.

In 1882 Porter wrote to Twain that he was doing well, but a year later he announced that if he received no commissions, he would have to come back to the United States.[42] He returned to Hartford with almost no funds in March 1884 and was to suffer monetary difficulties for the rest of his life. Porter continued to win praise from newspaper critics for his depictions of flowers and fruit, but his paintings brought low prices. In addition to being a great personal disappointment, Porter's rejection by the Paris Salon may have harmed his career, since American artists often got much publicity from exhibiting their Salon pieces. Nevertheless, upon his return to the United States, Porter sold enough paintings to be an independent artist, maintaining studios in Hartford, New York, and in his hometown of Rockville, Connecticut until his death in 1923.

HENRY O. TANNER AND HIS FOLLOWERS, 1891–1914

The remarkable career of Henry Ossawa Tanner (1858–1937) has been well documented in several dissertations and in a retrospective exhibition at and a catalog by the Philadelphia Museum of Art.[43] In brief, this son of an African Methodist Episcopal bishop emigrated from Philadelphia, where he had studied at the Pennsylvania Academy of Fine Arts in the early 1880s, to France and became an expatriate, as well as the most celebrated African American artist of his day. In 1881 an unidentified man offered to finance a study trip to Rome via London for the young painter; however, the journey did not materialize and Tanner did not go overseas until a decade later. In 1891 he went to Paris via London on his way to Rome, but after a week he was so enchanted by the city that he decided to make it his permanent home. Tanner studied with Jean-Paul Laurens and Benjamin Constant at the Académie Julian from 1892 to 1896. There he developed his signature style of luminous blue-green light in landscapes and biblical scenes. From 1894, his works were exhibited virtually every year in the Salon de Paris and in museums and galleries throughout the United States. In 1897 the French government purchased his painting *The Resurrection of Lazarus* (1896), which had won a third-class medal at the Salon, for the Luxembourg Museum. Among the numerous honors that followed were Tanner's election as an associate member, and later full academician, of the National Academy of Design in New York (1909), and as president of the Société Artistique de Picardie (Le Touquet, Paris-Plage, 1913), and memberships in the Paris Society of American Painters (1908) and the American Negro Academy in Washington, D.C. (1914).

As an internationally respected painter, Tanner naturally drew to France African American artists who hoped to benefit from his words of advice. From the late 1890s until Tanner's death in 1937, students flocked to his homes in Paris and Trépied. Those who made the trek at the turn of the century included Annie E. A. Walker, Meta Vaux Warrick Fuller, William A. Harper, and William Edouard Scott.

It seems that the first African American woman who went to Paris to study art was Annie E. Anderson Walker (1855–1926) in 1896. She was born in Flatbush, Brooklyn,[44] and presumably worked in the New York area during her early career. By 1883, Walker had moved to Washington, D.C., and married a lawyer, Thomas Walker.[45] In 1892, however, she began to take classes at Cooper Union in New York. It is likely that her professor, Thomas Eakins, told Walker how well his former pupil, Henry O. Tanner, was doing in Paris. No written communication between the African American artists exists, but it is highly probable that the two were aware of each other and met in France.

After receiving her diploma from Cooper Union in 1895, Walker studied at the Académie Julian from 1896 to 1902.[46] There, she worked from plaster busts of classical sculpture, as well as from live models. Walker excelled in pastel portraiture, and her three-quarters portrait *La Parisienne* (fig. 3) of 1896 was exhibited at the Salon that year.[47] Once back in the United States, however, she quickly faded into obscurity as a homemaker. Despite this, and her severe bronchial asthma, Walker continued to list herself as an artist in city directories[48] and offer drawing classes from her home.

While Walker was still in Paris, sculptor Meta Vaux Warrick Fuller (1877–1968) arrived. A native of Philadelphia like Tanner, Fuller won a three-year scholarship to the Pennsylvania Museum School for Industrial Art. She graduated with honors in 1899, winning the Crozer first prize in sculpture. Friends and professors urged Fuller to continue her studies abroad. She received her mother's consent after an uncle offered to ask Tanner to look after Fuller in France.[49]

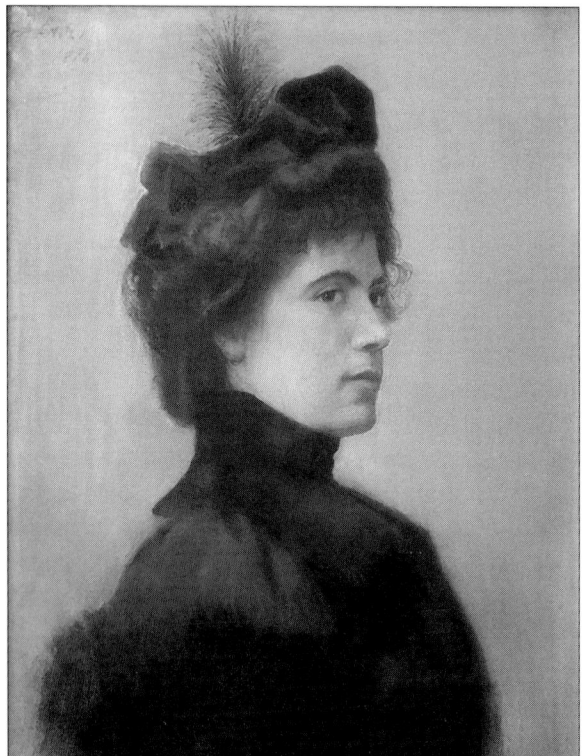

FIGURE 3
Annie E. A. Walker, *La Parisienne*, 1896, pastel on paper. 19¼ x 25½ in. Howard University Gallery of Art, Washington, D.C.

Like Porter and Tanner, Fuller passed through London en route to Paris. In England she heard the Fisk University Jubilee Singers perform and was deeply moved by the spirituals.[50] Later, she would be among the first to depict African American culture in sculpture.

In late October 1899 Fuller arrived in Paris. Tanner missed meeting her at the railway depot, but presented himself to her at the American Girls' Club the next day just as Fuller was writing a letter to the American consul expressing her indignation at being denied lodging at the club because of her race.[51] Fuller soon became a good friend of the Tanners.

The guilt-stricken director of the American Girls' Club placed Fuller in a hotel and introduced her to Augustus Saint-Gaudens. Upon the artist's advice, Fuller studied privately with Raphael Collin and subsequently worked at the Académie Colarossi with Injalbert, Gaugi, and Rollard. In 1902 Tanner served as one of the judges for the annual exhibition of the American Women's Art Association. At the very hostel that had refused her board, Fuller's bust *John the Baptist* (ca. 1901) was displayed; it was also reproduced in the *New York Herald* Paris edition.[52] Although many painters exhibited their work, the newspaper reported that Fuller had "the distinction of being the only sculptor represented."

One of Fuller's classmates at Colarossi was the German painter Paula Modersohn-Becker. It is likely that the latter's close friend Clara Westhoff Rilke, the wife of the poet and Rodin biographer Rainer Maria Rilke, arranged for Fuller to meet the celebrated sculptor Auguste Rodin.[53] In the summer of 1901 Fuller went to Rodin's studio in Meudon, bearing photographs of her work and a small clay sketch of *Secret Sorrow* (or *Man Eating His Own Heart*), a figure based on Stephen Crane's poem.[54] The master praised Fuller's efforts and invited her to return for further criticism. With Rodin's sponsorship, Fuller began to receive wider notice. The art dealer Samuel Bing exhibited twenty-two of her sculptures at his L'Art Nouveau Gallery in June 1902. *The Wretched*, a group of seven figures depicted with physical and mental disabilities, as well as other macabre pieces such as *Carrying the Dead Body* and *Oedipus*, earned Fuller distinction as a "delicate sculptor of horrors" from the French press.[55] Fuller later enlarged a plaster model of *The Impenitent Thief*, which she had exhibited at Bing's gallery. Although she never finished the piece, Rodin believed that it deserved a place in the Société Nationale des Beaux-Arts Salon, and he engineered its acceptance there in April 1903.[56] Fuller never saw that exhibition; with her mother's permission she had extended her stay in Paris by more than a year, then returned home in the fall of 1902.

Like Walker, Fuller found that her professional career slowed down considerably after her marriage, in her case in 1909 to the Liberian neurologist Solomon C. Fuller. Nonetheless, as a passionate believer in equal rights, she continued sculpting, receiving numerous commissions and awards from African American and women's groups. In 1922 the New York Making of America Exposition displayed her *Ethiopia Awakening* (perhaps first created in plaster in 1914) (fig. 4), a bronze sculpture of an upright woman wearing the headdress of an ancient Egyptian queen and shedding mummy cloths. This Pan-Africanist

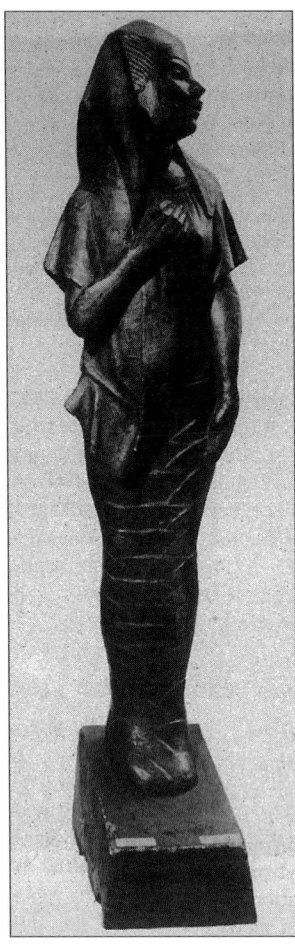

FIGURE 4
Meta Vaux Warrick Fuller, *Ethiopia Awakening,* ca. 1914–1920,
bronze, 67 x 16 x 20 in.
Art and Artifacts Division. Schomburg Center for Research
in Black Culture, The New York Public Library, Astor, Lenox,
and Tilden Foundations.

work symbolized the strength of womanhood, the emergence of nationhood, and the birth
of what Alain Locke would three years later call the "New Negro." Fuller's interest in her
African heritage was encouraged by the philosopher W.E.B. Du Bois, whom she had met in
Paris in 1900. He had been in France for the Pan-African conference and the Negro Exhibit
that he had arranged as part of the Paris Exposition. Du Bois had urged Fuller to depict their
black heritage and culture by making "a specialty of Negro types."[57]

It was not easy to respond to Du Bois's call for racially representative images. Those
who could afford to buy art, mostly bourgeois white people, were not interested in images of
sophisticated black people that might challenge the status quo. As Porter and Tanner had
discovered, such politically neutral subjects as landscapes, still lifes, and biblical scenes had a
much wider market appeal. Painters William Harper and William Edouard Scott were well
aware of this dilemma as they began their careers abroad.

William A. Harper (1873–1910) was an acclaimed landscape painter at the turn of
the century, thought by some to be "more creatively original than Tanner."[58] He completed
his best-known work, *Afternoon at Montigny* (ca. 1905, fig. 5), in France; it won a thirty-

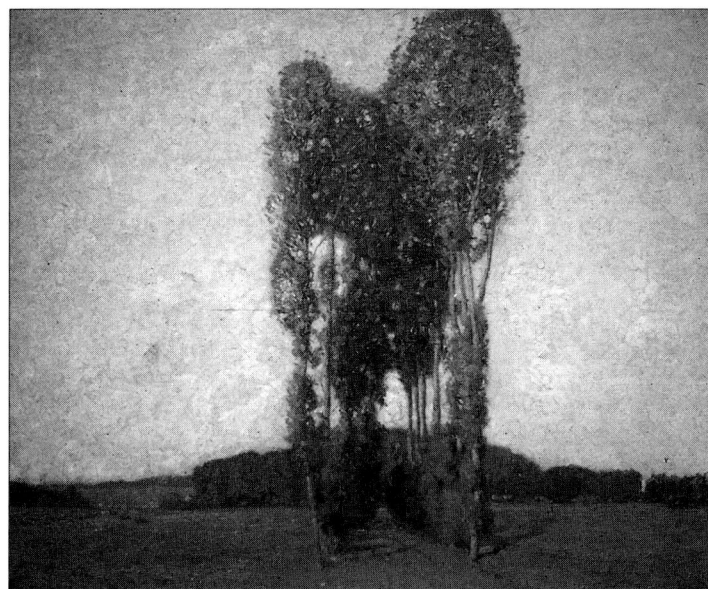

FIGURE 5
William Harper,
Afternoon at Montigny,
ca. 1905, oil on canvas,
23 x 28 in.
Howard University
Gallery of Art,
Washington, D.C.

dollar special prize for most worthy landscape at the Chicago Artists Exposition in 1905.[59]
Harper's work was included in numerous exhibitions thereafter, but his promising talent was
cut short by his premature death, at the age of thirty-five.

A Canadian by birth, Harper moved to Illinois in the early 1880s. He graduated
from the Art Institute of Chicago in 1900 with second honors.[60] That year three of his
paintings, *August, The Meadows,* and *Midday,* were seen by thousands at the institute and
praised as "among the most perfect in the exhibition."[61]

Like most of his classmates, Harper longed to study abroad, but lacked financial
support. He saved money while teaching drawing at the public schools in Houston, Texas.[62]
In 1903 he arrived in Paris and immediately threw himself into his studies at the Académie
Julian (see fig. 6). He rose before dawn to begin work, then went to the Louvre to copy
masterpieces by Millet and Dupré.[63] Harper's diligence so impressed his classmates Arthur
Krehbiel and Leon Gruenhagen, they nominated him for the American Art Association.
However, thirteen members argued strenuously against the recommendation and he was
never admitted.[64] About the same time, Tuskegee Institute offered Harper a position as
instructor of drawing.[65] Realizing that Harper's chances for success would be slim in the
segregated South, Krehbiel urged Harper to settle in Europe.

Harper must have considered expatriation, but he was suffering from severe financial
constraints. Bolstered by the exhibition at the Chicago Artists Association in 1904 of English
landscapes he had produced before going to France,[66] Harper returned to the Cornish coast
that spring after a short sketching trip to the Barbizon area, near Paris. He hoped to raise
funds with sales of more British and French landscapes and returned to Chicago in 1905 to
promote his work. That year, he won the Municipal Art League Prize from the Art Institute

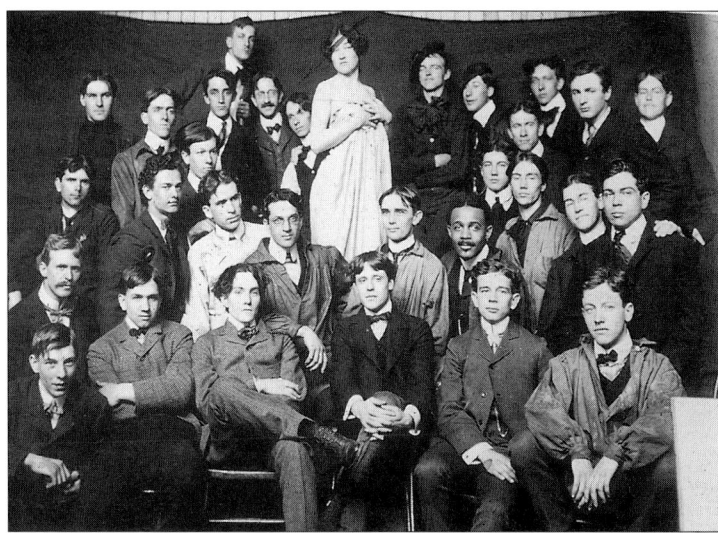

FIGURE 6
William A. Harper,
fourth from left in
the second row, at
Académie Julian, 1904.
Photo from
Robert Guinan,
*Krehbiel: Life and Work
of an American Artist.*

of Chicago.[67] In October, Harper first saw Tanner's works at the art institute.[68] In 1906 Harper's landscapes were included in three separate exhibitions and lauded in the press.[69] Apparently, Harper made enough money to continue his studies abroad, for he was back in Paris in 1907. This time he sought and received Tanner's criticism.[70]

Harper's funds ran out within a year and he went to live with or near his family in Decatur, Illinois. Continuing to exhibit his paintings despite failing health, in October 1909 Harper sought the benefits of a warmer climate in Cuernevaca, Mexico.[71] Five months later he died of tuberculosis at the American Hospital in Mexico City.[72]

One year after Harper left Paris in 1908, William Edouard Scott (1884–1964) arrived (fig. 7). The two may have heard of each other at the Chicago Art Institute; Scott was a student at the school from 1904 to 1908.[73] Otto Stark, a respected landscape painter and chair of the art department at Manual Training High School in Indianapolis, and who had studied in Paris, advised Scott to further his education at the institute and abroad.[74] Scott planned on becoming a sculptor, but partially supported himself through school as an illustrator for magazines such as *Redbook* and *Printer,* and as a muralist for five public schools in Chicago.[75] He won a number of awards, including the Frederick Magnus Brand first prize for pictorial composition.[76] After graduating from the Chicago Art Institute in 1908, he worked as an instructor at his former high school for one year to finance a two-year sojourn in France, Holland, and Italy.[77]

Like Tanner, Walker, and Harper, Scott studied at the Académie Julian (1909–1910). Like Harper, he soon suffered monetary problems. When Tanner learned of his predicament, he invited Scott to stay at his home in Etaples.[78] With Tanner's tutelage, Scott succeeded in showing three paintings at the Salon des Beaux-Arts at Toquet in 1911.[79]

Scott returned to Chicago for a short time to raise more money, then went back to Paris in late 1911. The following spring, his painting *La pauvre voisine* (The poor neighbor)

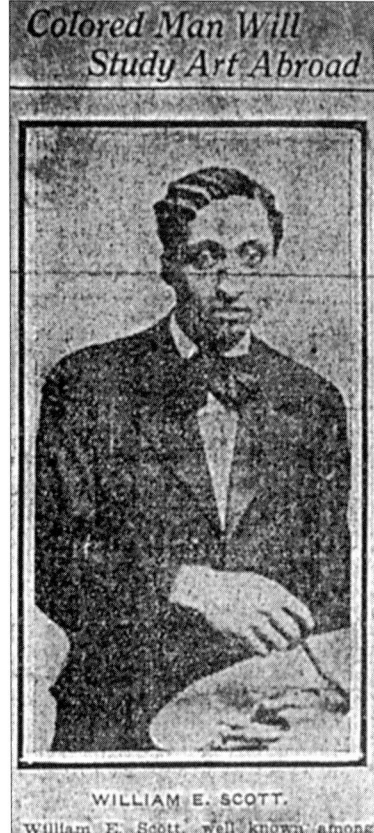

FIGURE 7
"Colored Man Will Study Art Abroad," with photograph
of William E. Scott, 1909. Newspaper clipping.

was accepted by the Salon[80] and commended by French journalists; it was reproduced in
newspapers, and even in full color on postcards.[81] No doubt the publicity played a major role
in the purchase of the painting by the Argentine Republic. The six-hundred-dollar income
allowed Scott to stay in France through the summer. In the fall of 1912, he exhibited twenty-
six of his paintings at the Indianapolis Otto Stark Studio. The show was an artistic,
commercial, and social triumph. A group of proud African Americans in Scott's hometown
purchased *Rainy Day, Etaples,* 1912, which depicts a street in the town where Tanner's
studio was located in Normandy, and presented it to the permanent collection of the Herron
Art Institute.[82] With this and other sales, Scott could afford his third trip abroad.

It is likely that Scott went to England at this time. In 1913 he exhibited *Silver Sun
at Boulogne* at the Royal Academy in London, as well as *Le connoisseur* at Salon La Loque in
France, and three paintings at the Salon de la Société Artistique de Picardie (Le Touquet,
Paris-Plage).[83] During this period, Scott studied for several months at the Académie
Colarossi during the summer, then for four months at the Académie Julian, and next for a
few months with Tanner. He completed his European training in April 1914.

Just three months after Scott's departure from France, two other African American artists, Laura Wheeler Waring (1887–1948), on the Grand Tour funded by a Cresson Travelling Scholarship from the Pennsylvania Academy of Fine Arts,[84] and (possibly) Robert H. Hemmings (1882–1955), who exhibited a painting, *Les deux soeurs*, at the Société des Artistes Français that spring,[85] fled Paris at the outbreak of the war in 1914.[86]

Tanner and his family were evacuated from the village of Trépied to England, but were able to return to France two weeks later. Unfortunately, the artist lost his creative spark. Instead, he volunteered with the American Red Cross from winter 1917 to June 1919.[87] One of Tanner's few wartime works, *Intersection of Roads, Neufchâteau, World War I* (1918) with its doughboy waving to travelers at twilight, signals a crossroads—a symbolic farewell to the nineteenth-century tradition of African American artists in Paris and a greeting to the twentieth-century adventure. By 1925, Tanner's active career was essentially over, but his international reputation soared, especially after he received the prestigious Cross of the Legion of Honor from the French government in 1923.[88] The renowned painter would remain a strong magnet for African American artists in Paris who sought his advice until his death in 1937.

The debut of African American artists in Paris was composed of three distinct periods. From 1830 until 1855, free men of color from French Louisiana in New Orleans studied at academies with European-born instructors and exhibited in Paris financed by their white fathers. Upon their return to the United States, Foy and Lion developed highly successful business ventures. Lion produced portraits of and Foy funerary monuments for wealthy whites, but they seem to have depicted virtually no African American subject matter.

From 1856 to 1890, self-taught midwestern and New England artists generally made brief stops in France and worked independently for years in England, Italy, Canada, and Haiti, financed by white (and abolitionist, ca. 1830–1865) patronage. None of them exhibited in France, but they achieved international reputations based in part on their experiences abroad. They executed landscapes and portraits, but their work also reflected their racial heritage: from Douglass's abolitionist paintings to Warburg's bas-reliefs, Duncanson's scenes from *Uncle Tom's Cabin*, Ball's daguerreotypes of Frederick Douglass and middle-class black Cincinnatians to Lewis's sculptures of Native Americans, African Americans, and Egyptians.

Finally, from 1891 to 1914, bourgeois, light-skinned African Americans from northern cities—Philadelphia, Indianapolis, Chicago, and Washington, D.C.—sojourned abroad, encouraged by their European-trained, white male university professors, and financed by some white supporters, but mostly by their families and their hard-earned savings. In the wake of Henry O. Tanner's international success, artists began to flock to Paris to attend classes at Julian and Colarossi academies and to exhibit their works at the Salon and other prestigious French galleries. Tanner produced primarily religious works and Harper and Scott produced mostly landscapes. Tanner and Fuller also did portraits, as did Walker, and some limited African American genre scenes. Study and exhibition in Paris won these artists solid, lifelong reputations that led to honors, scholarships, and private and high school teaching positions in the United States. While few of these pioneers ever knew one another personally, together they paved the way for the success of African American artists in Paris after World War I.

Many questions still remain regarding these pioneering artists in Paris that may never be fully answered. For instance, to what extent were they segregated from their European contemporaries, and was that isolation conditioned by others or self-imposed? With whom did they associate in Paris and how aware were they of the legacy of African Americans in that city? How did complicated attitudes toward race and nation in France impact the content and style of their work abroad? Why does so much of their art seem conservative, even retrograde, compared to the contemporary Parisian scene, especially at the end of the nineteenth century and the beginning of the twentieth? Similar issues, regarding those artists in Paris ca. 1922–1934, will be explored in depth in the following chapters.

2
THE ARTISTIC CAREER OF A NEAR EXPATRIATE:
NANCY ELIZABETH PROPHET IN PARIS, 1922–1934

*A*side from Henry O. Tanner and Albert Alexander Smith, both expatriates who would die in France, Nancy Elizabeth Prophet (1890–1960) spent more time in Paris—twelve years—than all of the other African American artists who were there between the world wars. In fact, the years of her arrival and departure, 1922 and 1934, flank those of the others. Along with Edmonia Lewis, who expatriated to Rome in the 1860s, and Meta Vaux Warrick Fuller, who studied in Paris, 1899–1903, she was one of the first African American sculptors to make a career abroad and receive critical international acclaim. As such, it would seem that Prophet would have been a magnet for other African American artists in search of guidance in France, but apparently she met only sculptor Augusta Savage, in 1929 in Paris at the request of Du Bois, and had little to do with her.

Prophet was a strong individualist with high ideals, yet also a lonely, insecure woman who relished solitude and was haunted by the threat of mediocrity and the reality of poverty. Often ill and on the brink of starvation for more than a decade, she nonetheless persevered and exhibited her work at prestigious Salons both in France and in the United States. Her meditative heads, figurative sculptures, and bas-reliefs were exhibited at the Salon d'Automne, the Société des Artistes Français, the Harmon Foundation, the Rhode Island School of Design—her alma mater—the Newport Art Association, the Boston Society of Independent Artists, and Fifty-Sixth Street Galleries in New York, among other places. Such influential, wealthy white women as Gertrude Vanderbilt Whitney, Eleanor Green, and Louise Brooks, in Newport, Providence, Boston, and New York, bought her sculptures. Yet this patronage was not enough to sustain Prophet, particularly in the wake of the Great

Depression. At the behest of W.E.B. Du Bois and John Hope, president of Atlanta University, Prophet left Paris to accept a teaching position at Spelman College in 1934.

While abroad, Prophet worked primarily in wood, favoring cherry, sycamore, ebony, and pear, as well as marble, but also in bronze, alabaster, granite, terra-cotta, plaster, and clay. She also lightly painted some of her bas-relief carvings, occasionally adding gold highlights. She made a conscious effort to document all of her work and in Paris diligently transported each piece to an arrondissement adjacent to her, to be photographed in black and white. Those images (now in the library at Rhode Island College), fewer than two dozen, in addition to fewer than ten of Prophet's works in ascertained collections, seem to be all that remain of most of her sculpture. Unfortunately, the photographed works are in the main undated and untitled, thus difficult to place chronologically and stylistically. Yet their subjects—meditative portraits of black men, as well as androgynous, and sometimes racially ambiguous, busts and figures—express two main themes of black modernism: modernity and romanticism.

Because no works made before the time Prophet lived in Paris, and only a few produced afterward, seem to be extant and because she died intestate and childless and the whereabouts of most of her papers and works is unknown, it is difficult to say how or even if her time abroad changed her entire oeuvre. Despite the records of Prophet's diary—composed of infrequent and brief entries—and numerous letters to Du Bois and a few others, there is still much information missing about those twelve years. What can be said, though, is that it is only after Prophet achieved recognition from the French through the acceptance of her work in Salons and critical reviews that audiences in the United States recognized her talent as well. It seems that only after Prophet had been in Paris for several years she began to depict black subjects. Yet American critics were more interested in these works because of her ethnic background than were the French, despite her protestations that she was "not a negro."[1] Prophet may have been involved in masking her identity in other ways; for instance, her name appears as the male "Eli" in an exhibition catalog in 1927. Whether this was by Prophet's choice or an error on the part of the exhibitors remains unknown, as does so much about the sculptor. An intensely private woman, she likely would have relished the continuing mysteries.

ARTISTIC BEGINNINGS: PROVIDENCE, RHODE ISLAND, 1890–1922

Elizabeth Prophet (fig. 8) was born Nancy Elizabeth Proffitt on March 19, 1890, in Warwick, Rhode Island, the second child of Rosa E. Walker Proffitt and William H. Proffitt.[2] It seems that Prophet changed the spelling of her surname after she went to Paris, perhaps as a way of disassociating herself from her family members, who were not particularly supportive of her artistic career. She may have also seen herself as a prophet, or at least as someone who was divinely inspired and gifted.

Prophet's paternal grandmother was Narraganset-Pequot Native American; she had bought her husband out of slavery. Prophet's father, originally from South Scituate, Rhode

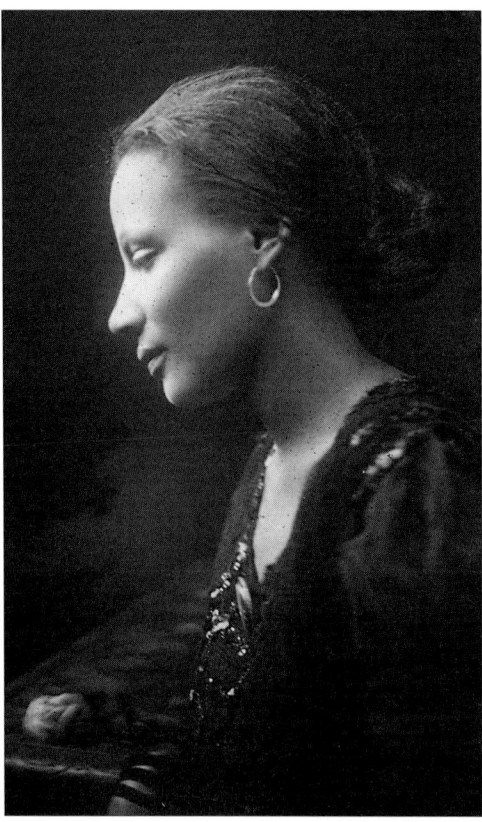

FIGURE 8
Nancy Elizabeth Prophet, ca. 1919.
Photographer unknown.
Nancy Elizabeth Prophet Collection,
James P. Adams Library, Rhode Island College.

Island,[3] worked initially as a horseman for the city of Warwick,[4] then later as a laborer
for the Providence Parks Department. Prophet's mother, a homemaker from Cranston,
Rhode Island, was of mixed African American descent.[5] Prophet's parents did not encourage
her in the visual arts. They reportedly considered art to be frivolous, and forbade it,
forcing their daughter to paint or draw secretly.[6] Although her parents did not support
her artistic goals, she apparently respected them, their "extraordinary energy, wisdom, and
activity."[7]

Little is known about Prophet's adolescence other than that she attended the
predominately white Saint Stephen's Church Episcopal in Providence.[8] She received her
primary and secondary education through the Warwick school system[9] and private tutors.[10]
From the age of fifteen, she was self-supporting, and paid for her education herself;[11] an
acquaintance of hers recalled that she worked as a housekeeper for a private family on the
fashionable East Side in Providence while a young woman.[12]

In September 1913 Prophet entered the Rhode Island School of Design (RISD),
paying the tuition "out of her menial savings"[13] and by working summers,[14] perhaps in the
school's kitchen.[15] It seems that Prophet's parents could not or would not help with her
college education; a newspaper article stated that she encountered "family indifference"[16]
in her early career. Apparently Prophet's parents maintained their bias against art and
discouraged her in her efforts, suggesting that she instead become a "maid-servant" or a

teacher "among her people."[17] Although Prophet made a mask of her father's face in her youth, he apparently never saw her art again until 1945, when he was eighty-eight years old.[18] The president of RISD, Eliza Greene Radeke (1857–1931), however, "gave generously toward her advancement."[19]

Prophet partly credited RISD for her later success, declaring that it was recognized abroad as a school of high standing.[20] Reserved and self-conscious, she worked diligently, keeping to herself.[21] L. Earl Rowe, then director of RISD, had her "progress constantly under observation" and found Prophet to be "a person of ability considerably above average . . . a person of imagination and ability."[22] Prophet seems to have been the only African American student at RISD,[23] but she was one of many women; most college-age men were serving in World War I. Few if any of Prophet's classmates objected to, or even much noticed, her presence, but one classmate noted that Prophet identified herself as Native American rather than African American; "She said she was Indian, but Yankees thought, oh yes, she's saying that because she doesn't want to say she's Negro."[24] Like the nineteenth-century sculptor Edmonia Lewis, who was also of Native American and African American descent, Prophet may have embraced her Native American identity more than her African American heritage because Native Americans were not enslaved to the same extent.

Among Prophet's instructors at RISD was Albert Henry Atkins (d. 1951), whose architectural sculptures adorned churches in Connecticut, New York, Massachusetts, Minnesota, Pennsylvania, and Washington, D.C.[25] Since Atkins had studied at Julian and Colarossi in Paris, he may have urged his pupils to study abroad as well.

On January 30, 1915, Prophet married Francis Ford, the son of a waiter, in an Episcopal ceremony.[26] He was thirty-four years old, she twenty-four. Ford's family had originally come from Maryland; he graduated from Hope High School in Providence in 1900. He was the only African American student to complete the classical course of study, and while there he also founded the school's athletic association. Prophet apparently felt ambivalent about the marriage; few people knew about their relationship[27] or the fact that Prophet's father helped support them.[28]

Although she had studied sculpture, Prophet graduated from RISD—as Elizabeth Proffitt Ford—in 1918 with a degree in freehand drawing and painting and a specific interest in portraiture.[29] She continued to take classes at RISD for one year.[30] For several years thereafter, Prophet tried to earn a living by making portraits, to no avail. One East Side resident recalled sitting for Prophet, but she never saw the portrait.[31]

It was difficult for Prophet to make money in the visual arts in Providence. Apparently, she continued to work menial jobs while creating work and submitting it to local exhibitions. When one white group accepted her work, with the proviso, however, that she not attend the opening and "mingle socially," Prophet withdrew her entry in protest.[32] Later, a wealthy American asked her to submit designs and prices for a fountain group. Hoping to economize, the patron suggested that Prophet use inexpensive materials. The artist refused the job, after responding that if she were able to commission a work of art, gold would not be too precious a medium for casting.[33] Frustrated with the lack of opportunities in Providence, she went to New York, but found little opportunity there, either.[34] In the summer of either 1921 or 1922, Prophet fled to Paris on the S.S. *La France* (fig. 9), leaving her husband behind.

IN SILENCE AND DISCONTENT: THE FIRST FIVE YEARS IN PARIS, AUGUST 1922–MAY 1927

The soul of me, let me not waver, or lose courage.
    —Prophet diary (April 3, 1926)

Prophet arrived alone in Paris on August 11 in either 1921 or 1922 with roughly 350 dollars.[35] She had saved 1,000 dollars for the trip, but lent about half of it "to a worthless brother" and paid for her fare and a few other things with the balance.[36] After obtaining a studio, at 36, avenue du Châtillon in Montparnasse, she took to her bed with nervous exhaustion and stayed there for the first two months. Prophet was so weak that she could hardly walk down the stairs to get groceries. She had hoped she would be friends with Mabel Tillinghast Gardner (b. 1892), who had a studio leading off the same courtyard. Gardner, a white woman, had been in the same high school graduating class as Ford[37] and had attended classes at RISD.[38] However, Prophet wrote, "She hated me the moment we met, so I closed the door on her, and decided to stay to myself. She is a person who is sick with envy."[39] In a moment of weakness, Prophet wrote to her husband asking him to join her, a decision she would later regret. "Two people instead of one in a strange land to live on three hundred and eighty dollars," she lamented, "neither speaking the language."[40] Ford paid for his voyage by selling furniture bought by Prophet's father that his wife had put in storage.[41]

As soon as she could stand again, Prophet went to work on her first piece of sculpture, "sick, but with a dogged determination to conquer" and "with a calm assurance and a savage pleasure of revenge." The physical activity gave her strength and confidence: "I remember how sure I was that it [the sculpture] was going to be a living thing, a master stroke, how my arms felt as I swung them up to put on a piece of clay. I was conscious of a great rhythm as they swung through the air, they seemed so long and powerful."[42]

Prophet worked on the sculpture in the studio of a French woman whose atelier, adjacent to the courtyard, was better lit. When the neighbor returned from classes at the Ecole des Beaux-Arts, she shared her five o'clock tea with cakes or toast with Prophet. This was practically the sculptor's only food. Unaware of her American acquaintance's indigence, the student "kept up a gay chattering and laughter" in which Prophet did her best to partake (a challenge, especially when just learning a new language), but, she recalled, "how empty I felt at times." Her pride kept her from taking the French woman into her confidence.

For a month Prophet labored on her sculpture in the morning, then all day the following month. Two weeks before the piece was completed, however, she ran out of money and food and her neighbor offered no refreshments. Desperate for sustenance, she waited until the French woman left the studio one morning, then stole a piece of meat and a potato from her neighbor's dog's food bowl. Later, she found the incident "humorous." She

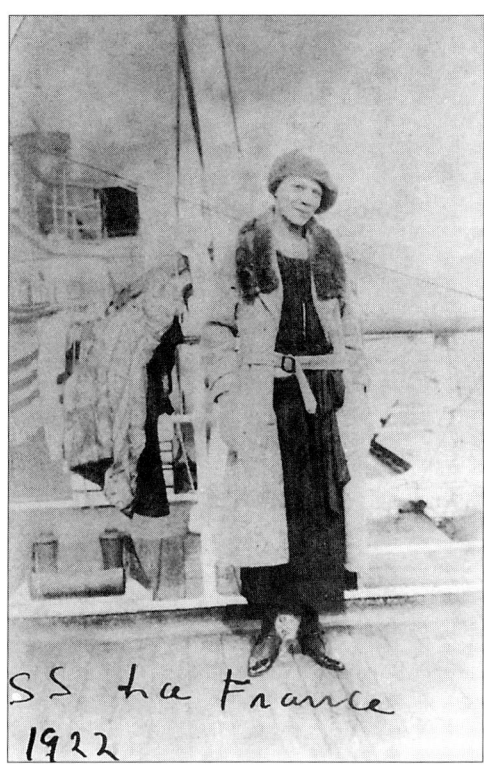

recalled: "For the first time in my life I was hungry, but this seemed of little importance in comparison to finishing the bust. It was even interesting to see how I felt each day, my mind was very clear[,] I could think with a great ease, though my belt was always dropping down around my feet." Prophet finished casting the bust (the identity if the subject is now unknown) in plaster at 2:00 a.m.

The day after Prophet finished her bust, Ellen Barrows, whom she had seen only once before (nothing else is known about Barrows's identity) called on her and invited her to dinner. Prophet gladly accepted and informed Barrows that she had not eaten for two weeks. During dinner, the lonely Barrows invited Prophet to live with her in Versailles and offered to give her a stipend so that she could travel to Paris daily to work in her studio. Prophet accepted. Barrows then tried to persuade Prophet to leave her husband (who had arrived in Paris) "since he was unfit to do anything" for her, but the sculptor was not ready to do so. She visited him every day (he stayed elsewhere in Paris), although she had decided that he was "a good man but completely helpless, without ambition, without hope, character, personality and of a fearful nature." After three months of living together, the women quarreled. It seems that Barrows wanted Prophet as an exotic companion who could lure men for possible romantic liaisons: "She wanted me for the attraction of men. I left her." In any case, Prophet moved into another studio with her husband. The proprietor of the building found Ford a position that paid a small wage and it seems the two were able to survive on that for some time.

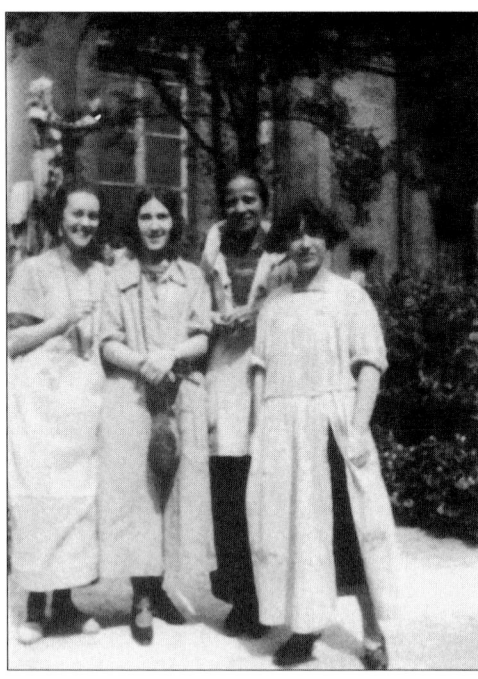

FIGURE 10
Nancy Elizabeth Prophet with classmates
at the Ecole des Beaux-Arts, Paris, 1924.
Nancy Elizabeth Prophet Collection,
James P. Adams Library, Rhode Island College.
Photographer unknown.

From the fall of 1922 or 1923 until the spring of 1924 or 1925 Prophet studied
with the noted sculptor Victor Joseph Jean Ambroise Ségoffin (1867–1925) at the Ecole
Nationale des Beaux-Arts (fig. 10). Ségoffin, officer of the Legion of Honor and winner of
the Prix de Rome in 1897, was a sculptor known for his numerous statues, tombs, and
portrait busts (of such painters as Léon Bonnat, H. Harpignies, and Félix Ziem), which were
frequently bought by the state.[43] Under Ségoffin's tutelage, Prophet completed two busts,
one of which may have been a wooden version of the bust she had created the previous year;
she wrote simply, "I cut the bust in wood."[44]

Prophet's wooden bust (identity and location now unknown) was exhibited in 1924
at the Salon d'Automne.[45] The Salon, once considered progressive and modernist, had been
founded in 1903 by a renegade group of French artists, the Nabis, from the Académie Julian,
but by 1920 many of the exhibitors were American.[46] A reviewer for the Paris *Herald* wrote
that the "numerous works by American artists and sculptors . . . if gathered together in one
of the halls [would] make an immense exhibition by themselves . . . to add to this American
invasion of artistic Paris."[47] In 1922, the *Herald* proclaimed that the Salon d'Automne
offered even more proof of "a vital art movement in the United States."[48] By 1923,
although the Salon continued to attract American participators, it had become more rigid in
its selections and censored the most radical elements. Many members of the Salon, such as
André Lhôte and Othon Friesz, were among the leading French academicians of the time.[49]
Thus, in 1924, Prophet's work was probably fairly realistic and not very progressive. As a
young woman finding her way personally and artistically, She may have deliberately avoided
producing avant-garde images, out of both fear of rejection from juries and a need for
conventional acceptance.

"Since then," Prophet wrote, "I have been continuously working, with very little to do with, but making peoples [*sic*] busts who would pose without pay."[50] After two years at the Ecole Nationale des Beaux-Arts, she believed that she could make more rapid progress working on her own under the supervision of masters. She bought sculpting tools—fine stone carver's tools made in Paris and in Italy[51]—one at a time and did all of the carving herself, unable to afford assistants.[52] The work was arduous and left coarse calluses on her slim-fingered hands.[53] Prophet received instruction in woodcutting from Oscar Waldmann (b. 1856), a noted Swiss German sculptor, and marble cutting from Kousouski, a Polish sculptor.[54]

Between 1923 and 1925, Prophet moved three times in search of inexpensive housing and, perhaps, to distance herself from her husband. She tried to sustain herself by growing vegetables near her self-described filthy shack outside of Paris. The place had no toilet or heat, and in the winter of 1924 water trickled down the walls and froze. "Many hours I sat on the couch in that cold wet studio trying to collect myself together,"[55] Prophet recalled. "Other places where there were public toilets in the court were so filthy that I could not enter them. I tried but each time they raised my stomach. Often I did not bathe regularly it was so cold + [*sic*] I was worn down with melancholia and worry always over money."[56] By the summer of 1925, Prophet was "ill from overwork, difficult living conditions, malnutrition." She wrote: "I was unable to stand up, my legs would collapse if I tried to. I had not had a full nights [*sic*] sleep for over a year, continued to go to the School of Beaux-Arts, and cut stone in my own studio in the afternoon. I had also begun making Batique [batik] with the hope of making some money. . . . Then I broke down, being all by myself all day, growing weaker and weaker each day."[57]

An acquaintance finally arranged for Prophet to be admitted to the American Hospital, against her will, for malnutrition. Upon noting her emaciated condition (evident even several years later in photographs of Prophet's thin face; see figs. 11 and 12), medical practitioners there accused her of being a drug addict and cautioned her not to exert herself for a year lest a relapse occur. Within three weeks, however, the artist returned to her shack, but "the horror of its poverty"[58] struck her so intensely that she had to move. Prophet sold some batik[59] and one woman gave her two thousand francs to help meet her expenses.

In the fall of 1925, Prophet took a six-month sublet on a studio on the famous rue Vercingétorix, where white American painters Maurice Sterne and Patrick Henry Bruce worked in 1904,[60] artists Per and Lucy Krohg lived in the former studio of Gauguin (at no. 6) in the 1910s,[61] sculptor Isamu Noguchi would work in 1927, and painter Stuart Davis would take over the studio of painter Jan Matulka at no. 50 in 1928.[62] Since Prophet never mentioned these artists (nor any others, European or American) in her diary or letters, it is not known whether she knew about or associated with them. Prophet moved into this studio alone, "with an attempt to leave" her husband.[63] She then began her first lifesize statue, *La volonté* (The will, or wish; apparently no longer extant). Prophet worked all day long, although the physical exertion obliged her to stop frequently; her legs gave way and she had strong nervous attacks.[64]

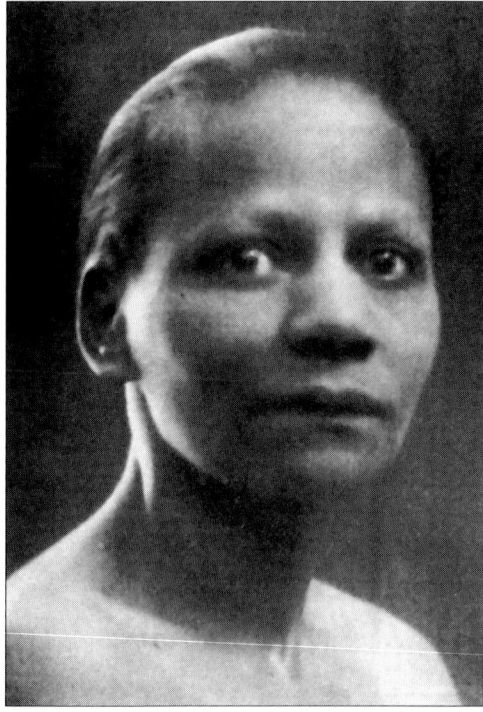
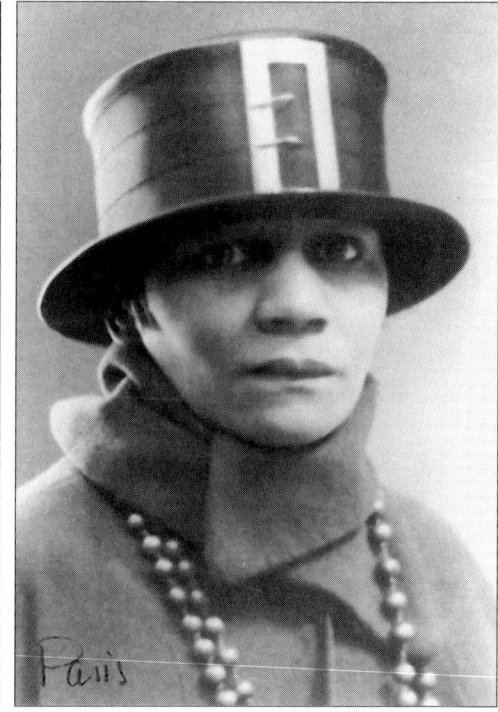

FIGURE 11
Photograph of Nancy Elizabeth Prophet,
ca. 1925–1929. From *Opportunity,* July 1930.

FIGURE 12
Nancy Elizabeth Prophet, ca. 1925–1929.
Nancy Elizabeth Prophet Collection, James P. Adams
Library, Rhode Island College.

In November 1925, by chance Prophet met a man by the name of Paul Berthier,[65] who planned on constructing a studio building at 147, rue Broca. She waited anxiously to hear about the cost and the final decision; "If that studio becomes mine it will be my first real studio in Paris, for during these three years I have been constantly moving about, living under all sorts of conditions."[66]

That same month, Prophet sculpted a portrait head of a man she had met in a café. The activity helped soothe her; she worked "with the most delicious sensation of rightness. Feeling that harmonic accord of my forces which I have been trying for years to attain."[67] The sculpture may well have been *Discontent,* ca. 1925–1929 (fig. 13), a fourteen-inch high head in pearwood. The androgynous visage has a strong Roman nose; thin, closed lips; pupilless eyes; and sunken cheeks. The head and neck are completely covered by a brownish-red cowl skimming the jaw line. The simple cloth suggests a makeshift wrap to ward off cold, or a nun's habit. The mood is of pain and unhappiness, but also stoicism, determination, and a strong spirituality. Prophet said that the work was "the result of a long emotional experience, of restlessness, of gnawing hunger for the way of attainment."[68] Poet Countee Cullen later described the work as "a face Dantesque in its tragedy, so powerful in the red polished cowl that envelops it that it might stand for the very spirit of revolt and rebellion."[69]

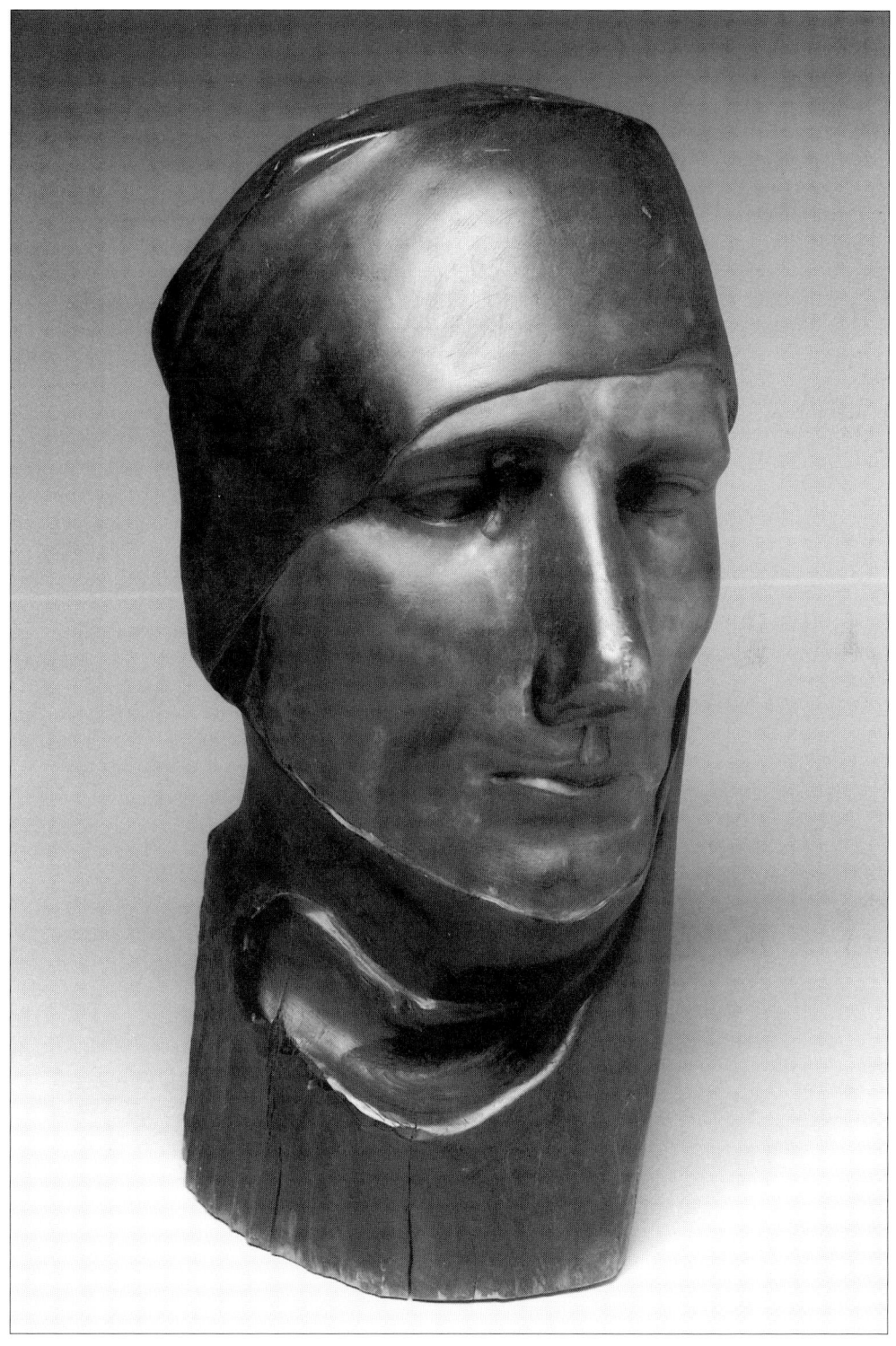

FIGURE 13
Elizabeth Prophet, *Discontent,* before 1930, stained and oiled wood, 14 in. (h)
Museum of Art, Rhode Island School of Design. Gift of Miss Eleanor Green and Miss Ellen D. Sharpe.
Photography by Erik Gould.

In November, Prophet began her second lifesize figure, which was particularly challenging because her studio was inadequate and the model was unattractive: "I arose fairly early and began to scan the studio, what a miserable place for a real model. I bustled around trying to scrape up the dirt to make a more fit setting for her. My work looked too poor for her to see. I hid the different things under cloths. The model arrived at 2, a model I thought for a master. She was really very ugly."[70] This piece may have been *Le pélerin* (The pilgrim, ca. 1925–1929, fig. 14). This eight-foot-high plaster statue depicts a person of uncertain gender with short hair.[71] The figure stands robed and rests the right arm at a right angle across the abdomen. As in the face of *Discontent*, the eyes are empty—there are no pupils—and s/he appears almost expressionless. With the head tilted slightly to the left, there is an air of melancholy and longing. Does the work represent Prophet's pilgrimage to Paris and her desire for recognition? Or was this lifesize work of the ugly model a different piece, perhaps a Venus-like untitled, half-nude figure (fig. 15)? This statue, too, has blank eyes and short, but fuller, hair. A long cloth draping her hips, this woman stands calmly, her left hand resting on her thigh.

In its subject matter, *Le pélerin* is reminiscent of medieval church statuary and represents a moment of nostalgia for the Middle Ages in French art also evident in the sculpture of Ossip Zadkine, who was often influenced by Romanesque and Gothic statuary, Constantin Brancusi, Henri Laurens, and Jacques Lipchitz.[72] Yet, the pilgrim in art traditionally wears a broad-brimmed hat, carries a staff, and a wallet on his shoulder. His special attribute, a scallop shell, frequently embellishes the hat or wallet.[73] Despite the work's title, the figure bears more of a resemblance to Francis of Assisi (ca. 1182–1226), founder of the Order of Friars Minor, or Franciscans. He apparently was a diminutive man, with ailing eyesight. The saint wore a brown or grey habit, its girdle distinguished by three knots, representing the religious vows of poverty, chastity, and obedience—conditions it seems Prophet endured, if not chose voluntarily.[74] Depictions of Saint Francis are easily recognized by the stigmata, the five marks corresponding to Christ's wounds on his hands, feet, and side. Prophet's sculpture has a slight physique and downcast eyes. Given the work's unknown location and sole documented photograph with its frontal view, it is not yet possible to discern whether the figure wears a knotted girdle. However, a stigma is clear on the back of the right hand.

Le pélerin also bears some resemblance to Rodin's *Burghers of Calais* (1886), particularly in the man holding the key to his hometown.[75] Both Prophet's and Rodin's figures wear close-cropped hair and simple, roughly modeled robes, and each is a convincing study in dignified resignation.

Like the work of (Emile) Antoine Bourdelle (1861–1929), a student of Auguste Rodin, Prophet's early figures and busts have an androgynous quality, with their close-cropped or cloth-covered hair, small breasts, heavy-lidded eyes, and enigmatic smiles. There is a difference, however, in that Bourdelle's works have much rougher surfaces, in contrast to Prophet's smooth, polished forms. Prophet may have been interested in the concept of androgyny, or at least the creation of her own identity and the control of her destiny; she

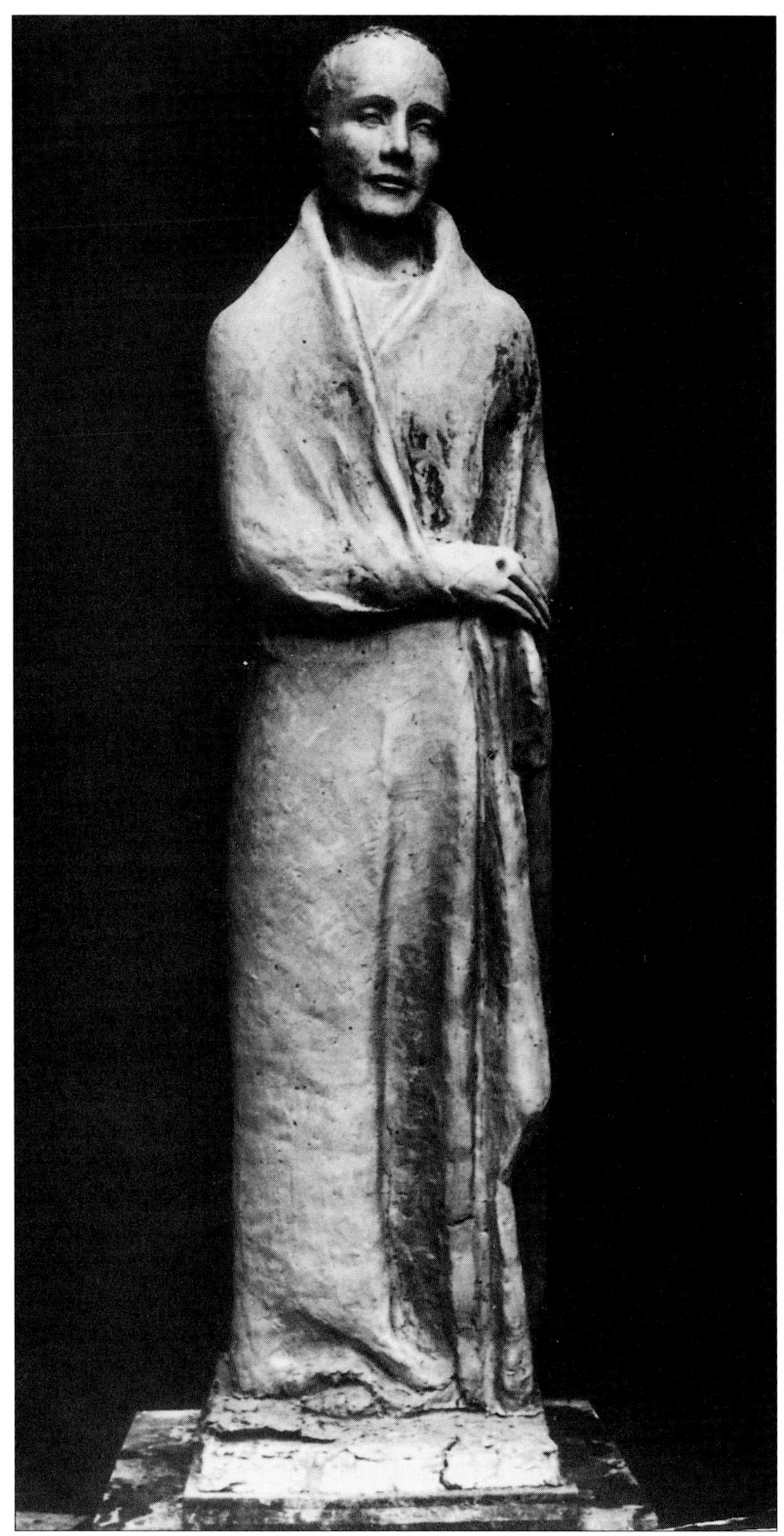

FIGURE 14
Nancy Elizabeth Prophet, *Le pélérin* (The pilgrim), ca. 1925–1929, plaster, dimensions and location unknown.
From a photograph in Nancy Elizabeth Prophet Collection, James P. Adams Library, Rhode Island College.

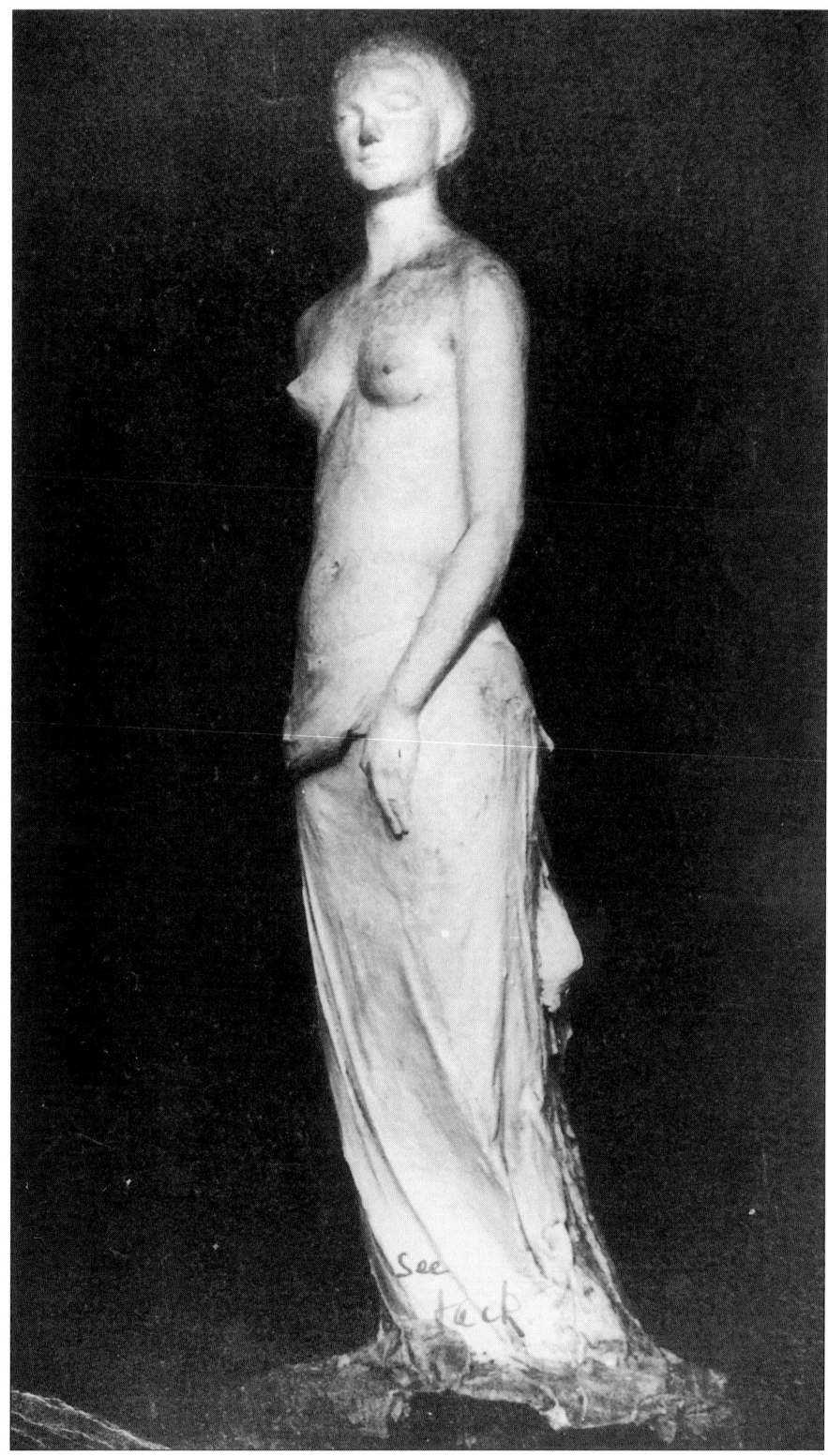

FIGURE 15
Nancy Elizabeth Prophet, Untitled half-nude female figure, ca. 1925–1929, plaster, dimensions and location unknown. From a photograph in Nancy Elizabeth Prophet Collection, James P. Adams Library, Rhode Island College.

would list herself, or be listed, by a man's name, Eli, in the Salon d'Automne catalog of 1927.[76] Could Prophet's unhappy marriage and her—initially—supportive relationship with Barrows have caused her to examine her sexuality more closely? Or was Prophet more interested in spirituality than physicality and seeking to express universal feelings with these androgynous figures? If so, her works recall certain characteristics of the Symbolist movement of the 1880s and 1890s. The Symbolists stressed the precedence of suggestion and evocation over direct depiction and explicit analogy and aimed to resolve the conflict between the material and the spiritual world. A series of Prophet's busts and head fragments in plaster (e.g., figs. 16 and 17) and clay have these qualities and also recall ancient Etruscan statues, as well as busts of the early Italian Renaissance, with their broad, calm foreheads and archaic smiles. By depicting few details and concentrating on facial expressions, Prophet imbued her works with a strong spiritual quality.

Ten days after Prophet began the unspecified lifesize work, she was disturbed by the appearance of her husband at her quarters. Ford visited her in December 1925, inebriated. "The man I married coming to see [me] with a great bunch of roses. There he lies on the couch now asleep. O God, O God, he came drunk"[77] was all Prophet wrote about the incident in her diary. She evidently believed he was envious of her.[78] Part of Ford's insecurity may have stemmed from weight gain; Prophet cryptically wrote, "I can appreciate the

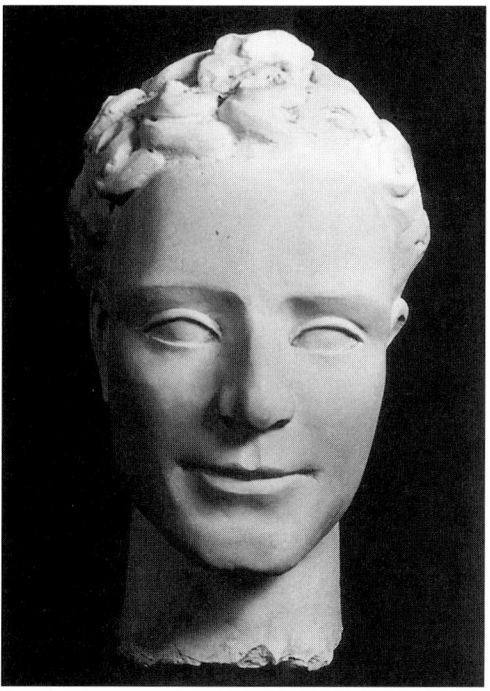

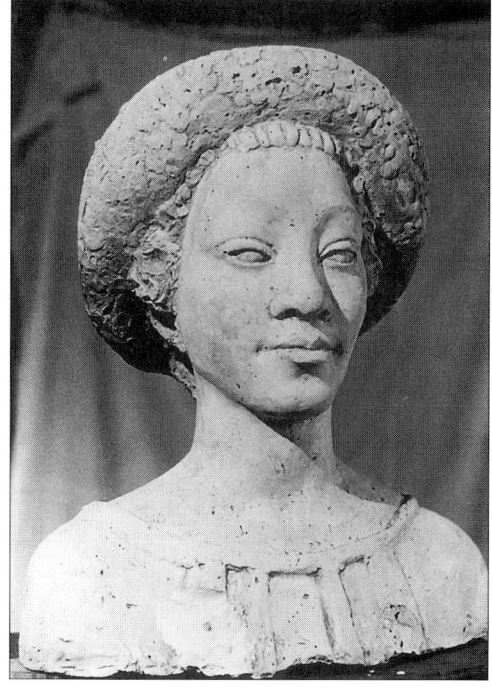

FIGURE 16
Nancy Elizabeth Prophet, Untitled head, ca. 1925–1929, plaster, dimensions and location unknown. From a photograph in Nancy Elizabeth Prophet Collection, James P. Adams Library, Rhode Island College.

FIGURE 17
Nancy Elizabeth Prophet, Untitled head, ca. 1925–1929, plaster, dimensions and location unknown. From a photograph in Nancy Elizabeth Prophet Collection, James P. Adams Library, Rhode Island College.

primitive beauty of the hippopotamus but I like not his humanized descendants."[79]
She tried to avoid thinking about her husband by working. "Cutting stone," she wrote.
"How I love it working alone, I feel so much in contact with myself."[80]

Few of Prophet's known works are of stone. The sculpture she refers to may
well have been *Silence* (ca. 1925–1929, fig. 18), the "companion piece" to *Discontent*,[81]
a woman's head in marble, or possibly white onyx, which Prophet said she created after
months of solitary living. The head is simple; there are no indications of eyebrows,
eyelashes, irises, or pupils, and the bobbed hair fits the head like a smooth helmet,
only slightly waved on the sides. The mouth and nose are of a medium size and the
facial expression is blank. The work held special significance for Prophet; she wrote
verses about it, one of which concludes, "Silence—the unifying quality of the body,
mind and soul."[82] Where silence is a Symbolist theme, the depiction of the head,

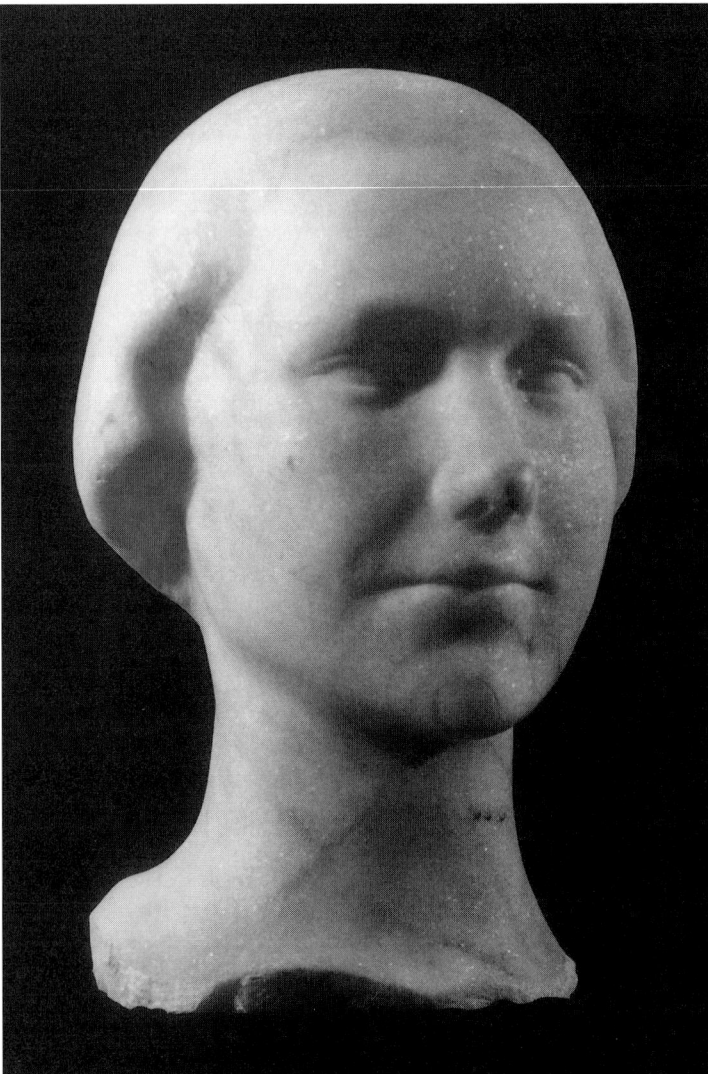

FIGURE 18
Nancy Elizabeth Prophet,
Silence, before 1930,
marble, 12 in. (h).
Museum of Art, Rhode
Island School of Design.
Gift of Miss Ellen D.
Sharpe. 30.092.

especially given the bobbed hair, is modern, reserved, and cool. It is Prophet's only known white-stone piece.

In March 1926, Prophet's spirits were uplifted by Berthier's news that he would promise her a studio if she could give him four thousand francs, a year's rent in advance. She borrowed the money.[83] She then spent a sad and lonely Easter by herself. Yet, she thought, "to think alone, and in silence[,] is beautiful. Not to be wholly oneself is death to the soul" (April 4, 1926). She cast two works in plaster, but was ashamed of them both and noted in her diary on April 6, 1926, that she would have to work more seriously on her development as an artist.

By then, Prophet had decided to leave her husband. "There is only one mode of conduct when with a fool, that is, be a fool. It is wiser to leave him" (April 6, 1926). Although the two lived apart, Ford remained in Paris for the following three years. Just four days after Prophet decided to leave her husband, she smashed *La volonté,* rationalizing, "I must not be guilty of doing with my work as I have formerly too often done with people. Trying to imagine there is good or overlook faults when in truth there is not enough to make a thing worth while [*sic*]" (April 30, 1926).

In May, Prophet went to a quiet beach, Le Crotoy, in Normandy for a short period while her studio was being built. Upon her return in June, she stayed in a small apartment for several weeks until the place was completed. During this time she was plagued by periods of loneliness and self-doubt and filled her diary with melancholic outpourings in her large, distinctive handwriting. She wrote that she was

> So hungry to work that it seems I must go completely insane. My head is full of ideas, a fever to execute. All day long I have sat here quietly thinking and planning. From time to time my eyes are forced to fall on a gas stove in the corner, a coal stove against the wall and a squalid sink in the middle of these two, which is embellished by a faucet with a rubber end that seems ready to squirt water at any instant, it[']s like a penis on the wall. The bedroom lies next with its great mahogany wardrobe with a beautiful glass, while the walls are lined with bedbugs, another little mirror in the kitchen. These two mirrors reflect to me my work hungry self. Otherwise the place suggests nothing, but to cook or clean and the poverty of my situation. O Poverty the curse of genius! (June 4, 1926)

Several days later, she continued her lament about her self-doubt:

> To be assailed by a desire which I will not give way to, or cannot without losing respect for myself. The anguish of three days [*sic*] bad work. Is that not enough without being obliged to fight against this thing that seems to be eating into my very entrails and dividing my thoughts in spite of my efforts against it. O Desire what a commanding force you are, how strong nature has made you, you come without love, unasked and unwished. When I think you are dead or sleeping you come rushing in with greater strength having been but in repose. (dated July 8, but probably June 8, 1926)

At the end of June, 1926 Prophet moved into a tiny two-room apartment at 147, rue Broca (today known as rue L. M[aurice]. Nordmann) in the thirteenth arrondissement, where she would live for the following eight years. Her atelier was at the end of a narrow passageway strewn with "the trampled and broken debris of the abandoned and frustrated travail of many transient sculptors."[84] Writer Robert McAlmon (1896–1956), author of *Being Geniuses Together, 1920–1930,* a work on literary life in Paris, lived on the same street, but it seems that the two never met.[85] Prophet partitioned off a corner of her studio in which to sleep and brightened her home with books. "They are all I have in the way of baggage," she commented, "and when I have arrayed them on a shelf, my house is furnished."[86] She also painted the walls a cool gray green to cover up a "howling yellow"[87] and hung curtains to hide the ugliness of the outdoor scenery. Later she described life in her cramped quarters: "I tried sleeping with my figures, but it was so full of dust that I almost smothered, so I partitioned off a little corner myself with old boards, and I've been in this one spot for six years."[88]

Prophet was finally settled in Paris. She continued, however, to have financial difficulties. The first work she made in her new studio she named *Prayer* (also called *Poverty,* 1926, fig. 19), which somehow made her feel at home. The nude woman stands in *contrapposto,* weight on the left leg, head thrown back. Her left arm hangs limply behind her back while her right one is bent as she rests her hand on her breast. About her ankles curls a serpent, which slithers up between her shins. Does the serpent symbolize the evil and power of money, or the desire that she wrote about that summer? The snake has many symbolic meanings that would have resonated with Prophet. As prudence personified, it is the attribute of Minerva, the goddess of wisdom. It is also the attribute of Logic, one of the seven Liberal Arts; Innocence; and Africa, one of the Four Parts of the World. The snake was also associated with Asclepius, the Greek god of medicine because of the sloughing of its skin, which was seen as a symbol of rebirth and healing.[89]

It is possible that Prophet's snake represents knowledge or sexuality from which the woman prays for deliverance. The reserved eroticism evident in the voluptuous figure, with its serpentine pose and rounded breasts, belly, hips, and thighs held in, coupled with the tilted-back head and closed eyes, prefigures that of Richmond Barthé's loincloth-clad female *African Dancer* (1933). The libidinal titillation also has ties to orientalist depictions of odalisques, from nineteenth-century artists such as Delacroix, Chassériau, Ingres, and Gérome, as well as Matisse in the twentieth century.[90] Yet Prophet's nude, bereft of an exotic setting and clothing, has a more universal quality, more akin to the 1925 classicist *Woman with Goat (The Shepherdess)* of Morice Lipsi (originally Lipsycc), a nude that also stands on a pedestal, clasps its hands/arms behind its back, and has an animal between its feet and shins (here, a goat's head). Lipsi had also studied at the Ecole des Beaux-Arts, in the 1910s, and also lived in Montparnasse. He was a resident of La Ruche (the beehive), an artist colony in the fifteenth arrondissement founded by the academic sculptor Alfred Boucher in 1902.[91] Prophet may have been familiar with Lipsi's solo exhibitions in several galleries in the 1920s, or even may have visited his studio. La Ruche housed numerous artists, many from eastern Europe, and many sculptors, including Ossip Zadkine and Moishe Kogan.[92] It seems likely that as a sculptor, Prophet at least knew of the popular colony. *Prayer* bears a striking resemblance to Michelangelo's marble *The Dying Slave* (1513–1516), which Prophet would have

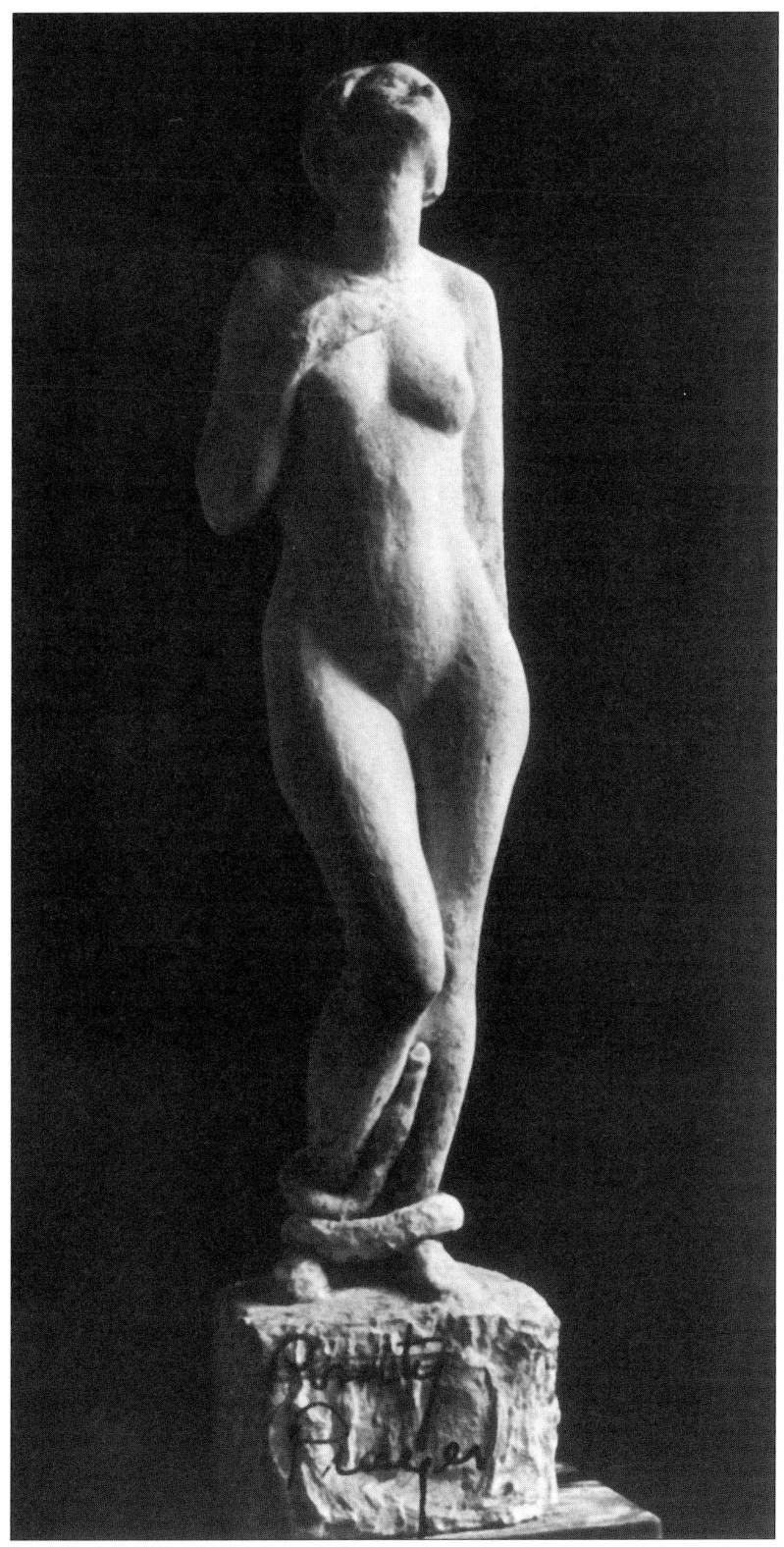

FIGURE 19
Nancy Elizabeth Prophet, *Prayer* (or *Poverty*), 1926, plaster, dimensions and location unknown.
From a photograph in Nancy Elizabeth Prophet Collection, James P. Adams Library, Rhode Island College.

seen at the Louvre.[93] While the arms are posed differently, *Prayer* is female, and the *Dying Slave* is male, both nudes stand in *contrapposto* on rough-hewn bases (Prophet's sculpture mirrors Michelangelo's), with their heads thrown back. Michelangelo's work, as one of some twenty figures of slaves, was intended for the tomb of Julius II. Both his figure and Prophet's seem to symbolize the struggle of the human soul to find release from the material body.

Prayer may also express a plea for a release from depression. Prophet wrote of her constant battle against melancholy and self-doubt:

> My days are spent with work, but battling [*sic*] with melancholia, nights of struggling without sleep. All my effort is exerted trying to bring about a harmonic action of my forces. This I try for hourly, minutely, and yet each day I seem to be farther off from doing what I would do.
>
> I am judge of my own works, that at least I am capable of, for my ideas or the vision of it and the execution of it are constantly side by side, there[']s no chance of mistake for the one never approaches the other.[94]

Prophet was very lonely in her new apartment. Even when she socialized with others, she felt empty afterward: "Why laugh or jest with fools only to be saddened and ashamed of oneself when left alone" (July 20, 1926). She decided not to have any more illusions about people:

> For three days I have felt something taking possession of me. Today I have a peculiar sense of having been emptied of something. There is a loss, what is it? The evening comes and quiet thought. The illusions for people have gone. It is this the loss. I feel a cold calm indifference and acceptance of a truth. There will be no more disappointments. I must grow now to be more worthy of the real souls whom I shall meet when I am ready.   (July 26, 1926)

Yet these admonitions to herself could not overcome her loneliness. A month later, she dressed up for a conversation with imaginary friends:

> Work. Quit work at 5.
>
> I have changed my clothes putting on a lovely green silk dress, feeling gay and well. I sit on the couch cheerily feeling myself among the people and setting I so much love, beauty, understanding, and harmony of thought and feeling. There comes a feeling of sadness[,] of desperate loneliness. How joyful would it be if these voices, these faces, these rugs and hangings would but speak aloud, and show themselves, instead of but misty formless things created and living only in my imagination.
>
> I sit here—to love, to relax, for just this hour that I wish it. The thing began at my feet—it has crept up to my neck and soon it will cover my head. O God the smothering blanket of reality.   (August 29, 1926)

In September 1926, she was in even more severe financial straits. She wrote passionately about her poverty in her diary:

> How swiftly the happy days slip by, it's only the unhappy ones that linger and drag. Almost a month has fled, a month of battles fought and won with all the glory that comes with success.

Days of spiritual freedom, days of harmony in body and soul, days when the body was healthy and heard [*sic*], days of passion and desire, days of sadness and of joy. Days of laughter and days of tears. Nights of sweet sleep and pleasant awakening. Days of plenty, and then days of want. Poverty, detestable poverty, how you trail behind me ever screeching out your presence. Think you to ever make me a subject of your kingdom? Never! Though I die of hunger I shall never bend the knee to your majesty for I am not of your race. And yet what new phases of poverty are there for me to learn. Going without eating is common, to regain my health and strength only to lose it through fasting, it comes as a periodical occurrence so frequent that neither interests or frightens me. Poverty, weary not yourself in trying to humiliate me.

Sometimes the face of life becomes but a mocking leer.

Poverty, your grace, I accept your challenge.   (September 19, 1926)

Often hungry and going without sleep, Prophet persevered in sculpting. A model named Povisipkine posed for a bust without payment. By November, the piece (now apparently lost) was finished, but Prophet was haunted by the threat of mediocrity and hid the work on its pedestal with a black cloth, "draped in mourning to hide it from my own eyes that seek so much a beautiful thing. . . . To have worked and then to learn I have been guided by delusion" (November 22, 1926).

Very little is known about what Prophet experienced during the first six months of 1927; she wrote only four brief entries in her diary then. The first was a rambling thought on "love, the genii of life." Two others concerned instances that moved her visually. The morning of January 29 offered a brief escape from her woes: "This morning as I awakened the studio was filled with a strange rosy light. I jumped out of bed[,] ran to the window and there across the heavens stretched in marvelous length a joyous rainbow. It lasted but a moment and then was gone" (January 29, 1927).

The titles of some of Prophet's early work, such as *Poverty, Discontent,* and *Bitter Laughter* (ca. 1925–1929, location unknown),[95] surely reflect her physical and emotional pain, often hungry, alone, and unsure of herself in a foreign land, in states that transcend issues of ethnicity. Yet the universal can have dimensions of particularity just as the particular is often more universal than it would seem. That is, critics have discerned and can discern issues dealing with racial matters in these works as well.

The poet Countee Cullen would say that Prophet's *Laughing Man* (reproduction not found location unknown; possibly the same work as *Bitter Laughter*), a figure in pure white marble, "might be taken to exemplify the unfathomed laugh of her race at a world it does not understand and which can never understand it."[96] He—and Prophet—may have been thinking of similarities between the work and Langston Hughes's poem "Minstrel Man," published in Alain Locke's *The New Negro* (1925):

Because my mouth
Is wide with laughter
And my throat
Is deep with song,
You do not think

I suffer after
I have held my pain
So long.
Because my mouth
Is wide with laughter,
You do not hear
My inner cry,
Because my feet
Are gay with dancing,
You do not know
I die.[97]

It is more likely, however, that the source of Prophet's *Laughing Man* comes not from the work of an African American poet, but from that of a French novelist. In February 1927, the French celebrated the 125th anniversary of the birth of Victor Hugo, author of *Homme qui rit* (The man who laughs, or The laughing man, first translated into English in 1869). In 1902, when the French celebrated the centennial of Hugo's birth, African American Meta Vaux Warrick Fuller (who was in Paris then) produced a sculpture called *The Laughing Man*. It is unlikely that Prophet knew of this; most of Fuller's work was destroyed in a studio fire in 1910. Nonetheless, the two may have been drawn to the subject for similar reasons. The main character, Gwynplaine, was a carnival freak and mountebank. As historian Judith Nina Kerr has noted, Gwynplaine's laugh, in Hugo's words, was a visible constant in life (as skin color was and is for African Americans); the "laugh which he had not placed on brow he was powerless to remove. His laugh had been stamped indelibly on his face."[98] Kerr suggests that Fuller would have found further similarities between Gwyplaine's plight and that of people of color: "Cruel stereotypes and crude caricatures of Afro-Americans, some insidious and all destructive, were everywhere" (126). White artists often depicted Black people as stereotypes, such as the "Sambo" character—a slow, lazy, but fun-loving dullard with bug eyes, very dark skin, thick lips, and a wide grin. Likewise, it "was Gwynplaine's laugh," Hugo wrote, "that so excited the mirth of others" (126).

Hugo also wrote that "although Gwynplaine's face laughed; his thoughts did not. . . . The exterior did not depend on the interior" (126). Hughes may have been inspired by this idea to write "Minstrel Man," as was perhaps another African American poet, Paul Laurence Dunbar, as revealed in his bitter lines about masking:

We wear the mask that grins and lies,
It hides our cheeks and shades our eyes,—
This debt we pay to human guile;
With torn and bleeding hearts we smile,
And mouth with myriad subtleties.

We smile, but, O great Christ, our cries
To thee from tortured souls arise.
We sing, but oh, the clay is vile
Beneath our feet, and long the mile:
But let the world dream otherwise,
We wear the mask.   (126–127)

Kerr suggests that the real tragedy of the story of Gwynplaine was the consequence of the public's attitude toward his "mask." Whenever he tried to speak, laughter from the crowd was inevitable. In the same manner, popular stereotypes fostered the idea that because people of color were less than human, their thoughts and feeling were not worth serious consideration (126–127). Like Fuller—who chose not to concentrate exclusively on "Negro types," which Du Bois had suggested she do—Prophet, it seems, may have been commenting on discrimination within the context of generally acceptable visual images, here in the allegory of Hugo's *Laughing Man.*

On May 14, 1927, the sight of a peasant in a café in Paris inspired Prophet. The artist preferred to create sculptures from life, but more often had to work from imagination for lack of money to pay sitters. Sometimes, however, she was able to persuade men she met in cafés to model for her.

An Argentine friend apparently modeled for *Poise* (also known as *Buste en marbre,* ca. 1926–1929, fig. 20). *Poise* is the nude bust of a man cut in heavily veined white marble. In this work, known only by a black-and-white profile shot, the man appears resolute with his square chin and closed mouth. Showing similarities to the head of *Discontent,* the cheeks are sunken, the nose is Roman, and the eyeballs are blank, without irises or pupils. Indeed, the profile is akin to those of Roman busts of Augustus Caesar. With his broad forehead and large skull—the short hair is indicated only by a smooth raised layer; in fact, the head appears almost bald—the subject of *Poise* seems to be a man of great intelligence, sensitivity, and restraint. Although the shoulders are relaxed, the throat muscles are tensed. Prophet later explained that the quality of poise "is necessarily compounded by inner intensity and outer calm."[99] In 1940, she would write an essay that reiterated her high regard for poise. She believed that artists should act as role models by embodying the principles of art: "The principles of the arts which are form, rhythm, harmony; and the abstract qualities, some of which are poise and courage; are factors which no civilized man who aspires to be educated can live successfully without attaining."[100] Prophet always strove to attain those "abstract qualities"; the titles of some of her works, such as *Poise* and *Silence,* reflect this ambition.

Other heads of men sculpted by Prophet are equally intense, such as *Head of a Cossack* (ca. 1926–1929, fig. 21). This portrait head, sculpted in wood, has a visage quite similar to that of *Poise,* but the softly polished brown wood exudes greater warmth. The Cossack is identifiable by his tall, plain, columnar hat. The Cossacks were expert equestrians of the steppes of southern Russia and of the Ukraine. Did a Cossack actually sit for this work or did Prophet adapt an image she had seen in a publication?

A similar query can be posed for *Reptile Woman* (ca. 1925–1929, fig. 22). Her face is square and hard, set off by bobbed, slightly wavy hair with bangs. The reptile woman's heavy-lidded eye sockets are mysteriously empty and she wears an enigmatic smile. The bust of this woman in clay bears the English title of a common circus figure in France, a *femme serpent,* a woman who performed with snakes. Yet the portrait gives virtually no indication of the woman's profession. Is the thin vertical shaft beneath her chin a reptilian fold of skin or merely a prop to hold up her head as she rests her folded, bare arms on an upraised platform?

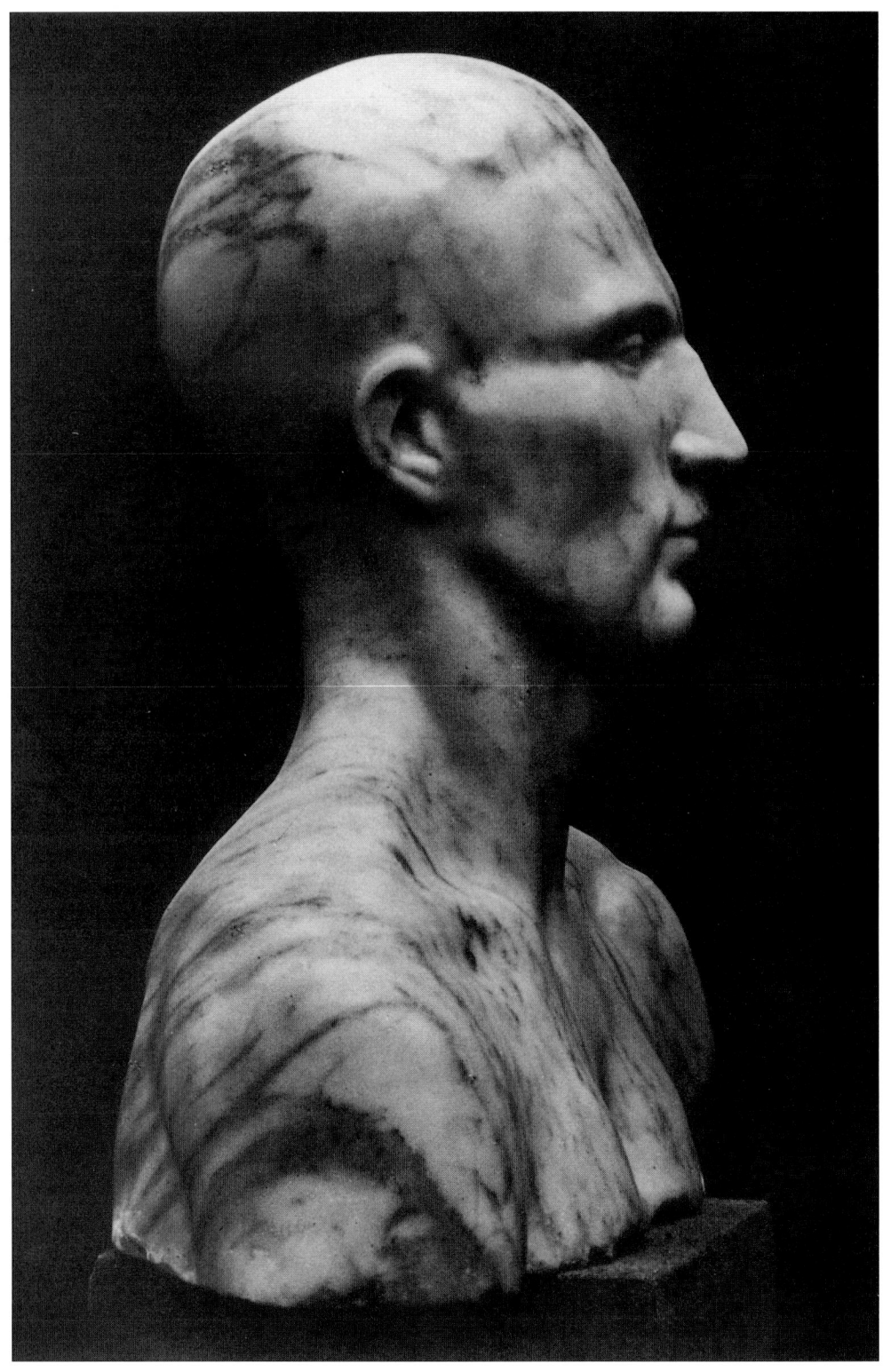

FIGURE 20
Nancy Elizabeth Prophet, *Poise,* ca. 1926–1929, marble, dimensions and location unknown.
From a photograph in Nancy Elizabeth Prophet Collection, James P. Adams Library, Rhode Island College.

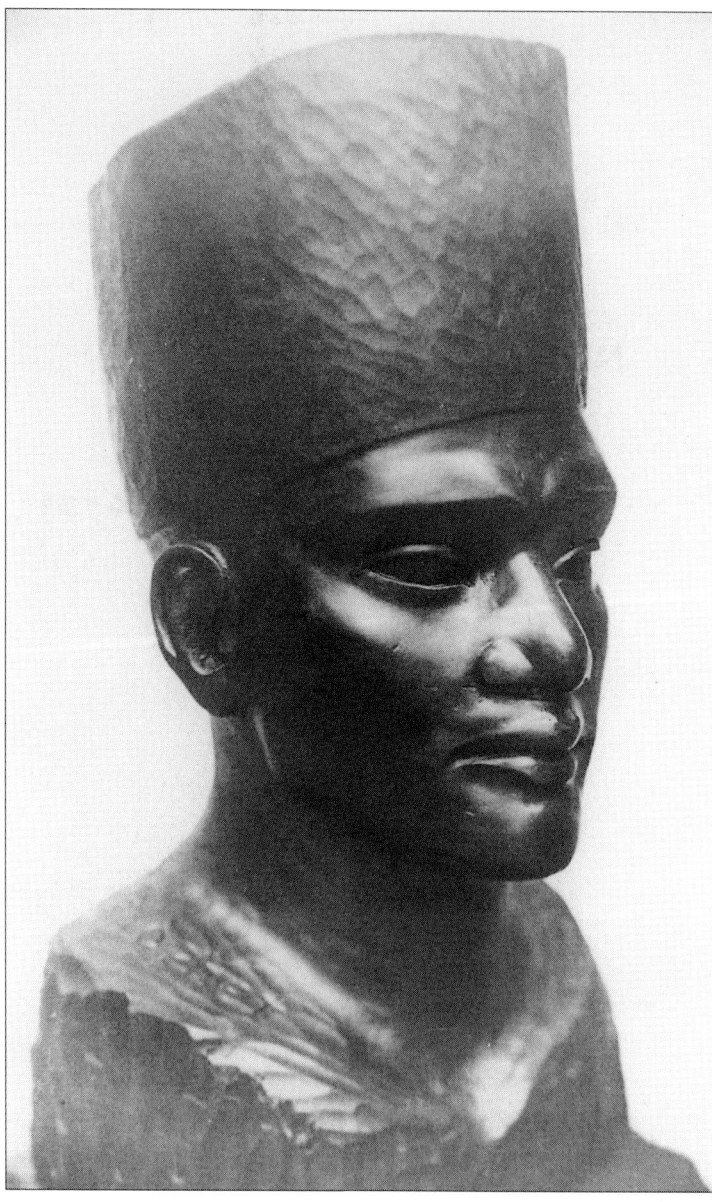

FIGURE 21
Nancy Elizabeth Prophet,
Head of a Cossack,
ca. 1926–1929,
wood, dimensions and
location unknown.
From a photograph
in Nancy Elizabeth
Prophet Collection,
James P. Adams Library,
Rhode Island College.

The back of the photograph bears an inscription, "for Dad." No further clues exist about this curious work, which seems never to have been exhibited.

PATRONAGE AND EXHIBITIONS IN PARIS AND THE UNITED STATES, 1927–1929

Although Prophet had initially disliked Mabel Gardner, she seems to have befriended her to a degree. Gardner was a very generous, albeit eccentric, woman.[101] She apparently contacted several wealthy persons on Prophet's behalf, including a translator of children's stories,

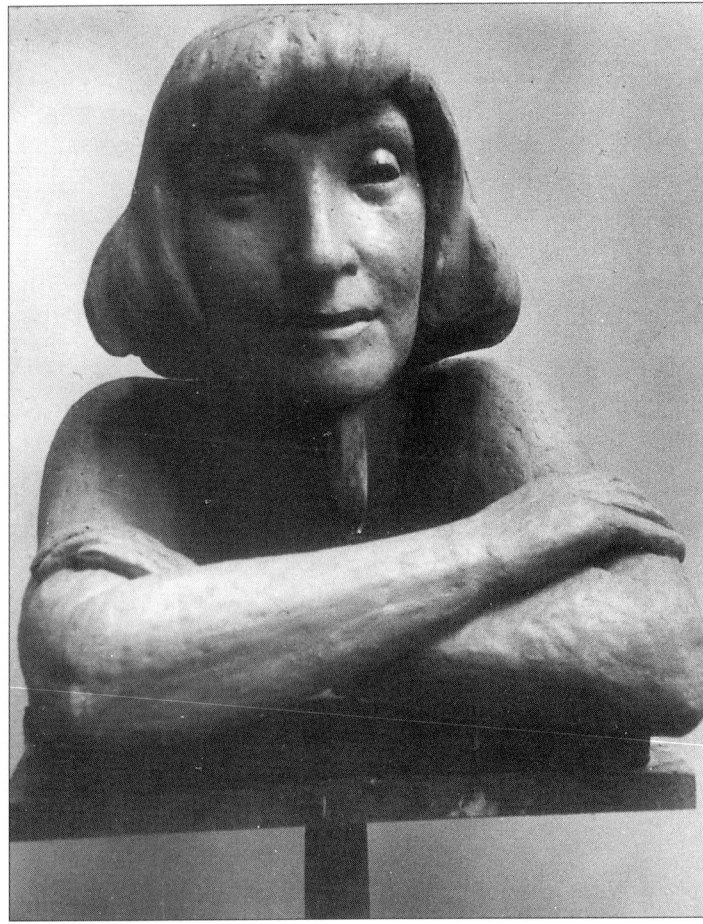

FIGURE 22
Nancy Elizabeth Prophet,
Reptile Woman,
1925–1929, clay,
dimensions and
location unknown.
From a photograph
in Nancy Elizabeth
Prophet Collection,
James P. Adams Library,
Rhode Island College.

Louise W. Brooks of Boston (not to be confused with the contemporary film star Louise Brooks).[102] Brooks then solicited the aid of several philanthropists in Providence who responded by providing funding (the details are not known) in 1927, 1928, and 1931.[103] Prophet recounted the patronage differently, saying that it came from an organization called the Students Fund of Boston. In her diary, she included a copy of the letter she wrote to Brooks:

> My Dear Miss Brooks
> Mable [*sic*] Gardner has told me of your love and interest in sculpture and what you and she are trying to do for it through me.
> I have decided to write you myself, something I am afraid I should hesitate to do, were not circumstances pressing me too cruelly. Also Mable G. writes, "She is the first person I have met who understands and is so spirited.["] This gives me courage. I can write to you as though I were writing to myself.
> I want to work. This is no vain ideal that I am favoring myself with, no distraction through which I seek to make life more agreeable and time pass more

quickly, but a fire that burns in me, a force which compels my obedience and I am only obeying a command which is stronger than myself, even in the face of what may seem discouraging conditions. I cannot stop, I must go on.

Someday people will realize that this is my medium of expression, that it is still possible to say something through sculpture, that a sculptor may yet live again.

I do not complain of difficulties. I am not afraid to face them, the contraire. I know that each one of life[']s problems I am able to overcome makes me bigger and richer for my work. I like to match myself with life[']s forces, but this thing money or the lack of it is too crushing, it keeps me from working when I should be expressing that which I learn from each day lived. It staggers me, sickens me . . .

I am a fighter, determined and nonretreating. I stop only when I drop . . .

I must continue to work. People like my things and if they like them shall I not someday be able to take care of myself? I want to. I expect that of myself, shall respect myself more when I can, but at this moment I seem not to be able to, and I am sad, almost ashamed to ask. Sculpture is an expensive medium, I know, but I have not chosen my medium of expression, it has chosen me.

What more can I say? I want to work, I want to work. I must work. I live for that alone.

Forgive me I beg you for writing like this, for I[']m driven to desperation.[104]

She wrote an addendum to this entry in 1936, noting that Laura Heathfield, Brooks's secretary, secured thirty dollars a month for two years from the Students Fund of Boston (nothing else is known about this small organization). Then, "it stopped as suddenly as it began at the end of that time without warning."[105] If Prophet was grateful for the money, she expressed it in an odd way; her next diary entry was a gleeful (or perhaps wistful) insight: "To have glimpsed the secret of Power!"[106]

Gardner also contacted a number of other older, well-to-do white women who had never married and had no children, such as Eleanor Burgess Green (1870–1954), informing them of Prophet's plight and urging them to buy her work. (Apparently, either Gardner had brought several pieces with her or Prophet had shipped them to her hometown.) Green, the founder of the Providence District Nursing Association and a volunteer social worker, had been first lady of Rhode Island when her unmarried brother, Theodore Francis Green, was governor.[107] Although she had never met Prophet, Green was interested in her in part because Green had attended the same church as had Prophet's aunt in the 1890s.[108] Green bought *Head of a Negro* (ca. 1926–1927, fig. 23) on May 18, 1927, and called it one of her "art treasures." She wrote that the work "has called forth high praise from my family and relations, as to fineness in conception, powerful workmanship, and its living quality."[109] The piece is a coarsely chiseled head in golden brown wood of a black man. As seen in the subjects of most of Prophet's portraits, the lips are firmly closed; the short, smooth hair fits like a cap; the forehead is broad, high, and smooth; and the gaze is directed straight ahead. Here, however, Prophet rendered the eyes realistically, with dark irises, thin eyelids, slightly knit brows, and, below the eyes, slight bags. The expression is determined and aggressive. *Head of a Negro* has sometimes

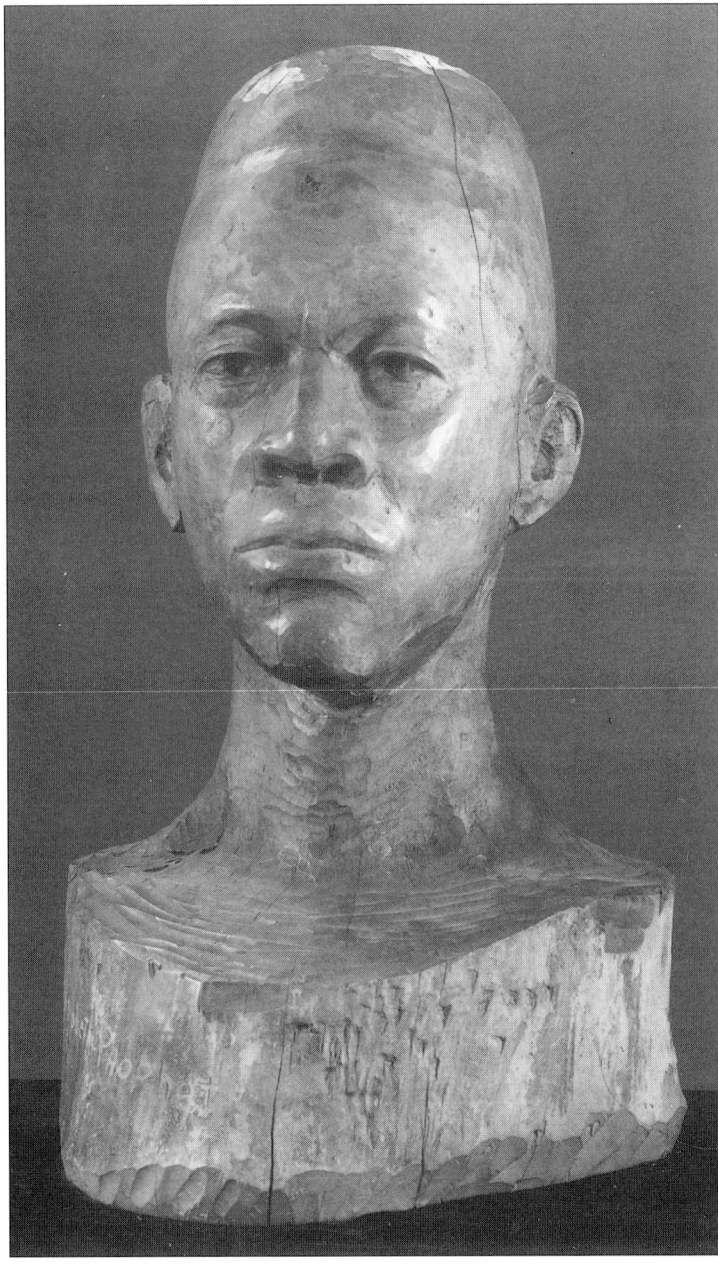

FIGURE 23
Nancy Elizabeth Prophet,
Head of a Negro,
ca. 1926–1927, wood,
20½ in. (h).
Museum of Art,
Rhode Island School
of Design. Gift of Miss
Eleanor B. Green

been called *Portrait of Roland Hayes,*[110] and it does, indeed, resemble the famous
African American tenor (1887–1977). Prophet attended a party given by Hayes in
New York in December 1929, but it is not known whether she knew him before this
time.[111]

A friend of Green's, Ellen D. Sharpe, of a prominent Rhode Island family, bought
the marble version of *Silence,* as well as a black man's head carved in wood. If the latter piece

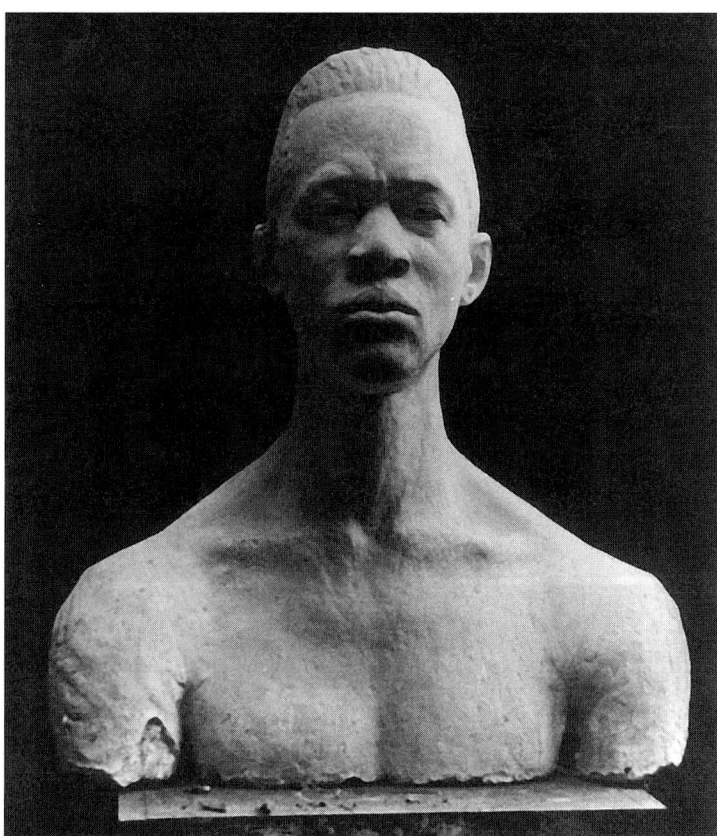

FIGURE 24
Nancy Elizabeth Prophet,
Head of a Negro,
ca. 1925–1929, plaster,
dimensions and location
unknown.
From a photograph
in Nancy Elizabeth
Prophet Collection,
James P. Adams Library,
Rhode Island College.

is the *Head of a Negro* (ca. 1925–1929), whose frontal photograph is in the library at Rhode Island College (fig. 24), it is a powerful work that depicts the nude bust of a black man with an intense facial expression and firmly set closed mouth. His nostrils are flared, his eyebrows knit, and his long neck muscles tensed, a study in anger, fortitude, or both. It is likely that Sharpe and Green were friends of Eliza Radeke—who also remained unmarried and childless—as well. Radeke, who as president of RISD had given Prophet financial support, was a member of the advisory council of Pembroke College (the women's college at Brown University)[112] and Sharpe would donate twenty-five thousand dollars to the Pembroke College dormitory fund in 1940.[113] Sharpe would also communicate with Prophet by mail for the next several years. Unfortunately, none of their correspondence seems to have survived.

Little else is known about Prophet's life from the spring of 1927 to the fall of 1928, other than her exhibiting *Tête de jeune fille* (location unknown) at the Salon d'Automne in November 1927. The exhibition catalog indicates that this work was a painting, rather than a sculpture: as noted earlier, Prophet had stated that in Paris she had painted for a year before switching to sculpture. Prophet is listed as male; "PROPHET (Eli), né à Providence, Rhode Island, U.S.A. Américain."[114] Either the French committee made a mistake or Prophet deliberately submitted her work under a male name, thinking it would increase her chances of acceptance. The listing certainly raises questions about the ways in which Prophet viewed herself, the ways that she wanted others to view her and her work, and the possible connection between her gendered persona and her androgynous busts and figures. One also wonders about the extent to which Prophet might have been aware of the activities and beliefs of such avant-garde lesbian women in Paris as Gertrude Stein, Romaine Brooks, and Natalie Barney, who enjoyed cross-dressing and exploring the conventions and boundaries of gender and sexuality.

The beginning of 1928 found Prophet still working in isolation. There were only two diary entries that year, both from January: "Haunting for the beauties of paradice [*sic*] in the midst of a burning hell" (day unspecified) and "How quiet the world is and how lonely" (January 15, 1928). Later, she penned a poem in her diary, which is found following entries from 1932 but which she dated 1928 (it is not known why Prophet rearranged this dating system):

> Like some dusky raven
> Waying through the night
> With a gruesome graveyard to cheer his appetite.
> Long after dawns the morning
> With a mocking clear blue sky.

The poem suggests that Prophet continued to suffer from hunger, that she was a night bird, and that she felt as though clear weather mocked her desperate situation. Her identification as a "dusky raven" is revealing. The bird is characterized by its lustrous black feathers (Prophet usually wore her straight black hair pulled back tightly in a bun), intelligence, and the power to utter articulate sounds in a hoarse, ominous voice—perhaps a reference to her often cryptic diary entries. Further, the verb *raven* means to "to prowl hungrily" or "to have a voracious appetite."[115] Prophet was no doubt familiar with Edgar Allan Poe's famous poem whose stanzas conclude, "Quoth the raven, Nevermore!" It is possible that the sculptor's metaphoric cry of "never" was against hunger.

The archaic term *dusky* had multiple meanings and synonyms, such as characterized by little or inadequate light, shadowy, crepuscular, nocturnal, swarthy, sooty, hidden, veiled, secret, occult, blurred, lackluster, and dirty.[116] It has also been used to describe the complexions of people of African or Native American descent. Prophet may have been drawn to both the colloquial and metaphorical connotations of the adjective.

Little is known about the following nine months in the artist's life. In the fall of that year, on October 9, 1928, Prophet sent photographs of her work to the Harmon Foundation—one of the only organizations in the country that exhibited works by African American artists and gave them monetary awards—hoping to get a fellowship. She reported that she was entirely without funds.[117] African American expatriate painter Henry O. Tanner wrote a strong letter of recommendation for aid on her behalf to the Harmon Foundation, praising her artistic potential: "Of the many, many students over here either white or black I know of none with such promise as Mrs. Prophet."[118] Apparently, the two had known each other for some time, but how or when they met is not documented. Tanner also urged Prophet to return to the United States to try to sell her work in person.[119] She was ineligible for the competition, however, because the date for entry as a candidate for awards and the exhibition had already passed, in September.[120]

Patrons aided Prophet by buying and exhibiting her work. Sometime in 1928, Brooks bought *Head of Roland Hayes* (if Green's *Head of a Negro* is also a portrait of Hayes, as suggested earlier, then Prophet may have made at least two portraits of the singer).[121] It may also have been during that year that Brooks's secretary visited Prophet's studio and confirmed that it was indeed "a bare place at the end of a blind alley, inadequately heated."[122] Clearly, if this is the place for which Prophet paid four thousand francs, she got a poor bargain. Also, in October 1928, *Silence* and *Head of a Negro,* which Sharpe and Green loaned, respectively, appeared in the Rhode Island School of Design fiftieth-anniversary show of art by former students and teachers.[123]

In February 1929, the Boston Society of Independent Artists (hereafter, BSIAI) exhibited Prophet's *Head of a Cossack* and a wooden head of a black man (which may have been lent by Brooks, Sharpe, or Green).[124] "The latter," the *Boston Evening Transcript* of February 16 declared, was "a powerful thing, one of the few outstanding things in the show." The BSIA exhibition was only in its third year in 1929. Like the Society of Independent Artists in New York, the BSIAI was most likely a nonjuried, nonaward event open to the public in which many artists participated.[125] For instance, in the 1931 exhibition, 237 works were shown by 116 artists.[126] While not particularly prestigious or well known, the society at least afforded Prophet an exhibition opportunity and a wider audience.

In March 1929 she sent her first piece to the Société des Artistes Français,[127] a group by then long considered an anachronism since it was the "Old Salon" from the nineteenth century—that is, not progressive. Yet the Salon still attracted many American participants.[128] *Buste d'homme,* a marble bust of a man (possibly *Poise*), was exhibited by the society beginning on April 1 and was favorably reviewed by the periodical *L'Art Contemporain.*[129] A French critic found the execution of the piece "virile and expressive as life." Prophet translated the review:

> The hand of Elizabeth Prophet is firm and strong. It ignores all affectation and works like a masculine hand energetic and sure. Her style is powerful, her composition skillful.
> Elizabeth Prophet is a sculptor of race: one feels it in everything, in her work, in the firmness of her will, in her independence. One has called her one of the most expressive sculptors of her country and of her time. That is easily possible.[130]

If the exhibited work was *Poise,* it is surprising that the critic would have called Prophet "a sculptor of race," since the subject of the piece looks more of European than of African descent. Perhaps the writer made this declaration based on a personal meeting with the sculptor rather than on the work itself.

On April 10, 1929, Ford left his job as an itinerant chef in France and went back to the United States, his fare paid by Prophet.[131] She noted the departure of her husband with relief: "The man I married leaves for America. I am able to send him away at last + with the help of the sale of a piece of my work. This represents an epoch in my life, a greater strength obtained."[132] By way of acknowledging the death of the relationship, she listed herself as a widow on the Harmon nomination form the same year.[133] She made the separation official in June 1932 by obtaining a legal affidavit to change her surname from Ford back to Prophet.[134] She also made a notary statement in 1946 disinheriting Ford, claiming that he had been a moral and financial handicap to her, that her father had supported them at the beginning of their marriage, and that she had never given birth to any child by him or anyone else.[135] It is unclear whether she ever divorced Ford.

In May, Prophet wrote to the Harmon Foundation once more for application blanks, indicating that she planned on traveling to the United States in the latter part of summer.[136] In June, when white banker Otto Kahn (1867–1934)—for whom the Harmon Foundation's major prize was named—traveled to Paris, Prophet invited him to see her work on exhibition at the Société des Artistes Français. A note from his secretary confirmed that he would do so that month, but there is no record of his reaction to Prophet's sculpture.[137] Kahn was a wealthy and generous patron; he served as president and chair of the board of the Metropolitan Opera Company, vice president of the Philharmonic Symphony Orchestra, member of the visiting committee for the department of art and archeology of Princeton University, and director of the American Federation of Art, and he was involved in many other similar organizations.[138] Clearly, Prophet was hoping to attract his attention and patronage. She did, at least, capture the attention of L. Earl Rowe, director of the Rhode Island School of Design, who attended the opening of the Société des Artistes Français and admired "one of her fine portrait heads in stone."[139] The following year, Rowe would write a letter of recommendation on Prophet's behalf to the Guggenheim Foundation.

At the end of June 1929, Prophet filled in the nomination blank for the Harmon Awards. She listed her high school as "the College of serious thought & bitter experience, situated on the Campus of Poverty & Ambition" and her position since leaving school as that "of a silent worker in the state of solitude."[140] In addition to Rowe, Sharpe and Green wrote letters of recommendation. Sharpe had never met Prophet, but communicated with her by mail and found her to be "a person of unusually refined nature—& she has much imagination & temperament. Has always shown herself most appreciative of encouragement & assistance."[141]

Sometime during the summer of 1929, poet Countee Cullen, who was W.E.B. Du Bois's son-in-law, visited Prophet in her studio and interviewed her for *Opportunity*, the magazine founded by the National Urban League. The article would appear in the July 1930 issue, accompanied by photographs of Prophet and her works *Head of a Negro* (fig. 24) (labeled, perhaps erroneously, *Bust of Roland Hayes*), *Silence,* and *Discontent.* Cullen was struck by Prophet's theatrical gestures and slender, copper-colored body when he first met her in Tanner's studio. He wrote that she swept into the room, "revealing her Indian ancestry in her straight, unbending gait; unleashing her Negro blood in a warm smile."[142] Apparently, Prophet paid close attention to African American cultural life. Cullen reported that eight years abroad "with little or no contact with her own had not chilled her ardor for them [African Americans], nor lessened her sense of belonging to them. She knew what they were writing, in what plays they were acting, what new opportunities they were seizing."[143]

On July 2, Cullen invited Prophet, "a lady of charming manners," to tea as his guest of honor in celebration of her exhibition at the Société des Artistes Français in Paris.[144] At his apartment, Prophet may have met some of Cullen's African American artist friends, such as painters Palmer Hayden and Hale Woodruff, but there is no record of this. Yet the day before, Woodruff and entertainers Gertrude Curtis, Bessie Miller, Zaidee Jackson, and Caska Bond attended a small party at Cullen's where they played cards and listened to such gramophone music as Duke Ellington's "lowdown" recordings. It seems likely that these guests returned not only for Prophet's tea, but also for the Independence Day celebration on Montmartre, Louis Coles's birthday party, Zaidee Jackson's cocktail party, and a Martinican ball.[145] Cullen may well have encouraged Prophet to attend these events too.

Prophet apparently felt at ease with Cullen and admired his writing. She later wrote to him, arguing for sincere, original African American artistic expression:

> I don't want to appear like the hateful critic who stands on the outside criticizing everybody's effort, but I[']m in the ring too you know, so please let me howl from time to time.
>
> Always when I find myself criticizing other people I suddenly come sneaking back to have a look at my own things and so the criticism reverts back upon myself.
>
> What I want is one man to take the whole race upon his shoulders + under the stress of that weight, with his individual voice, to hurl out in poignantly convinceing [sic] manner the soul of that race.
>
> I don't see any reason why at this late day anybody should start writing a book just to show that anybody can mass together some thousand words after a certain composition any more than a sculptor has any reason to be vulgarizing art by piling up material that has nothing to say. If you say that this is the beginning of writers, I object. It is not the beginning of literature, it is the end. When a man has something to say he has need of no man[']s method[.] It comes out a spontaneous expression of his own soul + so it is useless for us to be proud of showing that we can build up a form like other people if that form has no other reason to be.
>
> Every year in the salons we see sculpture + paintings as well as books done by people who have learnt how to do them, and the result is most evident proof that these people have no reason to do what they do. All is there with the art + message lacking, that which is most important, is not found.
>
> It seems to me that the Negro has something more than petty grievances and prejudices or light pleasure to express. I do believe that underneath there is something more vital. Indeed in your poetry one senses this, but not in these novels. . . . When the Negro had not education he sang the spirituals. Now that he has it, it should only facilitate the expression. There should be the same sincerity and ardour [sic].

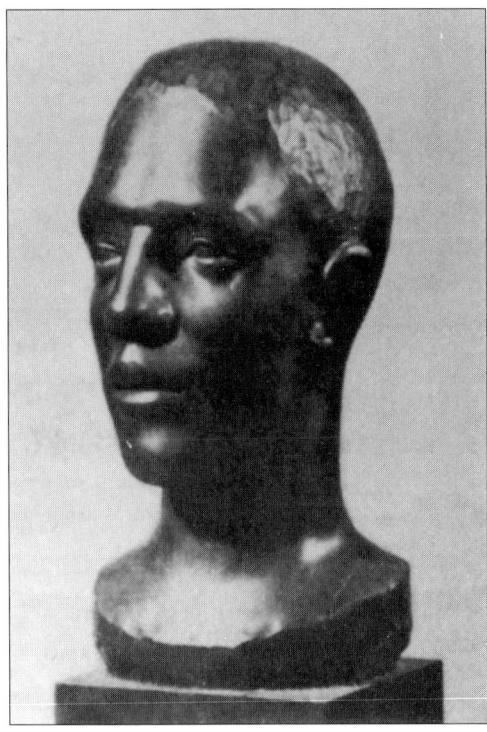

FIGURE 25
Nancy Elizabeth Prophet, *Head in Ebony,*
ca. 1926–1929, ebony, dimensions and
location unknown.
From a photograph in Nancy Elizabeth Prophet
Collection, James P. Adams Library, Rhode Island
College.

We know too well that comfort + success often brings [*sic*] about contentment +
yet it seems hard to believe that the race has gone so far that an individual could
become content. The state of a race should be the state of its individuals.

Now that I have gotten rid of all this spleen I beg you to forgive me. Tear up the
letter and throw me aside as a too temperamental solitary crazy woman.[146]

Prophet chose her words carefully. She identified with Cullen as an artist ("it is useless for us
to be proud"), but spoke of the Negro in the third, rather than first, person. Throughout her
life, she grappled with her mixed ethnicity, proud of her African heritage yet loath to call
herself "negro."

W.E.B. Du Bois, aware of Prophet's quandary with racial categorization, was
likewise circumspect in his choice of words with her, as we shall see in the following pages.
(As was the case with Tanner, it is not known when Du Bois and Prophet first met or
began communicating.) In the summer of 1929, he wrote to the artist, asking her to
advise a "colored" sculptor who would be studying in Paris, Augusta Savage.[147] Prophet
acknowledged his request to be Savage's "guide + consular," but informed him that she was
in bed with a sprained back and that he should not expect too much from her. Yet two days
later, on September 14, 1929, Prophet welcomed Savage in her studio and "found her very
sweet."[148] She arranged for Savage to work in her first atelier at 36, rue Châtillon in
Montparnasse.

On September 15, *La revue moderne illustrée* ran an article on Prophet, along with a
reproduction of *Head in Ebony* (ca. 1926–1929, fig. 25). The work is very similar to *Head of*

a Negro, but of harsher appearance, with blank eyes in polished, heavy, black wood. The
French critic noted that Prophet's sculpture, "a particularly virile art," retained "a certain
coldness which is not only due to the materials used in its realization, but also to the manner
in which the marble, the bronze, or the wood, is worked."[149] The critic marveled at the way
in which Prophet escaped the difficulty of breathing life into inert matters: "Whether it be a
finely engraved *Head in Ebony* on which alights every sort of reflection; whether it be the
charming head of a young girl fashioned with pure lines and in all the grace of adolescence,
the busts of Elizabeth Prophet are full of enticement and character. This American sculptress
has understood how to draw from her subjects the maximum output without having recourse
to the forms of caricature."[150] No doubt Prophet was pleased with the review.

VISIT TO THE UNITED STATES: OCTOBER 1929–AUGUST 1930

Shortly after her meeting with Savage, Prophet shipped four cases of statuary containing one
work each[151] to New York and returned to the United States in October 1929 to promote
her art,[152] her voyage apparently sponsored "through the generosity of some friends in Paris,
who felt that Americans should see what she is doing."[153] Once the boat reached New York
in November, however, Prophet was extremely anxious about being in America again after
seven years abroad. She was numb with anxiety and wished she had died at sea:

> The boat landed. . . . When I hear myself speaking I wonder why some power does
> not strike me dumb, + if I even try to laugh I am stunned by the stupidity of my
> effort.
> I have landed here without a single emotion. It speaks to me in no way + I feel
> not the least a part of it. . . . I adored that great + powerful ocean. . . . I would have
> been content + flattered to be lapped up by its powerful + cruel tongues. A rapturous
> moment in the armes [*sic*] of a love like that. O God! What a recompense. What a
> shame not to have been taken by the sea.
> Lone? I feel so indifferent since parting with the sea. . . . "He whom the Gods
> would destroy they first make mad."[154]

Despite her inner sense of terror and loneliness, as a guest of the Du Bois family for
several months she was immediately lionized in social circles and attended a Christmas party
given by singer Roland Hayes, visited various people in New York, and sketched at the
Metropolitan Museum of Art.[155] Prophet would also socialize with such notables as writers
Owen Dodson, Harold Jackman, and others.[156] Despite the warm reception, she yearned to
be back in France and by herself. She wrote to Cullen about her uneasiness with her renown:
"What is dear Paris doing these days? I long to be there in the solitude of my own studio, I
do not like being famous, Cullen. A man should be famous after he has been dead a hundred
years. That is a man. How he must work + try to think, one senses the need of it here so
terribly, deeper thought. I pray that I do not depress you with my philosophy, but I cannot
think of other things."[157]

Yet Prophet had much to celebrate in New York. *Head of a Negro* (also called *Negro
Head*), lent by Green, won the $250 Otto Kahn Prize for sculpture in 1930. Along with

Silence, lent by Sharpe, it was exhibited in New York at the International House on Riverside Drive early that year. Prophet said that *Head of a Negro* represented "the determination and aggressiveness" she felt when she began the struggle of earning her living by art.[158] Among the Harmon jurors were painters Victor Pérard and George Luks, art critic George Hellman, and sculptor Meta Vaux Warrick Fuller. It is not known whether she met these people, but juror and sculptor Karl Illava presented Prophet with the prize of the third annual national exhibition of fine arts on February 9, 1930.[159]

This was probably the only Harmon Foundation exhibition Prophet ever attended, and it afforded her one of the first chances she had to view the work of other African American artists. Little sculpture was on display there, but she could have seen Savage's acclaimed *Gamin* and five pieces by Sargent Claude Johnson. Yet it is unlikely that Prophet would have felt a strong affinity for Johnson's idealized, angular, symmetrical busts and masks. Besides Savage, the only other African American women sculptors who exhibited in Harmon Foundation exhibition shows were Meta Vaux Warrick Fuller, in 1931 and 1933, and May Howard Jackson, in 1929, yet there is no evidence that Prophet ever saw any of their work.

Prophet, like most people in the early twentieth century, was also probably unaware of those women sculptors who preceded her, black or white. Even if she had heard of Edmonia Lewis and the other, white members of the "White Marmorean Flock" in Rome in the nineteenth century, she most likely never saw work by them because it was not readily available in museums or galleries. It is possible that she had some awareness of contemporary sculptors Bessie Potter Vonnoh, Evelyn Longman, and Janet Scudder; Scudder lived just outside of Paris in Ville d'Avray from 1913 to ca. 1939. And it is likely that she saw Anna Hyatt Huntington's equestrian monument, *Joan of Arc,* which won honorable mention at the Paris Salon of 1910 and was cast in bronze in 1914, on Riverside Drive where the Harmon Foundation held its exhibition.

While in the United States, Prophet carried off several artistic coups. She became a member of and exhibited her works at the Salons of America at American-Anderson Galleries in New York[160] (April 22–May 8, 1930), the 56th Street Galleries,[161] Milch Galleries,[162] and the Boston Society of Independent Artists.[163] Mr. Brummer, director of the 56th Street Galleries, which exhibited nine of her works,[164] was so impressed with Prophet's work that he promised her a solo exhibition in 1931 or 1932.[165] On April 4, Prophet was the featured speaker, presumably at an African American women's group.[166]

Through the 56th Street Galleries in New York, Prophet sold *Discontent* to Sharpe and Green jointly for one thousand dollars. They then donated the work to the museum of art at Prophet's alma mater, Rhode Island School of Design, for its permanent collection, which Prophet duly noted in her diary.[167] However, the gallery's commission was a third of the sale and Prophet still needed funding to continue living in France.

Prophet confided to Du Bois that for her to live and work and buy materials in Paris, it would cost her two thousand dollars a year.[168] She applied for a Guggenheim Foundation Fellowship to complete some large statues in marble and other works that she had already begun in Paris, with the intent of bringing them to the United States for exhibition within three years.[169] Du Bois sent letters of recommendation on Prophet's behalf to the Guggenheim Foundation, the Harmon Foundation, and banker Otto Kahn.[170] He wrote to Kahn:

> Mrs. Du Bois while in Paris to visit her daughter urged Mrs. Prophet to come to America and offered her the hospitality of our home. She has made her sleep, rest and eat and be quiet these few months. I wish we could do more for Elizabeth Prophet as her character and genius is worth it. But we can't. Naturally, idleness and waiting is getting her nerves on edge. She is eager, almost wild, to be at work. But she can't. She landed in America with $15 and I loaned her $175 to pay for transporting her busts. This she promptly repaid from the Harmon prize and bought needed clothes with a part of the rest. . . .
>
> I trust you will forgive this importunity but my excuse is great interest in Elizabeth Prophet and my deep faith in her future.[171]

In April, Kahn promised to send 250 dollars in addition to the 250 already given in his name for *Head of a Negro*.[172]

In May, Du Bois wrote to Albert C. Barnes, director of the Barnes Foundation, a museum of outstanding modern European and African art in Merion, Pennsylvania.[173] He also asked Barnes to contribute to Prophet's fund, but Barnes apparently did not reply.

Du Bois's next strategy was to approach the Rosenwald Foundation in late May; he typed up a letter of request and a budget of expenses on Prophet's behalf for her to sign. The request was that the Rosenwald Foundation pay at least the deficit for one year's work, with the possibility of applying for funds to cover a second year's work.[174] Unfortunately, Prophet did not receive this aid, either, but the foundation encouraged her to reapply in early February 1931.[175]

While Du Bois worked to find Prophet funding, she visited friends in Providence. There, art critic Nell Occomy declared her to be "the only artist of the colored group who is doing note worthy [*sic*] [work] in Paris." She stated that the sculptor had endured much privation, "but Elizabeth has steeled herself against such suffering as long as the urge to create was satisfied. That look of steel has become a definite part of Elizabeth, and is more pronounced because of her Indian ancestry."[176] Prophet likely would have reveled in this description of her.

Initially, she had hoped to remain in the United States permanently, but as the effects of the Great Depression became more evident, she decided to return to France, where it was less expensive to live.[177] By the end of June, when Kahn had still not sent the funds he had promised, Prophet wrote to him asking if she could have the money soon so that she could return to Paris in July or August. She also indicated that Louise Brooks, as well as a Miss Helen D. Wright of Providence were tentatively offering at least 500 dollars.[178] After waiting two months, with none of these funds ever coming through, Prophet sailed back to France in August 1930 with just 500 dollars.[179]

THE PATRONAGE OF DU BOIS AND THE CHAMPIONS

In early September, Prophet applied again to the Harmon Foundation, this time indicating that she would send a bust in bronze, if the transportation expense were not too great.[180] She also asked Brooks to lend her *Study* (or *Head*) *in Ebony*[181] and Du Bois to lend *Poise*.[182]

In November, Du Bois wrote to Prophet urging her to reapply to the Rosenwald Fund and the Guggenheim Foundation, and he thanked her for a catalog she had sent him from Chez Plon that contained some information on Africa.[183] Prophet must have written to Du Bois on a more personal matter, because in early December, he wrote to her regarding her prospective marriage, apparently, to a white man:

> I am venturing to write to you concerning the question which you asked. It is so difficult in these matters to give advice. If there is real affection and compatibility, and in addition to this, a clear chance of income sufficient to reasonable needs, then I think that the matter of race should play absolutely no part. On the other hand, if there is doubt on any of these points, it would be unwise to marry simply on account of loneliness or need of sympathy and companionship. You would soon weary of that sort of thing.
>
> This advice is very vague and indefinite but knowing you as little as I do, it is about all that I can offer.[184]

Nothing else was ever mentioned about the marriage prospect (it is odd that Prophet's letter would be missing from the files of Du Bois, who fastidiously kept everything), but Prophet included a cryptic section in her letter to him a month later: "In reading it [Du Bois's letter] perhaps I shall love you again. I read your little note and feel myself weakening to it, but my heart tightens again. I want to love you always, and I know what life has been to you but remember that I have suffered and suffer. Let us not strike each other."[185]

Had the two been clandestine lovers during Prophet's stay with his family in New York? It is impossible to say, but Du Bois clearly had deep affection for her; in addition to all of the efforts he made on her behalf, he signed a letter in November, "with love and best regards"[186] rather than his customary "with best regards" and in 1931, Prophet would begin signing her letters to him "with love." In August 1931, she wrote, "Tonight I will write you because I am not cross and scolding the world and because tonight I love you."[187] Regardless of their possible amorous feelings for each other, the two remained amicable toward each other the rest of their lives.

In the middle of December 1930, Prophet wrote to Du Bois with instructions on how she wanted *Poise* to be exhibited at the Harmon Foundation. She was afraid that the work would be placed too low, and asked him to make sure that it was put "almost a head higher than a man's head, standing."[188] She also wanted him to know exactly what the French critics meant when they used the word *nerveuse* to describe her work: "The word (style, *nerveuse*) which is translated, brawny, lusty, powerful [*sic*]. It is the word nervose [*sic*] which corresponds to the english [*sic*] nervous and there is none of this in my things. There is entirely the contrary, and absolute quiet and calm as you will see as you see more of my things."[189]

In a postscript dated five days later on the same letter, Prophet begged Du Bois to find her financial aid:

> Do please try and get me some help[,] something to live on until I can get enough work done to get on my feet. For this hard living is beginning to tell on me and will kill me if it has to go on. I am in bed with the grippe and it drags on because I can afford no care whatever. I was working on a piece of work which one of the galleries asked me for, but with this grippe I am too weak to cut marble and I am so worried for I have about seventy[-]five dollars left.
>
> Try and help me if you can. I shall see that you are not sorry by honest and creditable work and my sincere appreciation. Sometimes it seems that no one understands what a serious artist goes through.[190]

Prophet also told Du Bois that she had met some influential French people, and she sent him two books.

Du Bois responded several weeks later that he had delivered *Poise* to the "Harmon folk." He also expressed pleasure that she had met some "French folk of importance." "The thing is important in itself," he wrote, "and, of course, will have tremendous influence in America. In art, especially, we are absolutely subservient to the judgement of the French."[191] In March 1931 Prophet again submitted a work to the Société des Artistes Français. When the exhibition opened on April 1, her *Buste marbre* was included.[192] Unfortunately, it is not known which marble bust this was. Nevertheless, as reported in the NAACP magazine *Crisis*, French critics praised Prophet's work; in 1931 Jean Patézon wrote in *Le rayonnment intellectuel:* "Elizabeth Prophet has a broad and grand vision, which is a guarantee of the quality of her work. Her vision follows her thought which is original and with no outward influences and this is what makes her work so strong and expressive."[193]

Prophet was "penniless again"[194] that spring, but fortunate enough to have "some wonderful friends" in Edouard and Julia Champion (these must have been the "French folk of importance" about whom Prophet had earlier written to Du Bois; it is not known how she met them). Edouard Champion (1882–1938) was a well-known author of more than twenty books, including a multivolume anthology of French comedy. He and his wife supported Prophet by paying for her room and board; they also sought "big money" on her behalf.[195]

In contrast, Prophet was apparently frustrated not only with Du Bois's largely futile efforts to obtain financial backing for her but also with what she perceived to be a lack of recognition of her achievements by Americans, both black and white. In turn, Du Bois was upset by her misunderstanding and ignorance of the severity of the Great Depression. It is worth quoting from his letter at length:

> I am disturbed by the evident fact that you are in some way hurt by my own actions and by the attitude of colored and white America. I hope, however, you will not let this feeling go too far.
>
> First of all, I am sure you must realize that no one, either in France or America, appreciates you as an artiste [*sic*] more than I do. Secondly, it is also true that the colored people of America, so far as they know about you, are proud of your work,

and all things considered, you had a marvellously fine reception by the white artistic world.

On the other hand, perhaps you do not understand what a difficult year this has been in America. Under ordinary circumstances, I think it would have been possible to secure aid and support for your work, but we have in the United States today at least six million men and women workers idle, and perhaps the number reaches ten million, no one knows. . . .

. . . Remember that I, even in prosperous times, have very little chance to solicit our white philanthropy in the United States. Most persons who have wealth and are in the habit of giving us subscriptions, are inimical to my attitude and particularly to my frank and unpopular writing and talking. I do not know rich people. I am not persona grata to the great Foundations, so that even in good times, I cannot do much for those who need and deserve help, while in bad times like this, I am quite powerless.

From this, I think you can understand how it has happened that you have been left to struggle alone. . . .

On the other hand, do not blame me and do not blame the colored people of the United States. We are still curiously helpless. When eventually you triumph, as I am sure you will, it will not be altogether wrong to give people of colored blood here a part of the glory. They are a kind-hearted and sympathetic folk but they are ignorant and inexperienced.

. . . You cannot expect colored people to appreciate you unless they know how much you are appreciated by those who are connoisseurs.[196]

Prophet seems not to have answered this letter.

Du Bois and Prophet had a mutually beneficial relationship in that she was able to send him hard-to-obtain French periodicals and historical material. However, he clearly did more for her—by continuously seeking funding for her and supporting her career—than she did for him. After the 56th Street Galleries closed for the summer in 1931,[197] Du Bois stored a bronze version of *Silence* for Prophet in his office and often commented on it in his correspondence to her.[198]

THE COLONIAL EXPOSITION OF 1931

In August, Prophet wrote excitedly to Du Bois about the Colonial Exposition, which had been open since May 6, 1931. The Colonial Exposition was an enormous, almost Disneyesque display on the subject of France's colonies throughout the world—the North African territories of Morocco, Algeria, and Tunisia; the vast area of French West and French Equatorial Africa; Madagascar; French Indochina; the French West Indies; and the Pacific dependencies. The exposition was a carefully orchestrated international spectacle that involved the participation of Britain, Belgium, Portugal, Italy, Japan, and the United States and was intended to draw public attention to the glory, diversity, and resources of overseas France. For six months, more than thirty-three million visitors from all over the world flocked to the eastern fringe of Paris, where the exposition was held, in the

Bois de Vincennes. In scale and attendance, the Colonial Exposition was "the most spectac- ular colonial extravaganza ever staged in the West."[199]

The dominant theme of the exposition was the mutually beneficial work of French colonialism, meant to stress that France was neither the exploiter of colonial societies nor the agent of miscegenation and decadence, as was claimed by Germany.[200] The exposition articulated and defended the current colonial theory and the policy of association rather than assimilation. The exposition planners thus reproduced as many details as possible of the cultures and lifestyles of the peoples whom France had colonized, rather than making reference to the dissemination of the French language among the empire's subjects or the adoption of French customs and dress. The French government imported colonial peoples to Paris to exhibit their arts, crafts, and natural products and to perform in purportedly authentic architectural re-creations, such as African dwellings and Indochinese temples, that had been designed by French architects. Most of these structures, in fact, were ridiculously enlarged to complement the monumental scale of the exposition's layout. More than just an enormously entertaining amusement park, the exposition was a great agent for the circulation and exchange of valuable information regarding all aspects of metropolitan- colonial relations. During the course of the event, the French held more than one hundred congresses and published nearly three thousand reports.[201] The exposition had many important effects—colonial service became a more attractive career for young men; colonial and "exotic" literature flourished; French jewelry designers introduced new lines of adornment of colonial inspiration; directors made movies that were affirmative of the French colonial experience; Vietnamese and North African restaurants sprouted throughout the city; and the Permanent Colonial Museum, now the Musée des Arts Africains et Océaniens, established in the wake of the exposition, provided continuous publicity on behalf of the empire.[202]

Prophet found the Colonial Exposition "very instructive and of rare beauty." She reported that many people visited it daily and "learned much about the people of color." Yet she did not seem to be critically aware of the propagandistic nature of the extravaganza and never commented on France's attitude to its colonies.

One of the buildings that Prophet, as a sculptor, would have most enjoyed was the highly publicized Palais des Bois Coloniaux, where designer furniture made of colonial wood, such as streaked ebony, palm wood, and burl ash, was on view. Art historian Romy Golan has argued that this exhibition acted as a catalyst for the shift toward a neorustic aesthetic: "The 'style colonial,' the modern rustic, and the proliferation of surrealist objects after 1931, all belong to a regime in which the reflective (namely specular) surfaces of highly polished and lacquered art deco furniture and objects, as well as the chillingly metallic sheen and dematerializing effect of glass in modernist design, gave way to the tactile."[203] Prophet would have appreciated this shift that affirmed her own use of "tactile" materials. She had previously worked in wood, stone, clay, and plaster, and apparently she exclusively sculpted in wood throughout the remainder of her years in Paris. Of course, this may not have been entirely her choice; it is unlikely that she could afford to work in large blocks of marble or to have pieces cast in bronze.

More than by the display of colonial resources, Prophet was especially moved by the African busts on view. At the exposition, she wrote to Du Bois, one could see

> men and women from real savage [illegible] with a swell developement [*sic*] that is unusual among the average European. I mean heads that are of such a mental development that are rarely seen among Europeans. Heads of thought and reflection, types of great beauty and dignity of carriage. I believe it is the first time that this type of African has been brought to the attention of the world of modern times. Am I right? People are seeing the aristocracy of Africa.[204]

In this letter, she also informed Du Bois that she continued to get a monthly food allowance from the Champions, who were at Le Touquet, spreading her "propaganda over the two continents."

Both the grandeur of the Colonial Exposition and the support of the Champions likely inspired Prophet to produce her best-known work, *Congolais* (ca. 1931, fig. 26), a powerful cherrywood head of a Masai warrior. The encounter with African sculptures and peoples, as well as the display of colonial wood may well have given Prophet the incentive to sculpt the piece. With its smooth, expansive brow, closed lips, and heavy eyelids, the head imparts a sense of majesty and dignity. Nevertheless, like Prophet's earlier work, such as *Head of a Negro, Congolais* depicts a type rather than a portrait of an individual. Masai men, from Kenya and Tanzania in East Africa, were known as cattle herders, lion hunters, and fierce warriors with distinctive coiffures that often included a single plait of beaded hair on the forehead. Here, Prophet depicted a "noble savage," but a savage, nonetheless. This warrior, however, depicted as bodiless and weaponless, with eyes half-closed and without elaborate war makeup or earrings, appears to a white audience as a nonthreatening, rather romantic symbol of exoticism. For Prophet, however, the significance was probably deeper. She may have been familiar with Joseph Thomson's popular account of his exploration through East Africa, *Through Masai Land,* first published in 1885 and available commercially and in French libraries. Thomson's book extolled the Masai for their bravery, their disdain for menial labor, and their tall, slender bodies and thin lips, which the British saw as hallmarks of aristocracy.[205] Why, then, would Prophet choose to name as Congolese—in other words, from the west of the continent—her depiction of an East African? It is unlikely that the Masai were represented in the French Colonial Exposition, since Kenya and Tanzania were British mandates. Prophet may have simply grafted the term onto the image out of ignorance. In truth, between the lack of decent publications on Africa and the vogue for the mere surface qualities of West African art at the time, she probably knew little about Africa, like most people in the early twentieth century. Writer Countee Cullen eloquently addressed this dilemma in his poem "Heritage," in which he ponders the gulf of three centuries between his life and that of his ancestors, asking at the end of each stanza, "What is Africa to me?"[206]

The suggestion that *Congolais* is a self-portrait is tantalizing,[207] and the bust's facial features do resemble Prophet's own, although the nose is slighter thinner than hers. Perhaps Prophet longed for the control and bravery of Masai warriors, or the esteem in which the British held them. While the distinctive braided coiffure marks the bust as male—Masai

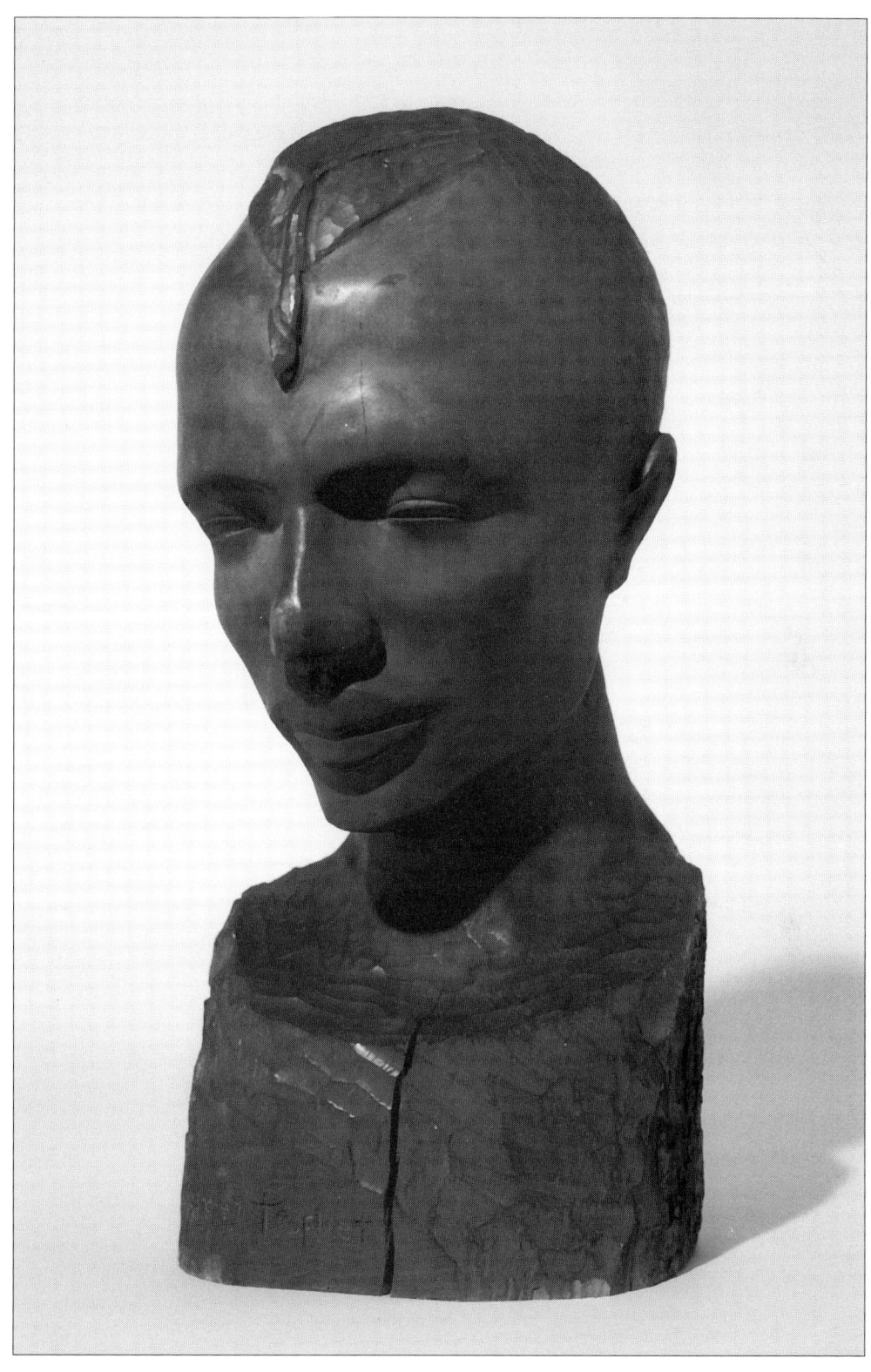

FIGURE 26

Nancy Elizabeth Prophet, *Congolais* (or *Congolaise*), ca. 1931, wood, 17⅛ x 6¾ x 8¹/₁₆ in. Photograph copyright © 1999 by the Whitney Museum of American Art, purchase 32.83.

women never wore their hair this way—the visage is androgynous and the work is sometimes called *Congolaise,* making it unclear what Prophet really named the piece. She may have enjoyed the resulting confusion and ambiguity.

SEVERAL BAS-RELIEFS AND PROPHET'S LAST EXHIBITION IN PARIS

In November 1931 Prophet reported that she had produced several works to show the Champions, including a large bas-relief of "that strangely beautiful female with the marvelous headdress in the *Croisière noire.*" It is likely that she was referring to George Specht's photograph *Nobosodrou, femme Mangbetu* (ca. 1924), published in the book *La croisière noire* (1927), a copy of which Prophet had sent to Du Bois.[208] This stunning image had inspired Aaron Douglas, whose drawing of a woman's head graced the cover of *Opportunity* magazine in May 1927, and the white American artist Malvina Hoffman, who produced a bronze bust titled *Mangbetu Woman* in 1927.[209]

Unfortunately, the location and title of Prophet's interpretation of the Mangbetu woman are unknown. Reproductions of three of her other wooden bas-reliefs exist, but they seem more concerned with spirituality and less with African sculpture. Yet all of the bas-reliefs may have been influenced by the sculpture of Alfred Janniot at the Colonial Exposition, at least in their form; the genre was relatively new to Prophet, who had always worked in the round. Janniot's huge frieze in low relief embellished the four exterior walls of the Palais des Colonies, the only permanent building in the exposition and that which became the Permanent Colonial Museum, today the Musée des Arts Africains et Océaniens. Titled *The Colonies' Contribution to France,* the bas-relief depicts the organic abundance of the colonies—flora and fauna, jungle scenes, crowds of fisherfolk and hunters, and shiploads of goods docked at Marseilles, Bordeaux, Le Havre, and Rouen—overseen by the female allegories of Peace, Justice, and Liberty, though not Equality.

In contrast, Prophet's bas-reliefs are not smooth, densely packed scenes of plenty, but rather slight, rough-hewn, contemplative portraits of individuals. In the October 1932 issue of *Crisis,* there is a reproduction of an untitled piece that depicts a man's head in profile surrounded by a halo (a good-quality image is unavailable). Another work, *Peace* (ca. 1928–1931, fig. 27), shows a woman's head in profile before a golden halo or an orb of light (possibly the sun). She has blank eyes but faces two enormous flowers. The third bas-relief, *Facing the Light* (ca. 1928–1931, fig. 28) seems to be much larger than the first two; it is 5 feet 6 inches by 17 inches. In this horizontal piece appear the heads and shoulders of four people. Three women—perhaps all the same woman—who wear buns or French twists, like the woman in *Peace,* bow their heads away from three rays of a large sun on the right, eyes closed. A curly-haired man in the center, however, looks directly into the bright star. These works are enigmatic, but all seem to deal with meditation, prayer, or a reckoning with one's self.

Prophet offered to send Du Bois photographs of her work only if he would promise not to show them to anyone, stating in a letter to him, "I believe that if I had money to work with I should avoid all show of my things, simply live my life and work, letting my things be

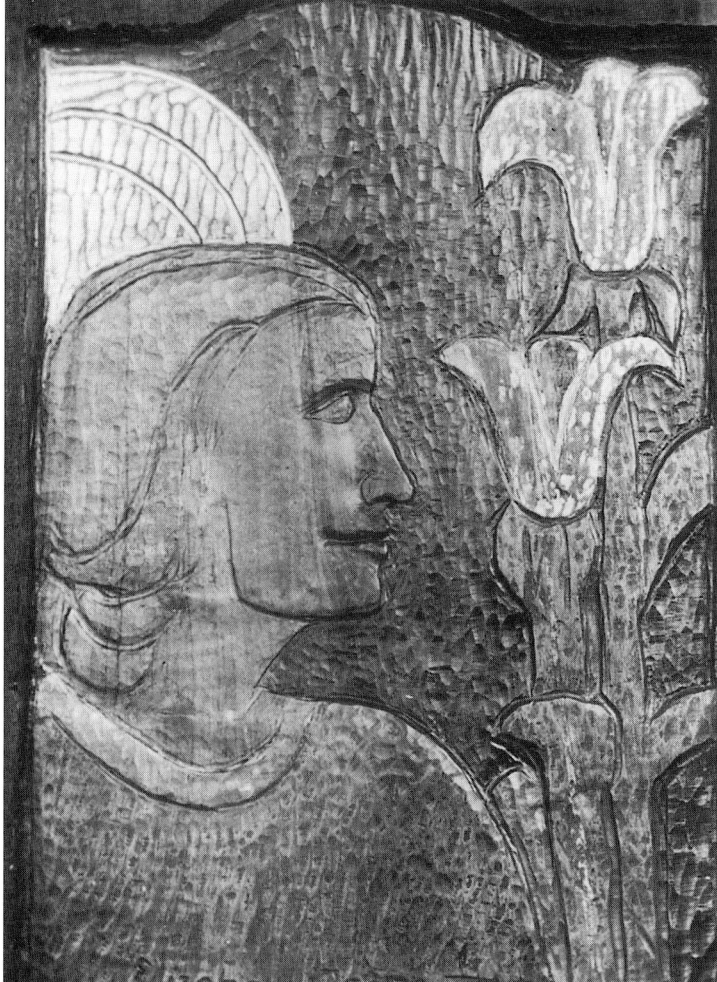

FIGURE 27
Nancy Elizabeth Prophet,
Peace, ca. 1928–1931,
painted wood, dimensions
and location unknown.
From a photograph in
Nancy Elizabeth Prophet
Collection, James P.
Adams Library, Rhode
Island College.

FIGURE 28
Nancy Elizabeth Prophet,
Facing the Light,
ca. 1928–1931, painted
wood, 5 ft. 6 in.
Black Heritage Society.
From a photograph in
Nancy Elizabeth
Prophet Collection,
James P. Adams Library,
Rhode Island College.

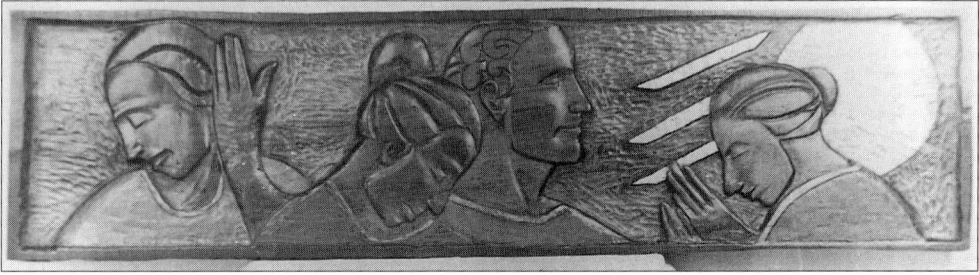

shown after I am gone, it would please me better."[210] In this letter she also encouraged Du
Bois to come to France: "How delightful it would be for you to come to Paris, Beautiful
Paris! and Wonderful France! and all because of the greatness of the French. It is the only
well poised nation of the day. . . . It is a great pity that the french [*sic*] are so little understood
by other people for they have much that others should learn. It is a people with the power
of reason and it is that that has put them in their superior position. It is a Nation Elite. The

frivolity of the french only exists in the minds of other people who have never known the french, nor understand them."

In December, Du Bois replied that he would love to see reproductions of Prophet's sculpture. He also said that he would be unable to make it to Paris, after all, because the depression was so bad.[211] Prophet might have suspected as much; the same day, she wrote in her diary: "Voici le [*sic*] vie dans toute sa beauté et tragede [tragédie], tous ses desapointe-ments [désappointements] et ses desespoirs [désespoirs]."[212] (This is life, in all its beauty and tragedy, all its disappointments and despair.)

In March 1932 Prophet sent two more works to the Société des Artistes Français. The exhibition opened again on April 1 and included her *Violence* and *Buste ébène*.[213] *Violence* (location unknown) reportedly depicted a man whose cap and scarf were tinted violet.[214] *Buste ébène*, mentioned earlier as *Head in Ebony* (fig. 25), looked much like *Head of a Negro*. Despite this acceptance in another French cultural venue and her impending second trip to America, she grew depressed again. In April, she wrote in her diary, "Sweet Death, the lover of weary souls."[215] It seems that Prophet had lost her drive and vision. She apparently produced nothing of substance after 1931 and she never exhibited in Paris again after 1932.

SECOND TRIP TO THE UNITED STATES: MAY 1932–FEBRUARY 1933

In May 1932, Prophet returned to New York on the S.S. *Lafayette* once more to promote her art there.[216] She apparently stayed with the Du Bois family in Harlem again,[217] but she wrote of her distaste for the neighborhood in her journal: "Harlem night where there is no light / Transition / From Paris to the sordid filth of Harlem."[218] But Prophet did not linger in Harlem; soon she was feted in Manhattan, Newport, and Providence.[219]

In July 1932 she was officially elected a member of the Art Association of Newport by its council, just in time for her works to be displayed in the twenty-first annual exhibition by that group (July 8–August 6),[220] along with work by forty-one other artists. Of the 201 works exhibited, five were Prophet's, *Silence, Poise, Peace, Congolais*, and *Discontent*, the last of which winning the Richard B. Greenough grand prize of seventy-five dollars for being "true sculpture in every sense of the word."[221] Prophet found the reception on July 8 "joyous, frank, and wholehearted."[222] Yet critics were quick to racially categorize the artist. The *New York Times* reported that "an Indian woman, Anne Elizabeth Prophet," had won the award. Headlines in the *Art Digest* and the *Newport Herald* announced, "Negress Wins the First Prize at Newport" and "First Prize for Indian Woman."[223] Ironically, the NAACP magazine, *Crisis*, which Du Bois edited, was the only periodical to compare Prophet's work to those of European masters; it declared that some said that no such work had been seen since Donatello and the artists of the Italian Renaissance.[224]

Some of the highest society members in New England admired Prophet's work: Mrs. William Vanderbilt, Mrs. William Randolph Hearst, Mrs. Vincent Astor, the countess Cocini, and the Sterners. Gertrude Vanderbilt Payne Whitney (1875–1942), herself a sculptor, was most impressed with *Congolais* and privately viewed the work three times. In July Prophet waited "with great anxiety for a sale."[225] On August 6, Whitney purchased the work for the Whitney Museum of American Art.[226] Whitney later wrote to Prophet to ask her when she intended to return to the United States and she suggested that Prophet "cut a head in marble" for her.[227] That fall, Whitney offered to share her Newport studio with Prophet.[228] It does not seem, however, that Prophet ever did either.

Once the art association exhibition closed, Prophet's work was then shown for a week in August at the antique shop (which existed from 1930 to about 1937)[229] of Schuyler L. Parsons (1892–1967)[230] on John Street. The exhibition was cosponsored by Parsons and by interior and set designer Casey Roberts and "attracted a large contingent of art lovers in Newport and environs throughout the week."[231] Part of the exhibition's popularity, no doubt, had to do with the elite, monied crowd with whom Parsons associated (many of these notables are mentioned in *Untold Friendships,* his autobiography) as well as Prophet's ethnic heritage, which wealthy whites may have perceived as exotic and curious. Although Parsons believed that there was a "highly respectable Negro colony in Newport,"[232] it is unlikely that he associated with any of its residents; he "could never tell one black from another and made some awful mistakes."[233]

From October 31 to November 19, 1932, the Robert C. Vose Jr. Galleries in Boston exhibited Prophet's sculpture and Casey Roberts's paintings. It is possible that Tanner had written to the Vose Galleries on Prophet's behalf; he had had a solo exhibition there in January 1921.[234] Loaned works included *Silence, Discontent, Head of a Negro, Congolais, Study [Head] in Ebony,* and *Head in Bronze.* Works for sale were *Poise* ($2,000), *Violence* ($1,000), *Youth* ($800), *Bitter Laughter* ($1,000), and *Peace* ($300).[235] Newspapers duly noted Prophet's success. Art critic Albert Franz Cochrane described her as "a charming artist and excellent technician" whose "textures have a pleasing tactile quality."[236] She seems to have basked in the glory and may have considered staying in the United States; she had her tools shipped from Paris to New York.[237]

Prophet left Boston for New York to request further aid from various institutions. Brooks's secretary, Laura Heathfield, had written a long letter of recommendation to the Carnegie Corporation on her behalf without her knowledge. Heathfield felt that given backing, she could be "another outstanding colored genius."[238] Heathfield concluded by saying that she would write to Prophet and tell her to call on Frederick Keppel (1875–1943), African American president of the corporation, but warned him, "She is very modest and will not say one-half about her work that it deserves."

When Prophet did meet with an administrator of the Carnegie Corporation (the administrator's identity is not known; it was not Keppel) in December 1932, her only plea was for the opportunity to work. Roberta Fansler, an art adviser, informed her that the corporation did not make grants to individual artists to enable them to work, but she suggested that the sculptor apply to the Guggenheim Foundation and the newly founded American Sculptor Painter Foundation.[239] Apparently, she also suggested that Prophet teach at an African American university.

One week later, Prophet returned for another meeting with the same staff member to say that she had reconsidered the possibility of teaching. Although she wanted to devote all of her time to sculpting, she believed that she could offer students something. She mentioned possible courses in art history and appreciation, as well as studio courses in stone-cutting, batik, drawing, painting, and anatomy. She hoped to begin teaching during the spring semester of 1933 at Spelman College or Hampton Institute; she had received the address of the president of Hampton Institute from Du Bois a year before.[240] Fansler believed that Prophet was one of those artists who "make superb teachers because they care so much about their subjects, know so much about them, and combine with their knowledge sensitiveness and sympathy."[241] Fansler recommended that the Carnegie Corporation pay her salary of $1,500 for one semester or $2,700 for two.

Enthused by the idea, Keppel contacted President Florence Read at Spelman College (later part of Atlanta University) with the proposal that Prophet spend a semester getting undergraduates interested in the arts, rather than teaching formal courses. He felt that she could do "something like what Robert Frost did when he spent a year at Amherst sometime ago."[242] Read was delighted by the proposal: "In fact, it is difficult for me to restrain my enthusiasm sufficiently to send a calm reply by mail. I feel like telegraphing or telephoning you, and throwing my hat in the air!"[243] The Carnegie Corporation voted approval of the necessary funds on January 11, 1933, only to receive a letter from Prophet the following day informing them that she was going back to Paris to carry out a commission (identity now unknown) that she had just received.[244] "I beg you to understand that each day lost is a month to me," Prophet wrote. "I thought that if I took your position I would sacrifice my work for the time, but the visit to Philadelphia gives me a small command, and the Whitney sale makes my departure possible. Forgive what seems like instability please."[245] She shipped her works to France and returned to Paris in February 1933. She did not apologize to Read for the change in plans, but later wrote to the Carnegie Corporation that Read could keep the photographs of her work that Keppel had sent for her perusal.[246]

LAST DAYS OF PRIVATION IN PARIS, 1933–1934

Apparently, 1933 was a grim year for the sculptor. Prophet received no fellowships and exhibited no works. Yet she persevered—in May, she reported that she was "hard at work cutting stone" on a twelve-hundred-pound block of stone.[247] In June, she wrote a brief note to Tanner to inform him of her return to Paris and to invite him to look at her sculpture.[248] There is no record of what she experienced or of her activities during the following five months.

In November, the police hounded the artist for avoiding import taxes and threatened to seize her belongings.[249] After she appealed to the minister of fine arts, the minister of finance granted her three hundred dollars to cover expenses. On November 28, in her diary she wrote, "If it had been a million frances [francs] I should not feel more happy and encouraged." Her funds were dwindling, and her landlord and concierge heated her studio on credit and provided her with food, as she also noted on that day. This arrangement would last throughout the winter. On November 30, she recorded in her diary that on that Thanksgiving Day, Julia Champion surprised her with "many good things" for a feast.

In early 1934 Prophet reactivated her 1930 application to the Guggenheim Foundation. She informed the foundation that she planned on having a solo exhibition in five years, stating: "I have a very profound conviction that I have something very great to offer to America in Artistic [sic] sculpture."[250] She requested funds to execute four large statues in marble and wood that she already had in sketch form, and to complete several other smaller works. Those who wrote letters of recommendation on Prophet's behalf were editor Edouard Champion, animal painter and government architect Francis Jacques (b. 1887), and director of the Academy of France in Rome and sculptor Paul Landowski (1875–1961). All admired Prophet's diligence as well as her sculpture. Champion declared that Prophet, whose work was encouraged by Jacques, Landowski, and Bourdelle, highly merited an award. He also emphasized her poverty and stated that she lacked proper materials to complete her work. Jacques, who had visited Prophet's studio in 1933, found her best work in "serious, profound subjects, in which she succeeds in appealing to the imagination of the spectator."[251] Landowski was particularly impressed with the personal treatment of *Le pélerin* and *Congolais,* which he must have seen either in person several years before or in photographs.

In February 1934 Du Bois wrote to Prophet that he was trying to find her financial support. He had told John Hope, president of Atlanta University, that "a person who is doing artistic work, and particularly a colored person, needs the freedom and inspiration of Paris."[252] At the end of the month, Prophet began to tear down partitions of her studio that closed off the small corner where she had lived for nine years. The landlord had rented her a small studio upstairs (with what money or credit is not known), which she planned on using for living quarters so that the entire downstairs space could be used for work alone. "This means at last a bit of quiet to think and work, after nine years of complete hellish bedlam [sic] going on over my head all day and all night made by the lowest kinds of brutes and *debauché* [*débauchés,* or debauched persons]."[253]

By the end of March, Prophet had still not completed her renovations, but she worked frantically from 6 a.m. to midnight each day to overcome the severe blow of once again not having received a Guggenheim Fellowship. She put two coats of paint on the walls and ceiling and split all of the wood from the partitions for winter heat. Now, however, she was ten thousand francs in debt to her landlord, Madame Chamtou.[254] Despite this, Chamtou lent Prophet five thousand more francs in April so that she could pay a few bills and have electricity and plumbing installed in the studio (April 9, 1934). In May, the studio, "quite charming and restful" (May 5, 1934), was nearly finished. Prophet began a new, large statue, *Le prince Sublil* [sic], a work of "just defiance," in plaster. She felt she could continue with her life and work, but she was not sure how: "I am going on, where?—Somewhere. Money?—" (May 5, 1934).

On May 5, the Champions took Prophet to dinner and apparently were appalled by her destitution. Prophet wrote, "I understand too well. My situation is too difficult. The friendship is withdrawn" (May 5, 1934). Just over a week later, she would write, "Life is so long" (May 14, 1934). By June, she had no food whatsoever: "Begins again the .00 diet." In the middle of the month, someone gave the artist a few presents that seemed to tease her appetite: "Gift of a lovely velvet wrap, how soft to touch, raspberry color, how pleasing to the eye, buttons set with *brillants*, how coquettishly they sparkle. Package of tea, jar of fruit, orange marmalade, how enticing to an empty stomach, no meat, no bread. These things awaken an appetite, recall a stomach, which was almost forgotten. I no longer care it seems. Yet how ironical" (June 16, 1934). Three days later she commented, "And after a time one can reach a point where just to caress, and gaze, upon a lovely velvet wrap, can, and must become—nourishment" (June 19, 1934). Two days after this she noted, "Orange marmalade and tea make a bad diet" (June 21, 1934).

In July, several people came to Prophet's aid. A man named Mario and his sister Erma gave her a nourishing dinner on the first, as did a Miss Grey on the ninth (more definitive identities of these acquaintances are not known.)[255] On the tenth, Erma informed Prophet with embarrassment that she had no more food or money for her. Prophet's last diary entry was July 19, 1934, in which she reported that she had had only one meal with Miss Grey since the tenth. Somehow, she reconciled with Julia Champion, who lent her the money to pay for the rent in July. The last sentence in her diary was "I feel well and calm."

Fortunately, although they had been rebuffed once, administrators at Spelman College were still interested in hiring her. Finally, with the encouragement of Du Bois who called her "our greatest Negro sculptor,"[256] and at the request of John Hope, she began teaching at Spelman in the fall of 1934. Her salary of two thousand dollars was sponsored by the Carnegie Corporation.[257]

Prophet's pedagogical activities eclipsed her sculpture. Early in 1940 she outlined her philosophy on the interaction of art and life in an article published in *Phylon* magazine. The sculptor firmly believed that the mark of civilized people was the degree to which they embraced the arts:

> If the purpose of art is to give aesthetic pleasure, that objective has not been fulfilled until some higher aesthetic quality has been reflected in the lives, habits, and manners of the people. The artist has always had a strong educational influence, and the obligation of the modern artist is no less today than it was in the Golden Age of Greece or the Renaissance of Italy. Intelligent America and her educators are well aware of this and are attempting to give some cultural education to the people, for this can no longer be neglected if America is to take her place in the civilized world.[258]

Convinced of her obligation to society, Prophet devoted herself to teaching while she was at Spelman, at the expense of her own art. It seems that she did not produce anything remarkable after her Paris years.

Prophet, along with painter Hale Woodruff, whom Hope had wooed away from France in 1931, built up Atlanta University's art department for ten years, until 1944, and continued to exhibit her work, but only sporadically. The last two decades of her life were marked by depression, poverty, and obscurity. In the late 1940s, she took odd jobs in New York, then she returned to Rhode Island to take care of her ailing father. After he committed suicide, she was hospitalized for psychiatric care at the Rhode Island State Hospital, 1951–1955, where she did needlework.[259] Next, she did benchwork at the Community Workshops of Rhode Island.[260] Prophet yearned to return to Europe and, in 1957, applied, unsuccessfully, to the Guggenheim and Louis Comfort Tiffany Foundations for fellowships. In July 1960, she wrote to her old benefactor Julia Champion how she longed to go back to Paris.[261] She had lost touch with Champion over the years when the government had restricted communications during World War II. Prophet never mailed the letter. She succumbed to a heart attack in December 1960. A man for whom she had worked as a housekeeper for six months, Edward J. Carley, hastily raised funds to save her from a pauper's funeral.[262]

3
PAINTING SEASCAPES AND "NEGRO CHARACTERS":
PALMER HAYDEN IN PARIS, 1927–1932

*I*n *Modern Negro Art* (1943), African American art historian James Porter lambasted Palmer Hayden's cartoonlike representations of black people of the 1930s as "one of those ludicrous billboards that once were plastered on public buildings to advertise the black minstrel face."[1] Hayden's characteristic dark-skinned figures with exaggerated facial features seem to play right into racist stereotypes. Yet the artist from rural Virginia documented contemporary African American life not only as he experienced it, but also as he saw it in the manner of popular cultural images in minstrel shows and penny postcards. Few artists, black or white, had much access to dignified depictions of blacks in fine art in the early twentieth century. Although Hayden's style reflected popular imagery, his representations of African American families, workers, churchgoers, soldiers, and legendary heroes are both humorous and respectful. As such, his narrative, sympathetic paintings are radical departures from contemporary, stereotypical images. Yet Hayden's appropriation and utilization of racial stereotypes may well have been, in part, a response to the expectations and demands of white patrons and French critics—who as early as 1927 published glowing reviews of his humorous African American genre scenes—as well as to the larger context of modern primitivism.

Perhaps because Hayden was the least academically trained of the artists who went to Paris and did not attend classes abroad, he was the most uniquely qualified to create paintings with a distinct folk sensibility. Hayden first won acclaim as a Postimpressionist marine painter in New York and continued depicting seascapes during his five-year stay in France. While abroad, he also developed his figurative painting, focusing on Breton peasants and fisherfolk. More important, he developed his signature style as a gently witty commentator on popular African American culture—from savvy cardplayers to the legendary John Henry. In Paris, Hayden also had his first exposure to other black peoples and cultures. There, he would paint his vision of West Indians at the Bal Nègre nightclub, West Africans at the Colonial Exposition of 1931, and West African sculpture in a domestic setting.

FROM "A WHISTLE STOP ON THE POTOMAC"
TO CITIES ALONG THE EAST COAST, 1890–1912

Under a mellow new moon on January 15, 1890, in the small town of Widewater, Virginia, "a whistle stop on the shore of the Potomac River"[2] Peyton Cole Hedgeman—Palmer Cole Hayden's original name—was born with a portion of the amniotic sac over his face. His mother, Nancy (Nannie) Belle Cole Hedgeman, was a devout Baptist who had great hopes for her thirteen children. The superstitious side of her believed that Hayden's caul meant that he seemed especially destined for greatness—or at least, good luck.[3]

Hayden's grammar school teachers at the local one-room country school encouraged him to develop his drawing talent. One instructor told him, "Keep at it and you'll be a famous artist."[4] However, he never received a formal secondary education. Instead, he went to work on the Potomac River at a young age, hauling sand and packing herring in barrels.[5] Hayden yearned to be a musician and hoped to earn enough money to buy a saxophone or a violin one day.[6] He would later express this longing in his painting *Moonlight at the Crossroads* (n.d.), a self-portrait as a child holding a fiddle at an intersection, uncertain of which way to turn.[7]

Hayden's father, James Hedgeman, was illiterate; he served as a tour guide for fishers and hunters who mostly came from Washington, D.C.[8] He was a great storyteller and often dramatized the legend of John Henry.[9] Like Henry, Hedgeman was a strong, confident man. He bragged to his sons that he had once squeezed a bear to death when a direct gunshot failed to kill the animal. Expecting his children to be equally self-sufficient, Hedgeman declared that his boys would have to leave home at the age of sixteen.[10]

Around 1906 Hayden went approximately forty miles north to Washington, D.C., to live with his aunt and study commercial art. In the early 1910s, he worked for the Ringling Brothers Circus as a roustabout—erecting and dismantling tents, keeping the grounds, and tending to the animals and circus equipment. Ringling Brothers managers noted Hayden drawing circus performers at night and asked him to produce posters, cards, and other graphics for publicity. Hayden enjoyed drawing the "kinkers," an old circus term for performers—clowns, trick bicycle riders, trapeze artists, and a contortionist called the Frog Man. Making these circus scenes gave him extra income; he recalled, "I made a lot of money at it."[11] The images would form the basis of his lifelong, signature, carnival-like style. When the circus went south at the end of the season, he returned home. Dismayed by the way her son had been living, Hayden's mother urged him to join the army to "see the world under a more honorable environment."[12]

INFANTRY REGIMENT SERVICE
AND WORLD WAR I, 1912–1920

Nancy Hedgeman's advice to her son, to find an honorable job, was with Hayden when he traveled to New York in the fall of 1912. He believed that being in the military would give him sufficient leisure to concentrate on his art: "I always thought army men had a lazy time of it. In that case, I thought I would have plenty of time to draw."[13] While working as a sandhog in a shaft for the Catskill water conduit, he decided to join the Twenty-Fourth Infantry Regiment. He was told that he needed a letter of reference, so he asked the timekeeper at the shaft, who listed his name as Palmer C. Hayden, rather than Peyton C. Hedgeman. Hayden left it as it was, afraid to tell the recruiters about the mistake.[14]

In November 1912, Hayden took on his new name and became a private in the U.S. Army. Whether or not the name was the artist's choice, Hayden may have welcomed the change as a symbol of an altered identity, a not uncommon phenomenon on the part of artists moving to a new environment. About the same time, he began to list his birth date as 1893 instead of 1890. It was not until 1958 when the New York Department of Motor Vehicles questioned the discrepancy in dates on a driver's license application that Hayden acknowledged his true birth date.[15] Determining one's own identity seemed to run in the family; Hayden's father had been named Hedge, but altered it to Hedgeman sometime between 1900 and 1910.[16]

Hayden was assigned to a garrison post in the Philippines with the all-black Company A, Twenty-Fourth Infantry Regiment. While he served on the islands of Panay, Negros, Luzon, and Corregidor, Hayden made many pen-and-ink drawings of Filipinos and of his fellow soldiers. His sketches came to the attention of two of his superiors and he was assigned to military cartography; his duties were mostly making road maps.[17] Soon General Frederick H. Funston awarded him a commendation for his artistic skill.[18] Military officials were pleased with Hayden's industry and earnestness; apparently, most privates drew only pornographic images.[19] In 1914, Hayden was discharged in San Francisco with a train ticket to Washington, D.C., and "returned to New York with a pocketful of money and a yearning to go to Europe to study art."[20]

By the time Hayden made it to the East Coast, World War I had begun. He enlisted with a detachment of black calvary men (part of the Tenth Calvary) stationed at West Point. There, he was responsible for taking care of the horses that cadets were learning to ride. Hayden's enlistment ended in 1917, but soldiers were not permitted a discharge, the United States having entered the war in Europe. While at West Point, he paid ten dollars a month from his eighteen-dollar monthly salary for a correspondence course in drawing. He frequently drew his fellow calvarymen and African Americans in Newburgh, a nearby off-duty center. He also sketched landscapes in the Hudson Valley, when he was allowed to go horse-back riding wherever he pleased.[21]

FIRST ARTISTIC SUCCESSES: NEW YORK, 1920–1927

After nine years in the service, Hayden was honorably discharged from the army and he returned to New York in 1920. He lived in Manhattan and worked at the Station P Custom House from May 2, 1920, to at least May 1922.[22] He began as a substitute mail carrier, then switched to night duty in order to attend summer school at Columbia University, from July 6 to August 13, 1920. He took two classes in art structure (probably design and composition) and one in drawing and painting, for which he received grades of C.[23]

Although he was only an average student, Hayden had at least one of his works exhibited in a group show at the 135th Street branch of the New York Public Library in August 1921.[24] This important exhibition of 198 works was probably Hayden's first exposure to other African American artists. Those who were represented included Henry O. Tanner, Laura Wheeler Waring, William Edouard Scott, and Meta Vaux Warrick Fuller, all of whom had studied in Paris.

Hayden also exhibited his work at the Society of Independent Artists (SIA) in New York on a regular basis in the early 1920s. This "no jury, no prizes" exhibition series (1917–1944), offered one of the few major venues where African Americans could exhibit their work in the early twentieth century, perhaps because their identity was not always known; works were mailed or brought in by members, who paid an annual ten-dollar fee.[25] Albert Alexander Smith and Rex Gorleigh (both of whom worked in Paris in the 1930s) also showed work with the SIA, as did thousands of white artists, such as Alexander Calder. From 1919 to 1929, each year in March, the exhibitions were held at the Waldorf Astoria.[26]

In 1922, the SIA showed two of Hayden's scenes of the Philippines, *Batangas, P.I.* and *Calumpang River.*[27] Two years later he exhibited a work that recalled "a vivid memory of a visit to Australia," probably a side trip from the Philippines,[28] *Jungle Night*, as well as a painting documenting the area where he would move next, *Greenwich Street.*[29] While apparently no reproductions of Hayden's works at the SIA are available (and the locations are unknown), at least the titles give us some indication of the kind of early work he produced. He continued to be an aspiring landscapist, but he was also developing a strong interest in narrative and figurative art, as evidenced by a series of illustrations of Hiawatha that he sold in 1923. The story of the Native American, immortalized by poet Henry Wadsworth Longfellow in 1898, was further popularized by the black British composer Samuel Coleridge-Taylor, around 1900. It is not known which version Hayden illustrated.

In the early 1920s, Hayden enriched his artistic education by visiting museums and galleries. Years later, he recalled seeing only Marcel Duchamp's *Nude Descending a Staircase* (1912) at the Whitney Museum of American Art during this time, which made a great impression on him because it was so perplexing.[30] He could not discern the nude in the work, even when it was pointed out: "I thought it was like one of those picture puzzles in the newspaper, where you draw a line from one dot to the next to get the picture."[31] Few works seemed to make a deep impression on Hayden. He said, "I don't like anybody else's work. I've been to many galleries and seen many artists' work and none of them make me say 'I want to paint like him.' Isn't that funny? I don't understand."[32] However, in January 1924, Hayden saw Tanner's solo exhibition at the Grand Central Galleries in New York and was impressed both by Tanner's works and his international success. He hoped to meet the master one day.[33]

In 1924 Hayden lost his job as a mail carrier through absenteeism. He moved to a tiny attic room with a skylight at 29 Greenwich Avenue, located behind a women's jail.[34] He moved to Greenwich Village because he wanted to be near other artists, but his shyness prevented him from forming many friendships. He did, however, become close to Cloyd Boykin, another African American artist from Virginia. The two met daily to talk and sometimes watched each other paint. Boykin and his wife, Maria, lived in a mid-Manhattan building where he was a janitor, but they soon moved into the building where Hayden resided.[35] Years later in Paris, Hayden would portray his friend in *The Janitor Who Paints* (1931). Boykin may have helped Hayden find some of the part-time work he did cleaning windows, polishing brass, and tending furnaces on an hourly basis for prosperous apartment dwellers. In this period, chance acquaintances with two such employers changed Hayden's life forever. He explained, "At this time in my life, Fate or Luck prepared the way for serious study and application of my art."[36]

Victor Semon Pérard (1870–1957), art instructor of life classes for twenty years at the Cooper Institute, now Cooper Union, hired Hayden to clean his studio during off hours, and gave him instruction in oil painting. No doubt Pérard reaffirmed Hayden's desire to study abroad; he himself was educated at the Ecole des Beaux-Arts in Paris, as well as at the National Academy of Design and the Arts Students League in New York. Hayden occasionally accompanied Pérard, a married man without children, on weekends to his home in New Jersey. Together, they would go to the Atlantic coast to sketch *en plein air*.[37]

While Hayden favored seascapes, Pérard probably encouraged him to also develop his skills in drawing animals and the human figure. Working primarily in pencil, pen, and ink, Pérard illustrated children's books, such as Washington Irving's *Rip Van Winkle* (1933) and produced more than twenty how-to books in drawing, such as *Drawing Horses* and *Faces and Expressions*. In his textbook *Anatomy and Drawing* (1936), he insisted, "Every figure artist finds sooner or later . . . that his work needs strengthening through a well grounded knowledge of anatomy."[38] Yet Pérard also stated: "The ability to construct figures from the imagination rather than to depend entirely on models is a distinct aid to the draftsman. . . . The student of anatomy should therefore test his skill by making memory drawings and by applying his knowledge to compositions of his own fancy."[39] From Pérard, then, Hayden learned about anatomical drawing, perspective, narrative art, drawing from life, and drawing from the imagination.

Another significant employer was Alice Miller Dike (1863–1930), daughter of the founder of Dike Woolen Mills.[40] A reserved, wealthy woman in her early sixties who had never married, Dike hired Hayden in 1923 to move furniture. When she learned that he was trying to become an artist, she asked to see his work. She was so impressed with his talent that she borrowed a painting to display above her mantelpiece and told him, "Keep it up. Maybe someday I can help you."[41]

During the summers of 1925 and 1926, Hayden kept house at the cottage of a New York woman (most likely Dike) in Boothbay Harbor, Maine.[42] He had written to Asa Grant Randall (1869–?), the founder of the Commonwealth Art Colony, that he was interested in exchanging labor for artistic training;[43] he would receive room and board as part of a "working scholarship."[44] Hayden worked mornings and attended classes in the afternoons.[45] He recalled, "That was the real turning point for me. Randall was the instructor, and I began to realize things, to make better connections about everything."[46]

On weekends, Hayden went to Portland and Haverstraw, Maine, to paint. His earliest known oil paintings (which survive only in poor black-and-white photographs), are *Haverstraw Brick Yards* and *Along the Kenebac River, Maine* (both 1925, 16 x 20 in.).[47] The former seems to depict two men standing in front of a steep-roofed building while the latter depicts a small dwelling on a peninsula in the river, with a tall tree on the right. Both images suggest calm and stability.

The titles of the works that Hayden exhibited at the Society of Independent Artists in the mid-1920s suggest that he was beginning to develop narrative more strongly in his art.[48] It is impossible to tell whether any of these images included African Americans. Until this time, it seems, Hayden was reluctant to paint images of black people, especially of rural folk: "My mother used to sing spirituals all day long. And while I was ashamed of them, and then you got away from home, you don't want to be a Negro folk at all, you know, those expressions and old stuff—you try to forget it, you drop it."[49] Hence, in the early part of his artistic career, he largely concentrated on landscapes and seascapes.

Perhaps through the influence of Pérard or Dike, Hayden had his first solo exhibition at the Civic Club on 12th Street, from April 3 to April 15, 1926.[50] The Civic Club was the only upper-crust New York association without race or sex restrictions, where African American intellectuals met with white liberals.[51] It was there that the New Negro movement had been launched just two years before. On March 21, 1924, Charles S. Johnson invited young writers, including Eric Walrond, Jessie Fauset, Gwendolyn Bennett, Countee Cullen, and Langston Hughes, to attend an informal gathering in honor of Jessie Fauset's novel, *There Is Confusion.* More than a hundred people came to hear and see Johnson, Du Bois, James Weldon Johnson, Carl Van Doren, Horace Liveright, and others as Locke introduced them.[52] Hayden may have met these writers around that time. He would associate with several of them later in Paris.

Fifteen of Hayden's works were shown at the Civic Club. They were mostly landscapes and marine studies, including *Sheepscot* and *Haverstraw,* but at least one work was figurative, *Nude with Child.*[53] While none of these paintings is extant, it is possible to get a sense of Hayden's early work and its reception from two writers. An American critic for the Parisian magazine, *La revue du vrai et du beau,* probably first saw Hayden's work at the Society of Independent Artists exhibition in 1925. Part of his review of Hayden, published that December in Paris, was translated and reprinted in the small Civic Club catalog: "One of the strong characteristics of the art of Palmer C. Hayden is an exceptionally vibrant sincerity, added to his very rare gift as a colorist, his light, yet sure touch, raise this artist's work to a level rarely equalled."[54] A critic for the *New York Herald Tribune* agreed with Chabrier's assessment of Hayden's sure use of color and also favorably reviewed the exhibition.[55]

Several months after Hayden's exhibition at the Civic Club, Dike saw an announcement at church concerning Harmon Foundation Awards for Negro Artists.[56] She encouraged Hayden to enter five of the waterfront scenes he had just exhibited.

Among the judges for the Harmon Foundation's first awards was Laura Wheeler, the only African American artist on the judges' panel and not yet married to Waring, of Cheyney State College in Pennsylvania. The finalists in the competition were Hayden and Hale Woodruff. Wheeler favored Hayden; she wrote to Harmon administrator George Haynes, "My choice is between Hayden and Woodruff, with the leaning towards Hayden because his subjects seemed to have required much more restrained painting. His limitations set for himself seemed more subtle."[57]

Thus in December 1926 Hayden won the first prize of a gold medal and four hundred dollars for *Boothbay Harbor* (a good reproduction is unavailable), an impressionistic marine study of sailboats docked near a boathouse on a wharf.[58] He was thrilled with the award, but declared that he would not let it "swell his head" and that he would continue to live in his overcrowded, six foot studio-bedroom at three dollars a week, because he "would rather have the paints and canvas than more room."[59]

Hayden decided that the time had finally come for him to study abroad, but he knew he didn't have enough funding: "I wanted to go to Paris, first of all. I didn't know how I was going to go. I didn't know the first thing about it, to tell you the truth. I made up my mind I was going to Paris that year. And I didn't have one buffalo nickel. I wanted to go there and study art."[60] Dike agreed that her protégé should study in Europe and sold stock shares to raise the money.

On February 19, 1927, Hayden excitedly wrote to William Harmon informing him of Dike's generous patronage. "I wish to tell you of the great kindness of Miss Alice M. Dike of 77 Park Ave. a lady for whom I work and who sponsored my candidacy for the award. She is so much pleased because of my receiving the award and appreciate[s] so highly the meritous [meritorious] value and the lofty purpose for which they are given, that she has given me the sum of $3000.00 in addition to the $400 that you gave with the awards, to finance me in my future studies abroad."[61]

Preparations for Hayden's departure began immediately. The Harmon Foundation took care of nearly all arrangements, from trying to get him private French lessons[62] to establishing contacts with African American artists who had studied abroad. Since Waring had studied in Paris in 1914 and again from 1924 to 1925, Harmon's assistant, George Haynes, asked her for "counsel and advice to guide him in getting in touch with the most reliable and responsible people and organizations who will help him on in the development of his art."[63] Waring personally met with Hayden and told him how to get in touch with Tanner in Paris.[64] Haynes also wrote to Tanner, asking him to recommend "the best contacts for securing the sort of instruction and encouragement [Hayden] needs." Haynes described Hayden in glowing terms: "Mr. Hayden has had a very unique career . . . devoting all of his time and soul for the last ten or twelve years to trying to get an opportunity to paint. . . . From all the testimony we have, Mr. Hayden is a young man of sterling character with a potential ability as an artist of a very high quality."[65]

On the day of Hayden's departure, the Harmon Foundation sent out a press release announcing: "Negro Housecleaner Will Study Art in Europe." The article stressed Hayden's economically disadvantaged background and the sacrifices he made to paint. On less than five dollars a week, Hayden said, "I paid $3.50 for my room and occasionally, when money was scarce, I had to let a day go by without eating."[66] The Harmon Foundation emphasized Hayden's strong work ethic, noting that the artist continued to scrub floors and wash windows almost until the hour of his departure.

African American painter Aaron Douglas deplored the Harmon Foundation's emphasis on Hayden's position as a janitor and what he described as the foundation's vacuum-cleaner approach to the arts:

> Neither streets, houses nor public institutions escaped. When unsuspecting Negroes were found with a brush in their hands they were immediately hauled away and held up for interpretation. They were given places of honor and bowed to with ceremony. Every effort to protest their innocence was drowned out with big-mouthed praise. A number escaped and returned to a more reasonable existence. Many fell in with the game and went along making hollow and meaningless gestures with brush and palette, but . . . the Negro artists have emerged.[67]

Several other artists, among them Romare Bearden, would also condemn the Harmon Foundation for its seeming lack of standards in its evaluation of fine art and its valorization of self-taught artists.[68]

On March 12, 1927, Hayden sailed third class on the S.S. *La France*. He planned to take art classes in Paris, then travel throughout Italy, Spain, England, and Germany: little did he know that he would spend the following seven years in France.

TAKING LESSONS, MEETING TANNER, AND GETTING REVIEWED, 1927

When Hayden arrived in Paris on March 26, 1927, he obtained a room at the Hôtel Jeanne d'Arc at 57, rue Vaneau in Montparnasse, where Laura Wheeler Waring had stayed in October 1924. A few days later, he searched the advertisements in the *New York Herald Tribune* for inexpensive French lessons. Finding an address not far from the hotel, Hayden went to the home of Mademoiselle Renée Martine, the daughter of a naval officer. Martine would teach Hayden her native language for more than a year.[69] She told him how to request a smaller, less expensive room at the hotel, and soon Hayden relocated to what was probably a maid's chamber on the top floor beyond the reach of the elevator.[70]

Frustrated by the language, Hayden longed to pass as a Martinican or another French subject so that he could easily blend in the new environment. His tutor quickly told him, however, that it was to his advantage to be American. The French treated their colonial subjects with less respect and addressed them in the familiar. When Hayden found this was the case from firsthand experience, he deliberately carried a copy of the *New York Herald Tribune* so that people would surmise that his native language was English.[71] While Hayden intended to stay away from Americans as much as possible, it was easy to communicate with them, and so his French did not develop as quickly as he had expected.

As Waring and Fuller had recommended, Hayden visited Henry O. Tanner to get his advice on his art and life in France. He found Tanner to be shy, courteous, and reluctant to say anything discouraging. When Hayden showed him his work on several different occasions, he remembered that "he usually made some complimentary remark, but I didn't continue to go to him for that because he was not a teacher and he didn't like to talk too much. I don't really know whether he thought they were good or bad; he never did say. I can't recall anything specific that he said about my work."[72]

The two discussed media, such as Tanner's experiments in mixing glazes, and the kind of composition board from the United States on which he painted. Tanner also gave Hayden many tips on dealing with French people, on "how to live with them. I remember he told me when I was getting a studio to be sure and tip the concierge when I moved in because otherwise she might tear up my mail."[73] Hayden would visit Tanner several times over the following years for further advice.

Within a month of his arrival in Paris, *La revue du vrai et du beau* published another glowing article about his work, "L'oeuvre de Palmer Hayden." Staff writers found it "an artistic and subtle pleasure to follow his development, for throughout all his steady progress forward, the artist retains that original personality that captivated our American critic."[74] What critic Raymond Sélig seemed to like most about Hayden was his humor; he recalled seeing *Roast Duck for Supper*, "a humorous scene," at the SIA, and *Pickaninnies*, "a rustic scene, full of humor," this latter portraying two African American boys sitting on a fence watching a woman milk a cow at sunset.[75] But Sélig also admired Hayden's use of color. He described *Clorinda*, a nude female bather in a soft green woodland startled by a frog as she enters a pond, as comparable to the work of Rubens, in its contrasts of "flesh" tones with clear greens. In fact, referring to the accompanying illustrations of *Boothbay Harbor* and *Port*, Sélig declared of Hayden's palette: "It is always in his use of delicate coloring in the manner of the impressionists that Palmer Hayden's style stands out most clearly, but through it all, how keenly one feels his thorough knowledge of technique! How one senses the solidity, the values, under the lovely range of blues and lavenders, the happy gradation of which makes the charm of his canvases. What flawless design!" Yet Sélig predicted great things for Hayden not because he was a fine colorist, but because he was an African American and "he paints all the gentleness, the tenderness, the force of his race. The paintings of Hayden will make his name famous. It is fitting that we publish the story of his life as an example to the artists of tomorrow. What energy! What faith in art and in himself! Palmer Hayden is a negro."[76]

It is not known what Hayden thought of Sélig's evaluation of him, but the positive review regarding his humorous "Negro folk" scenes might have influenced him to paint similar works several years later. The Harmon Foundation immediately turned the article which Hayden sent them into a press release, "Critic Compares Technique of Negro Artist to Rubens" and circulated it in New York periodicals.

The foundation's assistant for public information, Evelyn S. Brown, wrote to Hayden congratulating him on the publication and asked him to send information "in some detail, what your present arrangements are for art lessons and the like."[77] For unknown reasons, Hayden ignored this request and did not communicate with the foundation again until the end of November.

In the meantime, Hayden decided against formal art lessons, perhaps on the recommendation of his tutor: "I remember this, too, the lady in Paris said, 'Don't waste your time in art schools.' I've never forgotten that, maybe I should have forgotten it, but I don't believe so much in art schools because there's a whole lot to learn about painting, but not so much to be taught. So I said, well, I'm going to take her for her word . . . and so I didn't go to the art schools in Paris. I didn't go to the Chaumière where all the other painters go."[78]

Martine introduced Hayden to an old family friend, Clivette Lefevre (life dates unknown), an instructor at the Ecole des Beaux-Arts whose sculpture was exhibited at the Luxembourg Museum. Lefevre told Hayden his work looked promising and that his dark, grayish palette reflected the atmosphere of Paris. The professor accompanied Hayden on several excursions throughout the city, pointing out various sights that he thought would make good compositions: "One day it was raining cats and dogs and that old man, he was walking with a cane and he walked all around through the Latin Quarter and he said, 'See this here, that would make a good composition' and I made several of them."[79] Hayden painted at home and, for several months, occasionally took work to Lefevre's studio for criticism. He filled sketchbooks with graphite drawings of typical tourist sights in and near Paris, such as the Pont-Neuf, artists painting along the Seine, Empress Josephine's stables—which would have been of special interest to this ex-groom—and Versailles. This was a typically romantic tourist approach to French culture; Woodruff and Smith would paint such scenes, as well.

After the initial confusion of arriving in Paris and finding his way around, it did not take long for Hayden to adjust to life abroad, especially since he had Dike's gift of three thousand dollars. He was determined to catch up on the good life. In his sketchbook, he drew an autobiographical record of his journey to France (untitled, fig. 29). On the right, in an outline of the United States, a police officer towers over two prone black figures— echoing the image in a well-publicized photograph of a similar scene in Chicago in 1919; just months after Hayden had returned to the United States from serving in World War I in the

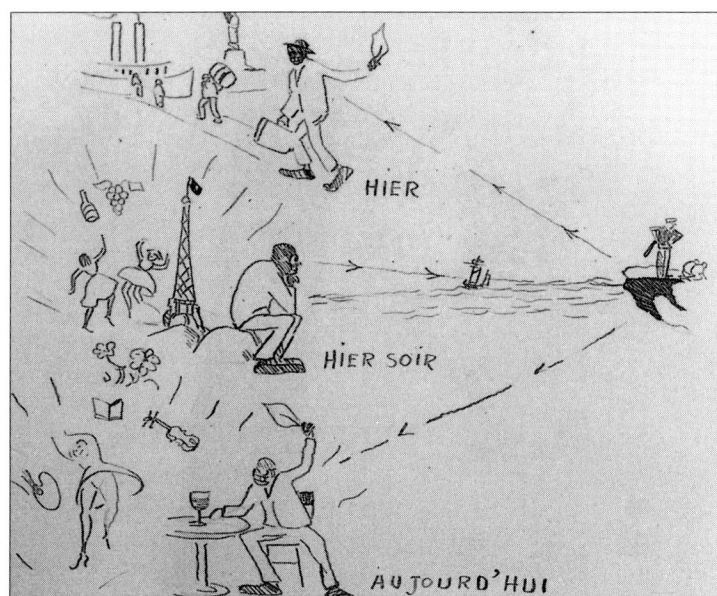

FIGURE 29
Palmer Hayden,
Untitled sketch [*Hier . . .*]
in sketchbook, ca. 1927,
graphite on paper,
4 x 6 in.
Palmer Hayden Papers.
Archives of American Art,
Smithsonian Institution,
Washington, D.C.

Philippines, race riots had erupted throughout the country, during the Red Summer of 1919. On the left, three vignettes depict Hayden's response to the situation. *Hier* (yesterday) was when he gladly boarded a ship to France. *Hier soir* (last night) he sat sadly at the base of the Eiffel Tower with his back to the lures of Paris—wine, women, and music—and contemplated going back home. *Aujourd'hui* (today), however, he enjoys his freedom and grant money, drinking at a nightclub, watching a cancan dancer, and envisioning a plethora of cultural opportunities, symbolized by a floating palette and brushes, a book, and a violin. In fact, the artist did spend his money freely on expensive clothing and nightclub entertainment.

BAL NÈGRE

One of Hayden's favorite nightclubs was the Bal Colonial, better known as the Bal Nègre, at 33, rue Blomet, which first opened in 1928. It is likely that West Indian employees who occupied the Hôtel Jeanne d'Arc had told him about the place. Bal Nègre was one of the most chic places in Paris, packed every night with pleasure seekers: "Elegant women would descend from stylish automobiles to dance to syncopated music with handsome young men from the French West Indies or French West Africa. The black vogue was not only a triumph for jazz and the new dance rhythms; it was also a triumph for black culture."[80] Like the West Indians and Hayden, a new generation of Surrealist artists, among them Robert Desnos, Georges Malkine, and André de la Rivière, frequented the Bal Nègre, but Hayden apparently never met the three men, who were his neighbors.[81] In 1927, the group had moved to 45, rue Blomet, Joan Miró's old studio. Hayden himself, frustrated after two months of looking for an inexpensive studio, had taken a rather costly room down the street from the Hôtel Jeanne d'Arc at 16, rue Blomet.[82]

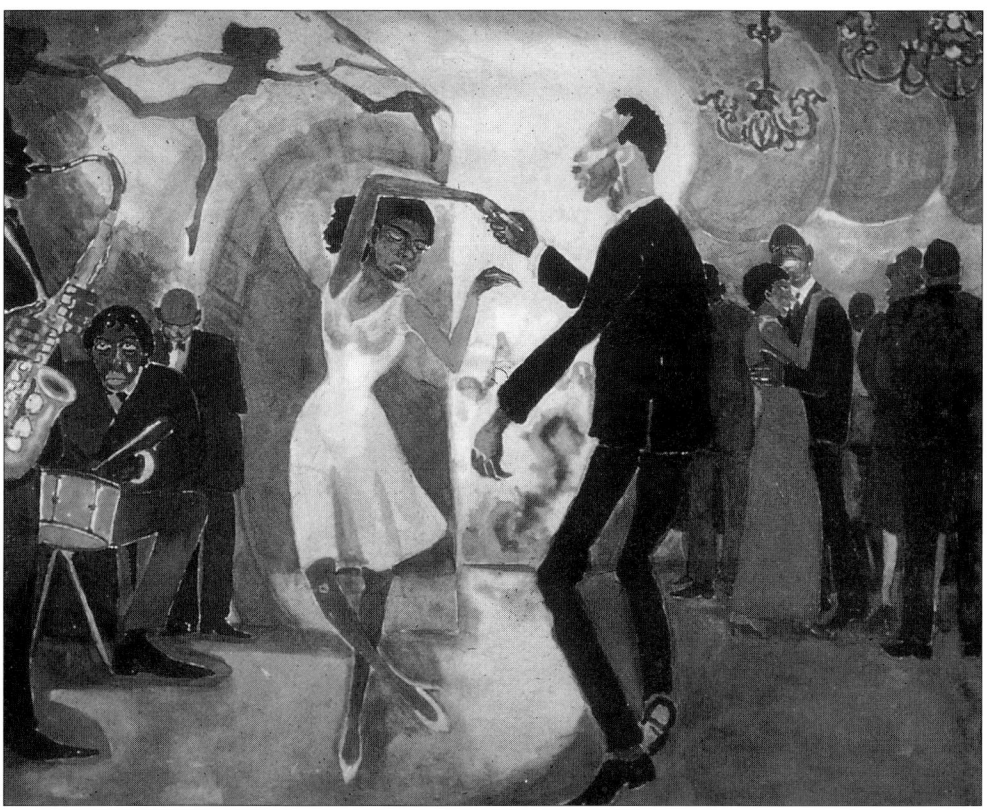

FIGURE 30
Palmer Hayden, *Bal jeunesse,* ca. 1927, watercolor on paper, 14 x 18 in.
With permission of Meredith and Gail J. Weight Sirmans.

One of the first watercolors that Hayden completed in Paris, *Bal jeunesse* (Youth dance, ca. 1927, fig. 30), is modeled after the Bal Nègre, with its black jazz band in front of a cool, blue mural of silhouetted female nudes holding hands and leaping over a red arch. Genteel black—possibly West Indian—patrons in modest evening wear dance slowly beneath gold chandeliers on the right. In the center, a tall, mustached man, Hayden perhaps, twirls a coffee-colored woman in a short, white gown on a reddish-brown dance floor. With its cool background palette of muted blues and controlled linear drawing, *Bal jeunesse* stands in stark contrast to depictions of the Bal Nègre produced by white artists, such as the French humorist and caricaturist Goursat Sem (1863–1934).[83] In Sem's watercolor sketches, such as *Le bal de la rue Blomet* (fig. 31), tall, coal black, lascivious men with outsized lips tightly squeeze short white women, swaying on a crowded dance floor. While Hayden also drew a similar scene in his sketchbook, *Bal noir de Paris* (fig. 32), his sketch is more of a cartoon than a caricature. Most of Hayden's men are the same size as the women and they lack the distorted facial features of Sem's male dancers. Further, Hayden's women seem more down to earth, with nappy hair, medium-sized, even plump, bodies, head ties, and plainer dresses, with one in a plaid skirt,[84] unlike Sem's bobbed white revelers in slinky gowns. Hayden, who

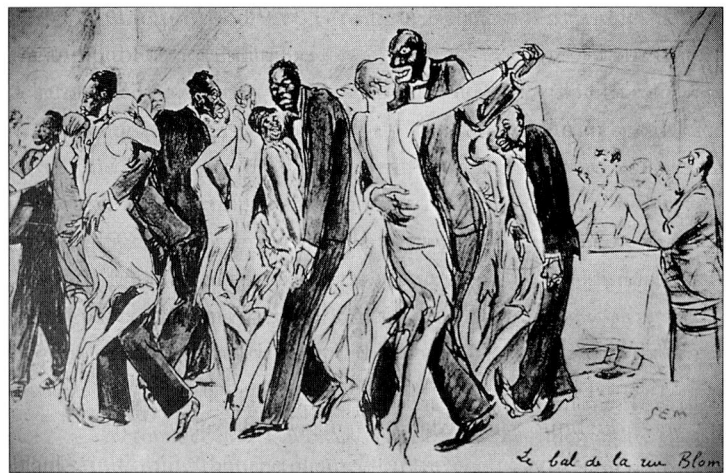

FIGURE 31
Sem,
Le bal de la rue Blomet,
n.d., pen and ink and
watercolor on paper,
dimensions and location
unknown.
Reproduced from
Janet Flanner,
An American in Paris.

FIGURE 32
Palmer Hayden,
Bal noir de Paris
(in sketchbook),
ca. 1927, graphite
on paper, 4 x 6 in.
Palmer Hayden papers.
Archives of American Art,
Smithsonian Institution,
Washington, D.C.

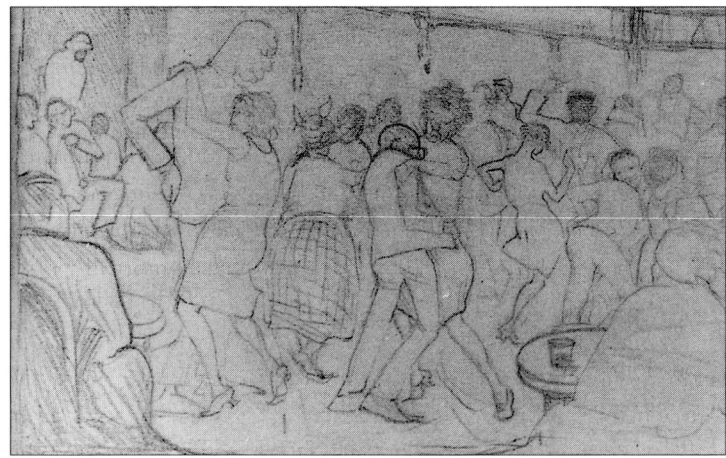

felt at home at the Bal Nègre, would frequent the nightclub for years, as would other black artists and writers, such as Hale Woodruff and Claude McKay. In 1928, Countee Cullen and Harold Jackman performed the beguine there, a ballroom dance similar to the rumba, and based on a dance from Martinique and Saint Lucia. Cullen recalled the exotic atmosphere:

> The music is a weird sort of playing, a mélange or cross between modern jazz and the residue of old West Indian folk pieces. The most primitive notes of all are contributed by a player who shakes with varying modulations a leather box filled with pebbles. . . . As an American Negro [*sic*] we are somewhat startled to find that our dark complexion avails us naught among these kindredly tinted people. Language must be the open sesame here, and it must be French. . . . The dancing for the most part is harsh and slightly reprehensible, faintly suggestive of the antics of some of the New York night clubs. In the midst of it all, however, one couple, as if disdaining such modern contortion, glides along slowly in an old Martinique step. . . . They are perhaps the remnants of what the Bal Colonial was before the tourists "discovered" it, perhaps somewhat analogous to what the Harlem clubs were before downtown New York found them amusing.[85]

It is not known whether Cullen, Jackman, Woodruff, McKay, or Hayden attended the elaborate costume party, Bal Ubu, called "the last ball in Montparnasse,"[86] at Bal Nègre in February 1929. However, journalist J. A. Rogers recalled a night of dancing with novelist Eric Walrond, Zaidee Jackson, and a group of other African Americans there after a cocktail party in July 1929: "Then on to the Martiniquan ball to complete this week of fun. Here some of our group can do a mean bout of ringing and twisting, along with the Martiniquans doing their delightful dance—the beguine."[87] Led there by Hayden and Woodruff, who first met in the fall of 1927 in Paris, Hayden helping Woodruff locate a room, sculptor Augusta Savage would later dance the beguine at the famous Bal Nègre, too.

BRITTANY

During the summer of 1927, Hayden left behind the boisterous nightclub scene in Paris to paint along the Brittany coast. He most likely went there on the advice Henry O. Tanner. Tanner had spent his vacations in Brittany with classmates during the summers from 1891 to 1894.[88] Hayden does not seem to have visited Pont-Aven, site of the artist colony that formed around Gauguin from 1885 to 1898, but chose instead to base himself in Concarneau, an offshoot of Pont-Aven approximately eight miles to the west. The old fishing port, dubbed Sardineopolis by American marine painter Alexander Harrison,[89] also developed into an international art colony in the 1880s. Eminent Continental painters who worked there were Jules Breton, Kroyer l'Hermite, Alfred Guillou, Paul Du Bois, and Jules Bastien-Lepage. English and American painters were Edward Simmons, Aubrey Hunt, Stanhope-Forbes, and C. P. Grayson. By the 1920s, Concarneau had nearly lost its allure as an artist colony (it was on its way to becoming France's third largest harbor, known for its production of tuna and fabric), but its history and rugged beauty still attracted young painters.

In the nineteenth century, Breton peasants were popular subjects in figure paintings by the French artists Jean-François Millet and Jules Breton. Tanner painted such images, too. It was at Concarneau that he completed *The Bagpipe Lesson* (1892–1893), a genre scene of an old man teaching a young boy how to play the Scottish instrument beneath a blossoming apple tree. Like his predecessors', Hayden's drawing of Breton peasants focused on the fisherfolk: "What I was doing then, I was painting the fishermen and their wives along the quais in Brittany. You know, where the fishermen come down in with their catch, mostly tuna fish, or big fish like that, and they go out and stay out a week or two weeks out in the ocean where their wives always know when they're coming back so they come down to meet 'em, bring 'em fresh change of clothing. They congregate on the piers where the boats line up and they all make very interesting compositions."[90] Hayden made numerous graphite sketches and watercolors of fisherfolk (such as *Fishing Scene, Brittany; Sale, Concarneau* [*sic*]; *Colored Sales* [*sic*], *Brittany; Unloading Fish-Brittany*). However, he apparently produced few oil paintings of them.

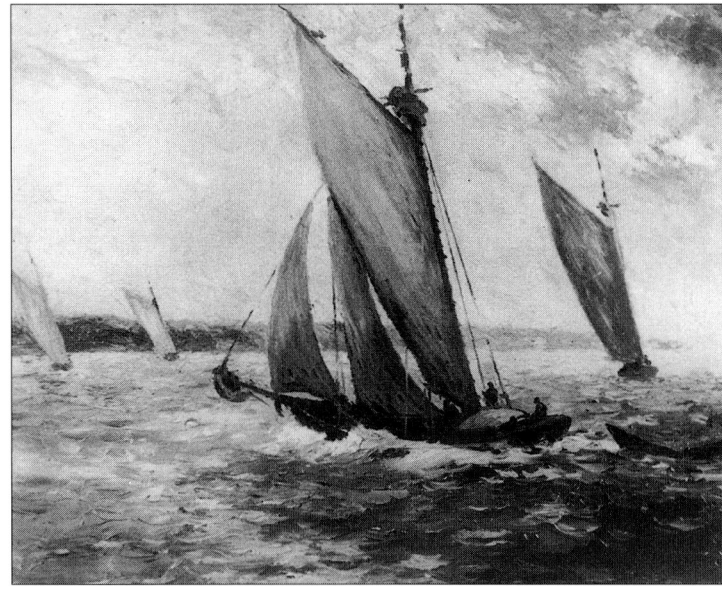

FIGURE 33
Palmer Hayden,
The Schooners, ca. 1927,
oil on canvas, dimensions
and location unknown.
From a photograph
in the National Archives;
used with permission.

Hayden produced several somewhat awkward oil paintings of seascapes along
the Bay of Biscay, such as *Le quay* [*sic*] *Port Luis, The Schooners,* and *St. Servan* (good
reproductions of the first and last are unavailable). *Le quay Port Luis* is a bird's-eye view of
several figures on a pier looking at two large docked boats with their masts unfurled. Three
smaller boats are also tied to the jetty and several others appear on the horizon. On the wharf
in the left foreground is a small building, a horse and cart, and a pile of logs. In contrast
to the busy activity of this work, *The Schooners* and *St. Servan* are seascapes that minimize
human presence. *The Schooners* (known only by a black-and-white photograph, fig. 33)
depicts four three-masted boats on a choppy sea. All lean to the left, two on the distant left
horizon, one a bit nearer on the right, and the fourth in the center, its mast and sail bisecting
the composition. Unlike *The Schooners,* with its dramatic movement, *St. Servan* depicts a
quiet harbor scene of two docked boats (whose bare cruciform masts look like telephone
poles) in front of a row of buildings. While this work is also only known through a black-
and-white photograph, it seems that Hayden has painted coarsely with a muted Impressionist
palette; one-third of the composition is devoted to the shimmering reflections of the masts
in the calm water. He seemed to work in an "American" Impressionist style, with a bright,
cool palette.

Hayden may have found the atmosphere of the rocky, tree-lined coast of Brittany
comparable to the coast of Maine where he had painted in the mid-1920s. The town of
Concarneau probably reminded him of Boothbay Harbor with its mild weather and cool
tonality, "a beautiful silvery gray."[91] Art historian James Porter later commented on the
appropriateness of this silvery tonality in Hayden's seascapes: "Hayden prefers to paint his
pictures in bleak, unfriendly tones, meticulously graduated. It is impossible to say whether he
has a sense of color since all his paintings leave an impression of silvery, reticent value, an
effect particularly unpleasing in his work involving figures, for then the usage suggests a

debilitated kind of impressionism. Still, no one can deny the effectiveness and artistic correctness of his greenish-gray palette. Where applied to a study of sailing ships at sea or tied up in misty harbors, such tonality seems perfectly appropriate and right."[92] Hayden's choice of colors may have been his version of Tanner's renowned bluish green palette. Upon his return to Paris, Hayden showed Tanner his painting of a little fishing boat going out to catch sardines in Brittany (it is not known which work this was). After Tanner critiqued the work, Hayden immediately made corrections. He kept and cherished the painting the rest of his life because Tanner had critiqued it.[93] He may have also used the work as a color model for other pieces.

SOLO EXHIBITION AT
GALERIE BERNHEIM-JEUNE

By the fall of 1927, Hayden believed he should have a solo exhibition and apparently approached the prestigious Galerie Bernheim-Jeune with the proposition. Lefevre was incensed over the idea and declared that Hayden was not ready for an independent show. When Hayden persisted, Lefevre announced that he would never aid him again.[94]

Galerie Bernheim-Jeune was, and still is, located in an elite neighborhood of the Right Bank on the corner of avenue Matignon and rue Faubourg Saint-Honoré. A family of art dealers from Besançon, who had been active since the late eighteenth century, owned the gallery. The family became famous for championing avant-garde artists; Alexandre Bernheim exhibited the work of the Impressionists in 1874 at his Paris gallery and when Bernheim's sons took over the business, they organized the first exhibition of Van Gogh's work in 1901. Altogether they mounted hundreds of exhibitions, displaying the work of leading artists such as Bonnard and Vuillard (1906), Cézanne (1907), Seurat (1908), Matisse (1910), the Italian Futurists and the douanier Rousseau (1916), Vlaminck (1921), Modigliani (1922), Utrillo (1923), and Pascin (1925); the drawings of Dufy, Cézanne, and Seurat (1926); and works by Van Gogh, Utrillo, and Bonnard (1927).[95] American painter Gerald Murphy also had a solo exhibition at Bernheim-Jeune at the end of the 1920s, and he considered it to be "the crowning success of his meteoric career."[96]

With such an impressive roster of artists, it seems likely that Hayden initiated the contact with the gallery rather than the other way around. In fact, he paid two thousand francs to have his works shown for two weeks, from November 7 to 18, 1927.[97] While the gallery circulated an invitation for the event, it did not publish a catalog.[98] Along with several seascapes, Hayden may have exhibited some scenes of African Americans. These images probably would have most interested the Bernheim-Jeune brothers, who had promoted the stiff, figurative, but exotic, work of the self-taught artist Henri Rousseau. Such work would have also interested the group of artists who surrounded Picasso, because it fell outside of the realm of "high art" and European tradition.[99] Clearly, there was a sharp split between Hayden's traditional landscapes and his caricaturist figurations of blacks. Perhaps Hayden was consciously producing for the marketplace, hedging his bets with two distinct approaches.

Hayden later reported that the newspapers gave him favorable reviews, but none of these have come to light and virtually nothing is known about the exhibition. The overall experience must have been rather deflating; Hayden later admitted that he wasn't really ready for a solo show at the time. Combined with the loss of money to mount the exhibition, the lack of public attention to the show, and his continuing frustration in learning French, he was beginning to wonder what he should do next in France, or if he should even stay there.

"PAINTING PARIS RED" AND PUTTING HIMSELF IN THE RED

One week after the exhibition at Bernheim-Jeune closed, Hayden wrote to Haynes on the pretext of thanking him for the announcement of the coming Harmon Foundation exhibition, which was sent via Hale Woodruff.[100] Although Hayden suggested that his works had been well received by the French press, he did not bother to send any reviews or even mention the name of the gallery. Rather, he indicated that he would send works similar to those displayed (at Bernheim-Jeune) for consideration by the foundation: "I've already shown a few things like the ones that I shall send for your exhibition, and I am fortunate enough to say that they were favorably commented on by the critics here."[101] In the same letter, Hayden explained his silence during the previous seven months:

> Now as I haven't wrote to you since I've been here, as to what course I've taken in my studies here, [sic] Well the truth is, I don't know anything even as yet to tell you in that respect. I suppose I've spent about half my time since I've been here trying to find a studio which [is] the next thing to impossible in Paris. I've been studying here so far mostly through observations. The art schools here are not attractive, so I hardly think I shall attend one. . . . So I think I shall work on in this way for a while, until I can see farther as to whether it would be best to take a course in a school or simply travel a bit and see things.
>
> And I am quite sure there are many places I could like much better than I do this particular city.[102]

Without waiting for Haynes's reply, Hayden wrote him another letter six days later informing him that he and Woodruff had placed several works in the hands of a shipper for submission to the Harmon exhibition. The three oil paintings Hayden sent were *A Home in Bretagne*, *St. Servan*, and *The Schooners*.

After writing the first letter to Haynes, Hayden must have realized that he had never answered Evelyn Brown's letter from the previous May. On December 5 he reiterated to her much of what he had written to Haynes, but added that having found "things here in general so much to my disliking," he planned to go to England in the near future: "Of course I don't know, but I believe that I would not feel that I was such a stranger there and would get more out of my studies, being able to speak and read the language, and talk with people to some satisfaction."[103] To complicate matters, he did not pay close attention to his funds, which were supposed to last for two years: "I spent my money like a mad man, I lived it up, my $3,000 didn't last very long."[104] Hayden believed he had "hit the jackpot" with Dike, so he "caught up on some good living . . . in Paris."[105] He had apparently exhausted most of his money on food, wine, and entertainment, going to cafés and nightclubs with Woodruff, Countee Cullen—whom he had met at the Harmon awards ceremony, Cullen winning the first award in literature—Harold Jackman, Claude McKay, and others. Later, he spent money entertaining women, too; Aaron Douglas mentions that Hayden had a very attractive French girlfriend in 1930.[106] In addition, he indulged in fine clothes. Around the fall of 1927, Woodruff sketched a bust of Hayden looking down, pensively perhaps, or in the midst of sketching or reading (this sketch, on microfilm at the AAA, would not photograph well). Hayden was a dashing figure, wearing a jacket and tie and with his hair neatly brushed to the side.[107] Woodruff recalled, "I was also impressed by the elegance which characterized Hayden's presence and appearance . . . he wore hand-made shoes; he didn't wear a necktie nor an ascot—he wore a foulard. It was a rich scarf-like tie stuck with a diamond horseshoe pin!"[108] Hayden's dapper wardrobe made such an impression on his friends that a year later, Jackman wrote to Cullen, "Does Palmer Hayden still dress so 'English'?"[109]

Hayden did continue to dress extravagantly and to party until the wee hours of the morning. He must have believed that his luck would hold out and that the Harmon Foundation would award him another prize soon. Apparently, he decided to stay in France rather than go to England to await his fate.

NOUS QUATRE À PARIS

During the winter of 1927–1928, Hayden frequented the cafés La Coupole, La Rotonde, and Le Dôme, at 102, 105, and 108, boulevard du Montparnasse, respectively. Built on a former coal yard and decorated by thirty-two artists—including Fernand Léger, Moishe Kisling, Othon Friesz, and Marie Wassilieff, who painted the five-meter high columns and a large mural on the back wall—La Coupole became an overnight success when it opened on December 20, 1927 and its patrons went through 1,500 bottles of champagne in two hours. Among the regulars were Derain, Foujita, Kisling, Pascin, Kiki, and Man Ray.[110] In 1928, the artist Stuart Davis discovered that "anyone could go to the Coupole . . . sit all night for a six-cent café-crème, write all the letters he wanted on cafe stationery, and play chess or cards in the bargain."[111] Ironically, Hayden sketched the interior, with its decorative columns, devoid of patrons, its tables and chairs empty (*Café La Coupole,* fig. 34), but he later developed the sketch into a watercolor (reproduction unavailable) that featured French clientele, *A Corner in La Coupole* (1937).

During World War I, La Rotonde, located on the northwest corner of the boulevards Raspail and Montparnasse, had been a favorite haunt of Picasso, Modigliani, Rivera, Léger, Apollinaire, and later, "second wave" Jewish artists, among them Chagall, Soutine, Lipchitz, Kisling, Zadkine, and Pascin.[112] However, after its owner, who had

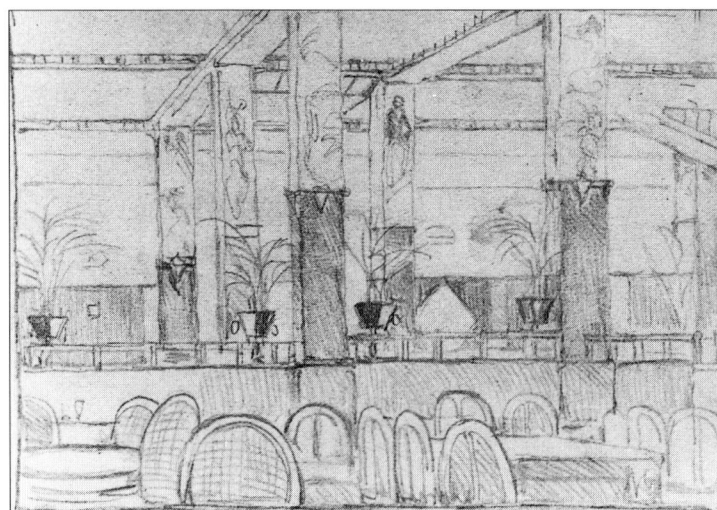

FIGURE 34
Palmer Hayden,
Café La Coupole
(in sketchbook),
n.d., graphite on paper,
4 x 6 in.
Palmer Hayden Papers.
Archives of American Art,
Smithsonian Institution,
Washington, D.C.

sympathetically supported poor artists by providing foreign-language newspapers and allowing clients to linger for hours over a single cup of coffee, sold the place in 1920, La Rotonde lost its vigor. Nevertheless, American tourists continued to patronize the place. At La Rotonde, Hayden sketched the head of a white woman wearing a chic hat; he called her "la plus jolie dame dans la Rotonde."[113] She may have been Kiki (née Alice Prin), the famous Montparnasse model and entertainer.

Le Dôme was *the* favorite meeting place of Americans in the 1920s, including writers Ernest Hemingway, who described it in *A Moveable Feast,* and Henry Miller, painter Jules Pascin, and photographer Man Ray. The group came to be known informally as "Dômiers."[114] They could listen to jazz, dance the Charleston, and get Quaker Oats there on demand.[115] African Americans enjoyed Le Dôme, too; in 1924 writer Claude McKay associated with white Americans as "a kind of sympathetic fellow-traveller in the expatriate caravan."[116] Yet when he met Jean Toomer there briefly, he wrote that he "could not like him in that awful atmosphere at the Dôme."[117] In the 1930s, Albert Alexander Smith would perform in jazz bands at the café and at La Coupole.

Opened in 1898, Le Dôme was a fancy café, furnished with marble-topped tables, leather banquettes, and mirrored walls facing the busy boulevard du Montparnasse. Two billiard tables were installed in the back room in 1902 behind the elaborate zinc bar. American art students who lived nearby set up a continuous poker game there that continued until the end of World War I.[118] Hayden recalled fond memories of cardplaying, perhaps at Le Dôme: "Eric Walrond . . . we used to play cards together all night in the cafés in Paris. There's a part of the cafés there . . . set aside especially for people who want to play cards, not gambling but . . . checkers and chess . . . bélote is a French card game something like bridge . . . so we'd hang out there, Countee, another West Indian [McKay, a Jamaican?], Dr. Dupré, all of them students. I was supposed to be a student, but I didn't do too much studying."[119] The back room in Le Dôme—or perhaps La Coupole—may have been the setting for Hayden's *Nous quatre à Paris.*

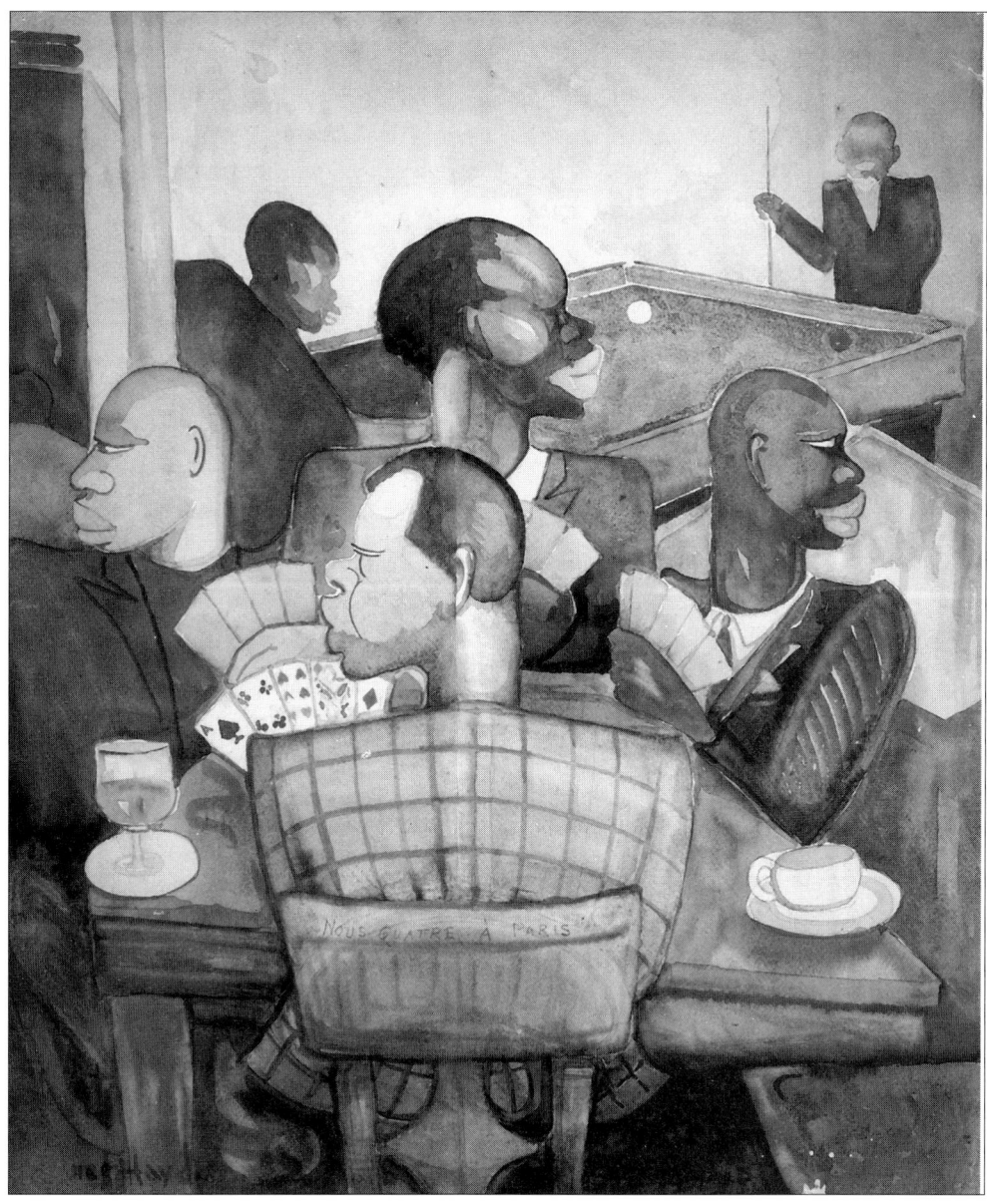

FIGURE 35
Palmer Hayden, *Nous quatre à Paris*, ca. 1928–1930, watercolor on paper, 21⅞ x 18 in.
Metropolitan Museum of Art, Purchase, Joseph A. Hazen Foundation, Inc. Gift 1975 (1975.125).

The watercolor *Nous quatre à Paris* (ca. 1928–1930, fig. 35), may be an imaginative self-portrait of Hayden with Walrond, Cullen, and Woodruff (or possibly McKay) as savvy, suited card sharks in a pool hall.[120] Given their similar facial features and hairstyles—two bald, two neatly trimmed, but with receding hairlines—it is impossible to ascertain the identity of each figure, since none of the men was bald. The image testifies to the strong sense of community Hayden had with his artist and writer friends in Paris, and the cosmopolitan fun they so often enjoyed together. The title reflects comfort with the French language, and it, along with the composition, suggests a kind of intimate camaraderie possible only at that time and in that place.

The four have their ubiquitous Parisian beverages, red wine and café crème, at their elbows, on the left and the right corners of the table around which they are gathered. In the foreground, the man in the plaid jacket with his back to the viewer— on whose chair back the title of the work is written—and his partner to the left look suspiciously toward a left entranceway while their companions look in the opposite direction. Thus, the composition is perfectly balanced on vertical and horizontal axes. The men's rounded heads, especially the gleaming bald heads of the men on the left and right, mimic those of the two pool players and the balls on the tilted pool table in the background. The cardplayers' heads form a four of clubs, echoing the second card held by the figure in the foreground. Although they are brown-skinned, Hayden hints that in demeanor, these men are as black as the ace of spades, the first card borne by this same figure. The card is held in front of his left shoulder, the spade pointing diagonally to the heart of the black-suited man on the left, visually and symbolically linking the players. *Nous quatre à Paris* is one of Hayden's most sophisticated and witty works, yet it never appeared in any of the Harmon exhibitions, possibly because its playful typecasting might have offended both white and black audiences in New York. Although Hayden's physiognomic exaggerations had a discomforting resemblance to nineteenth-century racist imagery and certain stereotyped items of twentieth-century material culture, as Richard Powell has pointed out, "so did many of the writings of Zora Neale Hurston, the 'Hokum blues' recordings of various musical groups and the 'downhome' antics of Louis Armstrong, Bill 'Bojangles' Robinson and other black performers. This tendency towards a humorous and expressionistic image of black culture was a terrain that many of the more radical artists were willing to enter in order to infuse their art with the totemic allure of 'the folk.'"[121]

Hayden enjoyed poking fun not only at himself and his friends but also at modern art. A pencil sketch, *Moderne* (fig. 36), depicts a bearded man, who may be European, placidly painting, seated before his canvas and easel on the cobblestoned bank of the Seine. Around the periphery of the drawing are a steamboat on the river, a wagon (or electric trolley car), and Notre Dame. Crowded about the artist, however, is a four-headed monster with enormous ears, multiple eyes, and men's and women's legs. Behind the figure a fish perches on two legs in a tree. The apparitions have both Cubist and Surrealist characteristics. Clearly, Hayden thought of these art movements as bizarre and laughable. Although he acknowledged that "all of my subjects, people, are from pure imagination," he also stated, "Cubism and that sort of painting I never was interested in because I couldn't tell a story."[122] Hayden's work would remain firmly in the realm of landscapes and narrative scenes for the rest of his life. In self-defense, people sometimes ridicule what they fear or do not fully understand. Hayden's lampoon of "moderne" art not only reveals his reaction to the current art scene in Paris, but also reflects the sentiments of most other African American artists, such as Prophet, Bennett, Waring, and Smith, who

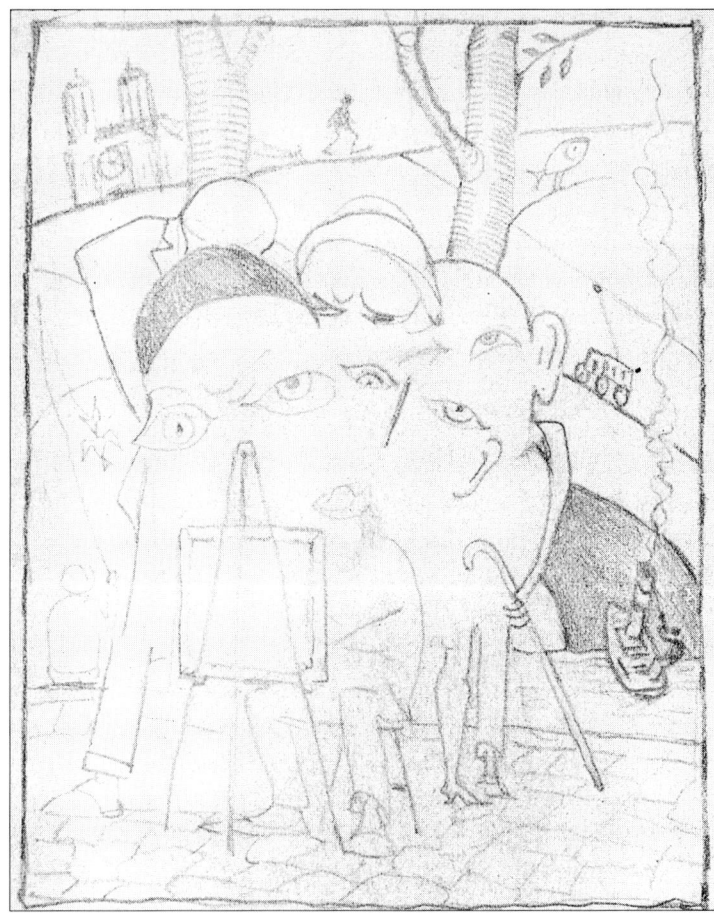

FIGURE 36
Palmer Hayden,
Moderne (in sketchbook),
ca. 1928, graphite on
paper, 4 x 6 in.
Palmer Hayden Papers.
Archives of American Art,
Smithsonian Institution,
Washington, D.C.

steadfastly avoided experimentation with the avant-garde. Their choices of style were, no doubt, prompted in part by such white institutions as the Harmon Foundation which valorized more conventional approaches and subjects such as seascapes, as Hayden well knew.

WOOING THE FOUNDATIONS, 1928

The first few months of 1928 went by before Hayden acknowledged the Harmon Foundation for its inclusion of his three seascapes in its January show and the reproduction of *The Schooners* in the catalog. Brady had sent him the publication in January and implied that William Harmon was pleased that he had sent in seascapes rather than portraits: "Mr. Harmon regretted very much that so many of the pictures that were sent this year were portraits which, while interesting, do not make it so readily possible to develop the economic side which we have in mind."[123] Brady also cautioned Hayden that sales would be difficult for those artists who placed high prices on their works. On March 18, 1928, Hayden wrote to Haynes, rather than Brady, thanking him for news regarding the exhibition. He was gratified that *The Schooners* was reproduced not only in the catalog, but also in the *Evening Post;*

Tanner had given him a copy of the newspaper. At the same time, Hayden informed Haynes that he could not afford to pay the duty charges on frames incurred by New York customs, because his funds were exhausted. To cover the expenses, he asked that the Harmon Foundation try to sell his paintings by slashing the prices he had set by two-thirds; *St. Servan* and *A Home in Bretagne* would now be 75 dollars instead of 250 and *The Schooners* would be 100 dollars rather than 300.

The week after Hayden wrote to Haynes, he realized that it would be very difficult to remain in France much longer without additional money. He wrote to Mary Brady on March 25 that he intended to return to the States in the fall and exhibit his works there. To help him make it through the intervening months, he requested a loan of five hundred dollars. Brady was infuriated by the entreaty, believing that Hayden had ample funds for two years abroad. Not wanting Hayden's behavior to become public knowledge, she decided to deny him the loan, but first asked Haynes's opinion on the matter.[124] Because Hayden did not follow Haynes's advice to be thrifty and instead exhibited "a lack of ordinary common sense," Haynes said he would have to make the best of it.[125]

Although Hayden regretted not getting the loan, he wrote back that he was also a bit relieved. He had been annoyed that every press notice mentioned the amount of Dike's gift:

> And of course I would be foolish to try to make anyone in the U.S. believe anything but that I've used it up "painting Paris red" during the short time of one year since I've been here. But if one comes to Paris of today and tries that, he will find that he's used up about three thousand dollars worth of paint in a few weeks and Paris would still be recognizable. But it would take volumes to tell the many difficulties I had in doing things when I first got here and they were nearly all costly, and I choosed [*sic*] to pay my way along in many cases because it is not good to make to make too many friends "right off the jump" especially in a strange country.
>
> And as to the cost of living abroad, but few persons in America today know that in Paris, studios for artists (painters) rent for a much higher price than apartments of the same grade and they are very scarce at that.
>
> I was told, before I came here, all sorts of weird tales, of how easy it would be to find a studio and how cheap they would be, etc. But I walked the streets day after day searching for one at a low price, and I wanted to get out of the hotel and get to painting the thing I came here to do, so I gave up the chase and [have] taken one for a higher price than I ought to have, so that is one item which accounts for the vanishing of some of the three thousand, and there were others.[126]

Hayden closed this letter with fond regards for Brady and the "lofty cause and helpful purpose of the Harmon awards," but did not communicate with the foundation again for another year and a half.

Meanwhile Hayden apparently tried to get funding from other sources. Well aware of the grants that artist Archibald Motley and writers Countee Cullen and Eric Walrond had received, Hayden applied to the Rosenwald and Guggenheim Foundations, as well, but to no avail: "When you're over there in Europe, it's harder than heck for you to get scholarships

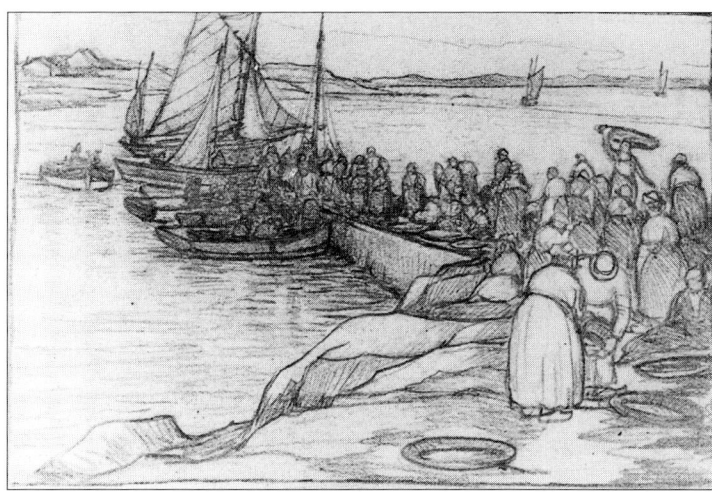

FIGURE 37
Palmer Hayden,
Untitled sketch in
sketchbook, n.d., graphite
on paper, 4 x 6 in.
Palmer Hayden papers.
Archives of American Art,
Smithsonian Institution,
Washington, D.C.

than back here, you see, but over there, they might give you one to go over there . . . if he's
over there already, why should we give him one to go over there, you see."[127]

During 1928, Hayden continued to see Woodruff often. The two hoped that they
might be able to rent and share a small studio together in Montparnasse, but they gave up
the idea after searching for several months.[128] When Martine discovered Hayden's financial
situation, she offered to let him stay at her place until his luck changed. Her mother had died
during the year, and since her brother and sister were both married, she had a five-room
apartment to herself.[129] Hayden moved in with his tutor sometime after April 1928 and lived
at 11, rue Rousselet in the seventh arrondissement for the following four years.[130] The same
spring, Woodruff moved to a suburb of Paris, Malakoff-sur-Seine, and shared a small house
with three other American artists.[131]

There are few records of what Hayden did in France in 1928; it is likely, however,
that the artist spent a great deal of time in Brittany. Woodruff reported in August that
Hayden was "on the coast painting,"[132] and his sketchbooks are filled with harbor scenes and
seascapes. His drawing technique improved considerably, as is evident in some of his sketches
of dockside fisherfolk (fig. 37). It is intriguing that while Hayden used the same simple linear
treatment in all of his figurative works, he never seems to have exaggerated the physiognomy
of white Americans or Europeans.

PRODUCING AND SELLING MORE SEASCAPES, 1929–1931

Since staff members of the Harmon Foundation had not heard from Hayden during most of
1928, but were anxious that their first gold-prize winner continue to be represented, they
showed *The Schooners* and *St. Servan* again in the 1929 exhibition, and reproduced the latter
work in the catalog. Meanwhile, Haynes continued to inquire about Hayden through
Woodruff. In March 1929 Woodruff wrote letters to both Haynes and Brady informing

them of Hayden's progress. "Hayden lives near me and we see each other occasionally. He is doing some very good things in the way of fishing boats and port scenes, the sort of things that seem to have such an appeal to him. I tried to persuade him to send over some of his works this year but he thought it best to await the outcome of the pictures he already has there. But I feel sure that the exhibition next year will have a chance to include several of his canvases."[133]

Concerned about Hayden and perhaps worried that he had taken offense at her chiding, Brady helped him out by selling several of Hayden's paintings and buying one for herself. On July 20, Hayden thanked Brady and offered to give her a small oil painting rather than the watercolor she had purchased for the same price. Apparently, Brady had written that she preferred his work in oils; he commented, "I also agree entirely with what you say in regards to the merits of my work in water colour and oil painting but am compelled to work sometimes in the former because the material for such is less expensive."[134] He continued to paint watercolors in Brittany, staying at the Hôtel de Bretagne Beuzec-Conq in Concarneau during the summer of 1929.

In October, Woodruff wrote again that he had tried to persuade Hayden to enter the competition, but to no avail. Finally, a bit of flattery and the possibility of more prize money must have got to Hayden through Woodruff. Haynes wrote to Woodruff on November 8, "I am delighted to receive your letter stating that you have started your paintings and regret that Hayden does not see his way clear to accept your spirit and follow your example in sending pictures. Certainly one who has received the first award should continue to keep in touch with the enterprise, if that helped him to public recognition, in order to be a party to stimulate others who need the same sort of help[,] besides we have a prize each year for the best piece put on exhibition."[135]

On December 2, Hayden wrote to Evelyn Brown that he was sending five watercolors for exhibition consideration. This time, he was careful to prepay all charges. Four of the works were marines, *Concarneau, Port Louis, Flotte de pêche* (Fishing fleet), and *Le matin* (The morning). Their French titles indicate Hayden's growing comfort with the language. The fifth work, *Portrait,* was the image of a young lady, perhaps one Miss Martha Tur, who lived in New York; most likely, she had met Hayden while abroad. Hayden wrote that she should come to the foundation office to claim the work, but pay one-fifth of the charges the foundation paid in getting the paintings from customs.[136] All five works would be exhibited at the Harmon Foundation in 1930. Hayden informed Brown that she might keep one of the four marines as a token of his appreciation of her kindness in looking after the recent sale of *The Schooners*.[137] A few weeks later, he was delighted to receive another check for a hundred dollars for the sale of *St. Servan*.[138]

Brady and Brown were not Hayden's only staunch supporters; Cullen was well aware of Hayden's financial situation and supported him by buying his oil painting *Parisian Landscape* (1928, fig. 38).[139] Despite the title, Hayden's landscape is a rural scene with rolling hills, a dirt road, thinning trees, and scattered houses. Cullen also urged others to buy

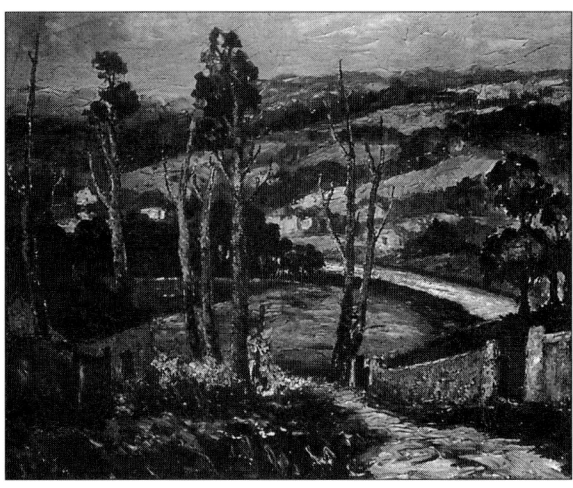

FIGURE 38
Palmer Hayden, *Parisian Landscape*,
1928, oil on canvas, 18¾ x 22⅝ in.
Countee Cullen Collection, Hampton
University Museum, Hampton, Virginia.

Hayden's work; in a letter dated December 29, 1929, Jackman asked Cullen about a painting from Hayden.[140] It is not known whether he bought a work, however.

In 1930, Hayden reported that several of his paintings were shown at the Salon des Tuileries, but his name does not appear in the exhibition catalog.[141] It may have been over-looked, however; in that year, 907 artists exhibited 2,947 works there.[142] In size and intent, the Salon was similar to the Society of Independent Artists in New York. Modernists from the Salon d'Automne and progressive members who had seceded from the Société Nationale des Beaux-Arts founded the Salon in 1923 to offer artists exhibition opportunities without jury and prizes.[143]

By the middle of 1930, repercussions of the Great Depression had hit France. In a series of four graphite vignettes on a single page (too light in tone to reproduce well), Hayden documented his initial reaction to the situation in his sketchbook. In the first, he empties his pockets before a ship and two porters who demand, "Votre billet ou l'argent. Autrement allez au pied" (Your wallet or money. Otherwise, walk). Next, Hayden begs on bended knee to a smiling woman whose skirt bears the title "Dame Fortune." The third scene depicts Hayden sitting near the Eiffel Tower listening to three men singing the blues near skyscrapers. He writes, "J'attend toujours des mauvaise[s] nouvelles de chez moi" (I'm always waiting for bad news from home). Across the ocean waft snippets of his compatriots' lament—"Blues . . . hard times . . . no work . . . Wall Street crash." The last scene, titled "Alors, je reste" (So, I rest), shows Hayden sleeping peacefully in Paris amid its famous landmarks—the Pont-Neuf over the Seine, the Hôtel des Invalides, Notre Dame, and the Eiffel Tower.

Although Hayden seems to have made light of the Great Depression in these draw-ings, he depicted a more somber self-portrait in the watercolor *Palmer Hayden Shaving/The Lean Years of Paris* (1930, fig. 39). Here, in a barren space with a grayish background, the artist stands naked, bending slightly at the waist to peer with one sleepy eye into a circular cosmetic mirror in the foreground before a large, shallow cream-colored basin. The vessel

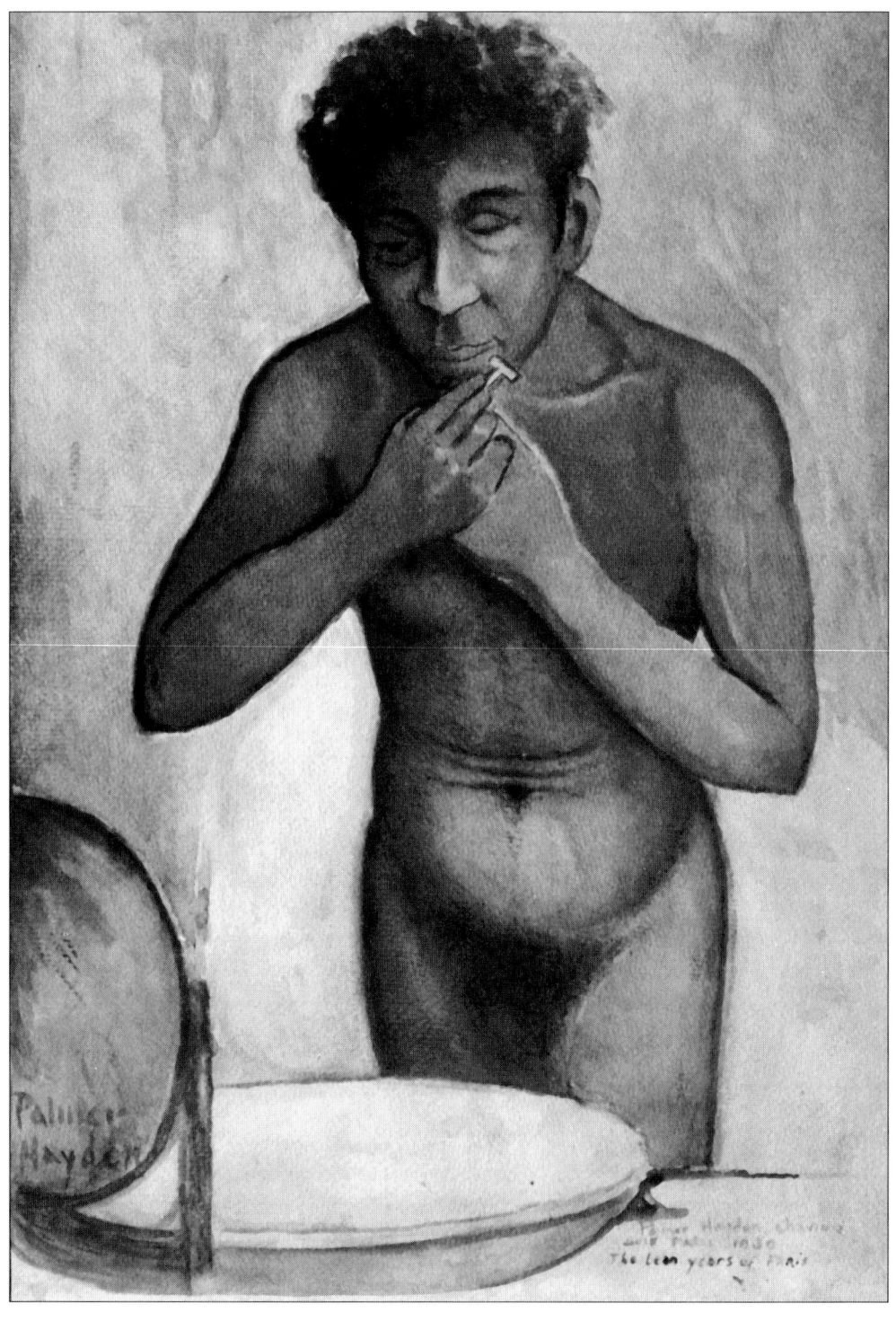

FIGURE 39
Palmer Hayden, *Palmer Hayden Shaving/The Lean Years of Paris,* 1930, watercolor on paper, 18 x 12½ in.
Courtesy of John P. Axelrod, Boston, Massachusetts.

rests atop a plain, thigh-high surface. Hayden appears weary and out of shape, with uncombed hair, dark shadows under his eyes, and flaccid arm, chest, and stomach muscles. He shaves thoughtfully, drawing the razor carefully below his lip with his right hand, his left hand holding his chin. Signed twice, on the mirror in the lower left and in the lower right, as part of the title, this is a remarkably intimate self-portrait of a man who seems vulnerable, yet calm. In its softness and slightly rounded belly and breast, Hayden's body seems almost androgynous. The lack of visible genitalia in the hairy groin flanked by pressed thighs pronounces this effect, yet this approach is likely more of an attempt at modesty than a study in ambiguous sexuality.

Palmer Hayden Shaving may well be the first black nude by an African American artist, and the first serious, nonromanticized black nude by any painter. It is such a radical departure from Hayden's typical cartoonlike figures that one wonders whether he produced more works like this, or whether this was an instance when the artist paused to contemplate his future in France with dwindling resources. The dry watercolor application emphasizes his enforced frugality, yet the slightly upturned corners of his mouth suggest that he savors pleasant memories.

By June 1930, he wrote to Brady that it was necessary for him to return to America at once and asked her to try to sell one of his paintings to pay for his passage. Hayden requested that she make arrangements for him with the American Aid Society in Paris, which could offer reduced rates on ship tickets for Americans who needed transportation home.[144]

Brady did not respond to Hayden's request, but informed him that several of his works had been framed and were hanging in the office. She suggested that he send more oil paintings unframed and rolled up to save on transportation expenses. Brady planned on framing the last set of works Hayden had sent and exhibiting them in the fall. She also hoped he could produce works over the summer that would have as strong an appeal as his *St. Servan* and *The Schooners:* "*Schooners* has a certain mystic quality that gave a very definite personality to the picture. While I would be the last one to suggest that you follow in a given mold, I do hope you can send us some things in the fall that will have the depth of your genius behind them."[145]

Hayden did send six seascapes and landscapes to the Harmon Foundation that fall, after traveling to small fishing villages in Brittany again during July and August. In early 1931, all six works were exhibited: *Auray—bâteaux de pêche* (Auray—fishing boats), *Le Rousseau* (possibly an homage to the "naive" French painter), *Les filets bleus—Concarneau* (The blue nets—Concarneau), *Vers le rivage* (Toward the shore), *Baie de la forêt* (Opening in the forest), and *Sortie des pêcheurs* (Departure of the fishermen). The latter work was published in the catalog. It and the first work listed are the only ones of which reproductions survive, and these poor and black and white, yet they were not singled out for additional merit by either the Harmon Foundation or the press.

At the end of September 1930, Hayden was back in Paris, but it seemed a dull place in contrast to the excitement there of a year ago. In the wake of the Great Depression, some artists had left the city in search of inexpensive housing: Woodruff, for example, went to Cagnes, as Hayden reported to Tanner in a letter.[146] Many others returned to the United States and the once overflowing cafés were now silent. Sculptor Mahonri Young recalled, "The difference at the Dôme between 1929 and 1930 was, for the Americans—who else was there?—the difference between night and day."[147] Hayden used the quiet time in the fall to produce a series of new, figurative works that recalled his rural origins.

PAINTING "NEGRO CHARACTER STUDIES," 1930–1931

On January 21, 1931, Hayden proudly wrote to Brady that he was sending her seven "Negro character studies"—*Telling the Young Folk, John Henry, The Janitor Who Paints, Gobble Race* (possibly *Watermelon Race,* 1930), *Au pious, The Boy from Home,* and *Red.* He wrote that they were "to my satisfaction very well commented upon by many who have seen them here including an able critic who holds a very important position in the Louvre Museum."[148] (Unfortunately, the identity of this critic is not known.) Hayden wanted "to advance farther into this particular line of work" while developing his marine painting. He also now hoped to stay abroad for another year.

Of these seven Negro character studies, only *The Janitor Who Paints* (ca. 1931, fig. 40) seems to have survived, and reproductions of the others have not yet surfaced (*The Boy from Home,* watercolor, is in a private collection). The oil painting depicts a man impeccably dressed in brown slacks, blue shirt, red-and-white polka-dot tie, and beret intently painting a woman and child in his cramped basement bedroom. Seated in a corner next to a garbage can, the artist-janitor fills the right side of the composition. On the wall behind him hang the tools of his trade, a feather duster and a broom. On the left, a young mother in a sleeve-less red gingham dress sits upright on a wooden chair casually holding her wide-eyed baby swaddled in white cloths. She has obviously taken care to dress up for her portrait—she wears red lipstick and fingernail polish, earrings and bracelets, and a lilac corsage. At the mother's feet is a sleeping cat—almost the mirror opposite of a cat Woodruff drew in Hayden's sketch-book at Le Dôme café in 1928—whose portrait, perhaps, hangs on the back wall above the mother's head. The alarm clock on the bedside table shows that it is 4:07 p.m.

With an overall scheme of warm orange browns and beiges, *The Janitor Who Paints* is a study in harmonious dualities. The right side is cooler and darker, and represents a traditional man's world of hard physical labor. The left side is warmer, brighter, and depicts a traditional woman's world of domesticity and decoration. Curvilinear forms—the rim of the garbage-can lid, the edge of the palette, the artist's shoulder, beret, and bedside—lead the eye around the room to the circular forms of the clock, the bedpost finial, the lightbulb, the water-pipe handle, the baby's head.

Art historians have suggested that *The Janitor Who Paints* is a self-portrait, based on Hayden's janitorial experience and his flair for dressing elegantly.[149] The artist proudly wore a beret and, as mentioned earlier, a foulard scarf and a diamond horseshoe pin. Yet, the image of the artist as a figure painter in a windowless basement does not jibe with Hayden's

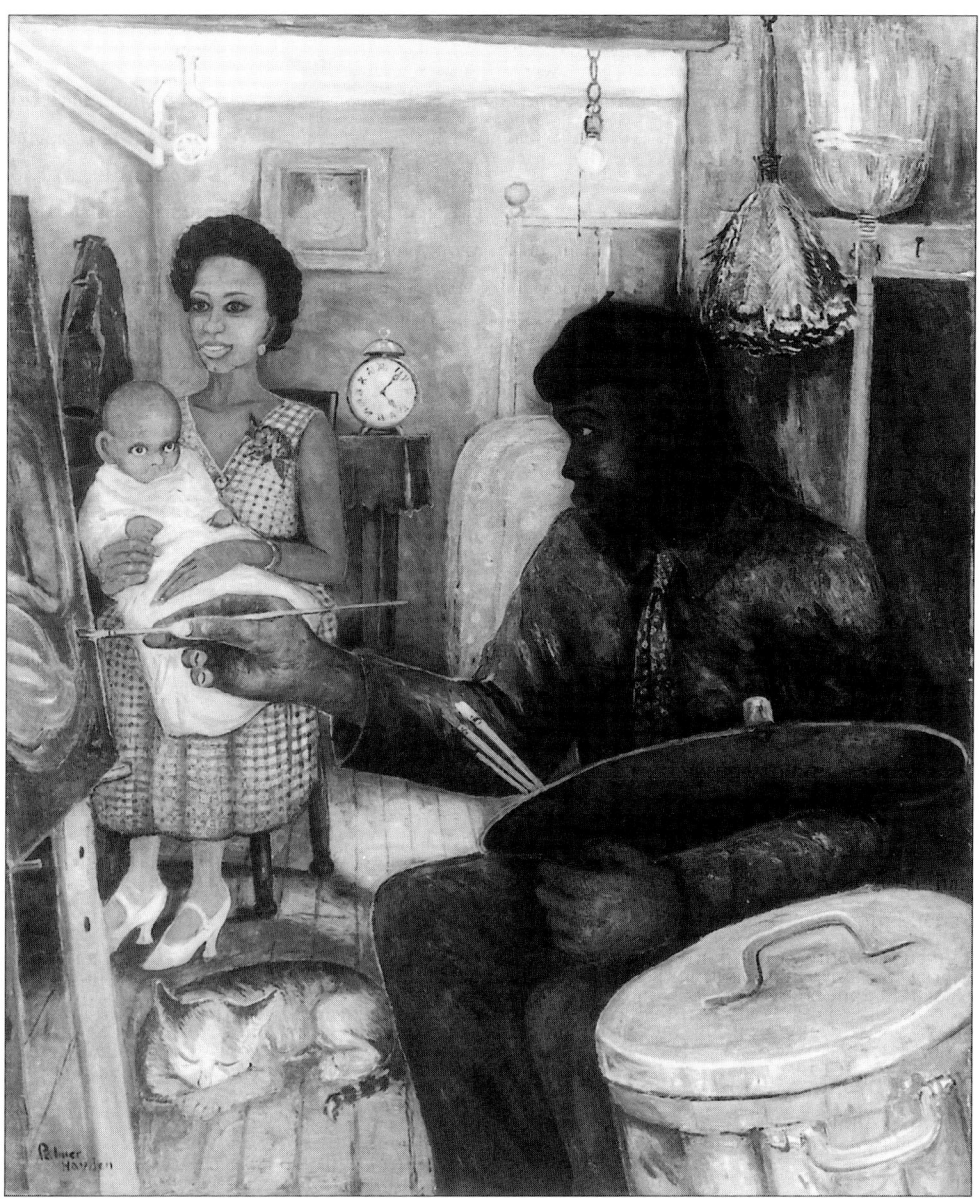

FIGURE 40
Palmer Hayden, *The Janitor Who Paints*, ca. 1931, oil on canvas, 39⅛ x 33 in.
National Museum of American Art, Smithsonian Institution. Gift of the Harmon Foundation.

earlier life as a marine painter who lived in an attic with a skylight. In fact, Hayden stated that the work was based on the life of Cloyd Boykin, who "had a place in a basement and I used to go and visit him because he was a good friend."[150] Hayden depicted his friend in a beret to symbolize his vocation: "It's sort of a protest painting. I painted it because no one called Boykin the artist. They called him the janitor."[151] Yet Hayden also alluded to his friend's paying job by including the alarm clock in the background, Boykin having to be alert for

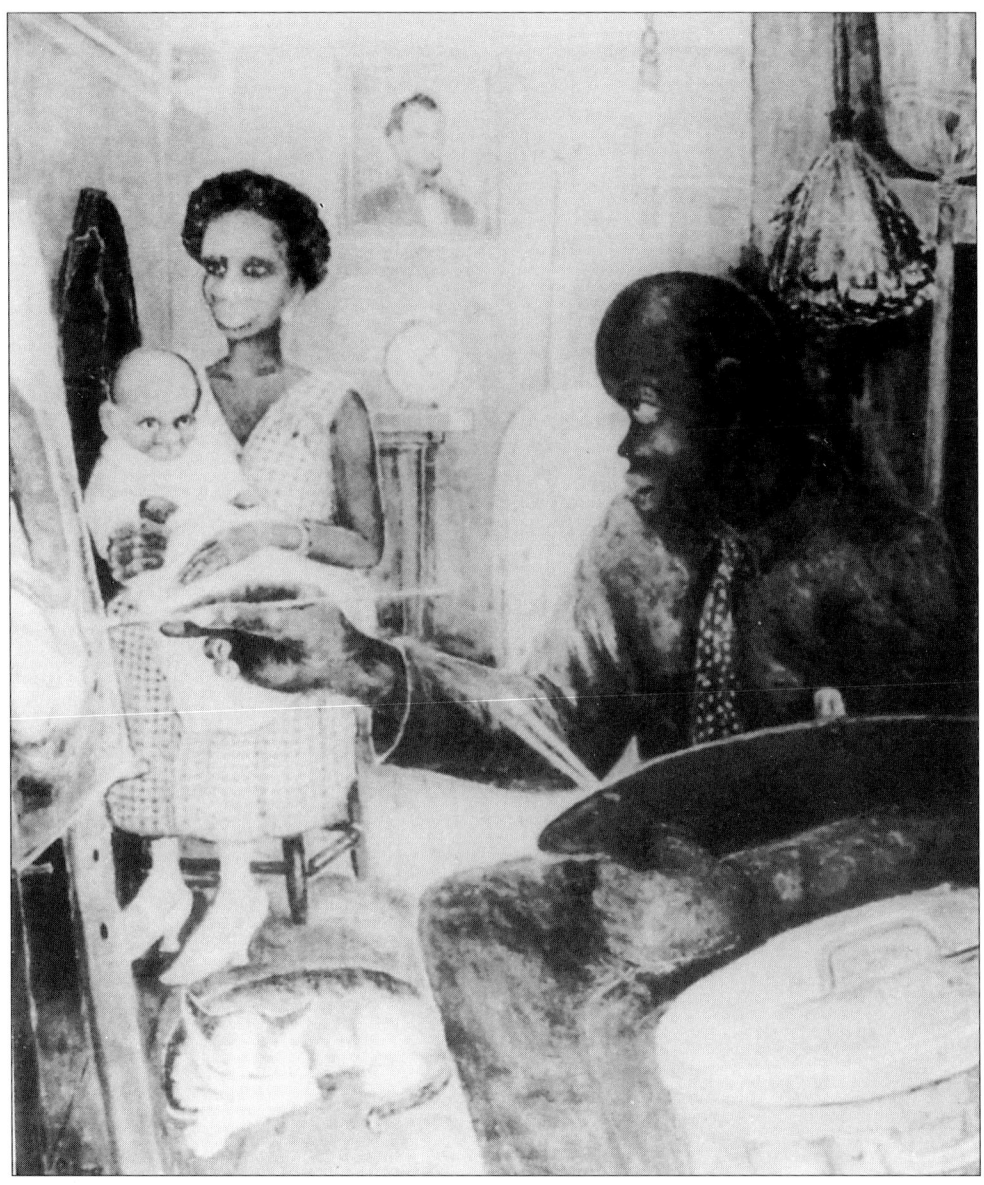

FIGURE 41
Palmer Hayden, *The Janitor Who Paints*, ca. 1930 (earlier version), oil on canvas, 39⅛ x 33 in.
National Museum of American Art, Smithsonian Institution, Gift of the Harmon Foundation.

packages delivered and tasks required at certain times. The subject of Boykin's double
portrait (the woman and her baby), within the painting had no particular meaning and the
two were not his own family, but Hayden explained that "all artists have been concerned
with painting the mother and child."[152]

     Hayden's finished version of *The Janitor Who Paints* is radically different from his
first conception (ca. 1930, fig. 41), visible in an X-ray scanning of the painting and in a

reproduction published in Locke's 1940 book *The Negro in Art*. Hayden had initially depicted "a minstrel-faced mammy"[153] with exaggerated lips, rather than the comely woman of the later version. The first janitor himself was a caricature, "a grinning monkey with fleshy lips and a head that has been distorted into a bullet-like shape"[154] (actually, in the earlier version, he does not appear to be grinning). On the wall in place of the picture of the cat was a painting of a three-quarters view, bust-length portrait of Abraham Lincoln, a reminder of his role of the "Great Liberator." Was Hayden mocking the white administration and audience of the Harmon Foundation by portraying African Americans as minstrel performers or was he just having fun? The question remains why Hayden painted such a stereotypes and then altered the scene to one of charming domesticity. Had his friends cautioned him against the images or did he make his own private decision to sweeten the piece? At any rate, Hayden must have realized that it would be easier to catch flies—patrons—with honey than with vinegar. Later, he insisted that "his works symbolically made reference to the comedy, tragedy, and pleasures of a black life-style."[155] The title of the painting also alludes to those aforementioned headlines that heralded Hayden, the housecleaner, as a Harmon Foundation prizewinner, such as "Painting by Negro Window Cleaner Takes First Prize at Art Exhibition" and "Negro Housecleaner Will Study Art in Europe."

Hayden also depicted a legendary black lifestyle in *John Henry* (location unknown). He may have first heard about the folk hero from his brother, a banjo player,[156] or his father, the storyteller. He was attracted to the subject because John Henry came from a similar background to his. Hayden recalled that "[the ballad] appealed to me chiefly because it told in sober words and tune the life and tragic death of a powerful and popular working man who belonged to my section of the country and to my own race. . . . The epic . . . dramatizes the beginnings of a movement of the Negro from agricultural into industrial labor in the development of industrial America."[157] It is significant that Hayden first painted this subject abroad. Once he had removed himself from his culture, he could see and appreciate it more clearly. But it was not just a matter of being outside of the United States, otherwise he might have painted a similar picture in the Philippines. The French valorized black culture, albeit in a vague and superficial way. Being in France heightened Hayden's awareness of the modernist preoccupation with primitivism and folklore. As Jeffrey Stewart has argued, "In the popular myth of John Henry, the Negro is eulogized precisely because he resists modernity. In order to enter the modernist discourse the African American had to do so as the primitive."[158]

Hayden found this concept affirmed when the American Legion held an exhibition of his work in Paris sometime in 1931, and he sold two paintings of ostensibly African American subjects, *Man with a Guitar* and *Campmeeting*.[159] Not only did Hayden sell at least these two works, but he also received several hundred dollars as a second installment of the veterans' bonus from the American Legion: "Then I had two hundred or three hundred dollars, I don't know what it was, but it was a lot of francs and I was up for a new suit, and a new old coat, give my landlord some money."[160] The unexpected income also meant that Hayden could stay abroad a while longer with his friends.

In the summer of 1931, Hayden often met with Countee Cullen, Harold Jackman, Harold Dingwall, and William White, this last the son of composer Clarence Cameron White.[161] Another of Hayden's companions was journalist-historian J. A. Rogers, who introduced him to Aaron Douglas. When Hayden told Douglas that he knew Tanner, Douglas asked him to arrange a meeting. One day, Hayden and Douglas were sitting in a large café and Tanner walked in with a white woman. Hayden told Douglas that he would tell Tanner that "another American Negro painter" wanted to meet him, but when he approached the table, Tanner coldly said to him, "Will you excuse me?" A few days later, Tanner apologized to Hayden and explained that his visitor, an elderly American woman, was nervous about being in a café because she thought they were all dens of sin. When Hayden approached, she was afraid that he was part of Tanner's "gang."[162] Hayden and Douglas visited Tanner at a later time.

Sometime in the summer or fall of 1931, Hayden attended the Colonial Exposition. He must have written something complimentary about the exposition to the office of the Commission of the United States of America, the International Colonial and Overseas Exposition at Paris; he received a brief letter of thanks for his "aimable pensée" from François Monod, French advisor and associate curator of the French National Museums.[163]

DEPICTING AFRICAN PEOPLE AND CULTURE AT THE COLONIAL EXPOSITION AND BEYOND

Hayden seemed most impressed by the performances of African drumming and dancing: "When we heard it first back in Paris, back in 1931, when we were there and the colonial exhibition came from Africa and they had these African drums and this rhythm of a dancing, well you know, it was something that now, everybody dances to the rhythm. . . . You don't call it a savage noise now."[164]

Hayden executed a watercolor series of the stunning performers. In one of the works, *African Dancers* (1931, fig. 42), two bald men in the lower left sit on the ground playing the large drums between their legs with their hands and small mallets. They, along with all of the costumed performers, look to the side, not unlike the cardplayers in *Nous quatre à Paris*. In the center, a dancer with caplike dreadlocks, arm bangles, a lavender fiber skirt, and conical breast shields leads two other dancers. The dancer just behind the first wears a large, striped mask, possibly of the Dogon people, with two horns. The group appears in a nondescript background that offers only the suggestion of a palm tree in the upper left. Rather than representing a particular people, Hayden has generalized this image and infused it with his own humor. All of the men have roundish heads with enormous foreheads, tiny squinting eyes, and outsized lips. In another watercolor, *African Dancer* (ca. 1931, fig. 43), the performer has a similar physiognomy, with the addition of a grin and a paunch. His clothing is more elaborate; he sports a round hat, hoop earrings, a clawlike necklace, sharply pointed breast cones, and a fiber skirt. He dances before the silhouettes of three cone-shaped buildings with sticklike projections that resemble mud mosques found in

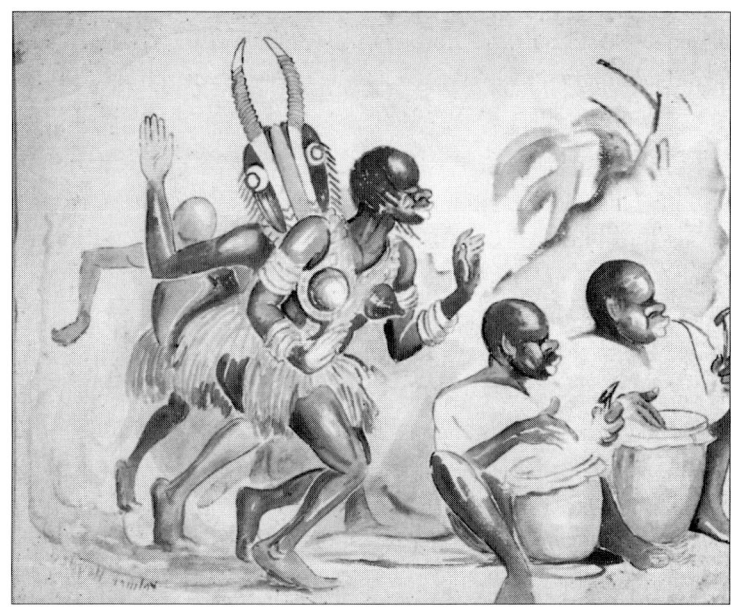

FIGURE 42
Palmer Hayden,
African Dancers,
ca. 1931, watercolor
on paper, 14½ x 18 in.
The Museum of
African American Art,
Los Angeles.

FIGURE 43
Palmer Hayden,
African Dancer,
ca. 1931, watercolor
on paper, 13 x 10½ in.
The Museum of
African American Art,
Los Angeles.

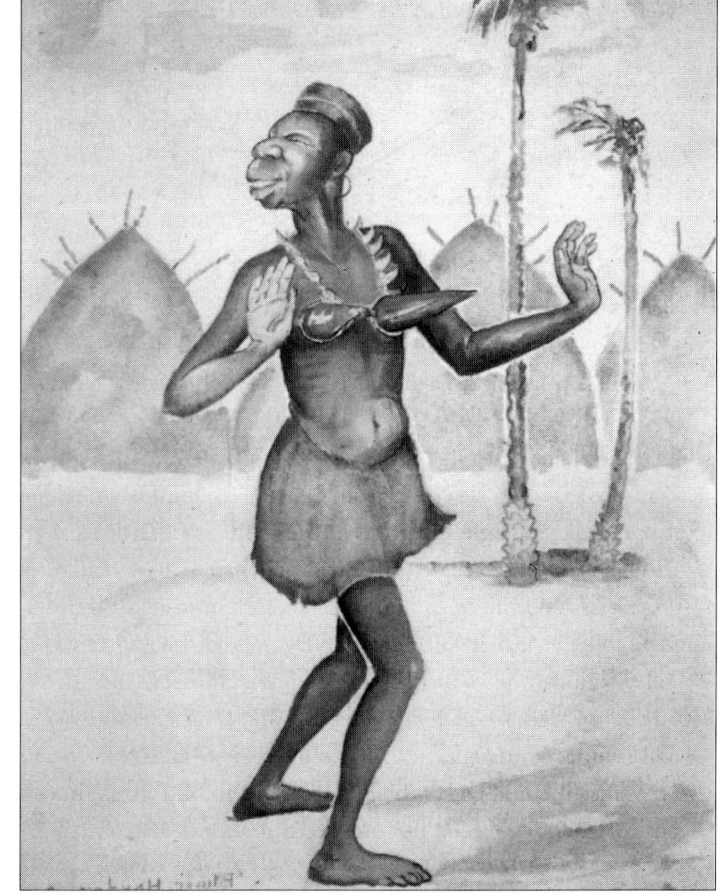

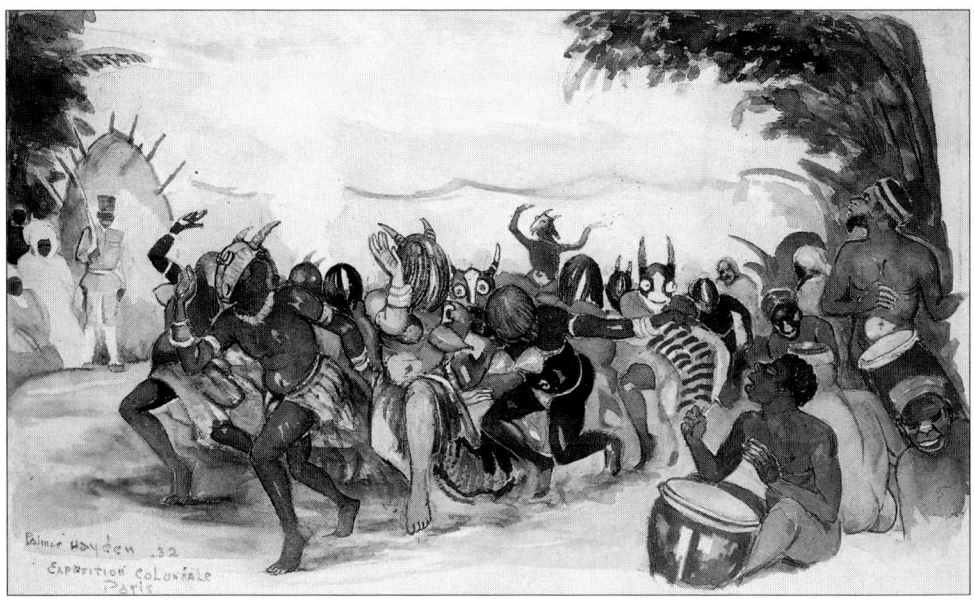

FIGURE 44
Palmer Hayden, *Exposition Coloniale,* 1932, watercolor on paper, 10 x 14 in.
With permission of Samella Lewis.

Timbuktu. In fact, such structures were re-created at the Colonial Exposition. A more
elaborate watercolor of African dancers featuring a mud mosque is *Exposition Coloniale*
(1932, fig. 44). This image includes at least three drummers in the lower right, a guard
wearing a European uniform on the left, and a procession of more than a dozen dancers,
some of whom wear fiber skirts, conical breast decorations, and horned wood-and-raffia
masks. Hayden's depictions of performances by Ivory Coast dancers are similar to those
seen in watercolors by the French artist Henri-Lucien Cheffer (1880–?) published in the
exposition catalog of July 1931 (fig. 45). Hayden's images, however, are more obviously
caricaturist in their physiognomic distortions.

    Hayden's appropriation of racist imagery is a complex and significant issue, and
one that continues to haunt African Americans today (witness the outrage by both blacks
and whites at the work of Kara Walker and Michael Ray Charles). It is difficult to ascertain
just how aware Hayden was of the power of such images, or what his intentions were in
using them. Because they are not excessively offensive, but rather have a sense of naïveté
about them, they seem to be made with affection and suggest the good-natured humor
and theatricality of the circus scenes of Hayden's paintings. But did this in part result
from a process in which Hayden, like so many others, had internalized white perceptions
of African American culture? Hayden could not escape the way in which the Harmon
Foundation perceived him—an unusually talented Negro janitor—and he clearly had
the Du Boisian double consciousness of being aware of his dual heritage. Was his
production of yet more stereotypes a form of vicarious suicide, caused by deeply ingrained
self-hatred? It seems unlikely, given Hayden's apparent easygoing personality, yet perhaps

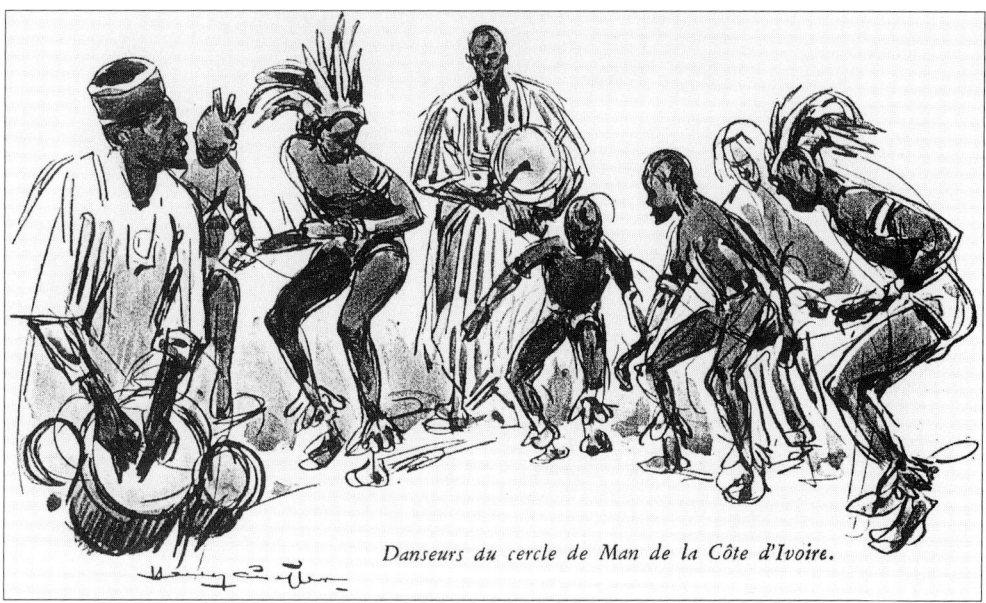

Danseurs du cercle de Man de la Côte d'Ivoire.

FIGURE 45
Henri-Lucien Cheffer, *Danseurs du cercle de Man de la Côte d'Ivoire,* 1931, dimensions and location unknown. Reproduced in *Exposition Coloniale Internationale de Paris 1931.*

he had a bit of the Stockholm syndrome, in which the captive identifies with the captor and perpetuates oppression when s/he in turn gains power. Or, maybe, in making exaggerated depictions of blacks, Hayden was exorcising his own personal race demons, as do some African Americans through collecting stereotypical black memorabilia.[165] If Hayden did or could not fully realize the implications of his imagery, he at least sensed its power to affect viewers in strong and memorable ways.

Although Hayden did not seem as moved by the African sculpture on display at the exposition as was Elizabeth Prophet, he was undoubtedly aware of its far-reaching influence on early twentieth-century European art. At about the time of the exposition, Hayden painted *Fétiche et fleurs* (ca. 1931–1932, fig. 46), his only known painting featuring African art. The work depicts a still life on a simple wooden table. In the back right, a sculpture of a Fang head rests on a Kuba textile draped diagonally across the table. To the left of the head is a round blue vase full of exotic golden, pink, and reddish orchids, the leaves of which partially obscure the base of the sculpture and almost seem to tickle its chin. In the foreground on the table a round light blue ashtray holds a single cigarette. Above a simple wooden chair in the left background of the compsition is a shelf, on which are a bowl and candlestick, both cropped by the side and top of the composition. On the right, a reddish curtain patterned with hollow blue ovals hangs behind the table, cropped both above and below.

Hayden first learned about African art from Alain Locke during one of his summer sojourns in Paris. He recalled that the experience was "an interesting discovery . . . a revelation,"[166] but he did not indicate whether Locke took him to flea markets, museums, or private collections, or merely showed him publications about African art. Like the faces of

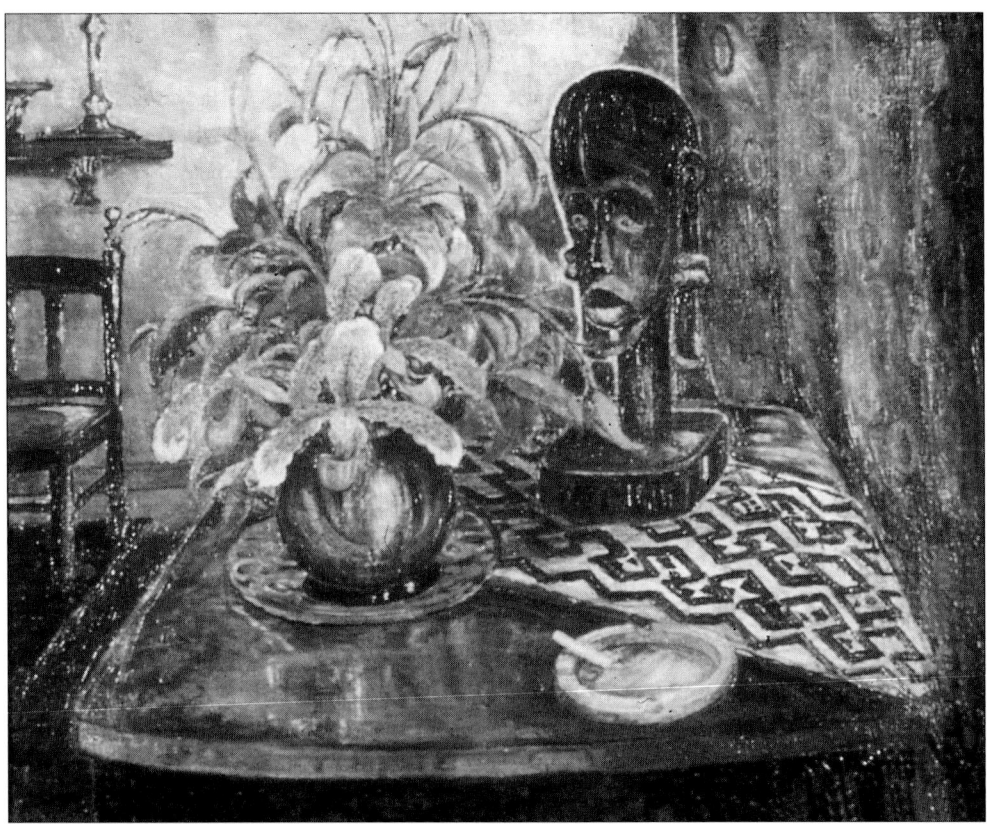

FIGURE 46
Palmer Hayden, *Fétiche et fleurs,* ca. 1931–1932, oil on canvas, 23½ x 29 in.
The Museum of African American Art, Los Angeles.

the African dancers, the Fang head in *Fétiche et fleurs* has a broad round forehead and full
lips, but a thin, angular nose and rounded eyes, as well as two decorative horizontal rolls
beneath the ears. The sculpture, further identified by the deep crack parallel to a vertical
incision in the forehead, is almost certainly the one that French writer Paul Guillaume first
owned, then sold to sculptor Jacob Epstein (1880–1959), and that is now the Metropolitan
Museum of Art (1979.206.229).[167] Had Hayden seen the Fang head in the home of
Guillaume or Epstein or did he copy it from a publication? The Fang head was published in
"Echoes," in *Les Arts à Paris,* no. 13 (June 1927). If Hayden was familiar with this image,
it might have also served as the prototype for the male head in *The Janitor Who Paints* or
the stylized heads in *Nous quatre à Paris.*[168] At any rate, the African artworks in *Fétiche
et fleurs* seem to be little more than decorative objects that bespeak an international
sophistication, even as their presence racializes the painting. Indeed, Hayden found no
other symbolic content in the images and never painted another such work. He said, "I
never had any desire to paint anything about Africa. I painted what Negroes, colored people,
us Americans do . . . we're a brand new race, raised and manufactured in the U.S. I do like
to paint what they did."[169]

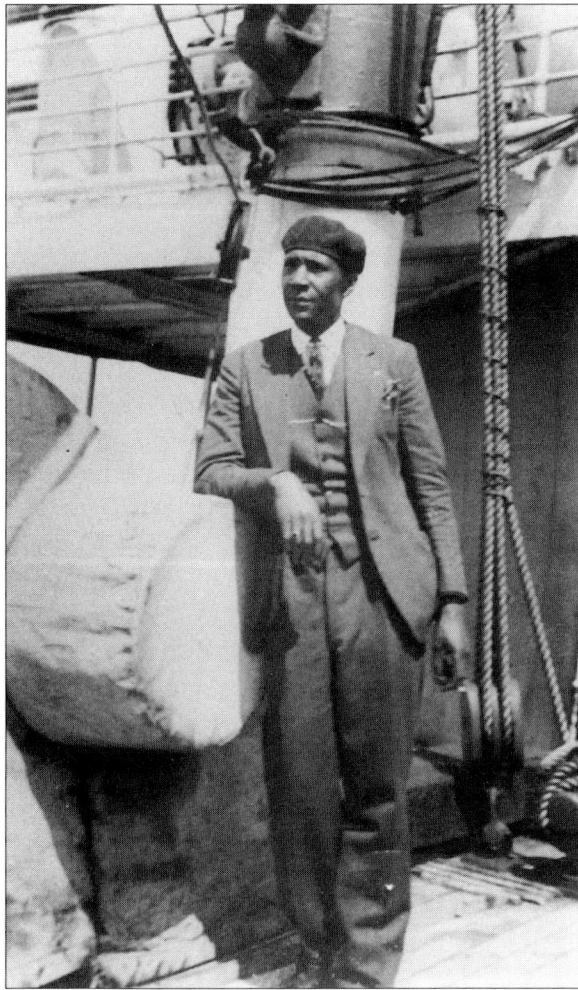

FIGURE 47
Palmer Hayden returning from Paris
on the S.S. *Majestic,* 1932.
Palmer Hayden papers.
Archives of American Art,
Smithsonian Institution,
Washington, D.C.

About the appropriation of African art by Europeans, Hayden said, "I just thought
it was, you know, something that they're trying now . . . something that would have no
importance whatever now."[170] He didn't feel that he had any special insight into African art:
"I don't know how much contact we have with the old world, Africa, so to speak. We can't
do much anymore than they can, anymore than a white painter can do."[171] Hayden's capital-
ization on the popularity of African art was a savvy, if somewhat uninformed, move; *Fétiche et
fleurs* won the John D. Rockefeller prize from the Harmon Foundation in early 1933 (there
were no prizes or exhibitions in 1932) and became Hayden's most reproduced painting.

Locke particularly admired Hayden's new style, calling it "more modernistic; more
decorative, high-keyed and in broken color."[172] Yet he wasn't quite sure how to categorize
Hayden's work; he gave him his own section in his book *Negro Art: Past and Present* (1936),
wedged in between the titles "The Traditionalists" and "The Modernists," explaining, "Not
ultra-modern in style, but far from the purely academic, Mr. Hayden's present work proves
him to be one of the soundest technicians among the younger Negro painters."[173] It is not

known what W.E.B. Du Bois thought of Hayden's work; no papers containing his comments on the matter seem to exist. However, given his agenda regarding racial uplift through the elite talented tenth, it is unlikely that Du Bois cared much for Hayden's sometimes awkward seascapes and his gently humorous depictions of rural African American folk.

FINAL MONTHS IN PARIS, 1932

Hayden's last year in Paris is a mystery; very little documentation about this time is extant, other than correspondence from December 1931 stating that Hayden offered William Harmon's wife, Katherine, a choice of his paintings as a gift. She selected one depicting old French houses near a wall.[174] Hayden may have abandoned his "Negro character studies" for a while and resumed his depictions of the French environment.

By the summer of 1932, Hayden felt that he had "lived out [his] time there [Paris] and wasn't getting anywhere there."[175] On August 10, 1932, he sailed home from Cherbourg on the S.S. *Majestic* (fig. 47), dressed in a three-piece suit and a beret. His passage was courtesy of the American Legion, which promised to pay back the American Aid Society for his transportation. In exchange for the fee, however, Hayden's passport was cut up.

4
THE EDUCATION OF A MODERNIST:
HALE WOODRUFF IN FRANCE, 1927–1931

Of all the New Negro artists in Paris, Hale Woodruff (fig. 48) was perhaps the most avant-garde. Although he began creating rather academic landscapes and depictions of French landmarks, he soon developed a Cubist-influenced style, then experimented with Expressionism, and finally, abstraction. This would launch him, in the 1940s, into Abstract Expressionism.

"A BLOSSOMING OF NEW PROMISES":
INDIANAPOLIS, 1918–1927

At the age of seventeen, in Nashville, Tennessee, Hale Aspacio Woodruff vowed that he would go to Europe to see the paintings of Henry O. Tanner, the internationally known African American painter whose works were often reproduced in *Crisis* magazine, which Woodruff read in the school library.[1] Ten years later, he would achieve his dream of studying in Paris.

After graduation from high school in 1918, Woodruff left Nashville with his friend George W. Gore to find work for the summer in Indianapolis. The teenagers chose the city because it was a large metropolis near Franklin, Indiana, where Gore's father was a minister. After viewing a student show at the Herron Art School, Woodruff was determined to enter the institution that fall, but instead was obliged to work for two years to save money for tuition and living expenses.

In the fall of 1920 Woodruff entered the Herron Art School, where he studied oil and watercolor landscape painting with William Forsyth (1854–1935), whom he found to be

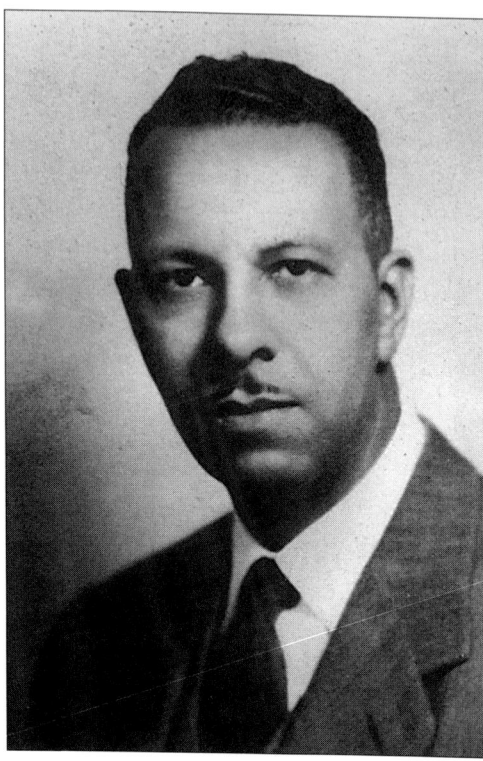

FIGURE 48
Hale Woodruff.
Photo courtesy of the Schomburg Center for
Research in Black Culture, New York Public Library.

"a very good teacher."[2] Forsyth, who had studied in Munich, painted quickly with a
generous amount of pigment, like his friend, William Merritt Chase. The members of an
active artists' colony in Brown County, south of Indianapolis, which sponsored frequent
exhibitions at county fairs, admired his style of painting. Woodruff sometimes worked
outdoors in the area, which boasted beautiful year-round scenery, but between work and
school, he had little time to go to the countryside. Because most of his landscapes were of
imaginary sites, Woodruff labeled himself "ultra-impressionistic"[3] and "Romantic."[4]

At the Herron Museum (later the Indianapolis Museum of Art), Woodruff gained
his first exposure to European masterpieces, such as Rubens's *Christ Giving the Keys to Peter*
(ca. 1613–1615),[5] from both the permanent collection and traveling exhibitions. He was
particularly moved by the "remarkable freshness" of Italian medieval paintings he saw in an
exhibition loaned to the Herron Museum by the Kress Foundation.[6] Woodruff was also
intrigued by the uproar occasioned by the presentation of a painting by Sidney Dickenson
(life dates unknown) to the museum. Dickenson showed a work that depicted a man with an
elongated body. The museum staff pronounced the piece "artistic blasphemy," but Woodruff
and other students liked its originality.[7]

In the early 1920s, Woodruff supplemented his income by drawing political
cartoons, at five dollars a piece, for the local African American newspaper, the *Indianapolis
Ledger.* Many of his cartoons depicted police brutality, lynchings, and segregation in
education and housing.[8] Whites in Indiana were generally known for their friendliness and

tolerance; they also, however, burdened black people living in the state with discrimination, segregation, and second-class citizenship. In Indiana, whites denied African Americans access to many restaurants, hotels, theaters, parks, and other public accommodations, and forced them to live in enclaves within the larger cities with inadequate urban services and amenities.

Many African Americans in Indiana lived with the threat of violence from the Ku Klux Klan. A large contingent of the Klan first appeared in the state in 1920, with membership reaching its peak in the summer of 1923, when it numbered about three thousand.[9] The Klan cloaked its hatred of African Americans through preaching patriotism and Protestant Christianity. The Klan newspaper, the *Fiery Cross,* published in Indianapolis, condemned Roman Catholics, Jews, immigrants, African Americans, immorality, and presumed threats to God and country. The African American newspaper the *Indianapolis Freeman,* vigorously criticized the Klan's tactics, which included marches to courthouse squares, burned crosses, organized boycotts of Catholic business-people, and rumors and threats.[10] While there was little actual violence and no reported lynchings in Indianapolis,[11] the intimidation produced fear and silence. By the late 1920s, public pressure for segregation forced the creation of an all-black high school, Crispus Attucks. Yet many people opposed the Klan, too, and soon after the *Indianapolis Times* won a Pulitzer Prize in 1928 for its crusade against the Klan, the group died out in Indianapolis.[12]

Although Woodruff was not directly affected by the Klan, he suffered from racial discrimination in that he was only able to find unskilled labor. His slight income was not enough to meet tuition expenses, so he appealed to his employer at the "colored Y" for an advance on his wages. When the art school found the proposition unacceptable, Woodruff had to withdraw permanently by 1923.[13]

Hoping for improved wages, Woodruff moved farther north, to Chicago. He briefly studied part-time at the Art Institute of Chicago, then dropped out after a few sessions, believing he could do as well on his own.[14] Finding living conditions no better in Chicago, Woodruff soon returned to Indianapolis.

Woodruff came back to his old position at the Senate Avenue YMCA with renewed respect; the institution had become one of the country's outstanding black branches and a cultural hub. The Y's "Chief," Secretary Fayburn E. DeFrantz, invited leading scholars, such as Charles S. Johnson, William Pickens,[15] Walter White, and W.E.B. Du Bois, to lecture there.[16] DeFrantz took a special interest in Woodruff and introduced him to some of the speakers, among them John Hope, president of Morehouse College, and Colonel Joseph H. Ward, director of the Veterans Hospital at Tuskegee, both of whom purchased Woodruff's work.[17] Hope had long been an art collector and owned many paintings by Edward Mitchell Bannister, the nineteenth-century landscapist.[18] He was greatly impressed with Woodruff's work, suggesting that the young artist consider a position as art instructor at Morehouse within a few years.[19]

The Y's Sunday afternoon "Monster Meetings" drew poets, artists, and musicians,[20] such as writer Countee Cullen and painter William Edouard Scott, both of whom befriended

Woodruff and urged him to study abroad. Scott had studied in Paris from 1909 to 1912. Upon his return to Indianapolis, his *La misère* took first prize at the Indiana State Fair.[21] Scott then developed a strong reputation as a muralist; in 1913 he completed murals at Schools 26 and 23, and in 1914, he painted murals in the Murdsal wing of City Hospital (now Wishard Hospital). In 1918 the city of Indianapolis purchased one of the works Scott had produced abroad, *A Rainy Night in Etaples*. Scott and Woodruff talked frequently about painting, and about Scott having met and worked with Tanner. They also discussed the many other African American artists and writers who were producing and publishing throughout the country. Woodruff viewed the tremendous creative activity as an awakening, "a blossoming of new promises in the twenties."[22]

Sharing evening studio expenses with artists Wilbert Holloway and John Wesley Hardrick—the only other African American students in a class of about forty at Herron[23]—over the years,[24] Woodruff continued to paint independently and had a solo exhibition at the Pettis Galleries in Indianapolis in 1923.[25] He also displayed his work in group exhibitions at the YMCA, the Annual Indiana Artists Exhibitions (*The Street Workers* and *The Red Sweater*, both no longer extant, appeared in the 1923 and 1924 exhibitions, respectively),[26] and the Herron Art Museum (1923, 1924, 1926).

In 1925 Woodruff submitted five paintings to the Amy Spingarn Competition at the *Crisis* under the fictitious name Icabod [*sic*] Crane.[27] One of his landscapes won the ten-dollar third prize for illustration.[28] These paintings so impressed Du Bois that he not only requested that Woodruff submit cover designs for the *Crisis* from time to time,[29] but he also hung them in his office and was, as he said, "loathe to depart with them" when the 135th Street branch library in New York requested them for a solo exhibition in 1925.[30]

From 1925 to 1926, Woodruff significantly aided the development of the Senate Avenue YMCA as its membership secretary. During that year, he was responsible for the largest membership for a black YMCA in the country.[31] To celebrate the membership drive, in the spring of 1926 Woodruff traveled with DeFrantz to Topeka, Kansas, where they stayed at the home of the Barker family. There, Woodruff met Theresa Ada Barker, a student at Washburn College. The two would court, largely by mail, for the following eight years until they married in 1934.[32]

In 1926, Woodruff won two major awards, one of which was a second prize for drawing (most likely for a landscape, either *August Wind* or *Laureate Autumn*, both now missing)[33] in the *Crisis* contest.[34] More significant, after Woodruff submitted four landscapes and a figurative work to the Harmon Foundation,[35] he achieved national acclaim by winning the bronze award for *Two Old Women* (fig. 49).[36] The oil painting depicts African American women from the waist up, their broad torsos filling the foreground. The woman on the left, clad in a dark hooded cape, looks directly at the viewer. The older woman on the right, wearing a plaid shawl and cap, looks off into the distance. The pair seem to be positioned in a nondescript setting, but the background is a busy pattern of thin, horizontal bands of color applied thickly to the canvas. One of the Harmon Foundation jurors, Francis Coates Jones,

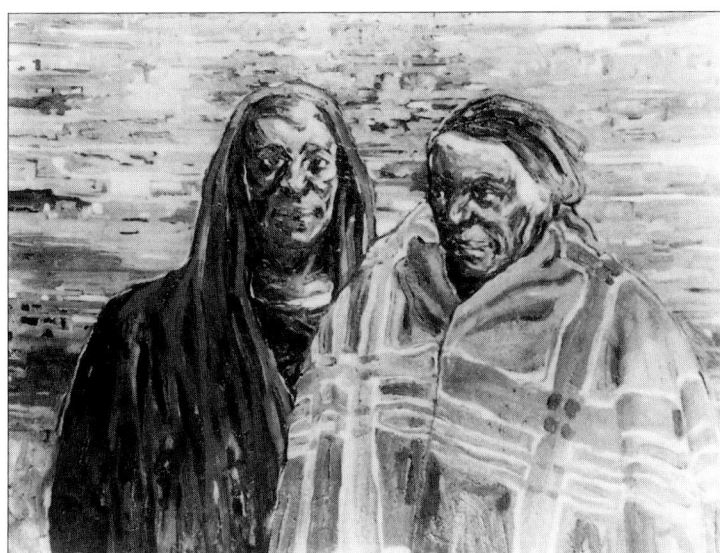

FIGURE 49
Hale Woodruff,
Two Old Women,
ca. 1926, oil on canvas,
dimensions and location
unknown.
Courtesy of
Kenkeleba Gallery.
Photo courtesy
of the artist via
Henry Henderson.

a prominent member of the National Academy of Design, felt that this work and the land-scapes demonstrated that Woodruff had "real promise" and that he "might be expected to develop in a fine way as he goes along."[37]

Woodruff planned to use the one-hundred-dollar award to help finance a two-year trip to Europe where he would study landscape painting in France, Italy, and Spain.[38] Several New Yorkers helped Woodruff raise additional funds for his journey. Walter White, assistant executive secretary of the NAACP in New York, was an enthusiastic promoter of many leading figures of the Harlem Renaissance, such as Countee Cullen, Rudolph Fisher, Nella Larsen, Claude McKay, and Dorothy West. He took special interest in Woodruff: "Button-holing wealthy white patrons of the arts and passing the collection plate among Harlem's affluent [residents] in order to send Woodruff to Paris for classes at the Académie Scandinave became routine for White."[39] White solicited the white banker and fine arts patron Otto H. Kahn, "without [Kahn] seeing any of Mr. Woodruff's work," to contribute $250 for each of the two years.[40]

The Harmon award brought Woodruff local acclaim and support, as well. Governor Edward Jackson—ironically "the leading Ku Klux Klanner of the State of Indiana"[41]—pinned a medal on the young artist. Members of the all-white Florentine Club of Franklin invited Woodruff to have an solo exhibition in their town.[42] They also performed a play written especially for the occasion in his honor to raise money for his trip and presented him with two hundred dollars. Woodruff was amazed by the patronage: "This was supposedly Klan country! Yet here they were giving me $150 [*sic*; it is not clear how much money Woodruff received] along with praise. Knowing the history and reality of the way we were treated day in and day out, it was virtually unbelievable!"[43] Other members of the commu-nity and friends also made small donations, and DeFrantz offered to try to sell some of the works Woodruff would make abroad.[44]

Among Woodruff's patrons in Indianapolis was Hermann Lieber, the owner of an art and photography supply shop at 24 West Washington Street.[45] Lieber offered to sell at least one of Woodruff's paintings each month. He had first befriended Woodruff when the artist brought some of his work to the little Pettis Gallery on the second floor of the shop. Sometime in 1921 or 1922 Lieber gave Woodruff one of the earliest books solely devoted to African art, Carl Einstein's *Afrikanische Plastik* (1921).[46] Lieber suggested that from it, the painter might be able to learn more about his cultural heritage. He said, "I want you to take this little book because it records the great work of your great people; African art."[47] Woodruff could not read the German text, but he was profoundly moved by the photographs of African sculpture:

> You can't imagine the effect that book had on me. Part of the effect was due to the fact that as a black artist I felt very much alone there in Indianapolis. I had heard of Tanner, but I had never heard of the significance of the impact of African art. Yet here it was! And all written up in German, a language I didn't understand! Yet published with beautiful photographs and treated with great seriousness and respect! Plainly sculptures of black people, my people, they were considered very beautiful by these German art experts! The whole idea that this could be so was like an explosion. It was a real turning point for me. I was just astonished at this enormous discovery.[48]

The gift initiated Woodruff's lifelong interest in African art, which would be further fueled in Paris.

Woodruff profusely thanked all those who had supported him. Apparently grateful for Cullen's long-distance words of encouragement, Woodruff sent him one of his paintings, explaining: "The picture is merely a slight token of my deep appreciation for the regard in which you seem to hold me. All my pictures are like children to me. Being the father of so many I can hardly take care of them all, so I have only appointed you guardian of one of the youngsters. My desire to go away in Sept. is gradually materializing and I'm sure I'll make the trip."[49] Cullen, who had been to Paris in the summer of 1926, was delighted for Woodruff. Months later he wrote: "While the two weeks I spent there were all too short, they were long enough to make me know how beautiful Paris can be. It is superfluous for one to say that I hope your work will have benefited by your stay there. I know it will."[50]

Before Woodruff left the country, he traveled to Chicago and viewed the permanent collection at the Art Institute of Chicago again. There, he admired the work of El Greco, perhaps because it reminded him of the daring elongation of the body that Dickenson had produced.[51] The reason for Woodruff's journey to Chicago may have been to deliver four of his canvases to the Art Institute, where they would be shown as part of *The Negro in Art Week* exhibition, November 16–December 1, 1927, sponsored by the Chicago Women's Club and committee on race relations. The exhibition included Woodruff's *Two Old Women, In the Garden, Snow Scene,* and *Twilight* (locations unknown).[52] From Chicago, Woodruff went to New York, where it is likely that he visited Cullen, Du Bois, White, and the Harmon Foundation staff before embarking for France.

On September 3, 1927, with a third-class $150 ticket, Woodruff sailed for Europe on the *Paris,* a French steamship. The art editor of the *Indianapolis Star,* Lucille Morehouse, noted Woodruff's departure with sadness: "Were it not that Mr. Woodruff said to me the day before he left "I shall return to Indianapolis, for it is my home," I would say that we are losing one of our most talented young artists—letting him go from us with scarce a recognition or a realization of his great gift as a painter. A few of us have followed his development within the last few years, studying groups of his paintings in exhibitions at the Pettis Gallery and at the colored branch of the Young Men's Christian Association."[53] Morehouse hoped to maintain ties with the talented young artist. She invited Woodruff to write and illustrate a series of descriptive articles on the art scene in France. For each of these, he would receive ten dollars.[54] Thus Woodruff left for Paris with the promise of some financial backing and high hopes.

SEEING AND PAINTING
THE SIGHTS IN FRANCE, 1927–1928

"I can't tell you how free I felt just being in the city," Woodruff was to comment later, reflecting on his impressions of Paris.[55] When he arrived there in the fall of 1927, he was most concerned about learning French, finding his way around the city, and meeting Tanner. Palmer Hayden, who had arrived in Paris five months before, located a room for him at 26, rue Rousselet in the seventh arrondissement in Montparnasse. Woodruff recalled the first night there: "I dropped my bag—and tried to rest a bit. Later that evening, I dragged out my English-French language book and undertook to learn something about the language I hoped to use. But—no use; I can now only remember the next morning—taxi horns and the sun coming through the window of that small room."[56] Over the following weeks, Woodruff would find Hayden "a very likable and congenial fellow" who relieved him "of embarrassment and the like—due to his knowledge of the city and the language."[57] Despite being overwhelmed by the new environment, Woodruff soon reported to Cullen that he found "Paris very beautiful and inspiring and life very pleasant."[58]

Woodruff immediately tried to visit Tanner, but found that Tanner had gone to Etaples for an indefinite stay. In the meantime, Woodruff sketched outside whenever the weather permitted. By the end of October, he had still not found an atelier; they were "very scarce and expensive."[59] Instead, he looked for a place to take classes. Knowing that Tanner had studied at the Académie Julian, Woodruff hoped to enroll there, but was disappointed to learn that the reputation of the institution had declined because its teachers seldom met with their students anymore. Woodruff chose, instead, to attend two smaller schools, the Académies Scandinave and Moderne, where leading modern painters worked directly with students.[60] The Moderne, which had begun in 1912 and resumed activity in 1920, had an impressive faculty in the 1920s—Othon Friesz, Raoul Dufy, Charles Camoin, Jean Puy, Fernand Léger, and Amédée Ozenfant. They encouraged students to go beyond Cubist formulas, emphasizing a personal approach to looking at objects.[61]

During his free time, Woodruff began to work on his assignment for the *Indianapolis Star* by writing about tourist attractions. His first article, "The Gardens of Luxembourg," without illustrations and written in a rather dry, reportorial manner, was not published until January 6, 1928. The others would appear over the following fourteen months as bimonthly features prefaced with an editorial note describing the author as "a Negro of Indianapolis," and illustrated by the artist's pen-and-ink drawings. Generally, these romantic sketches were devoid of people and centered on old French landmarks. As was the case with Hayden and Smith, it seems that Woodruff was awed by his opportunity to see these monuments in person and establish a connection to centuries of Western culture.

Woodruff's second article in the *Indianapolis Star,* "Artist Makes Forced Stop at Mendon [*sic*]," was more reflective and personal than his first. On his way to Versailles, he felt compelled to stop in the village of Meudon, just outside of Paris. He wrote that in the small, foggy town devoid of "English spoken" signs, "it suddenly dawns upon you that you are on French soil." Moved by the simple beauty of Meudon's large, old trees, he wrote, "Even visits to the Madeline and Notre Dame have not so inspired me as has this chapel of nature." The artist's sketch of houses and a church framed by bare tree branches illustrated his article, but Woodruff bemoaned his failure to capture the essence of the scene:

> Most of the day had been taken up by walking and sketching, so I decided to find my way out of the maze of little streets and start toward the station. In this attempt I found that I had walked to the extreme west end of Meudon, near the railroad but about a mile from the station. Here I found one of the churches, the sides and back of which were almost hidden by the eternal network of sprouts from the trimmed trees. The fog had never lifted during the whole day and to look at this age-old church through such trees and mists, there was formed a poem that requires one with more ability than I possess to put it on canvas.[62]

Other Parisian subjects about which Woodruff wrote were the Tuileries gardens near the Musée du Jeu de Paume and the Musée de l'Orangerie, the old bookstalls of the Seine, Montparnasse, the cave of the dungeons, and Notre Dame. Everywhere he went, Woodruff was deeply moved by the age and diversity of Europe and by its people. For instance, at Notre Dame, Woodruff described traces of countless visitors in the church's staircase: "We look around for something to see, but only the gray, black walls meet our eyes, the monotony of this blackness being broken only by names, initials and dates scrawled on every empty and accessible space. This has been done for hundreds of years and in many languages. . . . With our elbows on the sill, polished by the thousands of previous elbows, we pause here for a rest, look over the rooftops across the street—and reflect."[63]

Of all the Parisian sights, Woodruff was particularly impressed by the bridges. One of his first paintings abroad, *Paris Landscape* (1927, fig. 50, dedicated to Cullen), is a watercolor that depicts a small bridge spanning an icy brook. In the left foreground, the slender trunk of a nearly bare tree casts a purple shadow across the expansive snowy bank. Two like trees in the center casts their parallel shadows across the bridge and lead the eye to the background of a horizontal band of red and lavender woods, dappled by sunlight. It seems that

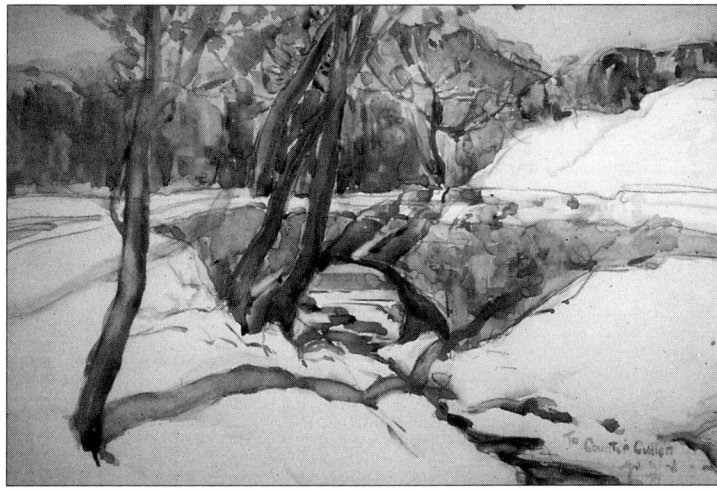

FIGURE 50
Hale Woodruff,
Paris Landscape, 1927,
watercolor on paper,
10½ x 12½ in.
Countee Cullen
Collection, Hampton
University Museum,
Hampton, Virginia.

Woodruff was developing his "ultra-impressionistic" style in the manner of Claude Monet. In the Musée du Jeu de Paume, Woodruff had seen Monet's memorial exhibition (1927) and had been overwhelmed by that artist's enormous paintings of water lilies and gardens; "I had never seen such color before!"[64]

Woodruff's fascination with the effects of sunlight on water is also evident in another painting of a bridge, *Pont-Neuf* (1927, location unknown), where blocklike patterns of color fill the lower third of the canvas. The oil painting is dominated by the structural solidity of a single, cropped arch and abutment that fill the upper portion of the composition. Pont-Neuf was the focus of Woodruff's third article, "Some Bridges of Paris." The artist admired the structure for its long history and role as an artistic gathering place:

> Perhaps the most painted bridge, not only in Paris but in the world, is Pont Neuf. It crosses the Ile de [la] Cite [*sic*], forming two sets of spans and joins the two extreme banks of the river. The Pont Neuf will turn the clock back many centuries for across it strode the escorts and guards of almost now forgotten kings. Upon it nearly falls the shadow of Notre Dame, which is drawn, painted and etched more than any other structure in all the world. Indeed that section of quais that surround the Ile de [la] Cite [*sic*] is a veritable outdoor studio for artists. . . . On any fair day one can find at least a dozen artists there working. One day I counted thirty-one.[65]

While Woodruff was interested in the social importance of the bridge, he was most interested in its aesthetic beauty:

> Pont Neuf affords the artist an opportunity to use more than the familiar and customary grays. Its color was at first apparently a yellowish tan—and it yet plays an important part in its present color. Copperish greens, purples and blues are also occasionally evident, though all the colors change with the sun. Masks, many in number, are the chief forms of ornamentation, yet every line, square and curve bespeaks beauty and symmetry. Near the Pont Neuf all along the walls of the quais are old as well as fresh smears of paint where the artists have cleaned their palettes and brushes after "doing" the famous bridge.[66]

The Pont-Neuf connects the Ile de la Cité with the Left Bank. There, not far from the bridge to the west, is a street that runs parallel with the Seine, the quai de Montebello. Woodruff painted a portion of the neighborhood along that street, as well. *Quai de Montebello* (1927, location unknown) depicts a cluster of buildings and bare trees behind an uneven wall plastered with posters. To the right of the entryway in the wall is a lamppost. Both this view and that of the Pont-Neuf are empty of people, in contrast to an early representation by Monet of the bridge surrounded by bustling activity. Instead of studies in light, color, and spontaneity, these works demonstrate Woodruff's interest in strong drafts-manship and structure. Further, the somewhat blocky nature of *Quai de Montebello* suggests Woodruff's growing interest in the work of Cézanne, which he had seen at the Musée du Jeu de Paume.

In December 1927, Woodruff sent *Pont-Neuf* and *Quai de Montebello* to the Harmon Foundation. Both works were included in the January 1928 show and the former was reproduced in the catalog, but Woodruff did not win any awards.[67] He was pleased, however, to learn that his old studio mate, John Wesley Hardrick, had won the bronze award.[68] Although Woodruff deeply appreciated the honor of having one of his paintings reproduced, he was disappointed not to have received another award and not to have sold either piece. He and Hayden had discussed the pricing of their work, but were not sure what to ask. He wrote to Mary Beattie Brady of the Harmon Foundation, "I must confess that I have never learned how to price my things as long as I've been painting."[69] William Harmon apparently had suggested a more reasonable pricing guide to Woodruff, who responded to this by expressing his appreciation of him and the foundation, in his letter to Brady:

> I honestly feel that the Harmon Foundation is doing a wonderful piece of work in bringing the achievements of the Negro before the public. Especially, with the economical point of view in mind, are its efforts of value to the artists. For artists, as you know, receive no great amount of remuneration for their works, even after they have "arrived." This is true not only among those of my own group but among artists of all other races as well. And I feel too much credit cannot be accorded Mr. Harmon and his associates for conceiving and launching the Harmon Awards.

As appreciative as Woodruff was for what the Harmon Foundation had already done for him, he was eager to win more accolades from it. In several letters, he reminded adminis-trators that he was now eligible only for first prize.[70] He added more modestly, "I occasionally turn out something that I can tolerate, yet I hope to have some representative and worthy pieces to offer."[71]

Woodruff also expected to earn money from the *Crisis* for illustrations, as Du Bois had suggested he do; he had quickly gone through the mere fifty or sixty dollars he had brought with him and had to ask his mother for an additional fifty dollars.[72] In December 1927, he made a departure from his customary landscapes and worked on an oil painting he considered naming *Six Artists,* "for it is composed of such a number of artists, each supposed to represent one of the fields of artistic endeavor in which the Negro is today engaged,"[73] these being "Architecture, Drama, Literature, Music, Sculpture, and Painting."[74] Before the work was completed, Woodruff wrote to Du Bois that he had such high hopes that it would

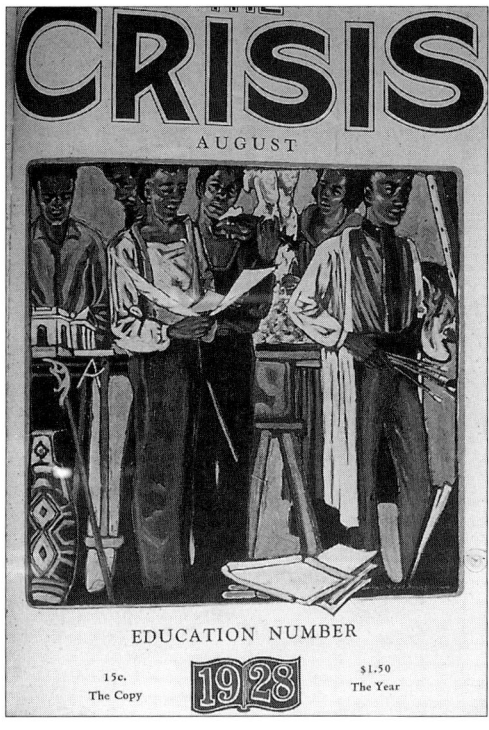

FIGURE 51
Hale Woodruff, *Untitled,* 1927–1928, oil on canvas, dimensions and location unknown.
From the cover of *Crisis,* August 1928.

serve as a cover illustration that he was already including lettering in the design. As with the Harmon Foundation, Woodruff was careful that he not appear too confident: "I shall not assume, should you thus favor me, that my effort will be accepted for publication, for no doubt you have a number of others to select from that are far more meritorious than mine. Yet I should be pleased to have you honor me with an acceptance. . . . I might add that the *Crisis* is one of my most worthy companions while I am here in Paris."[75]

Du Bois was pleased with Woodruff's proposal and suggested that he designate the painting for either the month of July or September.[76] The work was reproduced in green and blue on the cover of the August issue. No doubt the work was cropped; the space is tightly compressed and the title of the month was printed above the borders of the work. Left untitled, the final painting (1927–1928, fig. 51) depicts five figures standing at work. From left to right, a man stands before a model of a classical-looking building, thus representing architecture; a man with a mask peeping out behind his head writes with a quill on paper, doubling as drama and literature; a woman plays the violin, personifying music; another woman shapes a torso, symbolizing sculpture (Woodruff had possibly associated sculpture with women because of Prophet and Savage); and a man, wearing a smock and holding brushes and palette, paints, portraying painting. In the lower left is a large vase. In the center, large sheaves of paper spill out from the floor beyond the square frame of the composition. While Woodruff was probably disappointed that his work appeared altered in both size and color, he must have been pleased that it had won the Charles Waddell Chestnutt Honorarium first prize of twenty-five dollars for the month of August.[77] The money, no doubt, would help him to pay for art materials and museum admission fees.

STUDY IN MUSEUMS AND GALLERIES

Woodruff seems not to have been greatly affected by the classes he took at the Académies Moderne and Scandinave; in fact, he was disappointed to find that training consisted merely of drawing from the model, just as it had in Indianapolis.[78] Further, the teachers rarely commented on students' work and some visited the studios only weekly. Woodruff believed that "the [French] schools couldn't come up to the ones in the U.S., because the teachers were not as dedicated."[79]

Woodruff's artistic education abroad took place in the museums, galleries, and annual exhibitions. He stated, "To tell you the truth, I got my art education in the museums. I really credit my influences from seeing all kinds of art and artists in the museums."[80] In the Louvre, he admired the works of Rubens, Da Vinci, and Michelangelo,[81] but in the Salon des Indépendants held at the Grand Palais in early 1928, Woodruff was confronted with so many different styles and manners that he said the best one could do was state, "I like this" or "I don't like that." As he wrote in an article, "Local Artist Finds Painters Hard to Classify," in that Salon he found "bleak, dismal, perspective-less landscapes; bowls of fruit that do anything but whet your appetite and are only known as such by their titles; corpulent nude ladies who recline in grassy landscapes with turbulent seas in the background; streets of busy improportioned [*sic*] people with the house toppling over on them; such are the natures of works found among the 'conservatives.' . . . a number of them seem to have said to themselves, 'I am going to see just how badly I can paint.'"[82]

Woodruff was intrigued but overwhelmed by all of these new developments in art. In this article, he declared, "If one should attempt to keep pace with all of the different movements that are now evident in Paris, there would be little time for anything else." He felt that "since the time of Sisley, Manet, Monet, and Renoir," artists were trying to "carry their banner of revolt to the farthest extreme" and it seemed that that extreme was taking place in color:

> But now, today, you will find in Paris that many standard bearers of ultramodern art, seemingly tired of the principios [*sic*] and mannerisms of the impressionists, are seeking to express themselves in new and strange fashions. Some, on the other hand, are carrying the idea of impressionism to the extreme, employing wild and dazzling colors. Those who have given up the quest for atmosphere are now using dull, muddy grays and browns and blacks, while the most colorful note in their landscapes is an inky blue sky. Many are even wont to express peaceful clouds with great smears of black.

While Woodruff found these extremes perplexing, he went on to assert that modernists were "keen and sincere students" and that not all modern art was bad: "Thousands of worth-while pieces are unappreciated because they are misunderstood and find their final resting places in artists' attics and cellars, while things done in the styles with which we are familiar, sometimes not even good reminders of those styles, are sumptuously patronized." He concluded his article with a "wait and see" approach: "Although most of the modernists fail to impress me, I would not be justified in condemning any of them. I feel it is every artist's privilege to create whatever he desires in the manner that pleases him most. And who can say what works of art now being produced are worthy or unworthy. Only the test of time and elimination are capable of making such a decision."

Woodruff was not only interested in learning about contemporary art. He was also fascinated with the European appropriation of the forms of African art and African art itself. To this end, he frequently visited the Musée de l'Homme to view the works that had influenced Picasso, and he perused galleries that dealt in African art. Alain Locke encouraged Woodruff's interest. On one occasion in 1928, they went to a *marché aux puces* (flea market) to search for sculpture. Woodruff paid two dollars for his first pieces of African art; he bought a Bembe male figure and a Yoruba Shango staff.[83]

Woodruff was beginning to see how Cézanne's experiments with geometrical reductions would lead the way to an early-twentieth-century interest in African art; he said, "On seeing the work of Paul Cézanne I got the connection."[84] He went to the Jeu de Paume over and over to view Cézanne's work, being particularly impressed by *Boy in a Red Waistcoat* (ca. 1890–1895).[85] Later Woodruff stated, "Cézanne was my (European) image."[86] He recalled, "I went back again and again and, between the Cézannes and the African work, I was off and winging."[87] There was quite a contrast between the academically trained Woodruff, who embraced avant-garde painting styles—at least intellectually—and the mostly self-taught Hayden, who made fun of "moderne" art movements.

"A REAL INSPIRATION": MEETING HENRY O. TANNER

While Woodruff had been anxious to meet Tanner as soon as he went to France, he was unsure of his welcome; the master had not answered a letter Woodruff had written. Nevertheless, Woodruff visited Tanner's home in Etaples, a small Normandy town, in the early spring of 1928. By the time Woodruff had engaged a taxi from the railroad station, the sun was setting and the driver could not find Tanner's home, so Woodruff had to spend the evening in a small *auberge*. The next morning the taxi driver picked him up with exact directions.

After being elected chevalier of the Legion of Honor in 1923 and full academician of the National Academy of Design in 1927, Tanner was visited by so many Americans in Paris that he moved to the countryside for quiet. There he lived alone; his wife had passed away in 1925. Thinking Woodruff was a tourist, Tanner was initially reluctant to receive him. He subsequently relented, upon considering Woodruff's apparent youth and innocence.

Initially, Tanner briskly questioned Woodruff about his purposes and the American art scene. Both agreed that Americans, such as Childe Hassam and Alden Weir, seemed to be very much tied to the French context, painting Impressionist scenes.

Noting that Woodruff's landscapes were devoid of the human figure, Tanner spoke of the importance of the human form in all art. He suggested that Woodruff put figures in his compositions rather than just produce figure studies. He expressed his admiration for

Rembrandt's figurative work with its strong structural composition, dramatic lighting, and depth of human feeling. Tanner believed that French painting was indebted to seventeenth-century Dutch painting for these very qualities.

Tanner was curious about the working conditions of black artists in the United States. Woodruff told him that there was still widespread discrimination in "housing, jobs, education, and all the rest." He believed that artists were simply trying to raise themselves above such concerns to be judged solely on their humanity and artistic ability. Tanner concluded their conversation by approving of Woodruff's choice of an "artist-god," Cézanne, whom he called "a real master . . . in the tradition, yet . . . a real innovator."[88]

In the following months, Woodruff made a number of trips to the Luxembourg Museum to study Tanner's masterpiece *The Resurrection of Lazarus* (1896). Tanner's painting depicts Jesus calling Lazarus back to life after the man had been dead for four days. Jesus stands between Martha and Mary before a crowd of spectators in the burial cave. With its subtle pyramidal configurations, bursts of light, and richly textured surfaces, the work recalls the hallmarks of Rembrandt's style, but in a somewhat monochromatic palette, appropriate to the cave interior.[89] There is little tradition of images for Lazarus; art historian Dewey Mosby suggests that Tanner was drawn to the story because it—as does the biblical story of the other Lazarus, the beggar—deals with new life and redemption, and thus relates to the Emancipation Proclamation of 1863, which provided a rebirth for black slaves.[90] Tanner would have learned such metaphors from his father, an African Methodist Episcopal minister. *The Resurrection of Lazarus* received a superb critical reception at the Paris Salon of 1897. Soon thereafter, the French department of fine art purchased the work for the Luxembourg Museum, then the national museum for exhibitions by living artists. The literary scholar Michel Fabre stated, "When black American visitors saw his [Tanner's] paintings, bought by the French government, hanging in the Musée du Luxembourg, they were convinced that artistic talent is always rewarded in Paris."[91] Among the African Americans who made the pilgrimage to see the work at the museum were Booker T. Washington, Mary Church Terrell, Countee Cullen, John F. Matheus, and John Paynter, as well as a myriad of artists.[92] Woodruff himself never painted religious imagery, but he admired Tanner's draftsmanship and use of color, as well as his fame.

SELLING PICTURES OF FRENCH SIGHTS, 1928

In early 1928, to save money, Woodruff moved to 32, voie d'Issy in Malakoff-sur-Seine, a small suburb southwest of Paris, with three white Americans, Forrest Wiggins, Charles Law, and Robert Miller. The venture was agreeable to all; each had his own facilities, the rent was only eight dollars a month, and they could easily reach Paris by streetcar. They were still careful with their money, however, and lived primarily on rice pudding.[93]

In the following months, Woodruff traveled with Wiggins to tourist sights within a seventy-five-mile radius of Paris. In Orléans, the two visited the old cathedral of Saint-Croix and the home of Joan of Arc at 35, rue du Tabour. Woodruff carefully studied the medieval house with its small red bricks "overlaid with slabs of triangular areas."[94]

After the charm of Orléans, Woodruff and Wiggins found Beauvais, the tapestry center, a sad and ugly town. They made fun of it, and their continuing struggle with the French language, as a form of self-defense against "the world which was as strange to them as they were to it."[95]

In the summer of 1928, Woodruff painted along the English Channel while he lodged in Honfleur, a fishing village. Later, he wandered along the Eure River in the Beauce Valley, the location of Chartres Cathedral. He found the area picturesque: "The old houses in this section are as interesting as the life of the people and artists find here material for their canvases that they don't find elsewhere."[96] Woodruff himself painted the houses along the Eure in August and September. *Old Farmhouse in Beauce Valley* (fig. 52) is an oil painting from that year of a group of white, red-roofed farm buildings in a verdant landscape of tall trees. The vertical lines of the trunks balance the strong horizontals of the low roofs in the foreground and impart a feeling of harmony and stability, yet the light blue sky filled with fluffy white clouds recalls the spontaneity and atmospheric effects of Impressionist works. Another oil painting, *Medieval Chartres* (fig. 53), repeats Woodruff's interest in bridges and reflections on water. In this work, one arch and half of another with their reflections in the Eure River, broken by falling leaves from the tree branches at left, dominate the foreground in blocky patterns. The upper two-thirds of the composition is filled with a cluster of houses and extremely steep, snow-topped roofs. Here, Woodruff had been trying to adapt Cézanne's style, but he found that he was actually employing the triangular compositional precepts of painter Harold Haven Brown, which he had learned from Forsyth at the Herron. "Forsyth once pointed out that I had tilted a roof so much that it did not work well with the other triangles in the composition."[97] Here, however, the triangles

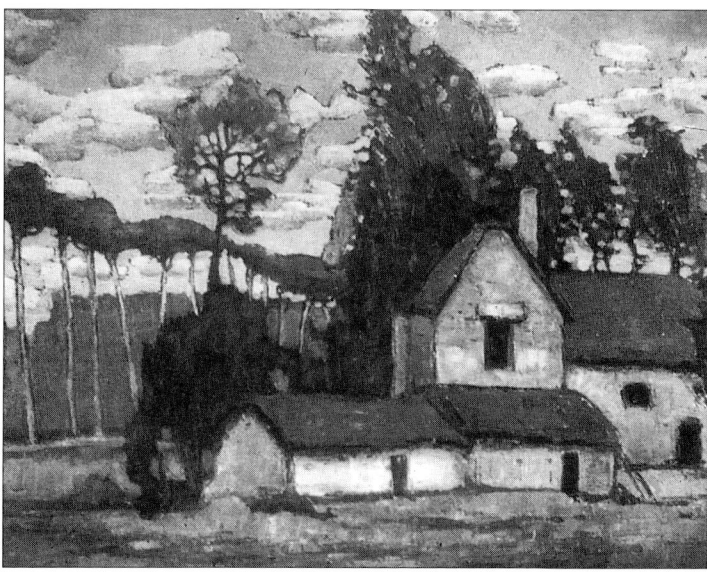

FIGURE 52
Hale Woodruff,
Old Farmhouse in Beauce Valley, 1928, oil on canvas, dimensions and location unknown.
Courtesy of Kenkeleba Gallery.

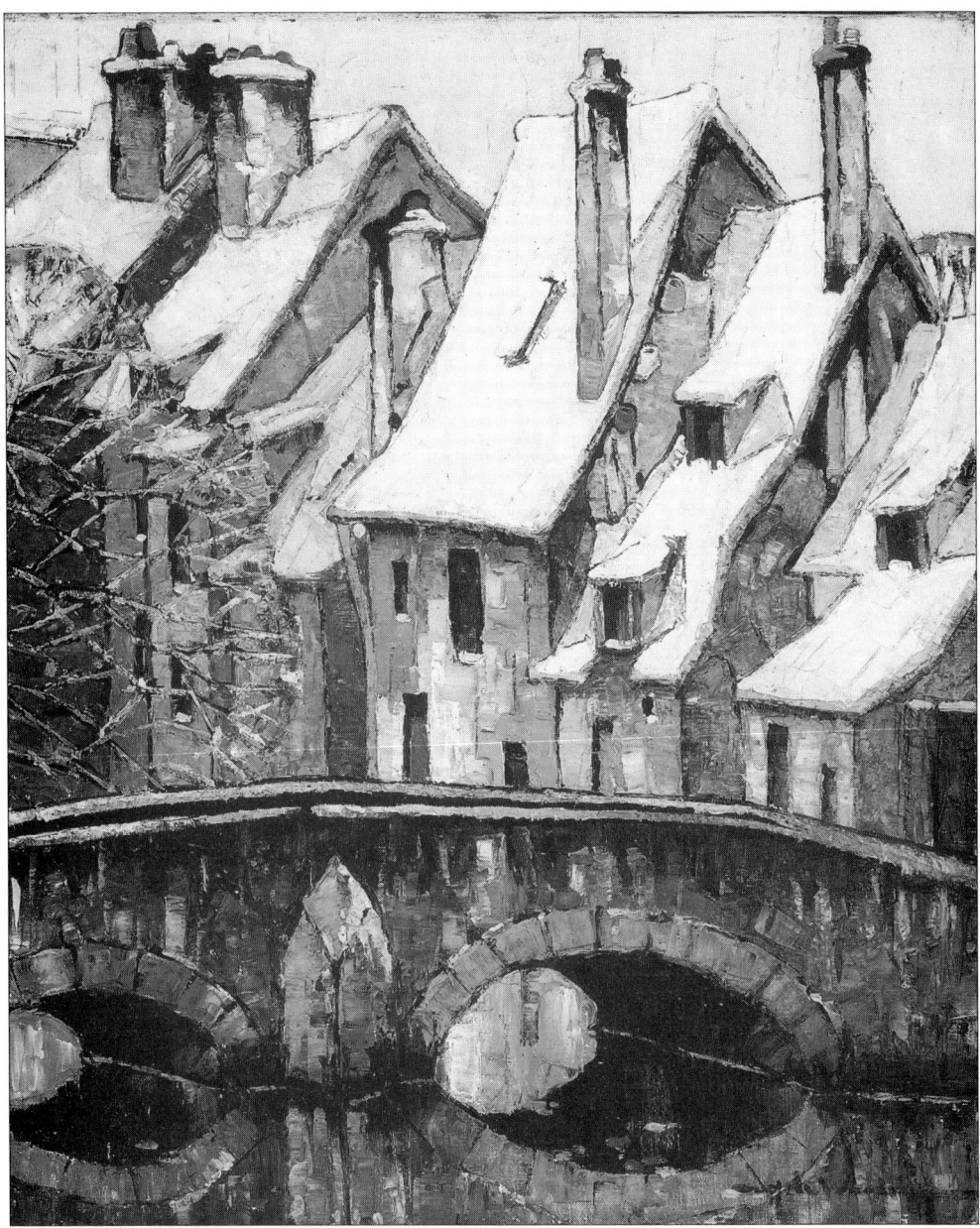

FIGURE 53
Hale Woodruff, *Medieval Chartres,* 1928, oil on canvas, 20 x 24 in.
Collection of Mr. and Mrs. Robert C. Davidson Jr.. Courtesy of Michael Rosenfeld Gallery, New York City.

do "work well," balancing out the curves of the bridge and its reflection. Woodruff
completed numerous other watercolors of the dwellings along waterways in the Beauce
Valley, such as *Chartres* (fig. 54), *House on a Canal,* and *Chartres* (fig. 55). These works,
while brilliant in color and well designed, are less experimental than the oil paintings and
more like nineteenth-century illustrations.

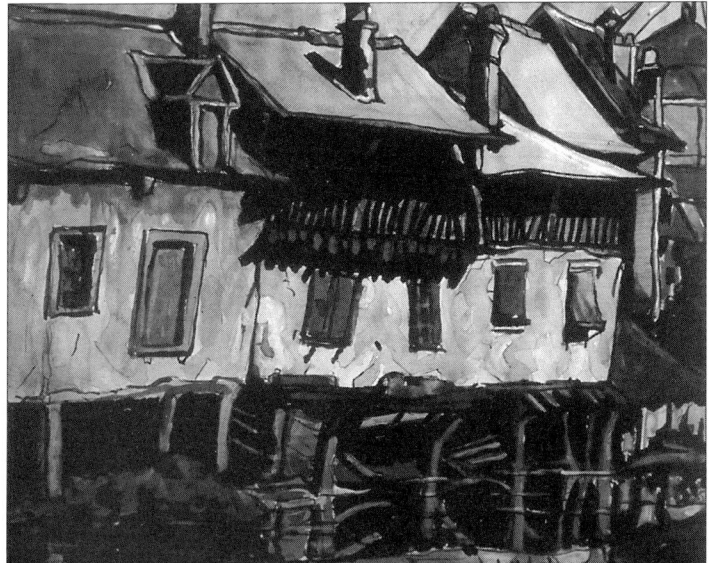

FIGURE 54
Hale Woodruff, *Chartres,*
1928, watercolor on paper,
18½ x 21⅜ in.
Countee Cullen Collection,
Hampton University
Museum, Hampton,
Virginia.

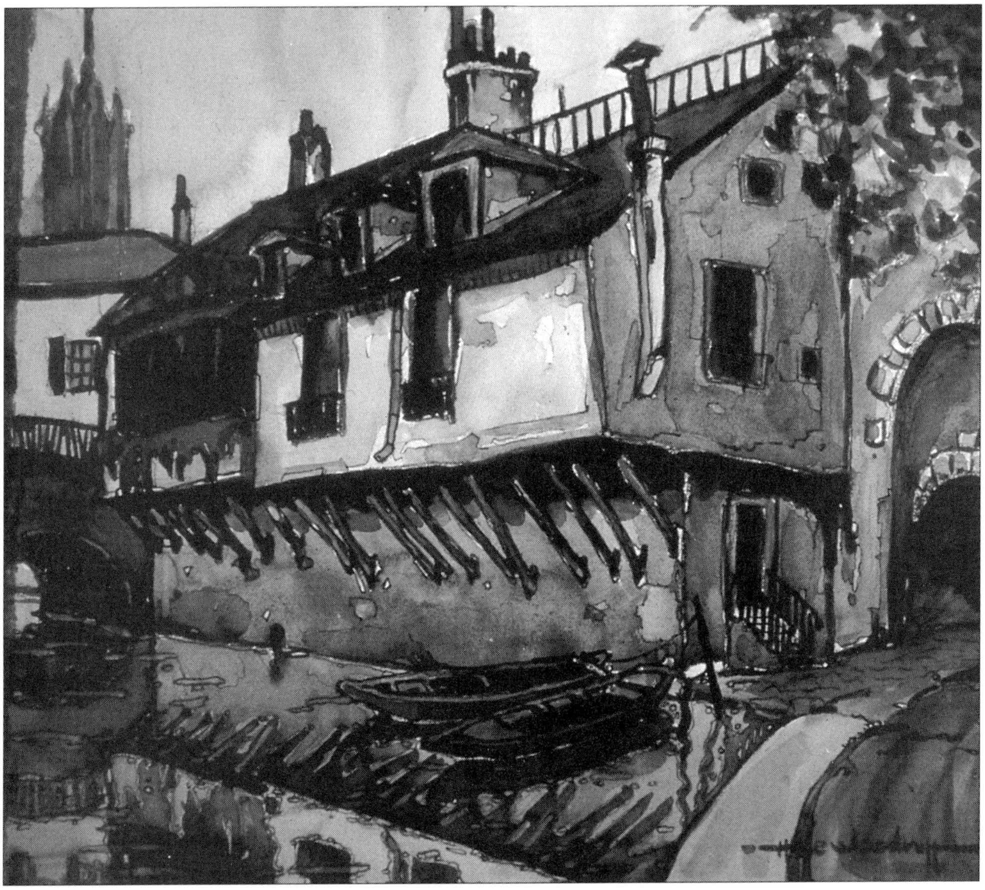

FIGURE 55
Hale Woodruff, *Chartres,* 1928, watercolor on paper, 16½ x 17¾ in.
Hampton University Museum, Hampton, Virginia

In the fall of 1928, Woodruff submitted four oil paintings, *Normandy Landscape, Old Farmhouse in Beauce Valley, Along the Eure at Chartres,* and *Medieval Chartres,* to the Harmon Foundation for its January 1929 show.[98] He desperately hoped that he would win first prize from the Harmon Foundation because, by the end of October, he was completely at the end of his resources. He was unable to get a job because he was not a French citizen and he was neither able to pay the rent nor eat for several days because his housemates had left the area. Woodruff made so little from sales in America that he had to continue "under the most unfavorable conditions."[99] It seems, in fact, that Woodruff sold only one work during the summer of 1928; Mrs. John D. Rockefeller bought a watercolor of a Paris scene from the Downtown Gallery, at 113 West Thirteenth Street in New York.[100] "Passing days of need and privation,"[101] his health suffered to such an extent that at times he could not paint. He was forced to borrow money from friends, including Locke, who lent him forty dollars in November.[102] That month, Cullen helped out by purchasing his portrait from Woodruff.[103] *Portrait of Countee Cullen* (ca. 1926–1928, fig. 56) shows the head and upper torso of the poet in a three-quarters position and with rather stiff posture, wearing a suit and bow tie. He appears engaged in thought, posed before a wall lined with books. To the poet's left at head level stands a small reproduction of the winged figure, Nike of Samothrace. The books and statue suggest that Cullen is a cultured, educated man who, inspired by Western thought and achievement, can reach victory. Through this small reproduction of the Greek statue that is on display at the Louvre, the painting also suggests Cullen's strong affiliation with France. As Arna Bontemps noted, "Cullen was the greatest francophile of us all."[104]

Several years later, Cullen's sonnet "To France" would appear in the August 1932 issue of *Opportunity*. He wrote about the country with deep gratitude for the freedom it offered:

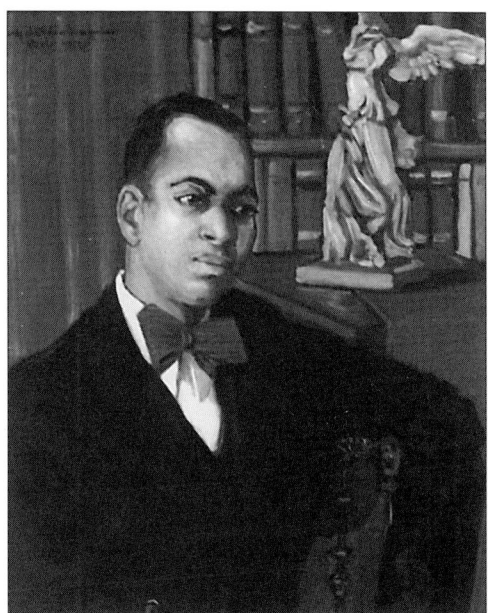

FIGURE 56
Hale Woodruff, *Portrait of Countee Cullen,*
ca. 1926–1928, oil on canvas, 31½ x 25½ in.
Amistad Research Center, Tulane University,
New Orleans.

As he whose eyes are gouged craves light to see,
And he whose limbs are broken strength to run,
So have I sought in you that alchemy

That knits my bones and turns me to the sun;
And found across a continent of foam
What was denied my hungry heart at home.[105]

It is likely that Woodruff, and all of the African American artists abroad, shared this strong feeling.

Despite aid from friends, Woodruff continued to be in severe financial straits. In February 1929, he wrote to Brady requesting a temporary loan of two hundred dollars and he applied to the Guggenheim Foundation for a fellowship.[106] It is not known whether Woodruff ever received the loan, but he did not receive the Guggenheim.

In February 1929, Woodruff borrowed trolley fare from his landlady to check his mail in Paris. He was delighted to find that all four of his works were exhibited by the Harmon Foundation, *Medieval Chartres* was reproduced in the catalog, and it and *Normandy Landscape* had been sold for a total of $135.[107] Helen Harmon, daughter of the late founder, purchased *Normandy Landscape* and Marthe Henriod, a young French student, bought *Medieval Chartres*. The foundation generously took no commission fee and paid customs and handling charges on the possibility that sales from the traveling exhibition of the other two works would cover the costs. Haynes and his wife were chagrined by the latter purchase because they had wanted it for themselves. Since "it was admired by many as a beautiful piece of art," Haynes hoped Woodruff would send over "another like it or something equally beautiful" for his home.[108] Haynes also suggested that Woodruff keep his prices as low as possible until he established his market.

Woodruff was very grateful for Haynes's interest in his work and planned on sending him a watercolor landscape similar to *Medieval Chartres*, because Haynes had admired the bridge, water, leaves, and snow in it. Woodruff remarked, "Somehow I've always enjoyed painting snow, and the effect of it on the ancient houses of France is truly inspirational."[109] Unfortunately, Woodruff took ill in early March and again in early June, so it was not until June 10, 1929, that he sent the work. Because he had received "favorable comments on it from several artists and critics," some of whom placed "it above the one similar to it that was sold to the young French woman," Woodruff requested $75.[110] Unhappily, the painting was not quite what the Haynes couple desired.[111] Woodruff was determined that they should get what they wanted and painted another scene of Chartres that seemed to meet their approval.[112]

"THE RACIAL VEIN OF ORIGINALITY": DEPICTING BLACK PEOPLE

While Woodruff was content that his work had sold, he was nonplussed when Locke wrote to him that the Harmon judges had made their decision before his paintings had arrived, which meant that he was ineligible for any of the awards. He lost no time in telling the French transporters what he thought of them, since he had submitted his pictures in ample time— more than six weeks in advance—for them to arrive in New York. He was determined to give a strong showing the following year not only by shipping works further in advance, but also by following the suggestion of Haynes to depict black people.

Haynes told Woodruff that he hoped to attract African American patrons, "members of your own group who are economically able to purchase art productions."[113] He noted that in 1928, Sargent Claude Johnson's terra-cotta head, *Sammy* (ca. 1927), was sold to Dr. Sadie Tanner Mossell Alexander of Harlem, Tanner's niece, and in 1929, African Americans had bought two still lifes, but all other purchases had been made by white people. That year, one work that elicited "a great deal of interesting comment" was Malvin Gray Johnson's *Swing Low, Sweet Chariot* (1929). Haynes asked of Woodruff, "Are you in your study doing anything along the line of expression out of your own background and environmental experience?" He suggested that the next works Woodruff send should include his "best production along this line."[114] Ironically, Haynes wanted Woodruff to learn from the European masters while in Paris, but he also wanted him to work on African American subject matter.

When Woodruff wrote to Brady at the end of March 1929, he let her, and Haynes, know that he would, indeed, produce "racial" works: "I have been thinking for some time of subjects of a more racial view than the things I've formerly sent and am at present working on such subjects."[115] A letter from Locke may have also prompted Woodruff to depict black people. While Locke admired Woodruff's *Normandy Landscape,* he had found the Harmon exhibition "quite poor and especially feeble in any strong racial vein of originality."[116] Woodruff also believed that African Americans needed to distinguish themselves in the fine arts: "The Harmon Foundation, I believe, is doing a wonderful piece of work toward furthering the interests in the achievements of the American Negro. Especially is this true in the field of Fine Arts, and happily so, for in this field, the Negro needs more encouragement and stimulation than in any other. I do not make this statement because I am an artist myself but because it seems to me that he has not done quite so much in painting and sculpture as he has done in other fields of endeavor."[117]

Woodruff may have felt that one way "American Negroes" could distinguish themselves in the fine arts was by depicting themselves, but he also felt the need to work in a more figurative vein for at least two other reasons. He took Tanner's advice about figurative painting to heart and he was not entirely satisfied with his landscapes: "As you know, I have painted mostly landscapes, drawing my subjects from the country around Indianapolis until coming here two years ago. I don't suppose I've ever painted an outstanding picture that I could single out from all the rest to you. In my opinion, so many of them have been bad and only a few fairly representative."[118] Additionally, Walter White, who visited Paris annually, encouraged Woodruff to experiment in new modes, but he cautioned him about going too abstract; "He mentioned, particularly, Gauguin's work, rich and beautiful in color and his distortions were less prominent that those of Cézanne."[119] Woodruff would follow the suggestions of all to a degree by doing figurative work and using more vivid hues.

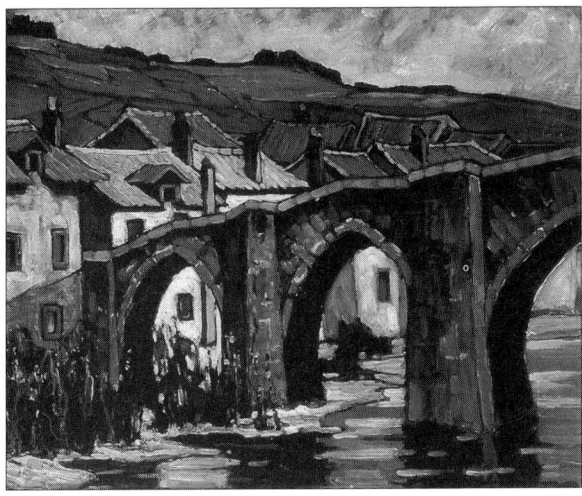

FIGURE 57
Hale Woodruff, *Bridge Near Avalon*,
1929, oil on canvas, 20 x 24 in.
Howard University Art Gallery,
Washington, D.C.

In 1929, Woodruff continued to produce tourist scenes, such as *Old Street, Paris* and *Bridge Near Avalon* (fig. 57), both of which would be included in the 1930 Harmon exhibition, but he also painted at least three works depicting black people. He explained, "I did this because I thought it would add more weight and significance to my submission."[120] Two, *Washer Women* (location unknown) and *Old Woman Peeling Apples* (fig. 58), both also in the exhibition, concern women doing domestic chores. The latter work is perhaps Woodruff's most Cézanne-like, with its wonderful still life of apples piled on large sheets of crinkly paper atop a severely tilted tabletop. At right, a seated middle-aged black woman calmly peels an apple and allows the curving peel to fall into a saucepot in her lap. The saucepot, like the tabletop, is dramatically tilted toward the viewer and echoes the rounded forms of the large white bowl in the upper center of the composition and the pitcher on the

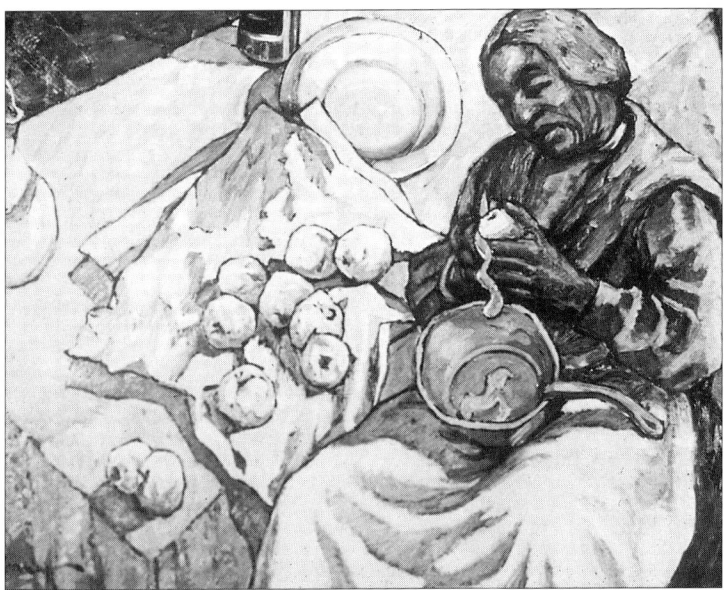

FIGURE 58
Hale Woodruff, *Old
Woman Peeling Apples*,
1929, oil on canvas,
location unknown.
Courtesy of Kenkeleba
Gallery. Photo from
National Archives
(200S-HN-WO–28).

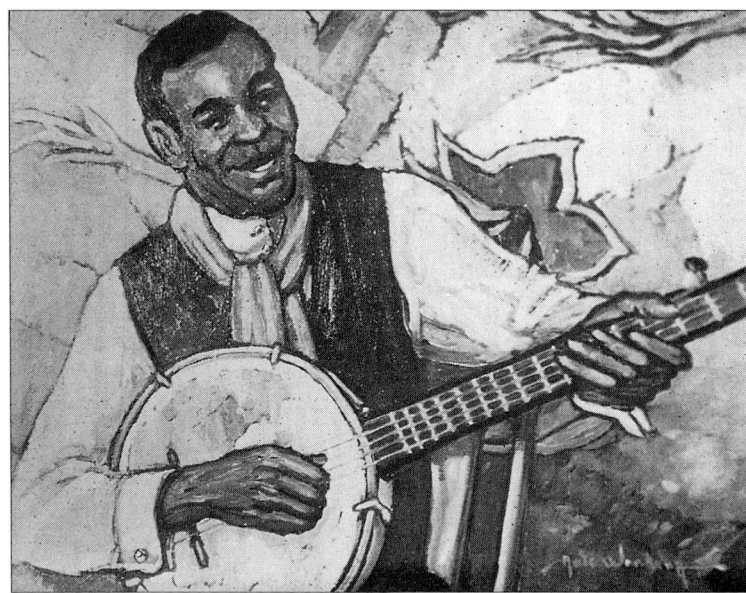

FIGURE 59
Hale Woodruff,
Banjo Player, 1929,
oil on canvas,
24 x 30 in.,
location unknown.
Courtesy of Kenkeleba
Gallery.

left. Like the figures in *Two Old Women,* this apple peeler wears a shawl and has a wide girth, but after whom is she modeled? She may be imaginary; Palmer Hayden was the model for the hands.[121]

The third figurative oil painting Woodruff produced in 1929 was the *Banjo Player* (fig. 59). Like the apple peeler, this musician has a mature face, is seated on a simple wooden chair, and remains anonymous, but he is apparently singing whereas she is silent and self-absorbed. His head and torso fill the composition on the left, the banjo's neck making a strong diagonal up to the right. Woodruff has delineated what could be construed as a stereotypical image—a one-dimensional, carefree banjo player—but he has infused the scene with references to modern European art. The banjo player is neatly dressed in a white, long-sleeved shirt, a tie, and a red vest, as is the subject in Cézanne's *Boy in Red Waistcoat,* and the background is a riotous pattern of arabesques and floral motifs. Woodruff's backdrop not only recalls the work of Cézanne; it prefigures some of the backgrounds the white writer Carl Van Vechten would use in the mid-1930s in photographing notable African Americans. Further, the subject was one earlier employed by Tanner with great success in *The Banjo Lesson* of 1893.

The combination was a hit: *Banjo Player* won honorable mention from the Harmon Foundation in 1930 and was reproduced in the catalog. Ironically, Woodruff may have inadvertently evoked a tradition of racist stereotypes. Four years later, African American artist Romare Bearden would condemn the low expectations of the Harmon Foundation for its attitude that, he declared, "from the beginning had been of a coddling and patronizing nature."[122] For all the success that Woodruff had with his landscapes and depictions of French cultural monuments, he, like Hayden, could not escape the expectations of white patrons that he racialize his paintings by drawing upon stock images of African Americans. Yet, like Hayden, Motley, Scott, and other African American artists, Woodruff had a genuine interest in and affection for black folk culture, from a different perspective. His dignified depictions of the old woman peeling apples and the banjo player have none of Hayden's cartoonlike humor, but rather indicate appreciation for their labor and talent. Nonetheless, Woodruff's portrayal of the musician could not help but also be informed by the dozens of African American banjo players, such as Albert Alexander Smith, who drew throngs of Europeans to French nightclubs. He must have been aware that they projected a sense of exoticism and nostalgia in their deliberate theatricality. It was precisely this aura of primitivism, of escape to a mythical time when ignorant blacks did not threaten to break the color line but instead happily served and performed for whites, that struck a responsive chord with certain factions of the Harmon Foundation and the white public.

Around 1930, Woodruff would meet Jean Renoir (son of Impressionist painter Auguste Renoir) in Cagnes-sur-Mer. One wonders if he had seen the French director's short film *Sur un air de Charleston* (1926), a fantasy of the redemptive power of the popular black dance step. In the film's post-Armaggeddon Europe, a white dancer, played by Renoir's wife, Catherine Hessling, teaches the Charleston to a visiting African aviator, played by the African American black minstrel and mime Johnny Hudgins. Renoir's implicit message, according to Richard Powell, was that "black creativity was modern society's only salvation and hope for human perpetuity."[123] While it is unlikely that Woodruff ever had such lofty goals for his banjo player, images of joyous performers (and the music itself) could, at least, offer a temporary, escapist palliative for weary urbanites. Since the nineteenth century, the banjo had acquired increasing popularity and was featured in black and white bands in the 1920s.

LEARNING THE LANGUAGE THAT ONLY MONTPARNASSE TEACHES, 1929–1930

Although Woodruff lived at 41, rue Lecourbe in the fifteenth arrondissement where it was less expensive, he spent most of his time in Montparnasse, which he believed "could well be called the hub of the art world. In its studios, ateliers, schools and let us not forget, its cafés, artists from every corner of the globe can be found."[124] Woodruff asserted, "One might be safe in saying that of the 50,000 artists living in the city, no more than 5,000 will be found outside of Montparnasse." In the evenings, "when the palette and chisel had been laid aside," Woodruff would meet fellow artists to "discuss, criticize and 'enthuse.'" Grouped around the little marble-topped tables drinking the ubiquitous café crème, patrons could "get an earful of practically every language spoken; Russian, German, Greek, Spanish, Arab, English, Czech, Chinese, and be assured, even French." But, it is here, Woodruff believed, that artists and students from every land come "to learn that language common to them that only Montparnasse teaches." Happily, "the coming student rubs elbows with the already arrived and there is found a genial spirit of 'live and let live.'"

Of all the cafés, Woodruff preferred to frequent the "old Café du Dôme," known to artists and students for more than a generation. Located at the intersection of the busy boulevard Raspail and the boulevard du Montparnasse, the café was close to the Académie Moderne, and just "a few paces away" from the Académie de la Grande Chaumière and the

Académie Colarossi. The café was also near three galleries, Le Portique, La Galerie d'Art Contemporain, and La Galerie du Montparnasse, that exhibited works by artists of the Latin Quarter. Not all artists were fortunate enough to be represented at such galleries, however. Woodruff reported that each October and April "the artist who can't afford to rent a gallery becomes a member of the 'Horde du Montparnasse' and shows in the Marcheaux Navets [turnip market]. . . . The sidewalks of the boulevard Raspail are turned into an open air gallery for three days. Here a hundred or so artists can sit the three days with a representative group of their 'turnips.' Sometimes a buyer stops. And if one doesn't stop, the artist seems as though he might wish he was permitted to cry his wares."[125] Despite the unfortunate circumstance of the turnip market, those artists, those "quarterites," Woodruff noted, were "all the more gay" every April when they attended the artists' ball in the beautiful Salle Bullier where the queen of the models was selected. Artists had several other exhibition opportunities, too; among them, the Salon des Refusés—for those artists whose works were rejected for the Salon d'Automne.

Woodruff found the white artists in Montparnasse amusing because they wore "Lord Byron ties, black hats and capes" and they refused to shave.[126] He frequently spotted artists Tsouguharu Foujita ("a familiar figure with his earrings and 'girlish' bob"),[127] John Graham, Man Ray, and Moise Kisling, and writers Ernest Hemingway, F. Scott Fitzgerald, Gertrude Stein, and Ezra Pound, but he never met them. He did meet Kay Boyle, Raymond Duncan, and Nancy Cunard, but it was only on a casual social basis. Nevertheless, Woodruff felt that the racial atmosphere in Paris was very tolerable: "But there was this rather exciting and challenging give-and-take between the blacks and whites. The whole problem of antipathy and challenge and name-calling didn't exist as it does today. We all recognized our problems and we faced them as artists."[128]

Woodruff's closest companions abroad were Countee Cullen—who influenced several people to buy Woodruff's paintings—Yolande Du Bois Cullen,[129] Eric Walrond, Claude McKay, Palmer Hayden, and Augusta Savage. He never met, however, William Henry Johnson, Albert Alexander Smith, or Archibald Motley Jr.[130] While these artists enjoyed greater freedom and tolerance than they had ever encountered in the United States, this "Negro colony" was not entirely free from racial strife, or what was interpreted as such. Once, while drinking coffee at Café La Coupole, McKay suggested he and Woodruff go to a nearby nightclub. When the two entered the establishment, they were informed that a private party was in progress and that a necktie was required of all guests. McKay was so upset about the occurrence that he brought a lawsuit against the club, and the place was suspended from doing business for the following six months.[131] It is unlikely that McKay would have had the same success in suing a white business in the United States in the 1920s.

Except for the incident at the nightclub, most of Woodruff's evenings were carefree. He often spent hours playing bélote, a French card game, with Hayden and others, and he attended many parties. A typical small soiree took place at Cullen's on July 1, 1929. "There was card-playing and gramophone music—especially low down recordings by Duke

Ellington."[132] Besides Woodruff, in attendance were entertainers, such as Gertrude Curtis, Bessie Miller and her daughter Olivette, Zaidee Jackson, and Caska Bond. The next day, a tea was given in honor of Elizabeth Prophet, who had just exhibited her work in Paris. Then the Fourth of July was celebrated with spare ribs and cabbage at Gertrude Curtis's place in Montmartre. A week of festivities concluded with dancing the beguine at the Martinican ball.

Yet the good times did not keep rolling. In the fall of 1929 when the depression hit the United States, Woodruff was concerned about finances and believed that he should return home, but he could not afford the passage fare. He knew it would be difficult to count on further sales of his paintings. In fact, Lieber had not sold anything of his. In November, Woodruff received a check for $71.25 for the sale of *Winter Calm*[133] (probably a watercolor landscape, based on the relatively small price)[134] to Henry Goodard Leach, who had seen the work at the 135th Street branch library, but few sales were forthcoming after that.

In the spring of 1930, Woodruff apparently had small exhibitions in Paris at two minor galleries, the Galerie Jeune Peinture and the Galerie Paquereau.[135] It does not seem as though the shows were reviewed, and if Woodruff sold anything, he let few people know. His health worsened and he needed a less expensive place to stay. In the summer of 1930, he moved to the South of France.

CUBISM IN CAGNES-SUR-MER, SUMMER 1930

Around July 1930, Woodruff drove to Cagnes-sur-Mer with Steven and Sophie Greene, whom he had met through Cullen. On the drive down, the couple "became very much attached" to Woodruff, who Steve decided was "a very sweet person indeed."[136] Upon their arrival, Woodruff dropped his bags at the depot and walked through the town. Cagnes-sur-Mer was a well-known magnet for artists, tourists, and socialites, with its idyllic scenery on the sun-drenched coast of the turquoise Mediterranean and its proximity to casinos in Monte Carlo, Nice, and Antibes. Woodruff was impressed by the village and quickly rented a large room with a cooking stove at one end of it, then searched for work to meet his living expenses.

Because Woodruff had no work permit, it was difficult to find a job. Cagnes was a bohemian world peopled not only by the rich and famous, among them American expatriates Harry Crosby and Gerald Murphy, but also by working-class French, vagabonds from around the world, and poverty-stricken artists and intellectuals like himself. Competition for jobs was stiff. Woodruff finally obtained a position as a road laborer, earning $1.30 a day by passing himself off as a North African. The labor—shoveling and moving rocks—was physically challenging, but the crew received midmorning, noon, and midafternoon breaks. Woodruff enjoyed his fellow crew members. Like them, he grew a beard, wore sandals, slung his lunch—a bottle of wine, a chunk of bread, and some cheese—in a sack over his back, and went swimming in the ocean. Woodruff's pay from the job covered his living expenses for several months.

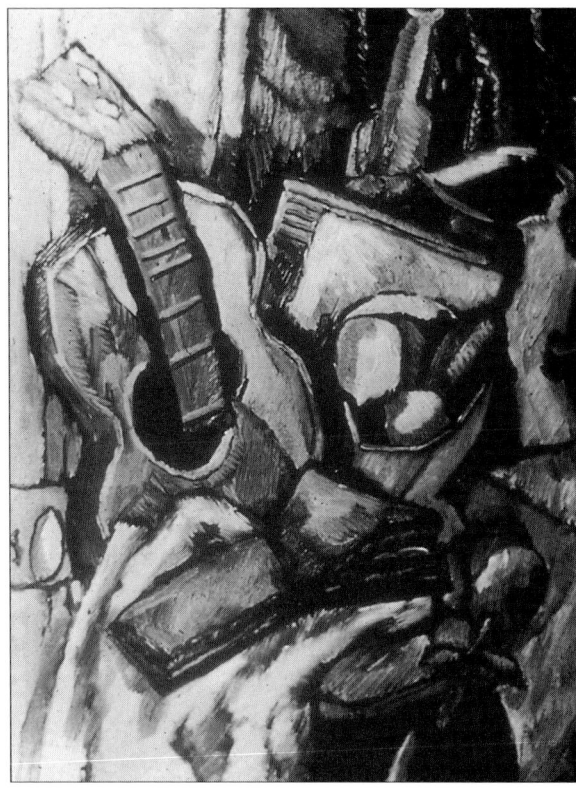

FIGURE 60
Hale Woodruff, *Still Life,*
ca. 1931, oil on canvas, 24 x 30 in.,
location unknown.
Courtesy of Kenkeleba Gallery.

Once Woodruff had saved some money, he was able to move into a much better place—a studio in a garden with orange, lemon, and fig trees. He would later comment, "I loved it all—olive and lemon trees, always productive, just outside the door. Hot? Yes! Beautiful? Yes! But seductive and rich? Yes!!!"[137] It may be the fruits of those trees that appear in one of Woodruff's first oil paintings in Cagnes, *Still Life* (ca. 1930, fig. 60). They are bunched together in a sack, possibly Woodruff's lunch bag, and on a table, along with a pitcher, wine bottle, and guitar. All the forms are angular and distorted, in the manner of Braque's and Picasso's early experiments that had led to Cubism.

Woodruff was delighted with his new studio at 34, rue Carnot, especially when he learned that it was the Expressionist painter Chaim Soutine's old atelier:

> I rented Soutine's old studio from Mme. Le Jeune who owned the building. She recalled to me how Soutine has dragged this tremendous beef carcass up the hill of Cagnes to his studio. He was set on painting it, inspired as he was, by the great painting of the same subject by the master Rembrandt. I knew the townspeople at Cagnes-sur-Mer—very nice but provincial citizens. They never understood Soutine, and Modigliani, who also lived there.
>
> As an occupant of Soutine's old studio I never sensed or observed the "vermin-infested floor" of the studio as mentioned in Genauer's article. The place was "in order" in accordance with usual concepts of French propriety. . . . Just before I left Cagnes I met one of the townspeople. He spoke of Soutine, of his warmth, of his

loneliness, of his yearning for friendship with just people, not necessarily artists whom he mistrusted.[138]

Although Woodruff knew of the strong influence Soutine had had on French culture and on William Henry Johnson, who had spent 1928–1929 in Cagnes-sur-Mer, he never felt compelled to work in his style: "I also felt the impact of Soutine's great work but in all cases, I never succumbed to it."[139] Soutine, Modigliani, and Renoir had all made the town their home at different times, attracted by the brilliant light and inexpensive lodgings.

Woodruff was well aware of Cagnes-sur-Mer's artistic heritage and its continuing attraction to creative visitors. He met a number of them at the small Hôtel de Colonie, where they often gathered in the evenings. Among Woodruff's acquaintances were the artist Victor Thal; Nigel and Suzanne Newton, of the English Winsor and Newton family, internationally known producers of artists' pigments; Joyce scholar Abraham Lincoln Gillespie, actors Gwen and Eva Le Gallienne, dancer Isadora Duncan, and composer George Antheil, "a true genius and a man of great human sensitivity."[140] Woodruff also met Jean Renoir, son of the great painter, whom he found warm and personable. Renoir showed Woodruff a number of paintings by Europeans, including several fakes of his father's works, and admitted that he was not always sure which ones they were because they had been copied so well. Another time, Renoir brought his father's famous model, La Belle Gabrielle, to the hotel.

One of Woodruff's acquaintances, Hilaire Hiler (1897–1966), the American painter, poet, musician, and owner of the Jockey Club in Paris, became a good friend. The two roamed Cagnes-sur-Mer, which Hiler dubbed "the garden spot of the world,"[141] and traveled throughout Provence. They saw Aix-en-Provence, where Cézanne lived; Arles, home of Van Gogh; Nice, where they toured the museums; and Marseilles, where they tasted the famous bouillabaisse.

Invigorated by the hot, beautiful climate of Provence, Woodruff worked feverishly, ten to twelve hours a day. He recalled, "The clock I punched then was the love and reverence for art and my employer was a burning desire to create and produce."[142] In the manner of Van Gogh, who had painted a scene of a corner of his dwelling in Arles, Woodruff painted a corner of his studio (location of painting unknown) and sent it to the United States, hoping to make some money. Nelson Jackson of the Urban League bought the work. Later, Woodruff, who thought it was "a fine piece," tried to buy the painting back.[143]

By August 21, just about three weeks after his arrival in Cagnes-sur-Mer, Woodruff had already painted several oil paintings and watercolors and was pleased with his progress; he felt that they exhibited "a decided step forward" with a "consistency and solidity" that seldom characterized his earlier pieces. He wrote to Locke that he was anxious for him to see his work and have one of his paintings: "The country here is so marvelous that I want to stay as long as possible. I'm sure I can accomplish something."[144]

One of Woodruff's oils, *Provençal Landscape* (1930, fig. 61), depicts that marvelous country, with its steep hills, dense foliage, terraced fields, and whitewashed, red-roofed homes. Only a sliver of silvery sky appears above this compact scene, which echoes Cézanne's

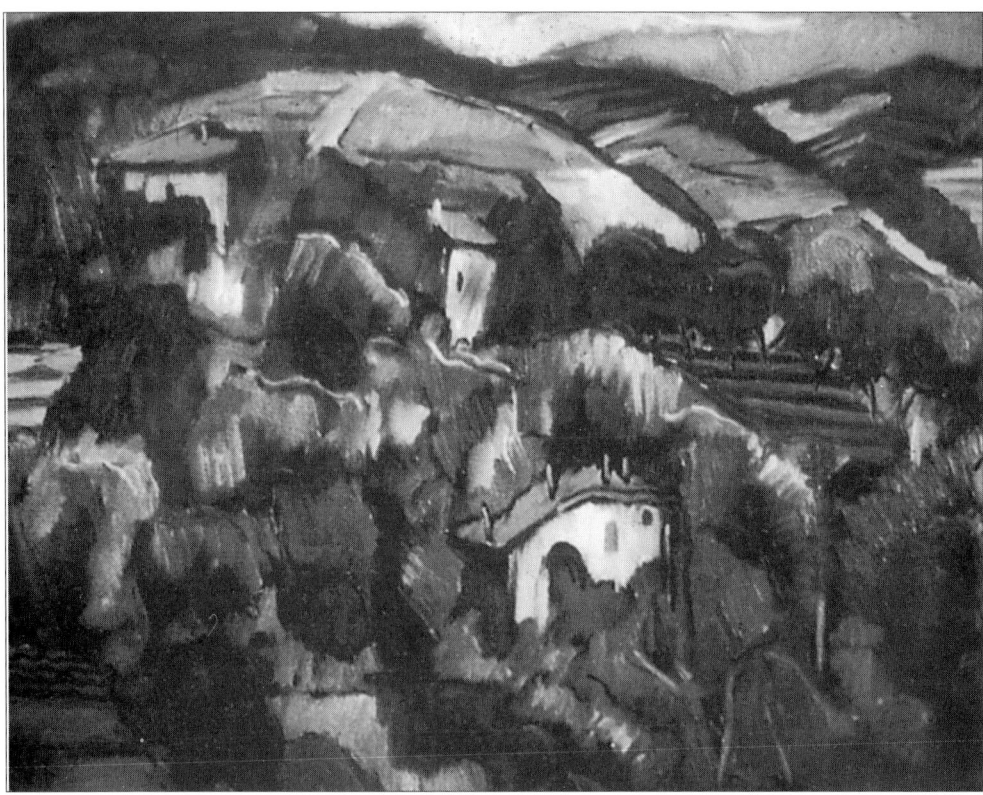

FIGURE 61
Hale Woodruff, *Provençal Landscape,* 1930, oil on canvas, dimensions and location unknown.
Courtesy of Kenkeleba Gallery.

treatments of the Mont Saint Victoire in its geometric reduction of forms. Woodruff's style had definitely evolved from the type of illustrations he had produced in Paris; now drawing and painting were one. Later, Woodruff explained his technique by quoting Cézanne, "When I draw I paint and when I paint I draw."[145] This process was also apparent in *The Cardplayers.*

The Cardplayers (1930, fig. 62)[146] is Woodruff's most daring and "moderne" French work. Woodruff's depiction of two figures playing cards in a café offers a unique interpretation of a subject explored by Cézanne in five canvases from 1890 to 1892. No doubt Woodruff had seen the last of these, of two men rather than the original five, in the Louvre. In this work, and the others, Cézanne used reverse perspective, a technique borrowed from Japanese woodcuts. Woodruff consciously tried to apply Cézanne's concepts to this composition[147] but he pushed the perspective further by "upending the tabletop, tilting it forward to a steeply raked angle, almost parallel with the picture plane, that recalls the flat, fragmented space of Picasso's Cubism."[148] Again, Woodruff was employing the triangular compositional precepts of Harold Haven Brown that he had learned at Herron.

In contrast to Cézanne's symmetrical balance on the side of the central axis of the wine bottle and the elimination of details, Woodruff's painting looks almost like a crazy quilt.

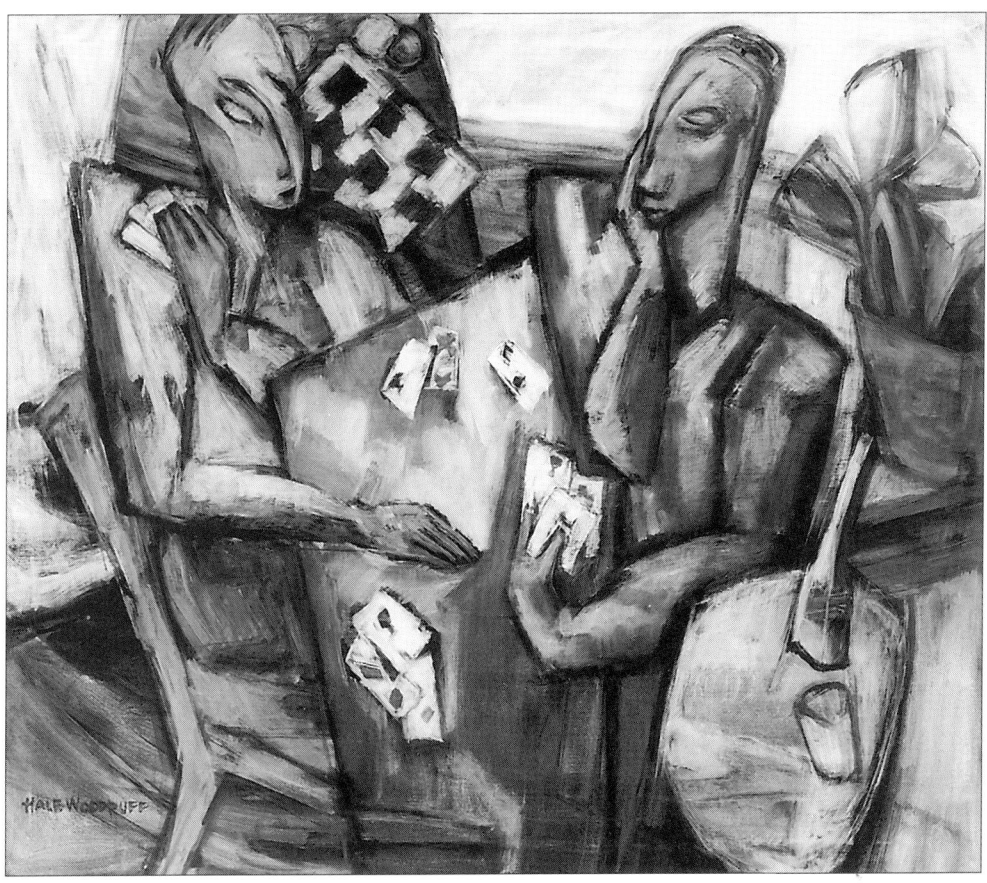

FIGURE 62
Hale Woodruff, *Cardplayers,* 1978 (after the 1930 original), oil on canvas, 36 x 24 in.
The Hewitt Collection, Courtesy the Bank of America.

The rigid angularity of the tabletop is emphasized by the sharp diagonals of the figures'
shoulders, a chessboard and table in the upper left, a blocky, bluish potted plant on the right,
and a skewed wine bottle on a roundish table in the lower right. Woodruff's palette also
departs from Cézanne's muted earth tones. Here, the colors are bold and strident—deep
blues, hot pinks, spring greens, and brash yellows.

      Far removed from the rustic simplicity and earthy realism of Cézanne's peasants,
Woodruff's cardplayers are even more abstract, with their contours reminiscent of West
African sculptures. Woodruff outstrips Picasso, who had given one of the figures in his
Demoiselles d'Avignon a masklike head; his cardplayers have long, bald heads, broad
shoulders, extra-long arms, and rough-hewn, pawlike hands. They are less naturalistic and
less traditionally gendered. These heads recall several works of African art in the book
Afrikanische Plastik, which Woodruff received from Lieber in the early 1920s, especially the
Fang head from Gabon (plate 21), but also the Bakongo knife handle (plate 41), and the
Yoruba mask (plate 44). Years later, Woodruff would articulate what he found most striking

about such sculptures: "The dignity of man, this is what I find in African sculpture. . . . There's always a very great sense of self. This is why you will find this very frontal, monumental, austere quality in all of their sculpture. It's never 'gut-bucket.' This is the kind of image that we should strive for. A self-image of the highest possible order, and the highest possible image of human dignity."[149] The cardplayers' heads also resemble portraits by Modigliani, with their linear noses, tiny mouths, and almond-shaped eyes. Woodruff believed that Modigliani's sources were African, too: "I felt Modigliani really dove into African sculpture and came out with something that, while it showed the influence of his African studies, nevertheless was his own art."[150]

While *The Cardplayers* certainly shows the influence of African and European art, it is nonetheless far from derivative. Rather, it is a unique product that pulls the two together to make a universal statement about intellectual thought and creativity. Later, Woodruff articulated what his discovery initiated: "The critics for a long time didn't understand African art until the black artist who understood the universality as well as the impact of its localization pointed it out. You see, any black artist who claims that he is creating black art must begin with some black image. The black image can be the environment, it can be the problems that one faces, it can be the look on a man's face. It can be anything. It's got to have this kind of pin-pointed point of departure. But if it's worth its while, it's also got to be universal in its broader impact and its presence.[151] Universal in its impact and presence, *The Cardplayers* is, as art historian Judith Wilson asserts, "a triumphant synthesis of African art and European modernism."[152]

The Cardplayers departs so strongly from Woodruff's previous work that it is clearly an indication that he has "gone modern." Whereas Hayden's *Nous quatre à Paris* is a genre scene, the sober tone of Woodruff's work gives it a monumental quality. The figure on the right cups his cheek in his palm in a gesture of contemplation while the figure on the left protectively shields his cards by pressing them against his chest. Floating above this figure's left shoulder is a chessboard, long a symbol of intellectual activity. Could it be that Woodruff knew that Cézanne associated cardplaying with modern painting? According to art historian Kurt Badt, it was widely recognized by the Impressionists that painting in a three-dimensional manner represented the old school while painting in the manner of playing cards, in other words, flat, represented the modern school. The critic Castagnary compared Manet's *Olympia* to a playing card; author J. E. Blanche quoted Degas as saying that the modern artists strove to paint "in the flat, flat as playing-cards"; and the critic Zola noted that Manet's detractors sneered that his pictures recalled Epinal's engravings, printed like playing cards.[153] If Woodruff was aware of this analogy, then he was clearly indicating his new artistic direction. In the fall, he confidently sent *The Cardplayers, Provençal Landscape, Still Life,* and *Head of a Woman* (location unknown) to the Harmon Foundation.

Woodruff knew that his roadwork would not last into the winter, so he tried to make additional money by sending four other works to Walter White for sale. At the end of September, White offered them to James Weldon Johnson, Carl Van Vechten, and Arthur Huff Fauset at Woodruff's "ridiculously low" prices.[154] At least Carl Van Vechten bought

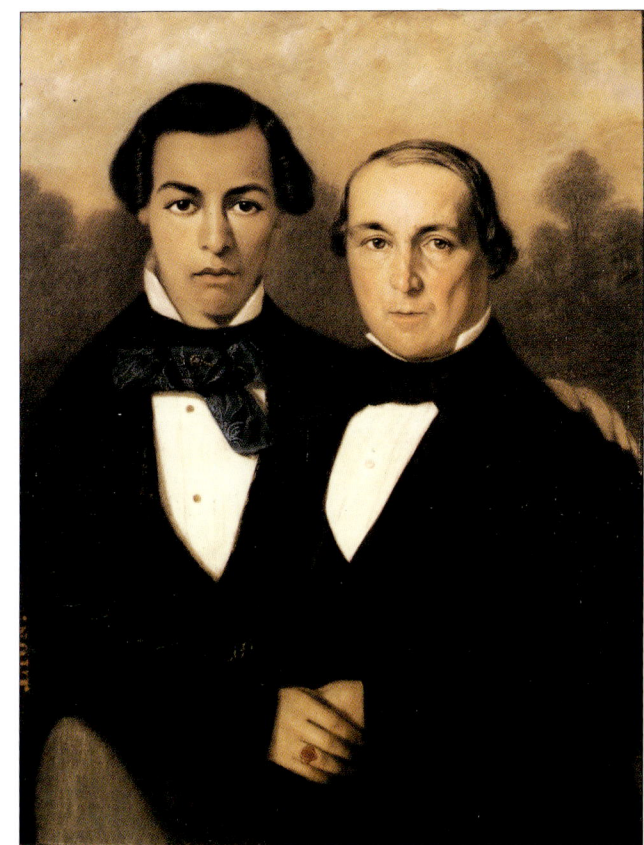

COLOR PLATE 1
Jules Lion,
Asher Moses Nathan and Son,
1845, pastel on paper, 26 x 36 in.
Owned by Mr. and Mrs.
Jack O. Brittain Sr.

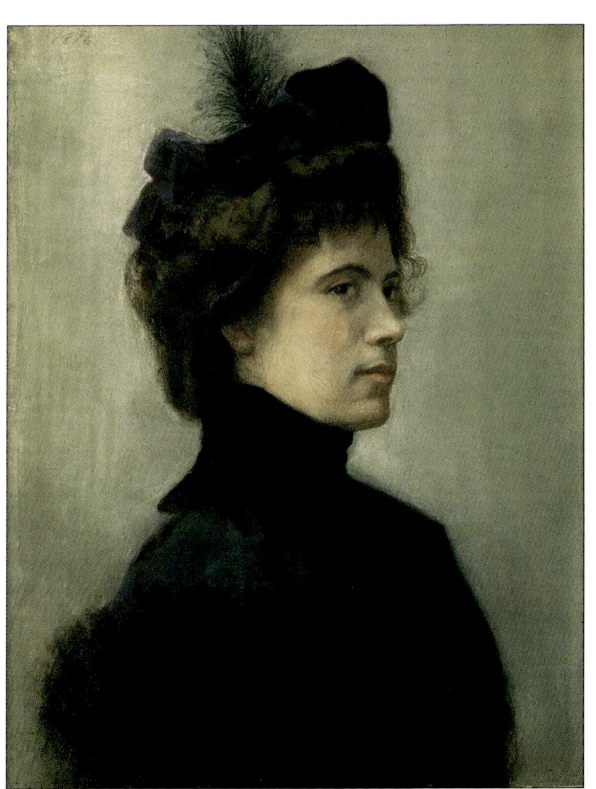

COLOR PLATE 2
Annie E. A. Walker,
La Parisienne, 1896,
pastel on paper. 19¼ x 25½ in.
Howard University Gallery of Art,
Washington, D.C.

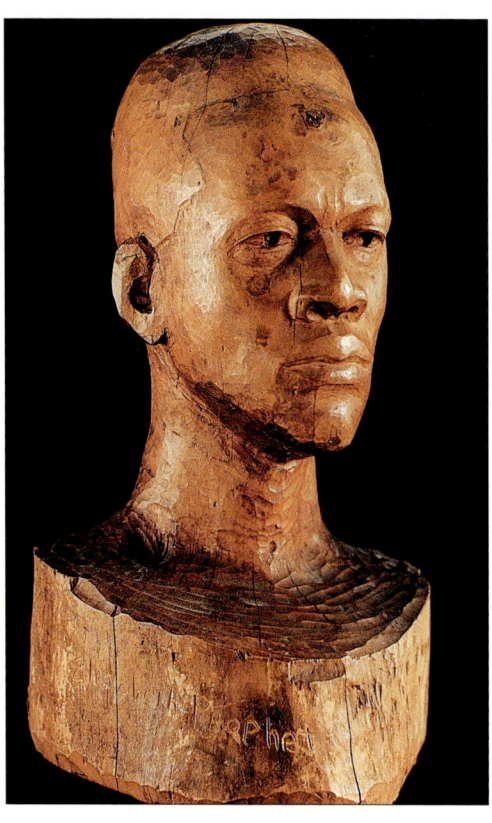

COLOR PLATE 3
Nancy Elizabeth Prophet,
Head of a Negro,
ca. 1926–1927, wood, 20½ in. (h).
Museum of Art, Rhode Island School of Design.
Gift of Miss Eleanor B. Green

COLOR PLATE 4
Nancy Elizabeth Prophet,
Congolais (or *Congolaise*),
ca. 1931, wood, 17⅛ x 6¾ x 8⅟₁₆ in.
Photograph copyright © 1999 by theWhitney
Museum of American Art, purchase 32.83.

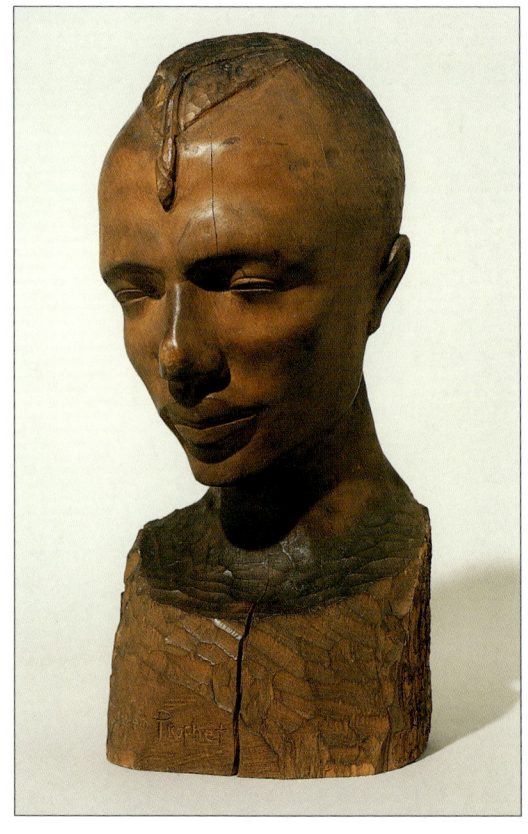

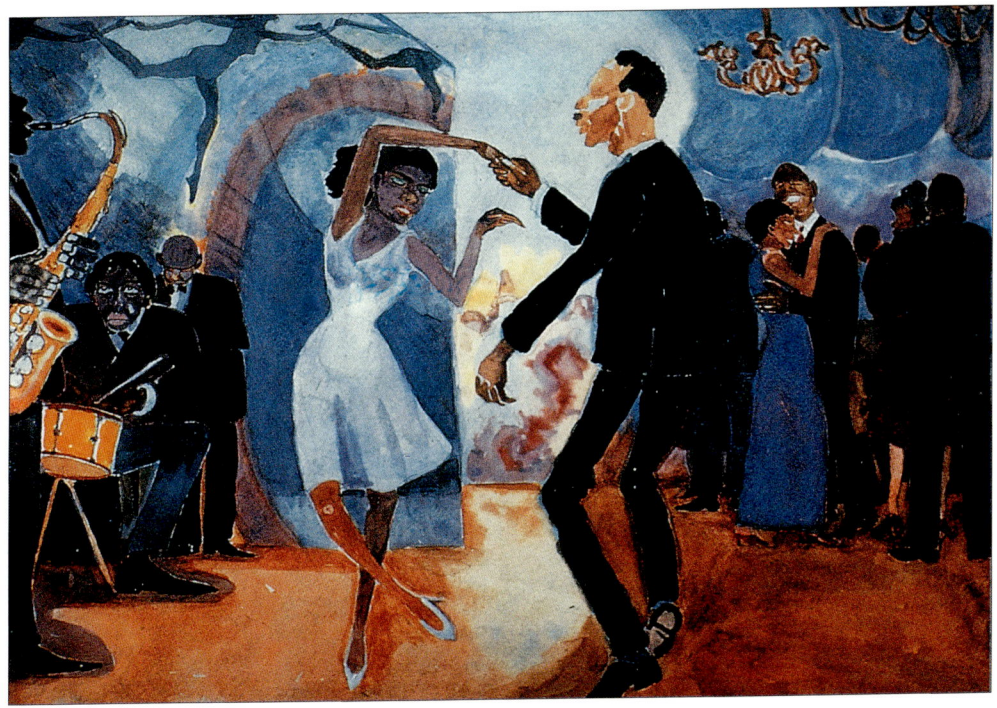

COLOR PLATE 5
Palmer Hayden, *Bal jeunesse*, ca. 1927, watercolor on paper, 14 x 18 in.
With permission of Meredith and Gail J. Weight Sirmans.

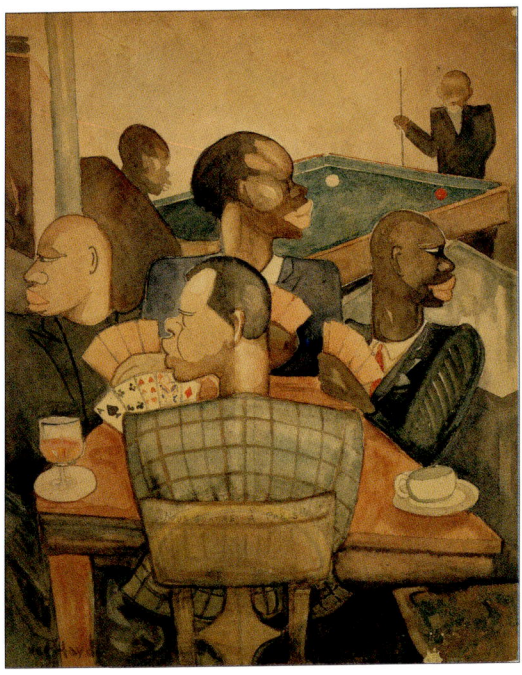

COLOR PLATE 6
Palmer Hayden, *Nous quatre à Paris,*
ca. 1928–1930, watercolor on paper, 21⅞ x 18 in.
Metropolitan Museum of Art, Purchase, Joseph A.
Hazen Foundation, Inc. Gift 1975 (1975.125).

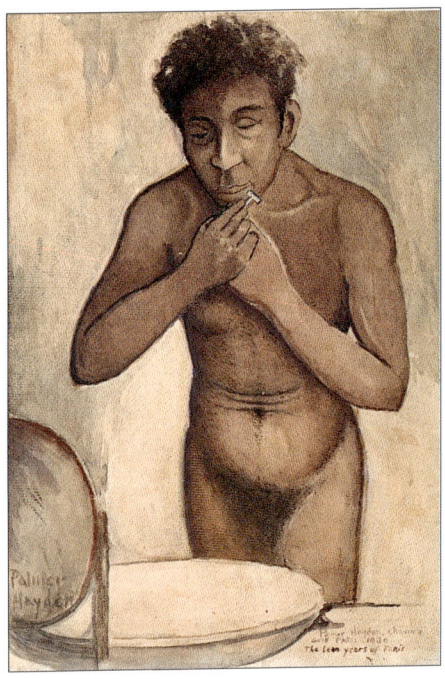

COLOR PLATE 7
Palmer Hayden, *Palmer Hayden Shaving/*
The Lean Years of Paris, 1930, watercolor on
paper, 18 x 12½ in. Courtesy of John P. Axelrod,
Boston, Massachusetts.

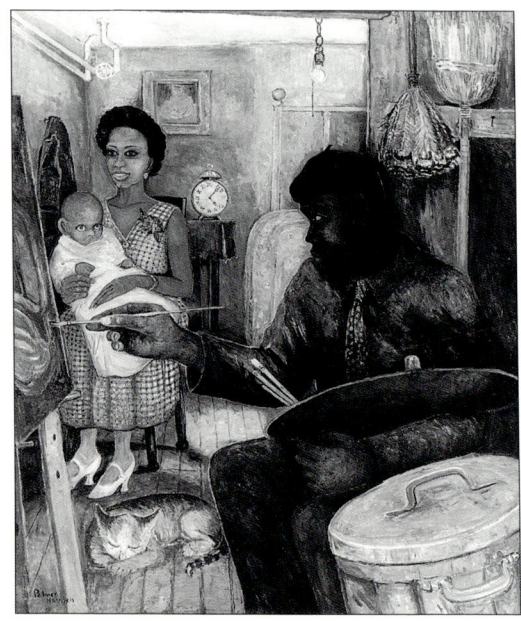

PLATE 8
Palmer Hayden, *The Janitor Who Paints,*
ca. 1931, oil on canvas, 39⅛ x 33 in.
National Museum of American Art,
Smithsonian Institution.
Gift of the Harmon Foundation.

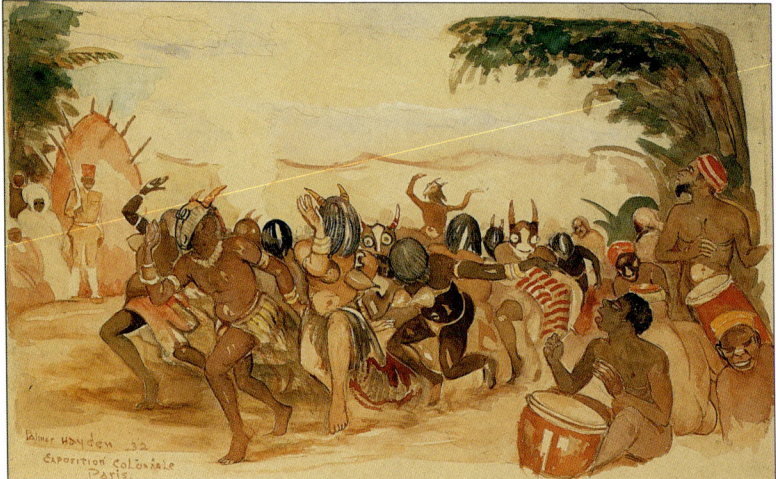

COLOR PLATE 9
Palmer Hayden,
*Exposition
Coloniale,* 1932,
watercolor on
paper, 10 x 14 in.
With permission
of Samella Lewis.

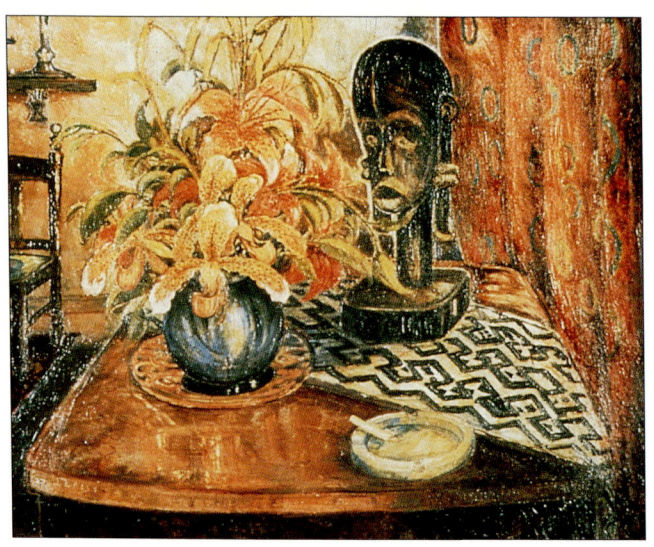

COLOR PLATE 10
Palmer Hayden, *Fétiche et fleurs,*
ca. 1931–1932, oil on canvas,
23½ x 29 in.
The Museum of
African American Art, Los Angeles.

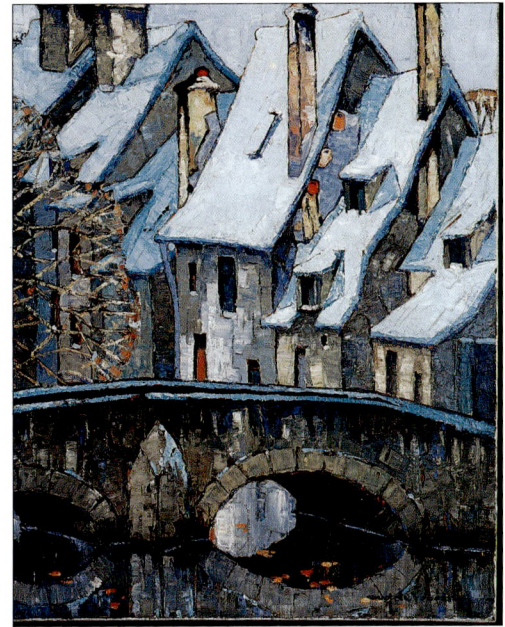

COLOR PLATE 11
Hale Woodruff, *Medieval Chartres,*
1928, oil on canvas, 20 x 24 in.
Collection of Mr. and Mrs. Robert C. Davidson Jr..
Courtesy of Michael Rosenfeld Gallery,
New York City.

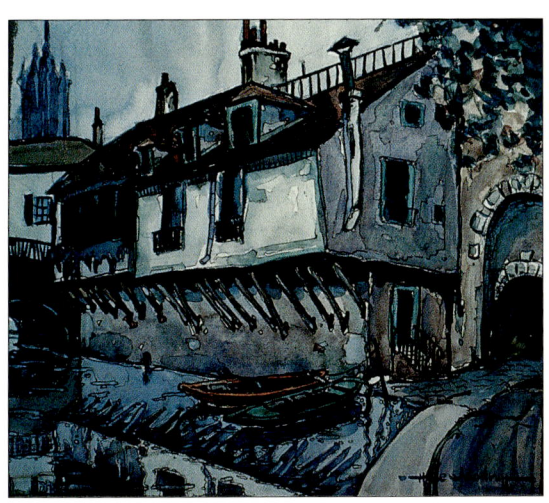

COLOR PLATE 12
Hale Woodruff, *Chartres,*
1928, watercolor on paper, 16½ x 17¾ in.
Hampton University Museum,
Hampton, Virginia

COLOR PLATE 13
Hale Woodruff,
Provençal Landscape,
1930, oil on canvas,
dimensions and location unknown.
Courtesy of Kenkeleba Gallery.

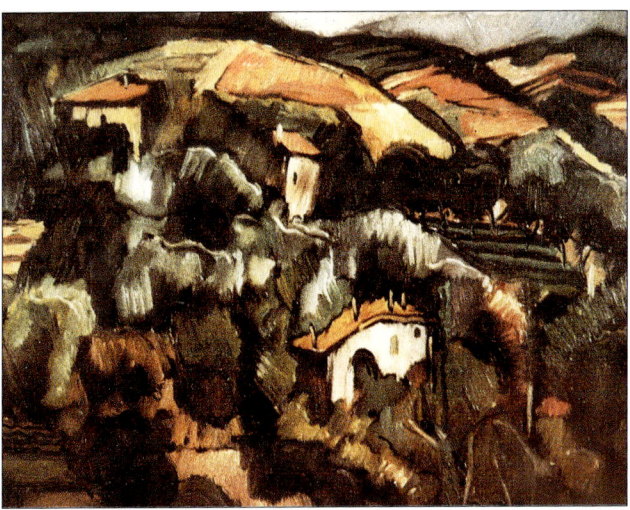

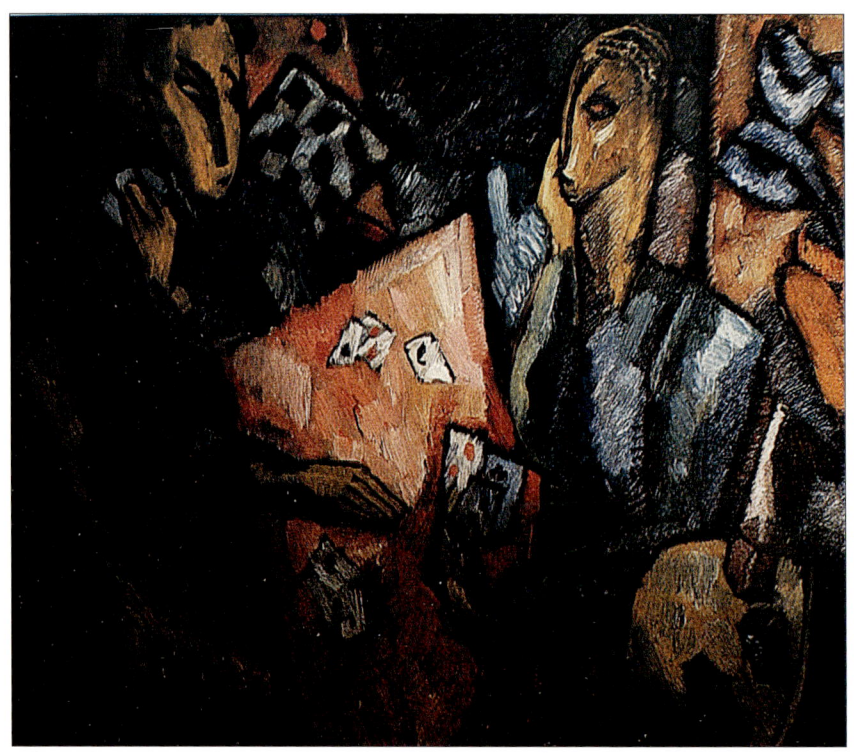

COLOR PLATE 14
Hale Woodruff, *Cardplayers,* 1978 (after the 1930 original), oil on canvas, 36 x 24 in.
The Hewitt Collection, Courtesy the Bank of America.

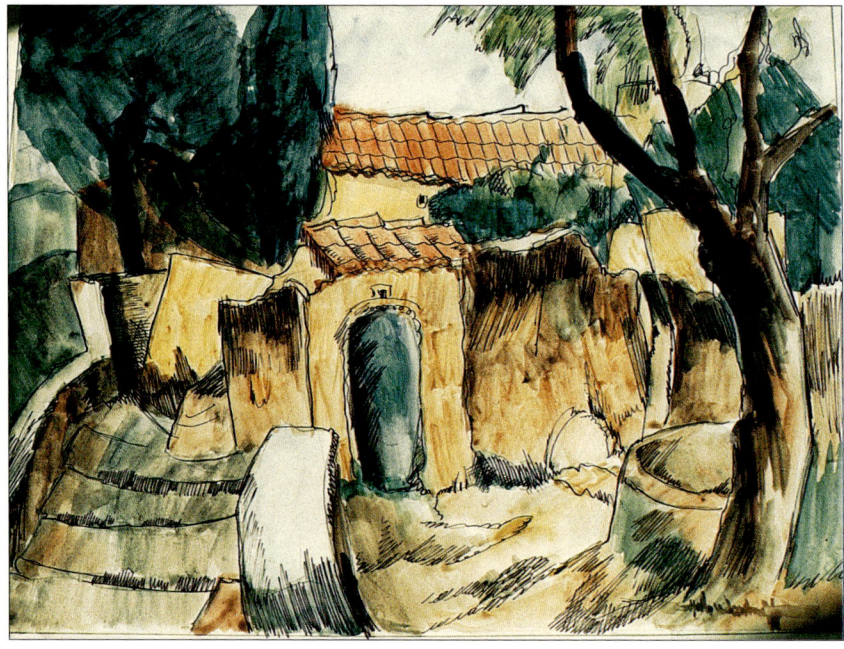

COLOR PLATE 15
Hale Woodruff, *Paysage du Midi,* 1930, watercolor on paper, 13 x 16¾ in.
James Weldon Johnson Memorial Collection of Negro Arts and Letters. Beinecke Rare Book
and Manuscript Collection, Yale University Library.

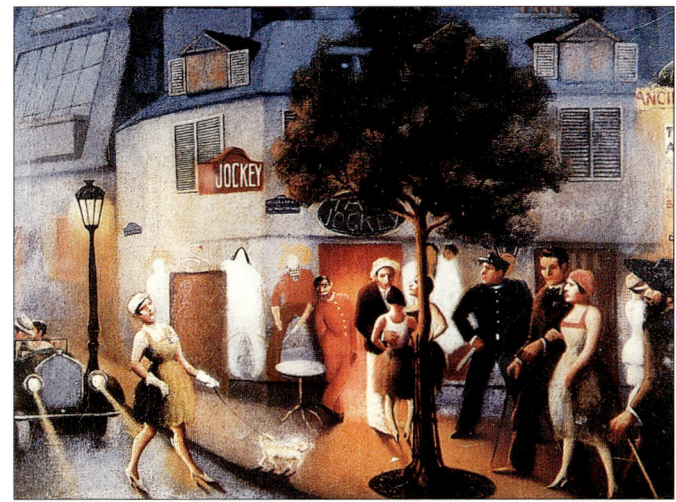

COLOR PLATE 16
Archibald J. Motley Jr.,
Jockey Club, 1929,
oil on canvas, 26 x 32 in.
Art and Artifacts Division,
Schomburg Center for Research
in Black Culture, The New York
Public Library, Astor, Lenox,
and Tilden Foundations

COLOR PLATE 17
Archibald J. Motley Jr.,
Café, Paris, 1929,
oil on canvas, 23⅝ x 28⅞ in.
Collection of Archie Motley
and Valerie Gerrard Browne.
Courtesy of Chicago
Historical Society.

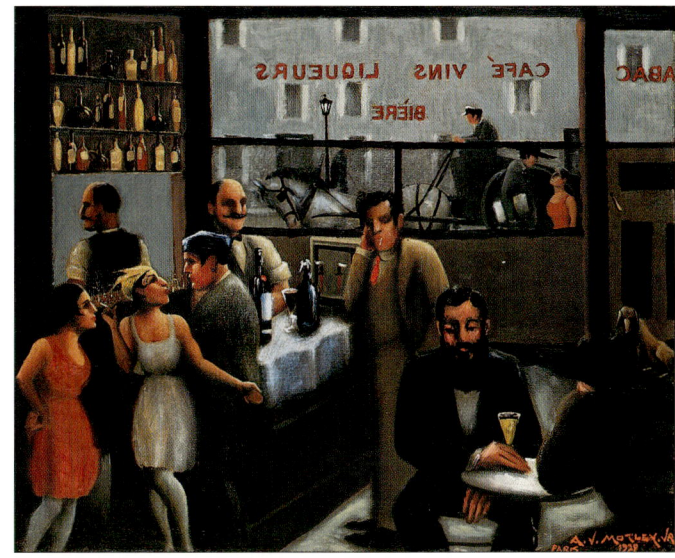

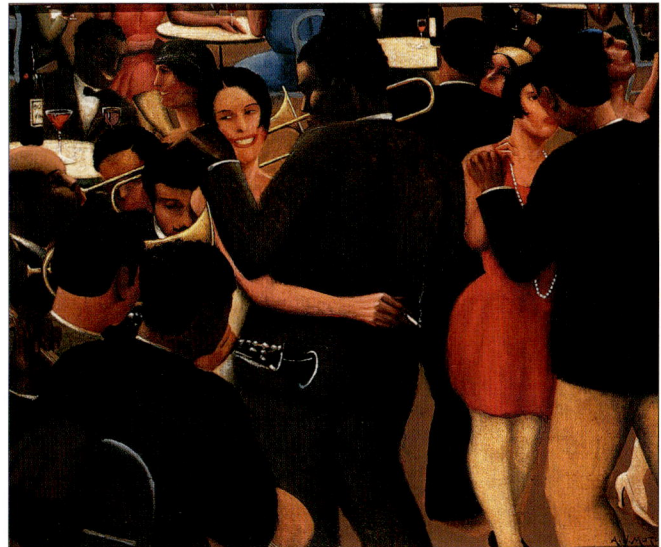

COLOR PLATE 18
Archibald J. Motley Jr.,
Blues, 1929, oil on canvas,
36 x 42 in.
Collection of Archie Motley
and Valerie Gerrard Browne.
Courtesy of Chicago
Historical Society.

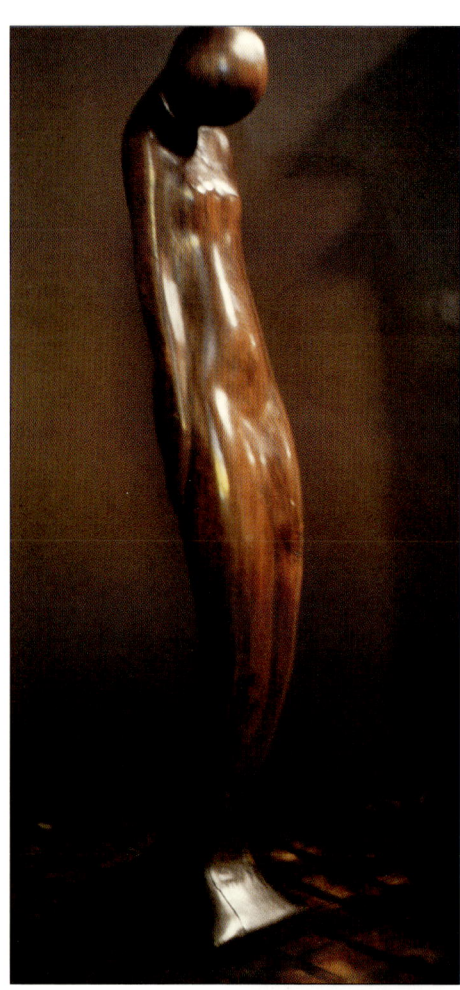

COLOR PLATE 19
Augusta Savage,
Fern Frond, ca. 1930–1931,
walnut, 10 in. (h).
Private collection, Paris.

COLOR PLATE 20
Albert Alexander
Smith,
Dancing Time, 1930,
oil on canvas,
22½ x 26½ in.
Hampton University
Museum,
Hampton, Virginia.

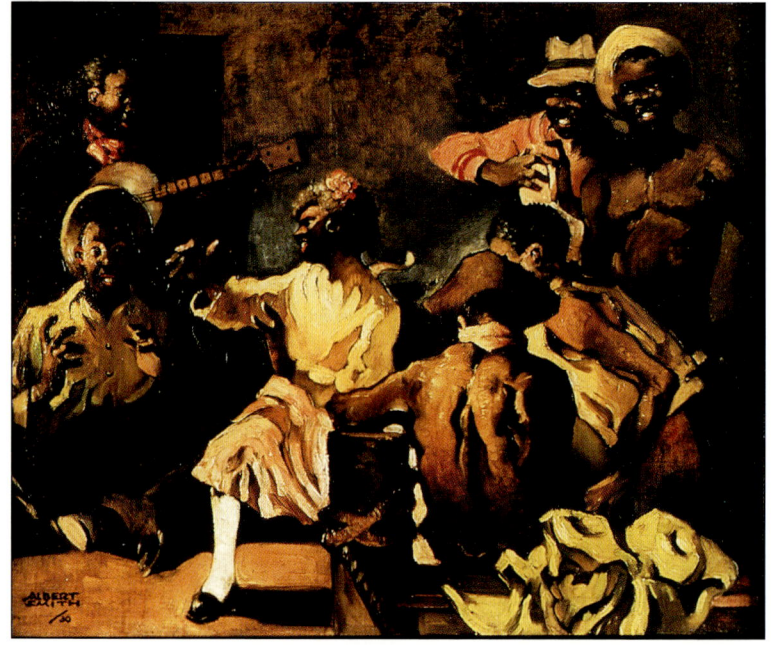

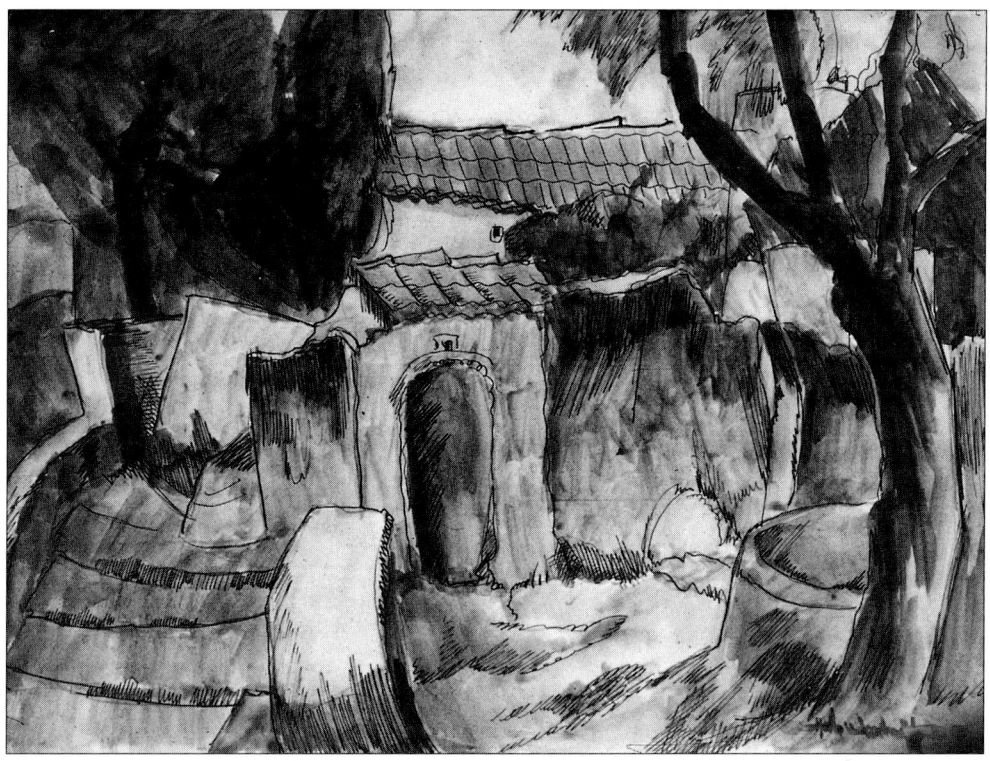

FIGURE 63
Hale Woodruff, *Paysage du Midi*, 1930, watercolor on paper, 13 x 16¾ in.
James Weldon Johnson Memorial Collection of Negro Arts and Letters. Beinecke Rare Book and Manuscript Collection, Yale University Library.

Paysage du Midi (fig. 63), a somewhat Cubist watercolor of a dwelling in the Provençal countryside.

In December, Woodruff wrote to Hannah Moriarta of the Harmon Foundation asking her to handle sales of his work during the coming exhibition, because his funds were quite low. He sent an additional four unframed and unmounted watercolors to be offered for twenty-five dollars each during the exhibition.[155] In the meantime, Woodruff economized by moving to a smaller place at 35, rue du Docteur Michel Provençal.

THE LAST SIX MONTHS ABROAD, 1931

On April 19, 1931, Woodruff commented, "I have studied and worked hard and I believe something will come out of it all." When Woodruff's new work was shown at the Harmon Foundation in early 1931, it elicited strong responses, both positive and negative. The positive responses primarily came from white writers and collectors. Edward Alden Jewell, the influential critic for the *New York Times,* saw a distinct French influence in Woodruff's work, especially in the Cubist structure of his *Head of a Woman* and *The Cardplayers,* "tributes to artists of the Picabia sort." Although somewhat skeptical of such a painting, the critic felt that it was, "at any rate, definitely modern in spirit."[156]

Author Ralph M. Pearson also admired the originality of Woodruff's *The Cardplayers*. He featured it in his book *Experiencing Pictures: Through Analysis of Ancient and Modern Works and through Practice of the Procedures Which Make Those Works Effective* (1932). Pearson cited the work in tandem with a watercolor by John Marin for its demonstration of emotion in art, "the one absolutely indispensable ingredient of authentic creative work."[157]

Other white viewers admired the boldness in all of the four paintings. Mrs. John Howells bought *Still Life* for two hundred dollars and Hannah Moriarta bought a watercolor for fifteen dollars. Several African American scholars, however, were less than thrilled with Woodruff's new direction. Du Bois called it "extremely modernistic" and stated that he did not like "that phase of his work."[158] Cullen, too, apparently was taken aback. Woodruff wrote to him: "So you didn't like the Harmon representation of mine. Well, old man, I've been working and studying and trying to find out things. I've been going through periods of different sorts. We can only see what will come out of it all!"[159] While Du Bois and Cullen did not care for Woodruff's new style—in part, because it did not promote racial uplift by depicting dignified black people—Locke and White, who were younger and more progressive than Du Bois, did, and they continued to support him. There was no consensus about the nature of what kind of art African Americans should produce, even among the few African American patrons of the early twentieth century.

One of White's friends, Nathan W. Levin, comptroller of the Rosenwald Fund, visited Woodruff in Nice around May. He was shocked by Woodruff's hunger when he took him out to lunch: "Mr. Woodruff tried his best to treat the meal as though it were an ordinary affair but he could not quite conceal that it was obviously the first good meal he had had in a long time."[160] Levin discovered that Woodruff was about to be ejected from the house where he was living. Upon his return to the United States, Levin visited White, told him the story, and gave him a personal check for ten dollars to send to Woodruff. White immediately wrote to Cullen and others, asking them to contribute a small sum.

Woodruff must have received some support from James Weldon Johnson, because he sent him an untitled ink-and-wash drawing of a still life (fig. 64), signed "with sincere appreciation." The sketch depicts a bundle of objects in front of a canvas turned to the back—a plaster clay torso, a zither, a palette, a jar of brushes, paint, and rapiers. In the lower right is a cat with slanted, almost Cubist eyes.

In mid-April, Woodruff received a check from sales through the Harmon Foundation after having had a very hard year and being forced to incur debt, despite aid from some French people. "The natives," he wrote, "have been splendid and I don't know what I would have done had it not been for them." He said that he wanted to return to the United States in the spring or summer, "yet it all depends on my getting the funds. That, alas! is always the great question." Although Woodruff continued to live hand to mouth,

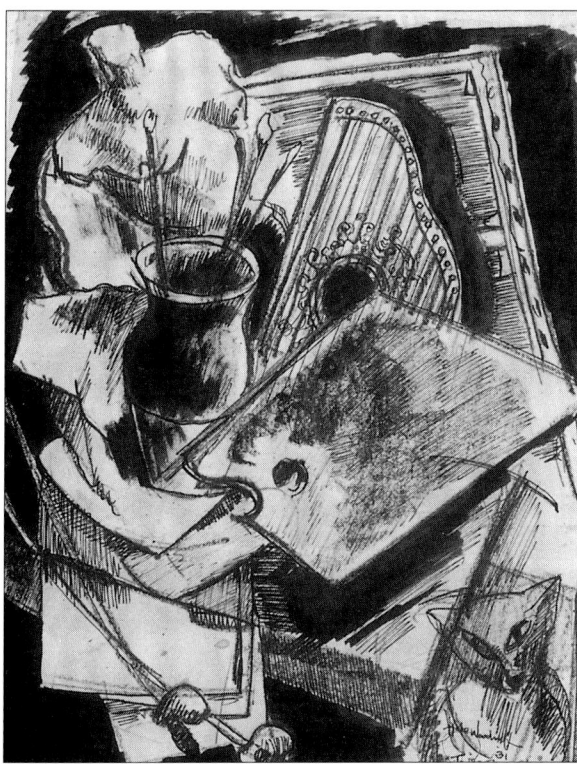

FIGURE 64
Hale Woodruff, *Untitled,* 1931, ink and
wash on paper, 15¼ x 12½ in.
James Weldon Johnson Memorial
Collection of Negro Arts and Letters.
Beinecke Rare Book and Manuscript
Collection, Yale University Library.

he believed he was maturing artistically: "I feel that I've made some progress. In quite a
different direction, however, as you may see from the paintings I sent over."[161]

    With the funding, Woodruff moved into the six-room house of a Russian artist,
whom he never met, furnished with a sundeck, hand-carved furniture, Belgian linens, and
beautiful silver and tableware. He also shared a studio with Hiler. Both artists benefited from
the relationship and they often discussed painting and color theory. Later, Hiler would write
several books on the subject, including *Some Directions and Dimensions of Color, Light Shades*
and *White and Scarlet Permutations* (dates unknown), *Why Abstract?* (1945), and *Notes on
the Technique of Painting* (1954).

    During Woodruff's last year in France, he had began to study "the theory and
science of art,"[162] especially fourteenth- and fifteenth-century media and methods of
painting.[163] He tried to perfect the usage of a water-wax medium and executed several
canvases with it, but was unsatisfied with the results. He hoped that such works would "resist
temperature, moisture, dryness, contact and time" and maintain "a permanent brilliance and
freshness."[164] When Woodruff returned to the States, he would apply to the Guggenheim
Memorial Foundation for a fellowship to carry on this work. In 1931, he also began to do
some work in gouache on wood. He believed that these pieces were "without doubt the
most promising things I've done. . . . I was really on the road to true accomplishment."[165]
One of these paintings may be *Abstract Composition* (1931, fig. 65), published in Locke's

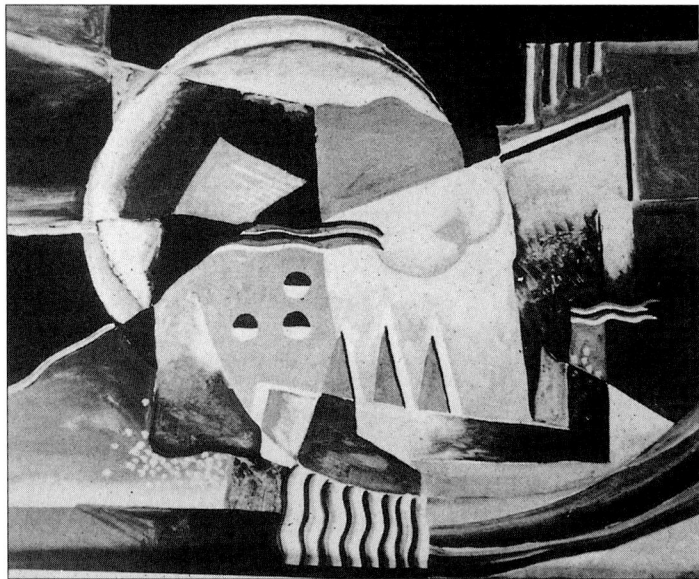

FIGURE 65
Hale Woodruff, *Abstract Composition*, 1931, oil on canvas, dimensions and location unknown. Courtesy of Kenkeleba Gallery.

book *The Negro in Art* (1940). This work (now missing) was reproduced in black and white; it seems, however, to have been painted thickly in vivid colors. The painting is a study in color, contrasts, and geometric forms—circles, semicircles, triangles, trapezoids, parallelograms—and organic shapes of bulging areas, wiggly lines, and undulating waves. In the center, three half-dark, half-light circles appear in a reverse L-shape to the left of three isosceles triangles. Without any representational imagery, *Abstract Composition* is Woodruff's first purely nonrepresentational piece.

In April 1931, Woodruff also produced his first mural (location now unknown). Together with Henri Julliet, a young French painter (about whom virtually nothing is known), for two weeks' board at a café, Woodruff covered more than three hundred square feet of wall space in the restaurant.[166] Apparently, the owner quickly grew tired of their eating in his café, but they continued to dine there until the agreement was fulfilled. The fresco murals depicted "the general spirit and character of this old town on the Mediterranean, Mecca for artists, tourists, and vacationists [*sic*]."[167]

Because Woodruff had received no money for his work on the frescoes, he was again in dire straits in May and felt that his "only way out" was to ask the Harmon Foundation or an associate of Brady's for a loan of four hundred dollars for his return fare to the United States. He had a number of debts "such as rent, board and quite a sum that I owe to my color and canvas dealer"[168] and he also had to pack and ship his paintings. The foundation did not produce a loan, but it did manage to sell more of his work; Amy Spingarn had bought a watercolor out of sympathy[169] and Woodruff received a check on June 5. Woodruff was deeply appreciative: "The arrival of the check for those sales was a godsend for I had long past [*sic*] the end of my rope. My debts had gone well beyond the 200 dollar mark and I didn't know what to do. I had made appeal but received no material results. Now I can look my grocer and dealer square in the face for a while."[170] But Woodruff still desperately needed funds and hoped that the foundation could find someone who would be willing to patronize him for a few months once he was back in the United States:

> Although I know of no other place where I can work so well as a Cagnes-sur-Mer, as conditions are good and life is comparatively cheap, I can't go on indefinitely like this.
>
> Before the depression I was able to sell paintings occasionally and I managed somehow to keep the wolf away. The sales at the exhibit are the first in many months. So you see how difficult it is. Perhaps I can find something to do in America though there are millions without work. In any case I hope you can do something for me.
>
> In view of the fact that work is so uncertain now at home, it may be possible that you could interest someone in my painting that they would help me out to the extent of a small sum per month. I could manage that way for a while—at least till I came to the place where I could go on independantly [sic]. There is much I can do now and I dislike the idea of having to give up my work just at this point.[171]

The Harmon Foundation reported again that it could not give Woodruff a loan, but that it would try to interest some patron in his plight.[172] To make matters worse, Woodruff suffered a badly twisted ankle in July. By this point, he was anxious to leave the Riviera and visit old friends. He wrote to Cullen that he hoped to see him shortly in Paris to give him "that belotte [sic] walloping that you're waiting for."[173]

During the summer, Hope, now president of Atlanta University, pressed Woodruff to accept a teaching position. He had heard about the artist's difficulties from DeFrantz. Hope had been watching Woodruff's progress, visiting him in France every summer. The painter finally agreed to teach and sailed back to the United States on September 10, 1931.

5
LONER IN PARIS:
ARCHIBALD J. MOTLEY JR., 1929–1930

"*R*IGHT HERE IN WONDERFUL AMERICA": CHICAGO, 1893–1929

Of all the African American artists who studied in Paris between the world wars, Archibald J. Motley Jr. (1891–1981) was the only one reluctant to go abroad. He recalled thinking: "I'm going to stay here, I'm not going anywhere, I'm not going to Europe. They're not going to chase me out of my own country. I'm an American. I'm proud of being an American. I don't give a damn what color my skin is, I'm going to stay right here and I'm going to fight it out, and I'm going to make my name right here. I'm staying right here in wonderful America."[1]

Specifically, Motley wanted to stay right in wonderful Chicago, his hometown since the age of two, when his family moved there from New Orleans after brief stays in Saint Louis and Buffalo.[2] And it was there that he "made his name," well before he ever went abroad.

By 1929, Motley's works had been displayed in Chicago for more than twelve years, beginning in December 1917 with his inclusion in the *Paintings by Negro Artists* exhibition at the Arts and Letters Society. Chicagoans also viewed his works at the Art Institute of Chicago (AIC) in 1921, 1922, 1923, 1925, the Galleries of Marshall Field and Company (1926, 1927), the Galleries of Carson Pirie Scott and Company (1926), and the Women's Athletic Club (1928).[3]

Motley's exhibition success was not confined to his hometown, however. His works were also shown in Springfield, Illinois, at the Art Galleries of the Illinois State Museum in 1926–1927 and 1929; Peoria, Illinois, at the Hotel Père Maquette in 1927; Newark, New Jersey, at the Newark Museum in 1927; Louisville, Kentucky, at the J. B. Speed Memorial

Museum in 1929; Albany, New York, at the Literary Roundtable of Albany in 1923; New York City, at the New Gallery in 1928, and the Harmon Foundation in 1929; and Washington, D.C., at the National Gallery of Art in 1929.[4] Compared with his African American colleagues, then, Motley had the most extensive exhibition history before going abroad.

This impressive exhibition history was, no doubt, a significant factor in the Guggenheim Foundation's decision to award Motley a fellowship in 1929 for study in Paris, apparently the only such fellowship given to an African American artist at that time.[5] The previous year, Motley had won the Harmon gold award for his painting *The Octoroon* (1902), from among 102 applicants.[6] Before that, his *Mending Socks* (1924), a portrait of his grandmother sewing, seated before a crucifix and near a still life on a round table, was voted the most popular work in the Newark Museum exhibition *Paintings and Watercolors by Living American Artists* in 1927.[7]

Motley's decision to study in Paris had been supported, directly and indirectly, by many white patrons, beginning with Frank W. Gunsaulus, president of the Armour Institute, who paid his first-year tuition at the AIC, the Midwest's most prestigious art academy which he attended[8] from 1914 to 1918. There he received a solid technical foundation in the French academic tradition. Students progressed from drawing in black and white to painting in color. They also studied elementary geometric forms and anatomical models, then copied casts of ancient and Italian Renaissance sculpture, before going on to work from live models.[9] Because Motley was already well trained in draftmanship, which he had learned at Englewood High School, he placed into the antique class upon his entrance.[10] His work—which consisted mostly of European American nudes and figure and still life studies—like that of all the pupils, was constantly reviewed and publicly criticized by teachers. Among Motley's most influential instructors were portraitist Karl Buehr (1866–1952), muralist and landscapist John Norton (1876–1934), and landscapist Albert Krehbiel (1873–1945), instructor of drawing and composition.[11] It is likely that Krehbiel, who had studied in Paris with William Harper, encouraged Motley to consider going abroad. He gave Motley a merit award for composition,[12] and he may also have supported him when he brought "colored models" to the institute.[13]

As mentioned in the introduction, Harper and William Edouard Scott had both studied at the AIC, Harper early on and Scott in 1904–1908. Other early African American students at the AIC were William MacKnight Farrow (1885–1967), who attended classes from 1908 to 1917, and Charles Clarence Dawson (1889–1981), who wanted to do "for the Negroes what Millet did for the French peasants,"[14] and who studied there from 1913 to 1917. Motley knew only Farrow personally, and not very well;[15] Harper had passed away in 1910 and Scott lived in Indianapolis. Works by Harper, Scott, Farrow, Dawson, and Motley (and by F. L. Holmes, Jesse Stubbs, Edward Knox, and R. M. Williams) were in the first exhibition of black artists in Chicago, presented by the Arts and Letters Society of Chicago in 1917. It is possible that this is the group whom Motley criticized in 1918 for their technical incompetence and stylistic derivativeness.[16] Other African American artists who studied at the AIC in the early 1920s included sculptor Richmond Barthé (1901–1989), who studied briefly with Motley; illustrator and portraitist Robert Savon Pious (1908–1983), who studied there in 1921; and painter Ellis Wilson (1900–1977), a student there from 1919 to 1923. All later developed their careers in New York.

Upon graduating from the AIC, Motley, like Woodruff, had difficulty finding a job commensurate with his artistic abilities. He had hoped to get portrait commissions, but quickly realized that few African Americans could, or were willing to, spend money on art. Motley then resolved to "paint pictures that anyone will buy, regardless of race, color, or creed,"[17] citing the religious paintings of Tanner for their universality. "If all Negro artists painted simply Negro types, how long would our Negro art exist?" he asked in 1918.[18] Yet he could not exist long in the job market for art either as a portraitist or genre painter. Throughout the 1920s, he supported his art while working odd jobs.[19]

In 1919, Motley returned to the AIC to audit a painting class taught by George Bellows (1882–1925), one of the few modern painters he ever acknowledged as an influence.[20] Motley was also influenced by the work of another white artist who depicted black subject matter, Wayman Adams (1883–1959), who switched from portraying sentimental stereotypes, such as the mammy, to sensitive portraits of African American intellectuals, such as Alain Locke, in the 1920s. But Motley believed that only African Americans could truly render "the soul and the very heart of colored people."[21] To that end, in the early 1920s, he made the decision to paint almost exclusively black subject matter for the rest of his life. He explained that ambition in 1933: "Subject matter plays a most important part in my art. It is my earnest desire and ambition to express the American Negro honestly and sincerely, neither to add nor detract, and to bring about a more sincere and brotherly feeling, a better understanding, between him and his white brethren."[22]

In the early 1920s, Motley explored his dual African and Creole heritage through a portrait series of family members that included his maternal grandmother, a "pygmy of former British East Africa"[23] who married a Frenchman. Motley's fascination with black skin tones also led him to what he called a "scientific"[24] inquiry of beautiful women of mixed racial ancestry. This portrait series included such paintings as *Mulatress with Figurine and Dutch Seascape* (ca. 1920), *Octoroon* (1922), and *The Octoroon Girl* (1925), on which Motley "worked diligently to give them the respect, dignity and honor they deserve. . . . I find in the black women such a marvelous range of color, all the way from very black to the typical Caucasian type."[25] Unknown to Motley, sculptor May Howard Jackson (1877–1931) also produced a like series of women and children in the 1910s and 1920s in Philadelphia. Many other African Americans explored images of people from mixed racial backgrounds, such as Dawson, whose *Quadroon Madonna* was shown in the Harmon Foundation exhibition of 1929.[26] In his early career, Motley also depicted the energy and excitement of the Jazz Age in black nightclub scenes such as *Black and Tan Cabaret* (ca. 1921), *Syncopation* (1924) (location of both unknown), and *Stomp* (1927).

Motley's depictions of contemporary black life and his background distinguished him from other African American artists in Chicago and from his compatriots in France in important ways. As Wendy Greenhouse has pointed out, he was "something of an outsider in the world he portrayed. Light-skinned, middle-class, and Roman Catholic, he belonged to a small minority in Chicago's black population." Rather than growing up in Chicago's Black Belt, also known as Bronzeville,[27] where 90 percent of Chicago's black residents lived, Motley lived in an adjacent white neighborhood where he and his sister were the only African American children to attend the local public elementary school, Perkins Bass.[28] Eventually, in 1924, he married a German American woman, Edith Granzo, who had lived across the street, dated him discreetly in high school, and accompanied him to Paris.[29] Motley was also unique in having a family who actively supported his decision—already made at the age of nine[30]—to be a fine artist frequently posed for him, and valued his education. Motley's mother was a schoolteacher and his father, a Pullman porter, had introduced him to Gunsaulus and shown him the American South when the two worked on trains together during school vacations in the late 1910s.[31] Further, his extensive recognition by the white artistic establishment separated him from the black community. Yet, as Greenhouse has demonstrated, Motley used his European-modeled training to celebrate contemporary black urban life. Even as a child, he studied and sketched what he called "characters," people in Black Belt pool rooms, churches, and other places where people socialized.[32] "The thing I was trying to do," he stated later, "was trying to get their [African American] interest in culture, in art. I planned that by putting them in the paintings themselves, making them part of my own work so they could see themselves as they are, I mean in a more conservative way. I've never cared about doing this modernistic art. . . . I've always wanted to paint my people just the way they are."[33]

Although Motley wanted to paint his people, he did not particularly want to associate with many of them, either in the United States or in France. As noted earlier, this was also the case with Prophet, as it was with Albert Alexander Smith, both of whom made disparaging remarks about the "race" and their disassociation from it. One wonders whether this lack of sustained interaction with other African Americans was in part a result of emotional distance caused by these artists' lighter skin (in the case of Motley and Smith). And yet, none of them ever had many friends; all valued their privacy and time alone or with loved ones, as do many artists of any background.

In 1922, African American artists, including Dawson and Farrow, who served as president, founded their own club, the Chicago Art League, and began to hold exhibitions at the Wabash Avenue YMCA. Five years later, the black Chicago Women's Club sponsored the event Negro in Art Week, which included an exhibition held both at the club and the AIC. Motley, however, only participated in Chicago Art League activities reluctantly and refused to show his work in the Negro in Art Week exhibition because "Negroes were putting out such poor work."[34] He was also disgruntled about their lack of support regarding his work. When he planned on submitting his images of contemporary black urban life *Syncopation, Mending Socks,* and *A Mulatress* (all 1924) at the AIC's 1925 annual exhibition, Farrow tried to discourage him.[35] Motley recalled, "So many colored artists discouraged me. My encouragement all came from white people."[36] Some of his closest friends were white, former classmates Josef Tomanek (1889–?) and William S. Schwartz (1896–1977), who offered him moral support[37] and backed his choice of entries. The 1925 exhibition marked the first time an African American artist had shown African American subjects at the AIC, according to Motley.[38] The works also won him two awards[39] and favorable reviews in the French press, these by Chabrier, who had also praised Hayden's work.[40] In 1926, after *Syncopation* was exhibited by the Chicago No-Jury Society of Artists, which was founded in 1922 for artistic radicals whose works were rejected by the AIC, Motley was asked to be the society's director.[41] He was the organization's only African American member.

Robert B. Harshe (1879–1938), director of the AIC and "a second father" to Motley,[42] was pleased that one of his preferred students was prospering artistically. On a personal trip to New York in 1927, he contacted two galleries about sponsoring Motley; both responded favorably. In early 1928, Motley exhibited twenty-six paintings, ten portraits, three works related to black music and dance, eight genre scenes, and five fanciful African scenes, painted at the suggestion of the gallery director, at the New Gallery for two weeks.[43] The exhibition was a commercial and critical success; twenty-two paintings sold and the *New York Times* favorably reviewed the show.

In the wake of the exhibition, Motley had a chance to network with other African American artists; Bessie Bearden, the New York correspondent for the *Chicago Defender* newspaper and mother of artist Romare Bearden, planned an elaborate black-tie event in his honor and invited sculptor Augusta Savage, painters Aaron Douglas, O. Richard Reid, Richard Bruce (Nugent), and Charles Alston. According to Edward Morrow, an adopted nephew of Bearden, Motley did not attend the gathering because he did not have the proper clothing.[44] However, Motley may have been apprehensive about the artists' reception of him, thinking they would not or did not appreciate his work. He felt that his exhibition "was very daring. I had the guts and the ambition to carry it through. So many colored artists discouraged me. . . . Now you take the average Negro, if they'd get out of that way of think-ing that 'Oh, I can't send that [paintings with black subject matter] in there because the white folks they're not going to have that . . .' They told me that when I was younger, when I sent in paintings like *Mending Socks.* . . . White artists, friends of mine, disagreed with them entirely." Motley had spent several hours every day in the gallery gauging people's reactions. Few African Americans visited the exhibition and none acknowledged the artist: "I didn't know them, they didn't know me. I didn't say anything to them, they didn't say anything to me."[45]

Further, Motley had heard rumors that the New York artists were jealous that it took an artist from Chicago to have a solo show in New York: "That group of New York artists, they're as jealous of me as they can be. . . . They've hated me ever since."[46] Motley was also embittered at the reaction of some of Chicago's wealthiest African Americans to whom Harshe had written letters asking for their support, without Motley's knowledge. Harshe reluctantly showed Motley the insulting responses from five men who thought that the white AIC director should "mind his own business."[47]

If Motley met with any African American artists or viewed any of their work in New York, he did not seem to esteem them or it. Later in life he stated unequivocally, "There was no Renaissance. . . . I think it was quite an advancement over the work that they had been putting out. . . . But the work did not reflect a Renaissance."[48] Motley was most disturbed by what he viewed as an overdependence by African American artists on the late nineteenth-century French tradition of painting:

> There exists entirely too much imitation and nor enough originality. . . . Our artists are entirely too much interested in and influenced by the modern school of French painting. In practically all exhibitions of our group, I have "seen" Renoir, Matisse, Corot, and many other Frenchmen imitated and poorly copied. Occasionally, I noticed here and there a futile attempt at the portrayal or depiction of our vibrant and rapidly progressing Negro Race. And this field is such as broad one, such an extremely interesting and important part of our American civilization. What a pity so many of our artists go in for pretty landscapes and pictures which have no bearing whatsoever on our group. The Negro poet portrays our group in poems, the Negro musician portrays our group in jazz, the Negro actor portrays our group generally with a touch of hilarity, comedy dancing and song. And now he is grasping for and is succeeding with that which is more serious in the theatre; the drama. All of these aforementioned portrayals are serious, original interpretations of the Negro. There is nothing borrowed, nothing copied, just an unraveling of the Negro soul. So why should the Negro painter, the Negro sculptor mimic that which the white man is doing, when he has such an enormous colossal field practically all his own; portraying his people, historically, dramatically, hilariously, but honestly. And who knows the Negro Race, the Negro Soul, the Negro Heart, better than himself?[49]

Although Motley befriended no African American artists in New York, he did forge a warm relationship with Mexican artist Miguel Covarrubias (1904–1957), whom he met at the New Gallery. After lunch, the two visited Covarrubias's solo exhibition at the Valentine Gallery, where he exhibited works depicting African, Caribbean, and Harlem subjects similar to those of musical entertainers in his book *Negro Drawings* (1927). Although the works bordered on caricature, Motley admired Covarubbias's daring, vibrant images.[50]

After seeing New York, Motley visited relatives in Pine Bluff, Arkansas, from the summer of 1928 to the late winter of 1929. When he returned to Chicago, he was sick with malaria and his family helped nurse him back to health.[51]

It is not known exactly how or when Motley learned about the John Simon Guggenheim Memorial Foundation or why he decided to apply to work in France. He may have been encouraged by favorable reviews he received in the French press, as mentioned above. Among those who sent Motley clippings of these articles was Du Bois, who also publicized Motley's achievements several times in the *Crisis*[52] and listed him as a credit in the "credit and debit" section of his column, "Opinion of W.E.B. Du Bois" in January 1926. He, along with Harmon administrators, may have prompted Motley to search for funding to cover the costs of going overseas.

The fellowships offered by the Guggenheim Foundation, established in 1925, were among the few given to African American artists in the 1920s. The awards were founded by

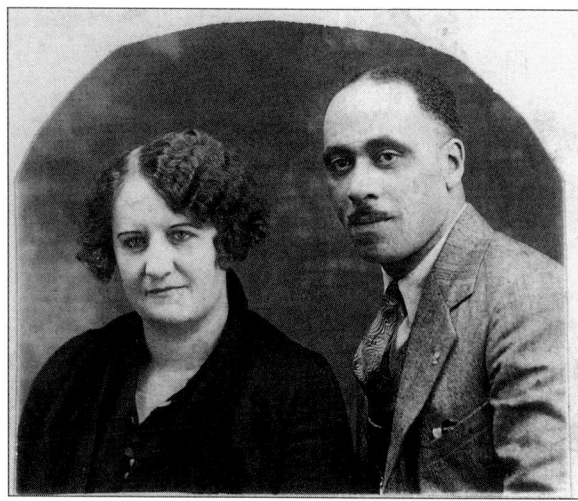

FIGURE 66
Edith and Archibald J. Motley Jr., 1929,
passport photograph.
Collection of Archie Motley and Valerie
Gerrard Browne. Courtesy of Chicago
Historical Society.

United States Senator and Mrs. Simon Guggenheim in memory of their son, who died in
April 1922, just as he had completed his preparation for college. The purpose of the foundation was to "promote the advancement and diffusion of knowledge and understanding, and
the appreciation of beauty, by aiding without distinction on account of race, color or creed,
scholars, scientists and artists of either sex in the prosecution of their labors."[53]

In his application to the Guggenheim Foundation, Motley stated that his primary
goal was to further develop his technique. He explained that he would "specialize in the
study of masterpieces in the Louvre, as to color composition, drawing and technique, laying
most stress on a serious study of the relationship of cold and warm light." Yet Motley was not
only interested in formal issues; he was also concerned with applying European techniques to
depictions of Negroes. He wrote,

> I would visit the Louvre every morning and do creative painting afternoons, or vice
> versa. I would paint compositions and genre-pictures, paintings depicting the various
> phases of Negro life. I would like to paint about twenty or thirty pictures . . . where
> the play of cool and warm light would be an important factor. To me it seems that
> pictures portraying the suffering, sorrow, and at times the childlike abandon of the
> Negro; the dance, the song, the hilarious moments when a bit of jazz predominates,
> would do much to bring about better relations, a better understanding between the
> races, white and colored.[54]

One wonders why Motley thought that scenes of "the childlike abandon" and "hilarious
moments"—he mentioned hilarity twice in "The Negro in Art"—of African American life
would bring about better race relations. Did he truly believe that such images would produce
a light-hearted response in all, or was he consciously playing into reassuring white stereotypes? As a fair-skinned man, did he not view himself as entirely "Negro?" At any rate, no
doubt Motley's goal of increased racial harmony appealed to the foundation's jurors. He was
awarded the fellowship in the spring of 1929. On July 18, 1929, Motley and his wife (fig.
66) left the New York Harbor on the steamer *Rochambeau* for France.[55]

In Paris, Motley's ambition to paint his people would lead him to switch from portraits of black family members, beautiful women, and southerners to those of persons from the broader African diaspora and to group genre scenes of Parisian urban life.

PAINTING NIGHTCLUBS AND CAFÉS IN PARIS, 1929

During their first two months abroad, the Motleys lived at the Hôtel Istria, at 29, rue Campagne-Première, in Montparnasse. Josephine Baker and Sidney Bechet had stayed at the same hotel on their first night in Paris when they were part of La Revue Nègre in 1925.[56] The small street was located in a prime area, connecting both the Boulevard du Montparnasse and the boulevard Raspail in the fourteenth arrondissement. Numerous artists had maintained studios on the rue Campagne-Première, including Sonia Delaunay, who settled there in 1906.[57] Motley had a distinct advantage over many white American artists and the other African American artists overseas in that he was already comfortable with the French language, having spoken a Creole version—"a mixture of poor Spanish, poor French and poor English"[58]—learned from his parents and grandparents at home. He understood most of what he heard; still, "you know, they talk so fast."[59] Unlike many artists in Paris, however, Motley chose not to take any art classes or receive any criticism. Buehr had told him not to study with anyone or to change his style[60] and Motley believed "I could do it much better my own way."[61]

Like most tourists, the Motleys became acquainted with Paris through sightseeing. They visited the Louvre, where Motley admired Rubens, Michelangelo, Rembrandt, Delacroix, and Hals;[62] the Musée Cluny; and many Parisian galleries.[63] One tourist site, the observatory built by Louis XIV, was just a few blocks from their hotel. One day while the couple was walking toward it, they passed two young white American boys sitting on a bench. Motley recalled:

> Just as we passed them, we were about ten feet away, one of them said, "Hey, you goddamned black nigger!" Oh, my blood just boiled. In France, too. Here I wouldn't have paid much attention to it. But in France. . . . You know, they had the idea that they could go over to Paris and carry all that shit over there that they couldn't carry on here. . . . I went back to where they were sitting. . . . When I was younger I was pretty husky and I put up a battle. When they said that I went back to where they were sitting and I said: I just want one of you to repeat what you said. Now I'm going to come back here and I'm going to beat the hell out of both of you, just say it once more. They looked at me, they looked like they were scared to death. And I would have fought it. It may have caused a little trouble. But they had no business calling me names like that. I wasn't bothering them. I was walking down the street with my wife.[64]

While unsettling, this was apparently the only racist incident the Motleys experienced during their year abroad; they found that the French treated them "so much better" than Americans did.[65] For the most part, in France the couple kept to themselves and, as was their wont in the United States, socialized with few people.[66] That feeling of isolation, self-imposed or not,

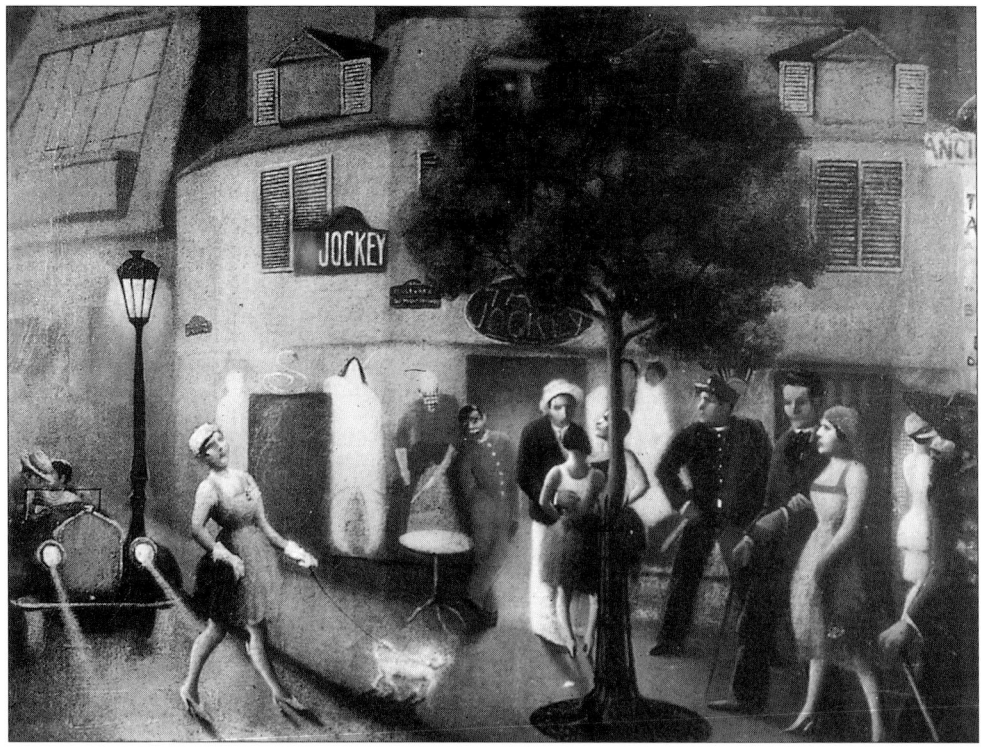

FIGURE 67
Archibald J. Motley Jr., *The Jockey Club*, 1929, oil on canvas, 26 x 32 in.
Art and Artifacts Division, Schomburg Center for Research in Black Culture, The New York Public Library,
Astor, Lenox, and Tilden Foundations

is present in the first few works Motley produced abroad, two of which depict outdoor scenes
and two indoor. These four works, painted in the fall of 1929, are genre scenes of Parisian
cafés and nightclubs and are filled with people from all walks of life.

Motley's first painting in Paris, *The Jockey Club* (fig. 67), depicts a place just a few
doors away from the Hôtel Istria at 146, boulevard du Montparnasse, the corner of the rue
Campagne-Première, the Jockey Club (later reestablished at no. 127). Started as Le
Caméléon by Alexandre Mercereau, the nightclub was taken over by an ex-jockey, Miller
(first name unknown), and the American painter Hilaire Hiler, who, as noted earlier, would
befriend Woodruff in Cagnes-sur-Mer in 1930, in November 1923. The new owners did
little to change the dingy interior, but Hiler decorated the place with posters and painted
figures of Mexicans, cowboys, and Native Americans on the exterior. Le Jockey quickly
became a magnet for artists where the flamboyant model Kiki performed her risqué songs
and dances until 1930, when the club ceased to exist.[67] Hemingway later described the club
nostalgically as "the best night-club that ever was."[68]

In contrast to the crowded interiors of night spots in his early Chicago cabaret
scenes, Motley depicts the Jockey Club from the exterior. In *The Jockey Club*, Motley shows

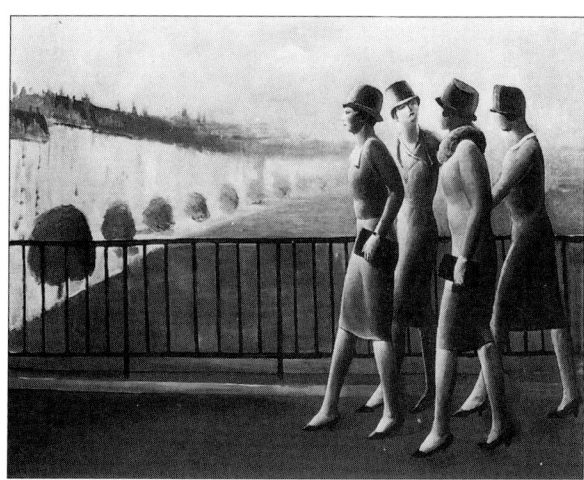

FIGURE 68
Guy Pène du Bois, *Americans in Paris,*
1927, oil on canvas, 28¾ x 36⅛ in.
The Museum of Modern Art, New York.
Anonymous gift. Photograph © 1999
The Museum of Modern Art.

twelve people mingling near the entrance to the cabaret, about half of whom anticipate the entertainment inside. On the left, beneath the stars and the soft glow of a lamppost, a couple neck in a convertible. The car's headlights illuminate the path of a strutting, young Frenchwoman in a short green dress who walks her white poodle toward a tall tree that bisects the composition just to the right of the club's entrance. The yellow glow of starlight, streetlights, car headlights, and the neon nightclub sign, coupled with the soft shades of blue and rose, elicit an ambience of romance and excitement. It is obvious that Motley launched immediately into his study of "cool and warm light," as evidenced here by the interplay of artificial and natural light. On the right, two young women, a man in a straw hat, a fashion-ably dressed couple, and a bearded man carrying a cane approach the front door. With their stiff, doll-like bodies, they formally recall the women in a painting by the white artist Guy Pène du Bois, *Americans in Paris* (1927, fig. 68),[69] and mark Motley's stylistic change from more painterly facture.

Flanking the entrance of the Jockey Club in Motley's painting are a gendarme on the right and a black, grinning doorman wearing a bright red, tight-fitting, brass-buttoned suit on the left. He leans against the door frame, right hand in pocket and left leg crossed in front of the right, peering at the incoming patrons. Although the doorman is framed by the glowing light from within and occupies the center of the composition, he is part of neither world, standing half inside the club and half outside. His placement at a nightclub largely populated by white Americans suggests the isolation and marginalization not only of black people within Paris, but also of African Americans within the United States. Further American references include Hiler's paintings of cowboys and Native Americans on the building's walls, which Motley has faithfully reproduced.

Motley's following three works avoided all references to American life. In compar-ison to the bustling nightlife in *Jockey Club, Café, Paris* (fig. 69) portrays a dull, gray Parisian afternoon. Here, Motley depicts a dark, crowded space where four patrons stand and smoke near the bar, the balding proprietor on the left, and two men sit and drink at a small table in the lower right. A series of interlocking, repeating rectangles shaped by the windowpanes, the

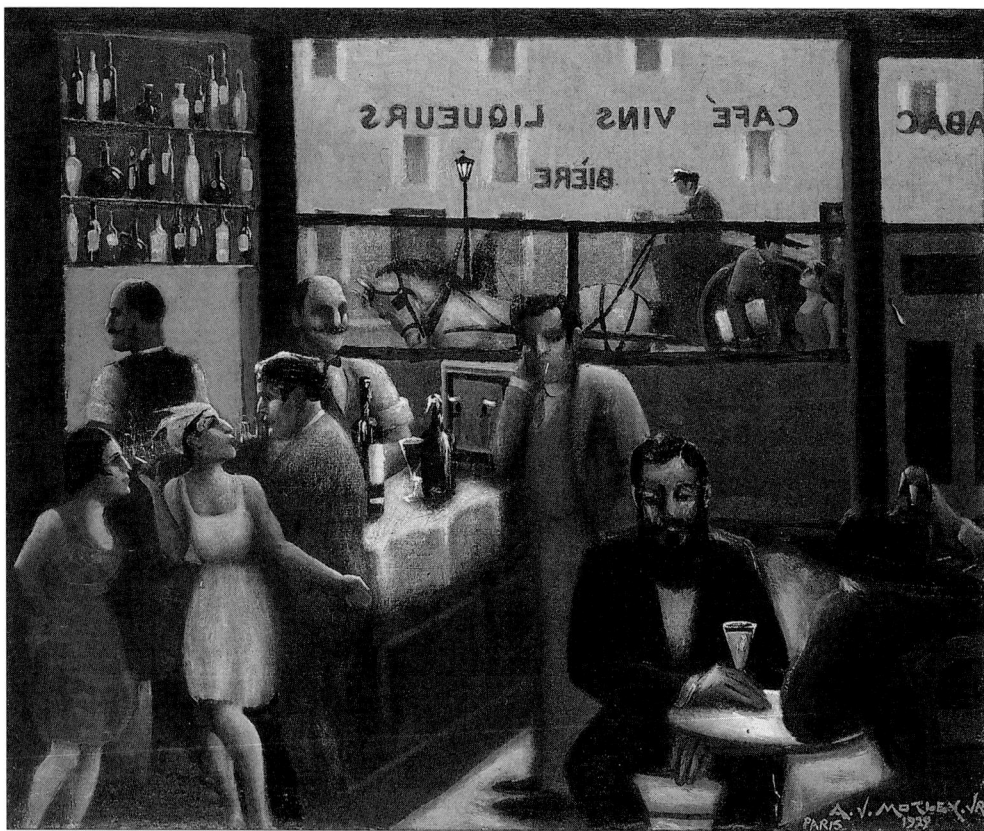

FIGURE 69
Archibald J. Motley Jr., *Café, Paris,* 1929, oil on canvas, 23⅝ x 28⅞ in.
Collection of Archie Motley and Valerie Gerrard Browne. Courtesy of Chicago Historical Society.

door design, the exterior wall of the café, the mirror behind the bar, and the shelves of liquor above it form the structure of the composition.

While there are pairs of people in *Café, Paris*—the couple outside, the two drinking men, and two young women in the lower left—all the patrons seem strangely alone and either melancholic or expressionless. Inside, no one looks at anyone else; all seem to stare blankly at a wall or down at the floor. It is as if everyone and everything is frozen in time, the characters incapable of registering reactions. The mirror behind the proprietor is even devoid of reflections. In fact, the entire work looks more like a still life composition than a genre scene. The cool palette of gray, blue, black, and brown with patches of subdued red under-scores the melancholic environment, just as the anonymous title suggests that this could be any small café anywhere in Paris frequented by native French folk rather than foreigners. The mood echoes that of some of the café scenes by Manet that Motley would have seen at the Louvre.

A similar still atmosphere is present in *Dans la rue, Paris* (fig. 70). Here, despite representing the teeming activity of an urban, outdoor scene of daily life, there are no

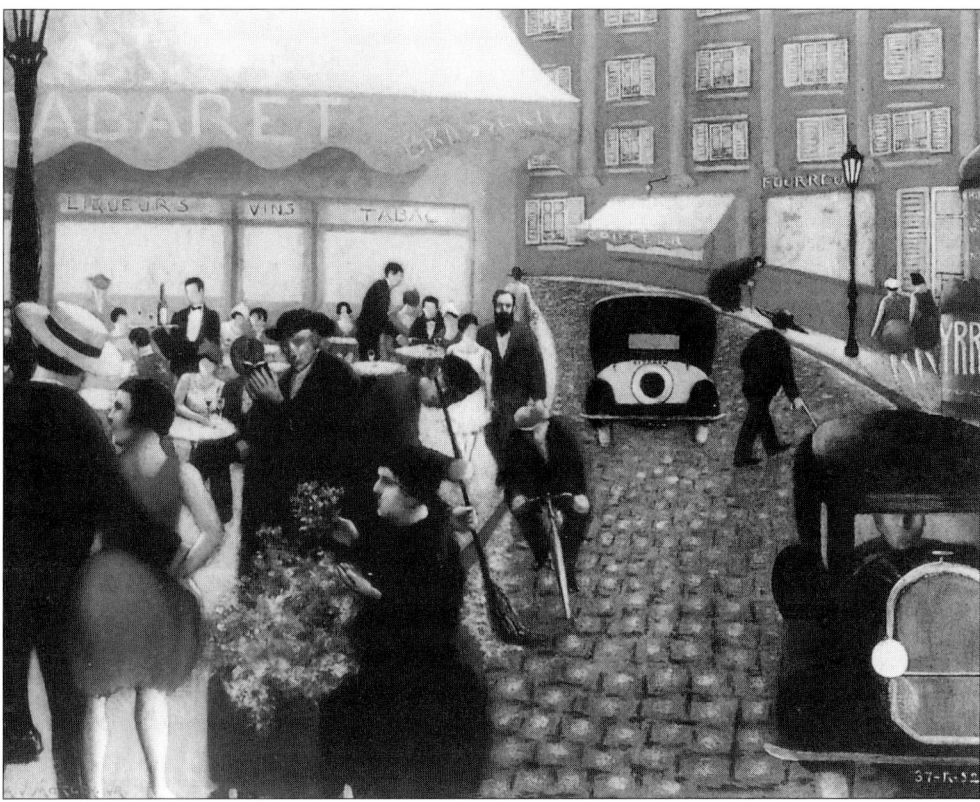

FIGURE 70
Archibald J. Motley Jr., *Dans la rue,* Paris, 1929, oil on canvas, 23¾ x 28½ in.
Art and Artifacts Division, Schomburg Center for Research in Black Culture, The New York Public Library,
Astor, Lenox, and Tilden Foundations.

shadows and few indications of motion. Like *Café, Paris,* too, this composition is divided in
half; but the palette is much lighter. On the left, pedestrians crowd a wide sidewalk in front
of an outdoor café, with a bold pink-trimmed awning bearing in yellow capital letters the
words "Cabaret, Brasserie," where two uniformed waiters serve patrons. On the right, a
bicyclist and a car approach the viewer down a steeply curving cobblestoned street. Behind
them, a man with a cane walks across the street in front of a black-and-yellow Citröen. Above
the man on the far sidewalk stoops a woman with her cane, while two young women walk
toward her past a kiosk. With their white hose and plain, sleeveless dresses, they could be the
same women in *Café, Paris.* They may be going to the *fourreur* (furrier) or the *coiffeur* (hair-
dresser) up the street. As in *Café, Paris,* the faces on all of the twenty-nine figures in *Dans
la rue, Paris* are expressionless or sometimes even lack facial features. Nonetheless, their
humanity is apparent in their actions.

As art historian Wendy Greenhouse has noted, Motley has balanced and paired their
ages and pursuits: the elderly man with the cane paired with the bicyclist who has just swerved
past him, a man bending over the street to sweep in front of the cyclist matched with a plump,

black-clad flower seller in the foreground who offers a bouquet to a pair of lovers in the lower left, and the walking lovers juxtaposed with a cleric absorbed in a prayer book. Motley enjoyed the implied narrative in such scenes filled with a cross-section of humanity. He said, "I think every picture should tell a story and I think if a picture doesn't tell a story then it's not a picture."[70] The story these images might tell us is the interest Motley had in French culture in his first few months in Paris, but also his sense of isolation and loneliness.

While the palette is brighter than that in *Café, Paris,* a cool blue-gray-and-black color scheme dominates, accentuated by flashes of bright yellow, red, and pink. A much stronger sense of pattern and texture is evident here, too, from the smooth, white tarp of the café awning to the coarse dense foliage in the flower-seller's cart, to the rough, bumpy surface of the cobblestoned street, to the rows of white-shuttered windows on the blue building across the street. One of Motley's earliest street scenes, *Dans la rue, Paris,* marked the beginning of a long series of street series he painted in Bronzeville (Chicago) in the two decades that followed.

Although Motley painted bustling cafés and nightclubs, he and his wife did not frequent the famous gathering places of white Americans such as the Jockey Club and the Dôme Café. Instead, they preferred the relatively quiet Kosmos Café next door to La Rotonde on the boulevard du Montparnasse and a small café almost on the outskirts of Paris in the sixteenth arrondissement. Motley remembered the latter place as the "Petite Café" (a name that has not been confirmed), located not far from the Bois de Boulogne or the Eiffel Tower. The café owner encouraged the artist to come every night, so Motley often sketched the clientele there while sipping a beer or a glass of wine. He may have recalled the success he had at the New Gallery, based in part on the director's suggestion that he "paint some pictures showing various phases of negro life in its more dramatic aspects—scenes, perhaps, in which the voo-doo element as well as the cabaret element—but especially the latter—enter."[71] From one of his sketches at the Petite Café came the basis of *Blues,* Motley's best-known work.

Blues (fig. 71) depicts a close-up scene of a "Black and Tan" nightclub packed with people from all over the African diaspora. Motley explained: "The idea is that there are no Americans in that painting, black or white. They are all either French, some of the dark ones are Senegalese from Senegal, some of the lighter ones come from Martinique or North Africa. But there are no white Americans. And they [American viewers] think that the black people there are Americans, but they're not."[72] Motley enjoyed the clientele at this cabaret exactly because they were not Americans. He explained, "I loved Paris, yes. It's a different atmosphere, different attitudes, different people. They act differently; they don't act like Americans."[73] Motley's interest in the variety of black skin tones is evident on faces ranging in shades from caramel to burnt sienna to mahogany. "Form is essential to me," Motley wrote, "only as a means of producing a pleasing composition; color being more important as an expression of the numerous shades and colors which exist in such great variety among Negroes."[74] Such diversity among people of different nationalities is united here in Motley's masterpiece by a common appreciation of American jazz. Motley had stated that one of his artistic goals was to inspire African Americans to appreciate their African heritage; however,

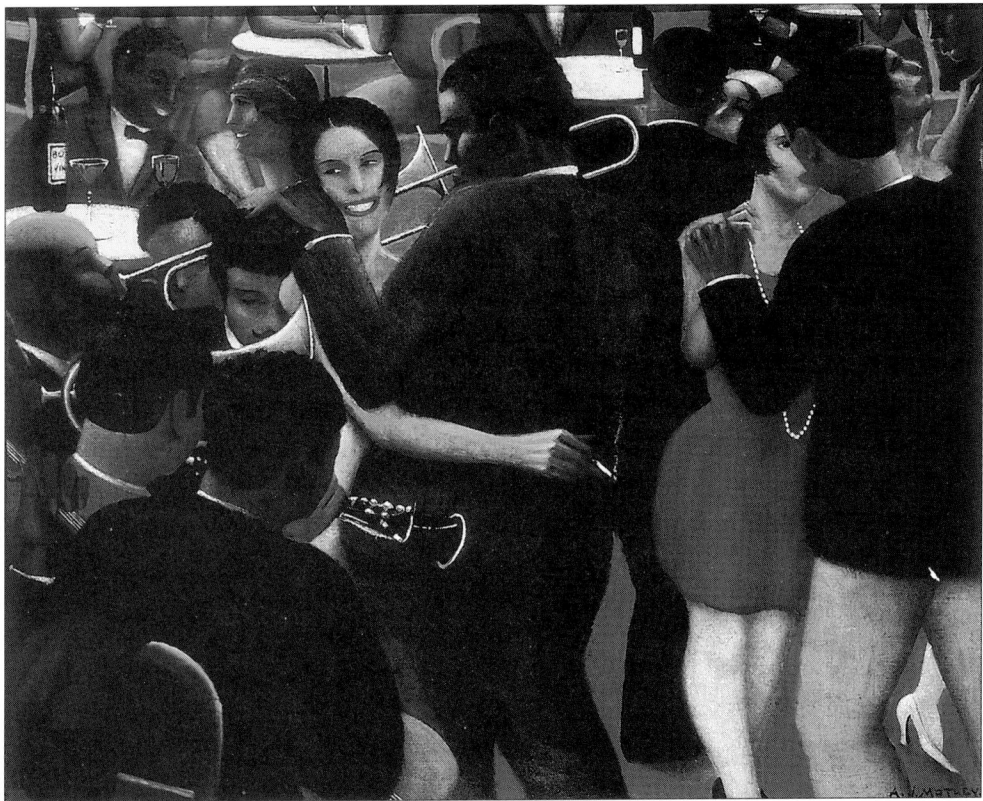

FIGURE 71
Archibald J. Motley Jr., *Blues,* 1929, oil on canvas, 36 x 42 in.
Collection of Archie Motley and Valerie Gerrard Browne. Courtesy of Chicago Historical Society.

as Jontyle Theresa Robinson points out, in Paris he ironically "found Africans [and others from the African diaspora] embracing American culture through its jazz and blues."[75]

The Petite Café was a fashionable nightclub for West Africans and West Indians who relished the rhythms of American jazz. In *Blues,* they almost become part of the music as couples sway into the embrace of a trombone, trumpet, and clarinet on the left. Dancers, seated onlookers, and musicians are crowded up against the picture plane so forcefully that they appear as an abstract pattern of flat, colored shapes and syncopated cadences. Rounded pairs of heads echo each other, from the back profiles of the clarinetist and guitarist in the lower left to the trombonist and onlooker just above them to the laughing couple behind and on across the composition to the right in four dancing couples. As art historian Richard Powell points out, these rhythms are not strictly symmetrical, but interrupted and fragmented, "almost to the point of evoking a quilt or, to a lesser extent, a synthetic cubist painting."[76] Powell likens the interruptions and reintroductions of Motley's compositional elements to the riffs and stop-time of a fellow New Orleans–born Chicagoan, jazz legend Louis Armstrong. Both artists created rhythmic intrigue through subtle beat accentuation and suspension against a fairly structured format, whether musical or visual.[77] *Blues* is an excellent example of Powell's theory of the blues aesthetic. He asserts that the blues aesthetic is defined by work produced by twentieth-century artists empathic with African American issues and ideals; who identify with popular or mass black American culture; who have an affinity with Afro-American derived music, rhythms, or both; and whose *raison d'être* is humanistic.[78] Further examples of the blues aesthetic would be Hayden's *Bal jeunesse* and *Nous quatre à Paris*.

The easy smiles of the patrons, the warm palette of primary colors in a sea of dark-jacketed men, and the casually cropped bodies and heads in *Blues* all contribute to atmosphere of spontaneity and lightheartedness. Here, Motley achieved his Guggenheim-application goal of depicting scenes of "the dance, the song, the hilarious moments when a bit of jazz predominates."[79] The artist himself, however, had few days of hilarity in Paris.

THE BLUES AND SHARKS: NOVEMBER 1929–MARCH 1930

Around October, 1929 Motley moved to 16, rue Simon Dereure in Montmartre, off of the horseshoe-shaped avenue Junot several blocks southeast of where Albert Alexander Smith, whom he never met, was living and several blocks northwest of Sacré-Coeur. He had found out about the newly constructed studio building along with Benjamin Greenstein (b. 1901), an American Jewish artist of Russian origin whom he had befriended. The building was one in three rows surrounded by a well-tended grassy area decorated with sculpture.[80] Greenstein settled in on the first floor, and Motley's place was on the second. His living quarters comprised a bedroom, kitchen, and bathroom, adjoined to a fifteen-by-nineteen-foot studio (Atelier 48), all with high ceilings.[81]

The move from Montparnasse and the Left Bank to Montmartre and the Right Bank was a significant one for Motley because it further isolated him from almost all of the other African American artists in Paris at the time, these being Hayden, Woodruff, Savage, and Prophet (who was in the United States from October 1929 to September 1930). Once, Hayden and Woodruff spotted Motley while eating dinner on a terrace in Montparnasse. When he walked into the restaurant and sat down, the two whispered to each other that they thought they knew who he was; they must have heard that Motley had won the Harmon gold medal in 1928 and had been on his way to Paris. Woodruff casually got up and walked past Motley, whose passport was lying open on the table. He came back to report that it was indeed Motley, but neither he nor Hayden made the effort to introduce themselves to him, for unknown reasons, and they never became acquainted. This hardly bothered Motley, who explained, "I think when you go to a foreign country, you don't go there to see Americans." He did not even make an effort to meet Tanner. It was not only African American artists whom Motley would have missed in Montmartre, however, but most artists. Ever since Picasso's move from the boulevard de Clichy to the boulevard Raspail, few serious artists visited the Butte, as Montmartre was known familiarly; almost all settled in Montparnasse. In fact, it was in Montparnasse that Motley bought all of his art supplies.[82] By November 6, 1929, Motley was further isolated in Paris because his wife had to return to the United States for treatment for an unknown illness.[83]

The following five months alone were very difficult for Motley. In his diary, which he began on January 1, 1930, he often mentions how much he missed his wife and cared about her: "I love her and I need her so damn bad" (January 12, 1930). Other entries are brief, but poignant outpourings of his loneliness, such as "A very blue day for me" (January 2, 1930), "Very tired and disappointed, no mail and no one to tell my troubles to. . . . Very lonely. Grey skies as usual in Paris" (January 4, 1930), and "Worked very hard to-day but had the 'blues,' terribly bad all day. A very lonely day, although the sun was shining. . . . It is hard to be alone a long ways from home" (January 26, 1930). Motley rarely ventured outside of his apartment, except to attend mass at Saint Joseph's,[84] pick up mail at the American Express office, and buy groceries, art supplies, and American newspapers, the *New York Herald* and the *New York Tribune*.[85] Although he had befriended Greenstein, he rarely socialized with him and did not attend his New Year's Eve party downstairs.[86] While Edith was away, it seems, Motley did not even visit any museums or galleries.

Perhaps Edith's presence in the United States prompted Motley to think more of his native country than before and "work like hell."[87] At any rate, in the late fall, he moved from painting scenes of Parisian life to depicting African American genre scenes, such as *Sharks (Playing Poker)* (finished in late fall, 1929) and four paintings in 1930, *Veterans* (finished January 15), *Spirituals* (painted January 21–February 16), *The Flight* (produced February 17–March 21), and *Refugees* (executed March 27–April 17). Unfortunately, there are no reproductions of these works (save possibly *Sharks*) and only very scant written documentation about them survives. In his diary, Motley noted when he worked on the compositions and when he finished them, but made few comments other than a few self-congratulatory remarks on paintings, such the following regarding *Veterans:* "Coming fine, want to finish it by Jan. 17th" (January 3, 1930), "Painted all day on painting called Veterans. Very interesting composition" (January 5, 1930), and "a very good picture I think" (January 15, 1930).

Motley never wrote about the artistic or intellectual movements in Paris. Instead, his brief diary entries describe his work schedule, the weather, his eating habits, and the names of the few places he frequented.[88] Typically, he stayed inside his apartment most of the time and worked with live models in the morning on sunny days for several hours without pausing or speaking.[89] In the afternoon, he worked on what he called "compositions." He recalled: "Composition was the thing I was more interested in than anything else because I felt that I could build up more paintings in composition and more salable things than I could with portraits and nudes. And I felt it was quite a trying thing."[90] One such composition, or genre scene, is *Sharks (Playing Poker)*.

In Porter's *Modern Negro Art* (1943), there is a reproduction of a work called *Playing Poker,* dated 1933, which may be *Sharks (Playing Poker)* mislabeled and misdated. Even if this is not the case, the similar title and theme may help us understand how Motley approached this subject. Here, ten men appear in constricted quarters. Just as in Hayden's *Nous quatre à Paris*—which Motley probably never saw, since he did not meet Hayden and it was not exhibited either in Paris or at the Harmon Foundation—four cardplayers dressed in suits and ties sit around the table, looking in opposite directions. The men at the left and rear exchange glances, as ostensibly do the man seated in front with his back to the viewer and the player at right. As in *Dans la rue, Paris,* Motley has given further pairings, instances of interaction, and balances, such as the cigarette-smoking cardplayer at right with the cigar smoker in the lower right, whose profile looking to the right balances that of the ubiquitous rotund, bald man looking to the left in the upper right, and the man whispering to another in the upper left, whose eyes shift to his right, as do the rear and right players.[91] A six-sided or octagonal lampshade (three side panels are visible), an empty frame, and an open door, all light-colored and without any decoration, dominate the upper portion of the composition. Further, Motley's setting is unspecified, in contrast to Hayden's Parisian references of the cup of café creme, the glass of wine, and the French title written across the back of the chair in the foreground. Further, unlike Hayden's portrayal of caricatured figures, Motley's depiction of realistic, absorbed cardplayers lacks humor. While Motley celebrated gaiety in such scenes as *Blues,* he eschewed any images that might have been viewed as cheap sight gags. In an essay called "How I Solve My Painting Problems," he wrote:

> For years many artists have depicted the Negro as the ignorant southern "darky," to be portrayed on canvas as something humorous; an old southern black Negro gulping a large piece of watermelon; one with a banjo on his knee; possibly a "crap-shooter" or a cottonpicker or a chicken thief. This material is obsolete and I sincerely hope with the progress the Negro has made he is deserving to be repre- sented in his true perspective, with dignity, honesty, integrity, intelligence and understanding. Progress is not made by going backward. The Negro is no more the lazy, happy go lucky, shiftless person he was shortly after the Civil War. Progress has changed all of this. In my paintings I have tried to paint the Negro as I have seen him and as I feel him, in myself without adding or detracting, just frankly being honest.[92]

Rather than Hayden's happy-go-lucky "darkies" just out to have a good time—as under- scored by the presence of alcohol and the absence of money or gaming chips—Motley has given us a more more naturalistic image of card sharks, swindlers who work by fraud, tricks, and strategems.

PORTRAIT TYPES FROM THE AFRICAN DIASPORA: JANUARY–MAY 1930

During the first few months of 1930, Motley produced three portraits of persons of African descent, two Martinicans and one Senegalese. Reproductions of the Martinicans apparently do not exist, and what little is known of the works comes solely from his diary. Apparently, the model for the first work, *Martinique Dancer,* was not a native of that island, but rather Miss Zaida, who was "a very pretty Haitian girl," as Motley noted in his diary (January 5, 1930), and who posed in a "Martinique costume." (How Motley found his models is a mystery.) Within a few days after he began the work in late January 1930, he noted, he was pleased with his progress and Zaida's "very interesting pose" (January 29 and 30, 1930).

At the same time that Motley painted *Martinique Dancer,* he worked mornings on *Martinique Youth,* another portrait of a Haitian, and finished the piece in three weeks

(January 18–February 9). A Mr. Garcia usually arrived at 8:00 or 9:00 a.m. to pose, but did not appear one day because of dull weather: "A very dark & dreary day," wrote Motley. "Waited anxiously for model. Wasted entire morning as he did not come. He thought the day was too dark for painting" (January 25, 1930). Nothing else is known about this work except that Locke counted it among Motley's best. "From Paris," he wrote, "some of his technically best compositions have come, among them, portrait study types like 'The Young Martiniquan.'"[93]

It is not clear why Motley chose to depict Haitians as Martinicans. One possibility may be that since Haiti was an independent nation and Martinique was a French colony, Motley, with his Creole heritage, may have felt more of an affinity with persons he associated more directly with French culture. Yet there were certainly Martinican and other black French models available in Paris, such as Julie Luce, a longtime resident of Montmartre who had come to Paris in 1902 to make a living as an actress.[94] She worked for Jules Pascin as a model, sometimes wearing his short silk shirts and long black stockings. Her daughter, Simone Luce (b. 1910), studied ballet, but because of her color was not accepted to the Opéra corps de ballet. Instead, she appeared throughout Europe as a music-hall performer. Both mother and daughter frequently socialized with Pascin, Kiki, and other well-known Montparnasse residents. Aicha was another renowned black model in Paris. Originally from the north of France, she joined the circus as a bareback rider at the age of six. At sixteen, she met Pascin and moved to Montparnasse. There, she associated with numerous celebrities, many of whom attended her banquet at La Coupole on October 2, 1929. Featured on the August 15, 1930, cover of the magazine *Paris-Montparnasse* in the turban she often wore, her exotic appeal is evident. Kiki proclaimed her "the splendid creole, a model much in demand." Certainly, the Luces and Aicha could command fees higher than those of most models—Pascin paid Julie forty francs—and it is unlikely that the shy Motley would have ever ventured to speak with these remarkable women, but there must have been other Martinican models who could have given his paintings more authenticity. Yet Motley stated that he did not actively seek out black models, because "there were not many of them. But those I found I painted."[95]

Senegalese, a portrait of a young man in European clothing, was supposed to be based initially on an actual Senegalese model, Mr. Diara, whom Motley described as "a very black fellow. A good type."[96] When the model could not pose in late February because of illness, Motley postponed the project until May. It seems that he then resumed the painting with a new model, Mr. Maurice, whose ethnic identity is unknown, but who was also "a very dark fellow," but a "poor fellow," too.[97] Motley seemed to be interested in the model's welfare; he paid him thirty francs, an apparently more than reasonable sum.[98] Because the work now belongs to a private collector who will not allow many scholars to view it or reproductions to be made of it, discussion of the piece must be limited to secondhand accounts. Apparently, in the portrait, the stark whiteness of the shirt accentuates the rich dark skin tones of the model, so it seems that Motley has continued his study of light. As before, however, he was not concerned with the personality or ethnic heritage/s of his model/s. As his comment "a good type" indicates, Motley was only concerned with formal issues in this portrait. It is not known whether he was even aware of the role that the Senegalese had played in the French military or informed of their current condition in Paris.

PORTRAITS OF MOTLEY'S WIFE AND MOTHER

On March 1, 1930, Edith Motley finally returned to the warm embrace of her husband in Paris. Motley wrote about this period in his diary. He declared, "I am surely happy. Talked, drank and finally to bed and a hot time all night. Everything is rosy" (March 1, 1930). The following day, the two skipped church, "drank & loved all day" with the help of a bottle of champagne and three bottles of red wine (March 2, 1930). The following two weeks were a time of "no painting." Motley was "taking a good rest after working so very hard" (March 4, 1930), but he also was ill for several days with a headache, stomachache, and indigestion—some of which was caused, no doubt, by too much wine; he sometimes ended diary entries with "No Vin Rouge today" (March 9–11, 1930). In fact, Motley suffered from these ailments almost weekly and treated them with "physics," rest, and hot baths.[99] This must have affected his productivity; he had hoped to produce twenty to thirty works while abroad, but only finished fourteen canvases. By May, he had difficulty envisioning new genre scenes: "Sat around & tried to visualize a composition. Could not think of a damn thing."[100]

On March 15, Motley began a new portrait, painting his wife standing nude from the hips up, completed in two weeks. *Nude (Portrait of My Wife)* (fig. 72) is a very frank portrait in which Edith poses calmly against a plain, but warm, brown background. Arms at her sides, looking off into the distance, she makes no attempt to either cover or accentuate her plump torso and sagging breasts, illuminated by a raking light from the left. Her auburn hair is stylishly cropped in a bob, but left straight, while her eyebrows are plucked into thin lines and her lips are carefully painted red. Edith's face is masklike and virtually expressionless, but her body is rendered with an almost photographic realism. As Greenhouse points out, this attention to surface detail was common in early Renaissance portraiture, of which Motley saw many examples in the Louvre.[101] The work was later exhibited by the Chicago Woman's Club, in 1933.

In April, Motley produced another, more conventional portrait of his wife. In *Portrait of Mrs. A. J. Motley, Jr.* (fig. 73), Edith sits formally, Motley choosing the pose, on a dark blue damask-covered armchair in a shadowy room.[102] As before, her expression is reserved, but here she stares almost icily into the viewer's eyes. Her makeup is the same as in *Nude,* but her curled hair is mostly hidden by a snug, simple hat—this perhaps because of an unfortunate bleaching job.[103] She wears a black long-sleeved dress, trimmed with a pink collar and cuffs, and a narrow belt with a square jeweled buckle, and she holds a pair of red gloves in her right hand on her lap.[104] About her shoulders lies an auburn fox stole. On Edith's left hand, which rests on the chair's arm, are two rings, a simple wedding band and, on her small finger, a large, dark stone. The clothing, no doubt, was the result of the first of Edith's many shopping binges in Paris.[105]

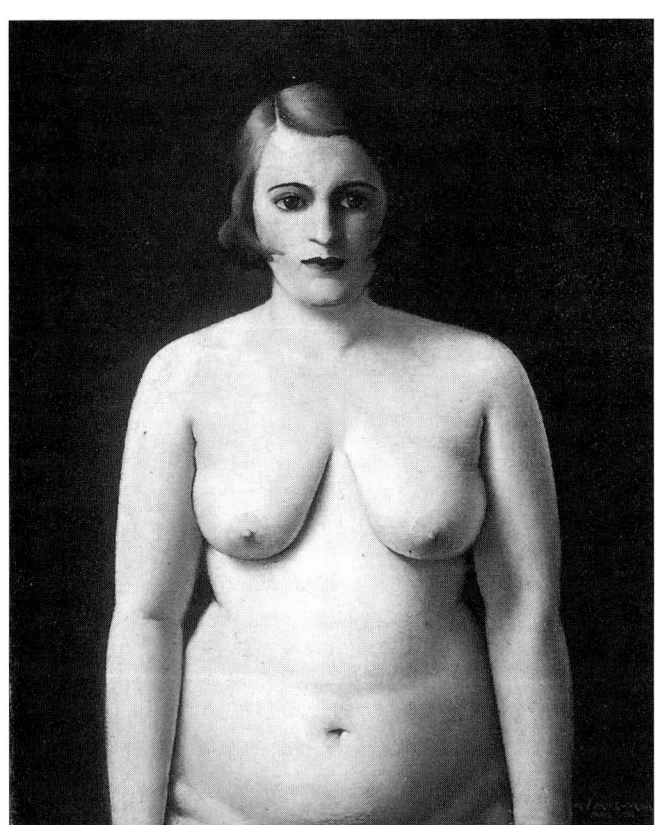

FIGURE 72
Archibald J. Motley Jr.,
Nude (Portrait of My Wife), 1930,
oil on canvas, 28¾ x 23½ in.
Collection of Archie Motley
and Valerie Gerrard Browne.
Courtesy of Chicago Historical
Society.

FIGURE 73
Archibald J. Motley Jr.,
Portrait of Mrs. A. J. Motley Jr.,
1930, oil on canvas, 39⅝ x 32 in.
Collection of Archie Motley
and Valerie Gerrard Browne.
Courtesy of Chicago Historical
Society.

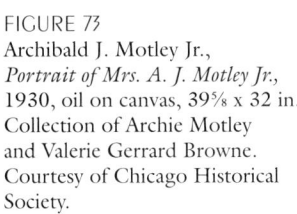

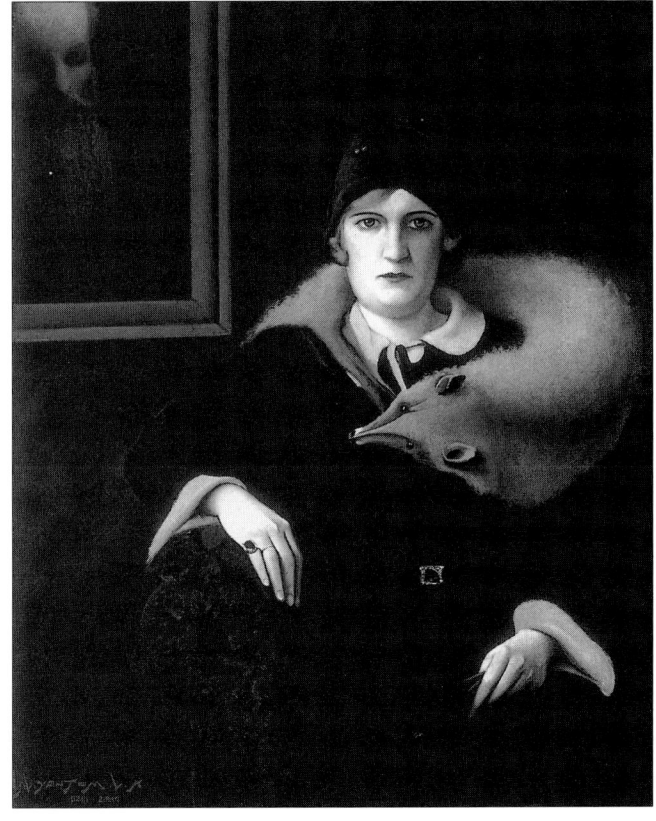

As Greenhouse suggests, this work may represent the type of conventional society portraiture through which Motley had hoped to make a living in the early 1920s.[106] With its dark tones, its somber mood, and even the dark gold-framed picture of a bearded, bald man in the upper right, *Portrait of Mrs. A. J. Motley, Jr.* recalls one of Motley's favorite portraits, *The Octoroon Girl* (1922). Edith may have found her almost forbidding look offensive, however; the work was never publicly exhibited during Motley's lifetime. Perhaps the two were already quarreling a bit then after their warm reunion; by the end of May, Motley wrote unhappily, "Edith shows her very nasty ways & and is quite disgusting. It seems she cannot control her temper which is a very sad thing."[107]

On April 25, Motley's mother arrived in Paris; she would live with him and his wife until they all departed France together three months later. The last work Motley produced abroad was *Portrait of My Mother* (location unknown; reproduced in the *Chicago Defender,* September 21, 1933, and in *The Art of Archibald J. Motley,* 20), about which nothing is known, other than that he completed the work in twenty days, finishing it on June 22, and later exhibited it with other work by "John Guggenheim Fellows" at the Grand Central Galleries in New York in 1931.[108] The three seemed to get along well and spent many hours shopping and playing cards together, rather than drinking in cafés, as did so many other artists.[109] Surprisingly, they did little sightseeing, but they did take walks on the avenue de Clichy and they all attended mass at Sacré-Coeur, from May 25 to July 13.

Realizing that his time abroad would be coming to an end soon, and perhaps finding an excuse to get away from his wife and mother for a few hours, Motley viewed art with Greenstein in June, at the Salon des Tuileries which was "very interesting"; at the Louvre, to see Delacroix; and at the George Petite Galleries, which had "some very good paintings".[110] While Motley was grateful for Greenstein's male companionship, he also found him annoyingly loquacious at times. One evening the painter "tried to talk the handle off a pot" (June 13, 1930) and another night he "talked & talked & talked" before leaving Motley's apartment at 12:30 a.m. (June 21, 1930).

During their last few weeks in France, the Motleys finally visited a few tourist sights, Versailles, Saint Germain, the Place de Tertre, and the Bois de Boulogne (June 30; July 4, 14, 16, 1930). They also saw *Faust* at the Opéra (July 12,1930) and a statue of Alexandre Dumas in the Parc Monceau, as well as his tomb in a Montmartre cemetery (July 3, 1930). Motley did not mention Dumas's identity as a black French writer in his diary, however, nor did he acknowledge in that volume any other evidence of black culture in Paris. In this sense, it was as if Motley hermetically sealed himself off from certain cultural issues while abroad.

Although Motley's work had already been favorably reviewed by the French critics who saw it at the AIC in 1925, it comes as no surprise that he chose not to submit any of his paintings to French establishments: he wanted to be known as an American artist and desired recognition in his own country. Upon his return, he would exhibit the works he had made in Paris at various small places in Chicago, such as the Olivet Baptist Church and Merchandise

Mart (1931), Women's Club, Knights of Pythias, Visitor's Exhibition, and Kroch's (1933), but also with the Harmon Foundation in New York (1931).[111]

When, in May, the Guggenheim Foundation had offered Motley a six-month extension of his fellowship if he would make reports and send photographs of his work,[112] he declined, saying that "a year was enough" and citing homesickness; "I always was a home body anyway."[113] Motley, his wife, and his mother returned to the United States on July 26, 1930.

6
"UNE FEMME SCULPTEUR NOIRE":
AUGUSTA SAVAGE IN PARIS, 1929–1931

$\mathcal{L}$ike Prophet, Augusta Savage (1892–1962) is an intriguing and perplexing subject because so much information about her life and art is missing (fig. 74). Of the seventy-plus works that she produced in her lifetime—a conservative estimate based on the titles published in newspapers and other periodicals—only nineteen small pieces could be located at the time of an exhibition of her work, which was shown along with that of the Harlem art schools, at the Schomburg Center for Research in Black Culture in 1988; nine of them were gifts to the center from the stepdaughter of Savage's daughter.[1] By her own count, Savage produced eighteen to twenty pieces during the two years she spent in Paris, from 1929 to 1931,[2] yet only three of the works are in ascertained collections in the United States and one is in a private collection in France. The others are known only by titles and descriptions found in various documents and several photographs in the Julius Rosenwald Fund Archives at Fisk University. This makes the establishment of an exact chronology of Savage's work problematic at best.

Of all the African American artists in Paris in the late 1920s and early 1930s, Savage was the best-connected to important leaders in Harlem and had the most financial backing. A resident of Harlem for eight years before she went abroad, she established her reputation early on, first as an amateur and then as a serious artist. She published her poetry in Marcus Garvey's newspaper, *Negro World,* and gave public readings of it at the 135th Street branch library, and she completed a four-year course of study in sculpture in just three years on a full scholarship at Cooper Union. The charge of racial discrimination directed against a committee of seven white men who denied Savage the opportunity to study at the Fontainebleau School in France in 1923 catapulted the young sculptor to momentary fame as it made head-

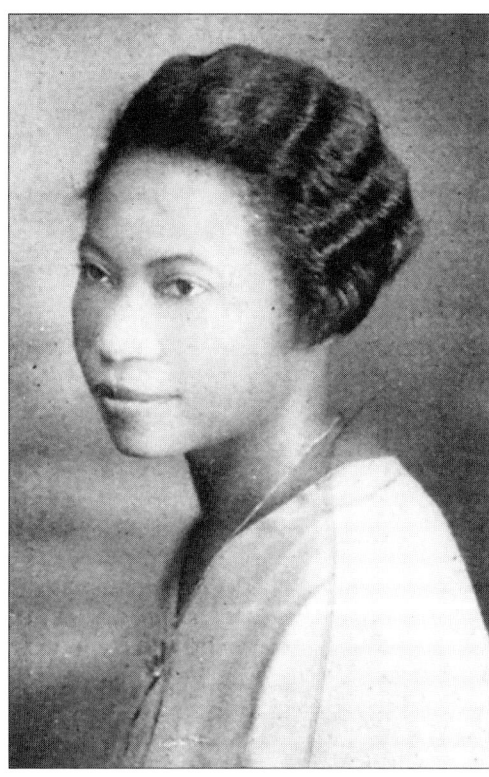

FIGURE 74
Photograph of Augusta Savage, ca. 1923.
From *Opportunity,* June 1923.

lines across the country. Several years later, W.E.B. Du Bois arranged a scholarship for her to study in Rome, but Savage could not afford the travel and living expenses. Finally, in 1929, through the aid of the Urban League, she received a two-year fellowship from the Rosenwald Fund, which was supplemented by a Carnegie grant and donations from friends and from African American teachers in Florida.

    In New York, Savage produced clay, plaster, and bronze portraits. In Paris, she expanded both her media and her subject matter, beginning to carve directly in marble and wood and sculpting nudes, dancers, African-inspired figures, and works symbolic of emotional states. These pieces, some of which were exhibited at the Salon d'Automne (1930) and the Société des Artistes Français (1931), were the most daring and original of her entire career. She produced two distinctive types of art while abroad—one nostalgic in its evocation of nineteenth-century romanticism and of African and Greek cultural history, and another quite modern in its subject matter and sleek design. Savage's success in Paris would bring her teaching positions, exhibitions, and commissions back in New York throughout the 1930s.

"THE BIRTHPLACE OF MANY HOPES AND FEARS": FLORIDA, 1892–1921

"At the mud pie age, I began to make 'things' instead of mud pies," Savage recalled.[3] As a child in Green Cove Springs, Florida, she often skipped school to fashion clay ducks. "Why I chose to make ducks, I don't know, we didn't raise ducks, although other people in town did."[4] From these humble beginning,s Savage launched a career in sculpture.

On February 29, 1892, Cornelia (Murphy) Fells, a laundress from South Carolina, gave birth to her daughter Augusta "at the dark of the moon."[5] Folklore had it that this was a sign that the sculptor would live to at least 102.[6] Savage was either the seventh child[7] or the third child and second daughter[8] of fourteen, nine of whom lived to maturity. Edward Fells, Savage's father, was a carpenter, fisherman, and farmer from Georgia who owned fifteen acres of land.[9] He was also a deeply religious, fundamentalist man who was fond of "good books"[10] and who assisted local Methodist ministers in conducting church services. Fells was disturbed by the sculptures Savage created, her "fashioning graven images in a godly house."[11] His stern disapproval and violent temper compelled Savage to hide her sculpture; "My father licked me five or six times a week and almost whipped all the art out of me."[12]

Perhaps as a means of escaping her father's wrath, Savage married John T. Moore in 1907, at the age of fifteen. Moore passed away a few years after the birth of their daughter, Irene Connie Moore, in 1908. Around 1915, Savage married laborer and carpenter James Savage, whom she divorced in the early 1920s.[13] Nothing else is known about their relationship.

Although Green Cove Springs was the seat of Clay County in northeast Florida, it was a tiny resort (population 1,719 in 1936),[14] centered around a spring that flowed at the rate of three thousand gallons a minute and that was impounded to form a large swimming pool. The town was a fashionable spa in the late 1870s and 1880s, and steamers from Charleston and Savannah brought passengers up the Saint Johns River to visit it. Among Green Cove Springs's notable guests were President Grover Cleveland (1885–1889), condensed-milk manufacturer Gail Borden, and chain-store magnate J. C. Penney. Penney bought property there, established a farm colony, and took an active role in the development of the town. With the advancement of railroads and resorts farther south, however, Green Cove Springs lost much of its out-of-state patronage.[15]

In 1915, Savage and her daughter moved with her family a few hundred miles south to West Palm Beach, where her father obtained a church position.[16] The city had been growing rapidly since the establishment of the railroad there in late 1894 that connected it to Miami in 1896.[17] After West Palm Beach became the county seat of Palm Beach County in 1909, the population more than quadrupled, from 1,700 in 1910 to more than 8,000 in 1920.[18] Many of the African Americans who lived in a colony west of the railroad found employment as gardeners and house servants on Palm Beach estates and in the hotels during the winter resort season.[19]

Since there was no clay soil in West Palm Beach, Savage could not sculpt as she had done before. One day, while driving in a wagon with Professor Mickens, principal of the public school that she was attending, Savage discovered heaps of soft clay in front of the Chase Pottery on the outskirts of town. Savage jumped off the wagon and begged the pottery owner for twenty-five pounds of clay.[20] With the gift, she sculpted an eighteen-inch-tall statue of the Virgin Mary (now lost) that won the approval of her father and his blessings for her artistic talent. Upon viewing the work, Mickens hired her, although she was still a student, to teach clay modeling at the school. Savage taught at the rate of a dollar per day for six months, working with clay that Chase donated.

In 1915, Savage requested and received permission from superintendent George Graham Currie to exhibit her work, mostly sculptures of farm animals, including a piece titled *Percheron Stallion*,[21] at the Palm Beach County Fair. There, she sold statuettes, charging from twenty-five cents to five dollars. Savage won a special prize of twenty-five dollars and an honor ribbon for her sculpture, the only work of its kind exhibited at the fair. Senator Thomas Campbell of Florida congratulated her and urged her to study art in New York.[22] From sales and contributions from Yankee tourists who also beseeched her to go to New York, Savage collected an additional $150. Currie then commissioned a bust of himself from her. He was so moved by the creation that he wrote the following poem about Savage:

> Augusta is a sculptress fine—
> A poetess as well;
> Her coal black hair and eyes that shine
> A soulful story tell.
>
> Her agile step, her lissome grace,
> Her happy, carefree mien,
> Proclaim her o'er her swarthy race
> A veritable queen.
>
> But other maids such attributes
> Might boast as well as her;
> And that she is common, Heaven refutes,
> Or else my muse must err.
>
> For out the fair Augusta stands,
> A mother though a maid;
> And subject to her art's commands
> Is pure and unafraid.
>
> With steady eyes she looks on me
> Then takes a lump of clay—
> When lo! another self I see,
> With all my faults away.[23]

Although Currie's well-intentioned, albeit weak, verse is condescending and somewhat racist, it describes the vibrant personality for which Savage became known. Currie sincerely admired Savage and promoted her artistic career. In turn, Savage thanked Currie for his support in a poem, "My Soul's Gethsemane":

> At the forks of life's high roads alone I stand.
> And the hour of my temptation is at hand,
> In my soul's Gethsemane
> I still have your faith in me,
> And it strengthens me
> To know you understand.[24]

In this verse, Savage compared her choice of staying with her family or moving north to a greater metropolitan area with Jesus' agony in the garden on the outskirts of Jerusalem where he wept, prayed, and was arrested.

Sometime in the late 1910s, Savage moved several hundred miles northeast, where she took classes for a year (1919–1920)[25] at Tallahassee State Normal School, which specialized in teacher training. She soon discontinued her studies there because she disliked spending valuable time translating Latin when she could have been sculpting.[26]

She then moved to Jacksonville, the largest city in Florida at the time, whose population grew explosively in the early twentieth century—from 28,249, in 1910 to 57,699 in 1920.[27] African Americans, who made up approximately 30 percent of the population by 1936, were largely engaged in domestic service or the unskilled labor market.[28] Others operated businesses that included restaurants, theaters, funeral establishments, and three insurance companies, one with assets of a million dollars in 1936. Among the town's notable residents were African American poets Paul Laurence Dunbar and W. E. Dancer, writers Thomas H. B. Walker and James Weldon Johnson, and composer J. Rosamond Johnson. James Weldon Johnson (1871–1938) wrote the lyrics for the Negro national anthem, "Lift Every Voice and Sing," when he was principal of Stanton High School, and had the work performed publicly for the first time in Jacksonville.[29] Savage would sculpt a large figural piece named after the anthem for the New York World's Fair in 1939. In Jacksonville Savage hoped to earn additional money to finance her artistic career by making portrait busts of wealthy African Americans.[30] When the "said rich folks refused to be 'done,'"[31] Savage was almost stranded after a four-month stay in the city,[32] but managed to travel to New York, moving north as part of the Great Migration, as had Palmer Hayden, Hale Woodruff, and Archibald Motley.

"A DETERMINATION TO LEARN SCULPTING": NEW YORK, 1921–1923

When Savage arrived in New York City in 1921, she came with little more than "a determination to learn sculpting in six months,"[33] $4.60, and a letter of introduction from George Currie to the well-known sculptor Solon H. Borglum (1868–1922), the brother of Gutzon Borlgum, the sculptor of Mount Rushmore, whom Currie had met while on a stay in New York.[34] For more than two decades Solon Borglum had worked in Paris, where he achieved fame for his images of cowboys and Native Americans; the French press hailed him as the "sculptor of the prairie."[35] Following his return to the United States at the end of World War I, Borglum established the School of American Sculpture in New York, in 1919. Realizing that Savage could not afford the high tuition at his school—"the young ladies who come here are the children of the rich and pay immense fees" he told her[36]—Borglum suggested that she try Pratt Institute and Cooper Union;[37] he had worked as a substitute teacher at Cooper Union in 1920 and knew that it was tuition-free.[38]

Savage went to Cooper Union accompanied by "a young colored man who, undaunted, 'spoke up for her.'"[39] Although 142 women were on the waiting list, the school's principal, Kate L. Reynolds, asked to see Savage's work after Savage presented Borglum's card. The day after Reynolds viewed Savage's portrait of an African American minister (which she had modeled overnight), she mailed her an acceptance letter.

Savage first took a class in modeling at Cooper Union for two weeks in October 1921. She then completed the second-year program in one month,[40] and would go on to complete the four-year program at Cooper Union in three years. Frederick Dielman, Director of Cooper Union, found Savage to be a popular student who experienced little, if any, discrimination: "Miss Savage's treatment at the hands of her fellow students, whether in the classes, in the lunchroom or in the social relations, has been as irreproachable as has been her [illegible] conduct: indeed it appears that she has been quite a favorite."[41]

In early 1922, Savage lost her position as a domestic servant for a family from whom she had been receiving room and board.[42] She was able to maintain a cheap, poorly lit room in Harlem (at 228 West 138th Street),[43] but she could no longer meet her living expenses. She was forced to quit school and go to work full time.[44] At the same time, she attended night school to earn the equivalent of a high school diploma.[45] Reynolds, who "nearly wept" at Savage's situation, helped her find temporary employment and then called a special session of the advisory committee, which awarded her Cooper Union's first working scholarship, covering rent, board, and transportation.[46]

In the winter of 1922, Savage advanced from a class in elementary freehand drawing to drawing from the antique and received an honorable mention.[47] After the usual preparatory training in modeling from casts she was advanced to the class for modeling from the living figure, where she studied under the direction of sculptor George T. Brewster (1862–1943). Like Borglum, Brewster had studied in Paris, but at the Ecole des Beaux-Arts, rather than at the Académie Julian, and exhibited at the Salon, in 1884.[48] A member of the National Sculpture Society (1898), Brewster was best known as a realistic portraitist; his bust of painter J. Carroll Beckwith (1852–1917) was exhibited at the National Academy of Design in 1917.[49] Brewster's statues adorned the State House in Providence, Rhode Island, and the U.S. Supreme Court, as well as the New York University Library, and the National Academy of Design.[50] Under Brewster's direction, Savage formally launched her career as a trained portraitist. She planned on executing busts of distinguished African Americans, such as A'Lelia Walker Wilson, daughter of Madame C. J. Walker, the millionaire owner of an enormous beauty and hairdressing company; the composer Harry T. Burleigh; and the late actor Bert Williams.[51]

To study photographs of her proposed subjects, Savage frequently visited the nearby 135th Street branch of the New York Public Library. There she also read about African art and the Garveyite movement. Marcus Garvey (1887–1940) was a charismatic Jamaican who immigrated to the United States. In 1914, he established the Universal Negro Improvement Association (UNIA) in New York to foster worldwide unity and pride in African heritage among black people. Rejecting any integration in countries where blacks were a minority, he urged a "back to Africa" movement. Garvey's brilliant oratory, the fabulous parades in which he and his followers dressed in military regalia, and his widely read newspaper, *Negro World* (1917–1934), made him one of the most influential black populist leaders of the early 1920s.

On October 7, 1922, Garvey's associate editor, Eric D. Walrond (1898–1966, born in British Guyana and raised in Barbardos and Panama), published an article on Savage in the *Negro World,* "Florida Girl Shows Amazing Gift for Sculpture." Walrond outlined Savage's biography and reprinted Currie's poem and that by Savage in response to it. He also linked Savage to Meta Vaux Warrick Fuller, "former pupil of Rodin," and declared that the black race had "another sculptress we can gloriously be proud of."[52] Savage was aware of Fuller's reputation, but apparently did not see any of Fuller's work until 1933, when it was on view in New York at a Harmon Foundation exhibition (or perhaps in 1926, when both women's work was exhibited in Baltimore; see below).

Sometime in the fall of 1922, Savage sculpted Garvey's bust (location unknown); he posed for her on Sunday mornings in his Harlem apartment. The work depicts the leader dressed in a suit, with a resolute expression.[53] Garvey sold reproductions of the lifesize bust and smaller versions to benefit the UNIA. Advertisements for the works appeared in his *Negro World:* "Critics declare that these bronze busts are the true likeness of the Honorary Marcus Garvey."[54]

On October 7, 1922, Savage published the following poem, "The Old Homestead," in *Negro World:*

I visited today the old Homestead,
Deserted now for many busy years,
Explored again with memory laden tread,
The birthplace of so many hopes and fears.

The windlass seemed to creak a doleful tune,
The mocking birds that used to sing so gay
Seem all forgetful of the month of June,
The time to sing their merriest roundelay.

The meadow that to childish eyes did seem
To stretch into the distance mile on mile,
Is but a glen, and now the raging stream.
Is just a little brook that tries to smile . . .

And down my time scarred cheek then crept a tear,
For those who sleep beneath the ocean's foam,
And then a sigh for other hearts so dear,
That rest so gently 'neath the sand of home.

The poem suggests that Savage returned to Florida to visit to her family—especially her daughter, whom she had left behind—in June 1922.[55] By the age of thirty, Savage had matured significantly and had experienced much loss and pain. Not only had three siblings and a husband succumbed to early death, but she had also lost a husband to divorce and had apparently suffered a prolonged separation from her daughter.

Savage continued to write and publish poetry in *Negro World,*[56] and she gave readings at the 135th Street branch of the New York Public Library. At one reading, on March 31, 1923, the following people were present—Gwendolyn Bennett, Langston Hughes, Countee Cullen, Eric Walrond, Arthur Schomburg, Sadie Peterson, and Ernestine Rose, the last a white librarian.[57] They may have inspired Savage to consider study abroad. Virtually all members of the group would go to Paris—Hughes in 1924, Bennett from 1925 to 1926, Schomburg and Cullen in the summer of 1926, and Cullen from 1928 to 1930 and in subsequent summers.

"NEGRESS DENIED ENTRY TO FRENCH ART SCHOOL," 1923

In early 1923, Savage applied for a scholarship from the French government for summer study at the Palace of Fontainebleau, France. She hoped to be one of the one hundred women chosen to study abroad. After receiving her application, the American Committee of Eminent American Architects, Painters and Sculptors—composed of seven white men[58]—informed her that, although they had received a letter of recommendation from the principal of Cooper Union, Savage needed two additional letters of recommendation. Before she could send them, however, the committee returned her thirty-five-dollar application fee and rejected her petition because she was "of the Negro race."[59] One of Savage's friends then explained the situation to Unitarian minister Alfred W. Martin (1862–1932), a German American leader of the Ethical Culture Society, who had been lecturing at the 135th Street branch library.[60] Appalled, both he and Ernestine Rose wrote to Ernest Peixotto (1869–1940),[61] the internationally known artist who had chaired the committee, and inquired whether Savage had indeed been excluded from the scholarship because of her race. Peixotto replied that Savage was denied because southern white women would have to sail on the same ship with her and work in the same ateliers.[62] "The refusal of the application was made in the girl's interest," Peixotto wrote. "Her presence in the school would be disagreeable to some white students and embarrassing to her."[63] He also wrote: "You can readily see that disagreeable complications would arise and the applicant in question would perhaps suffer most from these complications, and no matter how much we regret our action in depriving a serious student of the advantages of the school, we feel that we must take such action. Hoping you will try to understand our position."[64] After contacting New York newspapers to denounce Savage's exclusion, Martin sailed to France on April 28 to lay the full case before the French government, to no avail.[65] For weeks, articles about the controversy appeared in the *New York Amsterdam News, New York Herald Tribune, Negro World, New York Evening Post,* and *New York World.*

On May 3, W.E.B. Du Bois wrote to each of the committee members asking them to personally make a statement of the facts and explain their attitude toward Savage.[66] Of the seven, four responded. President of Beaux-Arts Architecture James Gamble Rogers (1867–1947) wrote immediately that he had not known anything about the situation until he read about it in the newspapers; he was not even aware that he had been on the committee. Based on the complaints he had received from Savage's friends, however, he would not recommend her for the scholarship even if he had the chance: "I have received a number of letters from friends of this young lady and from the language used in them I should be compelled to say that, judged by her friends, I do not think the young lady would be the kind that I could recommend to schools as a fitting companion for the teachers."[67]

Architect James Monroe Hewlett (1868–1941) was more conciliatory: "I think it is safe to say that there is not one [member of the committee] who is not sincerely desirous of seeing the fullest education opportunities given to the colored race." But, Hewlett insisted, "any race prejudice that manifested itself among the students might easily affect the entire morale of the School during its first year,"[68] and so he maintained his position. Architect Thomas Hastings (1860–1929) replied curtly that he had "no sympathy with keeping Miss Augusta Savage away from the Fontainebleau School of Arts because of Negro descent."[69]

Like Rogers, the sculptor Herman MacNeil (1866–1947) was not involved in the decision. But because he had high regard for the opinions of his fellow committee members, he defended their position and suggested that Savage's work may not have been of high quality. He added that he had "no greater joy than seeing the advancement of the colored race" because he had some "friends of color whose friendship" he prized as highly as that of any of his associates.[70] MacNeil was particularly embarrassed about the scandal, having briefly shared a studio with Tanner in Paris in 1893.[71] He went to view Savage's work at Cooper Union, then invited her to study with him in his studio at College Point, Long Island. She would receive his advice for about a year.[72] Like Brewster, MacNeil had studied in Paris, exhibited at the Salon, in 1890,[73] and was known as a sculptor of images of Native Americans.[74] He also executed numerous portraits and statues of American pioneers and frequently exhibited them at the National Academy of Design and the Art Institute of Chicago.

To support Savage and thank Du Bois for his defense of the artist, the librarian Sadie Peterson (Delaney) persuaded friends of the library to commission Savage to do a portrait bust of Du Bois. In the spring of 1923, Savage sculpted the bust (photograph unavailable), then presented it to the 135th Street branch of the New York Public Library in April.[75]

The uproar over the Fontainebleau decision continued for several weeks. About 150 people attended an indignation meeting at Saint Mark's Church on May 10, presided over by John Eustace Robinson (b. 1876), president of the Urban League. Mary D. Grout, Republican leader of the Fifth Assembly District, lamented "the narrow-minded Methodist view"[76] in drawing the color line. Savage also spoke at the meeting, stating that she had studied night and day to win the scholarship. The assembled group decided to ask President Harding to intercede and urge a reversal of the committee's decision. There is no documentation of the president's response.

Numerous other distinguished people such as German American Columbia University anthropologist Franz Boas (1858–1942); J. W. Brown, pastor of the A.M.E. Zion Church; Thomas O. Keefe, pastor of the Church of Saint Benedict the Moor (life dates are unknown); and secretary at Howard University, Emmett J. Scott (1873–1957), condemned the action of the committee. Scott went so far as to compare the incident to a recent Missouri lynching.[77] Boas wrote to Peixotto, "I cannot understand how the committee would be willing to expose itself to the ridicule of all Europeans by taking a stand dictated by narrow prejudice."[78] Reverend Brown attacked the committee members' patriotism: "Miss Savage's brother fought with the American Expeditionary forces overseas. It would be a slap at all talk about making this world safe for democracy if this young woman is denied the right to attend the Fontainebleau School of Fine Arts; it would be too obvious an incongruity."[79]

On May 20, Savage wrote a long letter to the editor of the *New York World* in which she challenged the racial discrimination she experienced:

> I hear so many complaints to the effect that Negroes do not take advantage of the educational opportunities offered them. Well, one of the reasons why more of my race do not go in for higher education is that as soon as one of us gets his head above the crowd there are millions of feet ready to crush it back again to that dead level of commonplace thus creating a racial deadline of culture in our Republic. For how am I to compete with other American artists if I am not to be given the same opportunity?[80]

Once newspapers publicized the controversy, Savage was inundated with anonymous letters warning her not to force herself onto the white race. She answered, "They seemed to have the notion that I must be a mulatto or octoroon, for that seems to me the only way in which I could possibly force myself into the white race. Now I happen to be unmistakable [unmistakably black], and that is obviously out of the question." She asked:

> Isn't it rather odd that such people should always suppose that when a colored girl gets a chance to develop her natural powers it must be that she will want to become white? It gets to be a tiresome task explaining to them that the desire to become better or more capable is a common quality of all human beings.
> I haven't the slightest desire to force any question like that of "social equality" upon any one. Instead of desiring to force my society upon ninety-nine white girls, I should be pleased to go to France on a ship with a black captain, a black crew and myself as sole passenger, if on arrival there I would be given the same opportunities for study as the other ninety-nine girls; and I feel sure that my race would not need to be ashamed of me after the final examinations.[81]

With her suggestion of a ship with a black captain and crew, Savage may have been thinking of Garvey's attempt to create an all-black steamship company, named the Black Star Line, to take African Americans to Liberia. She also pointed out the implications of her case for other African Americans and reiterated her brother's military service abroad:

> I don't much care for myself because I will get along all right here, but other and better colored students might wish to apply sometime. This is the first year the school is open and I am the first colored girl to apply. I don't like to see them establish a precedent. . . . Democracy is a strange thing. My brother was good enough to be accepted in one of the regiments that saw service in France during the war, but it seems his sister is not good enough to be a guest of the country for which he fought.[82]

Despite the uproar, the committee remained steadfast in its decision. The writer Jessie Fauset would immortalize Savage's case in her novel *Plum Bun* (1929), in which a young African American woman is denied a scholarship to the Fontainebleau because of her race. Fauset began writing the novel when she traveled to France in 1924.

LADY AUGUSTA SAVAGE, A GARVEYITE WIFE, 1923–1924

The Fontainebleau fiasco made Savage a temporary celebrity, and numerous people befriended her. Among them was Robert L. Poston (1890–1924), a writer for *Negro World* and secretary-general of the United Negro Improvement Association (UNIA) in 1922. He and Savage fell in love, and in June 1923, they married. Poston, a native of Hopkinsville, Kentucky, had studied at Walden University in Nashville and at Howard University and had served in the U.S. armed forces during the war.[83] Poet and literary critic, he had had a newspaper publishing career in Kentucky and Detroit before moving to New York in 1921 to become assistant secretary-general of the UNIA. Poston was passionate about the Garveyite movement and about righting inequalities. While the Fontainebleau controversy was going on, he declared in *Negro World:* "I accepted the Garvey program because of my patriotism towards America. . . . When a young American declares in favor of the Garvey program he is accused by the opposer [*sic*] of the program as being unpatriotic and disloyal. I am prepared to prove my loyalty as American—my right to dissent, to reform American policies if they are unequal."[84] Poston was an ambitious, highly energetic man who often traveled about the country and the world preaching Garveyite philosophy. Nothing is known about the brief courtship and marriage of Savage and Poston, but most likely it was intense.

Six months after their wedding, Poston sailed to Liberia as head of a UNIA delegation for talks with that country's government. On the return voyage, on March 24, 1924, he died of pneumonia. The UNIA gave him one of the most elaborate funerals it ever staged and posthumously elevated Poston to the rank of prince, the organization's highest honor. An article in *Negro World,* "Personalia: Lady Augusta Savage, the Wife of Our Late Secretary-General Sir Robert Lincoln Poston," reported that Savage then went to spend some time with her family in West Palm Beach and that she was expecting a child.[85] Just four months later, on July 21, 1924, Savage gave birth to a baby girl, Roberta L. Poston, who died ten days later. She stayed with her family for about a month, then returned to New York by September.[86] Savage never remarried, but kept her third husband's memory alive by speaking of him often. In retrospect, friend and painter Gwendolyn Knight explained, "He was a 'race man' and she was a 'race woman.'"[87] Savage did not believe in the back-to-Africa philosophy, but she agreed with the notions of racial pride and economic self-reliance.[88] Yet her interest in the Garveyite movement would wane considerably in 1925 when Garvey was convicted of mail fraud and jailed. In 1927 he was deported to Jamaica, where he died in relative obscurity in 1940.

Nothing is known about Savage's activities from the end of July 1924 until the spring of 1926. Perhaps she went back to work at a laundry and continued to sculpt in her spare time.

A CHANCE TO STUDY IN ROME, FIRST SOLO EXHIBITIONS,
AND PRIVATE STUDY, 1926–1929

In 1926 Savage exhibited her work at the sesquicentennial exhibition in Philadelphia, *America Welcomes the World* (June 1–December 1) and at the 135th Street branch of the New York Public Library, in April.[89] That month, Savage invited Du Bois to view her works on display at the library and asked for his candid opinion.[90] She invited him to sit for another portrait,[91] which he did in May.[92] He also labored to find a way for Savage to study in Europe. That spring Du Bois made arrangements with Countess Irene Di Robilant, of the Italian-American Society, for Savage to study at the Royal Academy of Fine Art in Rome. Di Robilant gave Savage funds to pay for materials and tuition, but the sculptor would have to pay for travel and living expenses.[93] After Savage met with the countess to thank her, the artist informed Du Bois:

> I found her exceedingly charming and very much interested in my work, although I think she was a trifle disappointed to find that I am a realist instead of a modernist, however we got on famously and she gave me some good sound advise [*sic*] concerning my proposed invasion of Italy. She has also offered me several letters of introduction to various people in Italy who might be of service to me. Thank you so much for introducing her to me. I am sure that her recommendations will be invaluable to me if I succeed in getting to Italy. My fund has not grown perceptibly since I saw you but I am getting a lot of encouragement.[94]

Although the Baptist Young People's Union Convention awarded Savage five hundred dollars a year for three years to help meet travel and living expenses in Rome, Savage could not raise enough money to make the difference. Unable to secure further funding, she declined the fellowship and wondered if she would ever study abroad.

The same year, Savage exhibited her work at the first show of the Baltimore Federation of Parent Teacher clubs at the Frederick Douglass High School in Baltimore. The tremendously successful exhibition, which included work by Fuller and Tanner, attracted more than fifty thousand visitors, according to the *New York Herald Tribune*. Among Savage's twenty-two works on display were portraits of Major Edward Bowes, vice president of the Metro-Goldwin Mayer Picture Company, and Theodore Upshure, an African American youth from Greenwich Village who was disabled and who was known in downtown art circles (both works are now missing), as well as a small bronze figure, *Green Apples* (ca. 1926, fig. 75).

Green Apples depicts a nude African American boy clutching his stomach, jackknifed in abdominal pain from having eaten too many green apples. The boy stands on tiptoe, one foot wrapped behind the other, as he grimaces, eyes and mouth firmly closed. The statue seems to be Savage's first genre work.

In the fall of 1926, Savage helped inspire *Fire!!* a bold periodical founded by African American writers Wallace Thurman, Langston Hughes, Zora Neale Hurston, and Richard Bruce Nugent. Savage did not contribute to the first and only volume, but her Saturday night parties formed the backdrop for Nugent's stream of consciousness prose poem, "Smoke, Lilies, and Jade":

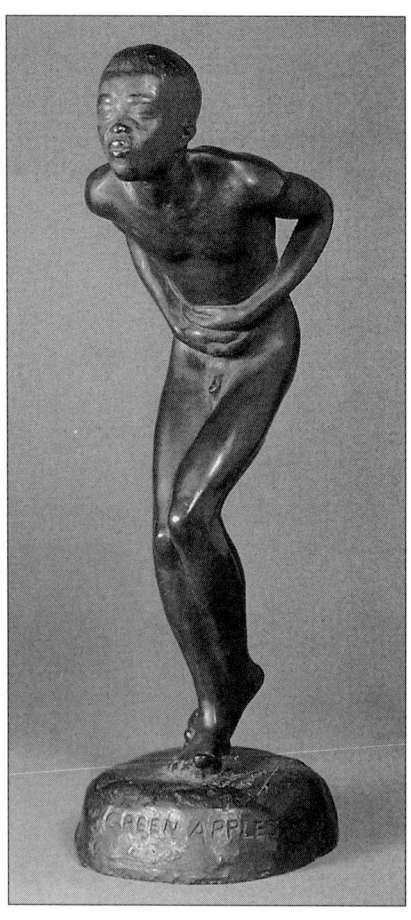

FIGURE 75
Augusta Savage, *Green Apples*, 1926, bronze, 15¼ in.
James Weldon Johnson Memorial Collection of Negro Arts
and Letters, Beinecke Rare Book and Manuscript Library,
Yale University Library.

At Augusta's party . . . Harold, Bruce, Connie, Langston . . . fy-ahs gonna burn
my soul . . . they were at Augusta's . . . Alex lay . . . half sat on the floor . . . sipping
a cocktail . . . such a dream, red calla lilies . . . Alex left down the narrow streets.
Fy-ah . . .[95]

Ironically, a warehouse fire destroyed virtually all copies of *Fire!!* which broke the
publishers both financially and morally. Savage was not directly involved with the periodical,
but she was close friends with its producers, and shared their excitement about New Negro
concepts.

In 1927 Savage began to study with Italian American sculptor Onorio Ruotolo
(1888–1966), former dean of the Leonardo da Vinci Art School on New York's East Side.
Ruotolo was best known for his realistic portraits of such notables as Enrico Caruso, Lenin,
Dante, Helen Keller, Theodore Dreiser, and Abraham Lincoln, whom he depicted holding an
African American baby in *The Father of a Race*. Savage would have found a kindred spirit in
Ruotolo, an artist and poet with similar experiences in life. He began sculpting as a child, as
had she, and had produced a religious work, in his case, a head of Christ; he left his small
hometown, Cervinara, Italy, to study in a large city, Naples; and he denounced injustice.[96]

Ruotolo came to the United States in 1908 and struggled for years to make a living. In 1920, shortly after he "arrived" by successfully sculpting a bust of Thomas Edison, he told the *New York Evening Post* that the American government must lend its backing to the cause of artists because "in many cases obscure and humble artists" are "paid starvation wages." He argued:

> There exists in the United States a proletariat of the brain—a proletariat composed especially of artists and not protected by any A.F.L. or I.W.W. It is ignored by the great majority of our people and even by those who call themselves patrons of the arts, art critics, and connoisseurs. The time has come when the Government must see that artists mean as much to our country as horses or pigs and should have the same protection. There is no reason why the day of Lorenzo the Magnificent should not return now in America and the artist be encouraged and backed by Uncle Sam himself and not petty individual patrons.[97]

Ruotolo was receptive to the artistic potential of people from all backgrounds. He insisted, "There is no national face of genius. Genius puts the same facial marks upon the man or woman of any race. Edison might be a Jew: His face is not typically American, as what face of genius is?" The sculptor found Savage "exceptionally talented and very progressive" and well as morally "very upright." "If properly assisted," he would later write, "I sincerely believe as an artist, that this girl will be a credit to her people and will gain some renown as a sculptress."[98]

Ruotolo might have advised Savage to study independently with another Italian American sculptor, Antonio Salemme (b. Gaeta, Italy, 1892–1955), at this time; she claimed him as one of her instructors.[99] Although Salemme, in the 1920s, had exhibited at the National Academy of Design, the Art Institute of Chicago, and the Society of Independent Artists, he would not have his first solo exhibition in New York until 1931.[100] Guggenheim Fellowships in 1932 and 1936 allowed him to study in Paris, where he exhibited at the Salon des Tuileries, the Salon d'Automne, and Galerie Zac. He was an expressionistic portraitist whose later subjects would include the explorer Sir Hubert Wilkins, the author Fannie Hurst, defense secretary James Forrestal, the publisher Thomas R. Coward, and President John F. Kennedy.[101] Nothing is known about the nature of Salemme's instruction to Savage, but it seems likely that he encouraged her to make her portraits more expressionistic than realistic. Little else is known of Savage's activities in 1927.

One of the works Savage produced in March 1927 was *The New Negro* (now missing), a small statue of an African American man kneeling in a fetal position. The *Chicago Defender* newspaper ran a photograph of Savage sculpting the piece in her home at 29 West 130th Street in Harlem—apparently, Savage moved often in search of inexpensive housing and space in which to work comfortably.[102] Undoubtedly, the inspiration for the work came from the title of Locke's eponymous 1925 anthology.

In 1928, the Harmon Foundation exhibited Savage's *Evening* and *Head of a Negro* (both now missing). That year, she sold some of her work, including a model for the Soldier's Monument in Philadelphia (lost).[103] It may have also been in 1928 that Savage began to teach soap sculpture to children in Harlem without charge, with the aid of materials from Proctor and Gamble.[104] James Gamble, the soap manufacturer, had aided another African American woman from Florida in her education efforts; he provided funds for building Mary McLeod Bethune's Daytona Educational and Industrial Institute in the late 1910s and early 1920s.[105] Savage apparently continued to work with the children in her home through the spring of 1929.[106] She was very proud of these students, some of whom continued their education at the secondary level; one boy subsequently attended the Ethical Culture School and another student went to Cooper Union.[107]

By the summer of 1928, Savage was a frequent guest at important social affairs. In August, she attended a classical piano recital at A'Lelia Walker's Dark Tower salon, along with Richard Bruce Nugent, Muriel Draper, Taylor Gordon, and musical arrangers Porter Grainger and John W. Work.[108] Walker opened the Dark Tower salon, named after Countee Cullen's column in *Opportunity*, in October 1927 at her fashionable apartment at 136th Street and Edgecombe in Harlem. She meant her home to be a place where artists could meet, eat, and discuss their plans and their work. However, the Dark Tower became a social forum for the elite. Nugent, who arrived without tie or socks, described the shock of the first night of the salon:

> Those engraved invitations should have warned them. . . . The large house was lighted brilliantly. There was an air of formality which almost intimidated them as singly and in pairs they arrived. . . . The great room and hall was a seething picture of well-dressed people. Everyone had worn evening clothes. One of the artists was nearly refused admission because he had come with open collar and worn no cravat, but someone already inside fortunately recognized him and he was rescued. . . . Colored faces were at a premium, the place was filled to overflowing with whites from downtown who had come up expecting that this was a new and hot night club.[109]

Nugent found the prices staggering, too: coffee was ten cents, lemonade twenty-five, and sandwiches fifty. He stated that the artists "left hungry."[110] They may have left with their stomachs empty, but their souls were uplifted. Savage could have met many other African American artists at Walker's place, including Aaron Douglas, whom the heiress had invited to decorate the room.[111] Savage would see Douglas again when he sojourned in Paris in 1930.

In the summer of 1928, Savage worked in a steam laundry to support her mother and father, the latter paralyzed by a stroke, who came to live with her.[112] In September, the Red Cross sent other members of her family to her after a hurricane destroyed their house. Her sister had broken her legs,[113] and her brother, Fred (a World War I veteran), had died while rescuing victims of the flood that had occurred after the storm.[114] For a while, nine people lived in Savage's three-room apartment at 284 West 137th Street in Harlem.[115]

Perhaps in an effort to seek help for her family, Savage visited Eugene Kinckle Jones, executive secretary of the National Urban League, at his office on Madison Avenue in mid-November 1928. Jones interviewed Savage, then dictated a three-page biographical statement about her to his secretary.[116] Two months later, Savage's paralyzed father burned to death; further circumstances of the tragedy are unknown. Savage paid for the funeral and burial. She seems to have produced little art at this time, no doubt because of the overwhelming nature of these events.[117]

At the end of March 1929, Jones wrote to Frederick Keppel, president of the Carnegie Corporation, in search of funding to further Savage's education.[118] Within a few weeks, Keppel suggested that Savage contact the Julius Rosenwald Fund about grant possibilities by writing to George Robert Arthur (1879–1950), the associate for Negro welfare for the fund, "himself a colored man."[119]

The chief stockholder and president of Sears, Roebuck and Company, Julius Rosenwald, founded an organization in the 1910s to aid economically disadvantaged whites and African Americans through university endowments, law and medical school construction, and graduate fellowships. By 1923, he had donated matching challenge grants to build modern YMCA buildings with swimming pools, bowling alleys, parlors, cafés, gymnasiums, readings rooms, boys' work departments, and dormitories in Manhattan, Brooklyn, Philadelphia, Indianapolis, Saint Louis, Cincinnati, Kansas City, Baltimore, Atlanta, Pittsburgh, and Detroit.[120] Savage immediately wrote to George Arthur that she wished to study in Paris for two years under sculptor Antoine Bourdelle.[121] Her letter of April 19 might have been instrumental in the establishment of the program of African American fellowships one weekend in April 1929. James Weldon Johnson worked out details of the program with fund president Edwin R. Embree (1883–1950) in Johnson's home.[122] On May 17, Johnson received word that the fund trustees had approved the decision. During its remaining twenty-five years of existence, the fund would award about one thousand fellowships to African Americans.[123]

While Savage awaited a response, Keppel introduced her to his friend the Italian American sculptor Victor D. Salvatore (1885–1965).[124] Like Ruotolo and Salemme, Salvatore was born in Italy, coming to the United States from Tivoli at the age of two, and exhibited his works at the National Academy of Design and the Art Institute of Chicago. Salvatore had studied at Cooper Union and the Art Students League and with Gutzon Borglum. He, too, was a realistic portraitist, whose subjects included Alexander Graham Bell, James Fenimore Cooper, and Abraham Lincoln. In 1918 Salvatore enlisted the support of artists in MacDougal Alley in New York, where his studio was located, to raise funds for war relief. The yearlong event raised more than $250,000 for relief organizations, including the Italian War Relief. The festival subsequently developed into an annual event on Washington Square. For the following twenty years, Salvatore directed the Greenwich House Work Shop (or Settlement), where disadvantaged children learned the rudiments of the arts, particularly woodworking and pottery.[125]

Salvatore was so interested in Savage's work that he promptly took her under his personal tutelage to better prepare her for study abroad. He suggested a program for a year's work—a half-lifesize figure, two heads, and a bas-relief with a study of classic bas-reliefs. He also recommended that "Miss Savage consider her future work largely in relation to her own people."[126]

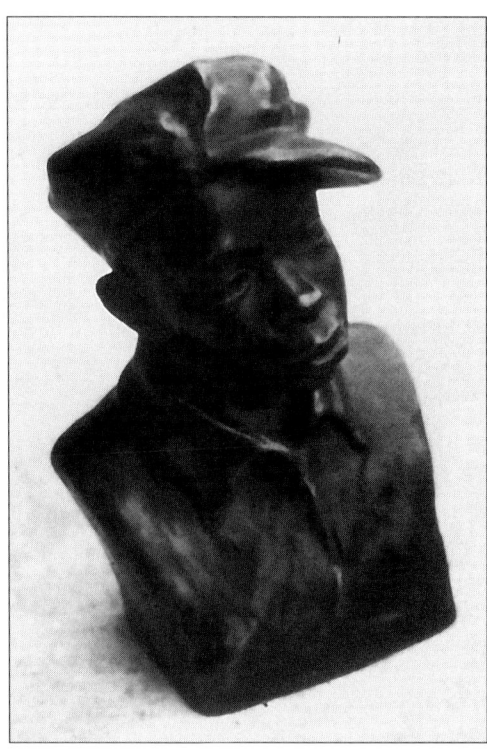

FIGURE 76
Augusta Savage, *Gamin*, 1929, bronze, 9 in. (h).
Howard University Gallery of Art,
Washington, D.C.

Sometime in the spring of 1929, Savage sold *Green Apples* to Harlem real estate broker John E. Nail (1883–1947). Nail had been instrumental in making the first arrangements for blacks to move into Harlem while it was still predominately white. A member of the National Urban League, he brought Savage's sculpture to the attention of Eugene Kinckle Jones, executive secretary of the league. The league then commissioned Savage to do a portrait of Jones (location unknown).

The same spring, Savage created *Gamin* (fig. 76). The lifesize bronze bust depicts a casually attired black boy about twelve years old. The model may have been the sculptor's nephew, Ellis Ford, who lived in Harlem, but the French word *gamin* describes a street urchin, a homeless or neglected child left to roam the streets.[127] Although the boy seems to be streetwise and has a sullen expression as he turns his head slightly to the right and gazes off into the distance, there is also a vulnerability in his face, with its expressive eyes, broad, sensitively modeled features, and prominent ears. The shoulderless bust, open-collared, wrinkled shirt, and broad-brimmed, crumpled cap contribute to the informality and appeal of this piece, which Savage replicated in several smaller, painted plaster versions. Jones and Nail brought *Gamin* to the attention of Embree and Arthur. Arthur then directed Charles Russell Richards (1865–1936), art director of the General Education Board of New York, to examine Savage's work.

Richards not only interviewed Savage in his office, but also obtained a letter of support from Brewster, interviewed Salvatore (who he said was greatly impressed with Savage's ability, at his studio) visited Savage in her home, and inspected the casts of ten pieces that were on view at the 135th Street branch library. Richards believed that Savage's work showed "exceptional ability and a fine feeling for sculpturesque form. There is nothing amateurish about her work. Even now it takes on a professional quality." He declared *Gamin* a definite success and recommended that Savage receive a scholarship, saying that the fund "would make no mistake in giving assistance to this young woman."[128] *Gamin* would be featured on the cover of *Opportunity* in June 1929 and exhibited at the Harmon Foundation in 1930. On May 20, 1929, Savage acknowledged receipt of a fifteen-hundred-dollar Julius Rosenwald fellowship to Arthur and requested an advance of five hundred dollars for mid-August so that she could leave for Paris on September 1.

Du Bois was delighted with Savage's award and asked her to write a brief essay about her life. In August, he published a one-page article, "Miss Augusta Savage: An Autobiography," in *Crisis*.[129] The piece prompted a letter to Savage from Baroness Seydewitz (life dates unknown) in England, who apparently asked to meet the sculptor. Du Bois was pleased with the news; he had known the baroness as a friend of the family for more than a decade.[130] It is not clear whether Savage ever met the baroness, but attention from nobility, however limited, probably thrilled her. Du Bois also gave Savage a letter of introduction to Tanner and wrote to Prophet on her behalf. He warned Savage to write to her before she arrived, because Prophet had "the artistic temperament." He further suggested, "Do not call without an appointment. She usually gets so absorbed in her work that she won't open her door to any visitor."[131] Du Bois also told Savage to get in touch with Countee Cullen at the Hotel Trianon.

During the summer, friends held farewell receptions for Savage at the Utopia Neighborhood House on West 130th Street and at Theodore Upshure's home on Waverly Place. They raised three hundred dollars to provide her with a wardrobe so that the money she received from the Rosenwald Foundation could be entirely applied to her studies.[132] Through the auspices of the Florida Agricultural and Mechanical College president, J.R.E. Lee, African American teachers taking a summer course at the Tallahassee State Normal School sent fifty dollars.[133] Guests and friends complimented Savage on her courage in the midst of her recent adversity. She replied, "I guess I was just a little pig-headed and did not want to consider myself licked."[134] Thrilled to begin a fresh life, on her passport application Savage listed her birth date as 1901, on paper becoming nine years younger than her actual age of thirty-seven that year, 1929.[135] Like Hayden and Prophet, Savage fictionalized part of her biography in the creation of a new identity. Perhaps the idea of going abroad, where virtually no one knew her, emboldened her to consider the journey as a fresh start, without familial burdens.

"TRYING TO DEVELOP AN ORIGINAL TECHNIQUE": PARIS, 1929–1931

Savage arrived in Paris in early September 1929. She missed Cullen at the train station, but took a taxi to the Hôtel Trianon, 22 avenue du Maine, where the owners remembered Du Bois's family and the clerk recognized Du Bois's stationery.[136] Writer J. A. Rogers helped her find a comfortable room in the fifth arrondissement at 50, rue des Ecoles, "after numerous adventures" in which she lost and later found one of her trunks. Savage then wrote to Tanner who answered that he would see her after he returned to the city from vacation (nothing is known about their meeting). Next she called upon Prophet: "I wrote to Mrs. Prophet and she answered very curtly that she could not see me, then she had a change of heart and wrote again and asked me to call, which I did and we became quite good friends. She had recently sprained her back which probably accounted for her first letter. Tanner wrote that he was on vacation and would see her as soon as he returned to the city."[137] Prophet and Cullen promised to look for a room for Savage. She soon settled in an apartment on a tiny street at 3, impasse de l'Astrolabe near the intersection of the rue de Vaugirard and the boulevard du Montparnasse, just a few blocks from Hayden's old apartment on the rue Blomet.

By September 22, Savage had found "a wonderful master in the person of M. [Félix] Benneteau[-Desgrois] at 5, rue de Bagneaux" who agreed to let her work in his studio. She wrote, "He speaks no english [*sic*] but we managed to understand each other and as I am learning french [*sic*] rapidly, that obstacle will soon be removed."[138] Benneteau-Desgrois (b. 1879), professor at the Académie de la Grande Chaumière, was a noted sculptor who had won the first Grand Prix de Rome in 1909, and exhibited his portraits of actors and politicians regularly at the Salon d'Automne, the Salon des Indépendants, and the Société des Artistes Français.[139] On November 1, he wrote a progress report for the Rosenwald Foundation stating that Savage had worked conscientiously with him for six weeks and that "the results she has obtained . . . deserve the greatest encouragement."[140] Benneteau-Desgrois believed that Savage was "very gifted, very artistic," and had no doubts that she would be accepted in the Société des Artistes Français in May. None of her works were exhibited there that spring, however.

By March, 1930, Savage had left Benneteau-Desgrois's studio to work on her own. She later explained to Arthur: "I have lately been trying to develop an original technique— as you suggested in your letter—but I find that the masters are not in sympathy as they all have their own definite ideas and usually wish their pupils to follow their particular method, so I have been working alone for the past three or four months only calling in a critic for suggestions which I have found better for me if I am to develop along the line that I have decided on for myself. My critic is away on vacation just now, but as soon as he returns I will ask him to write you a letter."[141] The critic was Monsieur Brunaleski (further identity unknown). Savage was never able to study with Antoine Bourdelle (1861–1929), as she had hoped, because the sculptor had died on October 1, 1929, just weeks after she arrived in Paris.[142] Savage also later stated that she had worked privately for one year under the direction of Charles Despiau (1874–1946) and Madame Hadjii (life dates unknown) at the Académie de la Grande Chaumière.[143]

As mentioned in the introduction to this volume, it is very difficult to date Savage's work abroad because of a dearth of information about the pieces. Nevertheless, based on her statement that she was "trying to develop an original technique" in June 1930, it seems that Savage's first sculptural efforts in Paris before that summer were probably fairly realistic figurative works in clay and plaster, such as *Bathing Boy* (ca. 1929–1930, fig. 77) and *Bust of*

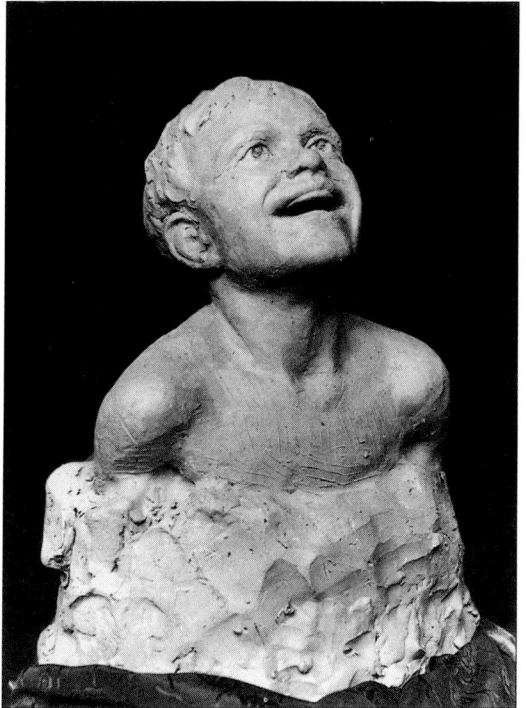 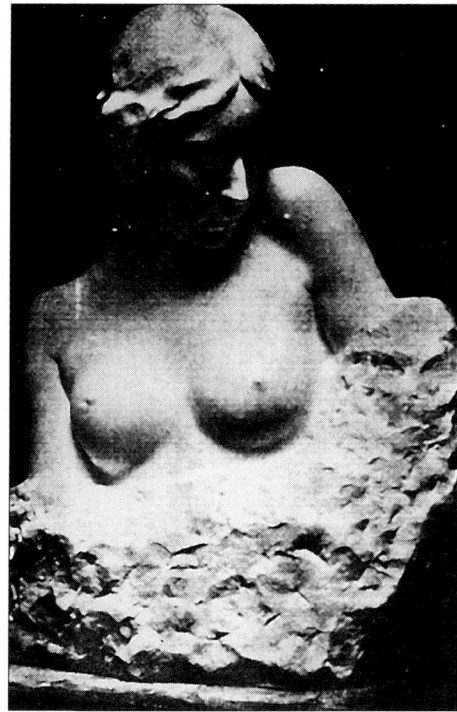

FIGURE 77
Augusta Savage, *Bathing Boy*, ca. 1929, clay,
dimensions and location unknown.
Photograph in the Rosenwald Collection,
Fisk University.

FIGURE 78
Augusta Savage, *Bust of a Woman*, ca. 1929, clay,
dimensions and location unknown.
Photograph in the Rosenwald Collection,
Fisk University.

a Woman (ca. 1929–1930, fig. 78). Despite its title, *Bathing Boy* depicts only the head and
bare shoulders of a young white boy who laughs with his head thrown back, his eyes and
mouth open wide. It is a fairly unremarkable piece. *Bust of a Woman* is more expressionistic
and evokes the romanticism of Bourdelle and Rodin. The piece is a bust of a nude young
white woman, her head slightly downcast to the left, her left shoulder upraised and her arms
at her sides. She seems to be awakening and emerging from a block of rough-hewn white
marble that outlines the area just above her elbows and just below her modest, firm bosom.

The subject and title of another one of Savage's presumably early works in Paris,
Terpsichore at Rest (or *Reclining Figure*, ca. 1929–1930, fig. 79), are intriguing. The work
depicts a seated young nude woman, her left leg bent inward on the ground crossed by her
bent, upraised right leg. With her left hand holding her right shin, she leans to the right on
her right hand pressed to the ground, head dropped. The woman's bobbed hair cascades
over her face like a loose helmet. The title of the work refers to the mythical Greek muse of
dancing, daughter of Jupiter and Mnemosyne. The name may also refer to the title of a short
chapter in *The Art of the Dance* by Isadora Duncan (1878–1927), published posthumously in
1928. This American dancer had astonished audiences in Paris, Berlin, New York, Budapest,
and Moscow by dancing barefoot in a revealing, modified Greek tunic with flowing scarves,

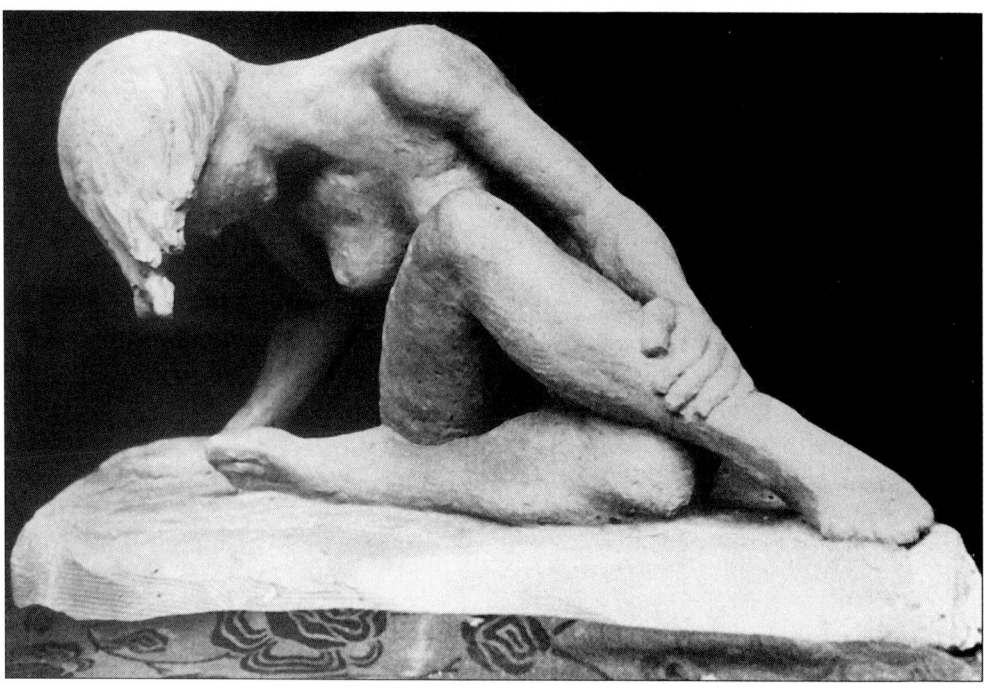

FIGURE 79
Augusta Savage, *Terpsichore (Reclining Woman)*, ca. 1929, clay, dimensions and location unknown.
Photograph in the Rosenwald Collection, Fisk University.

to complex music. Her concerts, schools, and dynamic personality greatly influenced modern
dance. Artists whom Savage admired, particularly Rodin and Bourdelle, adored Duncan and
produced numerous images of her. Savage may have emulated them by creating a work with
similar subject matter, guided by Duncan's own words. In "Terpsichore," a chapter in *The
Art of the Dance,* Duncan wrote: "Always the lines of a form truly beautiful suggest movement, even in repose. And always the lines that are truly beautiful suggest repose, even in the
swiftest flight. It is this quality of repose in movement that gives to movements their eternal
element."[144] Savage's *Terpsichore* also suggests movement in rest, as though the figure is only
pausing briefly. Further, the small breasts, strong limbs, and bobbed hair all echo the features
of Duncan's body. One wonders whether Savage knew that several of her colleagues had had
personal encounters with the dancer. In July 1927, William Aspenwell Bradley, the agent and
friend of most American expatriate writers, took NAACP official Walter White and his wife,
Gladys, to his apartment on the Ile Saint-Louis to meet Duncan, who performed to the first
recording made by Paul Robeson, "Go Down, Moses."[145] The following year Duncan
danced for McKay in her studio in Nice, and he then acted as her guide to the red-light
district of Marseilles.[146] And Woodruff had met Duncan at the Hôtel de Colonie in Cagnes-
sur-Mer around 1929.[147]

    Duncan's influence may be evident in another of Savage's figural works, *La
Citadelle—Freedom* (ca. 1930, fig. 80). The small bronze figurine, little more than a foot

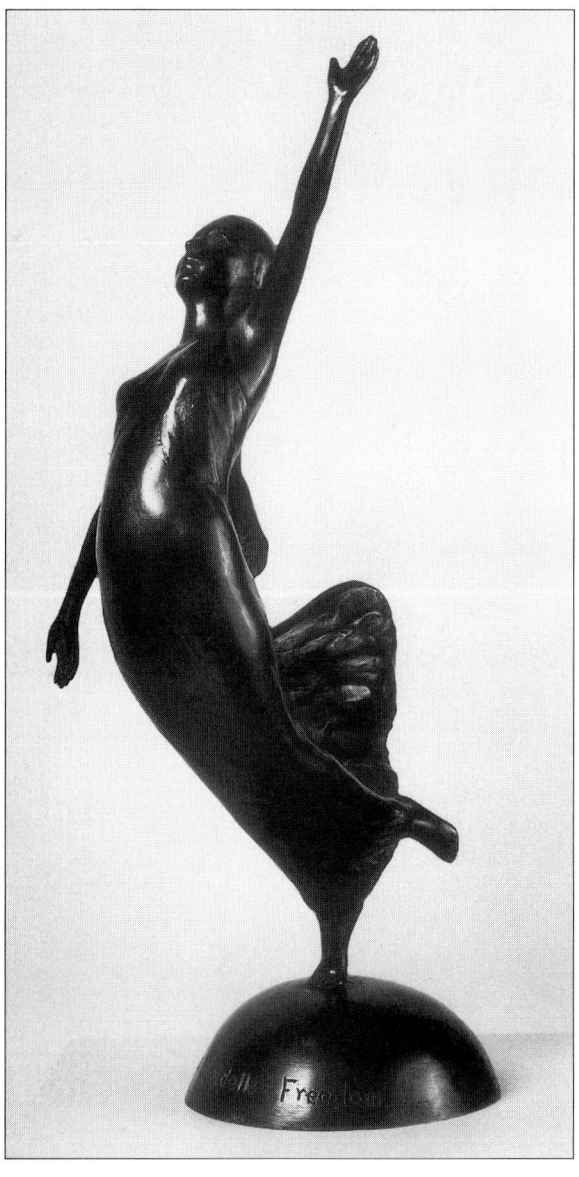

FIGURE 80
Augusta Savage, *La Citadelle—Freedom*,
ca. 1930, bronze, 14½ in. (h).
The Permanent Collection,
Howard University Gallery of Art,
Washington, D.C.

high, depicts a young woman standing on tiptoe on her right foot, her left foot flung out behind lifting her long, diaphanous tunic in a graceful swirl. The woman appears to be saluting something with her left, upraised arm, her right arm relaxed at her side palm forward, and her head tilted back. This lifted gesture of the head, Duncan said, was "one of the commonest figures [*sic*] in the Bacchic dances." She continued, "In this movement one senses immediately the Bacchic frenzy possessing the entire body. The movement underlying this gesture is in all nature. The animals, in Bacchic movement, turn back the head: in tropic countries, at night the elephants turn their heads; dogs baying at the moon, lions, tigers. It is the universal Dionysiac movement. The waves of the ocean form this line under a storm, the trees in a tempest."[148] With its fluid movement and loose gown, the figure evokes the energy

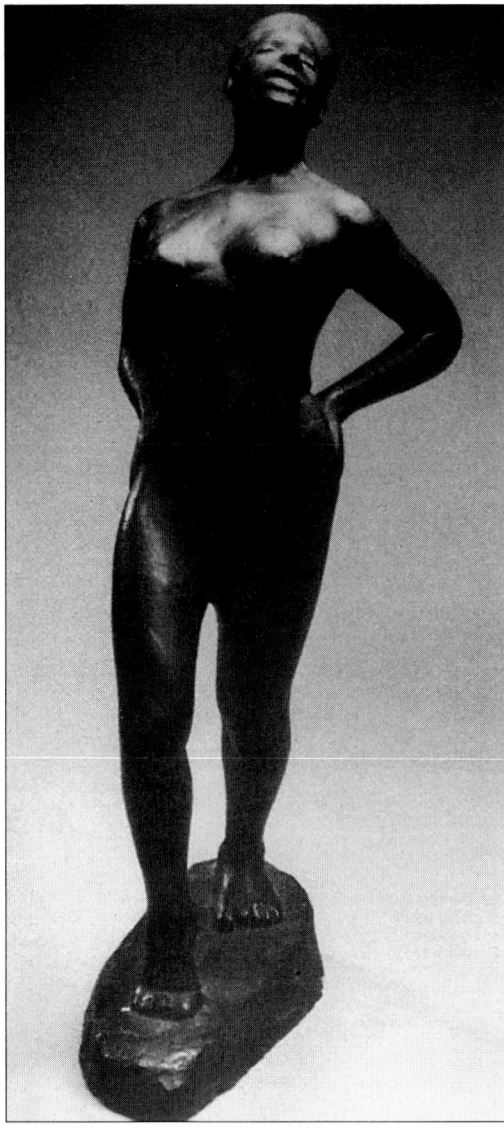

FIGURE 81
Augusta Savage, *Untitled*
(standing female figure), n.d., plaster,
18½ x 6¾ x 9⅜ in.
Collection of Lorraine Lucas.

and grace of Duncan. Its arclike silhouette, however, suggests a ship's masthead or even, given its small size, an automobile-hood ornament. Yet what is most intriguing about the piece is its title, which suggests the personification of freedom—or of Paris—as a woman who for Savage represents a citadel, fortress, or refuge. In Paris, she felt relatively protected from personal and financial hardship, at least for about two years, and free to create what she wished. The work's title as well as the gesture and simple clothing of the figurine also evoke Delacroix's painting *Liberty Leading the People* (1830). Rather than being a call to arms, Savage's dancing figurine may express an exuberant welcome to France.

        Savage produced another sculpture of a dancer in Paris that is now known only by its title, *Danseur nu* (ca. 1930). If this work depicted a woman, however, the title should have been *Danseuse nu*.[149] Along with a bronze work, *Nu* (also now known only by its title; perhaps fig. 81), which Savage exhibited at the Société des Artistes Français in 1931, it may have been among the first sculptures of nude black female bodies by an African American artist.[150]

The celebration of Josephine Baker's body in Paris since her first appearance there in 1925 with La Revue Nègre may have contributed to Savage's desire to depict beautiful, strong black women, but it was also the availability of black models willing to pose nude in Paris that allowed her to depict them with confidence. She informed one writer in France that in New York, "people of color, and in particular black models, refused to pose for her," but she did not say why.[151] Interestingly, McKay had worked as an artist's model, posing nude for painters in poorly heated Left Bank studios in 1923 while recovering from an illness that he had contracted in Russia. In his weakened state, he came down with pneumonia. There is no evidence that he ever modeled for any of his African American friends.[152]

The significance of Baker's success in Paris to African Americans and to the French perception of them cannot be denied. Not only was she a willing subject and participant in primitivist fantasies of Africans as carnal, sexual, and savage; her image was further distorted in an effort to capitalize on notions of desire; witness the racist and sexist images of the performer, caged and simianlike, in Paul Colin's lithograph portfolio *Le tumulte noir* (ca. 1927). As Richard Powell points out: "An almost universal ignorance of Africa, coupled with a legacy of exploitation of African peoples, created an atmosphere in which Westerners—usually taking their cues from Edgar Rice Burroughs novels and Hollywood jungle movies—saw "Africa" as either exotic and passionate or dangerous and fearsome."[153]

Intriguingly, despite Baker's fame, none of the African American visual artists in Paris ever seems to have been directly inspired by her. Virtually none of them, aside from Bennett, saw her perform, and they did not meet her, did not write about her, and did not depict her. Perhaps they were uncomfortable with her public persona and her primitivist connections, or perhaps they were too conscious of their conservative white patrons in the United States, who would have deplored such immodest behavior.

As a former Garveyite (or at least someone married to a prominent Garveyite leader), Savage would have been aware of the United Negro Improvement Association's movement to redefine Africa and make it a symbol of pride. The most striking works she produced abroad bespeak a strong sense of agency and strength, at the same time as they incorporate primitivist elements. These three plaster pieces, which I call the Amazon series,[154] are based on a single, female model of African descent. *Tête de jeune fille* (Head of a young girl, ca. 1930, known only by a photograph published in *La dépêche africaine*, fig. 82) is the nude bust of a young woman with broad facial features and coarse, curly, short hair. Head turned to the left, she gazes intently into the distance, lips closed. Her self-contained intensity is reminiscent of busts of African women by nineteenth-century French Romantic sculptors, such as Nicolas Cordier's *Vénus africaine* (1851) and Jean-Baptiste Carpeaux's *Pourquoi naître esclave* (1868), both of which were based on the same model, a former slave from the French colonies.[155] The model of *Tête* also appears as *The Amazon*

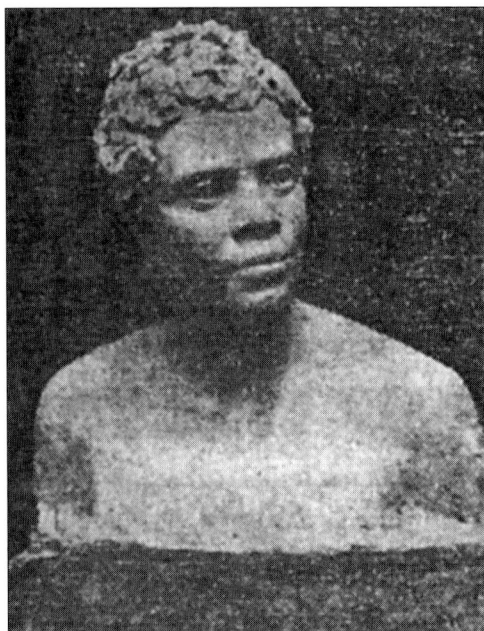

FIGURE 82
Augusta Savage, *Tête de jeune fille*, ca. 1930,
plaster(?), dimensions and location unknown.
Photograph from *La Dépêche Africaine*.

(ca. 1930, fig. 83) a bust of a nude female warrior holding a spear, and in *Mourning Victory* (ca. 1930, fig. 84), as a weaponless, standing nude who gazes at a severed head on the ground. The works are notable for their bold originality, their implied violence, and their mysterious significance.

The *Amazon* is a fully endowed female African woman, but Amazons were typically thought of as mythological Greek women who cut off one of their own breasts so they could more easily throw javelins. Perhaps Savage knew about Archibald Dalzel's book *The History of Dahomey, an Inland Kingdom of Africa* (1793), in which the explorer described the Dahomean king's female warriors, and was the first to call them Amazons.[156] The volume contains illustrations of the troops. One, titled "Armed Women, with the King at their head, going to War," depicts the guards topless save for loose loincloths.[157] The defenders were, in fact, the only thoroughly documented Amazons in world history. European visitors first referred to the women soldiers as Amazons in the 1840s.[158] The defenders of royalty and the palace existed since at least the eighteenth century.[159] The West African kingdom was once called a "small black Sparta" because residents of Dahomey aslo cultivated an intense militarism and sense of collectivism.[160] Moreover, both Spartan and Dahomean women prided themselves on bodies toughened from childhood by rigorous physical exercise. Yet Spartan females were raised to breed male warriors whereas these African Amazons were trained to kill them. Originally elite bodyguards to the king, the Dahomeans developed into a force six-thousand strong and were granted semisacred status.[161] They fought valiantly until the kingdom's final defeat by France in 1892.

Unlike the fantasized Amazons of antiquity, the Amazons of Dahomey never rode horses or any other animal, rarely used shields, and did not cut off their breasts. They vowed celibacy and thus did not produce children. Like their ancient forerunners, they lived by

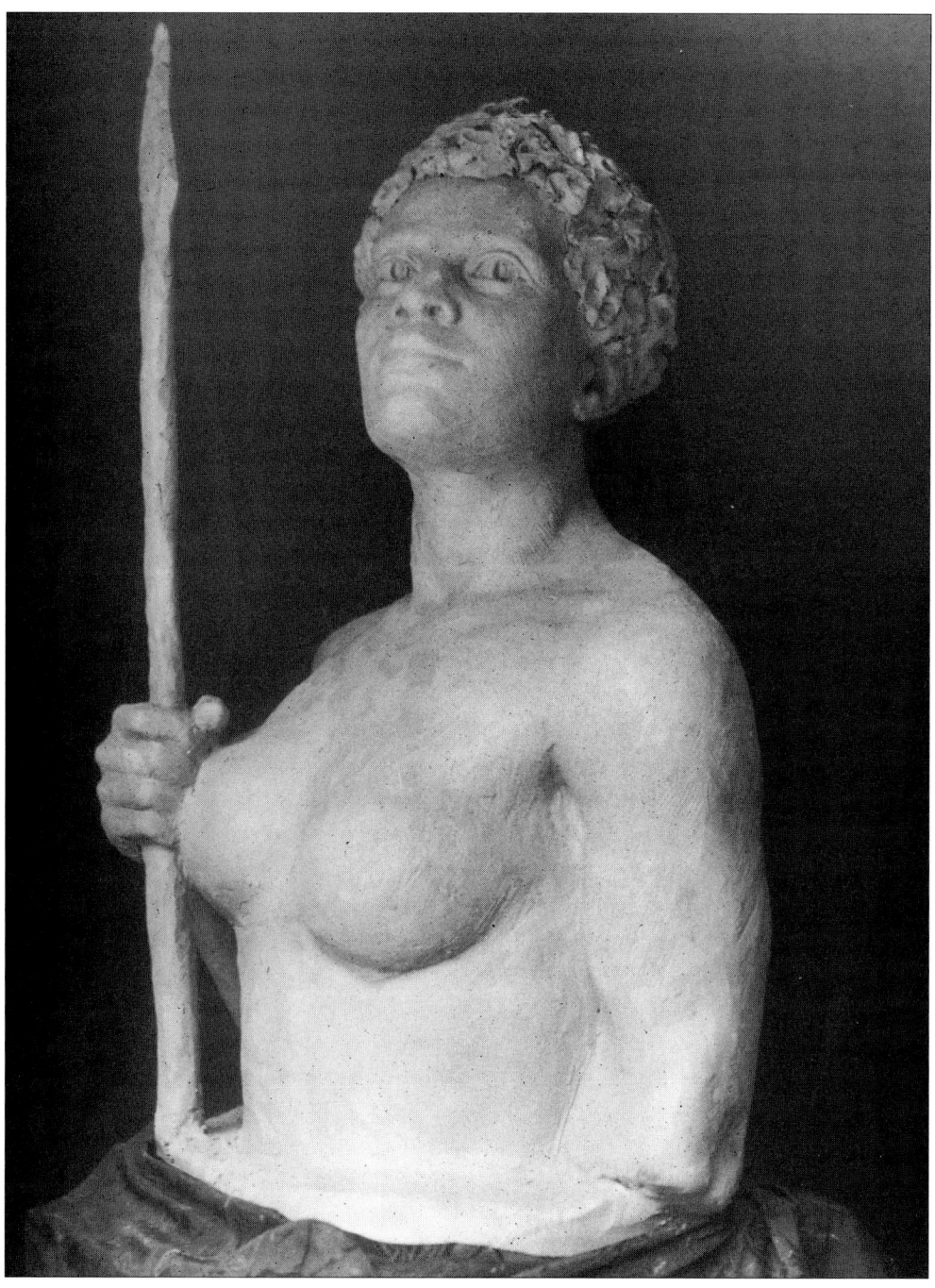

FIGURE 83
Augusta Savage, *The Amazon*, ca. 1930, clay, dimensions and location unknown.
Photograph in Rosenwald Collection, Fisk University Library.

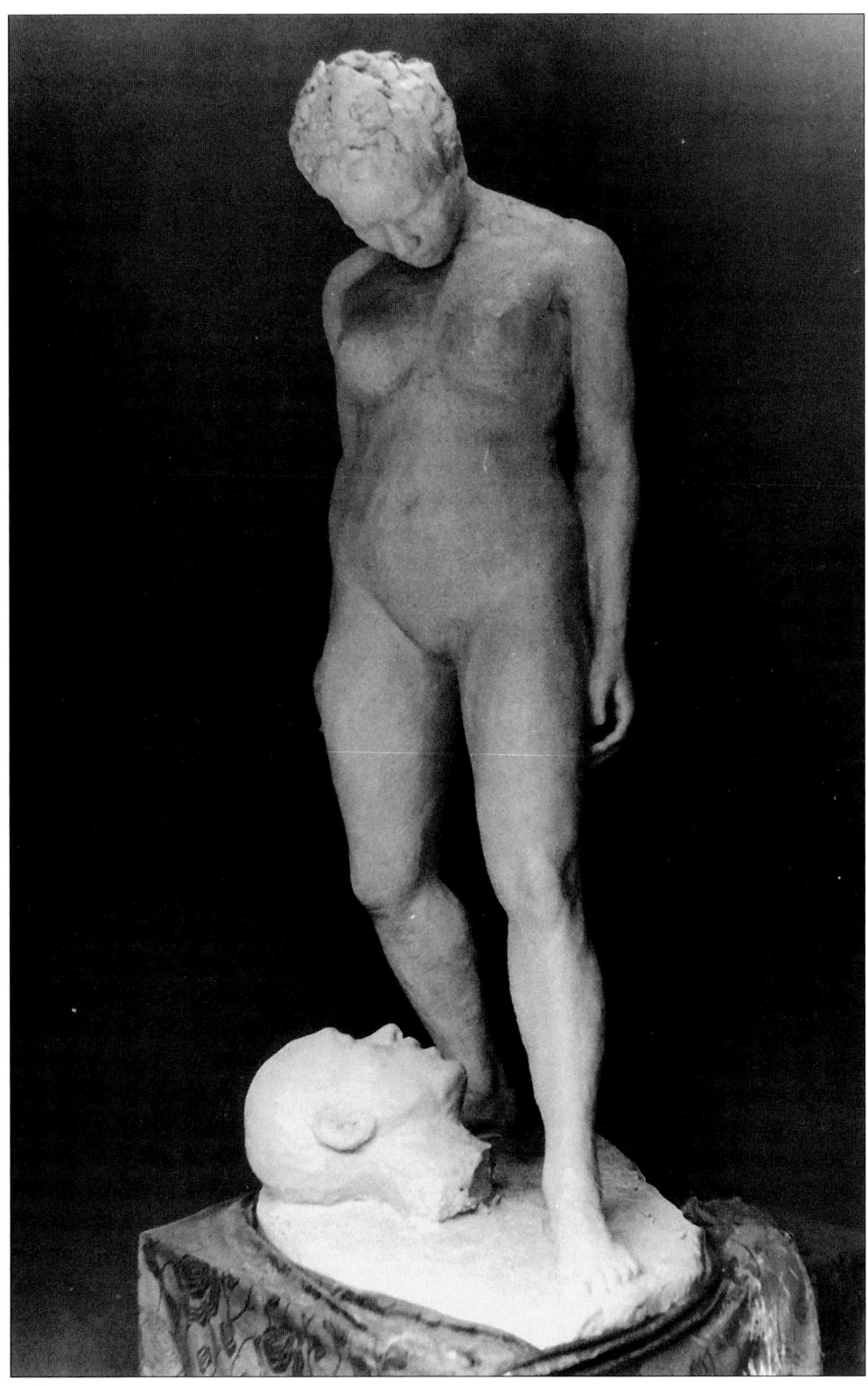

FIGURE 84
Augusta Savage, *Mourning Victory,* ca. 1930, clay, dimensions and location unknown.
Photograph in Rosenwald Collection, Fisk University Library.

themselves, but in royal palaces, not elsewhere autonomously. Further, they fought in an army with a male majority and were ultimately ruled by men.[162] The Amazons were recognized for their fierce, intrepid battle skills.

Savage's *Amazon* is a nude half figure, truncated at the waist. Her expression is similar to that of *Tête de jeune fille,* and her head is turned to the left, but with chin slightly uplifted. The warrior appears to be listening while standing at attention. Her breasts are full and round, but have no indication of nipples. Her left arm hangs at rest, yet she seems to have strong biceps. The soldier grasps a roughly modeled spear or pointed stick in her right hand. Dahomean Amazons mainly fought with muskets, clubs, and machetes, but did occasionally carry spears, lances, or assegais, which were light wooden javelins tipped with iron.[163] Savage's spear-wielding warrior is a far cry from typical French allegories of Africa, such as Carpeaux's *Les quatre parties du monde soutenant la sphère* (1872) in the Luxembourg Gardens. Here, the personified continent—whose features are not caricatured as are those of the blacks found in most European sculpture—is distinguished from her European, Chinese, and Native American sisters by a broken chain on one ankle, a reminder of slavery as well as a signal of liberation. Savage's *Amazon* never would have been a slave. Savage herself might have identified with the subject personally as an independent woman who was characterized by strength, boldness, perseverance, and nonreliance on men.

Contemporary scholars view the Greek myth of Amazons as an elaborate cautionary tale. In their patriarchal society, Greek men ruled, fought, hunted, farmed, and controlled marriage and reproduction. They saw their roles as natural, orderly, and civilized. Women were expected to obey, marry, keep house, rear children, and be modest and tame. Amazon society turned the status quo upside down, and appeared unnatural, disorderly, uncivilized, barbaric—and therefore doomed. It was a warning of what could happen if gender roles and values were reversed and women took charge.[164]

One wonders what other aspects of West African Amazons Savage found most intriguing. Clearly she, too, was challenging gender roles in a number of ways. She left home at an early age to pursue a career of which her father disapproved, attended college, allowed others to care for her young daughter while she traveled abroad alone as a widow, and enjoyed the company of male friends (Woodruff, Hayden, Cullen, and others). Further, she worked in sculpture, a field largely dominated by men. Yet the artist was not as stoic as the Amazons.

Mourning Victory may express Savage's discomfort with violence, and her anguish over death and separation. By the time she came to Paris, she had lost three husbands, several siblings, an infant daughter, and her father, and she had left behind her first daughter. But the depiction of a nude woman standing in *contrapposto* staring down at a severed adult male head gives few clues to its identity. Could the woman in *Mourning Victory* represent Salome, the New Testament figure who danced for the head of John the Baptist? Or is she Judith of the Apocrypha, who saved the city of Bethulia by cutting off the head of Holofernes? Could she be an Amazon reckoning with the violence and destruction of hand-to-hand combat? A possible source for this image is an illustration that appears in Frederick E. Forbes's *Dahomey and Dahomans* (London, 1851). Here a barefoot but clothed Amazon musketeer, a club and dagger tucked in her belt, holds a gun in one hand and a severed head by the hair in the other.

Beheading was the usual method of execution in Dahomey. Moreover, Amazons frequently decapitated and emasculated their victims with machetes or large, powerful razors. They either presented the enemies' heads and genitals to their leaders, or stuck the trophies on wooden stakes, iron spikes, hooks, or forks.[165] Some outer palace walls were adorned with the skulls of slain enemy soldiers.

The woman in Savage's *Mourning Victory* hardly appears to be a bloodthirsty or cruel warrior, however. She bears no arms and wears no battle gear. Head hung in apparent sorrow as she gazes at the face of the severed head, she seems weary and vulnerable. Her shoulders are slumped, her arms hang limply, her hips are tucked under, and her right leg is bent under the weight of her body and the moment of reckoning. Was the struggle worth the sacrifice? Was this truly a triumph?

The Amazon series represents a significant aspect of West African history. Images of Amazons became widely familiar in France through Dahomean ethnographic exhibitions at the Jardin d'Acclimation in 1891 and 1893 and when "100 Dahomeans and 25 Amazons" appeared at the 1892 Casino de Paris.

As proof of her progress, Savage sent photographs of the Amazon series and another work, *The Call* (ca. 1930, fig. 85), to the Rosenwald Foundation in May 1930. *The Call* portrays a nude young black man, his genital area discreetly covered by a cloth draped over his left leg between his spread thighs, listening intently and leaning forward slightly, hands pressed behind his hips on the boxlike seat, as he stares at a distant horizon. This work seems to be a more developed version of Savage's *The New Negro* (1927), another response to Locke's call for racially representative art.

Pleased with the photographs of her work, Arthur informed Savage that the fund had decided to renew her fellowship for another year at one thousand, eight hundred dollars. He wrote to her "as brother in the bond," on May 28, 1930, asking her to continue depicting black people:

> I hope you will continue to work primarily with negro [*sic*] models. I hope also that you will try to develop something original, born out of a deep spirituality which you, as a Negro woman, must feel in depicting modern Negro subjects. I even hope that you will not become too much imbued with European standards of technique, if they are going to kill the other something which in my opinion some Negro will eventually give to American art, maybe in sculpture, maybe in music, painting or literature. At any rate, *know* the culture and technique of other races, but do not simply be a copy of them at the expense of originality of your own. In my opinion there is just one field in which the Negro has an equal chance with the white man in American life and that field is art. If he follows standards of even the white Americans, which in turn have copied them from Europe, then the Negro can at best be but a bad copy of the copy. Maybe that is the reason why so much bad work is put out by our men.[166]

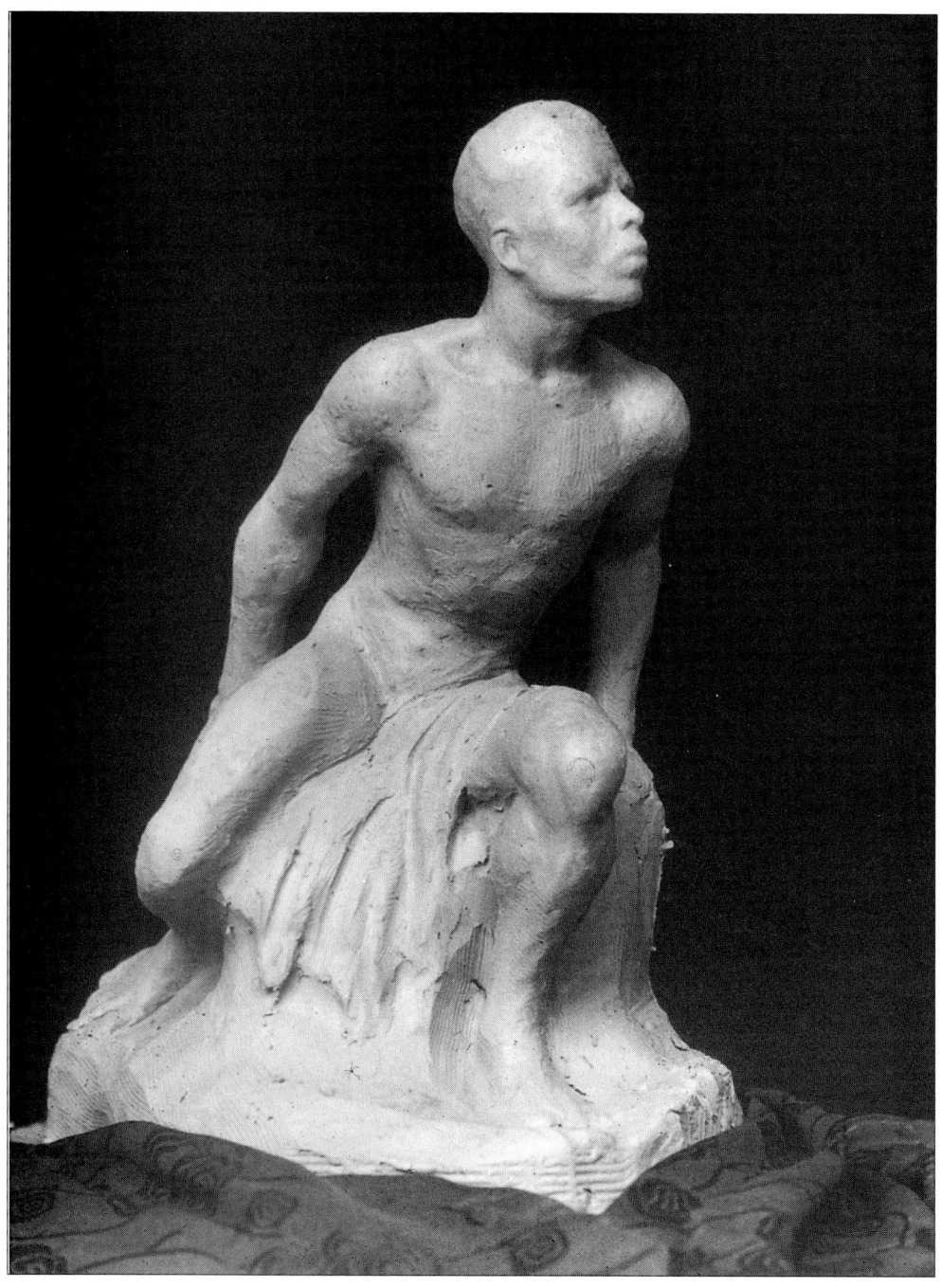

FIGURE 85
Augusta Savage, *The Call*, ca. 1930, clay, dimensions and location unknown.
Photograph in Rosenwald Collection, Fisk University Library.

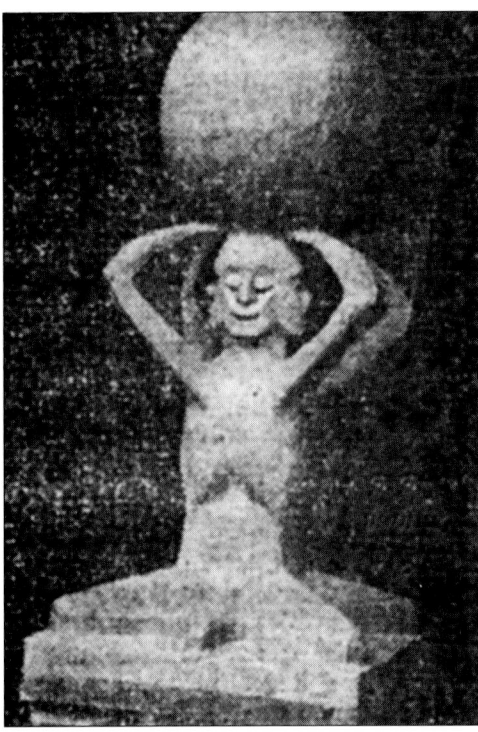

FIGURE 86
Augusta Savage, *Divinité nègre,* ca. 1930,
plaster (?), dimensions and location unknown.
From *La Dépêche Africaine,*
August–September 1930.

Savage was pleased with Arthur's "brotherly advice," and wrote to him that she was "glad that you are of my way of thinking."[167] But she also informed him that she was timid about showing her latest piece (identity unknown) because she was working in a "quite different" style and was concerned about its reception. Nevertheless, she considered it her "best effort so far" because several artists had been "almost unanimous in their praise." They urged her to have the piece cast in bronze and exhibited. Savage explained, "It is African in feeling but modern in design, but whatever else might be said it *is* original."[168]

Savage may have been referring to her *Divinité nègre* (ca. 1930, fig. 86), a small figurine in sharp planes with a four-sided woman's head, four folded legs that make a X, and four uplifted arms sustaining a globe.[169] The work may evoke an African power figure that Savage might have seen at the Musée de l'Homme, but it does not seem to be a copy of a single work of African sculpture. Instead, she claimed it was "a black divinity born of an imagination nourished by legends and readings about Africans"[170] (it is not known which African legends Savage had read). Aside from Palmer Hayden's well-known painting *Fétiche et fleurs* (ca. 1931–1932), itself little more than an acknowledgment of the vogue for things African according to Hayden, *Divinité nègre* is one of the few works produced by an African American artist as a literal response to Locke's directive to study the example of African art for inspiration.[171] However, Savage would later claim that she was "opposed to the theory of critics that the American Negro should produce African art." She emphasized the culture that black and white Americans shared: "For the last 300 years we have had the same cultural background, the same system, the same standard of beauty as white Americans. In art schools we draw from Greek casts. We study the small mouth, the proportions of the features and limbs. It is impossible to go back to the primitive art for our models." Yet Savage added that "there are certain traits and inherent racial characteristics which occur frequently in Negro artists' work which may approach the primitive," including "the sense of rhythm and spontaneous imagination."[172] *Divinité nègre* also appears Buddha-like in the pose of the legs, and multiple limbs are typical of Hindu sculpture. It seems that Savage invented her own "African" deity using multiple sources.

No doubt Savage was familiar with the work of sculptors other than Carpeaux, Rodin, and Bourdelle in Paris. Yet, generally, her style was more akin to theirs than to the Cubism of Jacques Lipchitz and Ossip Zadkine, the Classicism of Elie Nadelman's bronze nudes, the Art Deco found in the wood carving of Chana Orloff, the modernism in the daring combination of a formal hat and gloves with a nude male torso in Oscar Miestchaninoff's *Man in a Top Hat* (1922), or the sleek, aerodynamic forms of Brancusi. Her vision of New Negro art, while stylistically derivative of European art, was fresh and original in its depiction of black people and culture and reaffirmed by her personal encounters with those from the African diaspora in France.

Paris was a place where Savage could enjoy the company of other notable African Americans. Although Du Bois had advised her to cut off her English-speaking friends and try to speak nothing but French,[173] Savage frequently met with other compatriots. In the spring of 1930, John Matheus, a teacher of Romance languages and the private secretary to sociologist Charles S. Johnson, invited Savage out to dinner. Matheus and Johnson were members of an international committee on their way to investigate the charges of forced-labor practices in Liberia.[174] Savage also often had dinner and played cards with painters Hale Woodruff, Palmer Hayden, and Aaron Douglas and writer Countee Cullen. Delighted to talk with Cullen about literature again, Savage produced for him a witty and suavely generalized pair of small bronze bookends of unidentified men in bowler hats at *pissotières,* public urinals common in France (ca. 1930–1931, figs. 87 and 88). (One wonders if she was also slyly commenting on the way in which Cullen and his intimate companion, Harold Jackman, may have met some of their French male lovers.) Clearly, the expressionistic style and earthy subject matter of these works mark a strong departure from Savage's earlier realistic portraits of community leaders.

In June 1930, Savage reported that since the studios and schools were all closing for the summer, she hoped to take advantage of the vacation time by visiting other art centers. She requested that Arthur send her two fellowship installments at once for travel. Apparently, the Rosenwald Fund was unwilling to send Savage advance money for travel, but the Carnegie Corporation sent her some financial means for the purpose.[175] She seems to have viewed sculpture in museums, galleries, churches, and cathedrals in France, Belgium, and Germany at this time.[176]

During the late summer, Savage met Paulette Nardal, the West Indian editor of the bilingual magazine *La revue du monde noir* (Review of the Black World, 1930–1932),

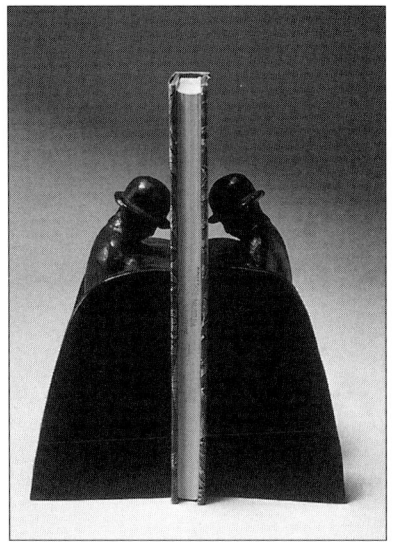
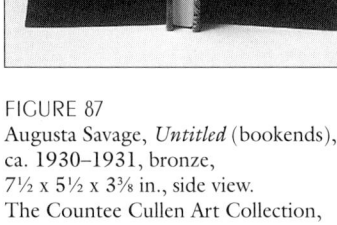
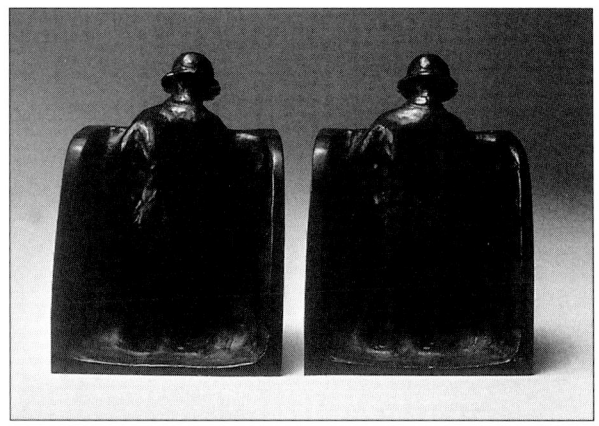

FIGURE 87
Augusta Savage, *Untitled* (bookends),
ca. 1930–1931, bronze,
7½ x 5½ x 3⅜ in., side view.
The Countee Cullen Art Collection,
Hampton University Museum,
Hampton, Virginia.

FIGURE 88
Augusta Savage, *Untitled* (bookends),
1930–1931, bronze,
7½ x 5½ x 3⅜ in., front view.
The Countee Cullen Art Collection,
Hampton University Museum,
Hampton, Virginia.

who had arrived in Paris in 1928. She founded the journal with Léo Sajous, from Haiti. They used the publication as a vehicle to discuss diasporic culture, ethnographic studies, Harlem Renaissance poetry ("la poésie du nègre nouveau"), the primacy of sensation and instinct, racial consciousness, and *Afro-latinité* (composite French-African identity).[177]

While still in Martinique, Nardal and her sister Jeanne saw themselves as French citizens and espoused the assimilationist views of their middle-class mulatto environment. Once they encountered the paternalistic and ethnocentric attitudes of some Parisians, who saw them as exotic women akin to Josephine Baker, they decided to battle white cultural chauvinism by publishing their own periodical about black achievements.[178] Their goal was "to create among the Negroes of the entire world, regardless of nationality, an intellectual and moral tie which will permit them to better know each other, to love one another, to defend more effectively their collective interests and to glorify their race."[179]

Paulette Nardal also held a literary salon with another sister, Andrée, from 1929 to 1934. There, African, Caribbean, and African American writers and artists met to discuss proto-Négritude ideas. It is not known, however, whether Savage ever attended those gatherings.

Nardal arrived at Savage's modest atelier just as the artist was stepping out. Savage had already covered up her works in progress with wet cloths, but she graciously unveiled them. Nardal was impressed with the sculptures and with Savage's charming personality: "She is a slender young woman with an extraordinarily soft voice of an unaffectedness that immediately makes her appealing." Nardal published a feature article on Savage, "Une femme sculpteur noire," in the August-September issue of Maurice Satineau's monthly newspaper *La dépêche africaine* (begun in 1928; nothing else is known about the publication or the publisher), accompanied by photographs of *Divinité nègre*, *Tête de jeune fille*, and *Gamin*. Just as writers had discerned "racial" qualities in Prophet's work, so Nardal found them in Savage's: "Her inspiration is of a racial order before all, something fairly rare among conquered and uprooted races. That is why she easily succeeds in the modern genre that is so imbued with Negro art." Nardal was particularly taken with the irony of *Green Apples* (ca. 1927, mentioned earlier). "Savage wouldn't be truly Negro if she didn't have a sharp sense of humor," she quipped with her own sharp wit, concluding on a flattering note: "We do not doubt that Augusta Savage's stay in Paris will be very profitable for her, and that the charming artist will find every success here which she merits for her originality, her fine talent, and her sincerity."[180]

In the fall of 1930, Savage succeeded in exhibiting a work called *Homme* (Man) at the Salon d'Automne.[181] This may have been the same work as *Martiniquaise* (Woman of Martinique, ca. 1930, fig. 89) or *Head of a Boy* (the title of this work is uncertain); an article in the *Chicago Whip* announced that Savage exhibited *Martiniquaise*, a black marble head there, but it also stated that she exhibited a nude figure at the salon.[182] While the Salon catalog only lists *Homme*—to make matters more confusing—Savage informed administrators of the Rosenwald Fund that she had three works exhibited at the Salon and she sent them the receipts to prove it, asking for their return so that she could claim her works at the close of the exhibition.[183] At any rate, Savage did produce a slightly larger-than-life, androgynous-looking head in black Belgian marble while she was in Paris. The head has an intense gaze, slender cheeks and nose, full lips, small ears, and a large, bulbous, bald head. It is especially this last feature that has led to confusion over the sexual identity of the piece (shades of Prophet's *Congolais*!); various writers have labeled reproductions of it *Head of a Boy*,[184] and others *Martiniquaise* (Woman of Martinique).[185] Whatever the sex and title of the piece, the smoothly modeled black marble head is a powerful image. With its hard, polished surface, intense stare, strong chin, and forward thrust of the neck, it expresses far more agency and assertiveness than Prophet's *Congolais*.

There is no other information about Savage's activities during the fall of 1930, but it may have been then that she created three pieces in wood; on January 8, 1931, she wrote to Keppel that she had been sculpting directly in this material. One of these works is *The Chase* (1930), a palm wood sculpture that depicts a fully outstretched panther, a black leopard, pursuing a gazelle up a steep sliver of cliff, with the animals' bodies hugging the angular rock's surface.[186] In this work, Savage returned to the subject matter of her youth, but she depicted wild African animals rather than tame barnyard creatures. It is not known whether she was cognizant of the leopard's high status among West African peoples, but she must have been aware of the prevalence of leaping gazelles in Art Deco design.[187] Savage's work does evince Art Deco qualities, with its sleek, streamlined, geometrically sharp planes

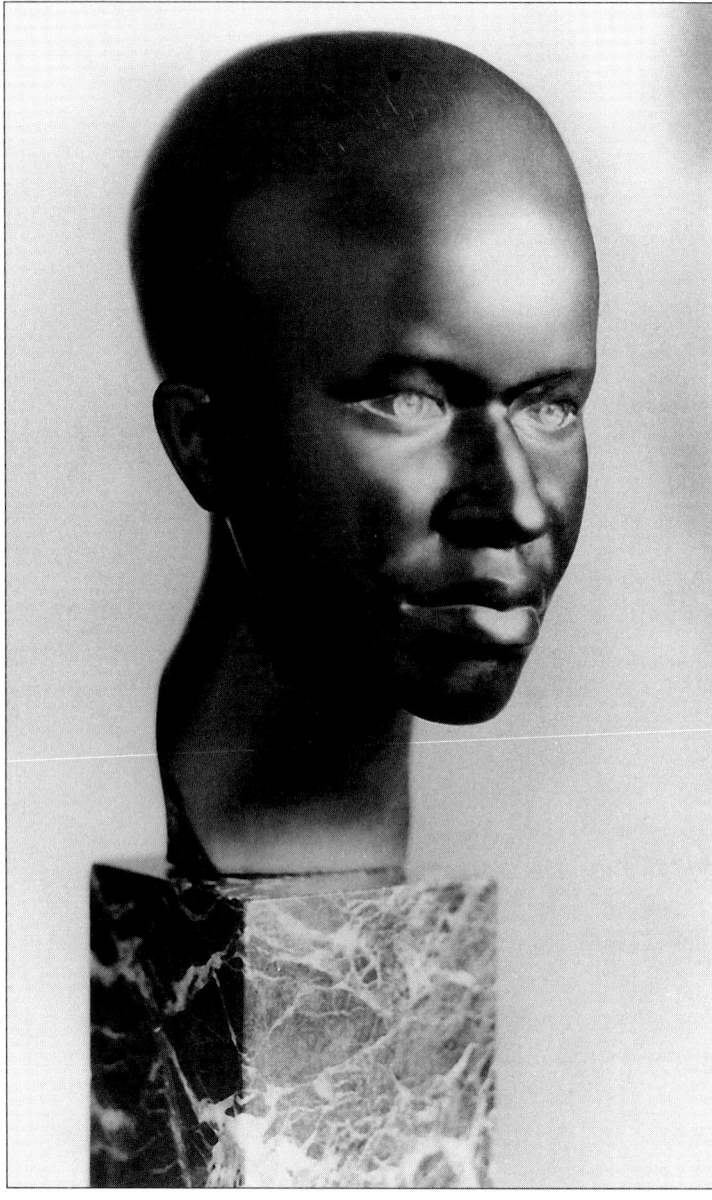

FIGURE 89
Augusta Savage,
Martiniquaise
(or *Head of a Boy*),
ca. 1930, black Belgian
marble, dimensions
and location unknown.
Photograph courtesy
of Harry Henderson.

and minimal degree of detail. One wonders if she had also seen Alfred Janniot's sculptural relief for the Palais des Colonies (1931) in the making: above one doorway a leaping lion claws a gazelle. The Harmon Foundation exhibited *The Chase,* along with *Bust* (unidentified; lost), in 1931.

Savage's work in wood seems to have become increasingly abstract, if she sculpted the teakwood *Envy* (good quality reproduction unavailable; location unknown) after *The Chase*. Savage's brother-in-law, T. R. Poston, later described *Envy* as a four-foot carving that "showed a shadowy figure of a woman with a crooked finger placed at the tip of her aquiline nose, frowning at the world before her. The minute detail, the hunched shoulders, the narrow chest, the clinging garments reveal the sheer poetry of the creator's conception and her every inch the artist."[188] *Envy* evokes Prophet's work (especially *Discontent, Bitter Laughter,* and *Prayer*) in its style and content, but it is not known how much of Prophet's work, if any, Savage saw. Savage would exhibit *Envy,* along with *Gamin* and *Martiniquaise,* at the tenth annual Spring Salon of American Art in 1932 at the Anderson Galleries, located at 30 East Fifty-Seventh Street. The Salons of American Art was an organization of artists founded in 1922 by Hamilton Easter Field, a renowned Brooklyn art patron.[189] The piece later received wide acclaim and was exhibited at the Women's National Exposition of Arts and Industries at the Grand Central Palace in France and at the Harlem festival in New York.[190]

Savage's most abstract work is *Fern Frond* (ca. 1930–1931, fig. 90), a small, polished figure of a standing woman in richly glowing black walnut gently unfurling herself, as if awakening. In concept, *Fern Frond* evokes Fuller's *Ethiopia Awakening* of ca. 1914 (see fig. 5), perhaps the first work by an African American to blend Pan-Africanism with the growing awareness of women's potential. *Ethiopia Awakening* depicts a standing young woman in an Egyptian headdress gently releasing herself from mummy cloths. Both sculptures bespeak rebirth and self-realization. Savage's piece, however, is utterly modern in its abstraction, and evokes a more universal idea of consciousness.

Charles Ratton (1895–1986?), the extremely influential French dealer of African art, whose advertisement appeared just below the article on Savage in *La Dépêche Africaine,* bought *Fern Frond* for his private collection.[191] Ratton played a decisive role in the diffusion of African art and the revision of ideas concerning it by recognizing certain stylistic regions that had previously been underestimated or unfamiliar; improving relations with museologists; donating seventy objects to the Musée de l'Homme; arranging for the celebrated exhibition of African art at the Galerie Pigalle in 1930; supplying African sculptures for exhibition at the Colonial Exposition; procuring African art masterpieces for the collections of Jacob Epstein, Baron von der Heydt, and Helena Rubenstein; and lending his collection of African art simultaneously to the Pierre Matisse gallery and the Museum of Modern Art in New York in 1935.[192] Unfortunately, nothing is known about the circumstances of the sale or even whether Savage and Ratton ever met. We may never know whether Ratton was drawn to Savage's work for its own merit or whether he selected it in part because she was black. Nevertheless, it may have been through his connections that Savage received recognition at the Colonial Exposition. Using an elusive article from the *Chicago Whip* as their source (the clipping has since disappeared from the Schomburg Research Center for Black Culture), several authors write that Savage executed an African figure in conjunction with the exposition (possibly a work in the Amazon series), but disagree on whether it received a medallion itself or whether it was selected for medallion reproduction.[193] Unfortunately, nothing else is yet known about Savage's involvement with or response to the grand event.

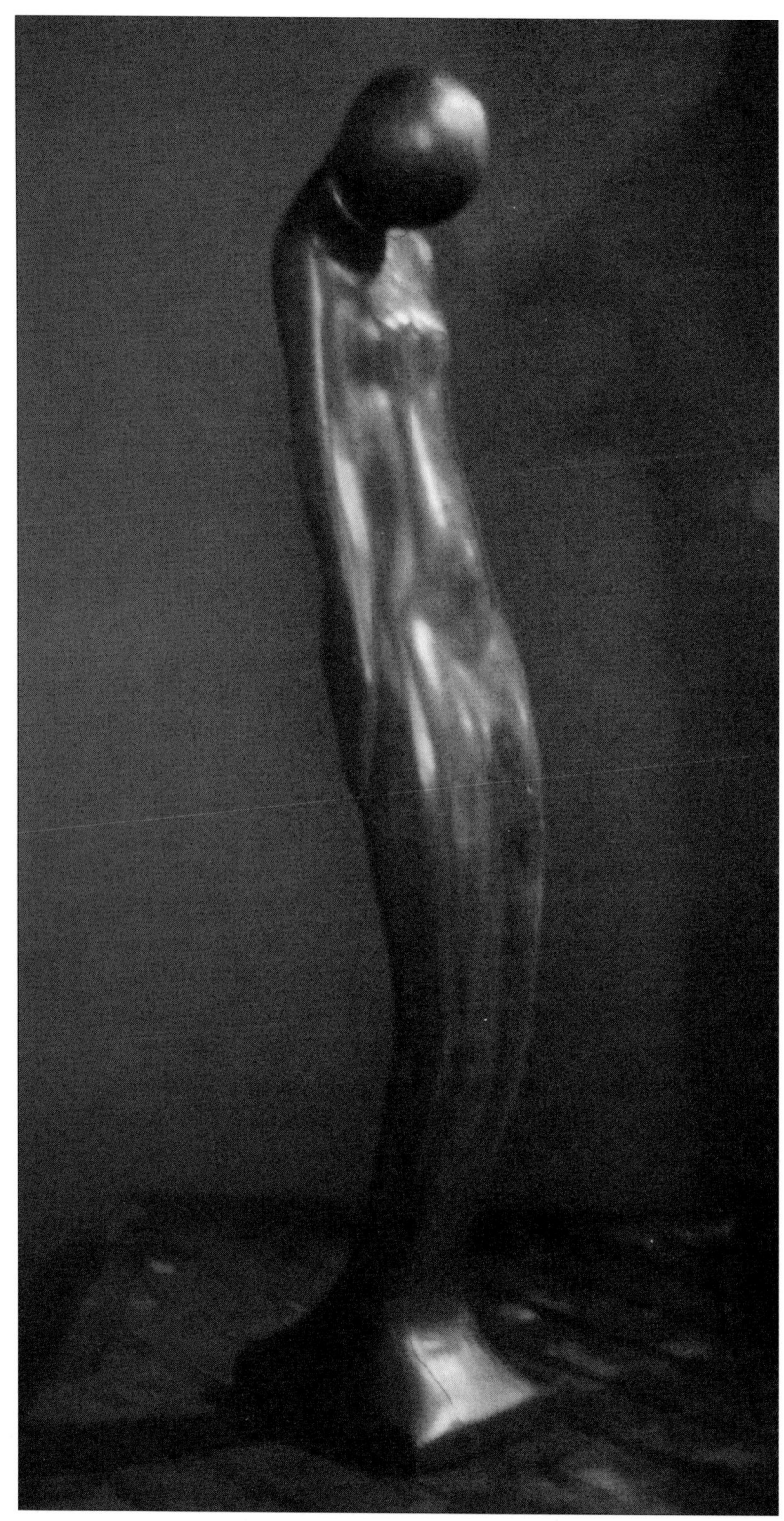

FIGURE 90
Augusta Savage, *Fern Frond,* ca. 1930–1931, walnut, 10 in. (h).
Private collection, Paris.

"MORE THAN AN ARTIST CAN RESIST": A SECOND EXHIBITION IN PARIS, 1931

By January 1931, Savage had moved to the outskirts of Paris, to 3, square de Châtillon, a few blocks from the Parc de Montsouris. Her new atelier was at 36, avenue de Châtillon, Prophet's former studio. Savage and Countee Cullen would sometimes go to the nearby Salon du Thé Vivier at the corner of avenue de Châtillon and rue d'Alésia.[194] After Cullen left Paris, Savage missed him greatly and wrote:

> I have been trying to decide whether I want to see you in Paris before I leave or see you in New York before you leave. I do want to do the beguine and play bellotte [belotte] (is that the way you spell it!) in New York.
>
> Sophie and Steve [Greene; the white couple befriended Cullen, Savage, and Woodruff] are like two kids waiting for Christmas. I think your week in Paris is going to be an orgy and I don't want to miss it, but unless something turns up soon I shall have to go home next month. Sob, sob, sob!!! I am trying to work up a case of homesickness, but without much success as the only one who could make Harlem bearable is you and you are coming back here so I shall be totally lost![195]

Savage wrote this letter to Cullen shortly after she had asked Keppel for additional funding. She believed that no further funds were forthcoming, and she would spend much of the spring of 1931 pleading for money from various members of both the Carnegie Corporation and the Rosenwald Fund. In early January, she had reported to the Carnegie Corporation that she had made much better progress than she had expected and was "sculpting directly on wood and marble." She mentioned that some friends who were visiting Paris the previous summer had very kindly donated a large piece of marble on which she was just beginning to work. Savage explained that she was running out of money and would have to return to the United States by the end of March, when she would receive her last Rosenwald check. She believed that she could not possibly finish all the pieces she had started before summer, and she predicted if she didn't "have a sufficient amount of work for exhibitions in America when I return in order to realize perhaps a little money, I shall be as badly off as when I started." She wondered whether she could get a Rockefeller scholarship if she showed her acceptance card from the Salon d'Automne and also could present letters of recommendation from several well-known sculptors in Paris; "I know that it is difficult for a girl to get a Fellowship because it is said that girls don't stick to their work, but surely my record for the past ten years proves me an exception to that rule, don't you think?"[196]

In the same letter Savage asked Keppel to recommend her for the Rockefeller scholarship because, she argued, "even six months more [abroad] will mean a great deal just now because if I have to return to America now there is not much chance of my coming back to Paris." She enclosed photographs of her entries to the Salon d'Automne as proof of her progress. Within a month, a reproduction of *Terpsichore* appeared in the *Baltimore Afro-American* newspaper (if this work appeared in the Salon, there is no record of it); Keppel may have forwarded a photograph of it.[197]

Keppel then apparently argued Savage's case to the Rosenwald Fund. Embree answered him: "We are pretty proud of our fellowship to Miss Augusta Savage and are entirely open-minded about an extension of it. We are writing asking her to give us a little statement about her work and needs. It was sporting of you to send a note. Appeals come to us all in plenty but a private tip from a friend about a useful thing to do is most helpful."[198] The Rosenwald Fund refused additional aid, however, which was "a great blow" to Savage.[199]

Savage then wrote to Arthur informing him that she planned on leaving Paris at the end of May. She stated that a friend in New York was working to get her an exhibition at Arden [Argent] Galleries, but that she had no other prospects, except the hope of an exhibition in Chicago. She was pleased that two of her works had been accepted for the Salon du Printemps, but was concerned that she would not be able to claim them until the middle of July. Savage stated, "My fellowship has been terribly inadequate for the kind of work that I am doing but I have managed to accomplish a lot and I am thankful. I hope that you will be pleased with the results."[200]

It is not known whether Savage actually exhibited works at the Salon du Printemps; a catalog for the exhibition does not exist. She may have confused it with the Société des Artistes Français exhibition, held that spring, where she showed three works. Two of Savage's works, in fact, the bronze *Nu* and the plaster bust *Martiniquaise,* the bust (both lost), mentioned earlier, were shown at the Société des Artistes Français in 1931.[201] On April 23, Savage wrote to Keppel that she had risked her fare back home in order to have the works cast in bronze, as she had a better chance of having them accepted that way (yet the catalog lists *Martiniquaise* as a plaster work; its medium distinguishes it from the other work of a Martinican, in black marble). She rationalized the decision by writing, "You will be pleased I am sure as it is a very great honor for me." Since she knew no one who could send the works to the United States and since she could not get the works back until July 15, after the exhibition closed, she paid her rent for another three months. Savage figured that if she sold one or both pieces she would be "all right."[202]

On May 1, Savage asked Embree for an extension on her fellowship until September. She explained that she had depleted much of her money by having several works cast in bronze: "Perhaps you will think that I acted unwisely, but I assure you that the chance of having work accepted by the Salon is more than an artist can resist. If you can make it possible for me to stay on a few months until after the Salon and in the meantime finish my other work I shall be very grateful as it would help me out of an awkward situation."[203] Embree agreed to the extension and had Arthur give her an additional $750 to carry her through until July, to cover the crating and shipping of her work, and to pay for her fare home.[204] Nothing else is known about Savage's final months in Paris.

ASSESSMENT OF SAVAGE'S PARIS YEARS

In September, Savage returned to New York with about twenty sculptures, "some of them quite large."[205] In October, she received an offer from a church in Chicago to exhibit the pieces, but apparently gave up the idea when she discovered that neither the church nor the Rosenwald Fund was willing to pay for transportation expenses. She was dismayed by the grim financial situation of the nation in the wake of the Great Depression. Fortunately, through the aid of Keppel, she received the position of teacher of sculpture at the Boykin Art School in Greenwich Village. She would sustain herself in various teaching positions throughout the 1930s—as founder and director of the Savage Studio of Arts and Crafts (early 1930s); instructor for an adult education project of the State University of New York, with aid from the Carnegie Corporation (1934); assistant supervisor for the Works Progress Administration Federal Art Project in the Uptown Art Laboratory (1936); and director of the Harlem Community Art Center (1937).[206] Many of Savage's students would become well-known artists, including Jacob Lawrence, Gwendolyn Knight, Norman Lewis, William Artis, and Ernest Crichlow. Savage continued to exhibit her work, at Anderson Art Galleries (1932), the Harmon Foundation (1933), Argent Galleries (1934, 1938), the State Museum of New Jersey (1935), her studio (1935), and the Uptown Art Laboratory (1936).

In 1936 the Rosenwald Fund asked Savage to fill out a form describing the benefits of her fellowship. She wrote:

> One of the greatest benefits I received from studying in Europe on this fellowship was a first-hand encounter with the sources of art (the opportunity to visit the galleries where world-famous works of art are on view). Another benefit I rec'd [sic] was the opportunity to study wood-carving and sculpture in the free manner in which it is taught in European schools as contrasted to the more formal, conventional type of training I had rec'd in America. After this time I was able to set up classes for young Negro students and pass on to them what I had learned while studying in Europe. . . . I feel that the very fact of a Negro's having won a Rosenwald scholarship serves to encourage other Negro artists, for many of the benefits I have received and the acclaim of my work has brought has been due to the fact of my having received such a scholarship. One example of this is the fact that I am the only Negro member of the National Association of Women Painters and Sculptors.[207]

Savage was elected to this association in 1934. She exhibited two works there that year, including *The Abstract Madonna* (lost), which African American art historian James Porter hailed as her forte for its "brooding and profound mood." Porter apparently did not think highly of the work Savage had produced in Paris. In 1940 he wrote: "From 1929 to 1932 there occurred a leveling off in her production. This was the result of the influence of studies abroad when she set aside her own convictions to learn techniques and to carve subjects that communicate a certain *joie de vivre*—but which also happen to be trivial. Not until she returned from Europe did she recapture the moods in which she created 'Gamin' and the remarkable head of W.E.B. Du Bois, now in the 135th Street New York Public Library—two productions that are truly masterful."[208]

Obviously, Porter was unaware of the remarkable strength and diversity of the art that Savage created abroad. Or perhaps, since he was a conservative artist himself, Porter did not appreciate her nonrealistic sculpture. In France, Savage's work became more expressionistic and modern and her subject matter included genre works, anonymous portrait busts, African-inspired figures of black men and women, an Amazon-woman series, exotic animals, dancing nudes, and figures symbolic of emotional and physical states of being. Being in Paris on fellowships truly afforded Savage the freedom to create what she wished.

7
PLAYING TO AMERICAN AND EUROPEAN AUDIENCES:
ALBERT ALEXANDER SMITH ABROAD, 1922–1940

Of all the African American artists who went to France between the wars, Albert Alexander Smith (fig. 91) was the most prolific. He produced at least 220 prints, drawings, and paintings. His productivity, however, spans twenty years abroad. Smith was the only African American expatriate besides Tanner who died in France, just three years after Tanner. Smith is further distinguished as the only African American artist who was a printmaker during this time and the only one who made his living as a musician. In fact, it was Smith's musical talent, rather than his artistic skill, that first took him overseas when he joined the 807 Pioneer Band and served in the American Expeditionary Forces during World War I.

Enthralled by the freedom he found in Europe, Smith moved there in 1920, after graduating from the National Academy of Design in New York. He maintained an apartment in Montmartre, but also traveled constantly throughout Europe with various bands and orchestras, as a jazz musician and singer. At the same time, after a year's study at the Académie des Beaux-Arts in Liège, Belgium, he achieved an impressive exhibition history. His prints and paintings were shown in Paris, Cannes, Brussels, New York, and Boston; they received awards from the Harmon Foundation; and they were frequently featured in the NAACP and National Urban League magazines, *Crisis* and *Opportunity,* respectively. Smith's works are significant for their social commentary on racism, their themes of global racial uplift, their exploration of human types and stereotypes, and their technical excellence. Perhaps the dominant motif in Smith's work is theatricality, or a sense of always being aware of putting on a show for diverse audiences. As a performer, Smith knew how to satisfy his customers. As an artist, he produced three distinctive genres: scenes of European landmarks

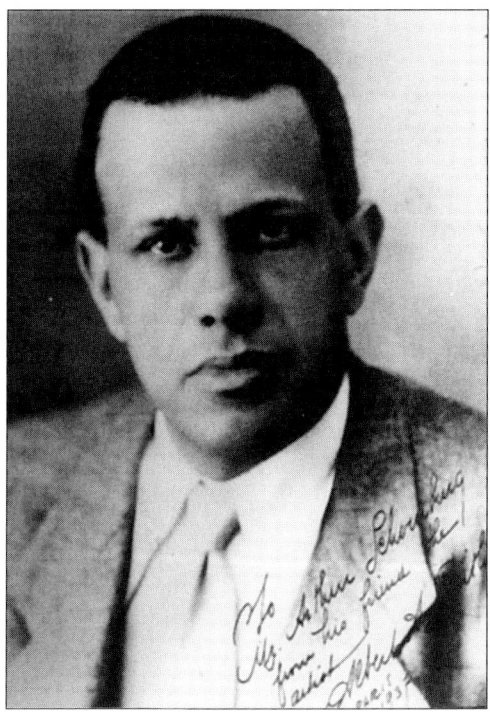

FIGURE 91
Albert Alexander Smith, 1937,
photographer unknown, dimensions unknown.
Art and Artifacts Division, Schomburg Center for
Research in Black Culture, The New York Public
Library, Astor, Lenox, and Tilden Foundations.

and character studies for the tourist market, images of a grand African past for illustrations to grace the covers and pages of *Crisis* and *Opportunity,* and black, Southern rural scenes for the Harmon Foundation and other white clients.

L'AMBITION AND THE REASON (FOR LEAVING NEW YORK), 1896–1920

Smith, born September 17, 1896, grew up in a black, middle-class neighborhood on the Upper West Side of New York City. Like Woodruff, Smith was an only child. His father, Alfred Renforth Smith, the lifelong chauffeur to Ralph Pulitzer, and his mother, Elizabeth A. Smith, a homemaker, were immigrants from Bermuda who were eager to see their child succeed in the United States. They encouraged his artistic talents early on, paying for music lessons (it is not known which instruments Smith played, but later he was recognized as a banjo player and guitarist) and praising his drawings of farm animals.[1] After graduation from Public School No. 70 in 1911, Smith attended the DeWitt Clinton High School for two years in a neighborhood where he socialized with African Americans, European Americans, and Hispanic Americans.[2] He seems to have had relatively carefree adolescent years and enjoyed "dances, parties, ice-creams, headaches, crushes, and a list of other weaknesses at the time youth was guilty of."[3]

     Smith began his formal art training in 1913 when he received a Wolfe scholarship to the High School of Ethical Culture, "the first Colored boy to win such an honor."[4] There, he studied drawing, watercolor painting, poster design, sculpture, and basket making with

Irene Weir. Next, according to Smith's father, the Art Students League accepted Smith's work, but refused him entrance "after finding out that he was a Negro."[5]

In 1915, Smith became the first African American student at the prestigious National Academy of Design.[6] He studied painting under Douglas Volk and Charles C. Curran, etching under William Auerbach-Levy, and mural painting under Kenyon Cox.[7] Smith won numerous awards at the NAD—honorable mention and the Suydam bronze medal in his first- and second-year antique classes (1915, 1916), two prizes from the academy poster competition; and the Suydam Medal for charcoal work in a life class (1917).[8] Unfortunately, none of these works seem to have survived.

When the United States entered the war in Europe in 1917, Smith enlisted in the 807 Pioneer Band and served overseas for two and a half months.[9] He was one of two hundred thousand soldiers who saw action and one of thirty thousand black combat troops who served in France.[10] The impressionable young musician-artist visited cathedrals in France and Belgium and worked as a cartoonist. Only one work from this period seems to have survived, a pen-and-ink drawing, *The Fall of the Castle* (1917, fig. 92). Here, a crowd of black men determinedly ascend a steep hill on top of which is perched a castle bearing the label "PREJUDICE." The drawing was published in the February 1920 edition of *Crisis* magazine with the following caption:

> It was a mighty Castle, with massive towers, walls of amazing thickness, and foundations that seemed to seek the very roots of earth. It was defended by armed hosts and vast beasts of the air. Men said it would never fall. They said God Himself had built it, to stand Forever and a Day. They laughed at the puny, black folk who attacked it daily, doggedly, with shovel and broom and stave. And yet—IT FELL. Why? It was built on SAND.[11]

Having served in the Great War for Democracy, Smith may have meant the *The Fall of the Castle* to represent his belief in the determination of black people to overcome racism not only in the United States, but throughout the world.

One of Smith's first prints, *L'ambition* (fig. 93), has a more constructive tone, although it also features a crowd. A square etching, *L'ambition* (dated January 14, 1919) depicts a bare-chested, fair-skinned, straight-haired young man in profile who leans backward and raises his outstretched arms to the glowing sun that emerges from behind a dark cloud in the upper left. Behind the central figure swathed in loose drapery, who rises above a group of people marching from a distant city, is a woman, perhaps a muse. With her head in the angle between the man's arms and chest, and her arms stretched out behind her, she offers compositional balance and inspirational support. The inscription in graphite on the lower left, "To Arthur Schomburg, a souvenir of Paris," may indicate that the work symbolizes Smith's own desire to distinguish himself artistically and rise above the crowd, a desire fueled by his glimpse of great art in France.

In fact, Smith was already distinguishing himself by working in printmaking. In July 1919, he received an honorable discharge from the army[12] and returned with renewed vigor to the National Academy of Design, where he was awarded not only the John Armstrong

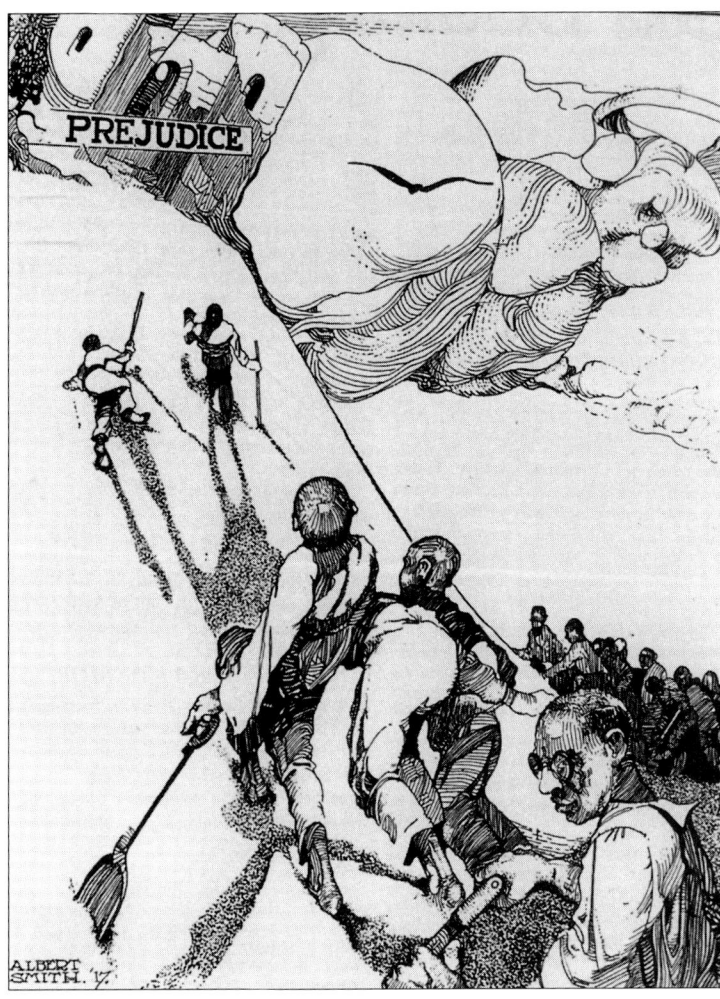

FIGURE 92
Albert Alexander Smith,
The Fall of the Castle,
1917, pen and ink on
paper, dimensions and
location unknown. From
Crisis, February 1929.

Chaloner Paris Foundation first prize, of twenty-five dollars, for painting from life—which
entered him in the competition for the Chaloner prize for study in Paris[13]—but also first
prizes in etching in his first and last years.

African slaves were active in printmaking in the colonies as early as 1724, but as
Leslie King-Hammond points out, slave anonymity makes it very difficult to trace individual
achievements.[14] Notable early printmakers include Robert Douglas Jr. (1809–1887), noted
for his lithograph *William Lloyd Garrison* (1833); Patrick Henry Reason (active ca.
1830–1845 in Philadelphia), who produced emblems and portraits for abolitionists; Jules
Lion (active ca. 1830–1865 in Paris and New Orleans), who is best known for his portrait
series of prominent Louisianians, such as Andrew Jackson; and Grafton Tyler Brown (active
ca. 1865–1890 in California and the Pacific Northwest), who executed stock certificates,
street maps, letterheads, diplomas, and panoramic views of western towns.

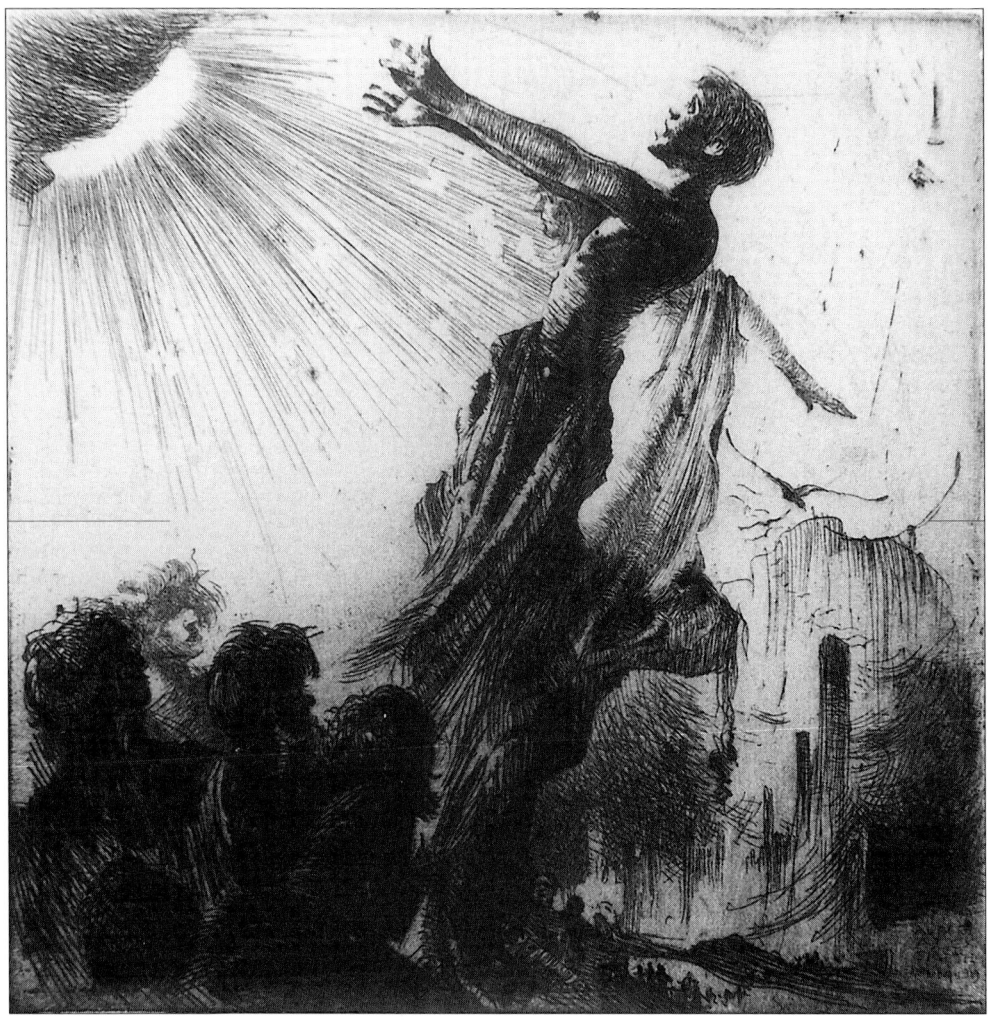

FIGURE 93
Albert Alexander Smith, *L'ambition*, 1919, etching, 11 x 11 in.
Art and Artifacts Division, Schomburg Center for Research in Black Culture, The New York Public Library,
Astor, Lenox and Tilden Foundations.

Like most artists, Smith was probably not aware of this history, however, nor of
the work of William McKnight Farrow, who attended the Art Institute of Chicago
(1908–1917), and produced lithographs in the 1920s and 1930s, until the Harmon
Foundation exhibited Farrow's prints in 1928, 1930, and 1931.[15] There is little other
evidence of African American printmaking in the early twentieth century until the mid-
1930s, when the Federal Art Project of the WPA provided the income and materials for
such activity, encouraged developments in lithography, and fostered the invention of
silkscreening and carborundum printmaking, this last invented by the African American
Dox Thrash (1892–1965).[16] Thus, for about two decades, Smith was one of the few
pioneer African American printmakers.

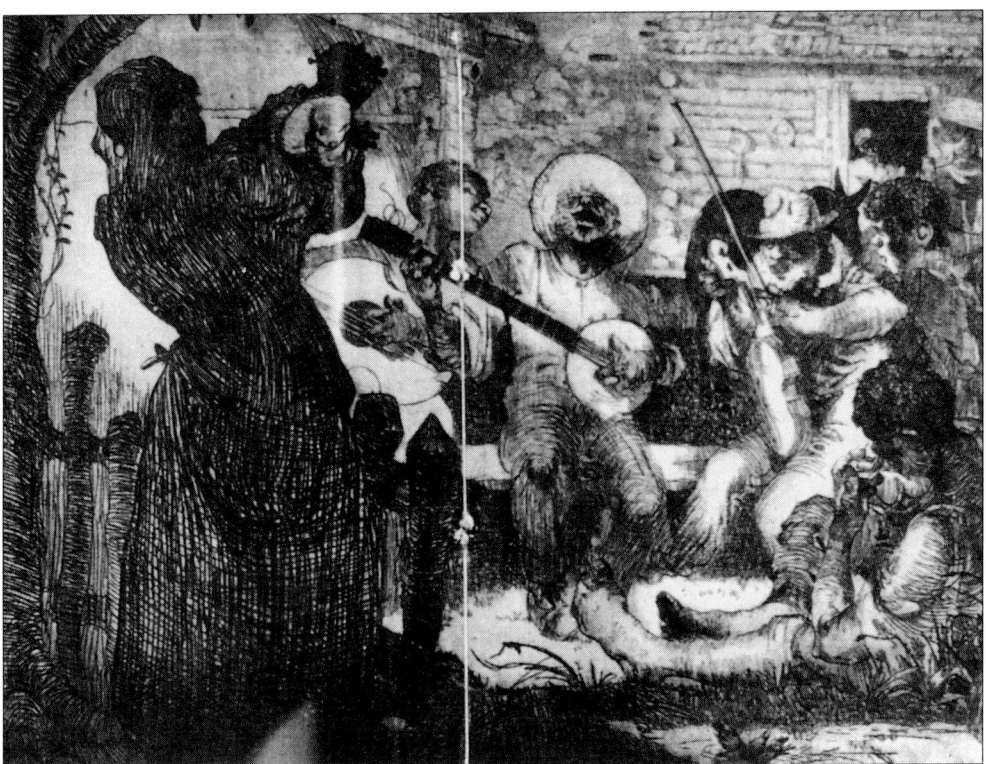

FIGURE 94
Albert Alexander Smith, *Plantation Melodies (Sud des Etats Unis),* 1920, etching, 9½ x 12½ in.
Art and Artifacts Division, Schomburg Center for Research in Black Culture, The New York Public Library,
Astor, Lenox and Tilden Foundations.

    In 1920, Smith's work shifted from the world of allegory to the world of African Americans in the South. *Plantation Melodies (Sud des Etats-Unis)* (fig. 94) depicts a group of people enjoying music at dusk in front of a log cabin. Four male musicians perform: seated on a bench are a young guitarist and two older, bearded men who play a banjo and fiddle, and in the right foreground sits a barefoot youth playing a harmonica. Between him and the cabin stand two men. In the upper right, a woman stands in the doorway. On the left, beneath a tree and in front of a picket fence, is the silhouette of a standing woman who holds a little girl aloft.

    It is not clear why Smith chose this subject matter. There is no evidence that he ever traveled in the South, although he may have done so briefly during his military training. Perhaps his travel abroad gave impetus to the work. It may be that Europeans who met Smith questioned him about the history of slavery, the birth of jazz, and life in the South. The parenthetical French title of the work suggests that Smith had a French-speaking audience in mind. At any rate, the work, striking in its unusual portrayal of southern black musicians as ordinary people performing for their own pleasure rather than as outlandish caricatures performing for whites, immediately won Smith acclaim.[17] The work was

published in *Crisis* magazine in August 1920, with a column devoted to Smith's achievements and the announcement of his study abroad, since June. *Plantation Melodies* may also
have been featured in the children's magazine *Brownies Book,* a short-lived publication by the
NAACP, from which it apparently won second prize.[18] Further, the print was exhibited by
the Society of Independent Artists (March 1922), the Tanner Art League (May 1922), and
the New York Public Library (1928). *Plantation Melodies* struck a chord with black and
white audiences alike, because it seemed to be a sympathetic treatment of the rural and folk-
loric, in the vein of work by other African Americans who were also depicting southern black
culture with seriousness, such as Tanner's *Banjo Lesson* (1893), some of Langston Hughes's
poetry, selected Bessie Smith lyrics, and Jean Toomer's novel *Cane* (1923).

   Conversely, Smith also produced horrifying images of the American South.
Two pen-and-ink drawings appeared in *Crisis* in 1920. One work, published in November,
takes its title from Psalms 135:17, *"They Have Ears but They Hear Not"* (reproduction
unavailable).[19] In this piece, an African American man whose wrists are chained pleas
in an all-white courtroom. Labels in capital letters clearly indicate the site and situation—
"SOUTHERN JUDGE," "SOUTHERN JURY," and "SOUTHERN LAW." In *The Reason (To the
North)* (fig. 95), published in March 1920, a black man in coat and tie, identified as a
"Southern Negro" by the label on the suitcase he carries, hurries away.[20] The reason for
his hasty departure is evident as he glances back at a white man gesturing toward a black
man hanging from a tree—a lynch victim. A banner streaming from the lapel of the Southern
Negro indicates his destination: "To the North."

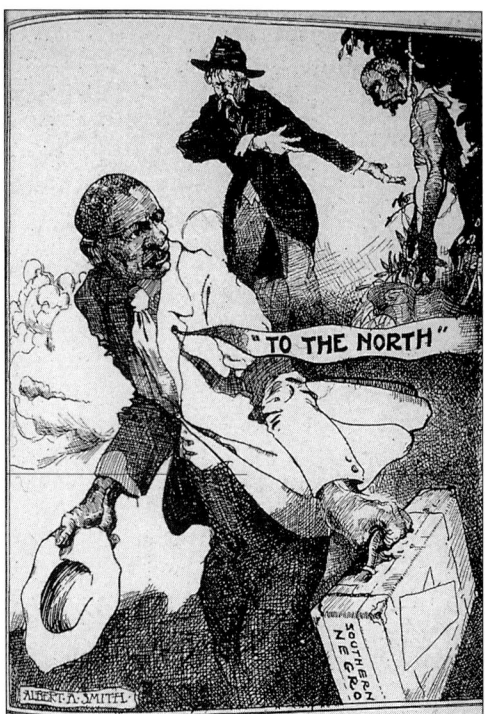

FIGURE 95
Albert Alexander Smith, *The Reason (To the North),*
1920, pen and ink on paper.
Dimensions and location unknown.
From *Crisis,* March 1920.

Participants in the Great Migration, such as the Southern Negro, found that racial discrimination was rampant in the North, as well. The discrimination that Smith had experienced in New York—at the Art Students League, for example, as well as at the National Academy of Design (Curran was apparently hostile to Smith),[21] and perhaps while working as a chauffeur[22]—may have been one of the reasons why, on June 12, 1920, Smith set sail for Europe, never to live in the United States again.

THE GATES OF OPPORTUNITY
AND SPEAKING OF FLAGS, 1920–1924

The years 1920 to 1926 were filled with traveling throughout Europe. Smith took on itinerant jobs as a musician with various bands. Unlike most of his colleagues, he had no financial backing for his sojourn abroad, although Schomburg sought financial aid for him from newspaper publisher Joseph Pulitzer, to no avail.[23] During his first two years overseas, Smith worked as "a musician by night and a struggling artist by day"[24] and mostly produced tourist or sightseeing scenes of streets, bridges, ports, and marketplaces in France and Luxembourg. He exhibited some of these etchings at the New York Public Library in 1921 and 1922,[25] and in the Tanner Art League exhibition, Washington, D.C., in 1922, where he won a gold medal.[26]

Smith spent the first half of 1922 in Italy, performing music and studying the works of Piranesi and Michelangelo in Rome, and other Italian masters in Naples and Pompei and in the Pitti and Uffizi galleries in Florence.[27] Again, he mostly produced tourist scenes of streets, bridges, rivers, and ports.

About this time, Smith's art took on a new direction and began to celebrate black achievements and racial uplift. This is evident in his print *René Maran* (1922, fig. 96), a half-length portrait of the noted black French author dressed in a suit and wearing wire-rimmed glasses. On the left behind him is a table upon which sit books, papers, pens in an inkwell, and a small statue of a man carrying a large globe on his head. In the lower right is Smith's name in capital letters above the date, 1922, and the name of the city where he made the work, Florence. In the upper left is the full title of the work in capital letters, "RENÉ MARAN/ AUTHOR OF/'BATOUALA'/PRIX GONCOURT/1921."

Maran, born in Martinique in 1888 and educated in France, became a colonial service official in Oubangui-Shari. There, he found the material for his "authentic Negro novel," *Batouala*,[28] which won the prestigious Prix Goncourt in 1921. The book's preface, with its critique of the abuses of French colonialism, influenced many black writers in the 1920s and 1930s, after its publication in English by Knopf in 1922. Among the visitors to Maran's modest salon were W.E.B. Du Bois, Walter White, Carter G. Woodson, Claude McKay, Jessie Fauset, Gwendolyn Bennett, Mercer Cook, Joel A. Rogers, and John F. Matheus. Maran's newspaper, *Les Continents,* cofounded in September 1924 with Dahomean prince Kojo Touvalou Houenou, a fervent Garveyite, featured articles on jazz, African civilizations, the abuses of colonial power, and poems by Hughes and McKay. It

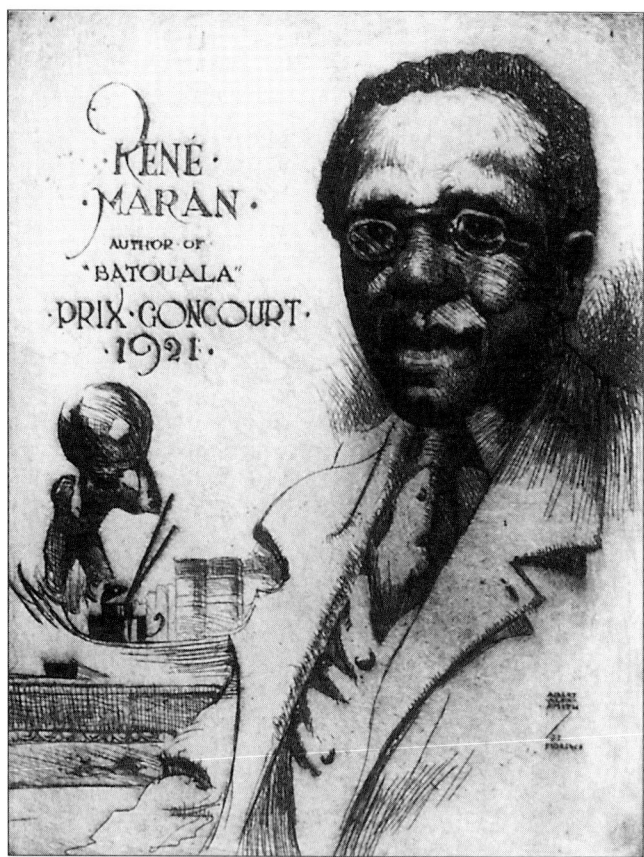

FIGURE 96
Albert Alexander Smith,
René Maran, Author of
"Batouala" Prix Goncourt, 1921,
1922, etching, 9½ x 12½ in.
Art and Artifacts Division,
Schomburg Center for Research
in Black Culture, The New York
Public Library, Astor, Lenox,
and Tilden Foundations.

would be the first in France to mention the incipient New Negro movement, publishing
Alain Locke's short article, "New African-American Poetry," in September 1924. Maran also
tried to get *The New Negro* published in France. Locke visited Maran every summer he went
to France and shared his interest in supporting the Nardal sisters' newspaper *La revue du*
monde noir.

Maran hoped that by publicizing black cultural achievements, he could help
rehabilitate the image of Africa and the Negro. Perhaps Smith believed that he could achieve
the same goals by creating images of notable black leaders; he would continue to create such
portraits throughout his life. Smith was particularly pleased with his rendition of Maran and
wrote to W.E.B. Du Bois, "Much has been heard of him; few have seen him, consequently he
should prove of keen interest to your readers."[29] Evidently Du Bois concurred; the painted
version was reproduced on the cover of *Crisis* in May 1922.

While Smith was in Paris, he executed a series of portrait etchings of great black
leaders, probably at the request of Schomburg, who not only wanted such images for himself
and the library, but who also may have believed that there would be a ready market for such
inexpensive portraits. Schomburg was an avid print collector; he also purchased a number of
etchings by African American William Ernest Braxton for his personal collection.[30] Smith

may have received reproductions of portraits of African Americans from Schomburg so that he could work from established likenesses. He executed portraits of the writers Phillis Wheatley and Paul Lawrence Dunbar, of the writer-educator Booker T. Washington, and of the abolitionists Bishop Richard Allen, Harriet Tubman, and Frederick Douglass. Smith produced not only portraits of these six, but also of the Haitian military leader Toussaint L'Ouverture, the British composer Samuel Coleridge-Taylor, the Russian poet Alexander Sergeyevitch Pushkin (fig. 97), and the French author Alexandre Dumas, père (fig. 98). Smith probably found likenesses of these celebrities in the Bibliothèque Nationale. At Schomburg's request, Smith conducted research there and frequently sent him references, as well as rare books and prints by and about black persons that he found throughout Europe.[31] Schomburg launched Smith (and others) on a lifelong quest to find, and purchase, where possible publications on black history and culture, at first for his personal collection, and later for the library that would be named in his honor. Most of the prints depict only the busts of these famous leaders or show them seated in three-quarters view. They are images of dignity, intelligence, and vision.

Related to this portrait series, and to *L'ambition,* is *Genius,* an engraving of 1922 (fig. 99). The "genius" in this composition, a bare-chested man who rises above the masses, looking heavenward while clutching a musical score, has a facial silhouette and hair that closely resembles those of the composer and pianist Samuel Coleridge-Taylor (1815–1912).

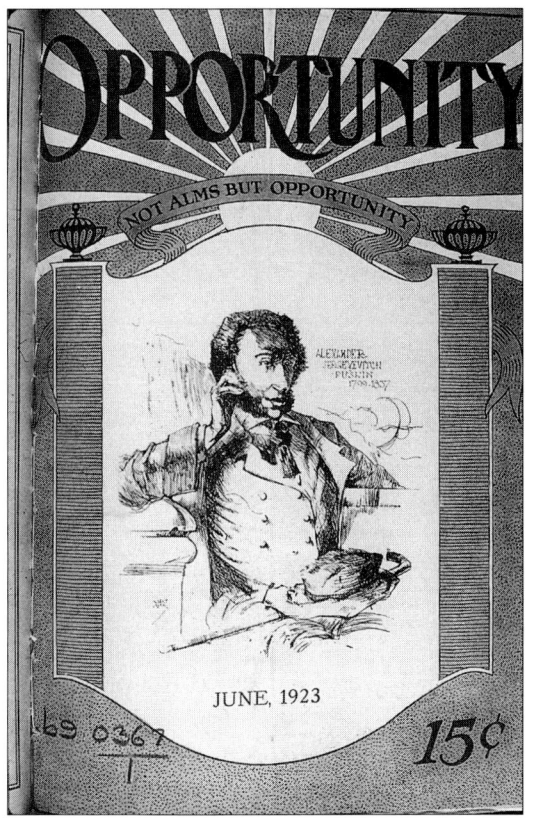

FIGURE 97
Albert Alexander Smith,
Alexander Sergeyevitch Pushkin (1799–1837),
1923, etching, 15 x 11⅝ in.
Photograph from cover of *Opportunity,*
June 1923. Art and Artifacts Division,
Schomburg Center for Research in Black
Culture, The New York Public Library,
Astor, Lenox and Tilden Foundations.

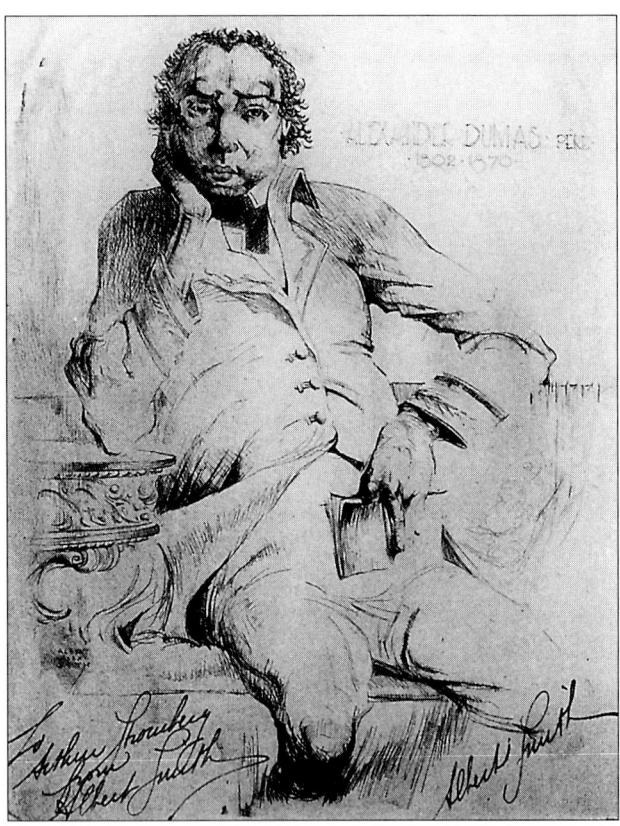

FIGURE 98
Albert Alexander Smith,
Alexandre Dumas, père (1802–1870),
1922, etching, 12½ x 9½ in.
Art and Artifacts Division,
Schomburg Center for Research
in Black Culture, The New York
Public Library, Astor, Lenox and
Tilden Foundations.

The son of a doctor from Sierra Leone and of a British woman, Coleridge-Taylor was best
known for his cantata *Hiawatha's Wedding Feast*. He also wrote *Twenty-Four Negro Melodies*,
inspired by the black American South. Aside from the physical resemblance to Coleridge-
Taylor, this "genius" could be anyone and may be an allegorical figure. In the background
on the right are skyscrapers, suggestive, perhaps, of Smith's hometown of New York. On
the left is a person playing a grand piano. Most significant, in the center foreground is a man
in a tuxedo and top hat. Since Smith often performed in this attire, the image may be a self-
portrait representing Smith's desire to rise above the masses—but as a musical performer
rather than as a composer.

Life in Europe, and particularly in France, offered Smith opportunities to distinguish himself as a musician and artist. His high regard for the French history of tolerance and
support is manifest in the drawing *Speaking of Flags (Liberté, egalité, fraternité)* (ca. 1923,
fig. 100). Here, France, personified as a haloed woman, stands in back of a black man dressed
in a suit, who marches forward carrying the tricolor flag. Across the middle of the flag is the
French motto Liberté, Egalité, Fraternité. In the lower right, a white man crouches with his
back to us, witnessing the procession. Smith may have been familiar with numerous similar
allegorical images of France as a divine guardian of freedom in such items of popular culture
as stamps, postcards, illustrations, and the like.[32]

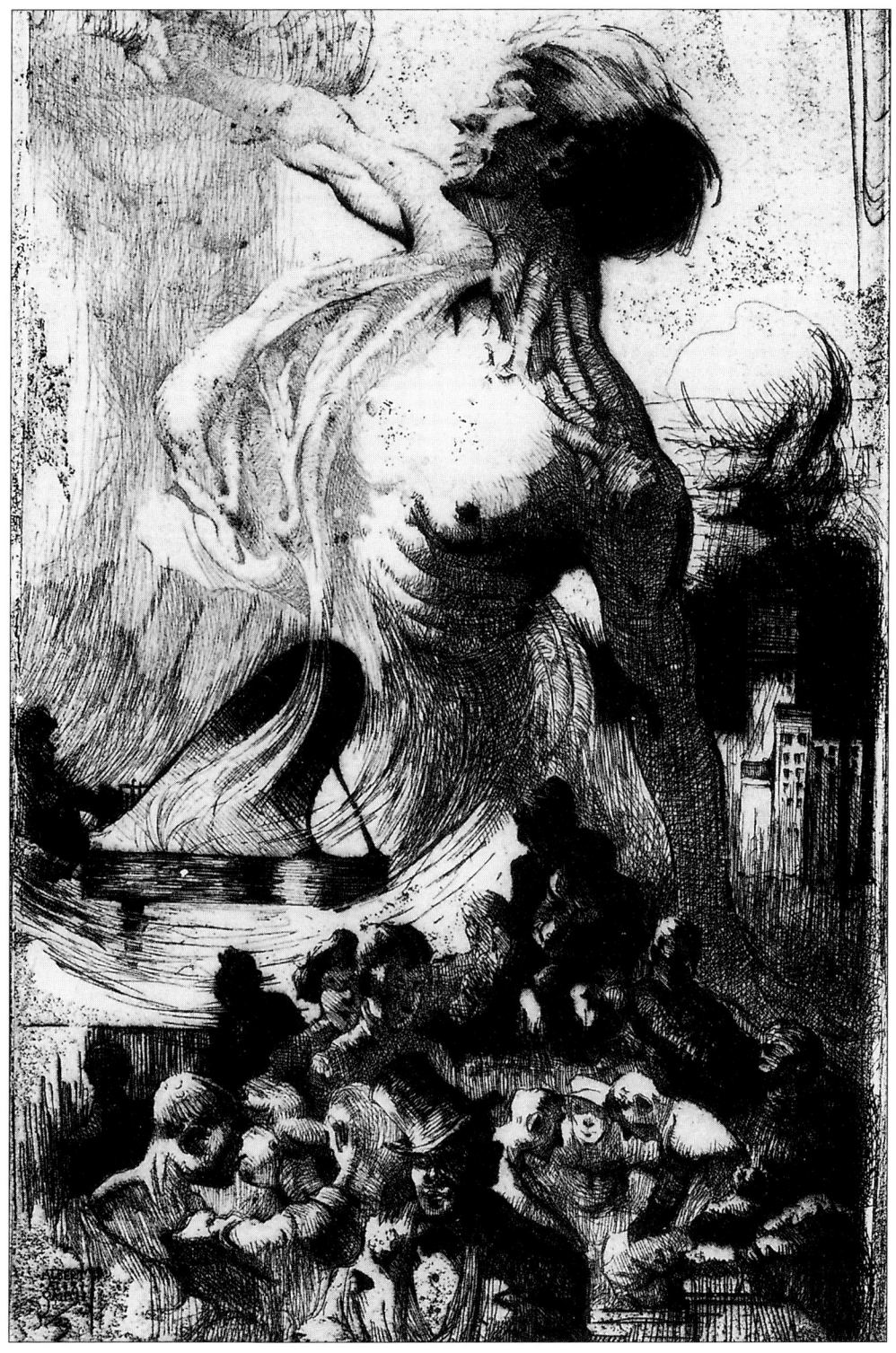

FIGURE 99
Albert Alexander Smith, *Genius,* 1922, engraving, 10¾ x 7⅛ in.
Art and Artifacts Division, Schomburg Center for Research in Black Culture, The New York Public Library,
Astor, Lenox, and Tilden Foundations.

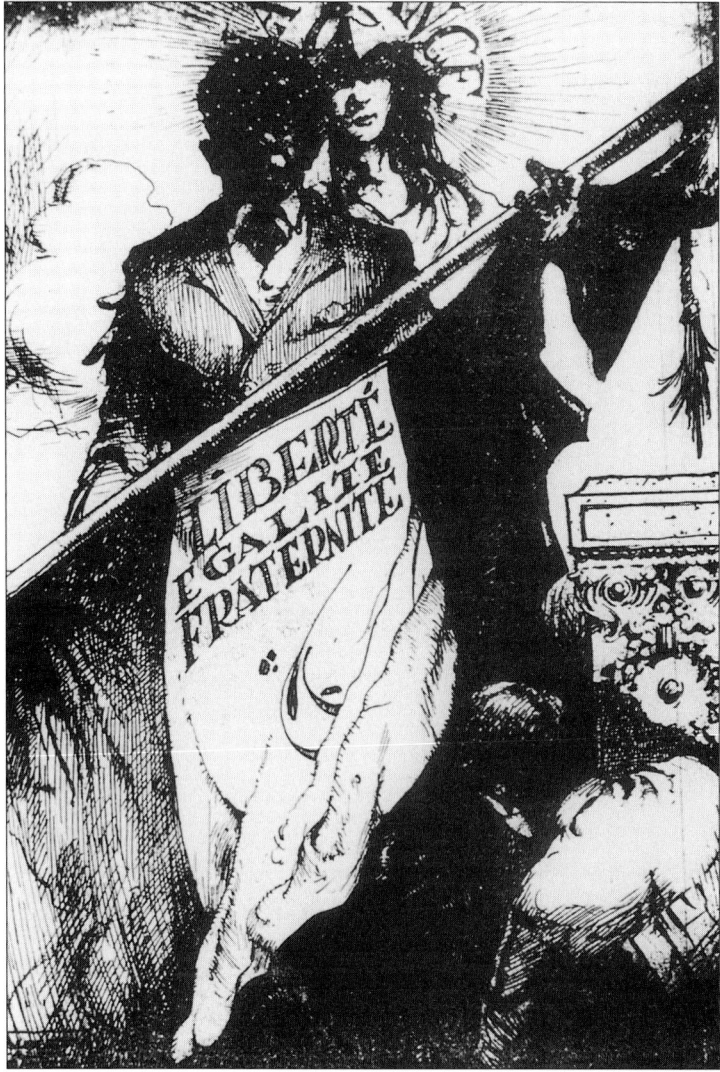

FIGURE 100
Albert Alexander Smith,
*Speaking of Flags
(Liberté, egalité,
fraternité),* ca. 1923,
pen and ink on paper,
dimensions unknown,
location unknown.
From the microfilmed
papers of W.E.B. Du Bois,
Library of Congress.

In the middle of 1922, Smith moved to 23, boulevard des Batignolles in the eighth
arrondissement of Montmartre. Montmartre, or "*Mo*-mart," as some black Americans called
it,[33] was, according to historian Tyler Stovall, "the undisputed center of black expatriate life
in Paris,"[34] even though, by 1924 "the number of black Americans . . . [there] remained
very small, probably no more than twenty-five or thirty individuals, virtually all musicians."[35]
Black musicians settled in the Butte, as Parisians called the top of the hill, because of the
many nightclubs nestled along the numerous narrow, twisting streets. Among the more
famous of these clubs were the Cosy Corner, the Palermo, Gerald's Bar, the Royal
Montmartre, and Zelli's. Foreign tourists seeking the shocks and thrills of Gay Paree often
ended their nights at the tiny square of place Pigalle, a center of prostitution and drugs, or at
the Moulin Rouge, where Impressionists had drunk and painted dancers. Among the African
American musicians who also lived in Montmartre after serving in World War I were Eugene
Bullard, Louis Mitchell, Palmer Jones, Cricket Smith, Sammy Richardson, and Opal Cooper.

Musicians and bandleaders who arrived later were Leon Abbey, E. E. Thompson, Sammy Richardson, Charlie "Dixie" Lewis, Maisie Withers, Bobby Jones, Gut Bucket, and Arthur Briggs. African American performers who opened their own nightclubs there included "Bricktop" Ada Louise Smith (The Music Box, then Bricktop's), Florence Embry Jones (Chez Florence), and Eugène Bullard (Le Grand Duc, frequented by Josephine Baker after her performances) where they offered champagne, jazz, and the Charleston. By the late 1920s, the African American community numbered several hundred, some of these residents opening their own small shops and restaurants, where they served fried chicken, American coffee, sausages, and hotcakes.[36] Historian Joel Augustus Rogers, who wrote several columns for the African American press relating his life in Paris, described the scene in 1929:

> The Boulevard de Clichy is the 42nd and Broadway of Paris. Most of the night life of Paris centers around it, and most of the colored folks from the States, too. If you hear that some friend from the States is in Paris, just circulate around this boulevard from the Moulin Rouge down Rue Pigalle as far as the Flea Pit, and it's a hundred to one shot you'll encounter him or her, at least twice during the night.
>
> Most of the colored folk live in this neighborhood. There is a surprising number of them, and it is increasing every year. Just now with the "Blackbirds" at the Moulin Rouge, this section of Montmartre reminds you more of Harlem than ever.[37]

At the beginning of the boulevard des Batignolles, Smith lived just steps from a major intersection, the place de Clichy, on the boulevard de Clichy. He was a man who cherished his privacy; perhaps that is why, by the mid-1920s, he moved northeast to a slightly quieter section of Montmartre, at 116, rue Lamarck in the eighteenth arrondissement.

While Smith would maintain his residence in Montmartre the rest of his life, during most of 1923 and 1924 he lived in Belgium, where he played the banjo in a band and studied the works of Rubens, Jordeans, and Rembrandt, in Brussels. Smith also studied etching and lithography at the Académie des Beaux-Arts in Liège and under the Belgian master François Maréchal (1861–1945).[38] Maréchal was one of the best-known painter-etchers of his time, noted for his landscapes, depictions of popular types from the Liège region in the manner of fellow Belgian printmaker Félicien Rops (1833–1898), and more than four hundred graphic works of plants and insects.[39] Under Maréchal's direction, Smith continued executing prints of tourist sites, such as a Japanese gate and a marketplace in Liège, the latter of which he exhibited along with *A Street in Rome* (fig. 101) at the Brooklyn Society of Etchers, December 1924–January 1925.

In 1923, Smith expanded his study of racial uplift by depicting glorious views of Ethiopia, having first begun his exploration of Ethiopian themes while in Florence, in *Visions of Ethiopia,* a drawing, of which no reproductions have been found, and *The Builders of the Temple,* published on the cover of *Crisis* in January 1924 (reproduction unavailable). The latter work depicts a frontal view of a deep temple porch, adorned with massive column, rich fabrics, and an intricately wrought arch and lamp. In the foreground are flowers, peacocks, and a group of turbaned, bare-chested young men. The image is one of opulence and grandeur. Published on the cover of *Crisis* magazine in August 1923, the earlier drawing

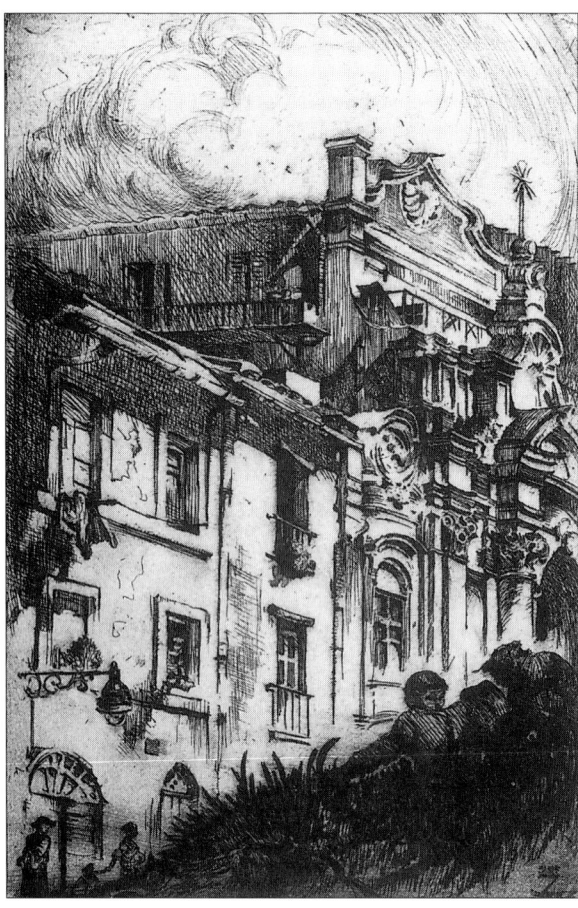

FIGURE 101
Albert Alexander Smith,
A Street in Rome, 1923,
etching, 12 x 9 in.
Hatch-Billops Collection, New York.

Ethiopia (1922, reproduction unavailable), depicts two men standing outside an entrance
flanked by Doric columns and topped by a sign announcing the name of the country.

It is no surprise that Du Bois would have approved of cover illustrations celebrating
the glory of Ethiopia. The country, formerly called Abyssinia, whose history reaches back at
least two thousand years, is the oldest independent state in Africa. Limited contact with the
outside world allowed it to escape colonization until the Italian occupation of 1935–1942. In
1896, the ancient kingdom, under the direction of Emperor Menelik II since 1889, defeated
an Italian expeditionary force in a battle at Adowa. Because the Italian army lost half its
power then, Ethiopia became known as a stalwart defender of black people everywhere. It
also "stood as a lone symbol of African autonomy at the height of the age of imperialism,
serving as a beacon of hope to Africans and African Americans in the early twentieth century,
as they began to imagine a postcolonial future."[40] The name of the country was often taken
to signify Africa in general. In the 1920s and 1930s, Ras Tafari, regent of the royal Ethiopian
court and later its ruler as Emperor Haile Selassie, initially resisted the presence of American
business in his country, then sought a closer relationship with the United States that would
include American arms and military advisers.[41] Later, the country would become a center of
Pan-Africanism.

Du Bois, who was the driving force behind the second Pan-African Congress in France in 1919,[42] was eager for artists to depict Ethiopian glory. The first such image seems to have been made in the 1910s by Meta Vaux Warrick Fuller, no doubt partially because of Du Bois's influence; he had visited the sculptor in Paris and urged her to make a study of "racial types." Like Smith, Fuller had produced a series of portraits of black people. While most of these images were of people Fuller personally knew, two, a plaster relief and a statuette (dated 1913 and 1914), both titled *Menelik II of Abyssinia*, commemorated the Ethiopian ruler's triumph. Shortly thereafter (ca. 1915–1921), Fuller produced one of her best-known works, *Ethiopia Awakening* (see fig. 5), a semi-Egyptian standing female figure emerging from mummylike swaths and a millennial sleep.[43] Fuller and Smith's visions of Ethiopia, then, suggest pride in African history, independence, and achievement, and the belief that the African country and its leader can stand as symbols of hope and an awakening consciousness for all black peoples.

It was significant that Smith's images would appear in the *Crisis* and *Opportunity* magazines, edited by Du Bois and Charles S. Johnson, respectively. These were two of the most widely read African American periodicals of the 1920s and 1930s. *Crisis*, founded in 1910, had a largely middle-class, African American audience; its circulation was sixty-five thousand in 1920, declining to less than thirty thousand by 1930 in the wake of the Great Depression.[44] In promoting *Crisis* as a literary journal, rather than an organizational periodical, Du Bois "did more than anyone else to prepare for the flourishing of Afro-American culture in the 1920s."[45] He wrote as a propagandist, believing that art needed to lead to racial uplift: "All Art is propaganda and ever must be, despite the wailing of the purists. I stand in utter shamelessness and say that whatever art I have for writing has been used always for propaganda for gaining the right of black folk to love and enjoy. I do not care a damn for any art that is not used for propaganda."[46] To meet this goal in part, Du Bois promoted two annual art and literature contests from 1925 to 1927, which were quite successful.

At the same time, *Opportunity,* founded in 1923, also sponsored similar contests from 1925 to 1927, and became an intense rival for *Crisis* from 1923 to 1928. *Opportunity* was the journal of the National Urban League, established in 1911 to meet the housing and occupational needs of southern black migrants. By 1927 the magazine reached the sizeable circulation of eleven thousand, but never became self-sufficient.[47] Johnson actively sought creative work with an announcement on the table of contents page for each issue until October 1925, when the large quantity of manuscripts and artwork received made it obvious that such advertisement was no longer needed: "'Opportunity' desires the following contributions: drawings, paintings and photographs for covers; fiction, poetry, local news of interest, with photographs; and authentic articles."[48]

Johnson and Du Bois were a study in contrasts in many ways. Johnson eschewed Du Bois's personal journalism, stating that the policy of *Opportunity* was "one of intelligent discussion rather than fireworks; of calm analysis rather than tears." While Du Bois insisted on art as propaganda, Johnson emphasized freedom and self-expression for writers. Yet both editors agreed on the promotion of African American culture, and both succeeded in rewarding many young writers and artists with publication, exposure, and monetary awards. By 1928, however, the terrain for both magazines was uncertain as they met monetary reversal and the little magazines began to proliferate. Du Bois had difficulty maintaining his editorial position, and Johnson resigned after the September 1928 issue to become chairman of the department of social sciences at Fisk University.[49] Du Bois's power over *Crisis* gradually declined until he, too, resigned to return to teaching at Atlanta University in 1934. Each in his own way, however, would continue to be a strong supporter of the arts and was instrumental in building up the art department at each of their respective institutions; Du Bois saw to it that Prophet was hired at Spelman, and Johnson supported Aaron Douglas's position at Fisk.

DEPICTIONS OF AMERICAN RACIAL DISCRIMINATION, INTERNATIONAL RACIAL UPLIFT, AND TOURIST SITES, 1924–1926

While Smith depicted scenes of a remote Ethiopian grandeur in the early 1920s (and would return to the theme in 1928), he also produced scenes of racial discrimination in the United States in *The Haunting Ghost of Negro Labor* (1925, fig. 102),[50] *Lords of Lynching* (1924, fig. 103),[51] and an untitled drawing (*Justice*) (1924, fig. 104).[52] The latter work is one of Smith's most eloquent statements on inequity in the United States. In this drawing, a black man sits forlornly in the lower left, surrounded by symbols of cultural enlightenment and achievement; in his hand is a palette, in his lap are a globe and an unidentified scientific or mechanical instrument, and scattered about him are books, papers, and scrolls. He stares silently at the scale tipped empty before him. On the right, Justice is personified

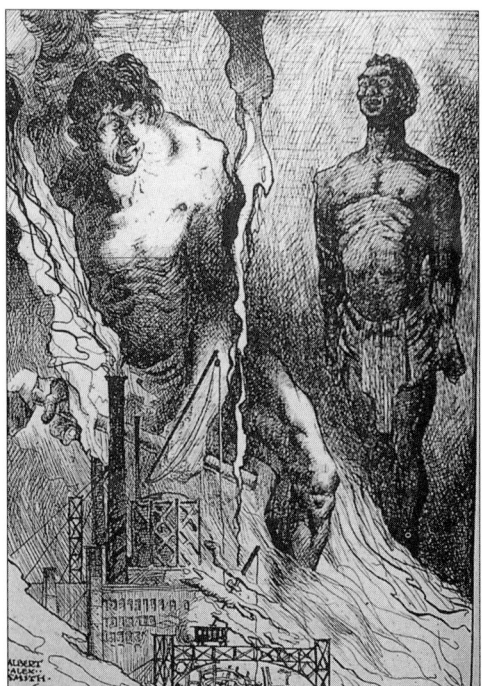

FIGURE 102
Albert Alexander Smith,
The Haunting Ghost of Negro Labor, 1925,
etching, dimensions and location unknown.
From *Crisis,* May 1925.

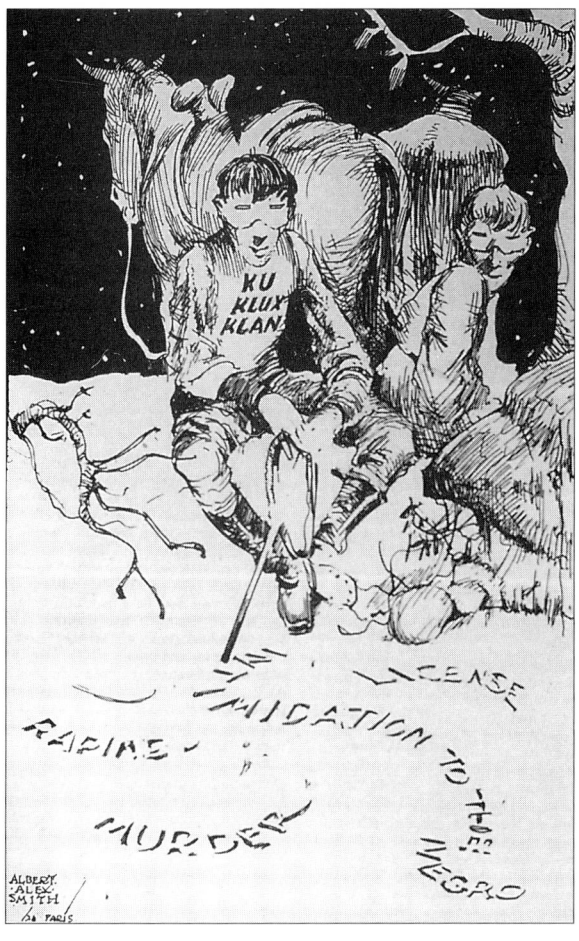

FIGURE 103
Albert Alexander Smith,
Lords of Lynching, 1924,
pen and ink on paper(?),
dimensions and location unknown.
From *Crisis*, February 1924.

as a classically robed, standing woman, her identity written on her blindfold, which is
lifted by a hand emerging out of the inky background. Justice's scales are tipped wildly
out of favor against the black man. Smith makes it clear that he has left behind this unjust
system; his signature, the date, and "Brussels" appear on a vase in the lower right. It may
have been in Brussels that Smith had his first solo exhibition. A short announcement in
Crisis magazine states that Smith "has held an exposition of his etchings and oil paintings
in Brussels."[53] Smith also wrote that he held a "private show" at the Galerie Royale,
Brussels.[54]

     As a student at the National Academy of Design, Smith would have been schooled
in visual allegory. His drawing of Justice can be linked to Samuel Jenning's painting of 1792,
Liberty Displaying the Arts and Sciences (fig. 105). Liberty, Justice's counterpart, is a white
woman, here dressed in contemporary, rather than Greco-Roman, clothing. She is seated
before a classical facade and at her feet are similar symbols of education—among them, an
artist's palette, globe, lyre, and books. Four freed slaves bow with gratitude in anticipation of
their opportunities. Yet it seems that only a chosen few may achieve full citizenship in the new
nation. In the background outside, unenlightened African Americans entertain themselves to

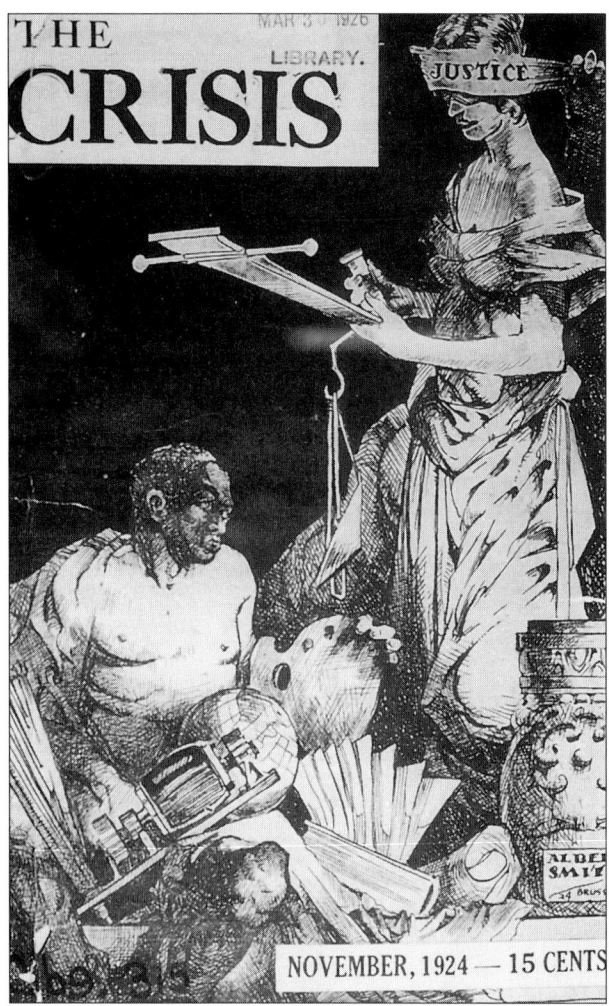

FIGURE 104
Albert Alexander Smith,
Untitled (Justice), 1924,
pen and ink on paper(?),
dimensions and location unknown.
From a cover of *The Crisis*,
November 1924.

FIGURE 105
Samuel Jennings,
*Liberty Displaying the
Arts and Sciences*, 1792,
oil on canvas,
60¼ x 73⅛ in.
The Library Company
of Philadelphia;
used with permission.

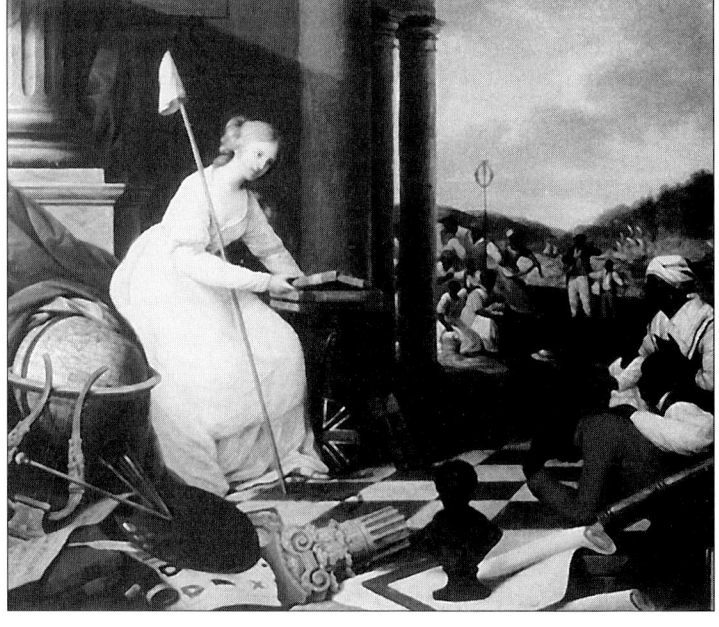

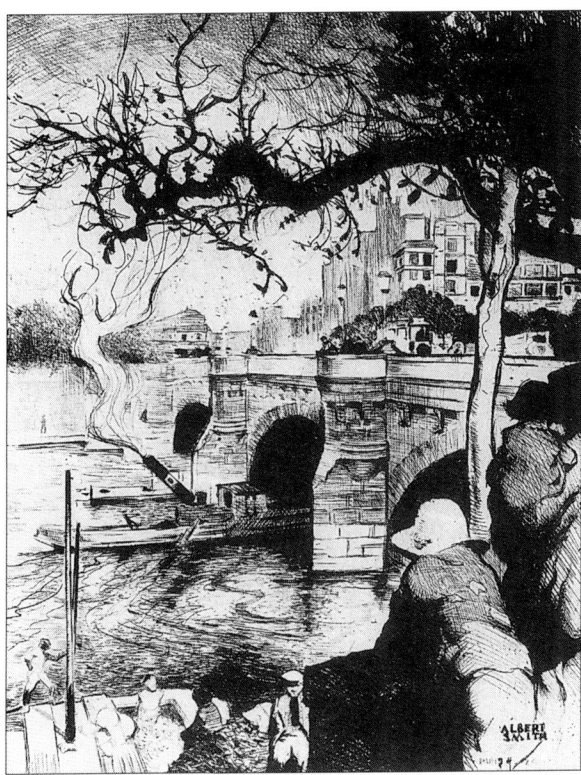

FIGURE 106
Albert Alexander Smith,
Pont Neuf, Paris, 1924,
lithograph, 10⅜ x 7⅜ in.
Art and Artifacts Division,
Schomburg Center for Research in Black
Culture, The New York Public Library,
Astor, Lenox, and Tilden Foundations.

the music of a stringed instrument, possibly a gourd fiddle, an Africa-derived precursor
of the banjo.[55] In both Smith's and Jennings's works, it seems that African Americans'
opportunities are entirely subject to the decisions of people of European descent.

From the middle of 1924 through 1926 while he lived in France, Smith continued
his three themes of racial discrimination, racial uplift, and tourist sites. His images of this last
include conventional etchings and drawings of the Pont-Neuf in Paris (fig. 106)[56] and of
marketplaces in Pau and Nice, such as his *Market Place, Nice, France,* in the south of France.
One of these missing drawings, *Place de la Monnaie, Pau, France,* would win an honorable
mention from the Harmon Foundation in 1928.

Smith's images of racial uplift include two untitled cover illustrations for *Crisis*
magazine in the summer of 1925. The first, published in June (fig. 107), depicts an
African American family, father, mother, and child, under the watchful protection of the
NAACP, whose banner is held aloft by a fair-skinned, winged, wreath-haloed woman.
The second, published in August, is an etching of great black leaders in the Western world
(fig. 108). The head of Samuel Coleridge-Taylor appears next to those of African Americans
whom the composer greatly admired—poet Paul Laurence Dunbar, some of whose poems
Coleridge-Taylor set to music; philosopher W.E.B. Du Bois; and abolitionist Frederick
Douglass, whose works Smith zealously studied. The illustration also includes images of
men whom Smith admired, painter Henry O. Tanner and writer Alexandre Dumas, who
both won success in Paris. The heads of these men appear in the clouds to a well-dressed

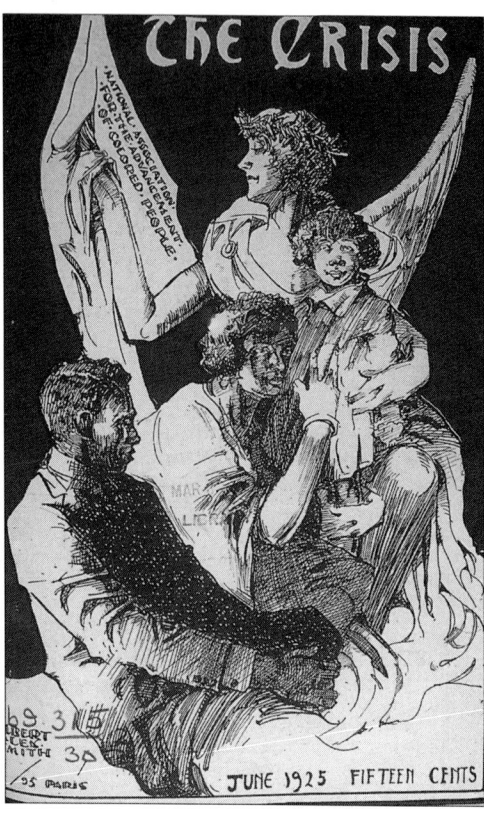

FIGURE 107
Albert Alexander Smith,
*Untitled (Negro Family under the Protection
of the NAACP)*, 1925, etching, 8¾ x 5⅞ in.
Photograph from cover of *The Crisis*, June 1925.

young black man, perhaps on his way to the small town in the distance. Ironically, he
pauses in a field beside a basket of cotton and a plow, symbols, perhaps, of the physical
labor he would like to leave behind in pursuit of more uplifting, mental work.

The gates of opportunity, however, while open to certain Africans in *Ethiopia*
and *Builders of the Temple*, are closed in the *Crisis* cover illustration by the same name
(*Gates of Opportunity*, reproduction unavailable) for which Smith won a prize from the
magazine in March 1926. Like the arch in *Builders*, the walls and portals in *The Gates
of Opportunity* are beautifully intricate, made perhaps of iron wrought by slaves. Here,
though, contemporary African Americans stand and sit forlornly in the hallway, staring
numbly ahead, bowing their heads in frustration, or stoically waiting before the closed
gates. These images of stasis contrast strongly with the violence in *Mob Rule,* a drawing
for which Smith won the Amy Spingarn honorable-mention prize for illustration in the
1926 *Crisis* contest.[57] Here, the meaning is unclear. Two black men, their backs in checked
shirts cropped by the lower-right corner of the composition, look up across what may
be the body of a white woman, beyond a startled World War I doughboy in the center,
who reaches for his hat, which has blown off, to a large, hideous face in the upper left.
The man's face has been beaten—his right eye is swollen, his front teeth are missing,
and his cheek is bandaged. Across his forehead is the term "MOB-RULE." Does this
hideous countenance frighten both white fighters for democracy and rural blacks with its

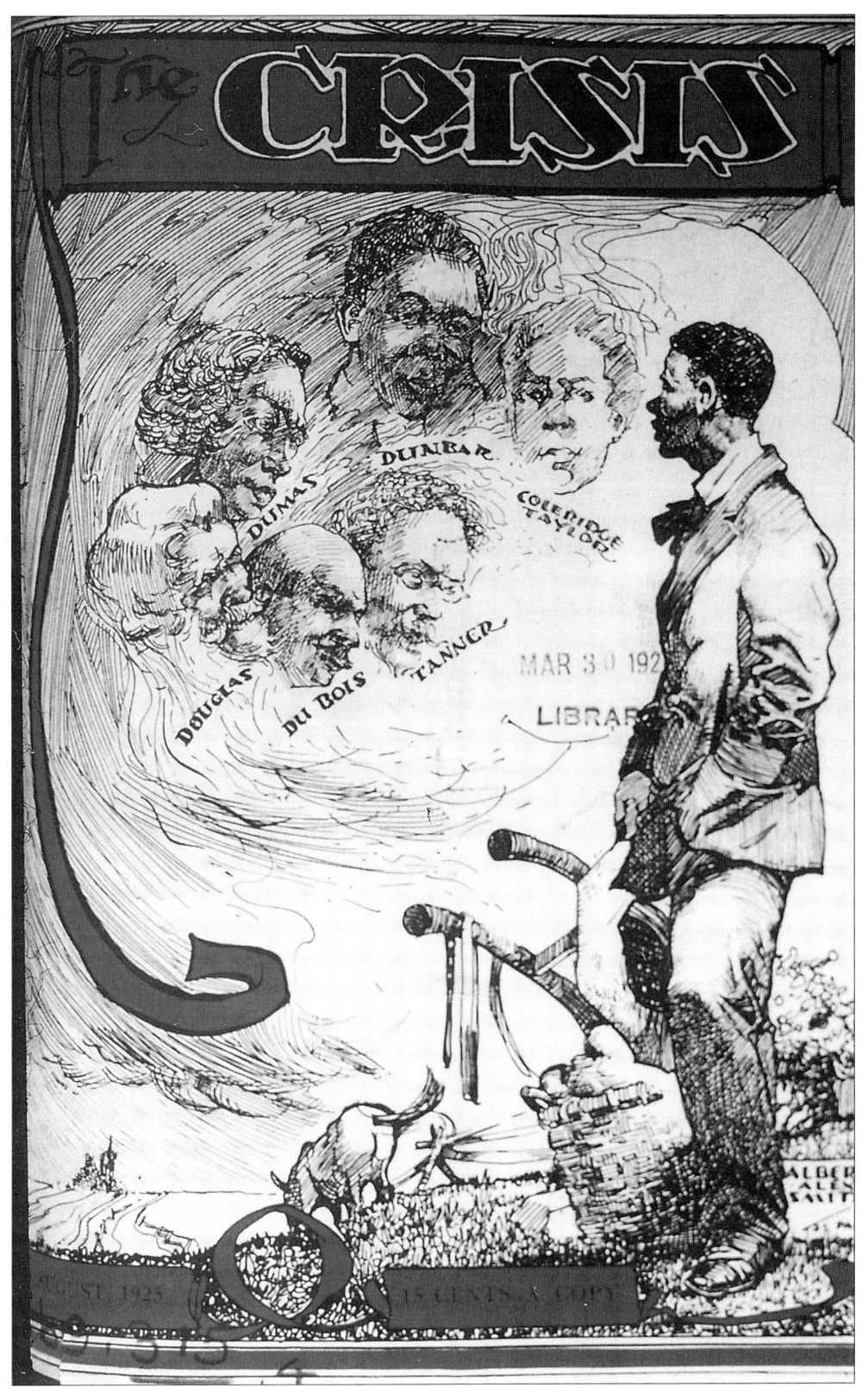

FIGURE 108
Albert Alexander Smith, *Untitled (Six Negro Leaders)*, 1925, etching, dimensions and location unknown.
From cover of *Crisis*, August 1925.

lawlessness and violence? Perhaps Smith is suggesting that both whites and blacks have much to fear from rioting mobs. Smith may have learned of the race riots in America from his parents, whom he had not seen in six years, until they visited him in Paris in the summer of 1926 at his three-room apartment at 116, rue Lamarck.[58] At any rate, it seems that Smith resolved to stay abroad, far away from such madness.

Yet it was in the United States that French critics discovered and admired the work of Smith. Like his compatriots, Smith frequently sent work back to the United States for exhibition. Unlike the others, however, Smith had an enthusiastic agent in his father. Alfred Renforth Smith eagerly promoted his son's work at every opportunity and badgered everyone he could to talk it up, buy it, and exhibit it. He even got an Episcopal clergyman from his hometown of Manhasset on Long Island to write a letter of recommendation to the Harmon Foundation for his son.[59] His persistence paid off; Smith's work was included in numerous, diverse American shows.[60] In 1925, he received a favorable review of the works he showed at the ninth annual Society of Independent Artists exhibition (March 6–29)[61] from *La Revue du Vrai et du Beau.* The French writer was particularly impressed with Smith's *Southern Melodies* (probably *Plantation Melodies* or *Southern Symphony*), *The Wrestler,* and *Exchange at Pau.* The writer concluded by prophesying a brilliant career for Smith.[62] Several months later, a critic for *Les Artistes d'Aujourd'hui* admired Smith's *Syncopation, Market Place of Liège, The Tiber,* and a view of Nice at the Independent Salon in New York. This writer believed that Smith, a "devil of a fellow," was able to fluidly work in several manners— "the modern school," art "allied to the very greatest," and "the second Flemish school."[63] It was not uncommon for French critics to peruse exhibitions in New York for review; the works of African American artists Allan R. Freelon, James Lesesne Wells, and Henry Bannarn, who never studied abroad, was also published in French periodicals.[64]

EUROPEAN TYPES, 1926–1928

From early 1926 to mid-1928 Smith focused primarily on depicting European types, encouraged, no doubt by Maréchal's success in this area. Where Maréchal, however, concentrated on the Walloon people in the industrial areas of southern and southeastern Belgium, Smith covered a wider range of Europeans, especially Spaniards and the French. In the first half of 1926, Smith traveled throughout Spain, to Seville, Bilboa, and Madrid, where he studied the works of Velazquez and Murillo at the Prado Museum. Over the next two years, he again spent several more months in Spain, in Toldeo, Pasajes, and Madrid. As before, Smith created scenes of the local markets, streets, churches, ports, and bridges, but he also depicted the common people at this time. In contrast to his portraits of individual black leaders whose names and life dates are prominently included in the composition, Smith's portraits of the Spanish seem to be largely of anonymous people almost reduced to caricatures, given the titles of such missing works as *Miser, Spain; Spanish Type; Beggars in Church, Madrid, Spain; Peasant Life in Spain; Spanish Musician;* and *Spanish Milkman.* Smith found the Spanish "a sad, unintelligent population" and "a proud, yet ignorant people."[65] Upon leaving the country, Smith stated, "It shall be with little regret that I shake the dust of Madrid, that I forget the odor of the bull-rings and the harsh voices of the señoritas."[66] Yet Rose Henderson, writer for the periodical *Southern Workman,* found these works fresh and unique: "His paintings show the Spanish influence in a way that is highly creditable to the artist's own individuality. He has not been in any sense a servile imitator, but there is a certain sharpness and richness, an alert clarity of emotion which allies him to the Spanish temperament. He has a strong decorative sense, plastic design, and sophisticated insight."[67] The jurors of the Harmon Foundation also admired Smith's depictions of popular types; in 1928 it exhibited *Spanish Type* and in 1929, *Beggars in Church, Madrid.* The latter work, along with prints of two Italian street scenes, and the head of a laughing boy, tied Smith for the bronze award; he split the prize money with Sargent Claude Johnson for Johnson's bust, *Sammy.*[68]

While in France, 1926–1928, Smith produced genre scenes of peasant life, such as *Selling Pigs, Normandy; Fishermen, France;* and *Washing Day, France.* Like his Spanish subjects, Smith's portraits of individual French people are of anonymous types categorized largely by working-class occupations, as suggested by their titles, such as *Le facteur* (mail carrier), *The Concierge, Book Vendor,* and *Fisherman in Trouville,* the latter shown at the Brooklyn Society of Etchers along with *Apaches, Montmartre,* in December 1928. Some of Smith's other titles of works are so general, such as *Patriarch, Comedians, Milk Seller,* and *Muscular Type,* that it is impossible to tell the nationality or ethnicity of their subjects. As for other nationalities, Smith painted a watercolor of one compatriot, *Portrait d'un jeune américain,* and he depicted two Russians, *A Russian Girl* and *Russian Pianist* (the media of these works are unknown, as are the location and reproductions of all the works). Smith probably produced his images of types, in runs of seventy-five to one hundred prints each, for a fickle tourist market that readily purchased inexpensive and simplistic images of peoples and places. He quickly learned that the prints that became bestsellers were those of famous European churches, marketplaces, and bridges, or character types.

In December 1927, Smith returned to the United States for an exhibition. Apparently, an art gallery on Fifth Avenue planned to exhibit his work, but three weeks later told him it was impossible to put the show on.[69] Only the titles of three oil paintings suggest that Smith painted them during that time, *My Bunk, A New York Corner,* and *New York Skyline.* The latter work depicts a cold, densely packed, uninhabited skyline across a calm harbor that fills the lower third of the canvas. It seems as though Smith is an ocean away from his former home. Just as he viewed tourist sites in Europe with an outsider's eye, so was he beginning to view the city of his birth and his native country as an outsider.

ETHIOPIAN MUSIC AND PLANTATION MELODIES, 1928–1933

In the early 1930s, Smith worked primarily in Paris, performing on radio and in hot spots such as the American hangout La Coupole, the trendy nightclub Zelli's, and the elegant Café de Paris. Curiously, few of Smith's works with musical imagery deal directly with his life in France. Only two undated etchings, from a few years earlier, depict the Parisian cabaret

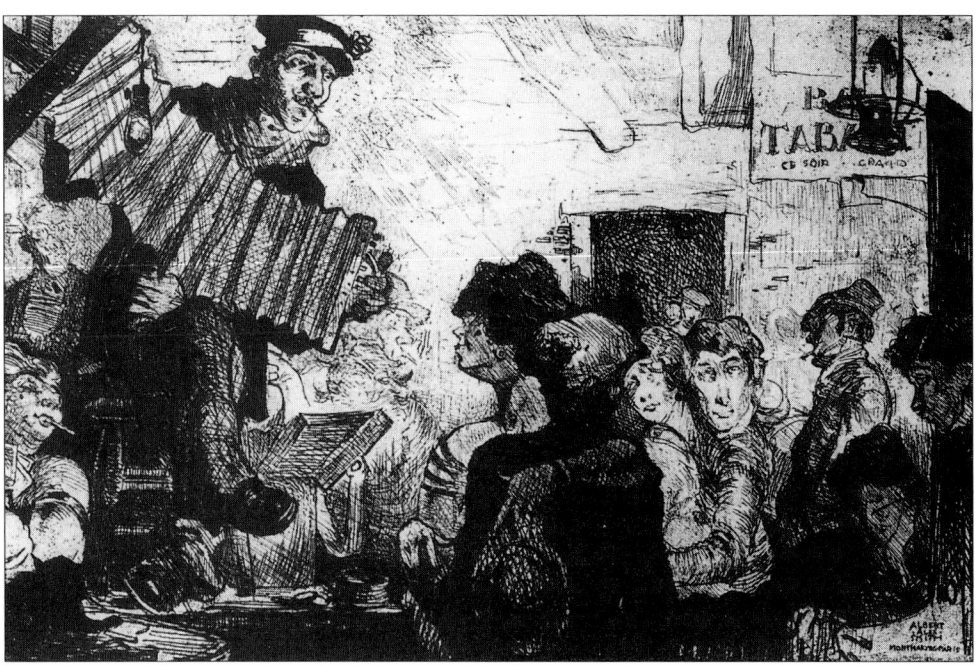

FIGURE 109
Albert Alexander Smith, *Montmartre, Paris,* 1928, engraving, 7¾ x 10¾ in.
Art and Artifacts Division, Schomburg Center for Research in Black Culture, The New York Public Library,
Astor, Lenox and Tilden Foundations.

atmosphere with which he was so familiar. *Montmartre, Paris* (fig. 109) shows people
listening to an accordion player in a low-ceilinged room. Similarly somber is *Bal Musette*
(fig. 110), the translation of which is "popular dance to accordion music." The shabby
furnishings and clientele of *Montmartre, Paris* and *Bal Musette* were typical of cheap cafés
where Smith sometimes spent his free time writing letters to Arthur Schomburg, director of
the 135th Street branch of the New York Public Library. Smith informed Schomburg that
many black people hung out and danced at such places; he called them "ordinary cafes where
the sons of Ham sway." "Here," he wrote, "all the Spades in Paris meet, fight, and share
their woes."[70] Smith might have been referring to the Flea Pit, a club popular with black
musicians. A *Chicago Defender* reporter described the place at the end of 1926 as "the headquarters for many of our well known artists, musicians, etc. in Paris . . . a combination of a
pool room, public bar, cigar stand . . . located on the . . . corner of Rue Pigalle and Rue
Bergère . . . if you happen to be in Montmartre you will in due time visit the Flea Pit."[71]

    Montmartre, Paris and *Bal Musette* depict no persons of African descent. Instead,
they feature French accordion players, who had lost popularity with upper-class Parisians,
now thoroughly seduced by the rhythms of "le jazz hot," introduced by African American
soldiers during World War I and popularized by Josephine Baker and *La Revue Nègre* in
1925. Smith learned to play the newly fashionable banjo in just three weeks and enjoyed
steady employment spreading the jazz craze throughout Europe (as seen with a band

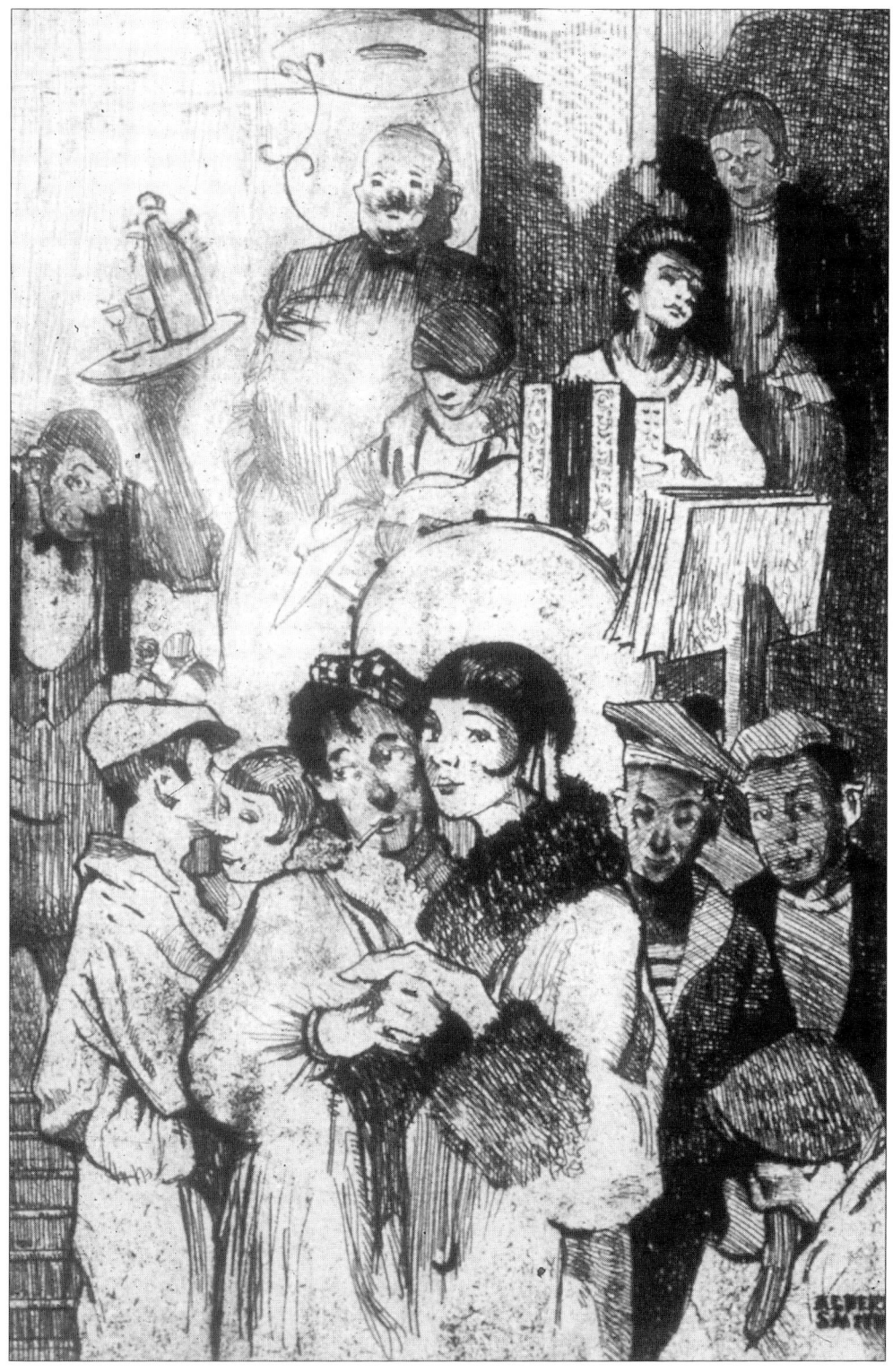

FIGURE 110
Albert Alexander Smith, *Bal Musette*, 1928, engraving, 11⅛ x 7¾ in.
Art and Artifacts Division, Schomburg Center for Research in Black Culture, The New York Public Library,
Astor, Lenox and Tilden Foundations.

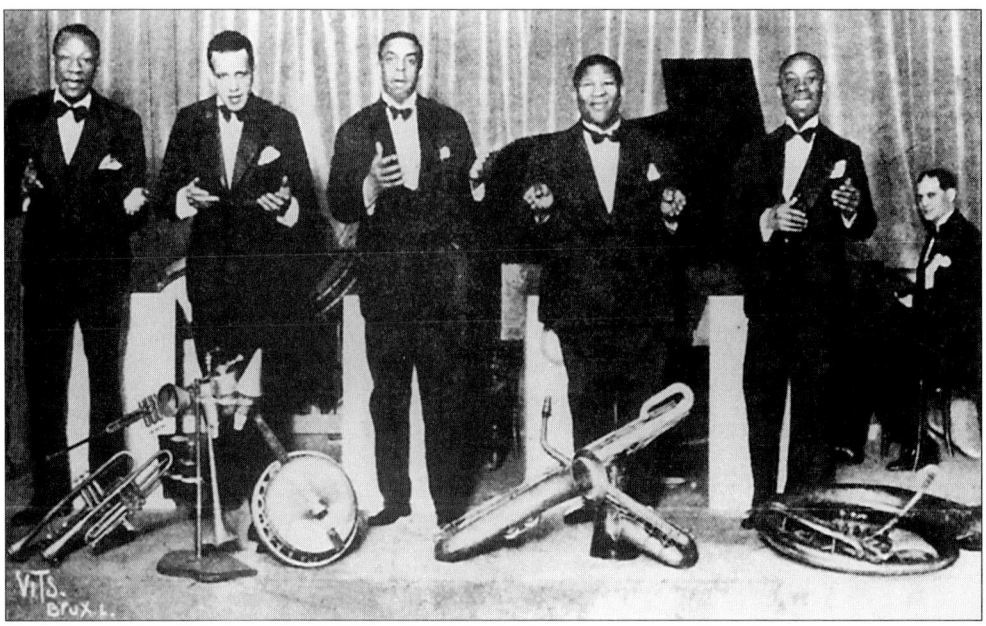

FIGURE 111
Albert Alexander Smith in Brussels with "Cat" Garland band (second from left behind banjo), 1932.
Frank Driggs Collection.

in Brussels in 1932, fig. 111). While none of his known works depict his working environ-
ments, at least nine prints and paintings highlight the stringed instruments Smith played, the
guitar and banjo. These images, however, are far from the sophisticated nightclubs where
Smith earned his bread and butter dressed in a tuxedo.

Struggling to make a living with two separate careers, Smith was torn between being
forced to sell his talents to catering to those who could pay for it and those who sought
positive racially representative images. His solution to the situation was unique. Smith's
career as a musical performer provided a rich source for his visual compositions. He produced
more than two dozen pieces depicting musicians, singers, and dancers. Almost half of these
feature working-class African American banjo players in a series he began in 1930. An astute
observer of popular culture, Smith used his musical and artistic talents both to profit from
common associations with the banjo and to elevate its status. Smith capitalized on the instrument in three ways—he played it in sophisticated nightclubs, he sold stereotypical images of
it to wealthy patrons, and he traced its African ancestry for appreciative African Americans.

Henry O. Tanner was perhaps the first artist to depict African American musicians
with honest warmth and dignity, in *The Banjo Lesson* of 1893 (fig. 112). The image of
a strong male figure as a serious, private educator was completely antithetical to earlier
depictions of comic, public minstrels. Tanner, better known for his luminous landscapes and
biblical depictions, painted just a handful of black genre scenes—and those only after he had
gained geographic and psychological distance from racial discrimination in the United States
as an expatriate in Paris since 1891.

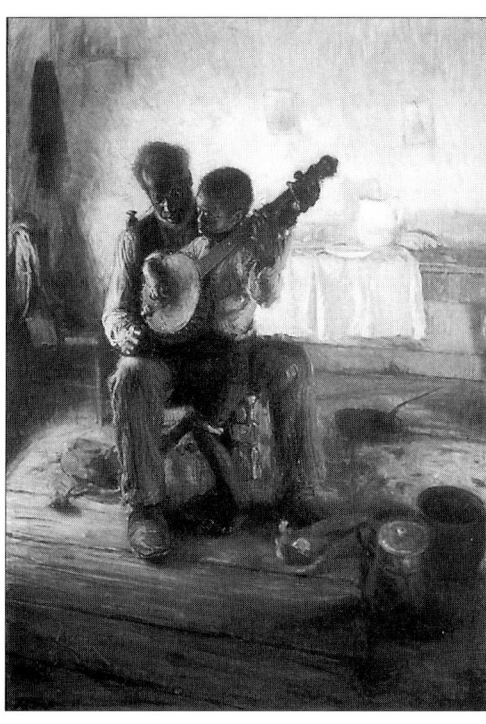

FIGURE 112
Henry O. Tanner, *The Banjo Lesson*, 1893,
oil on canvas, 49 x 35½ in.
Hampton University Museum, Hampton, Virginia.

Tanner and Smith both focused on the banjo, the rhythmic instrument that changed the face of American music at the turn of the century. After Scott Joplin published the score *Maple Leaf Rag* in 1899, musical compositions featured syncopation, rhythmic elaboration, and staccato arrangements for ragtime and cakewalk dance music. The banjo, played with a small flat pick, was the perfect percussive accompaniment to these snappy tunes and tango dancing. Rhythmic strumming of banjos and mandolins was the distinguishing sound of dance music by the Negro Symphony Orchestra, according to its leader, James Reese Europe. His group performed to large New York crowds in the 1910s. During the Great War, Europe directed the 369th Infantry Hell Fighters Jazz Band overseas.

After the war, the cultured, old-world melodies of waltzes and opera were rejected in favor of this newest American music—jazz. Soon, dances such as the Charleston and the Black Bottom became all the rage at home and abroad. Smith captured the musical mood of the 1920s with such titles and prints as The *Dancing Hour, A Tap Dancer, Syncopation,* and *Darktown Strutter.*

Although Smith's popular banjo earned him his living, he seems to have been ambivalent about its associations. In 1930, he created a series of works that depict banjo players in stock settings. Among these are the print *Do That Thing* (fig. 113) and the painting *Dancing Time* (fig. 114). Both feature a well-dressed little girl clapping her hands and dancing on a river dock to banjo music. The images are strongly lit and shadowed— *Dancing Time* in warm shades of brown and gold—in the manner of Rembrandt and Velazquez, artists whom Smith admired. Although realistically portrayed, the figures in both

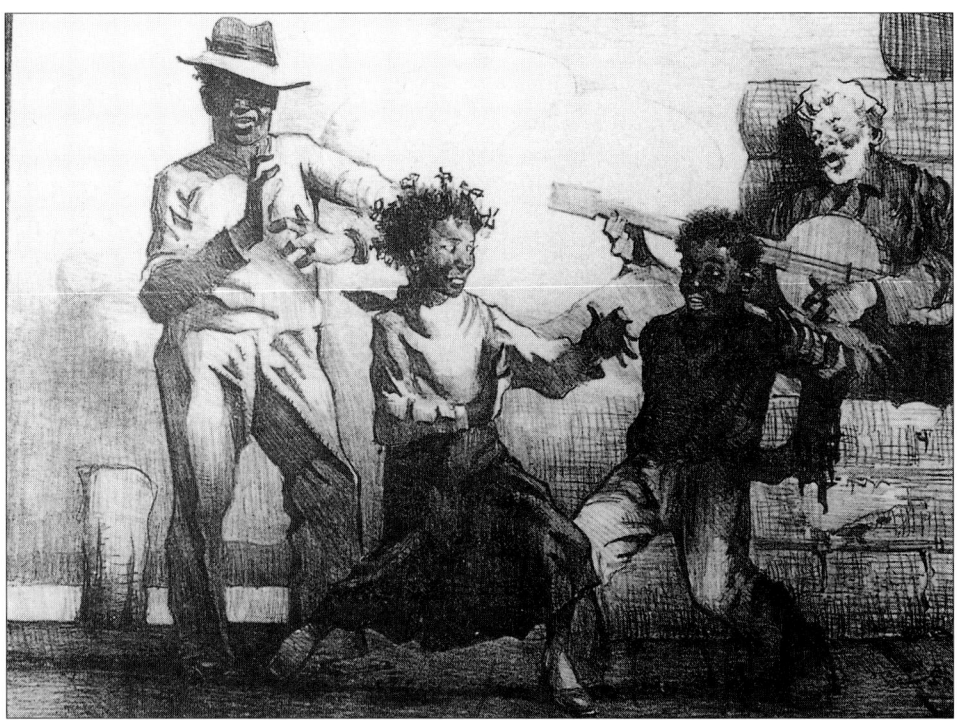

FIGURE 113
Albert Alexander Smith, *Do That Thing,* 1930, lithograph, 8¾ x 11½ in.
Art and Artifacts Division, Schomburg Center for Research in Black Culture, The New York Public Library,
Astor, Lenox, and Tilden Foundations.

works have a stiffness about them, their clothing frozen in unnatural angles. Such caricature
was common in the illustration style of the early twentieth century, but it may also reflect
Smith's discomfort with the subject matter. Some white northeastern Americans responded
favorably to the stereotypes in *Dancing Time;* the work appeared in an exhibition at the
Museum of Fine Arts, Boston, sponsored by the New England Society of Contemporary Art,
and was later reproduced in the magazine *Arts and Archeology.*[72]

That same staginess is evident in Smith's painting *Old Man River* and the print
Temptation; much of Smith's artistic and musical work was about performance and theatrical
presentation. Smith may have derived the imagery of *Old Man River* from Edna Ferber's
tremendously popular novel *Showboat* of 1926. The song *Old Man River* appeared in the
musical stage version of the book, and in the film in 1935, which featured Paul Robeson as a
"lazy southern darkie." As Jeffrey Stewart has pointed out, "what distinguished white usages
of Robeson's talents in the 1920s and 1930s was a symbolic return to the past, a past in
which the pre-industrial, pre-modern qualities of the Negro were both romanticized and
envied by the white author or viewer."[73]

In *Temptation* (1930, fig. 115), two amused workers watch a third fellow making
off with two enormous striped watermelons. Nancy Cunard, the British writer, recognized

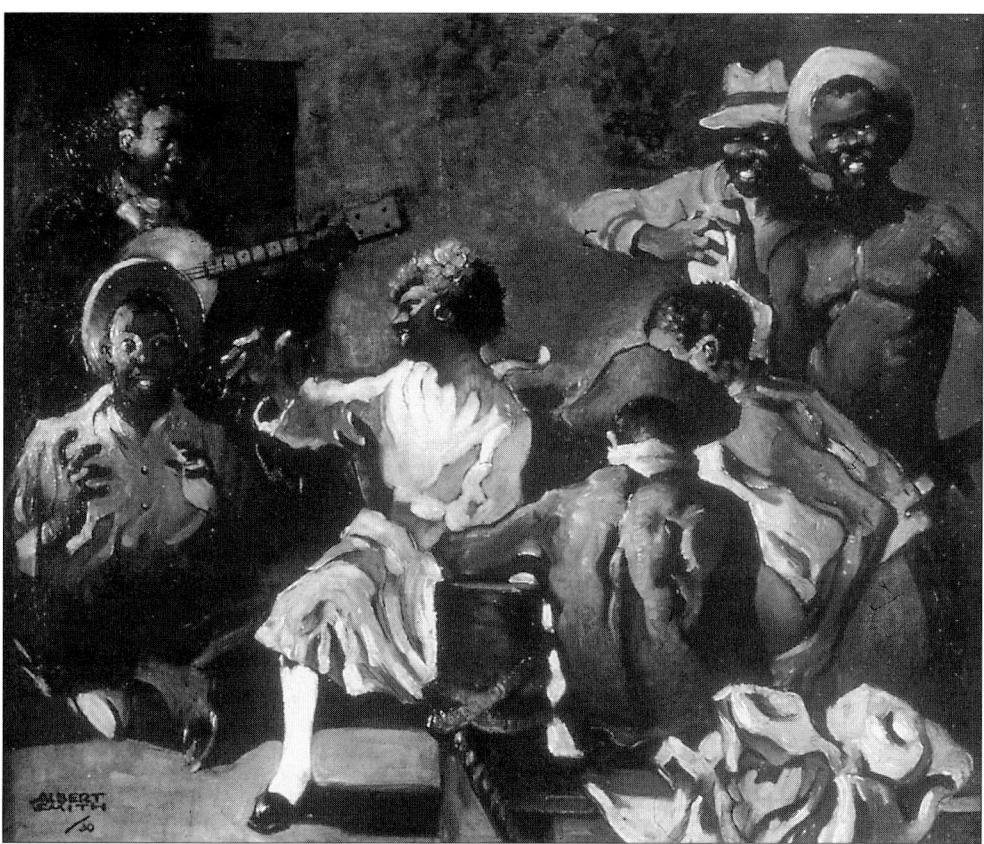

FIGURE 114
Albert Alexander Smith, *Dancing Time*, 1930, oil on canvas, 22½ x 26½ in.
Hampton University Museum, Hampton,Virginia.

the power of such formulaic images as *Temptation*. She wanted to publish the print in her
massive book of 1934, *Negro: An Anthology*, along with essays by leading writers and thinkers
such as Alain Locke, W.E.B. Du Bois, Langston Hughes, and Zora Neale Hurston. For some
reason, Cunard reconsidered her decision and the lithograph did not appear in this notable
volume.

　　　Temptation and *Old Man River* refer to a century-long association of African Americans with elements of southern life—the banjo, watermelon, cotton plantations, and river
work. By the mid-1920s, the banjo was developing a new image as a sophisticated instrument, but still retained strong racist associations. Claude McKay, the Jamaican-born writer
who left the United States to explore Europe, wrote *Banjo: A Story Without a Plot* in 1929
when he lived in France. The novel is set along the beaches of Marseilles, with most of the
characters of African descent. "Banjo" and "Goosey" are from the American South. Through
them, McKay describes some of the ambivalence black artists felt about the instrument:

　　　　　"Banjo! That's what you play?" exclaimed Goosey.
　　　　　"Sure that's what I play," replied Banjo. "Don't you like it?"

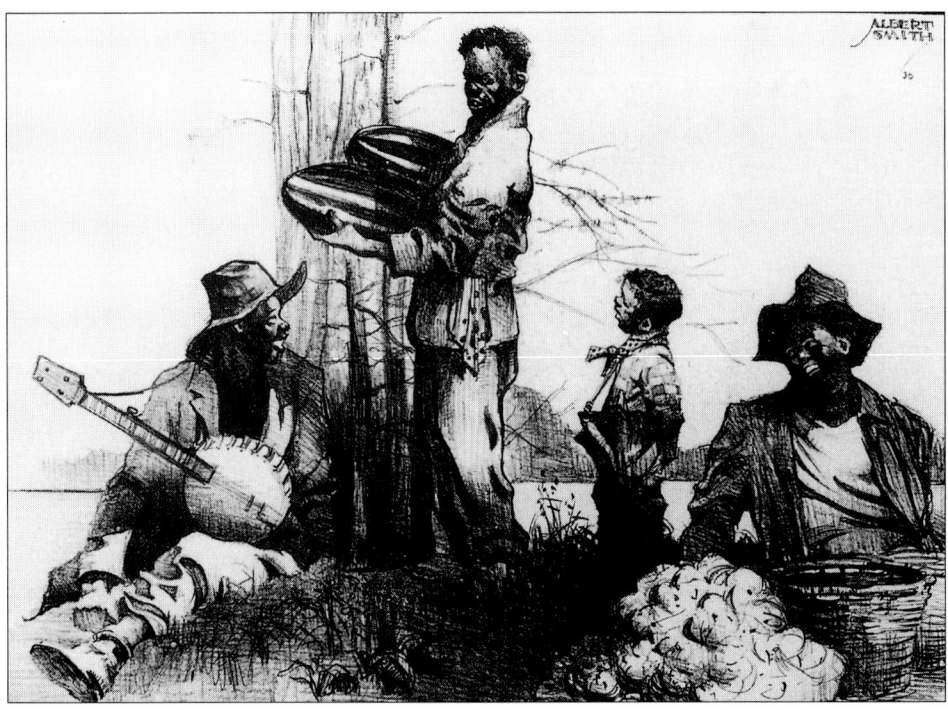

FIGURE 115
Albert Alexander Smith, *Temptation,* 1930, etching, 8 x 10⅞ in. Art and Artifacts Division, Schomburg Center for Research in Black Culture, The New York Public Library, Astor, Lenox, and Tilden Foundations.

"No. Banjo is bondage. It's the instrument of slavery. Banjo is Dixie. The Dixie of the land of cotton and massa and missus and the black mammy. We colored folks have got to get away from all that in these enlightened progressive days. Let us play piano and violin, harp and flute. Let the white folks play the banjo if they want to keep on remembering all the Black Joes singing and the hell they made them live in."

"That ain't got nothing to do with me, nigger," replied Banjo. "I play that theah instrument becaz I likes it. I don't play no Black Joe hymns. I play lively tunes . . ."[74]

Smith played "lively tunes," too, and deplored America's history of discrimination. Why would he, a well-educated expatriate living in France who was born and raised in New York, depict these stilted Southern scenes of blatant racial stereotypes? And why would he, like Hayden, showcase hackneyed images of black people at the very time when philosopher Alain Locke was issuing a call for positive portrayals of the New Negro? Racist imagery was often featured on the covers of sheet music that Smith studied as a boy at the turn of the century. One lithographed advertisement of 1899 for a minstrel group and the popular "coon song" "Hello! My Baby" (fig. 116) portrays a young man raking elements associated with the black South into a drumlike machine. Two "pickaninnies" crank out grinning, little black performers, including a raccoon chained to a banjo player. The implication, as music historian Karen Linn wryly suggests, is that "maybe little white girls are made of sugar and spice and everything nice and little white boys of frogs and snails and puppy dogs' tails but

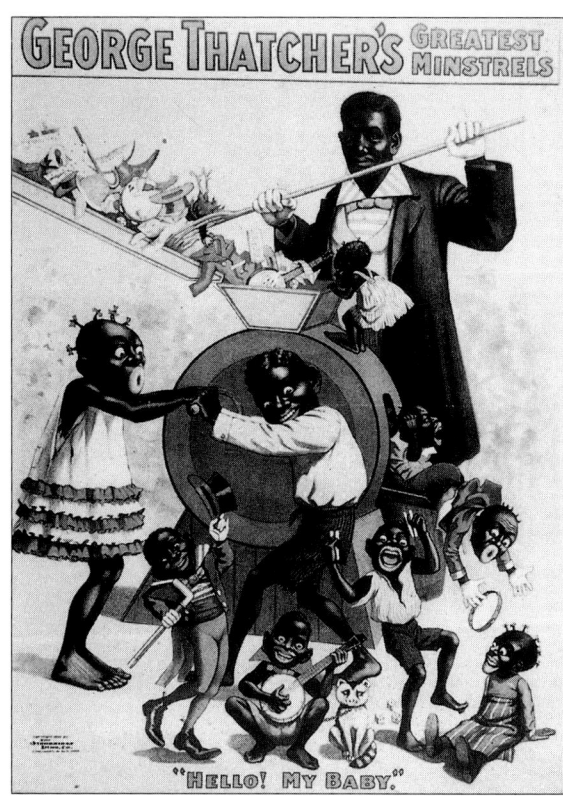

FIGURE 116
Strobridge Lithograph Company,
"Hello, My Baby!" 1899,
lithograph (cover of sheet music),
dimensions unknown.

little black children are made of banjos, chickens, watermelon, charcoal, minstrel clothes, dice, and tambourines."[75]

Smith may have created his southern scenes because of the large public demand for stereotypical images, a demand fueled by the music and movie industries. For example, Harriet Beecher Stowe's novel *Uncle Tom's Cabin* was made for the cinema at least seventeen times between 1903 and 1929. Universal Studios released its most lavish production in 1927, with a budget of almost two million dollars. White viewers flocked to see a world where all whites were aristocrats and all blacks were happy to serve them. Film reviewers were delighted with spectacle scenes in cotton fields and on riverboats. It is not surprising that white viewers wanted these images of the subservient "old Negro" (which Hayden and Motley also produced); they countered the threatening, real new Negro who was emerging and flooding northern cities during the Great Migration. According to Jeffrey Stewart,

> In that move north, the dominant refrain was a longing for the South, a note that is overwhelming in Jean Toomer's *Cane*, the short fiction of Rudolph Fisher, and in the short stories and novels of Zora Neale Hurston. . . . What is at issue here is nothing less than what W. B. Yeats and others searched for in the Irish Renaissance—a romantic re-engagement with a folk tradition that is still within reach historically and emotionally for an educated generation of cosmopolitans. . . . Negro history inevitably remains in the subconscious of American's most creative white people and the South remains in the subconscious of the recent black migrant.[76]

As the son of immigrants from Bermuda, Smith may not have regarded himself as African American. His negative attitude toward this community was certainly not limited to southerners; he disassociated himself from other African Americans as well, both physically and verbally. Smith lived in the northern section of Paris, in Montmartre, while his artist compatriots almost all lived near or across the Seine in Montparnasse, and he never went out of his way to meet them. His closest companions seem to have been a European woman, Jeanne Fevrier (perhaps his wife),[77] and her (or their) children.[78] Smith also often wrote disparagingly about African Americans, calling them "spades" and "corkers."[79] He admitted that his life in France had contributed to his attitude: "When you have tasted this part of the world and forget your color it is mighty hard to match your thoughts and steps with American tempos."[80] Like Motley, who was also fair-skinned and eschewed his black colleagues, Smith developed an elitism that cut him off from potentially enriching friendships with other African American artists.

Smith may have also envied African American artists who won success in the United States. He paid close attention to those who participated in the Harmon Foundation exhibitions and traveled abroad, as he did. Upon hearing that Palmer Hayden had quickly run out of his Harmon prize money in Paris, Smith complained to Schomburg: "So one of the flying-artist stars has been dimmed. Imagine running thru $3000 in so short a space of time. Just one more Negro gone wrong. I wish it had been my luck to fall into such money."[81] While Smith did win a bronze award from the Harmon Foundation at the end of 1929, he was rejected for a prestigious Guggenheim Fellowship. Knowing that Archibald Motley Jr. had received that prize, Smith dismissed his work perhaps out of jealousy or an aversion to modernism. He wrote, "Motley, Jr. stopped [in Paris for] a year and is painting worse than ever."

Smith was especially bitter about his defeats for prizes from both the Harmon and Guggenheim Foundations, in late 1928 and early 1929, not only because he needed the money, but because he believed that his old professor, Charles Curran, was responsible:

> As long as Mr. Curran judges at your exhibition I count myself as a defeated candidate in advance. And Curran's artistic animosity dates back to my school days when I purposely retired from his classes and his instructions to take a better teacher and a better painter. So a defeat at the Harmon Awards was certain—and if he judges again I expect another set-back. Currans [sic] doctrine has always been that a European painting education is not vital and he proves it by his judgements.
>
> During the space of four months I have suffered two defeats of great financial importance in my life and at both judgements Curran had to pass on my work. Were it not that I have an utter contempt for his ability and his work and his teachings, I would have left my brushes years ago, when as the first colored pupil in the National Academy School I came under his guidance.
>
> I have been a good sportsman all my life and defeats don't worry me much, for my life is a series of them—but I'm going to get on top, despite everything and everybody and when I do I am going to turn around and do a little white-washing myself.[82]

Smith also took note of the kinds of work that achieved honors from other white judges. Once he learned that Hale Woodruff, one of the first recipients of a Harmon award, won praise for the painting he submitted in 1928 called *The Banjo Player*, he may have concluded that depictions of the banjo would earn him accolades, too. He submitted *Silent Banjo* and *Dancing Time* and they were, in fact, included in the Harmon exhibition of 1931. In the meantime, Smith sought further exhibition opportunities in France and held solo shows at the Hôtel Beau Site in Cannes, February–March, 1930,[83] and at the Veterans Exhibition in Paris in 1932.[84]

Smith continued his study of the banjo and stringed instruments from Africa in other works. *Ethiopian Music* (fig. 117) refers to the strong African traditions of rich lyric sound and oral history. In this painting of ca. 1928, eleven men wearing traditional white robes gather to celebrate a religious feast, most likely the Christian Festival of Palms in Askum, the sacred city of Ethiopia. To the beat of slow, solemn drums, they will advance towards the cathedral. The second man from the left will lead the procession. He bears the staff of the sistrum, the top of which is cropped on the upper left by the edge of the canvas, this object a legacy of the ancient Eygptians. The musician on the left center plays the Abyssinian ten-stringed harp, the *beganeh*, believed to have been invented by King David. Smith depicts a similarly dressed musician playing another traditional stringed instrument

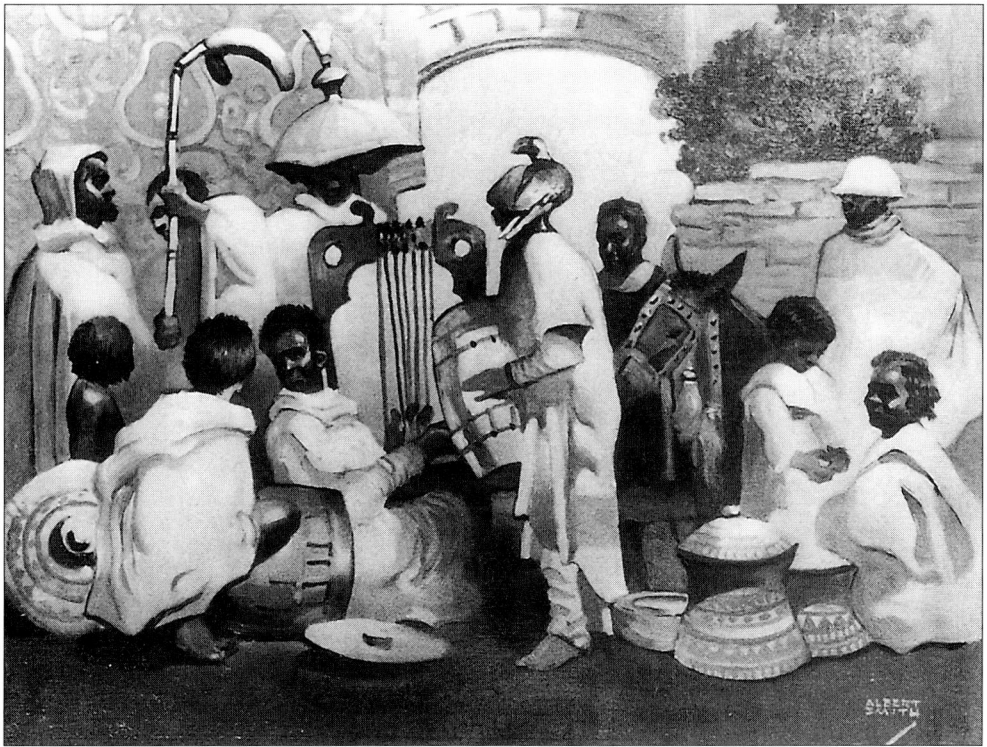

FIGURE 117
Albert Alexander Smith, *Ethiopian Music*, ca. 1928, oil on canvas, dimensions and location unknown.
From a photograph in the National Archives; used with permission.

in the pen-and-ink drawing *A Fantasy Ethiopia* (1928, fig. 118), in which Smith fuses his artistic, musical and intellectual passions. In the lower left, a painter, palette in hand, pauses to imagine wondrous images of Africa—colossal architecture, engraved stone tablets, and wild animals. In the center are two intent musicians. Along with the other emblems, they are framed by the silhouette of a large palette. Smith called his work *A Fantasy Ethiopia;* his composition, however, actually has historical accuracy. The obelisk on the left, parallel to the giraffe head, is the famous twenty-foot granite monolith at Askum, the city that ruled the entire area between the Roman Empire and Persia at the time of Jesus. The pattern behind the silhouette of the palette may be abstracted Greek letters from a stone nearby the obelisk. The inscription on this stone, dating from the fourth century C.E., describes the vast kingdom of the Askumites led by King Aizanes. The stone tablet in the right foreground is the fallen top of one of the many monoliths in Askum. Smith's source for these monuments may be the book *The Sacred City of the Ethiopians,* by J. Theodore Bent, of 1896, which the artist could have seen at the Bibliothèque Nationale. Smith's depictions of animals may also derive from sources in the French national library, such as Scottish explorer James Bruce's *Travels to Discover the Source of the Nile* of 1790 which contains many engravings of Ethiopian flora and fauna.

The central musician, with dreadlocks, plays the Abyssinian *chera masanko* or *masingo,* said to have been invented by Israel, the forefather of King David. This popular instrument is a rhomboid wooden sound-box tightly covered with skin, with a long neck and one or two strings. Wandering minstrels (*asmari*) played it with a bow at both sacred and secular feasts. As Smith well knew, the *masingo* was one of the forerunners of the banjo.

Smith symbolically traced the banjo's African lineage in the 1929 painting *Generations* (lost; reproduction unavailable). Atop a four-tiered stone structure, a man on the left plays the *masingo* while below, a bearded old man sits with his arms crossed around a banjo. Next to his feet is a bundle of cotton spilling down to the last tier. There, dressed in a Western shirt and pants, a wide-eyed young boy clasps one wrist as he hugs his knees to his chest. Hearing music, this African American boy may believe he has a strong African heritage, but he cannot see what is behind him, perhaps because he has no access to either books or education about African history. Whether numb from cotton-picking or paralyzed by uncertainty, he seems to wait anxiously for the future, staring and inactive. The dissonance created by the juxtaposition of diverse chronological and geographic images makes *Generations* one of Smith's most unusual paintings. Could this have been one of the works writer Rose Henderson critiqued after viewing it at a 1930 Harmon Foundation exhibition? She wrote that Smith's "plastic design and soft, rich colors are agreeable in this year's showing, as usual, but some of his compositions seem forced and deliberately eccentric, instead of conveying the sense of human directness which is evidently intended."[85]

Smith's images of song and dance are a small but significant part of his entire oeuvre, which included depictions of various European people and places. While he created ambivalent images of African American banjo players, he seems to have done this with a

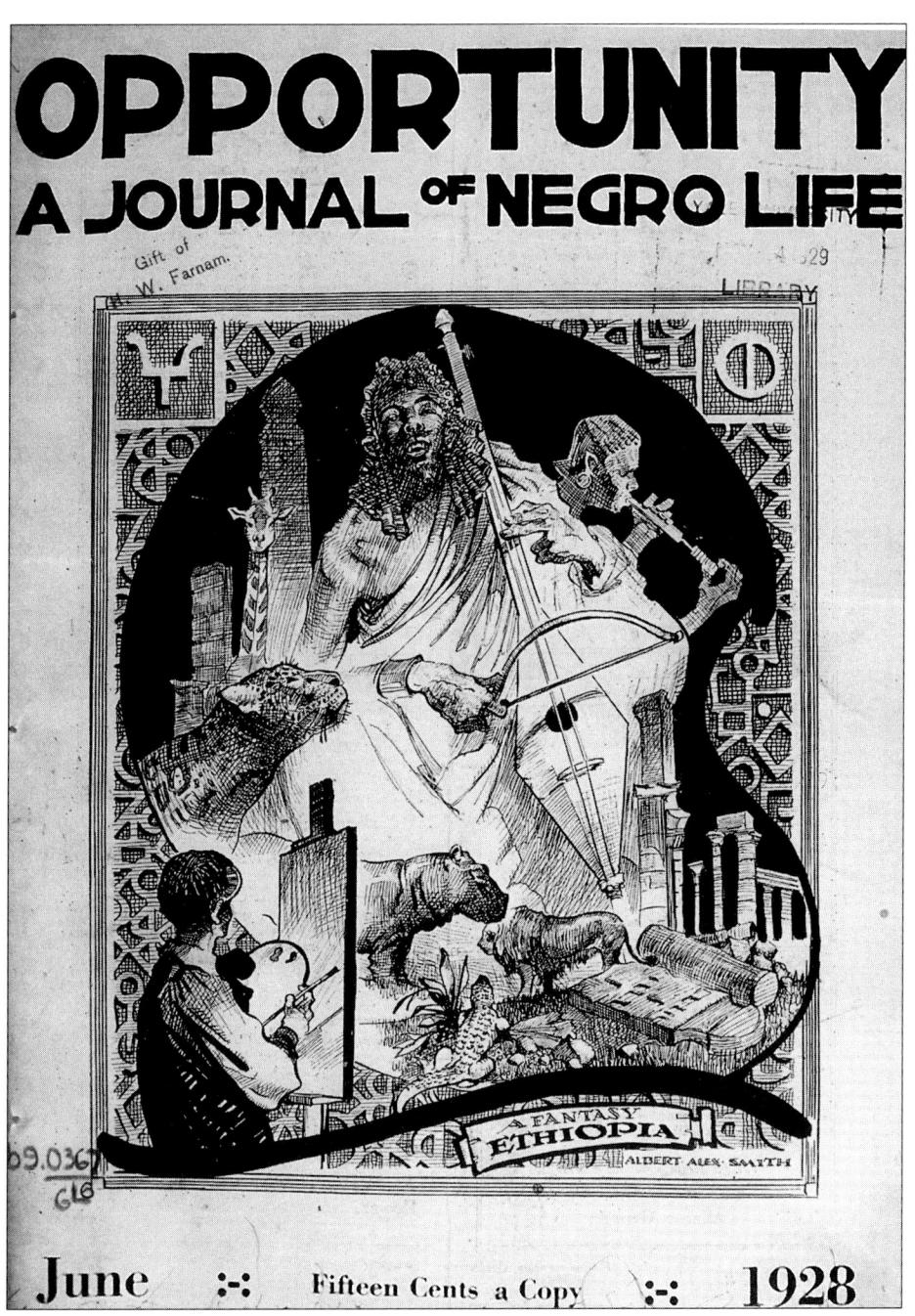

FIGURE 118
Albert Alexander Smith, *A Fantasy Ethiopia,* 1928, pen and ink on paper,
dimensions and location unknown. From the cover of *Opportunity,* June 1928.

primarily white, private audience in mind that could afford to buy his paintings and prints. Before he developed the banjo series in 1930, he was an optimistic young man who created powerful images of dignity for a large, public, predominantly African American audience via front covers for *Crisis* and *Opportunity* magazines. It was through those democratic vehicles that he denounced racism and declared pride in his heritage with various illustrations of Ethiopia's grandeur in 1923 and 1924, culminating in the rich African traditions of music and oral history in *A Fantasy Ethiopia* of 1928.

Clearly, then, Smith was a conflicted artist who made conscious decisions about his depictions of song and dance, carefully choosing specific imagery for separate audiences. While he played to the desires of a white public, he also responded to the requests of Schomburg and Du Bois, as well as to Locke's call for racially representative art, with dignified portrayals of African culture. Smith's performance on and depictions of the banjo were musical and artistic orchestrations, unique "call and response" systems.

CODA: A SON OF HAM IN EUROPE, 1934–1940

Like many artists who felt the effects of the Great Depression, Smith struggled to find ways to support his artistic production. After a short trip to Italy, where he executed more etchings of tourist scenes, in 1934, Smith applied to the Guggenheim Foundation for a travel grant. In his application, he emphasized his unique status as a printmaker: "As, practically, the only Negro etcher listed in the American Art Annual—I seek a Guggenheim Fellowship in order to develop my etching to the highest degree possible by research and study in leading museums of foreign capitals where examples can be studied first hand. My painting would naturally be a part of this development."[86]

Crushed by yet another rejection, Smith spent his last five years in France performing music. He seems to have produced little art from 1934 to 1936, yet he exhibited with the American Artists Professional League in Paris every year from 1935 to 1938.[87] Most of Smith's energy was spent performing at Zelli's and the Café de Paris, doing work for radio, and making recordings.[88]

In 1937, Smith's interest in portraiture may have been revived by Schomburg, who asked him to render a likeness of Tanner, after Tanner's death that year. During the following months, Smith produced another series depicting great black historic leaders, this time in watercolor. All of them seem to have been done after works that Smith viewed in the Bibliothèque Nationale, such as his portrait of African American playwright Victor Séjour (1817–1874) (fig. 119) from a cartoon by Etienne Carjat (1828–1906), or from photographs, such as the portrait of Tanner (fig. 120), from a snapshot from the 1920s lent by Tanner's son after his father's death on May 25. Whereas more than half of Smith's 1922 series, eleven works, is of African Americans, his ca. 1937–1938 series, nineteen works, includes only three, Séjour, Tanner, and Banneker. Smith executed portraits of some of the same men he had painted in 1922—Toussaint L'Ouverture, Pushkin, and Dumas. Apparently, Smith's interest in Dumas was heightened by the artist's

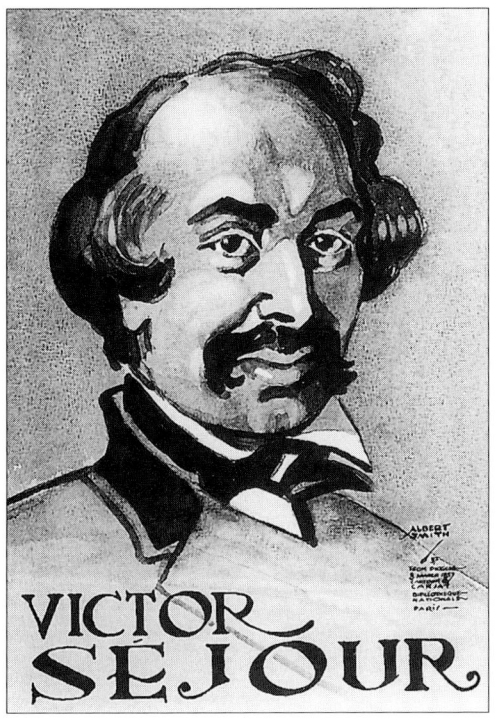

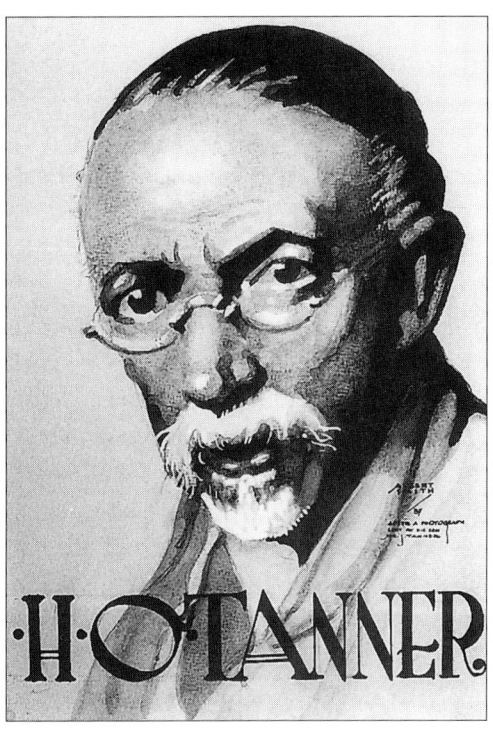

FIGURE 119
Albert Alexander Smith, *Victor Séjour,* 1937,
watercolor on paper, 12⅛ x 8⅝ in.
Art and Artifacts Division, Schomburg Center for
Research in Black Culture, The New York Public
Library, Astor, Lenox, and Tilden Foundations.

FIGURE 120
Albert Alexander Smith, *H.O. Tanner,* 1937,
watercolor on paper, 11⅜ x 8½ in.
Art and Artifacts Division, Schomburg Center for
Research in Black Culture, The New York Public
Library, Astor, Lenox, and Tilden Foundations.

travels. In the new series, Smith not only depicted Dumas and his father, but also Dumas
at the Châlet Monte Cristo and at his home in Villars-Cotterets. Smith also depicted
Cuban religious leader Archbishop Victoria; Haitian leader Christophe; Abyssinian leaders
Makonnen and Tahiti; Ethiopian leader Menelik II; Spanish artist Juan de Pareja; and the
French Soulouque, Bissette, Lethière, and Lislet Geoffroy.

Some of these works may have been featured in the Association of American
Professional Artists in Paris. Three of his paintings (identities now unknown) attracted a
critic for *La revue moderne illustrée* who admired "their vigorous composition, their color,
finally their general impression, luminous and bold, achieving at their height an ardeur [*sic*]
and optimism of better times."[89]

Shortly after completing this series, Smith became acquainted with Lois Mailou
Jones, who had received a General Education Board Fellowship to study in Paris, in
1937–1938. After her departure from France, the two communicated by mail several times,
Smith acting as the mentor on such matters as crating paintings and customs charges.[90] He
felt a kinship with Jones: "I am as ever your silent partner along this unusual road we have

both chosen."[91] Smith was anxious to know how Jones's landscapes and still lifes were accepted by white American audiences: "I thought you might have been 'thumbed-down' for not painting African subjects. That is all they expect us to be sufficiently capable of handling. . . . We can all take a good crack at African stuff but there are few of us that can paint a decent picture to hang along the walls with our white brethren."[92]

In 1939, Smith produced images with ostensibly Arabian themes; the titles of these apparently lost works are *Arabian Knight, A Daughter of Allah,* and *Dictator.* The reasons for the creation of these works are not yet known.

Smith was determined to take charge of his own destiny. He wrote to Schomburg, "Well, every failure is a whip to drive me on to further heights. I used to feel discouraged, but that feeling is gone now and as I can see it's a long and rough road, I must go on all the harder."[93] In his drive for success, Smith may have overworked himself. He died suddenly in France on April 3, 1940, only forty-four years old.

As an entertainer, Smith knew that in order to make a living, he had to give his predominantly white audience what it wanted. He explained to Lois Mailou Jones, "Our race is decidedly enthusiastic in paper praise but their enthusiasm ends where their pocket-book begins."[94]

Further, while Smith mingled with few African Americans in France and spoke disparagingly of his compatriots, privately he gloried in their shared racial ancestry and ironically subverted elements associated with racism in his music, art, and language. He turned a biblical curse—and subsequent racial slur—into an affirmative celebration. In the book of Genesis, Noah condemned Canaan, son of Ham, to be a "servant of servants." Hamitic-speaking peoples, however, ruled North Africa. Two years before his death, Smith announced to Schomburg that he, too, was proud to be "a Son of Ham."[95]

CONCLUSION

HOW YA GONNA KEEP 'EM DOWN ON THE FARM?

How ya gonna keep 'em down on the farm after they've seen Pa-ree?

How ya gonna keep 'em away from Broadway, jazz-in' aroun' and paintin'
the town?

How ya gonna keep 'em away from harm? That's a mystery.

They'll never want to see a rake or plow, and who the deuce can par-ley-voo
a cow?

How ya gonna keep 'em down on the farm after they've seen Pa-ree?

—World War I song, 1919; lyrics by Sam Lewis
and Joe Young, music by Walter Donaldson

Study and success in Paris were crucial to Nancy Elizabeth Prophet, Palmer Hayden, Hale Woodruff, Archibald Motley Jr., Augusta Savage, and Albert Alexander Smith in their establishment as some of the most significant leaders in the visual arts of the international New Negro movement in the 1920s and 1930s. In this challenging and stimulating environment, they proved their talent and enriched their visions, in the process forever changing their lives. Although the artists came from disparate backgrounds throughout the United States and their works differed significantly in style and content, they had much in common in class, origin, education, patronage, experiences, and achievements abroad, artistic development and subject matter, and careers. Paris provided a formidable, dynamic site for these intersections, and fostered a coming of age.

SHARED BACKGROUNDS

Prophet, Hayden, Woodruff, Savage, and Smith all came from working-class families; only Motley's background was middle class and he was perhaps the lightest-skinned. Motley, Woodruff, and Smith's parents encouraged their artistic tendencies, but Prophet, Hayden,

241

and Savage began their careers as artists without family support. While Hayden and Savage hailed from rural or nearly rural small, southern towns, they or their families shared the Great Migration experience with Motley and Woodruff. All, except Hayden, seem to have worked their way through four-year colleges in large, urban, northern centers—Prophet at Rhode Island School of Design, Woodruff at the John Herron Institute of Art, Motley at the Art Institute of Chicago, Savage at Cooper Union, and Smith at the National Academy of Design. All had white male instructors who had studied in Paris, urged their pupils to do the same, and helped them find financial support. Because these artists had to overcome numerous obstacles, none journeyed to Europe while undergraduates. All but two were in their thirties by the time they went abroad (Smith was twenty-four; Woodruff, twenty-seven; Prophet, thirty-two; Motley, Hayden, and Savage, all thirty-seven).

PATRONAGE

These artists earned the first awards ever established for African American artists and used them specifically to further their education in Paris. Hayden and Woodruff went abroad partially funded as the first Harmon Foundation awardees. Savage went supported by the first Rosenwald Fund for graduate fellowships for African Americans, and money from the Carnegie Corporation. The artists also received support from various African American groups, such as the National Urban League and the Baptist Young People's Union Convention, which sponsored Savage; and Walter White of the NAACP, who helped Woodruff; and many friends and interested well-wishers. Additionally, white patrons came forward to help the artists get to France—Alice Dike funded Hayden; Hermann Lieber, Lucille Morehouse, the Florentine drama club of Franklin, and banker Otto H. Kahn backed Woodruff; and Countess Irene Di Robilant and several Italian American sculptors aided Savage. And Motley received a one-year Guggenheim Fellowship, with an option for a six-month extension.

Once the artists were in Paris, many African American individuals and institutions actively promoted and publicized their achievements. W.E.B. Du Bois, in particular, created networks for Prophet, Savage, and Tanner, and he carried regular coverage on them and the others in *Crisis* magazine. Arthur Schomburg often held small exhibitions of the artists' work at the 135th Street branch of the New York Public Library. One of Schomburg's protégés was Smith, with whom he often corresponded. In exchange for the research Smith did and the material on black history he sent, Schomburg purchased Smith's prints. Alain Locke visited Woodruff and Hayden in Paris, introduced them to African art, and later published glowing evaluations of their work. Countee Cullen published an article on Prophet in *Crisis*, lent moral support to Savage, and purchased Woodruff's work. John Hope gave Prophet and Woodruff teaching positions in Atlanta upon their return to the United States. Numerous black periodicals published information on and work by the six—*Crisis, Opportunity, Negro World*, the *Baltimore Afro-American*, the *Messenger*, and the *Chicago Defender*, among others, in the United States, and *La dépêche africaine* and *La revue du monde noir*, which published one of Aaron Douglas's illustrations, *Forge Foundry*, in France. It was almost as if the six—or the ten, when we include William H. Johnson, Aaron Douglas, Laura Wheeler Waring, and Gwendolyn Bennett—were cultural ambassadors whose success in the French capital would prove to the world the competence of African Americans in the visual arts. This notion was also supported by the largely white Harmon Foundation.

The recognition that the Harmon Foundation gave to artists who studied in Paris is culturally and statistically significant. All but Savage received awards from the foundation. Prophet received the Otto H. Kahn prize; Hayden secured a gold award and a painting prize; Motley merited a gold award; and Woodruff and Smith both earned bronze awards and honorable mention. In fact, artists who studied in Paris—including William Edouard Scott, William Henry Johnson, Laura Wheeler Waring, and Lois Mailou Jones, who later went to Paris, 1937–1938—claimed more than half of the prizes. They won sixteen of the twenty-eight awards, or 57 percent; Prophet, Hayden, Woodruff, Motley, and Smith won eight, or 35 percent, of the awards. Additionally, of the 501 works exhibited by 123 artists, 142 (28 percent) were by artists who studied in Paris. Seventy-seven, or 15 percent, were by the six; sixty-five, or 13 percent, were by others who were abroad between the years of 1899 and 1938.

SHARED EXPERIENCES IN PARIS

When the six artists arrived in Paris, they followed similar educational paths. All except Smith settled in Montparnasse, and they often visited galleries and museums. All, apart from Smith and Motley, sought out the internationally-recognized Tanner for his advice on art and life in France. None, however, was interested in following the master's stylistic example, which they likely viewed as belonging to an older, outdated generation. All either attended classes at academies—Prophet went to the Ecole des Beaux-Arts, Woodruff took lessons at the Académies Scandinave and Moderne, Savage may have gone to the Académie de la Grande Chaumière, and Smith was enrolled in the Académie des Beaux-Arts in Liège—or studied with private instructors, in the case of Hayden and Savage.

The artists followed similar social patterns, as well. Each one, except Prophet and Motley, seemed to thrive on the nightlife, dancing in West Indian clubs, playing cards, drinking, and going to parties. All had little interaction with white French citizens or Americans. All traveled a bit throughout France or Europe, and all but Motley exhibited their work in Paris and shipped it back to the United States for exhibition. They kept abreast of U.S. news by reading the *New York Herald Tribune,* Paris edition, and *Crisis.* Everyone reveled in the freedom and relatively racially tolerant atmosphere of Paris; yet all, save Motley, struggled, at least initially, with the language and limited funds.

In Paris, four of the artists achieved recognition with exhibitions at prestigious institutions, and in some reviews. Prophet and Savage exhibited at the Salon d'Automne and the Société des Artistes Français, Hayden at the Galerie Bernheim-Jeune and American Legion headquarters (and perhaps the Salon des Tuileries), and Smith at the American Artists Professional League. Major French periodicals—*La Revue du Vrai et du Beau,*

La revue moderne illustrée des arts et de la vie, L'art contemporain—favorably reviewed the work of Hayden, Prophet, and Smith. Minor ones—*Chronique familiale du rayonnement intellectuel* and *La dépêche africaine*—lauded Prophet and Savage, respectively. Despite such approbation, the work of these artists seems to have had little lasting affect on anyone in Paris.

ARTISTIC DEVELOPMENT

The works that the six artists produced in Paris varied tremendously in style and content, not only when the artists are taken as a group, but also within the oeuvre of each. At first, almost all continued in the academic fashion in which they had been trained, producing landscapes and portraits. Most, however, then substantially expanded their approaches, subject matter, and use of materials.

Prophet and Savage, who had primarily produced realistic portraits in clay, plaster, and bronze, began to sculpt a wide variety of expressionistic images directly in wood and marble. Both created somewhat androgynous, nude figures expressive of emotional and physical states of being (e.g., Prophet, *Discontent;* and Savage, *Envy*). They also turned out African or generically black busts (Prophet, *Congolais;* and Savage, *Tête de jeune fille* and *Divinité nègre*) and black males (Prophet, *Head of a Negro;* and Savage, *The Call*). Prophet chiseled bas-reliefs, too, but Savage's range was broader. She also created dancing figures, an Amazon-woman series, genre works, and an exotic animal scene.

When Savage and Prophet returned to the United States, they continued to sculpt. Since little is known about Prophet's work both before and after Paris, it is difficult to assess the impact that her experience abroad had on her oeuvre. Savage's production was greatly curtailed by the demands of her teaching positions and directorships, but she created several large, striking, symbolic works in clay and plaster (*Realization* and *Lift Every Voice and Sing*) in the 1930s that received some critical acclaim. Her venture into abstraction, first seen in *Fern Frond* in Paris, was short-lived and seems to have reappeared only in *Abstract Madonna* (ca. late 1930s) in New York. Savage returned to the pragmatic practice of commissions, sculpting portrait busts of notable African Americans.

Paris had little effect on Motley's style, although he did develop a deeper understanding of the interplay between cool and warm light by studying the Old Masters in the Louvre. In terms of content, his depictions of Parisian street scenes, cafés, and nightlife prefigured his paintings of Bronzeville, Chicago, street scenes in the 1930s and 1940s. While there were few subjects that attracted all of the artists, Motley and Hayden were both interested in the depiction of jazz and cardplaying. Given the extreme popularity of black jazz in Paris, it might at first seem surprising that in the entire body of work created by African American artists in Paris, only two images of jazz-performing seem to exist, Motley's *Blues* and Hayden's *Bal jeunesse*. Both of these portray free-spirited, sophisticated black musicians and dancers in a nightclub. Jazz may have been one of the clichés that these artists hoped to avoid.

Ironically, Motley, Hayden, and Woodruff rendered a different stereotype of blacks in their depictions of cosmopolitan cardplayers. It was rare that several of the artists abroad depicted the same subject, but these three painters were all cardplayers themselves. Both Motley and Hayden portrayed four savvy, shifty-eyed black men dressed in suits. Where Motley's *Sharks (Playing Poker)* is set in a generic game room, Hayden's *Nous quatre à Paris* clearly takes place in Paris, as indicated by the title and the ubiquitous French drinks, red wine and café crème, on the table. Both scenes hint at the underhanded dealings of the demimonde as each contender slyly inspects his competitors or possible assailants. In Motley's work, the room fills with cigar and cigarette smoke while two men whisper conspiratorially in the background. Hayden's dark-skinned card players, with slanted eyes, cue ball-like spherical heads, and outsized lips, stare comically in opposite directions, two by two. With their uniformity of facial features and gestures painted in light watercolor washes, however, they demonstrate a good-humored collegiality—however racist it might appear—not evident in Motley's dark scene where every man is out for himself. In a sense, the works reflect the personalities of their creators; Hayden was a free spender who relished his nights out with the boys while Motley was a loner, suspicious of others' perceived stratagems.

In Woodruff's *The Cardplayers* two distorted "sharks'" heads echo the rounded profiles of Hayden's contenders, but they are hardly cartoon figures. Woodruff's Cubist approach is more intellectual, with its references to West African art in the players' alien faces, a thinker's game represented by the chessboard in the background, and the stylistic innovations of Modigliani and Cézanne. Of the three paintings, only Woodruff's was exhibited at the Harmon Foundation, but received little acknowledgment at the time.

Since four of Motley's works from Paris are either missing or are in inaccessible collections, it is almost impossible to know what they depicted, and especially given the vague titles of *The Flight, Refugees,* and *Veterans,* but it seems likely that *Spirituals* would have had some African American content. Such cultural content is amply evident in the work of Hayden and Smith, and to a lesser extent, of Woodruff.

In France, Hayden developed his signature, caricature-like style that had been first informed by the circus posters he had designed in the United States. Encouraged by the Harmon Foundation to depict Negro subjects, his work in Paris dealt for the first time, and then increasingly, with genre scenes of the African American working class, such as *The Janitor Who Paints* and *John Henry.* Hayden would continue working with this content and style throughout his life. Before he went abroad, Hayden painted landscapes and seascapes almost exclusively. Once in Paris, he expanded his repertoire to include depictions of an international colony of blacks, at the Bal noir, the Bal jeunesse, and the Colonial Exposition.

The Colonial Exposition prompted very different artistic creations from three African American artists in France. Hayden's watercolors series was a lighthearted, cartoon-like depiction of African dancers. Prophet's meditative bust *Congolais* may have been an appreciative response to the apparent but ambivalent respect Europeans gave African people and art at the exposition. Savage seems to have created an African figure (now lost) that won acclaim at the fair. Other African American artists, such as Aaron Douglas, attended the grand event, but it is not known whether the experience affected their work. Yet the exposition may have raised issues the artists dealt with at a later time. Like Woodruff, Hayden felt the influence of African sculpture on modern European art. Unlike Woodruff's sophisticated fusion of the two in *The Cardplayers,* Hayden's work was limited to a somewhat superficial depiction of a Fang head and Kuba textile in *Fétiche et fleurs.* Today, Hayden and Prophet are perhaps best known for *Fétiche et fleurs* and *Congolais,* despite their other remarkable productions, such as Prophet's *Head of a Negro* and *Discontent* and Hayden's *John Henry* series from the 1940s. The sculpture and painting, with their African subjects and French titles, lend a mystique and a cultural validity that continues to have resonance for both black and white people who uphold the tenets of European modernism.

All of the artists created works that referred to African cultures in some way. Except for Woodruff, they all depicted black people, whether real or imagined, from Ethiopia, Senegal, the Congo, Martinique, and Haiti. Hayden's images were cartoonlike; those of all the others were executed with sincere respect for the long history of their subjects, as well as some romantic longing for the grandeur of past black empires. The artists seem to have had limited and largely superficial personal contacts with West Africans and West Indians, yet at least they did meet with and depicted other black people rather than just appropriate their art forms, as had so many white Europeans and Americans.

Woodruff's work underwent the most changes while he was abroad. Like Hayden, he began his career as a landscapist. In Paris, with the encouragement to do figurative work from W.E.B. Du Bois, Walter White, Henry O. Tanner, and the Harmon Foundation, Woodruff painted a few canvases in a "racial" vein. *Washer Women, Old Woman Peeling Apples,* and *Banjo Player* were all black genre scenes, yet these were not New Negro images that would aid in racial uplift. Ironically, just as Woodruff was "going modern," *Banjo Player,* a work rife with allusions to an outdated minstrel tradition, won honorable mention from the Harmon Foundation in 1930. Like the work of William Henry Johnson, Woodruff's most daring innovations came after he left Paris for the south of France. In Cagnes-sur-Mer, he would produce the remarkable *Cardplayers* and several entirely abstract compositions. There, Woodruff also painted a mural in a restaurant and experimented with fifteenth-century fresco techniques. When Woodruff returned to the United States, he went back to representational imagery for more than a decade, in response, perhaps, to several factors: Regionalism, the Mexican muralist movement—Woodruff studied briefly with Diego Rivera—and the expectations of both black and white patrons for racially representative (propagandist) art. By the end of the 1940s, Woodruff's paintings were abstract and would remain so until he died in 1980. Woodruff's remarkable stylistic diversity carried him through successive waves of art movements and helped him achieve the most luminous career of the six artists.

In addition to renderings of European tourist landmarks and genre scenes, eleven of which the Harmon Foundation exhibited, Smith created numerous prints of southern African American genre scenes, among them *Old Man River* and *Plantation Melodies,* and sold both to Americans and Europeans. While some of his clichéd images may be amusing, they do not have the broad, slapstick humor of Hayden's paintings. Instead, Smith's depictions are deliberately theatrical and spring from his background as a musical performer. Like Savage, Smith also created portraits of famous black men. Unlike her busts modeled from life, his etchings, engravings, and watercolors were largely based on prints and photographs of deceased celebrities, such Dumas and Tanner.

That these artists created virtually no abstract work in Paris speaks to many complex issues. Among these are the choice to produce varied figurative and descriptive works as a means of documenting dignified images of people of color; a way to attract conservative patrons, both black and white, with stereotypes or stereotyical nuances; and, as art historian Catherine Bernard suggests, "the aesthetic acceptance of popular canons of representation, since pure or nonobjective abstraction was often seen as suspect and rejected by mainstream culture."[1]

THE IMPACT OF STUDY IN PARIS ON CAREERS IN THE UNITED STATES

Expatriation to France was always a possibility, yet all of the artists except Smith returned to the United States permanently. They came back for various reasons—because they could no longer afford to live in Paris (all but Motley); they felt they had gotten everything they could from the experience (Motley and Hayden); they missed their families and friends; and they wanted to be recognized as serious artists in their own country. Rather than returning to their hometowns, however, these international travelers migrated to bustling metropolises—New York, Chicago, Atlanta. Upon their homecoming, all excelled in the areas of education, exhibitions, and honors and awards.

Four of the six artists were among the first generation of African American college and university art professors. Woodruff and Prophet built the art department at Atlanta University. Woodruff also taught as a lecturer for the Association of American Colleges and as professor of art education at New York University, which honored him with the Great Teacher Award in 1966 and the status of professor emeritus in 1968. Savage taught in numerous capacities in the 1930s: as director of the Augusta Savage Studio of Arts and Crafts; leader of the Vanguard, a group of young intellectuals whom she left after a year in 1934 when its membership became communist-controlled; instructor of adult education classes at the State University of New York; assistant supervisor for the WPA Federal Art Project; director of the Harlem Community Art Center; director of the Salon of Contemporary Negro Art; and summer-camp art teacher for children in Saugerties, New York. The students of Woodruff, Prophet, and Savage, such as Jacob Lawrence, Norman Lewis, Wilmer Jennings, Hayward Oubre, Frederick Flemister, and Eugene Grigsby, as well as those of Lois Mailou Jones, including Elizabeth Catlett, Gwendolyn Knight Lawrence, and David Driskell, would become some of the best-known African American artists of the midtwentieth century.

Motley's teaching career was limited to one year, as visiting instructor at Howard University in 1935, and Hayden never taught. However, they each made a living working for the WPA Federal Art Project in the mid- to late 1930s, and their spouses supported them financially (Hayden married a white schoolteacher in 1940). After Motley's wife died in 1948, the artist worked for a manufacturer of shower curtains for nine years, then received social security benefits. Hayden earned an inconsistent income from various jobs and commissions.

In addition to Prophet, Woodruff, and Savage, many of the first generation of African American art professors studied in Paris in the 1920s or 1930s. They include Aaron Douglas (Fisk University), Laura Wheeler Waring (Cheyney State Teachers College), Rex Gorleigh (Harlem Art Center, the Southside Community Arts Center in Chicago, and the Princeton Group Arts Center), Selma Burke (Harlem Art Center, Selma Burke School of Sculpture in New York, Selma Burke Art Center in Pittsburgh), and Gwendolyn Bennett, James Porter, and Lois Mailou Jones (all Howard University).

All of the repatriated artists, particularly Woodruff and Motley, exhibited their work extensively. A brief list of the institutions that sponsored their art indicates the range and quality of their success. They include the Harmon Foundation, Argent Galleries, Frick Fine Art Gallery, National Collection of Fine Arts (Smithsonian Institution), Whitney Sculpture Biennials, Philadelphia Museum of Art's Sculpture International, Architectural League, Southside Community Art Center, Atlanta University Annuals, Bertha Schaefer Gallery, Art Institute of Chicago, Downtown Gallery, and museums throughout the country.

In addition to winning awards that took them abroad, the sculptors and painters earned important honors and commissions upon their return to the United States. Prophet was included in *Who's Who among American Women* in 1939. Hayden won the John D. Rockefeller Jr. prize for *Fétiche et fleurs* from the Harmon Foundation in 1933 and a commission to paint a black-soldiers series from the Creative Artists Public Service Program Foundation in 1973.

The U.S. Department of the Treasury commissioned Motley to paint a mural for the Wood River, Illinois, post office in 1937. In 1950, he received the Styletone prize for unusual composition with his painting *Gettin' Religion*. The National Conference of Artists paid homage to Motley in 1972, the School of the Art Institute of Chicago awarded him an honorary doctorate in fine arts in 1980, and President Carter honored him and nine other African American artists at the White House in 1980.

Savage became the first African American in the National Association of Women in Painters and Sculptors in 1934. She won honorable mention for *Realization* from the Architectural League the following year. In 1937, the New York World's Fair Board of Design commissioned her to create a large sculpture, *Lift Every Voice and Sing,* for the fair in 1939. She was one of four women, and the only African American woman, so honored. In 1939 the Women's Service League of Brooklyn bestowed upon Savage a silver medal as a pioneering woman whose work was featured at the fair.

Woodruff had the longest and most successful career of the six—he received a Rosenwald fellowship (1943), First Award from the High Museum of Art, Second and

Third Awards from the Diamond Jubilee Exposition in Chicago, and an Atlanta University Award and a Purchase Prize Award from Atlanta (dates of all these awards are unknown). He was named special delegate to the Dakar Festival of Negro Arts in Senegal (1966) and Distinguished American Abroad by the United States State Department (1966). He received an honorary doctorate from Morgan State College in Baltimore (1968) and recognition from the African-American Art Gallery Committee in Detroit (1978). He was also a member of the New Jersey Society of Artists, the Society of Mural Painters, the Committee on Art Education at the Museum of Modern Art, and the New York Council on the Arts.

Motley's *Blues,* Hayden's *Fétiche et fleurs,* Prophet's *Congolais*—these are several of the most indelible visual images of the New Negro movement, and all came out of Paris. The city, then the center of art-world production, at first offered hope as a site for more equal opportunities, and then validation of the artists' training, vision, and work. The achievements that Prophet, Woodruff, Hayden, Motley, Savage, and Smith made abroad assured them respected positions as visual arts leaders, reaffirmed racial pride—for themselves and all those who had a stake in their achievements—and paved the way for numerous other African American artists.

ENSUING GENERATIONS OF AFRICAN AMERICAN ARTISTS IN PARIS

Of the six, only Prophet and Hayden returned to France for brief visits in the 1930s and 1960s, respectively, as did others, for example, Lois Mailou Jones, who made the trip frequently until she died in the late 1990s. The French capital lured a new generation after World War II. Some, benefiting from the GI Bill, such as Romare Bearden, Ed Clark, Harold Cousins, and Herbert Gentry, sojourned abroad to study at Parisian academies and stayed but a few years in the 1940s, but returned again and again later in life. Others traveled on their own in the 1950s, such as Bob Blackburn, Larry Potter, and Ollie Harrington. Still others, among them Beauford Delaney and Barbara Chase-Riboud, like Smith, would become so enchanted with Paris in the 1960s that they became expatriates, and would earn positive critical attention internationally.

By the early 1960s, Abstract Expressionism was triumphant, and its birthplace, New York, was widely regarded as the new center of the art world. Consequently, as Valerie Mercer has pointed out, "American artists no longer considered it an imperative to go to Paris to study French culture or seek artistic freedom."[2] Yet those African American artists who ventured abroad in the postwar period, like those in the 1920s and 1930s, were motivated by many of the same factors: the American tradition of study in Paris, recommendations from teachers and friends, awareness of the debt of European modernism to African art, the quest for freedom, and hope of a refuge from segregation and racial turmoil as well as the threat of being accused of communism, especially during the Red Scare and the civil rights movement. Some were also unwilling to fight for the United States in the Vietnam War and were attracted to a more liberal, supportive atmosphere in France, as well as the greater possibility of European patronage and gallery representation. Unlike those who experienced Paris between the wars, these hopefuls had access to a much broader and more vibrant African diasporic community after World War II. This group included writers such as James Baldwin, Richard Wright, Chester Himes, William Gardner Smith, Hart LeRoy Bibbs, Ted Joans, and James Emmanuel, as well as musicians, scholars, entertainers, and enterpreneurs.[3]

Hundreds of other African American artists have been attracted to Paris in the ensuing decades, including Faith Ringgold, Sam Gilliam, Robert Colescott, and Raymond Saunders. Their pattern is more one of short visits rather than prolonged residencies, because of increased educational professional opportunities worldwide. Yet Paris remains a destination of choice. As historian Tyler Stovall has noted:

> African Americans engaged in the arts, especially music, literature, and visual art, still symbolize the black experience in Paris for many in both France and the United States. In spite of increased opportunities for black artists and intellectuals in America, the French capital has retained its ability to attract creative African Americans, offering physical beauty, cultural stimulation, and an enviable style of life. . . . The emphasis on both individual artistic freedom and the importance of black culture continues to make these artists central figures of a community whose members demand the right to be treated as blacks and simply as human beings at the same time. . . . The city symbolizes a hope for a color-blind society in which blackness will not be avoided but celebrated.[4]

What New Negro painters and sculptors found in Paris in the 1920s and 1930s was a sense of community in a diasporic black colony, albeit a small, loosely knit one. They discovered a shared history and similar goals, positive affinities with one another, and an awakening consciousness of their potential and freedom. These men and women made up not a Lost Generation of white literary expatriates, but a found community of black artistic pathfinders, who knew the French capital as a mainly hospitable citadel of *liberté, egalité, et fraternité*. Rather than discovering a color-blind society, however, they encountered a flawed, complex one that nonetheless threw into bold relief their twoness, Du Bois's term, as Americans and as Negroes, and that accepted, even embraced, that double identity. Knowledge of this helped to sustain Prophet, Hayden, Woodruff, Motley, Savage, and Smith as they struggled against racism in varying degrees the rest of their lives, at home and abroad. The Great War for Democracy had not, after all, radically changed race relations in the United States.

In 1925, Locke declared in *The New Negro:* "And certainly, if in our lifetime the Negro should not be able to celebrate his full initiation into American democracy, he can at least, on the warrant of these things, celebrate the attainment of a significant and satisfying new phase of group development, and with it a spiritual Coming of Age."[5]

Transformed through transplantation, this group underwent florescence abroad and attained a profound comprehension of "the soul-beauty of a race."[6] Individually and collectively, they used that knowledge to produce romantic, sophisticated, and potent images of the African diaspora and America's folk history, simultaneously looking backward and forward. In short, they created a black visual modernism, necessarily creolized. For these New Negro artists, Paris was irresistible, as an unequivocal muse, and as a place of pivotal significance.

NOTES

ABBREVIATIONS OF ARCHIVES AND LIBRARIES

AAA/SI   Archives of American Art. Smithsonian Institution, Washington, D.C.

AIC   Art Institute of Chicago

ALP/HU   Alain Locke Papers. Howard University, Washington, D.C.

AMP/CHS   Archibald J. Motley Jr. Papers. Archives and Manuscript Collection, Chicago Historical Society

CC/NY   Carnegie Corporation of New York

CC/NYPL   Countee Cullen Papers. New York Public Library

CCP/ARC   Countee Cullen Papers. Amistad Research Center, Tulane University, New Orleans

DP/LC   W.E.B. Du Bois Papers. Library of Congress, Washington, D.C.

GC/CU   Gumby Collection. Columbia University, New York

GMF   John Simon Guggenheim Memorial Foundation, New York

HFP/LC   Harmon Foundation Papers. Library of Congress, Washington, D.C.

HFR/NA   Harmon Foundation Records. National Archives, Washington, D.C.

JWJ/YU   James Weldon Johnson Memorial Collection of Negro Arts and Letters. Beinecke Rare Book and Manuscript Library. Yale University, New Haven, Connecticut

MSRC/HU   Moorland-Spingarn Research Center. Howard University, Washington, D.C.

RA/FU   Rosenwald Archives. Fisk University, Nashville, Tennessee

RIC   Rhode Island College, Providence

RISD   Rhode Island School of Design, Providence

SCRBC   Schomburg Center for Research in Black Culture, New York Public Library

WWC/LC   Walter White Collection. Library of Congress, Washington, D.C.

INTRODUCTION

1. Alain Locke, "The New Negro," in *The New Negro,* (1925; reprint, New York: Atheneum, 1980), 6.

2. W.E.B. Du Bois, *The Souls of Black Folk.,* reprinted in *Three Negro Classics* (New York: Avon Books, 1965), 214–216.

3. Richard J. Powell, "Re/birth of a Nation," in Richard J. Powell et. al., *Rhapsodies in Black: Art of the Harlem Renaissance* (Berkeley and Los Angeles: University of California Press, 1997), 23.

4. See Romy Golan, *Modernity and Nostalgia: Art and Politics in France between the Wars* (New Haven, Conn.: Yale University Press, 1995).

5. For more biographical details on these artists, see Theresa Leininger-Miller, "African American Artists in Paris, 1922–1934," Ph.D. diss., Yale University, 1995.

6. For more information about the experiences of these artists abroad, see my essay "Transatlantic Tradition: African American Artists in Paris, 1830–1940," in Asake Bomani and Belvie Rooks, eds. *Paris Connections: African American Artists in Paris* (San Francisco: Q.E.D. Press, 1992).

1   THE DEBUT OF AMERICAN ARTISTS

1. Charles East, "Jules Lion's New Orleans," *The Georgia Review* 40, no. 4 (1986): 913.

2. Michel Fabre, *From Harlem to Paris: Black American Writer in France, 1840–1980* (Urbana: University of Illinois Press, 1991), 9. See also Patricia Brady, "A Mixed Palette: Free Artists of Color of Antebellum New Orleans," *International Review of African American Art* 12, 3 (1995): 6–7.

3. Julien Hudson might also be included in this group. In 1900, Mrs. A. G. Durno asserted that Hudson (d. 1844) was "a very light colored man" without any documentation. Henry Rightor, ed., *The Standard History of New Orleans, Louisiana* (Chicago, 1900), 380–382. In 1938, a Works Progress Administration employee suggested that Julien Hudson's portrait of a young man (1839) with blue eyes and straight reddish brown hair was the self-portrait of a mulatto. Ethel Hutson, "Isaac Delgado Museum of Art," *Warrington Messenger,* September 1938, 19–20. Since then, most scholars have assumed that Hudson was of African American heritage, but no firm evidence has confirmed his racial identity. Hudson first studied under Antonio Meucci, an Italian miniaturist, in New Orleans. It is likely that the European-trained Meucci encouraged Hudson to go abroad. Hudson traveled to France twice, around 1831 and in 1837, when he studied in Paris with Abel de Pujol. Two of Hudson's other auto-graphed portraits, probably made in the United States, survive. They depict a young girl (1834) and Michel Fortier III (1839), the son of the colonel in charge of a free black corps at the Battle of New Orleans in 1815. For more information, see Patricia Brady, "Black Artists in Antebellum New Orleans," *Louisiana History* 32, no. 1 (1991): 7–9.

4. Patricia Brady, "Florville Foy, F.M.C.: Master Marble Cutter and Tomb Builder," *Southern Quarterly* 21, no. 2 (1993): 11. Brady's excellent article (9–19) is the most thorough study of Foy available, yet no illustrations of the marble cutter's funerary sculptures have yet been published.

5. Ibid., 14.

6. Brady, "Black Artists," 11 and East, "Jules Lion's New Orleans," 913.

7. East, "Jules Lion's New Orleans," 913.

8. Brady, "Black Artists," 16.

9. Regenia A. Perry, *Selections of Nineteenth-Century Afro-American Art* (New York: Metropolitan Museum of Art, 1976), unpaginated. Perry's suggestion that Achille was Jules's stepson is based on a notarial record of 1844 that lists Achille as Jules's son. However, the artist's obituary of 1866 "lists among his survivors a widow but no children."

10. Nathan left the bulk of his estate to "one Achille Lion, whom he [had] adopted as his son by a special act of the Louisiana legislature." Perry, *Selections,* n.p. Since Nathan's adoption of Achille required legislative action several years after the death of his wife, it seems that Achille was the product of an illicit union between Nathan and a woman of color.

11. Judith Wilson, "Optical Illusions: Images of Miscegenation in Nineteenth- and Twentieth- Century Art," *American Art* 5, no. 3 (summer 1991): 92.

12. Brady, "Black Artists," 5, 17, 18, 19, 26.

13. Fabre, *From Harlem to Paris,* 17–19.

14. Patricia Brady, "The Warburg Brothers: Sculptors," *The Historic New Orleans Collection Newsletter* 7, no. 3 (1989): 8–9. Also, for a fascinating account of Warburg's father, see Bertram W. Korn, *The Early Jews of New Orleans* (Waltham, Mass., 1969), 178–181.

15. Rodolphe Lucien Desdunes, "The Creole of Color in the Arts and the Liberal Arts Professions . . . ," in *Our People and Our History,* trans. Sr. Dorothea Olga McCants (orig. pub. as *Nos hommes et notre histoire,* 1911) (Baton Rouge: Louisiana State University Press, 1973), 69.

16. "A Creole Sculptor," *New Orleans Bee,* December 13, 1850, p. 3, col. 3.

17. Lois Marie Fink, *American Art at the Nineteenth-Century Paris Salons* (Cambridge, U.K.: Cambridge University Press, 1990), 402.

18. Patricia Brady, "Free Men of Color as Tomb Builders in the Nineteenth Century," unpublished manuscript, early 1990s, p. 10.

19. Brady, "Black Artists," 20, 22.

20. "A Colored Artist," *New Orleans Daily Crescent,* December 26, 1857, p. 4, col. 1 and "A Mulatto Sculptor from New Orleans," *The Daily Picayune,* December 26, 1857, p. 1, col. 5.

21. William H. Gerdts, "Celebrities of the Grand Tour: The American Sculptors in Florence and Rome," in Theodore E. Stebbins Jr., *The Lure of Italy: American Artists and the Italian Experience, 1760–1914* (New York: Harry N. Abrams, 1992), 68.

22. Ibid., 66.

23. Fink, *American Art,* 11.

24. Samella Lewis, *African American Art and Artists* (Berkeley and Los Angeles: University of California Press, 1990), 17–18.

25. Endorsement by Thomas Sully in letter from Sarah Grimké to Elizabeth Pease (August 25, 1839), in Gilbert Hobbs Barnes and Dwight L. Dumond, eds., *The Letters of Theodore Dwight Weld, Angelina Grimké Weld, and Sarah Grimké, 1822–1844,* 2 vols. (New York, Appleton, 1934), 2:792.

26. "I hear Robert Douglass is going to Haiti to reside. I hope his parents can cordially approve it." Letter from Sarah Grimké to Sarah Douglass (November 23, 1837), in Barnes and Dumond, *Letters,* 1:483 and "Our Friends in Hayti [*sic*]," *The Colored American* 2, March 3, 1838, 3.

27. Lewis, *African American Art and Artists,* 19.

28. Joseph D. Ketner, *The Emergence of the African-American Artist: Robert S. Duncanson, 1821–1872* (Columbia: University of Missouri Press, 1993), 71.

29. Ibid., 137–152.

30. Ibid., 167, 169.

31. *Daily Commercial,* January 12, 1857, p. 2, col. 7.

32. Deborah Willis, ed. *J. P. Ball, Daguerrean and Studio Photographer* (New York: Garland, 1993), xvi.

33. Ball visited the home of black abolitionist Charles Lenox Redmond in 1854. Ray Allen Billington, ed., *The Journal of Charlotte L. Forten* (New York: W. W. Norton, 1953), 241 n. 20. Art historian Juanita Holland suggests that Ball may have met painter Edward Mitchell Bannister then; Bannister's wife was related to the Redmonds by marriage. Juanita Holland, "Reaching through the Veil: African-American Artist Edward Mitchell Bannister," in *Edward Mitchell Bannister 1828–1901* (New York: Kenkeleba House, 1992), 58 n. 34.

34. Lynda Roscoe Hartigan, *Sharing Traditions: Five Black Artists in Nineteenth-Century America* (Washington, D.C.: Smithsonian Institution Press, 1985), 89.

35. Romare Bearden and Harry Henderson, "Edmonia Lewis," in *A History of African-American Artists From 1792 to the Present* (New York: Pantheon Books, 1993), 54–77.

36. "He was blue enough. He had not heard from certain parties upon whom he was somewhat dependent for his European trip, and things had gone awry considerably. I tried to cheer him up" (October 1881). Mary Armfield Hill, *Endure: The Diaries of Charles Walter Stetson* (Philadelphia: Temple University Press, 1985), 11.

37. Thomas P. Riggio, "Charles Ethan Porter and Mark Twain," in *Charles Ethan Porter* (Marlborough, Conn.: Connecticut Gallery, 1987), 78.

38. *Hartford Courant,* March 19, April 21 and 25, 1881; and *Hartford Evening Post,* April 13, 28, and 29, 1881, as noted in Hildegard Cummings, "The Hartford Artist," in *Charles Ethan Porter,* 64.

39. A private collector (telephone conversation with the author, May 1992) and Helen K. Fusscas, "The Paintings of Charles Ethan Porter," in *Charles Ethan Porter,* 28.

40. Telephone conversation with Helen Fusscas (December 21, 1994) regarding the auction of Porter's nudes and landscape.

41. Fusscas, "Paintings of Charles Ethan Porter," 30.

42. Riggio, "Charles Ethan Porter," 83.

43. Dewey F. Mosby et al., *Henry Ossawa Tanner* (Philadelphia: Philadelphia Museum of Art, 1991).

44. Certificate of Death, Annie E. A. Walker, no. 821322, District of Columbia, June 9, 1929.

45. Ibid.

46. Arna Bontemps, ed., *Forever Free: Art by African-American Women Artists, 1862–1980* (Alexandria, Va.: Stepheson, 1980), 138.

47. *Explication des ouvrages de peinture, sculpture, architecture, gravure et lithographie des artistes vivants exposés au Palais des Champs-Elysées* (Paris: Imprimerie Paul Dupont, 1896), 27.

48. For example, *Boyd's District of Columbia Directory* (Washington, D.C., 1901), 1058.

49. Judith Nina Kerr, *"God-Given Work:" The Life and Times of Sculptor Meta Vaux Warrick Fuller, 1877–1968.* Ph.D. diss., University of Massachusetts, 1986, 67.

50. Ibid., 72.

51. Ibid., 75.

52. As quoted in ibid., 129.

53. Ibid., 114–115.

54. Ibid., 115.

55. As quoted in William Francis O'Donnell, "Meta Vaux Warrick Fuller, Sculptor of Horrors," *The World Today* 13 (November, 1907): 1144.

56. Kerr, *"God-Given Work,"* 140.

57. Ibid., 128.

58. Alain Locke, *The Negro in Art: A Pictorial Record of the Negro Artist and of the Negro Theme in Art* (Washington, D.C.: Associates in Negro Folk Education, 1940; New York: Hacker Art Books, 1979), 132.

59. Florence Lewis Bentley, "William A. Harper," *Voice of the Negro* (February 1906): 118.

60. "William A. Harper," *Bulletin of the Art Institute of Chicago,* no. 4 (1910): 11.

61. Untitled, anonymous article, *Chicago Conservator,* February 16, 1901, n.p. Art Institute of Chicago Scrapbooks, vol. 13, 144..

62. Bentley, "William A. Harper," 121.

63. Arthur Krehbiel to Dulah M. Evans (January 24, 1904). Microfilm 4074, National Archives of American Art.

64. Ibid. (December 18, 1903).

65. Ibid. (March 20, 1904).

66. Peter Hastings Falk, ed., *The Annual Exhibition Record of the Art Institute of Chicago, 1888–1950* (Chicago: Sound View Press, 1990), 408.

67. "Colored Man Wins Position," *Chicago News,* February 6, 1905, Art Institute of Chicago Scrapbooks, vol. 20.

68. Tanner's *Abraham's Oak* (n.d.) and *The Good Samaritan* (ca. 1905) were exhibited at the Art Institute of Chicago in October 1905. Mosby, 43.

69. Bentley, "William A. Harper," 118.

70. Locke, *The Negro in Art,* 132.

71. Bentley, "William A. Harper," 11.

72. Report of the Death of an American Citizen, American Consular Service City of Mexico, Mexico (March 30, 1910). Enclosure no. 5 in dispatch no. 229, National Archives.

73. For a more detailed biography of Scott, see William E. Taylor, "Echoes of the Past: Artists' Biographies (Williams Edouard Scott, 1884–1964)," in William E. Taylor and Harriet G. Warkel, *A Shared Heritage: Art by Four African Americans* (Indianapolis: Indianapolis Museum of Art, 1996), 160–166.

74. William E. Taylor, "William Edouard Scott: Indianapolis Painter," *Black History News and Notes* no. 33 (August 1988): 4.

75. "Artist of Indian and Negro Extraction Attracts Attention With His Pictures," *Indianapolis Star,* November 17, 1912, 8.

76. Taylor, "William Edouard Scott," 4.

77. "Colored Man Will Study Art Abroad," *Indianapolis Star,* August 25, 1909, 32.

78. Francis C. Holbrook, "William Edouard Scott," *Southern Workman* (February 1924): 73. See also *Henry O. Tanner, William A. Harper, William E. Scott: A Mentor and His Influence* (Washington, D.C.: Evans-Tibbs Collection, 1985), 6.

79. *Indianapolis News,* December 9, 1911, page unknown.

80. *La pauvre voisine* is no. 1680, Société des Artistes Français, Le Salon 30è Exposition Officielle (Paris, 1912), 149.

81. Taylor, "William Edouard Scott," 5.

82. Holbrook, "William Edouard Scott," 74. Also, see Harriet G. Warkel, "Image and Identity: The Art of William E. Scott, John W. Hardrick, and Hale A. Woodruff," in Taylor and Warkel, *A Shared Heritage,* for description (18) and reproduction (20).

83. Taylor, "William Edouard Scott," 6, as noted in Taylor, "Echoes of the Past," 163, and 182 n. 23.

84. James Porter, *In Memoriam: Laura Wheeler Waring 1887–1948: An Exhibition of Paintings* (Washington, D.C.: Howard University Gallery of Fine Art, 1949), unpaginated.

85. "Music and Art," *The Crisis* 8, no. 3 (July, 1914): 111 (Hemmings also received a bronze medal for his watercolors at the exhibition at Ivry) and *Explication des ouvrages de peinture, sculpture, architecture, gravure et lithographie des artistes vivants exposées au Palais des Champs-Élysées* (Paris: Imprimerie Paul Dupont, 1914), 95.

86. It is not certain how long Hemmings stayed abroad or where he stayed while in France. He had been married from 1909 to 1915, perhaps to a Frenchwoman. He married Suzanne Heusch on July 25, 1924, in Paris and stayed abroad until World War II when he returned to his hometown of Boston, leaving Heusch behind. Correspondence from Solomon C. Fuller to author (July 16, 1990). Moreover, Hemmings's death certificate lists his second wife as Suzzane Hirsch. Registry Division, City of Boston (October 6, 1955).

87. Mosby, "The War Years and Late Work, 1914–1937," in Mosby et al., *Henry Ossawa Tanner,* 242–244.

88. Ibid., 244–245.

2   NANCY ELIZABETH PROPHET

1. "You must certainly know that I am not a negro, and though I am of mixed blood the two races which I represent are quite different from that which you wish your publication [*American Negro Art,* to be published in 1960] to represent." Letter from Prophet to anthropologist–art critic Cedric Dover (July 6, 1959). In the collection of George Proffitt.

2. Copy of Record of Birth no. 2029, Rhode Island State Department of Health, Division of Vital Statistics (copy issued December 8, 1955), collection of George Proffitt. Prophet was born in Warwick, but may have spent her childhood in West Warwick; a newspaper announcement stated that she was a native of that city. "Newport Art Prize Given Woodcarving," *New York Times,* July 9, 1932, p. 8, col. 4.

3. Copy of Record of Birth, Rhode Island State Department of Health.

4. Conversation with George Proffitt, a distant relative of Elizabeth Prophet (summer 1990).

5. Prophet stated that her mother was a "mixed Negro." Harmon Foundation questionnaire (July 14, 1938), HFP/LC.

6. Countee Cullen, "Elizabeth Prophet: Sculptress," *Opportunity* (July 1930): 204.

7. Harmon Foundation questionnaires (July 6, 1938, and July 14, 1938), HFP/LC.

8. Prophet, Harmon Nomination Blank (June 30, 1929), HFP/LC.

9. Harmon Foundation Nomination Blank (September 2, 1930), HFP/LC.

10. "Prophet, Elizabeth," *Standard Biographical Dictionary of Notable Women,* vol. 3 (Los Angeles: Richard Blank, 1939), 728–729. Also, applications to the John Simon Guggenheim Memorial Foundation, 1930, 1934, and 1941.

11. Prophet, application statement, 1957, GMF.

12. Blossom S. Kirschenbaum, "Nancy Elizabeth Prophet, Sculptor," *SAGE* 4, no. 1 (1987): 46.

13. Cullen, "Elizabeth Prophet: Sculptress," 204.

14. Prophet, application statement, 1941, GMF.

15. George Proffitt, conversation with the author (summer 1990).

16. "Sculpture in Wood Gets Special Prize," *Springfield Massachusetts Republican* (January 19, 1930): n.p.

17. "Can I Become a Sculptor? The Story of Elizabeth Prophet," *Crisis* (October 1932): 315.

18. "Negro Father, 88, Sees Famous Daughter's Work at Library," publication unknown (1945): n.p. From a clipping in the Artists Index, New York Public Library.

19. Laura Heathfield, Secretary to Miss Louise W. Brooks and Assistant Treasurer Student Fund, to Dr. Frederick P. Keppel, Carnegie Corporation (November 12, 1932), CC/NY.

20. "Women Artists' Work to Fore in Annual Exhibit at Newport," *The Providence Sunday Journal,* July 10, 1932, E:8.

21. As remembered by a white classmate whose identity remains anonymous. Kirschenbaum, "Nancy Elizabeth Prophet," 46.

22. L. Earl Rowe, letter of recommendation for Prophet to the Guggenheim Memorial Foundation, 1930.

23. A classmate recalled that Prophet "was the only colored girl there." As quoted in Kirschenbaum, "Nancy Elizabeth Prophet," 46.

24. Ibid.

25. Atkins taught at RISD 1909–1926. *Who Was Who in American Art,* 21. Other instructors at RISD in the late 1910s were Antonio Arino, Eliza Gardiner, Nancy Jones, Mabel Woodward, and Stacy Tolman, but it is impossible to discern from Prophet's transcript and school catalogs who taught what class to whom. Letter to author from Victoria Gianitsaris, archivist, RISD Library (September 1994).

26. The marriage license of Prophet and Ford is on file at City Hall in Providence, according to Kirschenbaum, "Nancy Elizabeth Prophet," p. 51, n. 7.

27. Kirschenbaum, "Nancy Elizabeth Prophet," 46.

28. So declared Prophet: "During our years of marriage, I was supported by by father. My father also supported Francis Ford." Notary statement (September 16, 1946). George Proffitt Collection.

29. Student's Record, Department of Freehand Drawing and Painting (transcript), RISD. Also, "Her special forte was portrait painting." Nell Occomy, *Providence Journal* (1930): n.p. As quoted in Kirschenbaum, "Nancy Elizabeth Prophet," 47.

30. Prophet, application statement to the Guggenheim Memorial Foundation, 1941.

31. As quoted in Kirschenbaum, "Nancy Elizabeth Prophet," 47.

32. Cullen, "Elizabeth Prophet: Sculptress," 204 and "Can I Become a Sculptor?" 315.

33. Cullen, "Elizabeth Prophet: Sculptress," 205.

34. "Can I Become a Sculptor?" 315. Also, L. Earl Rowe, letter of recommendation to the Guggenheim Memorial Foundation. Transcription on page 8 of records from 1930.

35. Prophet, application statement, 1941, GMF. Here, Prophet states that she arrived in Paris in the summer of 1921 with $350; in her diary, she claims that it was the summer of 1922 and that she had $380 (August 11, 1922). John Hay Library, Special Collections, Brown University, Providence. In the Guggenheim application, Prophet said that she painted for a year in Paris, then "discovered, however, that it was sculpture to which I wished to devote myself."

36. Prophet diary, entry dated August 11, 1922, but probably written later, based on a comparison of her handwriting with subsequent entries.

37. Kirschenbaum, "Nancy Elizabeth Prophet," 47.

38. Gardner attended evening modeling classes at RISD 1915–1916 and was a special student in 1916–1917 and 1918–1919. Letter to the author from Gianitsaris (September 21, 1994).

39. Prophet diary (August 11, 1922).

40. Ibid.

41. Notary statement (September 16, 1946). George Proffitt Collection.

42. Prophet diary (August 11, 1922). The quotes that follow are from this date in her diary.

43. E. Bénézit, *Dictionnaire critique et documentaire des peintres, sculpteurs, dessinateurs et graveurs de tous les temps et de tous les pays par un groupe d'écrivains spécialistes français et étrangers* (Paris: Librairie Gründ, 1976), 504.

44. Prophet diary (entry dated August 11, 1922).

45. Ibid. However, a listing of Prophet's work does not appear in the Salon d'Automne catalog for 1924; the work may have been entered late, after the catalog was already in press. The real reason for the omission is unknown.

46. Elizabeth Hutton Turner, *American Artists in Paris, 1919–1929* (Ann Arbor: University Microfilms Incorporated Research Press, 1988), 19.

47. "American Art Community Represented in Salon," *New York Herald* (Paris edition) (April 18, 1920): 2.

48. "Americans to the Fore at the Autumn Salon," *New York Herald* (Paris edition), October 31, 1922, 2.

49. Turner, *American Artists in Paris,* 44.

50. Prophet diary (entry dated August 11, 1922).

51. As noted by the (unnamed) sculptor who came into possession of Prophet's tools after her death. Kirschenbaum, "Nancy Elizabeth Prophet," 50.

52. "Nancy Prophet Wins Success as Sculptress," *Providence Evening Bulletin,* July 8, 1932, 10.

53. Ibid.

54. Prophet, application statement, 1941, GMF. Waldmann exhibited at the Société des Artistes Français annually from 1885 until his death and received a silver medal from the Exposition Universelle in 1900. Bénézit, *Dictionnaire critique,* 74. Nothing else is known about the Polish sculptor; he is not listed in Bénézit or Thieme-Becker.

55. Prophet diary (November 11, 1925).

56. Ibid.

57. Prophet diary (August 11, 1922).

58. Ibid.

59. In the 1920s, economic difficulties beset the textile industry in Europe and commercial batiks were no longer produced, so clients depended on handmade products. However, the demand for batik did not really grow until the establishment of the Republic of Indonesia following World War II when the Javanese batik industry was revitalized. Jack Lenor Larsen, *The Dyer's Art: Ikat, Batik, Plangi* (New York: Van Nostrand Reinhold, 1976), 9, 11. Prophet states that she sold batik for "fair prices." Application to the Guggenheim Memorial Foundation, 1941 and diary (August 11, 1922). Artist-writer Gwendolyn Bennett had also sold batik in Paris.

60. Turner, *American Artists in Paris,* 19.

61. Billy Klüver and Julie Martin, *Kiki's Paris: Artists and Lovers 1900–1930* (New York: Harry N. Abrams, 1989), 22, 84. Gauguin's studio was built in 1894 by the engraver Emile Delaune, 213.

62. Ibid., 186.

63. Ibid.

64. Ibid.

65. This may be the same Paul Berthier (1884–1953) who wrote *Réflexions sur l'art et la vie de Jean-Philippe Rameau (1683–1764),* published in 1957.

66. Prophet diary (November 11, 1925).

67. Prophet diary (November 19, 1925).

68. "First Prize for Indian Woman," *Newport Herald,* Saturday, July 9, 1932, n.p.

69. Cullen, "Elizabeth Prophet: Sculptress," 205.

70. Prophet diary (November 27, 1925).

71. The work is known only by photographs. In 1941, Prophet wrote to the GMF that she needed funds to execute the piece in wood.

72. Romy Golan, *Modernity and Nostalgia: Art and Politics in France Between the Wars* (New Haven: Yale University Press, 1995), 36.

73. James Hall, *Dictionary of Subjects and Symbols in Art* (New York: Harper & Row, 1979), 247.

74. Ibid., 131.

75. My thanks to Julie Aronson for suggesting the resemblance of *Le pèlerin* to depictions of Saint Francis and Rodin's *Burghers of Calais*.

76. "Prophet (Eli), né à Providence, Rhode Island, U.S.A. Américaine—147, rue Broca. 1778.—Tête de jeune fille," *Société du Salon d'Automne: Catalogue des ouvrages de peinture, sculpture, dessin, gravure, architecture et art décoratif* (Paris: Imprimerie Ernest Puyfourcat fils & Cie., 1927), 291.

77. Prophet diary (December 8, 1925).

78. "I pray that I may never become the victim of envy and jealousy, these low qualities bring nothing but destruction to the soul. Envy is the result of a poverty stricken soul." Prophet diary (December 21, 1925).

79. Prophet diary (December 23, 1925).

80. Ibid., (December 22, 1925).

81. "First Prize for Indian Woman."

82. As quoted in "Nancy Prophet Wins Success as Sculptress," *Providence Evening Bulletin*, July 8, 1932, 10.

83. Prophet diary (March 4, 1926). The quotes that follow are from Prophet diary. Dates are cited parenthetically in the text.

84. Cullen, "Elizabeth Prophet: Sculptress," 204.

85. Michel Fabre and John A. *Williams, Way B(l)ack Then and Now: A Street Guide to African Americans and Paris* (Paris: Centre d'Etudes Afro-Américaines, Université de la Sorbonne Nouvelle, 1992), 106.

86. As quoted in Kirschenbaum, "Nancy Elizabeth Prophet," 47.

87. Prophet diary (June 26, 1926).

88. As quoted in Kirschenbaum, "Nancy Elizabeth Prophet," 47.

89. Hall, *Dictionary*, 285–286.

90. For more information on the popularity of orientalism in Paris at this time, see Golan, *Modernity and Nostalgia*, 108–110.

91. Kenneth E. Silver and Romy Golan, "The Circle of Montparnasse: Jewish Artists in Paris, 1905–1945," in *The Circle of Montparnasse: Jewish Artists in Paris, 1905–1945* (New York: Universe Books, 1985), 24–25.

92. Ibid., 26.

93. Thanks to Julie Aronson for pointing out the similarity between Prophet's *Prayer* and Michelangelo's *The Dying Slave*.

94. Prophet diary (July 16, 1926). Quotes that follow are from Prophet diary. Dates are cited parenthetically in the text.

95. Little is known about *Bitter Laughter* other than a description of its "mild muscular contortion." Albert Franz Cochrane, "Once More the Independents Hold Forth on Beacon Hill," *Boston Evening Transcript*, February 16, 1929, 3:8–9.

96. Cullen, "Elizabeth Prophet: Sculptress," 205.

97. Langston Hughes, "Minstrel Man," in Alain Locke, ed., *The New Negro* (1925; reprint, New York: Atheneum, 1980), 144.

98. Judith Nina Kerr, "God-Given Work: The Life and Times of Sculptor Meta Vaux Warrick Fuller, 1877–1968," (Ph.D. diss., University of Massachusetts, 1986), 125–126. Page references to this source are cited parenthetically in the text.

99. "Nancy Prophet Wins Success as Sculptress," 10.

100. Prophet, "Art and Life," *Phylon: The Atlanta University Bulletin of Race and Culture* 1 (third quarter, 1940), 324.

101. As noted by the late Providence artist Gino Conti, longtime friend of Gardner. Kirschenbaum, "Nancy Elizabeth Prophet," 47. Gardner was also a successful artist; her sculptures were exhibited in the

Société des Artistes Indépendants in 1929 and critics often wrote about them in *La Revue Moderne Illustrée des Arts et de la Vie*, from 1930 to 1934.

102. Brooks translated *Heidi* (1884), *Rico and Wiseli* (1886), and *Grith's Children* (1887). *Allibone's Dictionary of Authors*, vol. 1 (Philadelphia: B.B. Lippincott, 1908), 218. Little else is known about Brooks; she appears in no other standard references and no information about her exists in the Bostonian Society. Letter to the author from Daniel McCormack, library assistant (October 14, 1994).

103. Heathfield to Keppel (November 12, 1932), CC/NY.

104. Prophet diary (June 7, 1927).

105. Prophet diary, addendum (1936).

106. Prophet diary, (June 10, 1927).

107. "Senator Green's Sister," *New York Times*, April 14, 1954, p. 29, col. 5. Theodore Francis Green also apparently sponsored Prophet; her work was listed as being in his collection in the *Spelman Messenger* (February 1940), n.p. From the collection of George Proffitt.

108. Eleanor Green, letter of recommendation to Harmon Foundation (October 4, 1930), HFP/LC.

109. Harmon letter of recommendation (October 4, 1930), HFP/LC.

110. See, for example, Cullen, "Elizabeth Prophet: Sculptress," 204.

111. At the time of this writing there is no biography of Hayes that outlines his concert schedule or describes his friends and acquaintances in depth. MacKinley Helm's biography, *Angel Mo' and Her Son, Roland Hayes* (Boston: Little, Brown, 1942), written as an autobiography, does not mention Prophet.

112. "Eliza G. Radeke Dies; A Leading Art Patron," *New York Times*, March 18, 1931, p. 25, col. 2.

113. "Gives $25,000 to Pembroke," *New York Times*, February 12, 1940, p. 15, col. 5.

114. *Tête de jeune fille* is listed as no. 1778 in *Catalogue des ouvrages de peinture, sculpture, dessin, gravure, architecture et art décoratif exposés au Grand Palais des Champs-Elysées du 5 Novembre au 18 Décembre 1927* (Paris, 1927), 291.

115. *Webster's New Twentieth Century Dictionary Unabridged*, 2d ed.

116. Microsoft Bookshelf, 1996–1997 edition.

117. Prophet to George Haynes (October 9, 1928), HFP/LC.

118. Tanner to Harmon Foundation (October 22, 1928), HFP/LC.

119. Prophet, application statement, 1941, GMF.

120. Haynes to Tanner (November 2, 1928), HFP/LC.

121. It is not known whether Prophet met Hayes in the 1920s while he was on tour in Europe or whether she made his likeness after a photograph.

122. Heathfield to Keppel (November 12, 1932), CC/NY.

123. *Exhibition of Work by Former Students and Teachers in Commemoration of the Fiftieth Anniversary of Rhode Island School of Design* (October 7–31, 1928). Exhibition catalog in the collection of George Proffitt.

124. I have been unable to locate the exhibition catalog for the Boston Society of Independent Artists, 1929, despite calls to the Boston Museum of Fine Arts Library, the Boston Archives of American Art, the Boston Public Library, and the Archives of American Art. In her 1941 application statement to the GMF, Prophet states that the head of a black man was titled *Head of a Negro*.

125. The Bostonian Society was unable to offer information on the Boston Society of Independent Artists, other than its initial date of 1927. It seems to have ceased to exist in the 1940s. Telephone conversation with librarian (October 1994).

126. *Catalog of the Fifth Annual Exhibition of the Boston Society of Independent Artists, Inc.* (Boston: Arch Print, 1931), unpaginated.

127. Prophet diary (May 30, 1929).

128. Turner, *American Artists in Paris*, 44.

129. *Buste d'homme* is listed as no. 3934, *Catalogue du Salon, Société des Artistes Français* (Paris 1929), 207.

130. Author, title, date, and page unknown, *L'Art Contemporain*. From a translation by Prophet, HFP/LC.

131. An acquaintance recalled that Ford worked as a chef in France. As noted in Kirschenbaum, "Nancy Elizabeth Prophet," 47.

132. Prophet diary (April 10, 1929).

133. Harmon application (April, 1929), HFP/LC.

134. Supplementary Affidavit Regarding Change of Name to be Submitted with Application for American Passport, Providence, Rhode Island (June 25, 1932). Collection of George Proffitt.

135. Notary statement (September 16, 1946). Collection of George Proffitt.

136. Prophet to Harmon Foundation (May 20, 1929), HFP/LC.

137. Copy of letter from E. Matke to Prophet (June 6, 1929), DP/LC.

138. For a full listing of Kahn's activities, see *Who Was Who in America*, vol. 1 (1897–1942), 655.

139. L. Earl Rowe to the Guggenheim Memorial Foundation, 1930.

140. Prophet, Harmon Nomination Blank (June 30, 1929), HFP/LC.

141. Sharpe, letter of recommendation to the Harmon Foundation (1929), HFP/LC.

142. Cullen, "Elizabeth Prophet: Sculptress," 204. Cullen was not the only one to comment on the Native American heritage of an artist in Paris. See, for example, "Indianapolis Artist of Mixed Negro and Indian Blood Winning Success in Paris," *Indianapolis News,* December 9, 1911, 2, regarding William Edouard Scott.

143. Cullen, "Elizabeth Prophet: Sculptress," 204.

144. "Beth Prophit [*sic*] is Hailed in Paris as Real Artist," *The Afro-American*, Saturday, August 3, 1929, 8.

145. Ibid.

146. Prophet to Cullen (day unspecified, 1929), CCP/ARC.

147. Telegram from Du Bois to Prophet (day unspecified, 1939), DP/LC.

148. Prophet to Du Bois (September 12, 1929; September 14, 1929), DP/LC.

149. As quoted in translation in Cullen, "Elizabeth Prophet: Sculptress," 205.

150. Ibid.

151. It cost $170.25 to ship the four cases of statuary on board the S.S. *Homeric*. John C. Fox Company to Prophet (December 3, 1929), DP/LC.

152. Prophet diary (October, day unspecified, 1929).

153. Heathfield to Keppel (November 12, 1932), CC/NY.

154. Prophet to Cullen (November 20, 1929), CCP/ARC.

155. Prophet's sketching permit from the Metropolitan Museum of Art (1930) is in the collection of George Proffitt.

156. Jackman to Cullen (January 10, 1930), CCP/ARC.

157. Prophet to Cullen (January 16, 1930), CCP/ARC.

158. "Negro Women Win Awards," (New York) *Women's Journal* (March, day unspecified, 1930): n.p. Also, "Negro Girl Wins Award for Carving," (Rockford, Illinois) *Register Gazette* (January 16, 1930): n.p. From clippings in HFP/LC.

159. Clipping from George Proffitt.

160. Prophet said that the Salons of America exhibited five of her works. Application statement to the Guggenheim Memorial Foundation, 1941.

161. The East 56th Street Gallery was opened in 1929 by the Roman Bronze Works foundry to showcase the sculptors whose works they cast, including Bessie Potter Vonnoh. My thanks to Julie Aronson for this information.

162. Prophet exhibited *Head* at Milch Galleries. Application statement, 1941, GMF. However, a clipping from *Parnassus* in George Proffitt's collection has a reproduction of *Discontent* that states that it was on view at Milch Galleries.

163. The work Prophet exhibited was probably the head of a Negro youth. Cochrane particularly admired such a piece at the Boston Society of Independent Artists (BSIA) several years prior to 1932 because it "stood out head and shoulders as one of the truly commendable pieces in any media shown in

the independent exhibition then on in Joy Street." Cochrane, "Once More the Independents," 4. Prophet's 1930 membership card in the BSIA is in the collection of George Proffitt.

164. The amount of works in the exhibition comes from Prophet's 1941 application statement to the Guggenheim Memorial Foundation. No catalog seems to exist.

165. Du Bois to Mary Beattie Brady (May 13, 1930), DP/LC.

166. A little clipping headed "Program" in George Proffitt's collection indicates that there was a lecture on early Staten Island abolitionists on March 7. Both this and Prophet's presentation were hosted by married women.

167. Prophet diary (April, day unspecified, 1930).

168. Du Bois to Haynes (December 30, 1930), HFP/LC.

169. Prophet to the Guggenheim Memorial Foundation, 1930.

170. "Everyone now depends on her getting a Guggenheim Fellowship," Du Bois to Tanner (January 13, 1930), DP/LC.

171. Du Bois to Kahn (April 21, 1930), DP/LC.

172. Du Bois to Kahn (April 23, 1930) and Du Bois to Haynes (December 30, 1930), DP/LC.

173. Du Bois to Albert C. Barnes (May 13, 1930), DP/LC.

174. Du Bois (under Prophet's name) to the Rosenwald Foundation (May 28, 1930), DP/LC.

175. Prophet to Kahn (June 24, 1930), DP/LC.

176. From "Art Corner," publisher, date, and page unknown. As quoted in Kirschenbaum, 47.

177. "R.I. Sculptress Wins Recognition," *The Providence Journal,* April 2, 1932, 8.

178. Prophet to Kahn (June 24, 1930), DP/LC.

179. Prophet diary (August 22, 1930).

180. Harmon nomination blank (September 2, 1930), HFP/LC and Prophet to Hannah Moriarta (September 4, 1930), HFP/LC.

181. Prophet to Moriarta (October 19, 1930), HFP/LC.

182. Prophet to Moriarta (November 16, 1930), HFP/LC.

183. Du Bois to Prophet (November 20, 1930), DP/LC.

184. Du Bois to Prophet (December 10, 1930), DP/LC.

185. Prophet to Du Bois (January 22, 1931), DP/LC.

186. Du Bois to Prophet (November 20, 1930), DP/LC.

187. Prophet to Du Bois (August 20, 1931), DP/LC.

188. Prophet to Du Bois (December 10, 1930), DP/LC.

189. Ibid.

190. Prophet to Du Bois (December 15, 1930), DP/LC.

191. Du Bois to Prophet (dated January 8, 1930, but this must have been 1931), DP/LC.

192. *Buste marbre* was no. 3905. *Catalogue du Salon, Société des Artistes Français* (Paris, 1929), 201.

193. Jean Patézon, as quoted in "Along the Color Line," *Crisis,* 308. This seems to come from *Chronique Familiale du Rayonnement Intellectuel* (July–August 1931). From a clipping in the collection of George Proffitt.

194. Prophet diary (March 1, 1931).

195. Prophet to Du Bois (March 11, 1931), DP/LC.

196. Du Bois to Prophet (May 18, 1931), DP/LC.

197. The 56th Street Galleries to Prophet (June 22, 1931) and Du Bois (July 7, 1931), DP/LC.

198. At the beginning of 1932, Prophet wrote that he could keep *Silence:* "I give it to you. Does her calm soothe you when you are tired[?]" Prophet to Du Bois (January 26, 1932). By the end of 1935, however, she made Du Bois type a note stating that the work belonged to her (December 18, 1935), DP/LC.

199. Prophet diary (July 14, 1931).

200. Thomas G. August, "The Circus Comes to Town," *The Selling of the Empire: British and French Imperialist Propaganda, 1890–1940* (Westport, Conn.: Greenwood Press, 1985), 145.

201. Ibid., 147.

202. Ibid., 150–152.

203. Golan, *Modernity and Nostalgia*, 117–118.

204. Prophet to Du Bois (August 20, 1931), DP/LC.

205. Joseph Thomson, *Through Masai Land: A Journey of Exploration among the Snowclad Volcanic Mountains and Strange Tribes of Eastern Equatorial Africa* (New York: Houghton, Mifflin, and Company, 1885), 272.

206. Countee Cullen, "Heritage," *The New Negro* (New York: Atheneum, 1968), 250–253.

207. Cochrane, "Once More the Independents," 4.

208. Prophet to Du Bois (August 20, 1931), DP/LC.

209. See Powell et al., *Rhapsodies in Black*, 26–27 for reproductions of all three of these images.

210. Prophet to Du Bois (November 14, 1931), DP/LC.

211. Du Bois to Prophet (December 18, 1931), DP/LC.

212. Prophet diary (December 18, 1931).

213. *Violence* was no. 3997 and *Buste ébène* was no. 3998. *Catalogue du Salon, Société des Artistes Français* (Paris, 1929), 206.

214. "Boston Art Notes," *Monitor* (November 4, 1932), n.p. From a clipping in George Proffitt Collection.

215. Prophet diary (April 24, 1932).

216. "Woman Artist," *Crisis* 39 (August 1932): 259.

217. Du Bois to Prophet (April 15, 1932), DP/LC.

218. Prophet diary (May 2, 1930).

219. Ibid., (June 2, 1932).

220. "Newport Art Prize Given Woodcarving: Special Ruling Made to Permit Rhode Island Woman, Now In Paris, to Receive Award," *New York Times,* July 9, 1932, 8:4. Also, "First Prize for Indian Woman." This article reports that the election was made on July 8, however, a letter from the assistant secretary of the Art Association of Newport to Prophet states that she was elected on June 14, 1932. George Proffitt Collection.

221. Maude Howe Elliott to Prophet (July 12, 1932), George Proffitt Collection and "Women Artists' Work to the Fore." The Greenough prize was offered by the granddaughter of the sculptor, Edith Blight Thompson.

222. Prophet diary (July 8, 1932).

223. "Negress Wins the First Prize at Newport," *Art Digest* (August 1, 1932): 14; "First Prize for Indian Woman," *Newport Herald*, n.p.

224. "Can I Become a Sculptor?" 315.

225. Prophet diary (July 24, 1932).

226. Ibid., (August 6, 1932). Along with Richmond Barthé's *Blackberry Woman* (1932), Prophet's *Congolais* (ca. 1931) was one of the first works by an African American sculptor to enter the Whitney Museum of American art.

227. Whitney to Prophet (n.d., from Breakers, Newport, Rhode Island), George Proffitt Collection.

228. "Can I Become a Sculptor?" 315.

229. Schuyler L. Parsons, *Untold Friendships* (Boston: Houghton Mifflin, 1955), 169 ff. Also, 206, when, in 1937, Parsons became the manager for Knoedler-Vernay Galleries in Newport.

230. Parsons was a retired New York sugar broker who had lived in Newport, New York, and Palm Beach. A 1914 graduate of Harvard University, he served in World War I with a British ambulance corps. "Schuyler L. Parsons," *New York Times,* November 23, 1967, 3:33.

231. "Three 'One-Man' Art Shows Held in Newport Last Week," *Providence Sunday Journal*, August 14, 1932.

232. Parsons, *Untold Friendships,* 157.

233. Ibid., 159. For Parsons' near, if not outright, racist comments on his servants and Gullah society, see 156–157, 159–163. Parsons believed that hearing spirituals, "an eerie form of entertainment," in Charleston gave him good background for acting as advisor to George Gershwin when he wrote *Porgy and Bess.*

234. Mosby and Sewell, *Henry Ossawa Tanner,* 49.

235. *Decorative Paintings by Casey Roberts and Sculpture by N. Elizabeth Prophet from October 31, 1932 to November 19, 1932* (exhibition list) (Boston: Robert C. Vose, Jr. Galleries, 1932), n.p.

236. Cochrane, "Once More the Independents," 4.

237. Du Bois to Prophet (October 31, 1932), DP/LC.

238. Heathfield to Keppel (November 12, 1932), CC/NY.

239. Roberta Fansler, Carnegie Corporation Memorandum of Interview (December 20, 1932), CC/NY.

240. Du Bois to Prophet (February 13, 1931), DP/LC.

241. Fansler, Carnegie Corporation Memorandum of Interview (December 28, 1932).

242. Keppel to Read (January 5, 1933), CC/NY.

243. Read to Keppel (January 10, 1932), CC/NY.

244. Keppel to Read (January 12, 1932), CC/NY.

245. Prophet to Keppel (January 10, 1932), CC/NY.

246. Fansler to Read (May 18, 1933), CC/NY.

247. Prophet to Fansler (May 6, 1933), CC/NY.

248. Prophet to Tanner (June 11, 1931), Henry O. Tanner Papers, Archives of American Art, roll D–306, frames 748–749.

249. Prophet diary (November 3, November 25, and November 28, 1933).

250. Prophet to the Guggenheim Memorial Foundation, 1934, GMF.

251. Francis Jacques to Guggenheim Memorial Foundation, 1934, GMF.

252. Du Bois to Prophet (February 8, 1934) DP/LC.

253. Ibid.

254. Prophet diary (March 30, 1934). Dates of diary entries are cited parenthetically in the text.

255. Miss Grey apparently helped Prophet in other ways. While in the United States, it seems that Prophet wrote to Grey asking her to get twelve duplicate photographs each of *Congolais* and *Discontent* from Bernes, Marouteau and Company, Photographers, and send them to 24 Gould Street in Newport. RISD files.

256. As quoted in Kirschenbaum, "Nancy Elizabeth Prophet," 51.

257. Read to Keppel (August 11, 1934) and Read to Robert Lester (April 3, 1935), CC/NY.

258. Prophet, "Art and Life," 325.

259. Statement to the Guggenheim Memorial Foundation, (June 28, 1957), GMF.

260. Prophet to the Guggenheim Memorial Foundation (May 20, 1957), GMF.

261. Prophet to Champion (July 22, 1960), collection of George Proffitt.

262. Kirschenbaum, "Nancy Elizabeth Prophet," 50.

3   PALMER HAYDEN

1. James A. Porter, *Modern Negro Art* (New York: Arno Press, 1969), 110.

2. As quoted from Hayden by his wife, Miriam, in Allan M. Gordon, *Echoes of Our Past: The Narrative Artistry of Palmer C. Hayden* (Los Angeles: Museum of African American Art, 1988), 11.

3. Nora Holt, "Painter Palmer Hayden Symbolizes John Henry," *New York Herald* (?), February 1, 1947, n.p. From a clipping in the AAA/SI. Also, microfilm 44, fr. 725 AAA/SI.

4. Ibid.

5. Hayden, tape-recorded interview with Harry Henderson and Romare Bearden (1972), collection of Harry Henderson (hereafter Hayden interview 1972).

6. Ibid.

7. Sam Norkin, "A Late Artist's Work Lives On," *New York Daily News,* April 15, 1973, Leisure section, 15, 27.

8. Hayden's father was listed as James Hedge, fisherman, in the 1900 census, Upper Aquia District, p. 7245B. Hayden was listed as "Paton," and his siblings or other people who dwelled in the house were Charlie, Willie, Claire, Kate, Mary, Nannie, and Jimmie.

9. Holt, "Painter Palmer Hayden," n.p.

10. Gordon, *Echoes of Our Past,* 11.

11. Ibid., 15.

12. Holt, "Painter Palmer Hayden," n.p.

13. *New York Evening World,* December 13, 1926, 8, HFP/LC.

14. Ibid. It has also been suggested that sometime during Hayden's military career, a commanding officer mispronounced his name and Peyton Hedgeman became known as Palmer Cole Hayden. David Driskell, "The Flowering of the Harlem Renaissance: The Art of Aaron Douglas, Meta Vaux Warrick Fuller, Palmer Hayden and William H. Johnson," in Mary Schmidt Campbell et al., *Harlem Renaissance: Art of Black America* (New York: Studio Museum in Harlem and Harry N. Abrams, 1987), 131. This information was reprinted in Gordon, *Echoes of Our Past,* 12.

15. Lawrence Epstein, supervisor, Bureau of Motor Vehicles, New York (November 25, 1958), microfilm 44, fr. 725, AAA/SI.

16. U.S. Census records, 1900 and 1910, National Archives.

17. Holt, "Painter Palmer Hayden," n.p. and Hayden interview, 1972.

18. *New York Evening World,* 8.

19. Hayden interview, 1972.

20. *New York Evening World,* 8.

21. Ibid., 158.

22. Microfilm 44, fr. 632, AAA/SI.

23. Transcript from the 1920 summer session at Columbia University, microfilm 45, fr. 279, AAA/SI.

24. Porter, *Modern Negro Art,* 94.

25. Clark S. Marlor, *Society of Independent Artists: The Exhibition Record, 1917–1944* (Park Ridge, N.J.: Noyes Press, 1984), 3, 14.

26. Ibid., 64.

27. Ibid., 288.

28. Raymond Sélig, "L'oeuvre de Palmer Hayden," *La revue du vrai et du beau* (April 25, 1927), n.p. Translated by Negro Awards Publicity department of the Harmon Foundation, HFP/LC.

29. Marlor, *Society of Independent Artists,* 288.

30. Hayden, tape-recorded interviews with Harry Henderson and Romare Bearden (May 22 and 29, 1969), collection of Harry Henderson (hereafter Hayden interview, 1969).

31. Bearden and Henderson, *A History of African-American Artists,* 162.

32. Hayden interview, 1972.

33. "I didn't meet him because we didn't meet big shots in my station then. He was a big shot. It's a little easier to meet big shots in Europe than it is in the United States." Hayden interview, 1972.

34. *Epworth League Herald,* n.d., n.p. From a clipping in the AAA/SI.

35. Bearden and Henderson, *A History of African-American Artists,* 159.

36. Holt, "Painter Palmer Hayden," n.p.

37. Hayden interview, 1972.

38. Victor Pérard, *Anatomy and Drawing* (New York: Victor Pérard, 1936), viii.

39. Ibid.

40. "Miss Alice M. Dike of Bronxville Dies," *New York Times,* November 9, 1930, p. 31, col. 2.

41. Hayden interview, 1972.

42. "He submitted five paintings . . . .also two landscapes of the country near Haverstraw, where he once worked in the summer cottage of a New York woman." Author and title of article unknown, *New York Evening World,* December 13, 1926, 8, HFP/LC.

43. Holt, "Painter Palmer Hayden," n.p.

44. Rosenwald application (1945), RP/FU.

45. Hayden interview, 1972.

46. Bearden and Henderson, *A History of African-American Artists,* 159.

47. Photocopies of microfilmed photographs are almost indiscernible. Microfilm 45, frames 224, 226, AAA/SI.

48. While Hayden showed a work titled *Landscape* in 1925, he also exhibited *Roast Duck for Supper.* Hayden's exhibition credits at the SIA the following year, *Through Washington Arch* and *Doin' th' Charleston,* most likely depicted scenes in New York. Marlor, *Society of Independent Artists,* 288.

49. Hayden interview, 1972.

50. Microfilm 45, fr. 40, AAA.

51. Lewis, *When Harlem Was in Vogue,* 90.

52. Ibid., 93–94.

53. The paintings in the exhibition at the Civic Club were *Boothbay Harbor No. 1, Boothbay Harbor No. 2, The Sheepscot, Autumn Leaves, Portland, Me., Haverstraw, The Yake, September, Bulls, Maine Mist, Linekin Bay, Nude with Child, The Steps, Up the River,* and *Fish Houses. Paintings by Palmer C. Hayden* (exhibition pamphlet) (New York: Civic Club, 1926), n.p.

54. Count Chabrier, "Palmer Hayden," *La revue du vrai et du beau* (December 1925): n.p.

55. Royal Cortissoz, "Random Impressions in Current Exhibitions," *New York Herald Tribune,* April 11, 1926, sec. 6, 10.

56. Hayden said this was the church that Adam Clayton Powell Sr. directed. Holt, "Painter Palmer Hayden," n.p.

57. Gary Reynolds, "An Experiment in Inductive Service: Looking Back at the Harmon Foundation," in Gary Reynolds and Beryl Wright, *Against the Odds: African American Artists and the Harmon Foundation* (Newark, N.J.: Newark Museum, 1989), 32.

58. David Driskell erroneously states that *The Schooners* won. "Mary Beattie Brady and the Administration of the Harmon Foundation," in Reynolds and Wright, *Against the Odds,* 64. However, he might have gotten his information from the error listed by Locke in *Negro Art: Past and Present* (New York, 1969), 60–61.

59. As quoted in the *Evening Post* by *Art Digest* (January 1, 1927): 7, in Fine, 121.

60. Hayden interview, 1972.

61. Hayden to William Harmon (February 19,1927), HFP/LC.

62. Olyve L. Jeter to Hayden (March 2, 1927). Because Mr. Jacque Duvoisin's rate was three dollars an hour and it was difficult to contact him (he had no telephone), it is unlikely that Hayden ever took French lessons from him.

63. George Haynes to Laura Wheeler (March 1, 1927), HFP/LC.

64. Hayden interview, 1972.

65. Haynes to Tanner (March 2, 1927), HFP/LC.

66. Harmon Foundation press release, "Negro Housecleaner Will Study Art in Europe," HFP/LC.

67. As quoted in Cedric Dover, *American Negro Art* (New York: Graphic Society, 1970), 31.

68. Romare Bearden, "The Negro Artist and Modern Art," *Opportunity* 12 (December 1934): 371–372.

69. Hayden interview, 1969.

70. Hayden interview, 1972.

71. Ibid.

72. Bearden and Henderson, *A History of African-American Artists,* 161.

73. Ibid., 161.

74. Raymond Sélig, "L'oeuvre de Palmer Hayden," *La revue du vrai et du beau* (25 April 1927): 16.

75. From Alice Miller's translation of an article in *La revue du vrai et du beau,* possibly December 1924 or January 1925. Microfilm 45, frames 272–276, AAA/SI. It is not known if or where *Pickaninnies* and *Clorinda* were exhibited.

76. Ibid.

77. Evelyn S. Brown to Hayden (May 20, 1927), HFP/LC.

78. Hayden interview, 1972.

79. Ibid.

80. Douglas Johnson and Madeleine Johnson, *The Age of Illusion: Art and Politics in France, 1918–1940* (New York: Rizzoli, 1987), 56–57.

81. Billy Klüver and Julie Martin, *Kiki's Paris: Artists and Lovers, 1900–1930* (New York: Harry N. Abrams, 1989), 152.

82. Hayden interview, 1972.

83. Known simply as "Sem," the artist was a member of the Salon des Humoristes and an officer of the Legion of Honor, and a well-known caricaturist. Entry in E. Bénézit, *Dictionnaire critique et documentaire des peintres, sculpteurs, dessinateurs et graveurs de tous les temps et de tous les pays par un groupe d'écrivains spécialistes français et étrangers* (Paris: Librairie Gründ, 1976), 258.

84. J. A Rogers described the West Indians' clothing at the *Bal Nègre* thus: "The dresses of the many colored women are also different. Their gowns have striking colors; they are flowing and reach out to the heels as in the good old days. Some wear bright-colored bandanas, tied so as to bring the kerchief to two points, which stick upward like the horns of a snail." As quoted in Stovall, *Paris Noir,* 97.

85. Fabre and Williams, *Way B(l)ack Then and Now,* 120–121.

86. Klüver and Martin, *Kiki's Paris,* 201.

87. Ibid., 121.

88. Mosby, *Henry Ossawa Tanner,* 38, 89.

89. David Sellin, *Americans in Brittany and Normandy, 1860–1910* (Phoenix: Phoenix Art Museum, 1982), 43.

90. Hayden interview, 1972.

91. Sellin, *Americans in Brittany,* 43.

92. Porter, *Modern Negro Art,* 109–110.

93. Hayden interview, 1972.

94. Hayden interview, 1969.

95. Bernheim-Jeune, *Petit Résumé Historique* (Paris: Bernheim-Jeune, ca. 1985), 18, 22.

96. Turner, *American Artists in Paris,* 145.

97. The receipt for this amount, dated October 21, 1927, is in the AAA/SI. Microfilm 45, fr. 278. Check dated October 21, 1927, microfilm roll 45, AAA/SI. At the then current exchange rate of 3.93 percent, this was $508.90.

98. Guy-Patrice Dauberville, director of the Bernheim-Jeune Gallery, to the author (15 May 1991). Also, the invitation is reproduced on microfilm roll 45, fr. 42, AAA/SI.

99. Turner, *American Artists in Paris,* 50.

100. Stoelting, *Hale Woodruff: Fifty Years of His Art* (New York: Studio Museum in Harlem, 1979), 13.

101. Hayden to Haynes (November 26, 1927), HFP/LC.

102. Ibid.

103. Hayden to Brown (December 5, 1927), HFP/LC.

104. Hayden interview, 1972.

105. *Southern Scenes and City Scenes* (New York: Studio Museum in Harlem, 1977): unpaginated.

106. Hayden interview, 1972.

107. Microfilm 44, fr. 489, AAA/SI.

108. Stoelting, "Hale Woodruff, Artist and Teacher: Through the Atlanta Years" (Ph.D. diss., Emory University, 1978), 28 n. 41.

109. Harold Jackman to Countee Cullen (22 November 1928), CCP/AC.

110. Klüver and Martin, *Kiki's Paris,* 167.

111. Ibid., 186 and Kenneth Silver and Romy Golan, *The Circle of Montparnasse: Jewish Artists in Paris 1905–1945* (New York: Universe Books, 1985), 42.

112. Silver and Golan, *Circle of Montparnasse,* 33.

113. Microfilm 45, fr. 400, AAA/SI.

114. Silver and Golan, *Circle of Montparnasse,* 72.

115. Turner, *American Artists in Paris,* 163.

116. Fabre and Williams, *Way B(l)ack Then and Now,* 109.

117. Ibid.

118. *Southern Scenes and City Streets,* n.p.

119. Hayden interview, 1972. The name of the doctor was inaudible on the tape, but see note 120.

120. Curator Lowery Sims said that Hayden's wife, Miriam, in a 1973 interview, identified the subjects as Hayden, Woodruff, Cullen, and Ernest Dupré (spelling uncertain), the latter a medical student at the Sorbonne. Telephone conversation with the author (August 6, 1998).

121. Powell, *Rhapsodies in Black,* 26.

122. Ibid.

123. Brady to Hayden (January 10, 1928), HFP/LC.

124. Brady to Haynes (April 4, 1928), HFP/LC.

125. Haynes to Brady (April 6, 1928), HFP/LC.

126. Hayden to Brady (April 21, 1928), HFP/LC.

127. Hayden interview, 1972.

128. Stoelting, "Hale Woodruff, Artist and Teacher," 28.

129. Hayden interview, 1969.

130. Hayden interview, 1972.

131. Stoelting, "Hale Woodruff, Artist and Teacher," 28.

132. Woodruff to Harmon Foundation (August 1928), HFP/LC.

133. Woodruff to Haynes and Brady (March 1929), HFP/LC.

134. Hayden to Brady (July 20, 1929), HFP/LC.

135. Haynes to Woodruff (November 8, 1929), HFP/LC.

136. Hayden to Brown (December 2, 1929), HFP/LC.

137. *The Schooners* was sold to Albert A. Harvey of Boston for $125. Brown to Hayden (November 11, 1929), microfilm 44, fr. 641, AAA/SI.

138. *St. Servan* was sold to Mrs. Theodore A. Greene of New Britain, Connecticut. Brown to Hayden (November 29, 1929). Microfilm 44, fr. 642, AAA/SI.

139. *Parisian Landscape* is now in the Countee Cullen collection at Hampton University, Virginia.

140. Jackman to Cullen (December 29, 1929), CCP/AC.

141. As listed in several sources, including Gordon, 14, 29.

142. Fernand-Demeure, *Petite histoire du Salon des Tuileries* (Paris: Goethe, n.d.), n.p.

143. Turner, *American Artists in Paris,* 42, 44.

144. Hayden to Brady (June 8, 1930), HFP/LC.

145. Brady to Hayden (July 30, 1930), HFP/LC.

146. Hayden to Tanner (September 25, 1930). Henry O. Tanner papers, microfilm D–306, fr. 620, AAA/SI.

147. Turner, *American Artists in Paris*, 179.

148. Hayden to Brady (January 21, 1931), HFP/LC.

149. Such as Campbell, *Harlem Renaissance*, 33.

150. Hayden interview, 1972.

151. As quoted in Bearden and Henderson, 159.

152. Ibid.

153. Mary Schmidt Campbell, introduction to *Harlem Renaissance*, 33.

154. Ibid.

155. Campbell, *Harlem Renaissance*, 133.

156. Hayden interview, 1972.

157. Benny Andrews, "Palmer Hayden, 1890–1973," *World Magazine*, no. 2 (July 21, 1973), front page.

158. Jeffrey C. Stewart, "Paul Robeson and the Problem of Modernism," in Powell et al., *Rhapsodies in Black*, 94.

159. Holt, "Painter Palmer Hayden," n.p.

160. Hayden interview, 1972.

161. Fabre, *From Harlem to Paris*, 85.

162. Hayden interview, 1972.

163. Microfilm 44, fr. 643, AAA/SI.

164. Hayden interview, 1972.

165. For a fascinating consideration of black memorabilia, and the reuse and modification of late-nineteenth- and early-twentieth-century racist imagery by African American artists, see "The Past Is Prologue But Is Parody and Pastiche Progress," a conversation between Karen C. C. Dalton, Michael D. Harris, and Lowery Stokes Sims, in *The International Review of African American Art* 14, no. 3 (1997): 17–29.

166. Hayden interview, 1969.

167. My thanks to African art historian Dominique Malaquais for supplying information about this piece.

168. My thanks to Richard Powell for this suggestion, and for prompting me to take a closer look at the Fang sculptures in William Rubin, *"Primitivism" in Twentieth Century Art* (New York: Museum of Modern Art, 1984).

169. Hayden interview with Henderson, 1966.

170. Ibid.

171. Hayden interview, 1972.

172. Locke, *Negro Art: Past and Present*, 66.

173. Ibid.

174. Brady to Hayden (December 1931), HFP/LC.

175. Bearden and Henderson, *A History of African-American Artists*, 164.

176. Microfilm 44, fr. 658, AAA/SI.

4   HALE WOODRUFF

1. Hale Woodruff, "My Meeting with Henry O. Tanner," *Crisis* 77 (January 1970): 7. Woodruff was born in Cairo, Illinois, on August 26, 1900. His mother, a domestic servant, moved with him to East Nashville, for unknown reasons, soon after his birth and the death of his father, George. Winifred Stoelting, "Hale Woodruff, Artist and Teacher: Through the Atlanta Years" (Ph.D. diss., Emory University, 1978), 1.

2. Bearden and Henderson, *A History of African-American Artists*, 201.

3. Transcription of "Harmon Prize Winner Sails," *New York Sun*, September 3, 1927, n.p. HFP/LC.

4. Woodruff interview with Al Murray, Archives of American Art, 1968, 10.

5. Woodruff, "My Meeting," 8.

6. Stoelting, "Hale Woodruff, Artist and Teacher," 5.

7. Ibid., 4–5.

8. Ibid., 4 and Woodruff interview, 1968, 3. Woodruff had already experienced segregation in housing; living in East Nashville meant that he was restricted to an area known as Crappy Shoot.

9. James H. Madison, *The Indiana Way: A State History* (Bloomington: Indiana University Press, 1986), 291.

10. Ibid., 293.

11. Between 1890 and 1930, there were ten reported lynchings in Indiana, but none of them were in Indianapolis. Ralph Ginzburg, *One Hundred Years of Lynchings* (Baltimore: Black Classic Press, 1988), 260.

12. Ibid., 294.

13. Woodruff's Reappointment file in the Rosenwald Archives states that he studied at the Herron, 1920–1923. Fisk University (Box 458, file 16).

14. Bearden and Henderson, *A History of African-American Artists*, 201.

15. It is possible that Pickens spoke about African American troops abroad during World War I. He wrote "How Colored Soldiers Defeated the Real Enemy at Granvillars," *Crisis* (November 1919): 200–203.

16. Stoelting, "Hale Woodruff, Artist and Teacher," 7.

17. Woodruff to Brady (June 20, 1929). HFP/LC.

18. Woodruff interview, 1968, 3.

19. Stoelting, "Hale Woodruff, Artist and Teacher," 56.

20. Black clubs and theaters on Indiana Avenue in Indianapolis thrived during the Jazz Age. Noble Sissle, born in Indianapolis in 1889, teamed with Eubie Blake to perform across the country, and they did a "record business" in their Indianapolis appearance in 1925. James H. Madison, *Indiana through Tradition and Change: A History of the Hoosier State and Its People, 1920–1945* (Indianapolis, Ind.: Indiana Historical Society, 1982), 364.

21. Benjamin Brawley, *The Negro Genius (A New Appraisal of the Achievement of the American Negro in Literature and the Fine Arts)* (New York: Dodd, Mead, 1937), 183.

22. Woodruff interview, 1968, 1 and 3.

23. Woodruff interview, 1968, 3–4. Holloway became a cartoonist for the *Pittsburgh Courier*. Bearden and Henderson, *A History of African-American Artists*, 201.

24. Woodruff to Brady (February 21, 1928). HFP/LC. In 1925 Woodruff's studio was at 46 North Penn Street, Suite 314. Woodruff to Du Bois (April 13, 1925). HFP/LC.

25. Woodruff, List of Public Exhibitions, RA/FU. It is not known which works Woodruff exhibited.

26. "Poetry and Painting," *Crisis* (May 1927): 84.

27. Woodruff to Du Bois (April 13, 1925), DP/LC.

28. Reynolds and Wright, *Against the Odds*, 14. W.E.B. Du Bois to Woodruff (August 17, 1925), DP/LC.

29. Du Bois to Woodruff (October 7, 1925), DP/LC.

30. Woodruff to Du Bois (November 7, 1925), DP/LC.

31. Stoelting, "Hale Woodruff, Artist and Teacher," 7.

32. Ibid.

33. Woodruff submitted these two landscapes, not identified by media, and a figure painting, *The Quadroon*, to the *Crisis* competition. Since the award was for drawing, it seems likely that Woodruff received it for one of the landscapes. Woodruff to Du Bois (April 28, 1926), HFP/LC.

34. "Poetry and Painting," 84.

35. Two of these were probably *Autumn Impression* and *A Day in June* (both 1926). Stoelting, 10, 11. Woodruff did not recall the titles of the others. Stoelting, "Hale Woodruff, Artist and Teacher," 8 n. 19.

36. Bearden and Henderson, *A History of African-American Artists,* 202.

37. Reynolds and Wright, *Against the Odds,* 31.

38. Press release, "Negro Artist Will Study in Europe," Harmon Foundation (ca. September 2, 1927), HFP/LC.

39. Samella Lewis, *African American Art and Artists* (Berkeley and Los Angeles: University of California Press, 1990), 139–140.

40. Ibid., from a letter from White to Claude McKay (January 26, 1924) (C–91), WWC/LC.

41. Woodruff interview, 1968, 5.

42. Crawford, "Hale Aspacio Woodruff," M.A. thesis, Howard University, 1972, 3.

43. As quoted in Bearden and Henderson, *A History of African-American Artists,* 202.

44. Woodruff to Brady (June 20, 1929), HFP/LC.

45. The source for the address is Woodruff to Brady (June 20, 1929), HFP/ LC.

46. Judith Wilson points out that Woodruff stated he was twenty or twenty-one years old when he received the Einstein book, which would place the occurrence somewhere between September 1920 and August 1922, when he would have turned twenty-two. Wilson, " 'Go Back and Retrieve It:' Hale Woodruff, Afro-American Modernist," in *Selected Essays: Art and Artist from the Harlem Renaissance to the 1980's* (Atlanta: National Black Arts Festival, 1988), 47 n. 14.

As Judith Wilson notes, Stoelting identifies the book as *Afrikanische Plastik,* Carl Einstein's second volume on African art. But Stoelting's footnotes say the work was published in Leipzig, which is where the first edition of Einstein's *Negerplastik* was published in 1915. The former book was published in 1921 in Berlin (not 1922, as Wilson maintains). Wilson, " 'Go Back and Retrieve It,' " 47 n. 14. Einstein, *Afrikanische Plastik* (Berlin: Verlag Ernst Wasmuth, 1921). Einstein, *Negerplastik,* 2d ed. (Munich: Kurt Wolff Verlag, 1920 [orig. pub. Leipzig: Verlag der Weissen Bücher, 1915].

47. Woodruff interview, 1968, 10.

48. Bearden and Henderson, *A History of African-American Artists,* 201.

49. Woodruff to Cullen (March 21, 1927), CCP/ARC.

50. As quoted in Fabre, *From Harlem to Paris,* 77. Cullen to Woodruff (October 17, 1927), CCP/ARC.

51. Woodruff, "My Meeting with Tanner," 9.

52. *The Negro in Art Week* (Chicago: Chicago Woman's Club, 1927), n.p.

53. Lucille Morehouse, "Hale Woodruff, Artist, Will Study in Europe," *Indianapolis Star,* August 28, 1927. From a clipping, AAA/SI.

54. Jane Allison, "OK, Museum, Why Not a Woodruff?" *Indianapolis News,* March 5, 1977, 5.

55. Woodruff to Romare Bearden and Harry Henderson, ca. 1971. As quoted in their *A History of African American Artists,* 118.

56. Stoelting, "Hale Woodruff, Artist and Teacher," 14.

57. Woodruff to George Haynes (October 24, 1927), HFP/LC.

58. Woodruff to Cullen (October 2, 1927), CCP/ARC.

59. Ibid.

60. Stoelting, "Hale Woodruff, Artist and Teacher," 14. It is not clear when Woodruff attended these schools. Although his reappointment file at the Rosenwald Foundation states that he studied at the Moderne in 1930 and the Scandinave in 1931, this seems unlikely given that he was in Cagnes-sur-Mer during those years and that in the spring of 1928 he told Tanner he was already studying at those places. RA/FU (Box 458, file 16).

61. Turner, *American Artists in Paris,* 38.

62. Hale Woodruff, "Artist Makes Forced Stop at Mendon [*sic*]," *Indianapolis Star,* January 27, 1928, n.p.

63. Woodruff, "Local Negro Artist Tells of View from Notre Dame," *Indianapolis Star,* April 2, 1928, 25.

64. As quoted in Wilson, " 'Go Back and Retrieve It,' " from George Preston's notebooks, 42 and 47.

65. Woodruff, "Some Bridges of Paris," *Indianapolis Star,* February 5, 1928, 6.

66. Ibid.

67. *Productions of American Negro Artists* (New York: Harmon Foundation, 1928), n.p.

68. "I feel quite certain that the award will mean much to him now for he has labored very hard for years with very little encouragement." Woodruff to Brady (February 21, 1928), HFP/LC.

69. Woodruff to Mary Beattie Brady (February 21, 1928), HFP/LC.

70. Ibid. and Woodruff to Haynes (March 19, 1928), HFP/LC.

71. Woodruff to Haynes (March 19, 1928), HFP/LC.

72. Crawford, "Hale Aspacio Woodruff," 3.

73. Woodruff to Du Bois (December 22, 1927). DP/LC.

74. Woodruff to Du Bois (April 6, 1928), DP/LC.

75. Ibid.

76. Du Bois to Woodruff (January 11, 1928), DP/LC.

77. "KRIGWA," *Crisis* (September 1928): 322.

78. Woodruff, "My Meeting," 8.

79. Anne M. Montero, "Village Artist Reflects on Career on Occasion of Museum Show," *Villager* (1977), n.p. From a clipping, AAA/SI.

80. Benny Andrews, "Hailing Hale Woodruff," *Encore American and Worldwide News* 7 (April 3, 1978): 31.

81. Woodruff said he went to Europe "as much for the museums as for the schools. . . . But the old masters, especially Michelangelo, inspired me." Montero, "Village Artist Reflects," n.p.

82. "Local Negro Artist Finds Painters Hard to Classify," *Indianapolis Star,* March 18, 1928, 31. The article was given its title by the newspaper.

83. Woodruff interview, 1968, 10. It is unclear whether Woodruff paid two dollars for one or both pieces.

84. Ibid.

85. Bearden and Henderson, *A History of African-American Artists,* 204. Here, listed as *Boy in a Red Vest.*

86. Woodruff to Edwin Coates (August 16, 1973), AAA/SI.

87. Ibid. and "KRIGWA," 322.

88. Woodruff, "My Meeting," 12.

89. Mosby, *Henry Ossawa Tanner,* 135.

90. Ibid., 136.

91. Fabre, *From Harlem to Paris,* 2.

92. Ibid., 36–37, 39, 89, 133, 143.

93. Bearden and Henderson, *A History of African-American Artists,* 204.

94. Woodruff, "A Lodging of Jeanne d'Arc," *Indianapolis Star,* May 27, 1928, 6.

95. As quoted in Stoelting, "Hale Woodruff, Artist and Teacher," 30.

96. Woodruff, "Travelers in France, Though Rushing for Time, Long to Linger in Chartres," *Indianapolis Star,* October 7, 1928.

97. Bearden and Henderson, *A History of African-American Artists,* 201.

98. Woodruff framed the works in Paris, for three reasons: it was inexpensive, he was concerned about troubling the foundation to do the work, and he thought it was easier to do it in France because the pictures and frames would both be measured in the same, metric, system. He requested that the foundation pay the customs duty in New York, which he would reimburse upon receipt of the statement. Woodruff to Haynes (November 15, 1928), HFP/LC. Later, the foundation would request him not to frame the works because it really was not less expensive.

99. Ibid.

100. Woodruff to Brady (June 20, 1929), HFP/LC. It is not known how Woodruff made the arrangement with the Downtown Gallery to promote his work.

101. Woodruff to Brady (October 26, 1928), HFP/LC.

102. "Do not worry about that $40—that can wait indefinitely. When you do have it, I will probably ask you to buy something for me in Paris." Locke to Woodruff (November 14, 1928), MSRC/HU.

103. "So they are painting you. Are you going to buy it when Woodruff is through?" Harold Jackman to Cullen (November 22, 1928), CCP/ARC. The work is now in the Countee Cullen Collection at Hampton University Museum.

104. As quoted in Fabre, *Black American Writers in France,* 76.

105. As quoted in Fabre, *From Harlem to Paris,* 85.

106. Brady to Woodruff (February 14, 1929), HFP/LC.

107. Haynes to Woodruff (February 14, 1929), HFP/LC.

108. Haynes to Woodruff (February 6, 1929), HFP/LC.

109. Woodruff to Haynes (March 3, 1929), HFP/LC.

110. Woodruff to Haynes (June 10, 1929), HFP/LC.

111. Woodruff to Haynes (September 1, 1929), HFP/LC.

112. Woodruff to Haynes (October 12, 1929), HFP/LC.

113. Haynes to Woodruff (February 14, 1929), HFP/LC.

114. Ibid.

115. Woodruff to Brady (March 20, 1929), HFP/LC.

116. Locke to Woodruff (January 15, 1929), MSRC/HU.

117. Woodruff to Brady (March 20, 1929), HFP/LC.

118. Woodruff to Brady (June 20, 1929), HFP/LC.

119. Stoelting, "Hale Woodruff, Artist and Teacher," 28.

120. Woodruff to Haynes (October 12, 1929), HFP/LC.

121. Bearden and Henderson, *A History of African-American Artists,* 204.

122. Romare Bearden, "The Negro Artist and Modern Art," *Opportunity* 12 (December 1934): 371–372.

123. Richard J. Powell, *Black Art and Culture in the Twentieth Century* (New York: Thames and Hudson, 1997), 57.

124. Woodruff, "Paris's Montparnasse," *Indianapolis Star,* February 17, 1929.

125. Ibid.

126. Ibid.

127. Ibid.

128. Ibid.

129. Woodruff first met Du Bois's daughter, Yolande, in August 1928 when she and her husband came to Paris. Du Bois asked Woodruff to advise her on "where and how to study." Du Bois to Woodruff (August 8, 1928), DP/LC.

130. Woodruff to Brady (June 20, 1929), HFP/LC.

131. Stoelting, "Hale Woodruff, Artist and Teacher," 38, 40. It is unclear whether the business was suspended from operation solely because McKay prosecuted.

132. Fabre, *From Harlem to Paris,* 141.

133. Woodruff to Haynes (November 20, 1929), HFP/LC.

134. Haynes to Woodruff (December 18, 1929), HFP/LC.

135. Woodruff to Evelyn Brown (April 9, 1935), HFP/LC.

136. Steve Greene to Countee Cullen (September 18, 1930), CCP/ARC.

137. Woodruff to Edwin Coates (August 16, 1973), AAA/SI.

138. Ibid.

139. Ibid.

140. Woodruff interview, 1968, 2.

141. Stoelting, "Hale Woodruff, Artist and Teacher," 48.

142. Woodruff to Locke (March 24, 1932), ALP/HU.

143. Ibid.

144. Woodruff to Locke (August 21, 1930), ALP/HU.

145. Woodruff, interview by Esther G. Robick (November 10, 1970), AAA/SI.

146. As Judith Wilson has noted, this illustration is not the original (oil on canvas board, 24 x 30 in.), which is not available. Wilson, "'Go Back and Retrieve It,'" 48. In 1978, Woodruff repainted the composition because the original had deteriorated badly. Mary Schmidt Campbell "Hale Woodruff: Fifty Years of His Art," in *Hale Woodruff: FIfty Years of His Art* (New York: Studio Museum in Harlem, 1979), 58 n. 7. The 1930 version is reproduced in Locke's *The Negro in Art*, 54 and Elsa Honig Fine, *The Afro-American Artist: A Search for Identity* (New York: Hacker Art Books, 1982), 124. The two versions seem to differ very little.

147. Bearden and Henderson, *A History of African-American Artists*, 201.

148. Wilson, "'Go Back and Retrieve It,'" 42.

149. Woodruff interview, 1968, 25.

150. Bearden and Henderson, *A History of African-American Artists*, 204.

151. Woodruff interview, 1968, 22.

152. Wilson, "'Go Back and Retrieve It,'" 42.

153. Kurt Badt, *The Art of Cézanne* (Berkeley and Los Angeles: University of California Press, 1965), 115.

154. White to James Weldon Johnson (September, 29 1930), JWJ/YU.

155. Woodruff to Moriarta (December 12, 1930), HFP/LC.

156. Edward Alden Jewell, "Work of Negro Artists on View," *New York Times,* February 17, 1931, 23.

157. Ralph M. Pearson, *Experiencing Pictures: Through Analysis of Ancient and Modern Works and through Practice of the Procedures Which Make Those Works Effective* (New York: Brewer, Warren and Putnam, 1932), 136.

158. Du Bois to the Guggenheim Foundation (November 21, 1940), DP/LC.

159. Woodruff to Cullen (ca. July 1931), CCP/ARC.

160. White to Countee Cullen (April 17, 1931), CCP/ARC.

161. Woodruff to Hannah Moriarta (April 19, 1931), HFP/LC.

162. Woodruff to Brady (June 5, 1931), HFP/LC.

163. Woodruff to Carl Van Vechten (October 26, 1932), JWJ/YU.

164. Ibid.

165. Woodruff to Locke (March 24, 1932), Alain Locke Papers, MSRC/HU.

166. Stoelting, "Hale Woodruff, Artist and Teacher," 54.

167. Woodruff to Evelyn Brown (April 9, 1935), HFP/LC.

168. Woodruff to Brady (May 5, 1931), HFP/LC.

169. Spingarn apparently did not care for Woodruff's work, but thought enough of him to support his efforts; Hannah Moriarta wrote to Evelyn Brown, "It may interest you to know, that although Mrs. Spingarn does not particularly like any of the watercolors, she felt it much better to buy something so as not to pauperize Woodruff." (April 28, 1931), HFP/LC.

170. Woodruff to Brady (June 5, 1931), HFP/LC.

171. Ibid.

172. Brady to Woodruff (June 23, 1931), HFP/LC.

173. Woodruff to Cullen (ca. July 1931), CCP/ARC.

5   ARCHIBALD J. MOTLEY JR.

1. Interview with Archibald J. Motley Jr. by Dennis Barrie (January 23, 1978), AAA/SI (hereafter Motley interview with Barrie), 33–34.

2. Jontyle Theresa Robinson and Wendy Greenhouse, *The Art of Archibald J. Motley, Jr.* (Chicago: Chicago Historical Society, 1991), 1, 39. See the essays by both Robinson and Greenhouse for full accounts of Motley's early years.

3. Robinson and Greenhouse, *Art of Motley,* 150.

4. Ibid.

5. Writer Richard Wright later received a Guggenheim to work on *Native Son.*

6. Reynolds and Wright, *Against the Odds,* 33.

7. As noted in Jontyle Theresa Robinson, "The Life of Archibald J. Motley Jr.," in Robinson and Greenhouse, *Art of Motley,* 5.

8. Gunsaulus had offered Motley a full scholarship to study architecture at the Armour Institute. When Motley turned down his offer, Gunsaulus was still impressed enough to pay for his first year's tuition at the AIC. Robinson, "Life of Motley," 3.

9. Robinson and Greenhouse, *Art of Motley,* 3–4, 49.

10. Ibid., 49.

11. Ibid., 50.

12. Motley interview with Barrie, 16.

13. Motley interview with Barrie, 18–19.

14. Reynolds and Wright, *Against the Odds,* 172.

15. Farrow helped Motley get a job dusting statuary at the AIC. Motley interview with Barrie, 14, 19.

16. Motley, "The Negro in Art," *Chicago Defender,* July 13, 1918, n.p. Motley did not identify those he critiqued.

17. Motley interview with Barrie, 26.

18. Motley, "The Negro in Art," n.p.

19. Elaine D. Woodall, "Archibald Motley, Jr.: American Artist of the Afro-American People, 1891–1928" (M.A. thesis, Pennsylvania State University, 1977), 29–30.

20. "The are no modern painters, with the exception possibly of George Bellows—none of them have ever influenced me." Motley interview with Barrie, 51.

21. Motley, "The Negro in Art."

22. Artist's statement by Motley in J. Z. Jacobson, *Art of Today: Chicago 1933* (Chicago: L. M. Stein, 1932), 93.

23. Motley interview with Barrie, 1. According to Robinson, Motley's maternal grandmother, Harriet Huff, was probably a descendant of the Dorobo (Ndorobo), people of small stature from East Africa who are possibly related to pygmies. Emily Motley, the artist's paternal grandmother, was of mixed descent, originally from Louisiana. Both of Motley's parents were from Louisiana. Robinson, "Life of Motley," 28 n. 1.

24. Motley, "How I Solve My Painting Problems" (1929), 5, HFP/LC.

25. Ibid.

26. Reynolds and Wright, *Against the Odds,* 172. For an excellent analysis of other images of products of American miscegenation, see Judith Wilson, "Optical Illusions: Images of Miscegenation in Nineteenth- and Twentieth-Century Art," *American Art* 5, no. 3 (1991): 89–107.

27. Greenhouse points out that the term Black Belt was first used in 1922 by the Chicago Commission on Race Relations. Its residents also called the area Bronzeville, a term found in a black newspaper in 1930. Wendy Greenhouse, "Motley's Chicago Context, 1890–1940," in Robinson and Greenhouse, *Art of Motley,* 59 n. 2.

28. Greenhouse, "Motley's Chicago Context," 34. Motley stated that when his family moved to the largely German, Swedish, and Irish district of Englewood around 1897, his was "the only colored family in the block." Greenhouse states that by 1920, however, nearly two thousand black residents lived in the

neighborhood (41). The Motley children attended two other elementary schools, Beale School, which seven other black children also attended, and Nicholas Copernicus School, from which they graduated. Robinson, "Life of Motley," 28 n. 4.

29. Ibid., 3.

30. Motley interview with Barrie, 11.

31. Ibid., 5.

32. Ibid., 9.

33. Ibid., 33–34.

34. Motley quoted in Woodall, "Archibald Motley," 113.

35. Ibid., 103–104, 108–111.

36. Motley interview with Barrie, 43.

37. Greenhouse, "Motley's Chicago Context," 51–52.

38. Archibald J. Motley Jr., "Autobiography," 9, AMP/CHS.

39. The awards were the Frank G. Logan Medal (bronze, second prize of two hundred dollars) for *Syncopation* and the Joseph N. Eisendrath prize for *Mulatress*. Motley interview with Barrie, 29, and Woodall, "Archibald Motley," 103.

40. Count Chabrier, "Expositions de l'Art Institute de Chicago, du No Jury Expositions et du Cincinnati Museum," *La revue du vrai et du beau* (February 10, 1925): 14–20 and Chabrier and G. Serac, "Expositions d'Amerique," *La revue du vrai et du beau* (July 10, 1925): 26–30.

41. Woodall, "Archibald Motley," 114.

42. Motley interview with Barrie, 34.

43. See Robinson and Greenhouse, *Art of Motley,* for a full discussion of these works, 11–13, 81.

44. Edward Morrow, quoted in Robinson, "Archibald John Motley, Jr.: A Notable Anniversary for a Pioneer," in *Three Masters: Eldzier Cortor, Hughie Lee-Smith, Archibald John Motley, Jr.* (New York: Kenkeleba Gallery, 1988), 42–43.

45. Motley interview with Barrie, 42.

46. Ibid., 34.

47. Motley, "Autobiography," 7–9.

48. Motley interview with Barrie, 42.

49. Motley, "The Negro in Art."

50. Robinson, "Life of Motley," 15.

51. Ibid., 17.

52. *Crisis* (February 1918; 1923; July 1925).

53. Introduction to *John Simon Guggenheim Memorial Foundation, Directory of Fellows, 1925–1967* (New York: John Simon Guggenheim Memorial Foundation, 1968), unpaginated.

54. Motley's Guggenheim Fellowship application, 1929, GMF.

55. Robinson, "Life of Motley," 17.

56. Michel Fabre and John A. Williams, *Way B(l)ack Then and Now: A Street Guide to African Americans in Paris* (Paris: Centre d'Études Afro-Américaines, Université de la Sorbonne Nouvelle, 1992), 114.

57. Kenneth E. Silver, Jewish Artists in Paris, 1905–1945, *The Circle of Montparnasse: Jewish Artists in Paris, 1905–1945* (New York: The Jewish Museum), 15.

58. Motley interview with Barrie, 51.

59. Ibid., 55.

60. Ibid., 17.

61. Ibid., 51–52.

62. Ibid., 51.

63. Motley to Moe (September 3, 1930), Guggenheim Foundation, New York.

64. Motley interview with Barrie, 52–53.

65. Ibid., 52.

66. The Motleys became accustomed to being shunned as a result of their interracial marriage; apparently Motley's parents-in-law, the Granzos, disowned their daughter. Only Edith's brother, Art, kept in touch with the couple. Robinson, "Life of Motley," 8.

67. In 1930, the Jockey and a group of other small buildings on the rue Campagne-Première were bought by Helena Rubenstein, who erected a modern apartment building on the site. Klüver and Martin, *Kiki's Paris*, 170.

68. As quoted in Tony Allan, *The Glamour Years: Paris, 1919–40* (New York: Gallery Books, 1977), 102.

69. The influential Washington, D.C., critic, Leila Mechin, first noted this similarity when she viewed Motley's *Mending Socks* and *Picnic at the Grove* in the traveling Harmon Exhibition of 1929. Leila Mechin, "Notes of Art and Artists," *Sunday Star*, May 19, 1929, sec. 2, 4, quoted in Reynolds and Wright, *Against the Odds*, 111, and figs. 62 and 63.

70. Motley interview with Barrie, 28.

71. George S. Hellman to Motley (May 7, 1927), CHS, as quoted in Robinson, "Life of Motley," 11.

72. Motley interview with Barrie, 55.

73. Ibid., 49.

74. As quoted in Woodall, "Archibald Motley," 93.

75. Robinson, "Life of Motley," 18.

76. Richard J. Powell, "The Blues Aesthetic: Black Culture and Modernism," in *The Blues Aesthetic: Black Culture and Modernism* (Washington, D.C.: Washington Project for the Arts, 1989), 26.

77. Ibid., 27.

78. Ibid., 21, 23. See the entire essay for more extensive elucidation of the blues aesthetic, 19–35.

79. Guggenheim application, GMF.

80. Motley interview with Barrie, 50.

81. Archibald J. Motley Jr. diary (1929–1930), undated, last page. Collection of Archie Motley and Valerie Gerrard Brown. Copy in AMP/CHS.

82. Motley diary (March 6, 17, 18; April 7; May 30; June 6; July 9, 1930).

83. Robinson, "Life of Motley," 31 n. 64.

84. It is not known which Saint Joseph's Motley attended; there are five of them in Paris. Since it took Motley approximately forty-five minutes to get to early mass, it is likely that it was the Catholic church for foreigners at which English was spoken, located in the eighth arrondissement at 50, avenue Hoche. Motley diary (March 9 and 16; May 4, 11, and 18, 1930).

85. Motley only mentioned the newspapers a few times, but did not comment on any current events. Motley diary (April 5, 13, 20, 1930).

86. "Going to retire early to-night as there was no rest for the weary last night. Studio party all night downstairs. B. Greenstein is now playing Casey Jones on his phonograph." Motley diary (January 1, 1930), AMP/CHS.

87. Motley interview with Barrie 49.

88. He visited the Coupole (February 7, 1930) and the Kosmos Café (February 9, 1930). Motley regularly attended mass at Saint Joseph's; "They asked me to serve Mass, but I have never served Mass in my life." Motley diary (February 16, 1930), AMP/CHS.

89. Motley diary (January–February, 1930), AMP/CHS.

90. Motley interview with Barrie, 22.

91. The short, fat, bald man in the upper right first appeared in *Stomp* (1921) and features in a number of Motley's other works. His identity or what he might represent is unknown. Robinson, "Life of Motley," 16. Perhaps the man is Motley's alter ego, expressive of a sense of isolation or alienation.

92. Motley, "How I Solve My Painting Problems," n.d., HFP/LC.

93. Alain Locke, *The Negro in Art: A Pictorial Record of the Negro Artist and of the Negro Theme in Art* (New York: Hacker Art Books, 1979), 69.

94. Klüver and Martin, *Kiki's Paris,* 225, passim.

95. Motley interview with Barrie, 56.

96. Motley diary (January 5, 1930), AMP/CHS.

97. Motley diary (February 17, 25; May 19, 28, 1930). "Dark fellow," (May 14, 1930). "Poor fellow," (June 20, 1930), AMP/CHS.

98. Motley diary (May 19, 1930), AMP/CHS.

99. Days Motley listed as being ill were March 9–11, 31; April 14, 20, 27, 29, 30; May 30; June 7, 12, 19–20, 27–28; and July 5, 11–12, 1930. Motley diary, AMP/CHS.

100. Motley diary (May 13, 1930), AMP/CHS.

101. Greenhouse, "Motley's Chicago Context," 96.

102. "I arranged her for a portrait." Motley diary (April 5, 1930), AMP/CHS.

103. "Edith went out and bought blonde preparation for her hair today." Motley diary (March 28, 1930), AMP/CHS.

104. Perhaps this dress was one Edith bought in Paris; Motley reported being unable to work on the portrait one day when Edith took the dress "to be fixed." Motley diary (April 28, 1930), AMP/CHS.

105. Motley recorded many instances of his wife buying dresses, gloves, hats, stockings, and coats, but he also purchased socks, shoes, spats, berets, and tailored suits. See Motley diary (March 3, 7, 8, 25; April 7, 11, 15, 18; May 3, 5; and June 11, 1930), AMP/CHS.

106. Greenhouse, "Motley's Chicago Context," 97.

107. Motley diary (Recapitulation of the month of May, probably written on May 31, 1930), AMP/CHS.

108. Robinson and Greenhouse, *Art of Motley,* 151.

109. Motley often played solitaire, but he also played card games with his wife and mother. It is not known whether one of the games was belote, which Hayden, Woodruff, and Savage enjoyed. Motley diary (May 16–18, 20, 24, 25; June 1, 2, 5, 6, 8, 10, 15, 16, 18, 20, 23, 24, 29; July 7, 1930), AMP/CHS.

110. Motley diary (June 17, 25, and 26, 1930), AMP/CHS. Dates from this diary are cited parenthetically in the text.

111. Robinson and Greenhouse, *Art of Motley,* 146.

112. This seems to be when Motley received the offer; he noted having received "a very nice letter from Mr. Moe to-day, Guggenheim secretary." Motley diary (May 10, 1930), AMP/CHS.

113. Motley interview with Barrie, 49.

6   AUGUSTA SAVAGE

1. Romare Bearden and Harry Henderson, *A History of African-American Artists From 1792 to the Present* (New York: Pantheon Books, 1993), 180.

2. Savage to George Arthur (October 19, 1931), RA/FU.

3. Savage, "Augusta Savage: An Autobiography," *Crisis* 36 (August 1929): 269.

4. "Courier Tintypes," *Pittsburgh Courier,* Saturday, May 5, 1934, 2:3.

5. Birth date from Savage's death certificate. Bearden and Henderson, *A History of African-American Artists,* 496 n. 1. Quote from "Courier Tintypes," 2:3.

6. "Courier Tintypes."

7. Savage, "Autobiography," 269.

8. DeWitt S. Dykes Jr., "Savage, Augusta Christine," in Barbara Sicherman and Carol Hurd Green, eds., *Notable American Women, The Modern Period: A Biographical Dictionary* (Cambridge, Mass.: Harvard University Press, Belknap Press, 1980), 627.

9. Juanita Holland, "Augusta Christine Savage: A Chronology of Her Life and Art, 1892–1962," in *Augusta Savage and the Art Schools of Harlem* (New York: Schomburg Center for Research in Black Culture, New York Public Library, 1988), 12.

10. Romare Bearden and Harry Henderson, "Augusta Savage," in *Six Black Masters of American Art* (Garden City, N.Y.: Zenith Books, 1972), 78.

11. Elton C. Fax, "Augusta Savage—An Appraisal," *American Society of African Sculpture Newsletter* 5, no. 2 (supplement, October 1962): 4.

12. As quoted from an unidentified newspaper clipping in Bearden and Henderson, *A History of African-American Artists*, 168.

13. Jessie Carney Smith, "Augusta Savage," in *Notable Black American Women* (Detroit: Gale, 1992), 980. Smith states that Savage married James Savage in 1915, whereas Bearden and Henderson, in *A History of African-American Artists*, 169, say that the marriage took place in the early 1920s and failed within a few months. None of the authors state their sources.

14. Federal Writers' Project of the Works Progress Administration for the state of Florida, *The WPA Guide to Florida: The Federal Writers' Project Guide to 1930s Florida* (New York: Pantheon Books [1984] ca. 1939), 352.

15. Ibid. This WPA guide also features Savage as a notable native of Green Cove Springs, 352.

16. Savage, "Autobiography," 269, and Bearden and Henderson, "Augusta Savage," 78.

17. Charlton W. Tebeau, *A History of Florida* (Coral Gables, Fla.: University of Miami Press, 1971), 287.

18. Federal Writers' Project, *WPA Guide*, 314.

19. Ibid.

20. Eric D. Walrond, "Florida Girl Shows Amazing Gift for Sculpture," *The Negro World* (October 7, 1922): n.p.

21. Holland, "Augusta Christine Savage," 12.

22. Walrond, "Florida Girl."

23. The poem was published in Currie's book, *Songs of Florida* (publisher and date unknown), Walrond, "Florida Girl."

24. Walrond, "Florida Girl."

25. Smith, "Augusta Savage," 980.

26. "Courier Tintypes," 2:3 and Bearden and Henderson, "Augusta Savage," 80.

27. Tebeau, *A History of Florida*, 341.

28. Federal Writers' Project, *WPA Guide*, 185.

29. Ibid., 186.

30. Lester A. Walton, "Negro Girl Gets Fund to Study Abroad: Prize Winner, Thwarted for Years, Will Now Go to Rome," publication unknown (ca. 1929). n.p. Clipping in SCRBC.

31. Savage, "Autobiography," 269.

32. Walton, "Negro Girl," n.p.

33. Ibid. It seems as though Savage left her daughter in Florida when she first moved to New York.

34. Walrond, "Florida Girl."

35. Janet A. Flint, *Solon H. Borglum, 1868–1922* (Washington, D.C.: National Collection of Fine Arts, Smithsonian Institution, 1972), n.p.

36. Walrond, "Florida Girl" and A. Mervyn Davies, *Solon H. Borglum: A Man Who Stands Alone* (Chester, Conn.: Pequot Press, 1974): 223.

37. Walrond, "Florida Girl."

38. Davies, *Solon Borglum*, 241.

39. Walrond, "Florida Girl."

40. Ibid.

41. Ibid.

42. Eugene Kinckle Jones, "Miss Augusta Savage" [a three-page, unpublished biographical summary] (November 11, 1928), RA/FU.

43. "Appeal Artists' Race Ban," *New York Times*, May 11, 1923, 17.

44. Savage, "Autobiography," 269.

45. Savage apparently attended night school for two winters. Jones, "Miss Augusta Savage," 2.

46. Walrond, "Florida Girl."

47. Frederick Dielman, Director of Cooper Union, to Du Bois (May 4, 1923), DP/LC.

48. Brewster exhibited *David avant le combat* at the Salon of 1884. Fink, 324.

49. Falk, *Annual Exhibition Record of the National Academy of Design*, 100.

50. *Who Was Who in American Art*, 76.

51. Walrond, "Florida Girl."

52. Ibid.

53. The work is reproduced in profile in Bearden and Henderson, *History of African-American Artists*, 171. The information regarding Garvey's sittings for Savage is in a letter from Amy Jacques Garvey to the authors (October 1,1970), 496.

54. *Negro World* (January 20, 1923), n.p.

55. "In order to come to New York to study, she had to break all relations with her family." Jones, "Miss Augusta Savage," 1.

56. Savage, "Supplication" (November 11, 1922), n.p. and "Rebellion," *Negro World*, n.d..

57. Eric D. Walrond, "My Version of It," *Negro World*, March 31, 1923, 4.

58. On the committee were Whitney Warren, Ernest C. Peixotto, President of the National Academy of Design Edwin Blashfield, Howard Greenley, Thomas Hastings, Herman MacNeil, and President of Beaux-Arts Architecture James Gamble Rogers. Savage, "Autobiography," 269.

59. "Famous Artists Draw Color Line against Student," Negro World, April 5, 1923, 3.

60. "Famous Artists," 3, and "Negress Denied Entry to French Art School," *New York Times*, April 24, 1923, 8:2.

61. A native of San Francisco, Peixotto was one of California's most accomplished painters. After study in Paris, he published *Our Hispanic Southwest* and *Romantic California* (dates unknown). Peixotto was also a muralist and did illustrations for *Harper's* and *Scribner's*. Doris Ostrander Dawdy, *Arts of the American West: A Biographical Dictionary*, vol. 1 (Chicago: Swallow Press, 1980), 179.

62. William A. Byrd, "The Color-Line in Art," *New York World*, April 30, 1923, n.p. and Peixotto to Ernestine Rose (April 23, 1923), DP/LC.

63. "Famous Artists," 3.

64. Peixotto to Rose (April 23, 1923), DP/LC.

65. "Harding Asked to Intercede," in "Exclusion Case," *New York World*, May 10, 1923, n.p.

66. Du Bois to Greenley, Hewlett, Peixotto, etc. (May 3, 1923), DP/LC.

67. Rogers to Du Bois (May 4, 1923), DP/LC.

68. Hewlett to Du Bois (May 29, 1923), DP/LC.

69. Hastings to Du Bois (June 7, 1923), DP/LC.

70. MacNeil to Du Bois (May 8, 1923), DP/LC.

71. Kathleen Jones and Sylvia Yount, "Chronology," in Dewey Mosby, Darrell Sewell, and rae Alexander-Mintner, *Henry Ossawa Tanner* (Philadelphia Museum of Art, 1991), 38.

72. "Augusta Savage Gets Fellowship," *New York Amsterdam News*, May 29, 1929, n.p. and Savage to Arthur (April 19, 1929), RA/FU.

73. MacNeil exhibited *M. le docteur E . . .*, a bust in plaster, at the Salon of 1890. Fink, 369.

74. For example, MacNeil received the Rinehart Scholarship for study in Rome in 1895 for *The Sun Vow* (1895), a sculpture of a seated, older Native American man watching the trajectory of an arrow shot by a young boy. The work received the silver medal at the 1900 Paris Exposition.

75. Cleveland G. Allen, "Miss Augusta Savage," *Opportunity* 1 (June, 1923): 25.

76. "Appeal Artists' Race Ban," *New York Times*, May 11, 1923, 17.

77. Bearden and Henderson, "Augusta Savage," 87.

78. Franz Boas to Peixotto, as quoted in "Harding Asked to Intercede in Exclusion Case," *New York World*, May 10, 1923, n.p.

79. "Negro Divine Raps Ban on Girl Artist," journal unknown, n.d., n.p., clipping in SCRBC.

80. Savage, "Augusta Savage on Negro Ideals," *New York World*, May 20, 1923, n.p.

81. Ibid.

82. "Protest Ban on Negro Student," journal unknown, n.d., n.p., clipping in SCRBC.

83. Tony Martin, *African Fundamentalism: A Literary and Cultural Anthology of Garvey's Harlem Renaissance* (Dover, Mass.: Majority Press, 1991), 352.

84. Robert L. Poston, "The Reason Why I Accepted the Garvey Program," *Negro World*, May 12, 1923, 4.

85. "Personalia: Lady Augusta Savage, the Wife of Our Late Secretary-General Sir Robert Lincoln Poston," *Negro World*, July 19, 1923, 12.

86. "Personal," *Negro World*, September 13, 1924, 13.

87. Conversation between Gwendolyn Knight and Hope Finkelstein (July 9, 1989). As quoted in Finkelstein, "Augusta Savage: Sculpting the African-American Identity" (M.A. thesis, City University of New York, 1990), 14.

88. Finkelstein, "Augusta Savage," 8. Unfortunately, the author did not indicate her source.

89. Savage, "Autobiography," 269.

90. Savage to Du Bois (April 11, 1925), DP/LC.

91. Savage to Du Bois (May, 7, 1926), DP/LC.

92. Du Bois to Savage (May 12, 1926), DP/LC.

93. Jones, "Miss Augusta Savage," 2.

94. Savage to Du Bois (May 7, 1926), DP/LC.

95. *Fire!!* 1, no. 1 (November 1926): 35.

96. Frances Winwar, *Ruotolo, Man and Artist* (New York: Liveright, 1949), 10–13.

97. "Artist Who Has Made Portrait Bust of Edison Says American Art Needs Government Backing," *New York Evening Post*, March 4, 1920, n.p.

98. Ruotolo to Jones (December 27, 1929), RA/FU.

99. Savage to Arthur (April 19, 1929), RA/FU.

100. Salemme's work at the AIC in 1930 was *Negro Spiritual*. Falk, *The Annual Exhibition Record of the Art Institute of Chicago, 1888–1950* (Chicago: Sound View Press), 781.

101. *Antonio Salemme* (New York: Robert Schoelkopf, 1964): n.p.

102. "Creator of Art," *Chicago Defender*, March 12, 1927.

103. Jones, "Miss Augusta Savage," 3.

104. Nell Occomy, "Who Is Who," *New York News*, June 1, 1929.

105. Glorida Jahoda, *Florida: A Bicentennial History* (New York: W. W. Norton, 1976), 86. The institute later became Bethune-Cookman College.

106. Charles Richards reported, "Some of the work of this group shows surprising talent and is a very high tribute to Miss Savage's fine instruction." Richards to Embree (May 8, 1929), RA/FU.

107. Savage to Keppel (January 8, 1931), RA/FU.

108. "Social Snapshot," *The Inter-state Tattler*, October 19, 1928, 4.

109. As quoted in David Levering Lewis, *When Harlem Was in Vogue* (New York: Oxford University Press, 1989), 169.

110. Ibid.

111. Lewis, *African American Art and Artists*, 168.

112. Walton, "Negro Girl."

113. Jones, "Miss Augusta Savage," 3.

114. "Sculptress Commissioned to Do Group," *Norfolk Journal and Guide*, October 19, 1929 and Savage, "Autobiography," 269.

115. *Norfolk Journal and Guide*, October 19, 1929, n.p. and Walton, "Negro Girl."

116. Jones, "Miss Augusta Savage," 3.

117. Jones, "Miss Augusta Savage," 3. It is not clear whether Savage's father died in January 1928 or 1929. While Jones's statement is dated in November 1928, the note about the death appears to be a postscript, which suggests that he died in 1929.

118. Jones to Keppel (March 25, 1929), RA/FU.

119. Keppel to Savage (April 15, 1929), RA/FU.

120. Beryl J. Wright, "The Harmon Foundation in Context: Early Exhibitions and Alain Locke's Concept of a Racial Idiom of Expression," in Reynolds and Wright, *Against the Odds*, 15.

121. Savage to Arthur (April 19, 1929), RA/FU.

122. Lewis, *African American Art and Artists*, 247.

123. Ibid., 169.

124. As implied in a letter from Jones to Arthur (April 19, 1929), RA/FU.

125. Salvatore also won a bronze medal at the Saint Louis Exposition in 1904, and exhibited two sculptures at the Armory Show in 1913. "Victor Salvatore, Veteran Sculptor," *New York Herald Tribune*, April 13, 1965, n.p. and "Victor Salvatore, Sculptor, Is Dead," *New York Times*, April 12, 1965, 35.

126. Richards to Embree (May 8, 1929), RA/FU.

127. Regenia A. Perry, *Free Within Ourselves: African-American Artists in the Collection of the National Museum of American Art* (San Francisco: Pomegranate Artbooks, 1992), 157.

128. Richards to Embree (May 8, 1929), RA/FU.

129. Savage, "Autobiography," 269.

130. Du Bois to Savage (August 12, 1929), DP/LC.

131. Du Bois to Savage (August 27, 1929), DP/LC.

132. Walton, "Negro Girl."

133. "Sculptress Commissioned to Do Group," n.p. and Walton, "Negro Girl."

134. "Sculptress Commissioned to Do Group."

135. Deirdre L. Bibby, *Augusta Savage and the Art Schools of Harlem* (New York: Schomburg Center for Research in Black Culture, New York Public Library, 1988), 27. Apparently, Savage had begun telling people she was younger than she actually was as soon as she came to New York; in 1922 she told Walrond she was twenty-one years old. In 1928, she persisted in the fib by telling Jones she was about twenty-seven. Jones, "Miss Augusta Savage," 1.

136. Savage to Du Bois (September 22, 1929), DP/LC.

137. Ibid.

138. Ibid.

139. Bénézit, 627.

140. Benneteau[-Desgrois] to Rosenwald Foundation (November 1, 1929), RA/FU.

141. Savage to Arthur (June 15, 1930), RA/FU.

142. Hans Vollmer, compiler, *Allgemeines Lexikon der bildenden Künstler des XX. Jahrhunderts* (Leipzig: E. A. Seemann, 1953), 285.

143. Savage did not indicate the nature of the relationship, and since the school does not have records dating back to the time, it is not possible to verify the information. Savage, Rosenwald review form (March 18, 1936), RA/FU.

144. Isadora Duncan, *The Art of the Dance* (New York: Theatre Arts Books, 1977), 90.

145. Fabre, *From Harlem to the Seine*, 136–137.

146. Ibid., 102–103.

147. Stoelting, "Hale Woodruff, Artist and Teacher," 47.

148. Duncan, *The Art of the Dance*, 91.

149. Paulette Nardal, "Une femme sculpteur noire," *La dépêche africaine* (August–September, 1930): 4.

150. *Danseur nu* was no. 3963. *Catalogue du Salon, Société des Artistes Français* (Paris: Imprimerie Georges Lang, 1931), 204.

151. Nardal, "Une femme sculpteur noire," 3. My translation.

152. Stovall, *Paris Noir,* 60.

153. Powell, *Black Art and Culture in the Twentieth Century,* 59–60.

154. Nardal wrote, "Augusta Savage dealt in the round with a series of busts of the Amazons [the people], with whom history seems obsessed." "Une femme sculpteur noire," 4. My translation.

155. Hugh Honour, *The Image of the Black in Western Art,* vol. 4, *From the American Revolution to World War I,* part 2 (Cambridge: Harvard University Press, 1989), 166.

156. "The rear he composed of a great number of women, armed like soldiers, having their proper officers, and furnished like regular troops, with drums, colours, and umbrellas, making at a distance a very formidable appearance." Archibald Dalzel, *The History of Dahomey, an Inland Kingdom of Africa, Compiled From Authentic Memoirs* (1793) (London: Frank Cass, 1967), 55.

157. Ibid., reprint London, 1967, opp. p. 54.

158. Stanley B. Alpern, *Amazons of Black Sparta: The Women Warriors of Dahomey* (New York: New York University Press, 1998), 11.

159. Ibid., 27.

160. Richard F. Burton, *A Mission to Gelele, King of Dahome,* ed. C. W. Newbury (New York, 1966), 111, quoted in Alpern, *Amazons,* 37.

161. Alpern, *Amazons,* 47, 73.

162. Ibid., 11–12.

163. Ibid., 12, 68.

164. Ibid., 8.

165. Ibid., 34. For further documentation of beheadings, see also 45, 65, 77, 103,107, 172, 177, 194, 195.

166. Arthur to Savage (May 28, 1930), RA/FU.

167. Savage to Arthur (June 15, 1930), RA/FU.

168. Ibid.

169. Published in Nardal, "Une femme sculpteur noire," 3.

170. Ibid.

171. Locke, "The Legacy of the Ancestral Arts," in *The New Negro,* 267.

172. "Noted Sculptress Expects Distinct, But Not Different, Racial Art," *Pittsburgh Courier,* August 29, 1936, 1:5.

173. Du Bois to Savage (October 9, 1929), DP/LC.

174. Michel Fabre and John A. Williams, *Way B(l)ack Then and Now: A Street Guide to African Americans in Paris.* (Paris: Centre d'Etudes Afro-Américaines, Université de la Sorbonne Nouvelle, 1992): 134–135.

175. New York World's Fair, Inc. News Release No. 226, 3, SCRBC, as noted in Finkelstein, "Augusta Savage," 22.

176. Bearden and Henderson, *History of African-American Artists,* 173.

177. For more information on Afro-latinité in *La revue du monde noir,* see chapter 7 in Philippe Dewitte, *Les mouvements nègres en France, 1919–1939* (Paris: Edition l'Harmattan, 1985). See also Catherine Bernard, "Confluence: Harlem Renaissance, Modernism, and Négritude: Paris in the 1920s–1930s," in *Explorations in the City of Light: African-American Artists in Paris, 1945–1965* (New York: Studio Museum in Harlem, 1996): 21–27, for more information on France's proto-Négritude movement, especially via the literary world.

178. Fabre, *From Harlem to Paris,* 151.

179. Paulette Nardal and Jeanne Nardal, "Our Aim," *La revue du monde noir* 1 (n.d.): 4.

180. Nardal, "Une femme sculpteur noire," 3. My translation.

181. Savage's *Homme* is listed as no. 1814 in the *Société du Salon d'Automne: Catalogue des ouvrages de peinture, sculpture, dessin, gravure, architecture et art décoratif* (Paris: Imprimerie Ernest Puyfourcat fils & Cie., 1930), 281. Savage's name is erroneously spelled Sauvage. The work is clearly by her, however;

the artist is listed as an American born in Florida who resides at 3, impasse d'Astrolabe. Savage stated that she had three works accepted in this salon, but the catalog only lists *Homme*. Savage to Dorothy A. Elridge (September 30, 1930), RA/FU.

182. Title unknown, *Chicago Whip* (August 15, 1931): n.p. (hereafter *Chicago Whip*), states that *Martiniquaise* appeared in the Salon d'Automne.

183. Savage to Dorothy Elridge (September 30, 1930), RA/FU.

184. Bearden and Henderson, *History of African-American Artists,* 180 and T. R. Poston, "Augusta Savage," *Metropolitan,* January 1935, 29.

185. "To Sculpture Group for World's Fair," *New York Times,* December 9, 1937, 2:6.

186. Location unknown; see *Art Digest* April 15, 1935, 19 for reproduction.

187. See, for example, the leaping gazelles and antelopes in Frederick Carder's architectural glass grille (1930s), René Buthaud's earthenware vase (1920s), in which the animal is paired with a nude black woman labeled "Afrique", and Paul Manship's *Pronghorn Antelope* sculpture (ca. 1914), in Alastair Duncan, *Art Deco* (New York: Thames and Hudson, 1988), 99, 105, 139.

188. Poston, 29.

189. As noted in Finkelstein, "Augusta Savage," 22.

190. Notes written on contact sheet, negative 1060e, Federal Art Service Project, SCRBC.

191. "Sculptress Commissioned to Do Group" states that Ratton, "director of the non-existant [*sic*] Trocadero in Paris," owned the piece. Ratton, however, was never director of the museum. I verified the work as belonging to him in the spring of 1991; the daughter of the dealer who acquired Ratton's estate after his death now has the work.

192. Jean-Louis Paudrat, *"From Africa," "Primitivism" in Twentieth Century Art,* vol. 1 (New York: Museum of Modern Art, 1984), 162–164.

193. Finkelstein, "Augusta Savage," 21; Bearden and Henderson, *History of African-American Artists,* 172.

194. Fabre and Williams, *Way B(l)ack Then and Now,* 118.

195. Savage to Cullen (February 27, 1931), CCP/ARC.

196. Savage to Keppel (January 8, 1931), RA/FU.

197. *Baltimore Afro-American,* February 14, 1931,: n.p.

198. Embree to Keppel (March 13, 1931), RA/FU.

199. Savage to Keppel (March 23, 1931), RA/FU.

200. Savage to Arthur (April 14, 1931), RA/FU.

201. *Catalogue du Salon, Société des Artistes Français* (Paris: Imprimerie Georges Lang, 1931), 204.

202. Savage to Keppel (April 23, 1931), RA/FU.

203. Savage to Embree (May 1, 1931), RA/FU.

204. Arthur to Savage (May 18, 1931), RA/FU.

205. Savage to Arthur (October 19, 1931), RA/FU.

206. Holland, "Augusta Christine Savage," 15–17.

207. RA/FU.

208. Porter, *Modern Negro Art* (New York: Arno Press, 1969), 139, 138.

7 ALBERT ALEXANDER SMITH

1. Statement by Alfred Renforth Smith to the Harmon Foundation, ca. 1929, HFP/LC.

2. In Smith's letter to Gladys E. Flynn (January 6, 1926), he asks her to give his kindest regards to his "many friends, Gladys and Lolita Fernandez among them." GC/CU.

3. Ibid.

4. Allen G. Cleveland, "Our Young Artists," *Opportunity* (June 1924): 24.

5. Alfred Renforth Smith, Statement to the Harmon Foundation, ca. 1929, HFP/LC.

6. James Lesesne Wells, who would also become a distinguished printmaker, would attend the National Academy of Design, ca. 1919–1921, followed by William Henry Johnson, 1921–1926. Reynolds and Wright, *Against the Odds*, 217, 267.

7. "Our Young Artists," 24.

8. Alfred Renforth Smith, ca. 1929. Also, "Our Young Artists," 24, which, however, reports that Smith won the Suydam Bronze Medal in the still life, rather than the antique, class.

9. Alfred Renforth Smith, ca. 1929. However, an untitled article states that Smith was abroad for one year. *Opportunity*, 1940, 208.

10. For more information on African American soldiers in World War I, see W. Allison Sweeney, *History of the American Negro in the Great World War* (Chicago: Cuneo-Henneberry, 1919); Arthur E. Barbeau and Florette Henri, *The Unknown Soldiers: Black American Troops in World War I* (Philadelphia: Temple University Press, 1974); Charles Williams, *Sidelights on Negro Soldiers* (Boston: B. J. Brimmer, 1923); P. J. Carisella and James W. Ryan, *The Black Swallow of Death* (Boston: Marlborough House, 1972); and Tyler Stovall, "Freedom Overseas: African American Soldiers Fight the Great War," in *Paris Noir*, 1–24.

11. *Crisis,* February 1920, 230.

12. "Our Young Artists," 24.

13. The Chaloner prize, called the Paris Prize Scholarship, formally established in 1919 and first awarded to John Ferris Connah on a biennial basis in 1921, was founded by John Armstrong Chaloner in 1890 to help Americans study art abroad. Originally, it offered $900 a year for five years for the support of an art student in Paris. In 1919, students who wished to compete for the Paris prize had to first win a monthly competition, each month of the school year of eight months, in drawing, painting, and composition. The competition was open to all American art students of either sex under thirty years of age, whether abroad or in the United States. A first prize of $25, a second prize of $15, a third prize of $10, and an honorable mention made up what became known as the Chaloner Concours. Smith won a first prize for painting during the season 1919–1920, but he did not win a major prize. The concours was eliminated in 1923–1924. Box 113 of 131, American Academy in Rome papers, Archives of American Art, Smithsonian Institution.

14. Leslie King-Hammond, "Black Printmakers and the W.P.A.," in *Alone in a Crowd: Prints of the 1930s by African American Artists from the Collection of Reba and Dave Williams*, 2d ed. (New York: Reba and Dave Williams, 1993), 16.

15. Reynolds and Wright, *Against the Odds*, 183, 285.

16. David R. Brigham, "Bridging Identities: Dox Thrash as African American and Artist," *Smithsonian Studies in American Art* 4, no. 2 (Spring 1990): 27–39. See also *Alone in a Crowd*, 4–5, 13–14, 55–56.

17. This latter is prevalent in a long tradition of nineteenth-century American art that depicted African American musicians. Examples include John Lewis Krimmel, *Quilting Frolic* (1813), William Sidney Mount, *Rustic Dance after a Sleigh Ride* (1830), Charles Winter, *Minstrel Show* (ca. 1830s–1840s), and Eastman Johnson, *Fiddling His Way* (1866).

18. "'Plantation Melodies,' an etching reproduced some time ago in the BROWNIES' BOOK, won for him the second prize [at the National Academy of Design] in 1918." "Our Young Artists," *Opportunity* (June, 1923): 24. However, according to a librarian at the Moorland-Spingarn Research Center, Howard University, neither a reproduction of *Plantation Melodies* nor a mention of it winning any prize appears in any of the *Brownies Book Magazine* (s), which existed only from 1920 to 1921.

19. *Crisis* (November 1920): 17.

20. *Crisis* (March 1920): 264.

21. Smith wrote that "Curran's artistic animosity dates back to my school days" when he dropped Curran's classes to take a better teacher. Smith to George Haynes (April 1, 1929). HFP/LC.

22. Harmon Foundation summary report, ca. 1940, HFP/LC.

23. Elinor Des Verney Sinnette, *Arthur Alfonso Schomburg, Black Bibliophile and Collector: A Biography* (Detroit: New York Public Library and Wayne State University Press, 1989), 69.

24. Arthur Schomburg to George Haynes (September 2, 1929), HFP/LC.

25. Ibid. Several sources also indicate that Smith also exhibited his works at the Paris Salon of 1921 (e.g., Guggenheim application, 1929, LC), but exhibition catalogs at the National Gallery of Art, Washington, D.C., show do not confirm this.

26. The following works were shown at the Tanner Art League: *The Market Place—Nice, Plantation Melodies, Study, Harmony, Fish Market, The Thinker, The Fair—Luxembourg, Mr. Hill, Bridgeport—Luxembourg*, and *Ship Building*. *Catalogue of the Third Annual Exhibition of the Tanner Art League* (Washington, D.C.: Dunbar High School, 1922), n.p. It is unknown which work won the award.

27. Statement to the Guggenheim Foundation, 1929. Manuscript Division/LC.

28. Fabre, *From Harlem to Paris*, 148.

29. Smith to Du Bois (February 3, 1921), DP/LC.

30. Sinnette, *Arthur Alfonso Schomburg*, 69.

31. Ibid., 92–93.

32. See, for example, reproductions in Kenneth E. Silver, *Esprit de Corps: The Art of the Parisian Avant-Garde and the First World War, 1914–1925* (Princeton, N.J.: Princeton University Press, 1989), 95–103.

33. Stovall, *Paris Noir*, 39.

34. Ibid., 47.

35. Ibid., 39.

36. Ibid., 47.

37. Joel Augustus Rogers, "The Boulevard de Clichy," in "The Paris Pepper Pot," *Pittsburgh Courier*, July 27, 1929, n.p., as quoted in Stovall, *Paris Noir*, 48.

38. It is not clear whether Maréchal taught at the Académie des Beaux-Arts in Liège. While well-respected during his time, it seems that Maréchal has not been the subject of much study outside of Belgium. No articles on him are present in the *Art Index* after 1984. His death date is not given in either Thieme-Becker or Bénézit.

39. Ulrich Thieme and Felix Becker, Hrsg., *Allgemeines Lexikon der bildenden Künstler von der Antike bis zur Gegenwart unter Mitwirkung von 300 Sachgelehrten des In- und Auslandes*, vol. 24 (Leipzig: W. Engelmann, 1907–50), 81.

40. Judith Wilson, "Will the 'New Internationalism' Be the Same Old Story? Some Art Historical Considerations," in Jean Fisher, ed., *Global Visions: Towards a New Internationalism in the Arts* (London: Kala, 1994), 68.

41. Sanford J. Ungar. *Africa: The People and Politics of an Emerging Continent* (New York: Simon & Schuster, 1986), 48.

42. David Levering Lewis, *When Harlem Was in Vogue* (New York: Oxford University Press, 1981), 7–8.

43. Wilson, "Will the 'New Internationalism,'" 69.

44. Abby Arthur Johnson and Ronald Maberry Johnson, *Propaganda and Aesthetics: The Literary Politics of African American Magazines in the Twentieth Century* (Amherst: University of Massachusetts Press, 1991), 35.

45. Ibid.

46. Du Bois, "Criteria of Negro Art," *Crisis* 32 (October, 1926): 296.

47. Johnson and Johnson, *Propaganda and Aesthetics*, 48.

48. Ibid., 49.

49. Ibid., 56, 63.

50. *Crisis* (June 1925): 76.

51. *Crisis* (February 1924): 169.

52. *Crisis* (November 1924): front cover.

53. "The Horizon," *Crisis* (September 1924): 215–216.

54. Guggenheim application statement, 1929. Manuscript Division/LC.

55. For a fuller discussion of Jennings's painting, see Albert Boime, *The Art of Exclusion: Representing Blacks in the Nineteenth Century* (Washington, D.C.: Smithsonian Institution Press, 1990), 21.

56. The Pont-Neuf, one of Paris's oldest bridges, was a popular subject with countless artists. Smith may have taken a particular interest in the site, too (as well as in rivers other than the Seine, such as the Tiber), because his professor, François Maréchal, was also noted for his etchings of the foggy Meuse River in Belgium. This work was exhibited by the Society of Independent Artists, along with *Puerta de Toledo, Spain,* in 1929.

57. *Crisis* (February 1927): 207.

58. "I want to welcome [Mother] properly, royally. In Paris, I have a three piece apartment that I keep always, so that if she came off the boat to-morrow, she could rest her head in a place called home." Smith to Gladys E. Flynn (January 6, 1926), GC/CU.

59. Harmon application, 1928, HFP/LC.

60. Among these shows was a solo exhibition of paintings of European sights at the New York Public Library, October 1–December 1, 1928. The cover of the two-page catalog states that the event was held "under the supervision of his father ALFRED RENFORTH SMITH." *Exhibitions* [*sic*] *of Paintings of France, Italy, and Spain* (New York: Public Library, 1928).

61. It is not known for certain that the French writer saw this exhibition. However, that is where *The Wrestler* and *Southern Symphony* were exhibited that year.

62. As reported in "The Horizon," *Crisis* (January 1926): 131. Smith seemed proud of this review. He wrote, "Now, artistically, I have not declined, neither in my ability or in my aims. French magazines have given me space, to the extent of a page in their publics [*sic*] eye." Smith to Flynn (January 6, 1926), GC/CU.

63. As translated in "Negro Artists," *Crisis* (December 1926): 107. I have been unable to locate the original French article.

64. See, for example, *La Revue Moderne* 30, no. 1 (15 janvier 1930): 22–23; 33, no. 1 (15 janvier 1933): 18–19; and 34, no. 18 (30 septembre 1934): 12–13.

65. Smith to Gladys E. Flynn (January 6, 1926), GC/CU.

66. Smith to Gladys E. Flynn (June 3, 1926), GC/CU.

67. Rose Henderson, "Exhibit of Painting and Sculpture by Negro Artists," *Southern Workman,* April, 1929, 166–167.

68. Reynolds and Wright, *Against the Odds,* 33, 286, 287.

69. Alfred Renforth Smith. Statement to the Harmon Foundation, ca. 1929, HFP/LC.

70. Smith to Schomburg (July 12, 1933), SCRBC.

71. As quoted in Stovall, *Paris Noir,* 48.

72. Jean McGleughlin, "Albert Alexander Smith," *Oppportunity* 18 (July 1940), 208. I have been unable to locate the *Arts and Archeology* reproduction.

73. Jeffrey C. Stewart, "Paul Robeson and the Problem of Modernism," in *Rhapsodies in Black,* 95.

74. Claude McKay, *Banjo: A Story without a Plot* (New York: Harcourt Brace Jovanovich, 1957), 90.

75. Karen Linn, *That Half-Barbaric Twang: The Banjo in American Popular Culture* (Urbana: University of Illinois Press, 1991): 53.

76. Stewart, "Paul Robeson," 95.

77. Smith called his companion "Madame Smith" in a letter to Lois Mailou Jones (December 25, 1938). AAA, SI microfilm roll 4371. However, Fevrier is listed as a friend in Report of the Death of an American Citizen (April 26, 1940), National Archives.

78. "I'm up here on the Normandie coast on my vacation. Whole family and dog. The Madame will be here at the seashore for two months." Smith to Lois Mailou Jones (August 13, 1939), AAA/SI.

79. Smith to his parents (January 7, 1935), HFP/LC. While it seems that Smith did not always identify himself as African American because his parents were West Indian, his usage of derogatory terms for African Americans may have been at times disparaging and at times affectionate, just as he alternately eschewed and embraced the term "son of Ham."

80. Smith to Lois Mailou Jones (December 25, 1938), microfilm roll 4371, AAA/SI.

81. Smith to Schomburg (April 18, 1931), SCRBC.

82. Smith to George E. Haynes (April 1, 1929), HFP/LC.

83. Memorandum to Smith from the Federal Council of Church of Christ in America (December 17, 1930), HFP/LC.

84. Smith also seems to have done some illustrations for a periodical by the American Legion; "I have made another sketch for a page-illustration for the editor." Smith to his parents (January 7, 1935), HFP/LC.

85. The other works included in this exhibition were the paintings *Friends, The Martyr, and Bilbas, Spain* (latter two works missing) and the lithographs *Down Home* and *Black and White*. Henderson found the latter work "agreeably sophisticated in pattern and point of view." Rose Henderson, "American Negro Exhibit at International House," *Southern Workman* (April, 1930): 167. Henderson might have also been referring to the painting *Friends*. About this work, the *New York Herald Tribune* commented: "Smith . . . has produced some pictures that reveal a keen appreciation of the spirit and aspirations of his race. Although his paintings are, for the most part, glossily suggestive of the old chromes of the 'God Bless Our Home' variety, they portray a quaintness of character which is perhaps best conveyed through that medium. His 'Friends,' a group portrait that includes two rural Negro men, a bright-eyed pickaninny holding a bunch of daisies, and a litter of puppies, is a vivid scene that would touch the heart of any Southerner." "News and Exhibitions of the Week in Art," *New York Herald Tribune* 7, January 12, 1930, 11. As quoted in Reynolds and Wright, *Against the Odds,* 112.

86. Smith, application to Guggenheim Foundation (1934), HFP/LC.

87. Summary in the Harmon Foundation files, HFP/LC.

88. Harmon Foundation summary report, ca. 1940, HFP/LC. I have been unable to find albums that Smith may have recorded with others.

89. Clement Morro, "Albert Smith," *La revue moderne illustreé des arts et de la vie* 38, no. 13 (15 juillet 1938): 14. Translation by the author.

90. Smith to Jones (July 19, 1939), microfilm roll 4371, AAA/SI..

91. Smith to Jones (August 13, 1939), AAA/SI.

92. Smith to Jones (December 25, 1938), AAA/SI.

93. Smith to Schomburg (October 12, 1939), SCRBC.

94. Smith to Lois Mailou Jones (August 13, 1939), AAA/SI.

95. Smith to Schomburg (May 3, 1938), SCRBC.

CONCLUSION

1. Catherine Bernard, "Confluence: Harlem Renaissance, Modernism, and Négritude: Paris in the 1920s–1930s," in *Explorations in the City of Light,* 25.

2. Valerie J. Mercer, *Explorations in the City of Light,* 40. See also 41–45.

3. For instance, a September 21, 1964, *Newsweek* article, "Negroes in Paris," states that there were fifteen hundred African Americans in the city at that time. In contrast, Stovall estimates that forty years earlier, in 1924, "the number of black Americans in Paris remained very small, probably no more than twenty-five or thirty individuals, virtually all musicians." Stovall, *Paris Noir,* 39.

4. Stovall, *Paris Noir,* 302, 303.

5. Locke, *The New Negro,* 16.

6. W.E.B. Du Bois, *The Souls of Black Folk,* reprinted in *Three Negro Classics* (New York: Avon Books, 1965), 216.

SELECTED BIBLIOGRAPHY

Please note: Every effort has been made to compile complete bibliographic information. Where page numbers are not indicated, the original citation was not found.

AFRICAN AMERICAN AND EUROPEAN-AMERICANS ABROAD

Alsop, Susan Mary. *Yankees at the Court: The First Americans in Paris.* Garden City, N.Y.: Doubleday, 1982.

Bainbridge, John. *Another Way of Living: A Gallery of Americans Who Choose to Live in Europe.* New York: Holt, Rinehart and Winston, 1968.

Benstock, Shari. *Women of the Left Bank: Paris, 1900–1940.* Austin: University of Texas Press, 1986.

Boyle, Kay, and Robert McAlmon. *Being Geniuses Together: A Binocular View of Paris in the Twenties.* Garden City, N.Y.: Doubleday, 1968.

Brinton, Crane. *The Americans and the French.* Cambridge: Harvard University Press, 1968.

Cleveland, Harlan, Gerard J. Mangone, and John Clarke Adams. *The Overseas Americans.* New York: McGraw-Hill, 1960.

"The Colored Americans in France." *Crisis* (February 1919): 167–168.

Cowley, Malcolm. *Exile's Return: A Literary Odyssey of the 1920s.* New York: W. W. Norton, 1934.

Cowley, Malcolm, and Robert Cowley. *Fitzgerald and the Jazz Age.* New York: Scribner Research Anthologies, 1966.

Crosby, Caresse. *The Passionate Years: An Autobiography.* New York: Dial Press, 1953.

Dulles, Foster Rhea. *Americans Abroad: Two Centuries of European Travel.* Ann Arbor: University of Michigan Press, 1964.

Dunbar, Ernest. *The Black Expatriates: A Study of American Negroes in Exile.* New York: E. P. Dutton, 1968.

Fabre, Michel. *From Harlem to Paris: Black American Writers in France, 1840–1980.* Urbana: University of Illinois Press, 1991.

———. *La rive noire: Le Harlem à la Seine.* Paris: Lieu Commun, 1985.

Fabre, Michel, and John A. Williams. *Way B(l)ack Then and Now: A Street Guide to African Americans in Paris.* Paris: Centre d'Études Afro-Américaines, Université de la Sorbonne Nouvelle, 1992.

Flanner, Janet. *An American in Paris: Profile of an Interlude between Two Wars.* New York: Simon and Schuster, 1940.

———. *Paris Was Yesterday 1925–1939*. Edited by Irving Drutman. New York: Viking Press, 1972.

Flanner, Janet, Virgil Thomson, Maria Jolas, Man Ray, John Levee, James Jones, and William Gardner Smith. "Then and Now, The Expatriate Tradition." *Paris Review* 34 (winter–spring 1965): 158–170.

Ford, Hugh. *Published in Paris: American and British Writers, Printers, and Publishers in Paris, 1920–1939*. New York: Macmillan, 1975.

———, ed. *Nancy Cunard: Brave Poet, Indomitable Rebel 1896–1965*. Philadelphia: Chilton, 1968.

The Franco-American Yearbook 1921. Paris: Edward Cantor, 1921.

Hansen, Marcus Lee. *The Atlantic Migration 1607–1860: A History of the Continuing Settlement of the United States*. Cambridge: Harvard University Press, 1951.

Huddleston, Sisley. *Back to Montparnasse: A Sequel to "Bohemian Literary and Social Life in Paris."* London: George G. Harrap, 1931.

Klüver, Billy and Julie Martin. *Kiki's Paris: Artists and Lovers 1900–1930*. New York: Harry N. Abrams, 1989.

Kreymbourg, Alfred. *Troubadour: An Autobiography*. New York: Liveright, 1925.

Laffont, Robert. *Man Ray: Autoportrait*. Translated from the English by Anne Guerin. Paris: Robert Laffont, 1964.

Lanoux, Armand. *Paris 1925*. Paris: Bernard Grasset, 1975.

Loeb, Harold. *The Way It Was*. New York: Criterion Books, 1959.

Longstreet, Stephen. *We All Went to Paris: Americans in the City of Light: 1776–1971*. New York: Macmillan, 1972.

Luhan, Mabel Dodge. *Intimate Memories*. Vol. 3, *Movers and Shakers*. New York: Harcourt, Brace, 1936.

Monnier, Adrienne. *The Very Rich Hours of Adrienne Monnier: An Intimate Portrait of the Literary and Artistic Life in Paris Between the Wars*. Translated by Richard McDougall. London: Millington Books, 1976.

Paris: Guide de la Rive Gauche. Publié sous le patronage des mairies des 6e, 7e, 14e, 15e Arrondissements. Paris: Prefecture de Police, 1931.

Paul, Elliot. *The Last Time I Saw Paris*. New York: Bantam Books, 1945.

Petit, Solange. *Les Américains de Paris*. Paris: Mouton, 1975.

Rumer, Thomas A. *The American Legion: An Official History, 1919–89*. New York: M. Evans, 1990.

Sellin, David. *Americans in Brittany and Normandy, 1860–1910*. Phoenix, Ariz.: Phoenix Art Museum, 1982.

Stebbins, Theodore E., Jr. *The Lure of Italy: American Artists and the Italian Experience 1760–1914*. New York: Harry N. Abrams, 1992.

Stovall, Tyler. *Paris Noir: African Americans in the City of Light*. New York: Houghton Mifflin, 1996.

Susman, Warren I. "Pilgrimage to Paris: The Backgrounds of American Expatriation, 1920–1934." Ph.D. diss., University of Wisconsin, 1958.

Turner, Elizabeth Hutton. *American Artists in Paris, 1919–1929*. Ann Arbor, Mich.: University Microfilms Incorporated Press, 1988.

Wilson, Robert Forrest. *Paris on Parade*. Indianapolis, Ind.: Bobbs-Merrill, 1925.

Wolff, Geoffroy. *Black Sun: The Brief Transit and Violent Eclipse of Harry Crosby*. New York: Random House, 1976.

AFRICAN AMERICAN ART HISTORY

Books

Bearden, Romare, and Harry Henderson. *A History of African-American Artists from 1792 to the Present*. New York: Pantheon Books, 1993.

Brawley, Benjamin. *The Negro Genius: A New Appraisal of the Achievement of the American Negro in Literature and the Fine Arts*. New York: Dodd, Mead, 1937.

Dover, Cedric. *American Negro Art.* New York: New York Graphic Society, 1970.

Fine, Elsa Honig. *The Afro-American Artist: A Search for Identity.* New York: Hacker Art Books, 1982.

Locke, Alain. *Negro Art: Past and Present.* New York: Arno Press, 1969.

———. *The Negro in Art: A Pictorial Record of the Negro Artist and of the Negro Theme in Art.* Washington, D.C.: Associates in Negro Folk Education, 1940; New York: Hacker Art Books, 1979.

Porter, James A. *Modern Negro Art.* 1943. Reprint, New York: Arno Press, 1969.

Salzman, Jack, ed. *Encyclopedia of African American Culture and History.* New York: Simon and Schuster Macmillan, 1996. Entries by Theresa Leininger-Miller: Aaron Douglas (vol. 2, 781–782), Meta Vaux Warrick Fuller (vol. 2, 1079–1081), William A. Harper (vol. 3, 1224–1225), Palmer Hayden (vol. 3, 1241), Augusta Savage (vol. 4, 2393–2394), and Albert Alexander Smith (vol. 4, 2491).

Willis, Deborah. *J. P. Ball: Daguerrean and Studio Photographer.* New York: Garland, 1993.

Exhibition Catalogs

Alone in a Crowd: Prints of the 1930s–40s by African-American Artists from the Collection of Reba and Dave Williams. New York: Washburn Press, 1993.

Bernard, Catherine. *Afro-American Artists in Paris: 1919–1939.* New York: Hunter College of the City University of New York, 1989.

Bontemps, Arna Alexander, and Jacqueline Fonvielle-Bontemps. *Forever Free: Art by African-American Women 1862–1980.* Alexandria, Va.: Stephenson, 1980.

Campbell, Mary Schmidt, et al. *Harlem Renaissance: Art of Black America.* New York: Studio Museum in Harlem and Harry N. Abrams, 1987.

Catalogue of the Third Annual Exhibition of the Tanner Art League. Washington, D.C.: Dunbar High School, 1922.

Driskell, David. *Hidden Heritage: Afro-American Art, 1800–1950.* San Francisco: Art Museums Association of America, 1987.

———. *Two Centuries of Black American Art.* Los Angeles: Los Angeles County Museums of Art, 1976.

Edward Mitchell Bannister, 1828–1901. New York: Kenkeleba House, 1992.

Explorations in the City of Light: African-American Artists in Paris, 1945–1965. New York: Studio Museum in Harlem, 1996.

Gelburd, Gail. *A Blossoming of New Promises: Art in the Spirit of the Harlem Renaissance.* Hempstead, N.Y.: Hofstra University, 1984.

Hartigan, Lynda Roscoe. *Sharing Traditions: Five Black American Artists in Nineteenth Century America.* Washington, D.C.: National Museum of American Art, 1985.

Henry O. Tanner, William A. Harper, William E. Scott: A Mentor and His Influence. Washington, D.C.: Evans-Tibbs Collection, 1985.

Leininger, Theresa. "The Transatlantic Tradition: African-American Artists in Paris, 1830–1940." In Asake Bomani and Belvie Rooks, eds., *Paris Connections: African American Artists in Paris.* San Francisco: Q.E.D. Press, 1992, 9–23. Translated by Lydia Rand as "La Tradition Transatlantique: Les Artistes Africains Américains à Paris, 1830–1940," 24–37.

McElroy, Goy C. *Facing History: The Black Image in American Art, 1710–1940.* San Francisco: Bedford Arts, 1990.

Perry, Regenia A. *Selections of Nineteenth-Century Afro-American Art.* New York: Metropolitan Museum of Art, 1976.

Powell, Richard J., et al. *The Blues Aesthetic: Black Culture and Modernism.* Washington, D.C.: Washington Project for the Arts, 1989.

———. *Rhapsodies in Black: Art of the Harlem Renaissance.* Berkeley and Los Angeles: University of California Press, 1997.

Reynolds, Gary R., and Beryl J. Wright. *Against the Odds: African-American Artists and the Harmon Foundation 1923–43.* Newark, N.J.: Newark Museum, 1989.

Taylor, William E. and Harriet G. Warkel. *A Shared Heritage: Art by Four African Americans.* Indianapolis, Ind.: Indianapolis Museum of Art, 1996.

Wright, John S. *A Stronger Soul Within a Finer Frame: Portraying African-Americans in the Black Renaissance.* Minneapolis: University of Minnesota, 1990.

Articles

Barnes, Albert C. "Negro Art and America." *Survey Graphic* 6 (March 1925): 668–669.

———. "Negro Art: Past and Present." *Opportunity* 4, no. 21 (May 1926): 148–149, 168–169.

Bearden, Romare. "The Negro Artist and Modern Art." *Opportunity* 12, no. 12 (December 1934): 371–372.

Brady, Patricia. "Black Artists in Antebellum New Orleans." *Louisiana History* 32, no. 1 (winter 1991): 5–28.

———. "Free Men of Color as Tomb Builders in the Nineteenth Century," unpublished manuscript, early 1990s.

Brigham, David R. "Bridging Identities: Dox Thrash as African American and Artist." *Smithsonian Studies in American Art* 4, no. 2 (spring 1990): 27–39.

Du Bois, W.E.B. "Criteria of Negro Art." *Crisis* (May 1926): 290–297.

———. "Opinion of W.E.B. Du Bois: In Black." *Crisis* (October 1920): 263–264.

Evans, Sally Kittridge. "Free Persons of Color." In Roulhac Toledano, Sally Kittridge Evans, and Mary Louise Christovich, eds., *New Orleans Architecture,* Vol. 4, *The Creole Faubourgs,* 25–36. New Orleans, La.: Pelican, 1974.

"Exhibit Raises Question Whether Negro Should Paint 'White.'" *Art Digest* (15 February 1931): n.p.

Henderson, Rose. "American Negro Exhibit at International House." *Southern Workman,* April 1930, 166–169.

———. "American Negro Exhibit at the New York Art Center." *Southern Workman,* May 1931, 214–217.

———. "Exhibit of Painting and Sculpture by Negro Artists." *Southern Workman,* April 1929, 165–168.

———. "First Nation-wide Exhibit of Negro Artists." *Southern Workman,* March 1928, 121–127.

———. "Negro Artists in the Fifth Harmon Exhibition." *Southern Workman,* April 1933, 176–179.

Hughes, Langston. "The Negro Artist and the Racial Mountain." *Nation* 112 (1926): 692–694.

Locke, Alain. "Advance on the Art Front." *Opportunity* 17 (May 1939): 132–136.

———. "African Art: Classic Style." *American Magazine of Art* (May 1935): 271–278.

———. "African Art in America." *The Nation,* March 16 1927, 290.

———. "The African Legacy and the Negro Artist." In *Exhibition of the Works of Negro Artists,* 10–12. New York: Harmon Foundation, 1931.

———. "The American Negro as Artist." *American Magazine of Art* 23 (September 1931): 210–220.

———. "Art or Propaganda." *Harlem* (November 1924): 12.

———. "A Collection of Congo Art." *Arts* 11 (1927): 60–70.

———. "The Concept of Race as Applied to Social Culture." *Howard (University) Review* (June 1924): 290–299.

———. "Freedom Through Art: A Review of Negro Art, 1870–1938." *Crisis* 45 (1938): 227–229.

———. "The Legacy of the Ancestral Arts." In *The New Negro,* 254–262 (1925).

———. "The Negro Takes His Place in American Art." In *Exhibition of Productions of the National Conference of Social Work,* 315–322. Chicago: University of Chicago Press, 1933.

———. "The New Negro." In *The New Negro,* 3–16, 1925.

———. "A Note on African Art." *Opportunity* 2 (May 1924): 134–138.

———. "To Certain of Our Philistines." *Opportunity* (May 1925): 155–156.

Porter, James A. "Negro Art on Review." *American Magazine of Art* 27 (January 1934): 33–38.

Schomburg, Arthur. "The Negro Digs Up His Past." In Alain Locke, ed., *The New Negro,* 231–237. 1925. New York: Atheneum, 1980.

Wallace, Michele. "Afterword: 'Why Are There No Great Black Artists?' The Problem of Visuality in African-American Culture." In Gina Dent, ed., *Black Popular Culture*, 333–346. Seattle, Wash.: Bay Press, 1992.

———. "Modernism, Postmodernism, and the Problem of the Visual in Afro-American Culture." In Russell Ferguson, Martha Gever, Trinh T. Minha-ha, and Cornel West, eds., *Out There: Marginalization and Contemporary Culture*, 39–50. Cambridge, Mass.: MIT Press, 1990.

Wilson, Judith. "Lifting the Veil: Henry O. Tanner's *The Banjo Lesson* and *The Thankful Poor.*" *Contributions in Black Studies,* 9/10 (1990–1992), 1992: 31–54.

———. "Optical Illusions: Images of Miscegenation in Nineteenth- and Twentieth-Century Art." *American Art* 5, no. 3 (summer 1991): 89–107.

———. "Will 'the New Internationalism' Be the Same Old Story? Some Art Historical Considerations." In Jean Fisher, ed., *Global Visions: Towards a New Internationalism in the Arts,* 60–78. London: Kala, 1994.

AFRICAN AMERICAN CULTURAL AND SOCIAL HISTORY

Achille, Louis. "L'Art et les noirs/The Negroes and Art." *La Revue du Monde Noir* 1 (1931): 28–31.

Aptheker, Herbert, ed. *The Correspondence of W.E.B. Du Bois.* Vol. 2, *Selections 1934–44.* Amherst: University of Massachusetts Press, 1976.

Baker, Houston A. *Modernism and the Harlem Renaissance.* Chicago: University of Chicago Press, 1987.

Berry, Mary Frances, and John W. Blassingame. *Long Memory: The Black Experience in America.* New York: Oxford University Press, 1982.

Cunard, Nancy. *Negro History Anthology 1931–33.* London: Wishart, 1934.

Driggs, Frank. *Black Beauty, White Heat: A Pictorial History of Classic Jazz, 1920–1950.* New York: William Morrow, 1982.

Du Bois, W.E.B. "Of Our Spiritual Strivings." In *The Souls of Black Folk,* 15–22. Greenwich, Conn.: Fawcett, 1961.

Geiss, Immanuel. *The Pan-African Movement: A History of Pan-Africanism in America, Europe, and Africa.* Translated by Anne Keep. New York: Africana, 1974.

Ginzburg, Ralph, ed. *One Hundred Years of Lynchings.* Baltimore: Black Classic Press, 1988.

Harris, Leonard, ed. *The Philosophy of Alain Locke: Harlem Renaissance and Beyond.* Philadelphia: Temple University Press, 1989.

Johnson, Abby Arthur, and Ronald Johnson. *Propaganda and Aesthetics: The Literary Politics of Afro-American Magazines in the Twentieth Century.* Amherst: University of Massachusetts Press, 1979.

Kellner, Bruce. *The Harlem Renaissance: A Historical Dictionary for the Era.* New York: Methuen; London: Routledge and Kegan Paul, 1984.

O'Grady, Lorraine. "Olympia's Maid: Reclaiming Black Female Subjectivity," *Afterimage* 20, no. 1 (summer 1992): 14–15, 23.

Rampersad, Arnold. *The Life of Langston Hughes.* Vol. 1, *1902–1941: I, Too, Sing America.* New York: Oxford University Press, 1986.

Sinette, Elinor Des Verney. *Arthur Alfonso Schomburg: Black Bibliophile and Collector.* New York and Detroit: The New York Public Library and Wayne State University Press, 1989.

AFRICAN ART HISTORY AND HISTORY

Alpern, Stanley B. *Amazons of Black Sparta: The Women Warriors of Dahomey.* New York: New York University Press, 1998.

Einstein, Carl. *Afrikanische Plastik.* Berlin: Wasmuth, 1921.

Haardt, Georges-Marie, and Louis Audouin-Dubreuil, *La Croisi ère noire.* Paris: Librarie Plon, 1927.

Ungar, Sanford J. *Africa: The People and Politics of an Emerging Continent.* New York: Simon and Schuster, 1986.

EUROPEAN ART HISTORY

Bénézit, E. *Dictionnaire critique et documentaire des peintres, sculpteurs, dessinateurs et graveurs de tous les temps et de tous les pays par un groupe d'écrivains spécialistes français et étrangers.* Paris: Librairie Gründ, 1976.

Bernheim-Jeune, Petit résumé historique. Paris: Bernheim-Jeune, ca. 1985.

Des artistes à La Coupole: Montparnasse, 1918–1940. Paris: Museée Bourdelle, 1990.

Explication des ouvrages de peinture, sculpture, architecture, gravure et lithographie des artistes vivants exposés au Palais des Champs-Elysées. Paris: Imprimerie Paul Dupont, 1896.

Exposition coloniale internationale de Paris, 1931: comprenant les matières du premier album de Mai, augmentées des 24 pages du numéro de L'Illustration du 27 Juin et des 20 pages du numéro de L'Illustration du 25 Juillet 1931. Paris: L'Illustration, 1931.

Fernand-Demeure, *Petite Histoire du Salon des Tuileries.* Paris: Goethe, n.d.

Golan, Romy. *Modernity and Nostalgia: Art and Politics in France Between the Wars.* New Haven, Conn.: Yale University Press, 1995.

Green, Christopher. *Cubism and Its Enemies: Modern Movements and Reaction in French Art, 1916–1928.* New Haven, Conn.: Yale University Press, 1987.

Hall, James. *Dictionary of Subjects and Symbols in Art.* New York: Harper & Row, 1979.

Honour, Hugh. *The Image of the Black in Western Art.* Vol. 4, *From the American Revolution to World War I,* part 2. Cambridge: Harvard University Press, 1989.

Janson, H. W., compiler. *Catalogues of the Paris Salons 1673–1881.* New York: Garland, 1977.

Milner, John. *The Studios of Paris: The Capital of Art in the Late Nineteenth Century.* New Haven, Conn.: Yale University Press, 1988.

Paris–New York. Paris: Centre National d'Art et de Culture Georges Pompidou, 1977.

Silver, Kenneth. *Esprit de Corps: The Art of the Parisian Avant-Garde and the First World War, 1914–1925.* Princeton, N.J.: Princeton University Press, 1989.

Silver, Kenneth, and Romy Golan. *The Circle of Montparnasse: Jewish Artists in Paris 1905–1945.* New York: Universe Books, 1985.

Thieme, Ulrich, and Felix Becker, Hrsg. *Allgemeines Lexikon der bildenden Künstler von der Antike bis zur Gegenwart unter Mietwirkung von 300 Sachgelehrten des In- und Auslandes.* Leipzig: W. Engelmann, 1907–1950.

Vollmer, Hans, compiler. *Allgemeines Lexikon der bildenden Künstler des XX. Jahrhunderts.* Leipzig: E. A. Seemann, 1953.

EUROPEAN AMERICAN ART HISTORY

Antonio Salemme. New York: Robert Schoelkopf, 1964.

Art Association of Indianapolis, Indiana. Various exhibition catalogs. Indianapolis, Ind.: John Herron Art Institute.

"Artist Who Has Made Portrait Bust of Edison Says American Art Needs Government Backing," *New York Evening Post,* March 4, 1920, n.p.

Boime, Albert. *The Art of Exclusion: Representing Blacks in the Nineteenth Century.* Washington, D.C.: Smithsonian Institution Press, 1990.

Davies, A. Mervyn. *Solon H. Borglum: A Man Who Stands Alone.* Chester, Conn.: Pequot Press, 1974.

Falk, Peter Hastings, ed. *The Annual Exhibition Record of the Art Institute of Chicago, 1888–1950.* Chicago: Sound View Press, 1990.

———, ed. *The Annual Exhibition Record of the National Academy of Design, 1901–1950.* Madison, Conn.: Sound View Press, 1990.

———, ed. *Who Was Who in American Art.* Chicago: Sound View Press, 1985.

Fielding, Mantle. *Dictionary of American Painter, Sculptors and Engravers.* Green Farms, Conn.: Modern Books and Crafts, 1974.

Fink, Lois Marie. *American Art at the Nineteenth-Century Paris Salons.* Cambridge, U.K.: Cambridge University Press, 1990.

Flint, Janet A. *Solon H. Borglum, 1868–1922.* Washington, D.C.: National Collection of Fine Arts, 1972.

Guinan, Robert. *Krehbiel: Life and Works of an American Artist.* Washington, D.C.: Regnery Gateway, 1991.

Guggenheim Memorial Foundation, John Simon. *Directory of Fellows, 1925–1968.* New York: John Simon Guggenheim Memorial Foundation, 1968.

Hoffman, Malvina. *Heads and Tales.* New York: Charles Scribner's Sons, 1936.

Marlor, Clark S. *Society of Independent Artists: The Exhibition Record, 1917–44.* Park Ridge, N.J.: Noyes Press, 1984.

Platt, Susan Noyes. *Modernism in the 1920s: Interpretations of Modern Art in New York from Expressionism to Constructivism.* Ann Arbor, Mich.: University Microfilms Incorporated Research Press, 1985.

Rubin, William, ed. *"Primitivism" in Twentieth Century Art.* New York: Museum of Modern Art, 1984.

"Victor Salvatore, Sculptor, Is Dead." *New York Times,* April 12, 1965.

"Victor Salvatore, Veteran Sculptor." *New York Herald Tribune,* April 13, 1965.

Winwar, Frances. *Ruotolo: Man and Artist.* New York: Liveright, 1949.

AMERICAN HISTORY

Barnes, Gilbert Hobbs, and Dwight L. Dumond, eds. *The Letters of Theodore Dwight Weld, Angeline Grimké Weld, and Sarah Grimké, 1822–1844.* 2 vols. New York: Appleton, 1934.

Dabney, Virginius. *Virginia, The New Dominion.* Charlottesville: University Press of Virginia, 1971.

Doyle, Don H. *Nashville in the New South, 1880–1930.* Knoxville: University of Tennessee Press, 1985.

Federal Writers' Project of the Works Progress Administration for the State of Florida. *The WPA Guide to Florida: The Federal Writers' Project Guide to 1930s Florida.* New York: Pantheon Books [1984], ca. 1939.

Fitzgerald, Ruth Coder. *A Different Story: A Black History of Fredericksburg, Stafford and Spotsylvania, Virginia.* Fredericksburg, Va.: Unicorn, 1979.

Madison, James H. *Indiana Through Tradition and Change: A History of the Hoosier State and Its People, 1920–1945.* Vol. 5. Indianapolis, Ind.: Indiana Historical Society, 1982.

————. *The Indiana Way: A State History.* Bloomington: Indiana University Press, 1986.

FRENCH CULTURAL HISTORY

Coloniales, 1920–1940. Boulogne-Billancourt: Musée Municipal de Boulogne-Billancourt, 1989.

Klüver, Billy and Julie Martin. *Kiki's Paris: Artists and Lovers, 1900–1930.* New York: Harry N. Abrams, 1989.

Lebovics, Herman. *True France: The War Over Cultural Identity, 1900–1945.* Ithaca, N.Y.: Cornell University Press, 1992.

Monfrin, Jacques. *Honoré Champion et sa librairie, 1874–1978.* Paris: Éditions Honoré Champion, 1978.

Rightor, Henry, ed. *The Standard History of New Orleans, Louisiana.* Chicago, 1900.

SELECTED SOURCES ON INDIVIDUAL ARTISTS

Gwendolyn Bennett

Bennett, Gwendolyn. "Wedding Day." 1926. Reprinted in Marcy Knopf, ed., *The Sleeper Wakes: Harlem Renaissance Stories by Women,* 48–54. New Brunswick, N.J.: Rutgers University Press, 1993.

Govan, Sandra Yvonne. "Gwendolyn Bennett: Portrait of an Artist Lost." Ph.D. diss., Emory University, 1980.

Leininger-Miller, Theresa. "Bennet, Gwendolyn." In John A. Garraty and Mark C. Carnes, eds. *American National Biography.* Vol. 2, 578–579. New York: Oxford University Press, 1999.

———. "Bennett, Gwendolyn (Bernette)." In Thomas Riggs, ed. *Black Artists,* 46–47. Detroit: St. James Press, 1997.

Aaron Douglas

Driskell, David. *Retrospective Exhibition: Paintings by Aaron Douglas.* Nashville, Tenn.: Carl Van Vechten Gallery of Fine Arts, Fisk University, 1971.

Kirschke, Amy Helene. *Aaron Douglas: Art, Race, and The Harlem Renaissance.* Jackson: University Press of Mississippi, 1995.

Florville Foy

Brady, Patricia. "Florville Foy, F.M.C., Master Marble Cutter and Tomb Builder." *Southern Quarterly* 31, no. 2 (1993): 9–19.

Desdunes, Rodolphe Lucien. *Our People and Our History.* Translated by Dorothea Olga McCants. Baton Rouge, La., 1973, 71.

Encyclopedia of New Orleans Artists, 1718–1918. New Orleans, La., 1987. S.v. "Foy, René Prosper" and "Pickhil, Alexandre."

Foy, Prosper. Papers. Howard-Tilton Memorial Library, Tulane University.

Glenk, Robert. *Handbook and Guide to the Louisiana State Museum.* New Orleans, La., 1934, 96.

New Orleans Daily Picayune, March 17, 1903.

Orleans Parish Notarial Archives. James Fahey, 29, 46; M. V. Dejan IV, 31.

Testut, Charles. *Portraits littéraires de la Nouvelle-Orléans.* New Orleans, La., 1850, 177–178.

Meta Vaux Warrick Fuller

Kerr, Judith Nina. *God-Given Work: The Life and Times of Sculptor Meta Vaux Warrick Fuller, 1877–1968.* Ann Arbor, Mich.: University Microfilms Incorporated Press, 1987.

William A. Harper

Bentley, Florence Lewis. "William A. Harper." *Voice of the Negro* (February 1906), 118–122.

"Colored Man Wins Position." *Chicago News,* February 2, 1905, n.p. Art Institute of Chicago scrapbooks, vol. 20.

"Report on the Death of an American Citizen, American Consular Service, City of Mexico, Mexico" (March 30, 1910). Enclosure no. 5 in dispatch no. 229, National Archives.

"William A. Harper." *Bulletin of the Art Institute of Chicago* 4 (July 1910), 11.

Untitled, anonymous article, *Chicago Conservator* (February 16, 1901), n.p. Art Institute of Chicago scrapbooks, vol. 13, 144.

Palmer Hayden

ARTICLES AND ARCHIVAL MATERIAL

Andrews, Benny. "Palmer Hayden, 1890–1973." *World Magazine,* no. 2, July 21, 1973, front page.

"Artists Meet." *New York Amsterdam News,* March 29, 1947.

"Babyish Bays." [New York periodical, other than the *New York Times*] January 1927. AAA/SI.

Chabrier, Comte. *La Revue du Vrai et du Beau,* December 1925.

Cortissoz, Royal. "Random Impressions in Current Exhibitions." *New York Herald Tribune,* April 11, 1926, sec. 6, 10.

Delaney, Joseph. "Reflection of Palmer Hayden." *Studio Museum in Harlem Quarterly Newsletter* 1, no. 2 (1974): cover.

Driskell, David. "The Flowering of the Harlem Renaissance: The Art of Aaron Douglas, Meta Warrick Fuller, Palmer Hayden and William H. Johnson," In Mary S. Campbell, David S. Driskell, David Lewis, and Deborah Willis-Ryan, *Harlem Renaissance: Art of Black America*. New York: Harry N. Abrams, 1987.

Epworth League Herald, February 12, 1927.

Evening Post, winter 1927 or 1928.

Holt, Nora. "Painter Palmer Hayden Symbolizes John Henry." February 1, 1947. AAA/SI.

"Housecleaner off for Study of Art: Negro Whose Sketches Won Harmon Prize Sails on France for Paris." *The World,* March 13, 1927, 7.

Interview with Palmer Hayden by Camille Billops, James V. Hatch, and James Adams, May 14, 1972. Hatch-Billop Archives, New York.

Interview with Palmer Hayden by Harry Henderson and Romare Bearden, 1972. Harry Henderson Archive, Croton-on-Hudson, New York.

Jewell, Edward Alden. "Art in Review: Sargent Johnson Wins Chief Prize at Exhibition by Negro Artists Sponsored by Harmon Foundation." *New York Times,* February 21, 1933, 22.

"Miss Alice M. Dike of Bronxville Dies." *New York Times,* November 9, 1930, 31.

"Negro Artist Wins Prize for Paintings." *New York Times,* December 8, 1926, 11.

"Negro Artists: Their Works Win Top U.S. Honors." *Life* 21 (July 22, 1946), 62–65.

"Negro, 33, Quits Scrub Bucket to Study Abroad." Clipping in AAA/SI.

Norkin, Sam. "A Late Artist's Work Lives On." *New York Daily News,* April 15, 1973, Leisure section, 15, 27.

Pérard, Victor. *Anatomy and Drawing.* New York: V. Perard, 1928.

Sélig, Raymond. "L'oeuvre de Palmer Hayden." *La Revue du Vrai et du Beau,* April 27, 1927, 16.

Trapp, William O. "Palmer C. Hayden Tells of Long Struggle to Become an Artist." *Evening World,* December 13, 1926.

"Victor Pérard, 87, Artist and Author." *New York Times,* July 10, 1957, 27.

CATALOGS

Driskell, David. *Palmer Hayden: The John Henry Series and Paintings Reflecting the Theme of Afro-American Folklore.* Nashville, Tenn.: Art Gallery, Fisk University, 1970.

Gordon, Allan. *Echoes of Our Past: The Narrative Artistry of Palmer C. Hayden.* Los Angeles: Museum of African American Art, 1988.

Paintings by Palmer C. Hayden. New York: Civic Club, 1926.

Sims, Lowery S. *The Many Facets of Palmer Hayden (1890–1973).* New York: Just Above Midtown Gallery, 1977.

The Studio Museum in Harlem. *Southern Scenes and City Streets.* New York: Studio Museum in Harlem, 1977.

Robert Hemmings

"Along the Color Line/Music and Art," *Crisis* 8 (July 1914): 111.

Daniels, John. *In Freedom's Birthplace.* 1914. Reprint, New York: Arno Press, 1969, 202.

Explication des ouvrages de peinture, sculpture, architecture, gravure et lithographie exposés au Grand Palais des Champs-Elysées (30 April 1914). Paris: Imprimerie Paul Dupont, 1914.

Fuller, Solomon C., Jr. Correspondence to Theresa Leininger (July 6, 1990).

Record of Death, Robert Hemmings. Registry Division, City of Boston. October 6, 1955.

Julian Hudson

George D. Coulon manuscript, Scrapbook 100, Louisiana State Museum.

Chase, Judith Wragg. *Afro-American Art and Craft.* New York: Van Nostrand Reinhold, 1971, 100.

Clark, Taylor. *Our Catalog of Fine Prints and Paintings*. New Orleans, 1984, 21.

Desdunes, Rodolphe Lucien. *Our People and Our History*. Translated by Dorothea Olga McCants. Baton Rouge: Louisiana State University Press, 1973.

Encyclopedia of New Orleans Artists, 1718–1918. New Orleans, 1987. S.v. "Meucci, Antonio."

Federal Writers' Project, WPA. *Louisiana: A Guide to the State*. New York, 1941, 177.

———. *New Orleans City Guide*. Boston, 1938, 105.

Glenk, Robert. *Handbook and Guide to the Louisiana State Museum*. New Orleans, 1934, 76.

Hutson, Ethel. "Isaac Delgado Museum of Art." *Warrington Messenger,* September, 1938, 19–20.

Kendall, John S. *History of New Orleans*. Vol. 2. Chicago, 1922, 656.

Looney, Ben Earl. "Historical Sketch of Art in Louisiana." *Louisiana Historical Quarterly,* 1935, 396.

Morton's Auction Exchange. *Third Annual Louisiana Purchase Auction*. New Orleans, 1983, lot 370.

New Orleans Bee, advertisement, June 6, 1831, p. 2, col. 6.

New Orleans Courier, December 3, 1831.

———, January 7, 1832.

———, January 10, 1832.

New York Times, June 7, 1876.

William Henry Johnson

Powell, Richard J. *Homecoming: The Life and Art of William H. Johnson*. Washington, D.C., and New York: Smithsonian Institution and Rizzoli, 1991.

———. "William H. Johnson: Expressionist and Artist of the Blues Aesthetic." Ph.D. diss., New Haven, Conn.: Yale University, 1988.

Lois Mailou Jones

Benjamin, Tritobia. *The World of Lois Mailou Jones*. Washington, D.C.: Meridian House International, 1990.

Jules Lion

L'Abeille de la Nouvelle-Orléans, June 6, 1831.

———, December 13, 1842.

———, November 25, 1843.

———, October 12, 1865.

———, January 10, 1866.

East, Charles. "Jules Lion's New Orleans." *Georgia Review* 40, no. 4 (1986): 914–916.

Encyclopedia of New Orleans Artists, 1718–1918. New Orleans, La., 1987. S.v. "Canova, Dominique"; "Lion, Jules"; "Navarre, Bisynthe"; "Nelder, Alexander"; "Monsseaux, Paul H."; and "Callico, Joseph Frédéric."

Hacker, John Burton, and Mary Louise Tucker. *The Louisiana Portrait Gallery*. Vol 1, *To 1870*. New Orleans: The Louisiana State Museum, 1979, 69, 122.

Huber, Leonard V., and Samuel Wilson Jr. *The Basilica on Jackson Square: The History of the St. Louis Cathedral and Its Predecessors, 1727–1965,* 29–34. New Orleans, La.: St. Louis Cathedral, 1965.

Korn, Bertram Wallace. *The Early Jews of New Orleans*. Waltham, Mass.: American Jewish Historical Society, 1969, 138.

Lawrence, John H. *L'Abeille de la Nouvelle-Orléans,* March 14, 1840, 2.

Leininger-Miller, Theresa. "Lion, Jules." In John A. Garraty and Mark C. Carnes, eds. *American National Biography*. Vol. 13, 717–718. New York: Oxford University Press, 1999.

Lion, Jules. Letter to Monsieur Le Président and to Messieurs les Membres du Comité de Construction de la Cathédrale St. Louis, New Orleans (December 8, 1850), 86–74-L, Historic New Orleans Collection.

Louisiana Courier, November 30, 1848. [Dominique Canova].

Nelson, William J., Jr. "The Free Negro in the Ante Bellum New Orleans Press." Ph.D. diss., Duke University, 1977, 84.

New Orleans Daily Picayune, March 20, 1840.

O'Neill, Charles Edwards. "Fine Arts and Literature: Nineteenth-Century Louisiana Black Artists and Authors." In Robert R. Macdonald, et al., eds., *Louisiana's Black Heritage.* New Orleans, La., 1979, 72.

Rouen, Bussière, "L'abeille de la Nouvelle-Orléans." *Louisiana Historical Quarterly* 8 (1925): 585–586.

Sheet music collection, The Historic New Orleans Collection.

Wiesendanger, Martin, and Margaret Wiesendanger. *Louisiana Painters and Paintings from the Collection of W. E. Groves,* 66, 67. New Orleans: W. E. Groves Gallery, 1971.

Archibald Motley Jr.

"Archibald John Motley, Jr." *Opportunity* 6 (April, 1928), 114–115.

Chabrier, Count. "Expositions de l'Art Institute de Chicago, du No-Jury Exposition et du Cincinnati museum." *Revue du Vrai et du Beau* 4 (February 16, 1925), n.p.

Chabrier, Count, and G. Serac. "Expositions d'Amerique." *La Revue du Vrai et du Beau* 4 (July 10, 1925).

Jewell, Edward Alden. "A Negro Artist Plumbs the Negro Soul." *New York Times Magazine,* March 25, 1928, 8, 22.

Motley, Archibald J., Jr. "Autobiography." Archibald J. Motley Jr. Papers, Archives and Manuscripts Collection, Chicago Historical Society.

———. "How I Solve My Painting Problems." 1929. Harmon Foundation Collection, Library of Congress, Washington, D.C.

———. "Paris Diary" (1929–1930). Collection of Archie Motley and Valerie Gerrard Browne; copy in Archibald J. Motley Jr. Papers, Archives and Manuscripts Collection, Chicago Historical Society.

Motley, Willard. "Negro Art in Chicago." *Opportunity* 18 (June, 1940): 19–22, 28.

Robinson, Jontyle Theresa. "The Art of Archibald John Motley, Jr.: A Notable Anniversary for a Pioneer." In *Three Masters: Eldzier Cortor, Hughie Lee-Smith, Archibald John Motley, Jr.,* 42–45. New York: Kenkeleba House, 1988.

Robinson, Jontyle Theresa, and Wendy Greenhouse. *The Art of Archibald J. Motley, Jr.* Chicago: Chicago Historical Society, 1991.

Woodall, Elaine D. "Archibald Motley and the Art Institute of Chicago: 1914–30." *Chicago History* 9 (spring 1979), 53–57.

———. "Archibald Motley, Jr.: American Artist of the Afro-American People, 1891–1928." M.A. thesis, Pennsylvania State University, 1977.

Charles Ethan Porter

Charles Ethan Porter, 1847–1923. Malborough, Conn.: Connecticut Gallery, 1987.

Nancy Elizabeth Prophet

"Along the Color Line." *Crisis* 38 (September 1931): 308.

"Anne Elizabeth Prophet Wins R. S. Greenough Prize." *New York Times,* July 9, 1932, p. 8, col. 4.

"Art: Woman Artist." *Crisis* 39 (August, 1932): 259.

"Awarded Greenough Memorial Prize: Miss Prophet's Picture 'Silence' Judged Best in Art Association Exhibit," *Newport Daily News,* July 8, 1932, 3.

"Beth Prophit [*sic*] is Hailed in Paris as Real Artist." *Baltimore Afro-American,* August 3, 1929, 8.

"Can I Become a Sculptor? The Story of Elizabeth Prophet." *Crisis* 39 (October, 1932): 315.

"Carving 'Discontent' Is Awarded Prize—Richard Greenough Memorial Prize—Given the Woodcarving Not 'Silence.'" *Newport Daily News,* July 9, 1932, 5.

Cochrane, Albert Franz. "A Sculptress Who Carves Her Own at Vose's." *Boston Evening Transcript,* November 2, 1932, 4.

———. "Once More the Independents Hold Forth on Beacon Hill." *Boston Evening Transcript,* Saturday, February 16, 1929, p. 3, col. 8–9.

Cullen, Countee. "Elizabeth Prophet: Sculptress." *Opportunity* 8 (July, 1930): 204–205.

Dover, Cedric. *American Negro Art.* Greenwich, Conn.: New York Graphic Society, 1960, 56.

"Elizabeth Prophet, Artiste Américaine." *L'Art Contemporain* (ca. 1929–1931): n.p.

"Elizabeth Prophet Names Among Famous Women in America." *Atlanta University Bulletin* (December, 1939): 11.

"Elizabeth Prophet, Sculptor." *Crisis* 36 (December 1929): 407, 427.

"Elizabeth Prophet, Sculpture Prize Winner." *Providence Evening Bulletin,* February 1930.

"Elizabeth Prophet Wins Prize for Head of Negro." *New York Times,* January 12, 1931, p. 26, col. 1.

"First Prize for Indian Woman." *Newport Herald,* July 9, 1932.

Four From Providence: Bannister, Prophet, Alston, Jennings. Providence, R.I.: Rhode Island Black Heritage Society and Rhode Island College, 1978.

Hughes, Katharine. "Vose Galleries Have Sculpture—N. Elizabeth Prophet Exhibits." *Boston Herald,* November 6, 1932, 9.

"In Social Circles." *Newport News,* July 21, 1932.

Kirschenbaum, Blossom S. "Nancy Elizabeth Prophet, Sculptor." *SAGE* 4, no. 1 (1987): 45–52.

Leininger, Theresa. "Elizabeth Prophet (1890–1960)." In Jessie Carney Smith, ed., *Notable Black American Women,* 890–897. Detroit: Gale Research 1992.

———. "Prophet, Nancy Elizabeth." In John A. Garraty and Mark C. Carnes, eds., *American National Biography.* Vol. 17, 903–904. New York: Oxford University Press, 1999.

———. "Prophet, Nancy Elizabeth." In Thomas Riggs, ed., *Black Artists,* 437–438. Detroit: St. James Press, 1997.

"Nancy Prophet Wins Success As Sculptress/Calls Courage Real Requisite for Achieving." *Providence Evening Bulletin,* July 8, 1932, 10.

"Negress Wins the First Prize at Newport." *Art Digest* (August 1, 1932): 14.

"Negro Father, 88, Sees Famous Daughter's Work at Library." Clipping. N.p., 1945, n.d. Artists Index, New York Public Library, New York.

"Newport Art Prize Given Woodcarving." *New York Times,* July 9, 1932, p. 8, col. 4.

"Newport Exhibition Marks Twenty-fifth Year of Group." *New York Herald Tribune,* July 10, 1932.

"Newport Ready for Art Show." *Providence Sunday Journal,* July 3, 1932, sec. D, 6.

Occomy, Nell. "Art Corner." N.p., n.d.

Patézon, Jean. "Elizabeth Prophet, artiste américaine." *Le Rayonnement Intellectuel* (July–August 1931).

Photograph of Prophet on cover of *Crisis* 39 (October 1932).

Porter, James. *Modern Negro Art.* New York: Arno Press, 1943.

Prophet, N. Elizabeth. "Art and Life." *Phylon: The Atlanta University Review of Race and Culture* 1 (third quarter 1940): 322–326.

Prophet, Nancy Elizabeth. "I Will Not Bend an Inch: Elizabeth Prophet's Struggle to Become an Artist" title given by editor Eliot Krieger to Prophet's diary; entire diary published), *Rhode Islander Magazine, Providence Sunday Journal* (July 10, 1994), 8–10, 12, 14–16.

"R.I. Sculptress Wins Recognition." *Providence Journal,* April 2, 1932, 8.

Sélig, Raymond, Jules de Saint-Hilaire, and Jean d'Humovain, "Les Salons des Artistes Français, de la Nationale et des Indépendants (Elisabeth Prophet)." *La Revue du Vrai et du Beau* (August 10, 1929): 7.

Société du Salon d'Automne: Catalogue des ouvrages de peinture, sculpture, dessin, gravure, architecture et art décorative. Paris: Imprimerie Ernest Puyfourcat fils & Cie., 1927, 291.

Who's Who in American Art. New York: R. R. Bowker, 1937, 341.

————. New York: R. R. Bowker, 1939, 423.

————. New York: R. R. Bowker, 1940–1941.

Who's Who of American Women. Chicago: Marquis Who's Who, 1939.

"Woman Artist." *Crisis* 39 (August, 1932): 259.

"Women Artists' Work to Fore in Annual Exhibit at Newport: Opening Marked By Award to R.I. Girl Sculptress." *Providence Sunday Journal,* July 10, 1932, sec. E, 8.

Augusta Savage

Allen, Cleveland G. "Miss Augusta Savage." SCRBC, clipping file.

————. "Our Young Negro Artists." *Opportunity* 1 (January 1923): 16.

"Artist Who Has Made Portrait Bust of Edison Says American Art Needs Government Backing." *New York Evening Post,* March 4, 1920, n.p.

"Augusta Savage." *Chicago Whip,* August 15, 1931, n.p., SCRBC, clipping file.

"Augusta Savage: An Autobiography." *Crisis* 36 (August 1929): 269.

"Augusta Savage Gets Fellowship." *New York Amsterdam News,* May 29, 1929.

"Augusta Savage Studies Under Master in Paris." *New York Amsterdam News,* November 13?, 1929, n.p.

Bearden, Romare, and Harry Henderson. "Augusta Savage." In *Six Black Masters of American Art,* 76–98. New York: Doubleday, 1972.

Bibby, Deirdre. *Augusta Savage and the Art Schools of Harlem.* New York: Schomburg Center for Research in Black Culture, New York Public Library, 1988.

Byrd, William A. "The Color-Line in Art" (letter to editor), *New York World,* April 30, 1923, n.p.

"Carving a Name for Herself." *New York Times,* March 20, 1939, n.p.

"Colored Sculptress Tells Story of Life." *Waterbury (Conn.) American,* December 2, 1935, n.p.

"Courier Tintypes." *Pittsburgh Courier,* Saturday, May 5, 1934, p. 2, col. 3. Copy in SCRBC, clipping file.

"Creator of Art." *Chicago Defender,* March 12, 1927, p. 2, col. 3.

Du Bois, W.E.B. "That Architectural Lie." *Crisis* 37 (June 1930): 209.

Exhibition of Sculpture by Augusta Savage. New York: Argent Galleries, 1939.

"Famous Artists Draw Color Line against Student." *Negro World,* May 5, 1923, 3.

Fax, Elton C. "Augusta Savage: An Appraisal." *American Society of African Sculpture Newsletter* 5, no. 2 (supplement) (October, 1962): 4–6.

Finkelstein, Hope. "Augusta Savage: Sculpting the African American Identity." M.A. Thesis, City Univeristy of New York, 1990.

"Harding Asked to Intercede in Exclusion Case." *New York World,* May 10, 1923.

Hayes, Frank. "Young Art Student Wins Prize for Sculptor [*sic*] Work." *Chicago Daily News,* 1929, n.p.

"Joe Louis Fans and Exhibits Figure in News of the Day: Envy." *New York Amsterdam News,* June 20, 1936, 13.

Nadral, Paulette. "Une femme sculpteur noire." *La Dépêche Africaine* (August–September 1930): 3–4.

"Negro Artist Fight Moves to France." *New York World,* May 12, 1926.

"Negro Artists Reveal Genius in Trenton Show." *Art Digest* (April 15, 1935): 19.

"Negro Students Hold Their Own Art Exhibition." *New York Herald Tribune,* February 15, 1935, 17.

"No African Art, Says Sculptress." *Afro-American,* August 29, 1936, n.p.

"Noted Sculptress Expects Distinct, But Not Different, Racial Art." *Pittsburgh Courier,* August 29, 1936, p. 1, col. 5.

Occomy, Nell. "Who is Who—Augusta Savage." *New York News,* June 1, 1929.

"Persons and Achievements to be Noted in March—Augusta Savage." *Negro History Bulletin* (March 2, 1939): 50, 51.

Poston, T. R. "Augusta Savage." *Metropolitan Magazine,* January, 1935, 28–31, 51, 66–67. Copy in SCRBC, clipping file.

————. "Harlem Will See Self as Others See It at Novel Show." *New York Amsterdam News*, February 9, 1935, 9.

Savage, Augusta. "Augusta Savage: An Autobiography." *Crisis* 36 (August 1929): 269.

————. "Augusta Savage on Negro Ideals" (letter to the editor). *New York World*, May 20, 1923. SCRBC, clipping file.

"Sculptress Commissioned to Do Group." *Norfolk Journal and Guide*, December 18, 1937, 4.

"Sculptress Makes Good in France." *Afro-American*, February 14, 1931, 10.

"Sculptress to Study Abroad: Talented Augusta Savage Awarded Rosenwald Fellowship." *Chicago Defender*, June 1, 1929, 2:6.

"Sculpture Group for World's Fair." *New York Times*, December 9, 1937.

"Seeks Exhibition of Augusta Savage Work." *New York Amsterdam News*, March 7, 1936, 5.

"Showing the 'Susie Q.'" *New York Journal of America*, December 9, 1937, n.p.

Smith, Jessie Carney. "Augusta Savage (1892–1962)." In Jessie Carney Smith, ed. *Notable Black American Women*, 979–983. Detroit: Gale Research Inc., 1992.

"Something New in Negro Art in America." *Washington Tribune*, August 25, 1936.

"Three-Hundred-Dollar Purse for Augusta Savage." *Afro-American*, August 10, 1929.

"To Live in Bronze." *New York Amsterdam News*, February 17, 1932.

"U.S. Folklore Gets a Place in Art of All Types." *New York Herald Tribune*, April 14, 1939, n.p.

Walrond, Eric D. "Florida Girl Shows Amazing Gift for Sculpture." N.p., ca. 1922, n.p. SCRBC, clipping file.

Walton, Lester A. "Negro Girl Gets Fund to Study Art Abroad." N.p., 1926, n.p. SCRBC, clipping file.

William Edouard Scott

"Along the Color Line." *Crisis* 4 (June 1912): 63–64.

"Along the Color Line." *Crisis* 7 (January 1914): 114.

"Along the Color Line: Art." *Crisis* 1 (January 1911): 8.

"Along the Color Line/Music and Art." *Crisis* 34 (June 1927): 124.

"Artist of Indian and Negro Extraction Attracts Attention With His Pictures." *Indianapolis Star*, November 17, 1912, 8.

"Colored Man Will Study Art Abroad." *Indianapolis Star*, August 25, 1909, 32.

"'Commerce.' Painting by Young Negro Artist, Who Leaves Chicago for Paris." *Chicago Record-Herald*, July 26, 1909, 4.

Hayes, Frank L. "Negro Artist Given Haiti Merit Award." *Chicago Daily News*.

Holbrook, Francis C. "William Edouard Scott, Painter." *Southern Workman* 52 (February 1924): 72–76.

"The Horizon: Music and Art." *Crisis* 16 (August 1918): 189.

"Indianapolis Artist of Mixed Negro and Indian Blood Winning Success in Paris." *Indianapolis News*, December 9, 1912, 2.

"Men of the Month: A Young Artist." *Crisis* 5 (March 1913): 224.

Morehouse, Lucille E. "Colored Artist Home from Study in Paris." *Indianapolis Star*, November 14, 1912, 13.

————. "New Interest Develops in Work of William Edouard Scott." *Indianapolis Sunday Star*, May 2, 1943, part 1, p. 19.

Perisho, Sally. *Woodruff, Hardrick and Scott*. Indianapolis, Ind.: Indianapolis Museum of Art, 1977.

Phillips, Bertrand. "William Edouard Scott (1884–1964)." *World Magazine*, November 3, 1973, M-6, M-7.

Rouzeau, Edgar T. "Compete with White Artists, Advises Wm. Edouard Scott, Who Has Done So." SCRBC, clipping file.

Stokes, Derrick. "Mural Painter Has Left an Impression in Indianapolis." *Indianapolis News,* February 26, 1990, D1, 3.

Taylor, William E. "William Edouard Scott: Indianapolis Painter." *Black History News and Notes,* no. 33 (August 1988): 4–7.

"William E. Scott, Artist, Gets Rosenwald Fellowship." SCRBC, clipping file.

Albert Alexander Smith

Allen, Cleveland G. "Our Young Artists." *Opportunity* 1 (June 1923): 24.

Exhibitions [*sic*] *of Paintings of France, Italy and Spain* [Albert Alexander Smith]. New York: Public Library, 1928.

"The Horizon." *Crisis* (January 1926): 131.

"The Looking Glass: Negro Artists." *Crisis* (December 1926): 107.

McGleughlin, Jean. "Albert Alexander Smith." *Opportunity* 18 (July 1940): 208.

Morro, Clement. "Albert Alexander Smith." *La Revue Moderne Illustrée des Arts et de la Vie* 38, no. 13 (July 15, 1938): 14–15.

———. "Albert Alexander Smith." *La Revue Moderne Illustrée des Arts et de la Vie* 39, no. 13 (July 15, 1939): 18–19.

"Negro Artists." *Crisis* (December 1926): 107.

"News and Exhibitions of the Week in Art." *New York Herald Tribune,* January 12, 1930, sec. 7, 11.

"Social Progress." *Opportunity* 3 (December 1925): 385–387.

Henry O. Tanner

Matthews, Marcia. *Henry O. Tanner: American Artist.* Chicago: University of Chicago Press, 1969.

Mosby, Dewey, Darrell Sewell, and Rae Alexander-Minter. *Henry Ossawa Tanner.* Philadelphia: Philadelphia Museum of Art, 1991.

Simon, W. A. *Henry O. Tanner: A Study of the Development of an American Negro Artist.* Ann Arbor, Mich.: University Microfilms Incorporated Press, 1961.

Eugène Warburg

Brady, Patricia. "The Warburg Brothers: Sculptors." *Historic New Orleans Collection Newsletter* 7, no. 3 (summer 1989): 8–9.

Christovich, Mary Louise, et al., eds., *New Orleans Architecture,* Vol. 3, *The Cemeteries.* Gretna, La., 1974, 92.

"City Intelligence: A Creole Sculptor." *New Orleans Bee,* December 13, 1850, p. 1, col. 3.

Conrad, Glenn R., gen. ed. *A Dictionary of Louisiana Biography.* Vol. 2, *N–Z.* New Orleans, La.: Louisiana Historical Association, 1988, 823–824.

Desdunes, Rodolphe Lucien. *Our People and Our History.* Translated by Dorothea Olga McCants. Baton Rouge, La.: Louisiana State University Press, 1973, 69–71.

"Duchess of Sutherland." In *Dictionary of National Biography.* Vol. 33, 152–153. London, 1885–1900.

Encyclopedia of New Orleans Artists, 1718–1918. New Orleans, La., 1987. S.v. "Garbeille, Philippe."

Ettinger, Amos A. *The Mission to Spain of Pierre Soulé, 1853–1855: A Study in the Cuban Diplomacy of the United States.* New Haven, Conn.: Yale University Press, 1932.

Gandolfo, Henri A. *Métairie Cemetery: An Historical Memoir.* New Orleans, La.: Published by Stewart Enterprises, Inc. 1981.

Gerson, Noel B. *Harriet Beecher Stowe: A Biography.* New York: Praeger, 1976.

Korn, Bertram Wallace. *The Early Jews of New Orleans.* Waltham, Mass.: American Jewish Historical Society, 1969.

"Leveson-Gower, Harriet Elizabeth Georgiana, Duchess of Sutherland." In Sir Leslie Stephen and Sir Sidney Lee, eds., *The Dictionary of National Biography.* Oxford: Oxford University Press, 1917, 1031–1032.

Malone, Dumas, et al., eds., *Dictionary of American Biography.* 20 vols. New York: 1928–1936. S.v. "Soulé, Pierre"; "Mercier, Charles Alfred"; "Mason, John Young"; and "Stowe, Harriet."

"Mason, John Young." *The National Cyclopaedia of American Biography Being the History of the United States.* Vol. 6, 1892, 1929. Reprint, Ann Arbor, Mich.: University Microfilms, 1967, 7.

New Orleans Bee, March 9, 1859.

New Orleans Daily Crescent, December 26, 1857, p. 4, col. 1.

New Orleans Daily Picayune, December 26, 1857, p. 1, col. 5.

Warburg, Eugène. Letter to Messieurs les Membres du Comité de Construction de l'Eglise St. Louis (February 12, 1851), 86-74-L. Historic New Orleans Collection.

Laura Wheeler Waring

James, Milton M. "Laura Wheeler Waring." In *Nine to the Universe: Black Artists.* Philadelphia: Black History Museum UMUM, 1983.

Porter, James. *In Memoriam: Laura Wheeler Waring 1887–1948: An Exhibition of Paintings.* Washington, D.C.: Howard University Gallery of Fine Arts, 1949.

Hale Woodruff

Allison, Jane. "OK, Museum, Why Not a Woodruff?" *Indianapolis News,* March 5, 1977, 5.

Andrews, Benny. "Hailing Hale Woodruff." *Encore American and Worldwide News* 7 (April 3, 1978): 31.

Campbell, Mary Schmidt. *Hale Woodruff: Fifty Years of His Art.* New York: Studio Museum in Harlem, 1979.

Crawford, Doris. "Hale Aspacio Woodruff." M.A. thesis, Howard University, 1972.

Fraser, C. Gerald. "Hale Woodruff Looks Back on Lifetime of Painting." *New York Times,* May 6, 1979, part 1, p. 69.

"KRIGWA." *Crisis* (September 1928): 312, 322.

Leininger-Miller, Theresa. "Hale A. Woodruff (1900–1980)." In Jessie Carney Smith, ed. *Notable Black American Men,* 1247–1250. Detroit, Mich.: Gale Research, 1999.

Montero, Anne M. "Village Artist Reflects on Career On Occasion of Museum Show." *Villager* 45 (August 25, 1977): 13.

Morehouse, Lucille. "Hale Woodruff, Artist, Will Study in Europe." *Indianapolis Star,* August 28, 1927, 7.

Murray, Al. Interview with Hale Woodruff. AAA/SI.

Perisho, Sally. *Woodruff, Hardrick and Scott.* Indianapolis, Ind.: Indianapolis Museum of Art, 1977.

"Poetry and Painting." *Crisis* (May 1927): 84.

Stoelting, Winifred. "Hale Woodruff, Artist and Teacher: Through the Atlanta Years." Ph.D. diss., Emory University, 1978.

Wilson, Judith. "'Go Back and Retrieve It:' Hale Woodruff, Afro-American Modernist." In *Selected Essays: Art and Artists from the Harlem Renaissance to the 1980's,* 41–49. Atlanta, Ga.: National Black Arts Festival, 1988.

Woodruff, Hale. "My Meeting with Henry O. Tanner." *Crisis* (January 1970): 7–12.

ARTICLES BY WOODRUFF IN THE INDIANAPOLIS STAR (1928–1929)

"The Gardens of Luxembourg." January 6, 1928, 4.

"Artist Makes Forced Stop at Mendon [*sic*]." January 27, 1928.

"Some Bridges of Paris." February 5, 1928, 6.

"Local Negro Artist Find Painters Hard to Classify." March 18, 1928, 31.

"Local Negro Tells of View From Notre Dame." April 22, 1928, 35.

"A Lodging of Jeanne d'Arc." May 27, 1928, 6.

"Garden of Tuileries Offer Vista of Enchanting Beauty." June 10, 1928.

"Old Bookstalls of the Seine." July 8, 1928, 5.

"Travelers in France, Though Rushing for Time, Long to Linger in Chartres." October 7, 1928, 9.

"The Cave of the Dungeons." November 4, 1928, 8.

"Paris's Montparnasse." February 17, 1929, 7, part 6.

FRENCH PERIODICALS

Art et Decoration, Revue Manuelle d'Art Moderne

Les Arts à Paris

Les Arts Plastiques

Les Continents, Bulletin de l'Effort Moderne

Bulletin de la Vie Artistique

Cahiers d'Art

La Revue du Vrai et du Beau

La Revue Moderne Illustrée des Arts et de la Vie

La Revue du Monde Noir

New York Herald Tribune, Paris edition

ARCHIVAL RESOURCES

Archives of American Art, Smithsonian Institution. Papers of Palmer Hayden, William Henry Johnson, Henry O. Tanner, Archibald Motley, and Hale Woodruff and materials on William Harper, Augusta Savage, Lois Mailou Jones, and Albert Alexander Smith in vertical files.

Carnegie Foundation, New York.

Harmon Foundation Papers, The Library of Congress, Washington, D.C.

Harry Henderson, Croton-on-Hudson, New York. Private files and tape-recorded interviews.

Hatch-Billops Archives, New York.

James P. Adams Library, Special Collections, Rhode Island College, Providence, Rhode Island. Documents on Nancy Elizabeth Prophet.

James Weldon Johnson Memorial Collection of Negro Arts and Letters, Beinecke Rare Book and Manuscript Library, Yale University, New Haven, Connecticut.

James Hay Library, Special Collections, Brown University, Providence, Rhode Island. Diary of Nancy Elizabeth Prophet.

John Simon Guggenheim Memorial Foundation, New York.

L. S. Alexander Gumby Collection of Negroiana, Columbia University Library, New York.

Madeline Murphy, Baltimore, Maryland. Private collection of diaries and papers of Laura Wheeler Waring.

Moorland-Spingarn Research Center, Howard University, Washington, D.C. Papers of Alain Locke.

National Archives, Harmon Foundation Records, Washington, D.C.

Rosenwald Archives, Fisk University, Nashville, Tennessee.

Schomburg Center for Research in Black Culture, New York Public Library, New York.

Studio Museum in Harlem, New York.

INDEX

(Page numbers in bold indicate illustrations.)

307

Soulé, Pierre, 4–5
Soulouque, 239
Southern Workman, 225, 286n.67
Southside Community Arts
  Center, 248
Soutine, Chaim, 130, 131
Spain, 73, 109
Specht, George, 58
Speed, J. B. Memorial, Museum,
  140–141
Spelman College, 17, 62, 64, 218
Spingarn, Amy, 138, 273n.169;
  Competition, 108, 222
Springfield, Illinois, 140
Square de Châtillon, 199
S.S. *Lafayette,* 60
S.S. *La France,* 20, 73
S.S. *Majestic,* 104
S.S. *Rochambeau,* 146
Stanhope-Forbes, 79
Stanton High School, Jackson-
  ville, 166
Stark, Otto, 12; Otto Stark
  Studio, 13
State Museum of New Jersey,
  201
State University of New York,
  247
Stein, Gertrude, 44, 128
Sterne, Maurice, 23
Stewart, Jeffrey, 230, 233,
  268n.158, 286nn.73, 76
Stoelting, Winifred, "Hale
  Woodruff, Artist and Teacher:
  Through the Atlanta Years,"
  xx, 267nn.108, 128, 131;
  268n.1; 269nn.6, 7, 8, 16, 19,
  31, 32, 35; 270nn.46, 56, 60;
  271n.95; 272nn.119, 131;
  273nn.141, 166; 281n.147;
  *Hale Woodruff: Fifty Years of
  His Art,* 266n.100
Story, William Wetmore, 5
Stubbs, Jesse, 141
Soutine, Chaim, 83
Stovall, Tyler, *Paris Noir,* xix,
  214, 259, 266n.84; 282n.151;
  286n.71; 287nn.3, 4,
Stowe, Harriet Beecher, 5; *Uncle
  Tom's Cabin,* 6, 14, 233,
  285nn.33–37
Students Fund of Boston, 40
Studio Museum in Harlem, xix
Sully, Thomas, 5
Sutherland, Duchess of, 5
Surrealists, 76, 86
Survey Graphic, xvi
Suydam Medal, 204

Tallahassee State Normal School,
  179

Tanner, Henry Ossawa, xix, xxi,
  7–14, 16, 44, 69, 70, 142, 243,
  247, 254nn.43, 68; 255nn.78,
  87, 88; 259nn.118, 120;
  261n.170; 263nn.234, 248; and
  Hayden, 73–74, 88, 98; and
  Prophet, 61–62; and Savage,
  154, 170, 173, 179, 180; and
  Scott, 7–12; and Smith, 202,
  221, **223**, 238, **239**; and
  Woodruff, 111, 117–118, 246;
  The Bagpipe Lesson, 79; *The
  Banjo Lesson,* 126, 208, 228,
  229, 268n.1; *Intersection of
  Roads, Neufchâteau, World War
  I,* 14; *The Resurrection of
  Lazarus,* 7, 118; papers of, xix
Tanner Art League, 208, 209,
  285n.26
Tanzania, 56
Taylor, William E., xiii, 254nn.73,
  74; 255nn.76, 81–83
Tenth Calvary, 68
Terrell, Mary Church, 118
Thal, Victor, 131
Thierry, Louis and Camille, 1
Thomson, Joseph, 56, 262n. 205
Tiffany, Louis Comfort Tiffany,
  Foundations, 65
Timbuktu, 100
369th Infantry (Harlem Hell-
  fighters) Jazz Band (WWI), 229
Thrash, Dox, 206
Thurman, Wallace, 173
Toledo, Spain, 224
Tomanek, Josef, 144
Toomer, Jean, 84; *Cane,* 208, 233
Trépied, 7, 14
Trocadero Museum, 283n. 192
Trouville, 225
Trumbull, John, 5
Tubman, Harriet, 211
Tuileries gardens, 112
Turner, Elizabeth Hutton, *Ameri-
  can Artists in Paris, 1919–1929,*
  xxi, 257nn.46, 49, 60; 259n.128;
  266nn.96, 99; 267nn.115, 143;
  268n.147; 270n.61
Tuskegee Institute, 11
Twain, Mark, 6–7, 253n.37
Twenty-Fourth Infantry
  Regiment, 68

Uffizi Gallery, 209
U.S. Department of the Treasury,
  248
U.S. Supreme Court, 167
United Negro Improvement
  Association (UNIA), 167, 168,
  172, 185
Upshure, Theodore, 173, 179

Uptown Art Laboratory, 201
Urban League. *See* National
  Urban League
Utopia Neighborhood House
  (New York), 179
Utrillo, Maurice, 81

Valcour, B., 1
Valentine Gallery (New York),
  145
Vanderbilt, Mrs. William, 60
Van Doren, Carl, 71
Van Gogh, Vincent, 81, 131
Van Vechten, Carl, 126, 134,
  135, 273nn.163, 164
Velazquez, Diego, 224, 229
Versailles, 21, 75, 112, 160
Veterans Exhibition (Paris), 235
Victoria, Queen, 6
Vinci, Leonardo da, 116;
  Leonardo da Vinci Art School,
  174
Visitor's Exhibition (Chicago),
  161
"Visual Arts Encounter: African-
  Americans and Europe, A"
  conference (Paris, 1994)
Vlaminck, Maurice de, 81
Volk, Douglas, 204
Vonnoh, Bessie Potter,
  260n.161
Vose (Robert C. Vose Jr.)
  Galleries, 61, 263n.235
Vuillard, Edouard, 81

Walden University (Nashville),
  172
Waldman, Oscar, 23
Walker, A'Lelia, 167, 176
Walker, Annie E.A., 8, 14,
  254nn.44, 45; *La Parisienne,*
  8, 9
Walker, Kara, 100
Walker, Madame C. J., 167
Walker, Thomas H.B., 166
Walrond, Eric, 71, 79, 84–85,
  88, 128, 168, 169; "Florida
  Girl," 278nn.20, 22, 23, 34,
  36, 37, 39–41; 279nn.46, 51,
  52; "My Version of It,"
  279n.57
Warbourg, Daniel, 4
Walton, Lester, "Negro Girl Gets
  Fund to Study Abroad,"
  278nn.30, 32, 33; 280nn.112,
  115; 281nn.131, 132
Warburg, Eugène, 1, 4–5, 14; *Un
  portrait,* 4; *Un jeune pêcheur
  jouant avec un crabe,* 4; *Portrait
  de S.E., le ministre des Etats-Unis
  à Paris,* **4**

ABOUT THE AUTHOR

THERESA LEININGER-MILLER is associate professor of art history and director of graduate studies at the University of Cincinnati and the recipient of numerous fellowships and awards. She received her Ph.D. from Yale University and has published articles, exhibition catalog essays, and reference entries on African American art and delivered many papers at conferences, universities, and museums.